INTERPLAY

The Process of Interpersonal Communication

THIRTEENTH EDITION

Ronald B. Adler
Santa Barbara City College

Lawrence B. Rosenfeld
University of North Carolina at Chapel Hill

Russell F. Proctor II
Northern Kentucky University

New York   •   Oxford
OXFORD UNIVERSITY PRESS

Oxford University Press is a department of the University of Oxford.
It furthers the University's objective of excellence in research,
scholarship, and education by publishing worldwide.

Oxford New York
Auckland Cape Town Dar es Salaam Hong Kong Karachi
Kuala Lumpur Madrid Melbourne Mexico City Nairobi
New Delhi Shanghai Taipei Toronto

With offices in
Argentina Austria Brazil Chile Czech Republic France Greece
Guatemala Hungary Italy Japan Poland Portugal Singapore
South Korea Switzerland Thailand Turkey Ukraine Vietnam

For titles covered by Section 112 of the US Higher Education Opportunity Act,
please visit www.oup.com/us/he for the latest information about pricing and
alternate formats.

Published by Oxford University Press
198 Madison Avenue, New York, New York 10016
http://www.oup.com

Library of Congress Cataloging-in-Publication Data

Adler, Ronald B. (Ronald Brian), 1946–
  Interplay : the process of interpersonal communication / Ronald B. Adler, Lawrence
B. Rosenfeld, Russell F. Proctor II. — Thirteenth edition.
      p. cm.
  ISBN 978-0-19-939048-9
  1. Interpersonal communication. I. Rosenfeld, Lawrence B. II. Proctor, Russell F.
III. Title.
  BF637.C45A33 2015
  302.2—dc23
                                    2014028834

Printing number: 9 8 7 6 5 4 3

Printed in the United States of America
on acid-free paper

Brief Contents

Contents

CHAPTER 3 INTERPERSONAL COMMUNICATION AND THE SELF 68

CHAPTER 4 PERCEIVING OTHERS 106

FEATURES

PART TWO: CREATING AND RESPONDING TO MESSAGES

CHAPTER 5 LANGUAGE 138

CHAPTER 6 NONVERBAL COMMUNICATION 170

PART THREE: DIMENSIONS OF INTERPERSONAL RELATIONSHIPS

CHAPTER 9 DYNAMICS OF INTERPERSONAL RELATIONSHIPS 268

CHAPTER 10 COMMUNICATION IN CLOSE RELATIONSHIPS: FRIENDS, FAMILY, AND ROMANTIC PARTNERS 300

CHAPTER 11 COMMUNICATION CLIMATE 336

CHAPTER 12 MANAGING CONFLICT 366

Preface

Most of us who introduce students to the field of interpersonal communication search for the "sweet spot" that strikes a balance between academic rigor and user friendliness. The growing use of *Interplay* suggests that both professors and students have found that this book does a good job of finding that spot—connecting scholarship to everyday life and providing tools for understanding and enhancing communication in important relationships. We hope you agree.

In this edition of *Interplay*, we build on the proven approach that has served students and professors over three decades. The book's accessible writing style is based on the belief that even complicated ideas can be presented in a straightforward way. A variety of thought-provoking photos, sidebars, and cartoons make the subject more interesting and compelling than text alone can do. In terms of its scholarly grounding, in this edition, we cite more than 1,800 sources, about a third of which are new to this edition. Research and theory aren't presented for their own sake, but rather to support insights about how the process of interpersonal communication operates in everyday life.

NEW IN THIS EDITION

Although the overall structure of the book will be familiar to long-time users, several changes enhance its usability and keep the content up to date. The three most visible updates involve

- Expanded and updated coverage of **social media**: Throughout the book, we address the revolutionary impact of social media on personal relationships. An overview titled "Social Media and Interpersonal Communication" now appears in Chapter 1, where we introduce key terms and concepts. Expanded coverage of social media appears in the body of every chapter and also in sidebars, photos, self-assessments, and activities.

- Expanded and reworked discussions of **relational contexts**: We have thoroughly reworked coverage of communication in close relationships and moved it to Chapter 10. In addition to expanded treatment of communication among friends and family, this chapter includes a new section on "Communication in Romantic Relationships" in response to the requests of many readers.

- **Contemporary examples from film, television, and popular culture** with a corresponding **YouTube channel** to launch lectures: We have updated almost all of the film and TV examples in the book and added even more in this edition, along with other examples from today's world. Video clips for many of these examples and more are now available on a YouTube channel, accessible via the companion website at **www.oup.com/us/adler**

We have made many changes to individual chapters to address the latest communication research and changing communication practices. These include the following:

- In Chapter 2, we address the impact of **co-cultural factors**—including ethnicity, gender identity, age, and socioeconomic status—on interpersonal communication.
- In Chapter 4, we explain **perceptual biases** such as the primacy effect, the horns effect, and the fundamental attribution error.
- In Chapter 5, we discuss **gender effects** on language use (both in person and online).
- In Chapter 7, we introduce new research on **listening styles**.
- In Chapter 8, we include a new discussion of how **facilitative emotions** shape relationships.
- In Chapter 9, we devote more coverage to **relational maintenance** and **social support**.
- In Chapter 11, we now have **invitational communication** as an organizing principle for communication climate.

In addition to updates in the text proper, even a quick look at this edition will show that numerous changes in sidebars, boxes, and images help keep the book engaging and current:

- **Focus on Research** boxes cover new, timely subjects including interpersonal dimensions of tweeting, relational challenges of studying abroad, reflected appraisal in online postings, the negative consequences of fat talk, the different languages of texting and talking, exchanging advice online, cell phones and relational dialectics, and the implicit rules for Facebook friendships.
- **Dark Side of Communication** sidebars address problems including loneliness and the Internet, online hoaxes, the "Gaslight Effect," preferential treatment given to attractive people, abusive relationships, and updated looks at jealousy and cyberbullying.
- **Media Clips** use both television shows and films to dramatize how communication concepts operate in everyday life. New TV shows include *How I Met Your Mother* (transactional communication), *An Idiot Abroad* (intercultural competence), *The Big Bang Theory* (emotional intelligence), *Scandal* (nonverbal deception clues), and *Catfish* (online impression management). New feature films include *Her* (social media and intimacy), *The Way Way Back* (self-concept), *Stories We Tell* (personal narratives), *Our Idiot Brother* (family boundaries), *Bully* (aggression), and *The Hunger Games* (conflict).
- **At Work** boxes help readers apply scholarship to their careers. Topics include identity management in the workplace, the effects of swearing on the job, the role of touch in career success, and the value of cultivating social capital. A new box on organizational culture appears in Chapter 2.
- **Learning Objectives** now correspond to the major sections in each chapter, clarifying what information students need to know and where to find it.

- **Assessing Your Communication** instruments in every chapter help students understand how they currently communicate and provide a vision for interacting more effectively in important relationships. New instruments in this edition include measurements for the use of social media, online and offline self-disclosure, empathy, listening styles, and family communication patterns.
- At the end of each chapter, new **Check Your Understanding** summary points, questions, and prompts are linked to Learning Objectives. They help students evaluate how much they have learned and apply key concepts to their own lives.
- **Activities** now emphasize collaborative learning to enhance understanding.

DIGITAL AND PRINT ANCILLARY RESOURCES

In addition to the text, a variety of ancillaries provide resources for both instructors and students.

For Instructors

- The **Ancillary Resource Center (ARC)** at **www.oup-arc.com** is a convenient, instructor-focused, single destination for resources to accompany *Interplay*. Accessed online through individual user accounts, the ARC provides instructors with up-to-date ancillaries at any time while guaranteeing the security of grade-significant resources. In addition, it allows OUP to keep instructors informed when new content becomes available. The ARC for *Interplay* contains a variety of materials to aid in teaching:

  - An enhanced **Instructor's Manual and Computerized Test Bank** provides teaching tips, exercises, and test questions that will prove useful to both new and veteran instructors. The Instructor's Manual includes teaching strategies, course outlines, chapter exercises, discussion questions, and unit windups. The comprehensive Test Bank offers approximately 100 class-tested exam questions per chapter in multiple-choice, true/false, essay, and matching formats.
  - Newly revised **PowerPoint-based lecture slides**.
  - **Links to supplemental materials and films**.
  - *NEW!* A **YouTube channel of video clips** to launch lectures and provide examples tied to the text.

- *Now Playing: Instructor's Edition*, an instructor-only print supplement, includes an introduction on how to incorporate film examples in class, sample responses to the numerous discussion questions in the student edition of *Now Playing*, viewing guides, additional films, and references.
- **Course cartridges for a variety of e-learning environments** allow instructors to create their own course websites with the interactive material from the ARC and student companion website.

Contact your Oxford University Press representative or call (800) 280–0280 for more information on accessing these resources.

For Students

- *Now Playing: Learning Communication through Film*, available as an optional printed product, looks at contemporary and classic feature films through the lens of communication principles. Authored by Darin Garard of Santa Barbara City College, *Now Playing* illustrates a variety of both individual scenes and full-length films, highlighting concepts and offering discussion questions for a mass medium that is interactive, familiar, and easily accessible.
- The **companion website** at www.oup.com/us/adler offers a wealth of resources including exercises, flashcards for key terms in the book, interactive self-tests, and links to a variety of communication-related websites such as *Now Playing* online.

ACKNOWLEDGMENTS

The book you are reading wouldn't have been possible without the help of many talented people. We are grateful to the many colleagues whose suggestions have helped make this book a far better one:

Angie M. S. Anderson
Anoka-Ramsey Community College

Nancy Bandiera
Charleston Southern University

Sharon Beal
Long Beach City College/Chapman University

Constance Berman
Berkshire Community College

Sandra Bodin-Lerner
Kean University

Leeva Chung
University of San Diego

Kathleen Czech
Point Loma Nazarene University

Andrea M. Davis
University of South Carolina Upstate

Susan Fletcher
Hocking College

Lowell Habel
Chapman University

Brittany W. Hochstaetter
Wake Technical Community College

Joy A. Jones
Atlantic Cape Community College

Betty Kennan
Radford University

Shyla Lefever
Old Dominion University

Joey Pogue
Pittsburg State University

Rasha I. Ramzy
Georgia State University

Rachel Reznik
Elmhurst College

Patricia Smith Ollry
Concordia University Irvine

Julie Simanski
Des Moines Area Community College

Linda K. Stewart
Cochise College

Matthew Taylor
Lone Star College—Fairbanks Center

Lindsay Timmerman
University of Wisconsin-Milwaukee

Judith Vogel
Des Moines Area Community College

Emanuelle Wessels
Missouri State University

Interplay continues to benefit from the contributions of these colleagues who helped shape previous editions:

Marcanne Andersen
Anoka Ramsey Community College

Aurora Auter
University of Southwestern Louisiana

Heather Bixler
College of the Sequoias

Colleen Butcher
University of Florida

Kathleen Czech
Point Loma Nazarene University

Katrina Eicher
Elizabethtown Community College

Karyn Friesen
Lone Star College—Montgomery

Kristin K. Froemling
Radford University

Darlene J. Geiger
Portland State University

Debra Gonsher
Bronx Community College

Em Griffin
Wheaton College

Gail Hankins
Wake Technical College

Meredith Harrigan
SUNY Geneseo

Kristin Haun
University of Tennessee

Lisa C. Hebert
Louisiana State University

Shaorong Huang
*Raymond Walters College—
University of Cincinnati*

Beverly Merrill Kelley
California Lutheran University

Anastasia Kurylo
Marymount Manhattan College

Andrea Lambert South
Northern Kentucky University

Phil Martin
North Central State College

Tim Moreland
Catawba College

Mark Morman
Baylor University

Kelly Morrison
Michigan State University

Johance F. Murray
*Hostos Community College/
CUNY*

Noreen Mysyk
North Central College

Gretchen R. Norling
University of West Florida

Tracey Powers
Central Arizona College

Laurie Pratt
Chaffey College

Narissra Maria Punyanunt-Carter
Texas Tech University

Elizabeth Ribarsky
University of Illinois—Springfield

Gregory W. Rickert
Lexington Community College

Jennifer A. Samp
University of Georgia

Julie Simanski
Des Moines Area Community College

Debbie Sonandre
Tacoma Community College

Renee Strom
Saint Cloud State University

Dennis Sutton
Grand Rapids Community College

Lindsay Timmerman
University of Wisconsin—Milwaukee

Michael Wittig
Waukesha County Technical College

Gordon Young
Kingsborough Community College

We salute the team of hardworking professionals at Oxford University Press, led and inspired by the masterful John Challice; Mark Haynes, our hands-on Editor; Michele Laseau, Art Director; George Widmer, Senior Designer; David Bradley, Senior Production Editor; Lisa Grzan, Production Manager; and Paul Longo and Grace Ross, Editorial Assistants. We're also grateful for the oversight of Editorial Director Patrick Lynch and Director of Development Thom Holmes. Our Developmental Editors, Lauren Mine and Lisa Sussman, deserve special acknowledgment—a full account of their contributions would require a book of its own. Our thanks also go to Deanna Hegle for her copyediting talents and Susan Monahan for crafting the useful indexes. Sherri Adler chose the evocative photos that help make *Interplay* unique. We continue to value the legacy of our former editor Peter Labella.

ABOUT THE AUTHORS

Ronald B. Adler is Professor Emeritus of Communication at Santa Barbara City College. He is coauthor of *Understanding Human Communication*, Twelfth Edition (OUP, 2014); *Essential Communication* (OUP, 2015); *Looking Out, Looking In* (2014); and *Communicating at Work: Principles and Practices for Business and the Professions* (2013). In addition to his academic pursuits, Ron works with businesses and nonprofit agencies to improve communication among coworkers as well as with clients and the public.

Lawrence B. Rosenfeld is Professor of Communication Studies, University of North Carolina at Chapel Hill. His articles appear in journals in communication, education, social work, sport psychology, and psychology; and he is the author of books on small group, interpersonal, and nonverbal communication. His most recent book is *When Their World Falls Apart: Helping Families and Children Manage the Effects of Disasters* (NASW Press, 2010). In 2000, Lawrence received the Donald H. Eckroyd Award for Outstanding Teaching in Higher Education from the National Communication Association; and in 2006 received the Gerald M. Phillips Award for Applied Communication Research from the same national communication organization. In 2012, he received the William C. Friday Award for Excellence in Teaching from the University of North Carolina at Chapel Hill.

Russell F. Proctor II is Professor of Communication Studies at Northern Kentucky University (NKU). He teaches courses in interpersonal communication, interviewing, and communication pedagogy; and he won NKU's Outstanding Professor Award in 1997. Russ has also received recognition for his teaching from the National Communication Association, the Central States Communication Association, and the Kentucky Communication Association. In addition to his work on *Interplay*, he is coauthor (with Ron Adler) of *Looking Out, Looking In* (2014).

INTERPLAY

chapter 1

Interpersonal Process

CHAPTER OUTLINE

LEARNING OBJECTIVES

1.1 Recognize the needs that communication satisfies.
1.2 Explain the relational, transactional nature of interpersonal communication.
1.3 Identify characteristics of effective communication and competent communicators.
1.4 Understand the advantages and drawbacks of various social media communication channels in relation to face-to-face communication.

EVERYONE COMMUNICATES. Students and professors, parents and children, employers and employees, friends, strangers, and enemies—all communicate. We have been communicating with others from earliest childhood and will almost certainly keep doing so until we die.

Why study an activity you've done your entire life? First, studying interpersonal communication will give you a new look at a familiar topic. For instance, you may not have given much thought to the notion that you can't *not* communicate or that more communication doesn't always improve relationships—topics that we examine a few pages from now. In this sense, exploring human communication is rather like studying anatomy or botany—everyday objects and processes take on new meaning.

There is a second, more compelling reason for studying interpersonal communication. To put it bluntly, all of us could learn to communicate more effectively. In a nationwide survey, "lack of effective communication" was identified as the cause of relational breakups more often than any other reason, including money, relatives or in-laws, sexual problems, previous relationships, or children (National Communication Association, 1999). Ineffective communication is also a major problem in the workplace, as indicated by 62 percent of executives in a recent survey (American Management Association, 2012).

If you pause now and make a mental list of communication problems you have encountered, you'll probably see that no matter how successful your relationships are at home, with friends, at school, and at work, there is plenty of room for improvement in your everyday life. The information that follows will help you improve the way you communicate with some of the people who matter most to you.

WHY WE COMMUNICATE

Research demonstrating the importance of communication has been around longer than you might think. Frederick II, emperor of the Holy Roman Empire from 1220 to 1250, was called *stupor mundi*—"wonder of the world"—by his admiring subjects. Along with displaying administrative and military talents, Frederick was a leading scientist of his time, although some of his experiments were dramatically inhumane. A medieval historian described one:

> He bade foster mothers and nurses to suckle the children, to bathe and wash them, but in no way to prattle with them, for he wanted to learn whether they would speak the Hebrew language, which was the oldest, or Greek, or Latin, or Arabic, or perhaps the language of their parents, of whom they had been born. But he labored in vain because all the children died. For they could not live without the petting and joyful faces and loving words of their foster mothers. (Ross & McLaughlin, 1949, p. 366)

Fortunately, contemporary researchers have found less barbaric ways to illustrate the importance of communication. In one study of isolation, five participants were paid to remain alone in a locked room. One lasted for 8 days. Three held out for 2 days, one commenting "Never again." The fifth participant lasted only 2 hours (Schachter, 1959).

The need for contact and companionship is just as strong outside the laboratory, as individuals who have led solitary lives by choice or necessity have discovered. W. Carl Jackson, an adventurer who sailed across the Atlantic Ocean alone in 51 days, summarized the feelings common to most loners in a post-voyage interview:

> I found the loneliness of the second month almost excruciating. I always thought of myself as self-sufficient, but I found life without people had no meaning. I had a definite need for somebody to talk to, someone real, alive, and breathing. (Jackson, 1978, p. 2)

You might claim that solitude would be a welcome relief from the irritations of everyday life. It's true that all of us need time by ourselves, often more than we get. On the other hand, each of us has a point beyond which we do not want to be alone. Beyond this point, solitude changes from a pleasurable to a painful condition. In other words, we all need people. We all need to communicate.

PHYSICAL NEEDS

Communication is so important that its presence or absence affects health. Recent studies confirm that people who process a negative experience by talking about it report improved life satisfaction, as well as enhanced mental and physical health, compared with those who think privately about it (Francis, 2003; Sousa, 2002). A study conducted with police officers found that being able to talk easily with colleagues and supervisors about work-related trauma was linked to greater physical and mental health (Stephens & Long, 2000). And a broader study of over 3,500 people ages 24–96 revealed that as little as 10 minutes of talking, face to face or by phone, improves memory and boosts intellectual function (Ybarra et al., 2008).

In extreme cases, communication can even become a matter of life or death. When he was a Navy pilot, U.S. Senator John McCain was shot down over North Vietnam and held as a prisoner of war (POW) for 6 years, often in solitary confinement. POWs set up clandestine codes in which they sent messages by tapping on walls to laboriously spell out words. McCain describes the importance of keeping contact and the risks that inmates would take to maintain contact with one another:

> The punishment for communicating could be severe, and a few POWs, having been caught and beaten for their efforts, had their spirits broken as their bodies were battered. Terrified of a return trip to the punishment room, they would lie still in their cells when their comrades tried to tap them up on the wall. Very few would remain uncommunicative for long. To suffer all this alone was less tolerable than torture. Withdrawing in silence from the fellowship of other Americans . . . was to us the approach of death. (McCain, 1999, p. 12)

Communication isn't a necessity just for prisoners of war. Evidence gathered by a host of medical researchers and social scientists (e.g.,

Braithwaite et al., 2010; Cole et al., 2007; Fitzpatrick & Vangelisti, 2001; Holt-Lunstad et al., 2010; Mendes de Leon, 2005; Parker-Pope, 2010; Uchino, 2004) has shown that satisfying relationships can literally be a matter of life and death for people who lead normal lives. For example

- A meta-analysis of nearly 150 studies and over 300,000 participants found that socially connected people—those with strong networks of family and friends—live an average of 3.7 years longer than those who are socially isolated.
- People with strong relationships have significantly lower risks of coronary disease, regardless of whether they smoke, drink alcoholic beverages, or exercise regularly.
- Divorced, separated, and widowed people are 5 to 10 times more likely to need mental hospitalization than their married counterparts. Happily married people also have lower incidences of pneumonia, surgery, and cancer than single people. (It's important to note that the *quality* of the relationship is more important than the institution of marriage in these studies.)
- Pregnant women under stress and without supportive relationships have three times more complications than pregnant women who suffer from the same stress but have strong social support.
- Socially isolated people are four times more susceptible to the common cold than those who have active social networks.
- College students in committed relationships experience fewer mental health problems than those not in committed relationships.
- Close relationships offer opportunities for meeting touch needs—from a pat on the back to sexual intimacy—that provide mental, emotional, and physiological benefits (we explore this topic in detail in Chapter 6).

Research like this demonstrates the importance of meaningful personal relationships, and it explains the conclusion of social scientists that communication is essential. Not everyone needs the same amount of contact, and the quality of communication is almost certainly as important as the quantity. Nonetheless, the point remains: Personal communication is essential for our well-being.

IDENTITY NEEDS

Communication does more than enable us to survive. It is the way—indeed, the *major* way—we learn who we are (Fogel et al., 2002; Harwood, 2005). As you'll read in Chapter 3, our sense of identity comes from the way we interact with other people. Are we smart or stupid, attractive or ugly, skillful or inept? The answers to these questions don't come from looking in the mirror. We decide who we are based on how others react to us.

Deprived of communication with others, we would have no sense of identity. Consider the case of the famous "Wild Boy of Aveyron," who spent his early childhood without any apparent human contact. The boy was discovered in January 1800 while digging for vegetables in a French village garden. He could not speak, and he showed no behaviors one would expect in a social human. More significant than this absence of social skills was his lack of any identity as a human being. As author Roger Shattuck (1980, p. 37) put it, "The boy had no human sense of being in the world. He had no sense of himself as a person related to other persons." Only after the influence of a loving "mother" did the boy begin to behave—and, we can imagine, think of himself—as a human.

Contemporary stories support the essential role communication plays in shaping identity. In 1970, authorities discovered a 12-year-old girl (whom they called "Genie") who had spent virtually all her life in an otherwise empty, darkened bedroom with almost no human contact. The child could not speak and had no sense of herself as a person until she was removed from her family and "nourished" by a team of caregivers (Rymer, 1993).

Like Genie and the boy of Aveyron, each of us enters the world with little or no sense of identity. We gain an idea of who we are from the way others define us. As we explain in Chapter 3, the messages we receive in early childhood are the strongest identity shapers, but the influence of others continues throughout life.

SOCIAL NEEDS

Some social scientists have argued that besides helping define who we are, communication is the principal way relationships are created (Duck & Pittman, 1994; Hubbard et al., 2009). For example, Julie Yingling (1994) asserts that children "talk friendships into existence." The same can be said for adult relationships: It's impossible to imagine how they could exist without communication, which satisfies a variety of needs such as giving and receiving affection, having fun, helping others and being helped, and giving us a sense of self-worth (Rubin et al., 1988). Because relationships with others are so vital, some theorists have gone so far as to argue that communication is the primary goal of human existence. Anthropologist Walter Goldschmidt (1990) calls the drive for meeting social needs through communication "the human career."

There's a strong link between the quality of communication and the success of relationships. For example, children who grow up in strong conversation-oriented families report having more satisfying same-sex friendships and romantic relationships when they become adults (Koesten, 2004). Women in one study reported that "socializing" contributed more to a satisfying life than virtually any other activity, including relaxing, shopping, eating, exercise, television, or prayer (Kahneman et al., 2004).

Despite knowing that communication is vital to social satisfaction, evidence suggests that many people aren't very successful at managing their interpersonal relationships. For example, one study revealed that one quarter of the more than 4,000 adults surveyed knew more about their dogs

DARK SIDE OF COMMUNICATION
LONELINESS AND THE INTERNET: A DELICATE BALANCE

It's Friday night and you have no plans. You don't want to spend the evening by yourself, but it feels like a chore to go out and socialize. Instead, you hunker down in front of your computer and interact with others on the Internet—perhaps with friends, or maybe with strangers. Is that a good way to meet your social needs? The simple answer is "occasionally, but not regularly."

Research about online communication and loneliness presents a mixed bag. Connecting with others in cyberspace can help alleviate lonely feelings (Lee et al., 2013), particularly for those who find it challenging to get out and about (Cotten et al., 2013). On the other hand, there's a correlation between loneliness and what social scientists call a *preference for online social interaction* (Caplan, 2003). The cause-effect relationship isn't always clear, but research shows that lonely people prefer to interact with others online, which can lead to problematic Internet use, which can create a greater sense of loneliness (Kim et al., 2009).

The key to healthy communication lies in a principle we discuss frequently in this book: all things in moderation. When online communication complements and reinforces in-person relationships, it can be a wonderful tool for meeting social needs. When it mostly or completely replaces face-to-face interaction, there may be cause for concern. The Assessing Your Communication box on page 26 can help you determine whether your online and in-person communication are in balance.

than they did about their neighbors' backgrounds (Rochmis, 2000). Research also shows that the number of friendships is in decline. One survey (McPherson et al., 2006) reported that in 1985, Americans had an average of 2.94 close friends. Twenty years later, that number had dropped to 2.08. It's worth noting that more-educated Americans reported having larger and more diverse networks. In other words, a higher education can enhance your relational life as well as your intellect.

PRACTICAL NEEDS

We shouldn't overlook the everyday, important functions communication serves. Communication is the tool that lets us tell the hairstylist to take just a little off the sides, direct the doctor to where it hurts, and inform the plumber that the broken pipe needs attention *now*!

Beyond these obvious needs, a wealth of research demonstrates that communication is an essential ingredient for success in virtually every career. (See the At Work box on page 9.) On-the-job communication skills can even make the difference between life and death for doctors, nurses, and other medical practitioners. Researchers discovered that "poor communication" was the root of over 60 percent of reported medical errors—including death, serious physical injury, and psychological trauma (Joint Commission on Accreditation of Healthcare, 2008; Strachan 2004). Studies also show a significant difference between the communication skills of physicians who had no malpractice claims against them and doctors with previous claims (Rodriguez et al., 2008).

Communication is just as important outside of work. For example, married couples who are effective communicators report happier relationships than less skillful husbands and wives (Kirchler, 1988; Ridley et al., 2001)—a finding that has been supported across cultures (Rehman & Holtzworth-Munroe, 2007). And the effects of work–family conflict—a common occurrence that negatively affects marital satisfaction—can be mitigated with constructive communication (Carroll et al., 2013). In school, grade-point

● COMMUNICATION AND CAREER ADVANCEMENT   @WORK

No matter what the field, research confirms what experienced workers already know—that communication skills are crucial in finding and succeeding in a job. A survey of business leaders rated abilities in spoken and written communication as the most important skills for college graduates to possess (Supiano, 2013). Similarly, the National Association of Colleges and Employers (NACE) identified verbal communication skills as the quality employers seek most in job candidates (National Association of Colleges and Employers, 2010, 2013)—a finding that has been confirmed year after year in their reports. "Employers consistently place communication skills at the top of the list of key skills," says Marilyn Mackes, NACE executive director.

Once you're hired, the need for communication skills is important in virtually every career. Engineers spend the bulk of their working lives speaking and listening, mostly in one-on-one and small-group settings (Darling & Dannels, 2003). Accounting professionals spend 80 percent of their time on the job communicating with others, individually and in groups (Nellermoe et al., 1999). Oral and written communication skills are also vital in the computer industry, according to Silicon Valley employers (Stevens, 2005). Writing in *The Scientist* magazine, a commentator echoed this sentiment: "If I give any advice, it is that you can never do enough training around your overall communication skills" (Richman, 2002).

averages of college students are related positively to their communication competence (Hawken et al., 1991; Rubin & Graham, 1988). In addition, school adjustment, dropout rate, and overall school achievement are highly related to students' having strong, supportive relationships (Heard, 2007; Rosenfeld & Richman, 1999).

Psychologist Abraham Maslow (1968) suggests that human needs fall into five categories, each of which must be satisfied before we concern ourselves with the next one. As you read about each need, think about the ways in which communication is often necessary to satisfy it. The most basic needs are *physical*: sufficient air, water, food, and rest and the ability to reproduce as a species. The second category of Maslow's needs involves *safety*: protection from threats to our well-being. Beyond physical and safety concerns are the *social* needs we have already mentioned. Next, Maslow suggests that each of us has the need for *self-esteem*: the desire to believe that we are worthwhile, valuable people. The final category of needs involves *self-actualization*: the desire to develop our potential to the maximum, to become the best person we can be.

THE COMMUNICATION PROCESS

So far, we have talked about communication as if its meaning were perfectly clear. In fact, scholars have debated the definition of communication for years (Littlejohn, 2008). Despite their many disagreements, most would concur that at its essence, **communication** is about using messages to generate meanings (Korn et al., 2000). Notice how this basic definition holds true across a variety of contexts—public speaking, small groups, mass media, and so forth. Our goal in this section is to explain how messages and meanings are created in interpersonal communication and to describe the many factors involved in this complex process.

A MODEL OF COMMUNICATION

As the old saying goes, "A picture is worth a thousand words." That's what scientists had in mind when they began creating models of the communication process in the 1950s (Craig, 2009). These early models were simplistic and usually better suited for explaining mass communication than the interpersonal variety. They characterized communication as a one-way, linear event—something that a sender "does" by encoding a message and delivering it to a passive receiver who decodes it. This one-way process resembles an archer (the sender) shooting an arrow (the message) at a target (the receiver). Even in interpersonal settings, this linear approach sometimes makes sense. If you labor over a letter or e-mail to get the tone just right before sending it, your message is primarily a one-way effort.

Later models represented communication more like a tennis game, with people sending messages to receivers who responded with verbal or nonverbal **feedback** that indicates a response to the previous message. A back-and-forth chain of text messages seems to fit this description pretty well.

Over time, though, communication theorists have developed increasingly sophisticated *transactional communication models* in an attempt to depict all the factors that affect human interaction. No model can completely represent the process of communication, any more than a map can capture everything about the neighborhood where you live. Still, the model in Figure 1.1 provides a starting point for explaining the insights and principles discussed in the next section.

INSIGHTS FROM THE TRANSACTIONAL COMMUNICATION MODEL

Figure 1.1 reflects a number of important characteristics of transactional communication. As you read on, note how the following insights help explain the richness of this process.

Sending and Receiving Are Usually Simultaneous

Some forms of communication, such as e-mail, texting, voice messages, or "snail mail" letters, are asynchronous: There's a delay between when they are sent and received. But in face-to-face interaction, it's hard to distinguish sender and receiver. Consider a few examples:

- A teacher explaining a difficult concept to a student after class
- A parent lecturing a teenager about the family's curfew rules
- A salesperson giving a customer information about a product

The natural impulse is to identify the teacher, parent, and salesperson as senders, whereas the student, teenager, and customer are receivers. Now imagine a confused look on the student's face; the teenager interrupting

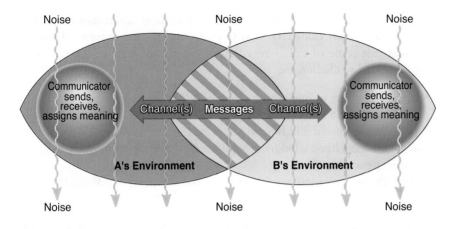

FIGURE 1.1 **Transactional Communication Model**

defensively; the customer blankly staring into the distance. It's easy to see that these verbal and nonverbal responses are messages being "sent," even while the other person is talking. Because it's often impossible to distinguish sender from receiver, our communication model replaces these roles with the more accurate term *communicator*. This term reflects the fact that—at least in face-to-face situations—people are simultaneously senders and receivers who exchange multiple messages.

Meanings Exist in and among People

Messages, whether they are verbal or nonverbal, don't have meanings in themselves. Rather, meanings reside in the people who express and interpret them. Imagine that a friend says, "I'm sorry," after showing up several hours late to a date. There are several possible "meanings" that this expression might have: a genuine apology, an insincere statement designed to defuse your anger, or even a sarcastic jibe. It's easy to imagine that your friend might mean one thing and you might have a different interpretation of it. The possibility of multiple interpretations means that it is often necessary to negotiate a shared meaning in order for satisfying communication to occur.

Environment and Noise Affect Communication

Problems often arise because communicators occupy different **environments** (sometimes called *contexts*): fields of experience that help them make sense of others' behavior. In communication terminology, environment refers not only to a physical location but also to the personal experiences and cultural background that participants bring to a conversation. You can appreciate the influence of environments by thinking about your beliefs about an important topic such as work, marriage, or government policies. Then imagine how your beliefs might be quite different if your personal history were different.

Notice how the model in Figure 1.1 shows that the environments of **A** and **B** overlap. This intersecting area represents the background that the communicators have in common. If this overlap didn't exist, communication would be difficult, if not impossible.

Whereas similar environments often facilitate communication, different backgrounds can make effective communication more challenging. Consider just some of the factors that might contribute to different environments, and to challenges:

- **A** might belong to one ethnic group and **B** to another.
- **A** might be rich and **B** poor.
- **A** might be rushed and **B** have nowhere to go.
- **A** might have lived a long, eventful life, and **B** is young and inexperienced.
- **A** might be passionately concerned with the subject and **B** indifferent to it.

Another factor in the environment that makes communication difficult is what scientists call **noise**: anything that interferes with the transmission and reception of a message. Three types of noise can disrupt communication. *External noise* includes those factors outside the receiver that make it difficult to hear, as well as many other kinds of distractions. For instance, loud music in a bar or a jackhammer grinding in the street might make it hard for you to pay attention to another person. *Physiological noise* involves biological factors in the receiver that interfere with accurate reception: hearing loss, illness, and so on. *Psychological noise* refers to cognitive factors that make communication less effective. For instance, a woman who is called "girl" may become so irritated that she has trouble listening objectively to the rest of a speaker's message.

Channels Make a Difference

Communication scholars use the term **channel** to describe the medium through which messages are exchanged. Along with face-to-face interaction, we have the option of using mediated channels such as phones, e-mail, and instant messages. The communication channel being used can affect the way a receiver responds to a message. For example, a typewritten love letter probably won't have the same effect as a handwritten expression of affection, and being fired from a job in person would likely feel different than getting the bad news in an e-mail.

Most people intuitively recognize that the selection of a channel depends in part on the kind of message they're sending. In one survey, Patrick O'Sullivan (2000) asked students to identify which channel they would find best for delivering a variety of messages. Most respondents said they would have little trouble sending positive messages face to face, but mediated channels had more appeal for sending negative messages (see also Feaster, 2010). You'll read much more about social media channels later in this chapter and throughout this book.

COMMUNICATION PRINCIPLES

In addition to the insights offered by the communication model, there are other principles that guide our understanding of communication.

Communication Is Transactional

By **transactional**, we mean that communication is a dynamic process that the participants create through their interaction with one another.

Perhaps the most important consequence of communication's transactional nature is the mutual influence that occurs when we interact. To put it simply, communication isn't something we do *to* others; rather, it is an activity we do *with* them. In this sense, communication is rather like dancing—at least the kind of dancing we do with partners.

Like dancing, communication depends on the behavior of a partner. A great dancer who doesn't consider and adapt to the skill level of his or her partner can make both of them look bad. In communication and dancing, even two talented partners don't guarantee success. When two skilled dancers perform without coordinating their movements, the results feel bad to the dancers and look foolish to an audience. You can probably think of people with whom you have difficulty communicating, and your exchanges are filled with awkward stops and starts—and misunderstandings.

Finally, relational communication—like dancing—is a unique creation that arises out of the way in which the partners interact. The way you dance probably varies from one partner to another because of its cooperative, transactional nature. Likewise, the way you communicate almost certainly varies with different partners. That's why competent communicators score high in adaptability, as we discuss later in this chapter.

Psychologist Kenneth Gergen (1991) captures the transactional nature of communication well when he points out how our success depends on interaction with others. As he says, "one cannot be 'attractive' without others who are attracted, a 'leader' without others willing to follow, or a 'loving person' without others to affirm with appreciation" (p. 158).

MEDIA CLIP
Transaction in Action:
How I Met Your Mother

The framing device for this TV series is that Ted (Josh Radnor) is in the future, describing to his children how he met their mother. Each episode chronicles the ever-evolving relationships he forges, maintains, or ends in pursuit of this woman. His core group of friends includes Marshall (Jason Segal) and Lily (Alyson Hannigan), a married couple who represent stability. Also in the group are Robin (Cobie Saunders) and Barney (Neil Patrick Harris), who are happily single in early episodes but eventually launch their own quests for lifelong partners.

Past events affect the dynamics of the group. For instance, Robin has been romantically involved with both Ted and Barney. Not only does that have an impact on Robin's ongoing relationships with these men, but it sometimes causes friction between Barney and Ted. What we see over the course of this series is that every interaction that takes place between the main characters plays a role in how they later relate to each other. This illustrates the irreversible, unrepeatable, and transactional nature of interpersonal communication.

Communication Can Be Intentional or Unintentional

Some communication is clearly deliberate: You probably plan your words carefully before asking the boss for a raise or offering constructive criticism. Some scholars (e.g., Motley, 1990) argue that only intentional messages like

"Let's stop this before we both say a lot of things we mean."

these qualify as communication. However, others (e.g., Baxter & Montgomery, 1996; Buck & VanLear, 2002) suggest that even unintentional behavior is communicative. Suppose, for instance, that a friend overhears you muttering complaints to yourself. Even though you didn't intend for her to hear your remarks, they certainly did carry a message. In addition to these slips of the tongue, we unintentionally send many nonverbal messages. You might not be aware of your sour expression, impatient shifting, or sigh of boredom, but others view them nonetheless.

Even the seeming absence of a behavior has communicative value. Recall the times when you sent an e-mail or left a voice mail message and received no reply. You probably assigned some meaning to the nonresponse. Was the other person angry? Indifferent? Too busy to reply? Whether your hunch was correct, the point remains: All behavior has communicative value. "Nothing" never happens.

In *Interplay* we look at the communicative value of both intentional and unintentional behavior. This book takes the position that whatever you do—whether you speak or remain silent, confront or avoid, show emotion or keep a poker face—you provide information to others about your thoughts and feelings. In this sense, we are like transmitters that can't be shut off.

Communication Is Irreversible

We sometimes wish that we could back up in time, erasing words or acts and replacing them with better alternatives. Unfortunately, such reversal is impossible. Sometimes, further explanation can clear up another's confusion or an apology can mollify another's hurt feelings, but other times no amount of explanation can erase the impression you have created. It is no more possible to "unreceive" a message than to "unsqueeze" a tube of toothpaste. The same is true of most electronic messages: Once you hit "send," they can't be taken back. Words said, messages sent, and deeds done are irretrievable.

Communication Is Unrepeatable

Because communication is an ongoing process, an event cannot be repeated. The friendly smile that worked so well when meeting a stranger last week may not succeed with the person you encounter tomorrow. Even with the same person, it's impossible to re-create an event. Why? Because both you and the other person have changed. You've both lived longer. The behavior isn't original. Your feelings about each other may have changed. You need not constantly invent new ways to act around familiar people, but you should realize that the "same" words and behavior are different each time they are spoken or performed.

Communication Has a Content Dimension and a Relational Dimension

Virtually all exchanges have content and relational dimensions. The **content dimension** involves the information being explicitly discussed: "Please pass the salt"; "Not now, I'm tired"; "You forgot to buy a quart of milk." In addition to this sort of obvious content, all messages also have a **relational dimension** (Watzlawick et al., 1967) that expresses how you feel about the other person: whether you like or dislike the other person, feel in control or subordinate, feel comfortable or anxious, and so on. For instance, consider how many different relational messages you could communicate by simply saying "Thanks a lot" in different ways. You can appreciate the importance of communication's relational dimension by looking at the photo on this page. This image says as much about the relationship between the two people as it does about what they're discussing.

Sometimes the content dimension of a message is all that matters. For example, you may not care how the directory assistance operator feels about you as long as you get the phone number you're seeking. In a qualitative sense, however, the relational dimension of a message is often more important than the content under discussion. This explains why disputes over apparently trivial subjects become so important. In such cases, we're not really arguing over whose turn it is to take out the trash or whether to play tennis or go for a swim. Instead, we're disputing the nature of the relationship. Who's in control? How important are we to each other? In Chapter 9, we explore several key relational issues in detail. For now, we turn our attention to the connection between relationships and interpersonal communication.

CHARACTERISTICS OF INTERPERSONAL COMMUNICATION

It's impossible to talk about *interpersonal* communication without discussing *relationships*. As we just noted, every exchange—even the most mundane— has a relational dimension. Visualize a brief conversation you've recently had with a cashier at the checkout counter. Was it friendly or indifferent? Rushed or more leisurely? Did the clerk seem genuinely helpful or superficial and mechanical? In every case, the messages exchanged between you and the cashier created and reflected some sort of relationship. In more meaningful relationships, communication is distinctive and nuanced—more *personal*. It's helpful, therefore, to view communication with others on a continuum, ranging from impersonal to interpersonal (see Figure 1.2).

Many of our interactions in life are relatively impersonal, but key relationships are characterized by highly interpersonal communication—at least enough of the time to keep the relationship meaningful.

Four features distinguish communication in highly interpersonal relationships from less personal ones:

- The first is *uniqueness*. Whereas impersonal exchanges are ritualized and governed by social rules, interpersonal exchanges are shaped by the nature and history of a particular relationship. For example, with one friend you might exchange good-natured insults, whereas with another

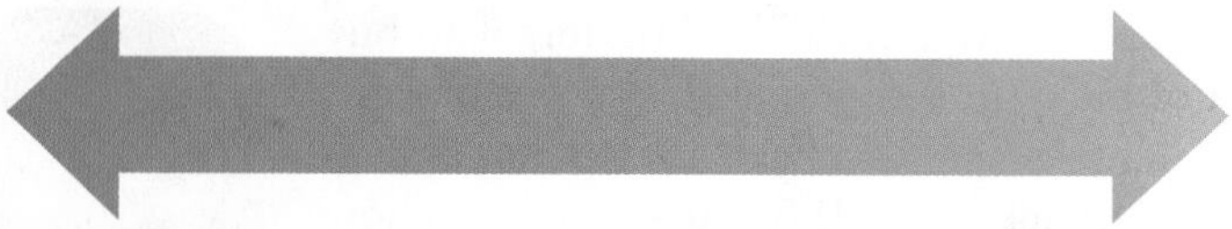

Highly Impersonal
(e.g., scheduling appointment,
answering phone survey)

Highly Interpersonal
(e.g., marriage proposal,
asking for forgiveness)

FIGURE 1.2 Impersonal–
Interpersonal Communication
Continuum

you are careful never to offend. Consider how you communicate with those closest to you, and you'll recognize that each relationship is defined by its own specific language, customs, and patterns.

- The second feature that distinguishes interpersonal communication is *interdependence*. Highly interpersonal communication exchanges reveal that the fate of the partners is connected. You might be able to brush off the anger, affection, excitement, or depression of someone with whom you share an impersonal relationship (such as a restaurant server you don't know), but in an interpersonal relationship the other's life affects you (if the same server is a close friend, you may empathize with his emotion).

- The third feature that distinguishes interpersonal communication is *self-disclosure*. In impersonal exchanges, we reveal little about ourselves; but interpersonal exchanges often include sharing important thoughts and feelings, and they reflect the communicators' comfort with one another. This doesn't mean that all highly interpersonal relationships are warm and caring or that all self-disclosure is positive. It's possible to reveal negative personal information: "I really hate when you do that!" But note you'd probably say that only to someone with whom you have an interpersonal relationship.

- The fourth feature that distinguishes interpersonal communication has to do with the *intrinsic rewards* of interacting. Communicators in relationships characterized by impersonal exchanges seek extrinsic rewards, payoffs that have little to do with the people involved. You listen to professors in class or talk to potential buyers of your used car in order to reach goals that have little to do with developing personal relationships. By contrast, you spend time in highly interpersonal relationships, such as relationships with friends and lovers, because of the intrinsic rewards that come from your communication: Just being with the other person is the reward. It doesn't matter what you talk about—developing the relationship is what's important.

Because interpersonal communication is characterized by the qualities of uniqueness, interdependence, self-disclosure, and intrinsic rewards, it forms just a small fraction of our interaction. The scarcity of interpersonal communication, however, contributes to its value (Mehl et al., 2010). Like precious and one-of-a-kind artwork, highly interpersonal communication is special because it is rare. It's even fairly scarce in close relationships, where much of our daily communication is comfortably mundane (Alberts et al., 2005). Those special relationships, however, provide the best opportunities

FOCUS ON RESEARCH
Interpersonal Dimensions of Tweeting

Twitter allows communicators to send short messages to a mass audience. It's tempting to think of tweeting as impersonal—but social scientists believe it's possible to create a sense of a personal connection through this social networking tool.

Communication researchers asked respondents to evaluate written messages from a local politician who was running for office. Some participants viewed the politician's words as an excerpt from a news article. Others viewed the same message as a Twitter feed from the candidate. The content was identical; only the formats differed. Those who read the Twitter version said they felt a greater sense of social presence and connection with the politician.

This was particularly true of participants with "less affiliative" (socially reserved) personalities. Moreover, those who viewed the Twitter version said they would be more likely to vote for the politician, in part because they felt a stronger bond with him.

The authors believe these results demonstrate the power of a communication channel to influence the perception of a message. When politicians interactively exchange messages with their Twitter followers, it enhances impressions even more (Parmelee & Bichard, 2012). Studies such as these show that electronic communication has far more interpersonal potential than was once predicted.

Lee, E., & Jang, J. (2013). Not so imaginary interpersonal contact with public figures on social network sites: How affiliative tendency moderates its effects. *Communication Research, 40,* 27–51.

to communicate interpersonally—and that's why we take a close look at them in Chapter 10.

COMMUNICATION MISCONCEPTIONS

Now that we've described what communication is, we need to identify some things it is not. Avoiding these common misconceptions (adapted from McCroskey & Richmond, 1996) can save you a great deal of trouble in your personal life.

Not All Communication Seeks Understanding

Most people operate on the flawed assumption that the goal of all communication is to maximize understanding between communicators. Although some understanding is necessary for us to coordinate our interactions, there are some types of communication in which understanding, as we usually conceive it, isn't the primary goal. Consider, for example

- *The social rituals we enact every day*. "How's it going?" you ask. "Great," the other person replies, even if he or she isn't actually feeling great. The primary goal in exchanges like these is mutual acknowledgment of one another's existence and value. The unstated message is "I consider you important enough to notice." There's obviously no serious attempt to exchange information (Burnard, 2003). An analysis of examples from Twitter shows how this social ritual to "keep in touch" can take place digitally as well as in person (Schandorf, 2013).

- *Many attempts to influence others.* A quick analysis of most television commercials shows that they are aimed at persuading viewers to buy products, not to help viewers understand the content of the ad. In the same way, many of our attempts at persuading others to act as we want don't involve a desire to get the other person to understand what we want—just to comply with our wishes.
- *Deliberate ambiguity and deception.* When you decline an unwanted invitation by saying "I can't make it," you probably want to create the impression that the decision is really beyond your control. (If your goal were to be perfectly clear, you might say, "I don't want to get together. In fact, I'd rather do almost anything than accept your invitation.") As we explain in detail in Chapter 3, people often lie or hedge their remarks precisely because they want to obscure their true thoughts and feelings.

More Communication Is Not Always Better

Whereas failure to communicate effectively can certainly cause problems, too much talking also can be a mistake. Sometimes excessive communication is simply unproductive, as when two people "talk a problem to death," going over the same ground again and again without making progress.

There are times when talking too much actually aggravates a problem. We've all had the experience of "talking ourselves into a hole"—making a bad situation worse by pursuing it too far. As McCroskey and Wheeless (1976, p. 5) put it, "More and more negative communication merely leads to more and more negative results." Even when relationships aren't troubled, less communication may be better than more. One study found that coworkers who aren't highly dependent on one another perform better when they don't spend a great deal of time talking together (Barrick et al., 2007). There are even times when no interaction is the best course. When two people are angry and hurt, they may say things they don't mean and will later regret. In such cases it's probably best to spend time cooling off, thinking about what to say and how to say it. Chapter 8 will help you decide when and how to share feelings.

Communication Will Not Solve All Problems

Sometimes even the best-planned, best-timed communication won't solve a problem. For example, imagine that you ask an instructor to explain why you received a poor grade on a project you believe deserved top marks. The professor clearly outlines the reasons why you received the low grade and sticks to that position after listening thoughtfully to your protests. Has communication solved the problem? Hardly.

Sometimes clear communication is even the cause of problems. Suppose, for example, that a friend asks you for an honest opinion of an expensive outfit he just bought. Your clear and sincere answer, "I think it makes you look fat," might do more harm than good. Deciding when and how to self-disclose isn't always easy. See Chapter 3 for suggestions.

Effective Communication Is Not a Natural Ability

Most people assume that communication is something that people can do without the need for training—rather like breathing. Although nearly everyone does manage to function passably without much formal communication training, most people operate at a level of effectiveness far below their potential. In fact, communication skills are rather like athletic ability. Even the most inept of us can learn to be more effective with training and practice, and even the most talented need to "keep in shape." With this in mind, we'll look at what's involved in communicating more competently.

COMMUNICATION COMPETENCE

"What does it take to communicate better?" is probably the most important question to ask as you read this book. Answering it has been one of the leading challenges for communication scholars. Although all the answers aren't in yet, research has identified a great deal of important and useful information about communication competence.

COMMUNICATION COMPETENCE DEFINED

Defining **communication competence** isn't as easy as it might seem. Although scholars continue to debate a precise definition, most agree that competent communication is both *effective* and *appropriate* (Spitzberg, 2000). To understand these two dimensions, consider how you might handle everyday communication challenges such as declining an unwanted invitation or communicating about a friend's annoying behavior. In cases such as these, *effective* communication would get the results you want. *Appropriate* communication would do so in a way that, in most cases, enhances the relationship in which it occurs. You can appreciate the importance of both appropriateness and effectiveness by imagining approaches that would satisfy one of these criteria but not the other. Effectiveness without appropriateness might achieve your goals, but leave others unhappy. Conversely, appropriateness without effectiveness might leave others content but you frustrated. With the goal of balancing effectiveness and appropriateness, the following paragraphs outline several important characteristics of communication competence.

There Is No Single "Ideal" or "Effective" Way to Communicate

Your own experience shows that a variety of communication styles can be effective. Some very successful communicators are serious, whereas others use humor; some are gregarious, others are quieter; and some are more straightforward, and others hint diplomatically. Just as there are many kinds of beautiful music or art, there are many kinds of competent communication. Furthermore, a type of communication that is competent in one setting might be a colossal blunder in another, and what one person thinks is competent may be seen by another as incompetent (Dunleavy & Martin, 2010). The joking insults you routinely trade with one friend might offend a sensitive family member, and last Saturday night's romantic approach would probably be out of place at work on Monday morning. This means that there can be no surefire list of rules or tips that will guarantee your success as a communicator.

In the Coen brothers' film *Inside Llewyn Davis*, the title character (Oscar Isaac) is a talented but interpersonally inept musician, struggling to make it in the 1960s Greenwich Village folk scene. He endlessly insults and imposes on his friends and family. "There must be someone in the five boroughs who isn't pissed at me," he laments. Spoiler alert: Davis's communication incompetence is not a career asset.

Flexibility is especially important when members of different cultures meet. Some communication skills seem to be universal (Ruben, 1989). Every culture has rules that require speakers to behave appropriately, for example. But the definition of what kind of communication is appropriate in a given situation varies considerably from one culture to another (Arasaratnam, 2007; Ulrey, 2001). On an obvious level, customs like belching after a meal or appearing nude in public that might be appropriate in some parts of the world would be considered outrageous in others. But there are more subtle differences in competent communication. For example, qualities such as self-disclosure and straight-talk that are valued in the United States are likely to be considered overly aggressive and insensitive in many Asian cultures where subtlety and indirectness are considered important (Kim et al., 1998; Yeh, 2010). We'll discuss the many dimensions of intercultural competence in Chapter 2.

Competence Is Situational

Because competent behavior varies so much from one situation and person to another, it's a mistake to think that communication competence is a trait that a person either possesses or lacks (Spitzberg, 1991). It's more accurate to talk about degrees or areas of competence.

You and the people you know are probably quite competent in some areas and less so in others. For example, you might deal quite skillfully with peers while feeling clumsy interacting with people much older or younger, wealthier or poorer, or more or less attractive than yourself. In fact, your competence may vary from situation to situation. This means it's an overgeneralization to say, in a moment of distress, "I'm a terrible communicator!" It's more accurate to say, "I didn't handle this situation very well, but I'm better in others."

Competence Can Be Learned

To some degree, biology is destiny when it comes to communication competence (Teven et al., 2010). Some research suggests that certain personality traits predispose people toward particular competence skills (Hullman et al., 2010). For instance, those who are agreeable and conscientious by nature find it easier to be appropriate and harder to be (and become) assertive and effective.

Fortunately, biology isn't the only factor that shapes how we communicate. Communication competence is, to a great degree, a set of skills that anyone can learn (Fortney et al., 2001). For instance, people with communication anxiety often benefit from interpersonal training sessions (Ayres & Hopf, 1993; Dwyer, 2000). Skills instruction has also been shown to help communicators in a variety of professional fields (Brown et al., 2010; Hyvarinen et al., 2010). Even without systematic training, it's possible to develop communication skills through the processes of observation and trial and error. We learn from our own successes and failures, as well as from observing other models—both positive and negative. And, of course, it's our hope that you will become a more competent communicator as a result of putting the information in this book to work.

CHARACTERISTICS OF COMPETENT COMMUNICATION

Despite the fact that competent communication varies from one situation to another, scholars have identified several common denominators that characterize effective communication in most contexts.

A Large Repertoire of Skills

As we've already seen, good communicators don't use the same approach in every situation. They know that sometimes it's best to be blunt and sometimes tactful; that there is a time to speak up and a time to be quiet.

The chances of reaching your personal and relational goals increase with the number of options you have about how to communicate (Pillet-Shore, 2011). For example, if you want to start a conversation with a stranger, all it might take to get the conversational ball rolling is a self-introduction. In other cases, seeking assistance might work well: "I've just moved here. What kind of neighborhood is the Eastside?" A third strategy is to ask a question about some situational feature: "I've never heard this band before. Do you know anything about them?" You could also offer a sincere compliment and follow it up with a question: "Great shoes! Where did you get them?"

Many people with disabilities have learned the value of having a repertoire of options available to manage unwanted offers of help (Braithwaite & Eckstein, 2003). Some of those options include performing a task quickly, before anyone has the chance to intervene; pretending not to hear the offer; accepting a well-intentioned invitation to avoid seeming rude or ungrateful; using humor to deflect a bid for help; declining a well-intentioned offer

FOCUS ON RESEARCH
How to (NOT) Antagonize Your Professor: Adapting E-Messages

Research shows that out-of-classroom communication (OCC) usually strengthens teacher–student bonds and improves learning. Most OCC exchanges used to take place in hallways and offices, but now they often occur online through e-mails (Young et al., 2011). A research team led by Keri Stephens investigated whether the writing style of student e-messages has an impact on their effectiveness.

The researchers asked college and university instructors to evaluate overly casual e-mails from students. These less-than-formal messages included a lack of openings/closings, incorrect punctuation and grammar, and shortcuts such as using "4" instead of "for." The findings aren't surprising. They include

- Highly casual e-mails lower instructors' appraisals of the students who sent them.
- Instructors are far less likely to comply with requests made in overly casual messages, compared with e-mails that are written more formally.
- Two violations that particularly bother instructors are e-mails not signed by the message sender and messages that include shortcuts such as "RU" instead of "are you."

Failing to adapt your message to the recipient runs the risk that your requests will backfire. This is important not only for student–instructor emails but also in every interpersonal interaction.

Stephens, K. K., Houser, M. L., & Cowan, R. L. (2009). R U able to meat me: The impact of students' overly casual email messages to instructors. *Communication Education, 58,* 303–326.

with thanks; and assertively refusing help from those who won't take no for an answer.

Just as a golfer has a wide range of clubs to use for various situations, a competent communicator has a large array of behaviors from which to choose.

Adaptability

Having a large repertoire of possible behaviors is one ingredient of competent communication, but you have to be able to choose the *right* one for a particular situation (Hullman, 2007). Effective communication means selecting appropriate responses for each situation—and for each recipient. The Focus on Research sidebar above describes how some college students don't adapt their messages when e-mailing instructors, creating a negative impression.

Ability to Perform Skillfully

Once you have chosen the appropriate way to communicate, you have to perform that behavior effectively (Barge & Little, 2008; Burleson, 2007). In communication, as in other activities, practice is the key to skillful performance. Much of the information in *Interplay* will introduce you to new tools for communicating, and the activities at the end of each chapter will help you practice them.

Involvement

Not surprisingly, effective communication occurs when the people care about one another and the topic at hand. Involvement has several dimensions. It includes commitment to the other person and the relationship, concern about the message being discussed, and a desire to make the relationship clearly useful.

Empathy/Perspective Taking

People have the best chance of developing an effective message when they understand and empathize with the other person's point of view (Baile & Constantini, 2013; Passalacqua & Harwood, 2012). Because others aren't always good at expressing their thoughts and feelings clearly, the ability to imagine how an issue might look from another's perspective suggests why empathy is such an important communication skill. And of course, it's not enough just to take another's perspective; it's vital to *communicate* that understanding through verbal and nonverbal responses (Kellas et al., 2013).

Cognitive Complexity

Cognitive complexity is the ability to construct a variety of different frameworks for viewing an issue. Imagine that a longtime friend seems to be angry with you. One possible explanation is that your friend is offended by something you've done. Another possibility is that something has happened in another part of your friend's life that is upsetting. Or perhaps nothing at all is wrong, and you're just being overly sensitive.

Researchers have found that a large number of constructs for interpreting the behavior of others leads to greater "conversational sensitivity," increasing the chances of acting in ways that will produce satisfying results (Burleson, 2011; MacGeorge & Wilkum, 2012). Not surprisingly, research also shows a connection between cognitive complexity and empathy (Joireman, 2004). The relationship makes sense: The more ways you have to understand others and interpret their behaviors, the greater is the likelihood that you can see and communicate about the world from their perspective.

Self-Monitoring

Psychologists use the term **self-monitoring** to describe the process of paying close attention to one's own behavior and using these observations to shape the way one behaves. Self-monitors are able to detach a part of their consciousness to observe their behavior from a detached viewpoint, making observations such as

"I'm making a fool out of myself."
"I'd better speak up now."
"This approach is working well. I'll keep it up."

It's no surprise that self-monitoring generally increases one's effectiveness as a communicator (Day et al., 2002; Turnley & Bolino, 2001). The President's Council of Economic Advisers maintains that greater "self-awareness, self-monitoring, and self-control" will help students be more successful when they enter the job market ("Preparing the Workers of Today," 2009, p. 10). The ability to ask yourself the question "How am I doing?" and to change your behavior if the answer isn't positive is a tremendous asset for communicators. People with poor self-monitoring skills often blunder through life, sometimes succeeding and sometimes failing, without the detachment to understand why.

It's worth noting that interpersonal competence isn't always just a matter of having the necessary "will and skill." Sometimes it can be hindered by **communication apprehension**: feelings of anxiety that arise in unfamiliar or difficult communication contexts. Although much of the research on communication apprehension is focused on public speaking anxiety (or "stage fright"), research shows that interpersonal settings can also be nerve-racking for some communicators (McCroskey, 2009). In Chapter 8, we take a close look at managing the kinds of debilitative emotions that usually accompany communication apprehension.

How does your behavior as an interpersonal communicator measure up against the standards of competence described in this chapter? Like most people, you will probably find some areas of your life that are very satisfying and others that you would like to change. As you read on in this book, realize that the information in each chapter offers advice that can help your communication become more productive and rewarding.

Although the qualities described here do play an important role in communicative competence, they can be ineffective when carried to excess (Spitzberg, 1994). For instance, one study found that too much self-monitoring can be detrimental to communication in intimate relationships (Wright et al., 2007). Even in less personal contexts, an excessive concern for appearance ("How do I sound?", "How am I doing?") overshadows the need to be faithful to one's true beliefs. Likewise, an excess of empathy and cognitive complexity can lead you to see all sides of an issue so well that you're incapable of acting. In other words, there is a curvilinear relationship among most of the elements described in these pages: Both a deficiency and an excess can lead to incompetent communication.

SOCIAL MEDIA AND INTERPERSONAL COMMUNICATION

Until a generation ago, face-to-face communication was essential to starting and maintaining most, if not all, interpersonal relationships. Other channels existed: the telephone (in an era of expensive long-distance rates and less-than-perfect technology) might have worked during temporary absences, and postal correspondence helped bridge the gap until the people involved could reconnect in person. Nonetheless, interpersonal communication seemed to require close physical proximity.

Now things are different. Obviously, face-to-face communication is still vitally important; but technology plays a key role in starting and maintaining relationships. The term that collectively describes all the channels that make remote personal communication possible is **social media**. You're using social media when you text message with friends or coworkers; post a tweet; exchange e-mails, texts, and instant messages; and when you use social networking sites such as Facebook. The number of social media technologies

has exploded in the past few decades, giving communicators today an array of choices that would have amazed someone from a previous era.

Social networking sites (SNS) provide a vivid example of the rapid changes in communication technology (Brenner & Smith, 2013). A generation ago, these sites didn't exist. As recently as 2005, only 8 percent of U.S. adults used them. By 2013, 72 percent of online adults were on social networking sites. Young adults have led the way, as almost 90 percent of Americans under age 30 are SNS users. Older communicators are coming aboard too. Out of 10 Internet users ages 50 to 64, 6 are now online social networkers, as are 43 percent of those ages 65 and older. It's not an overstatement to say that it's a new day and age in interpersonal communication.

And of course, getting on social networking sites is now easier than ever. As little as two decades ago, the biggest technological change in the lives of most Americans was a personal computer in the home. Today, cell phones and other mobile devices allow that computing power to be held in one's pocket, purse, or hand. Over a third of American adults own tablet computers (Zickuhr, 2013), and more than 90 percent own a cell phone (Duggan, 2013). These devices are important platforms for social networking. For instance, 81 percent of users send or receive text messages with their cell phones; 60 percent access the Internet with them; and more than 50 percent use their phones to email. The rise and ease of mobile devices means that our interpersonal communication with others is increasingly likely to occur through mediated channels. You can get a better understanding of the role social media play in your life by completing the assessment on page 26.

CHARACTERISTICS OF SOCIAL MEDIA

In many ways, mediated and face-to-face communication are similar. Both include the same elements described in this chapter—messages, channels, noise, and so forth. Both are used to satisfy the same physical, identity, social, and practical needs outlined on pages 5–9. Despite these similarities,

ASSESSING YOUR COMMUNICATION

Your Use of Social Media

Respond to each of the following statements using a scale ranging from 1 to 6, where 1 = strongly disagree and 6 = strongly agree. Consider inviting someone who knows you well to also rate you on each item.

For this assessment, the term "social media" refers primarily to social networking sites such as Facebook but also to text messaging, tweeting, instant messaging, and e-mailing.

_____ **1.** I feel disconnected from friends when I am not logged in to social media.

_____ **2.** I would like it if everyone used social media to communicate.

_____ **3.** I would be disappointed if I could not use social media at all.

_____ **4.** I get upset when I can't log in to social media.

_____ **5.** I prefer to communicate with others mainly through social media.

_____ **6.** Social media play an important role in my social relationships.

Adapted from Jenkins-Guarnieri, M. A., Wright, S. L., & Johnson, B. (2013). Development and validation of a social media use integration scale. *Psychology of Popular Media Culture, 2,* 38–50.

For scoring information, see page 35 at the end of the chapter.

communication by social media differs from the in-person variety in some important ways.

Leanness

Social scientists use the term **richness** to describe the abundance of non-verbal cues that add clarity to a verbal message (Otondo et al., 2008). Conversely, **leanness** describes messages that carry less information due to a lack of nonverbal cues. As you'll read in Chapter 6, face-to-face communication abounds with nonverbal messages that give communicators information about the meanings of one another's words. By comparison, most social media are much leaner. (See Figure 1.3.)

To appreciate how message leanness varies by medium, imagine you haven't heard from a friend in several weeks and you decide to ask, "Is anything wrong?" Your friend replies, "No, I'm fine." Would that response

Channel	Text	Voice	Audio-Visual	In-Person
Examples	E-mail, texting, letters, online posts	Phone calls, voice mail	Video conferencing, Skyping, FaceTime	Face-to-face interaction

Leaner ➤   Richer

FIGURE 1.3   Leanness–Richness Spectrum of Communication Channels

be more or less descriptive depending on whether you received it via text message, over the phone, or in person?

You almost certainly would be able to tell a great deal more from a face-to-face response because it would contain a richer array of cues: facial expressions, vocal tone, and so on. By contrast, a text message is lean because it contains only words. The phone message—containing vocal cues but no visual ones—would probably fall somewhere in between.

Because most mediated messages are leaner than the face-to-face variety, they can be harder to interpret with confidence. Irony and attempts at humor can easily be misunderstood, so as a receiver it's important to clarify your interpretations before jumping to conclusions. Adding phrases such as "just kidding" or emoticons like ☺ can help your lean messages become richer, but the potential for your sincerity being interpreted as sarcasm still exists. As a sender, think about how to send unambiguous messages so you aren't misunderstood.

The leanness of social media messages presents another challenge. Without nonverbal cues, online communicators can create idealized—and sometimes unrealistic—images of one another. As you'll read in Chapters 3 and 6, the absence of nonverbal cues allows communicators to manage their identities carefully. After all, it's a world without bad breath, unsightly blemishes, or stammering responses. Such conditions encourage participants to engage in what Joseph Walther (2007) calls **hyperpersonal communication**, accelerating the discussion of personal topics and relational development beyond what normally happens in face-to-face interaction. Research shows that online communicators self-disclose at higher rates and share more emotions than they would in person, often leading to a hastened (and perhaps premature) sense of relational intimacy (Jiang et al., 2011). This accelerated disclosure may explain why communicators who meet online sometimes have difficulty shifting to a face-to-face relationship (McEwan & Zanolla, 2013; Ramirez & Zhang, 2007).

It's important to remember that richer doesn't always mean better. There are times when a lean message is the best route to take. Maybe you don't want the other person to hear the quiver in your voice, see the sweat on your forehead, or notice the clothing you're wearing. Moreover, lean messages communicate less information about communicators' personal features. One study found that the text-only format of most online messages can bring people closer by minimizing the perception of differences due to gender, social class, race or ethnicity, and age (Hampton et al., 2009). When you want people to focus on what you're saying rather than your appearance, leaner communication can be advantageous.

Asynchronicity

As you read earlier, **asynchronous communication** occurs when there's a time gap between when a message is sent and when it's received. By contrast, **synchronous communication** is two-way and occurs in real time. In-person communication is synchronous, as are phone conversations. On the other hand, e-mail and voice mail messages are asynchronous. So are "snail mail" letters, Twitter postings, and text messages.

The asynchronous nature of most mediated messages makes them fundamentally different from synchronous communication. Most obviously, asynchronous messages give you the choice of not responding at all: You can ignore most problematic text messages without much fallout. That isn't a good option if the person who wants an answer gets you on the phone or confronts you in person.

Even if you want to respond, asynchronous media give you the chance to edit your reply. You can mull over different wording, or even ask others for advice about what to say. On the other hand, delaying a response to an asynchronous message can send a message of its own, intentionally or not ("I wonder why she hasn't texted me back?").

Permanence

What happens in a face-to-face conversation is transitory. By contrast, the text and video you send via hard copy or social media channels can be stored indefinitely and forwarded to others. The permanence of digital messages can be a plus. You can save and share the smartphone photos of your once-in-a-lifetime encounter with a celebrity. And if your boss e-mails you saying it's okay to come in late on Monday morning, you're covered if she later complains about your tardy arrival.

There can also be a downside to the enduring nature of digital messages. It's bad enough to blurt out a private thought or lash out in person, but at least there's no permanent record of your indiscretion. By contrast, a regrettable text message, e-mail, or web posting can be archived virtually forever. Even worse, it can be retrieved and forwarded in ways that can only be imagined in your worst nightmares. The best advice, then, is to take the same approach with mediated messages that you do in person: Think twice before saying something you might later regret. As one writer (Bennehum, 2005) put it, "Old e-mail never dies."

The characteristics of social media described in this section lead to certain advantages and disadvantages to communicating electronically, which are outlined in Table 1.1. As discussed earlier in this chapter, it's important to give thought to the best means for sending your personal and professional communication, because channels make a difference.

SOCIAL MEDIA AND RELATIONAL QUALITY

At first glance, social media might seem inferior to face-to-face interaction. As noted earlier, it lacks the rich array of nonverbal cues that are available in person. One observer put it this way: "E-mail is a way to stay in touch, but you can't share a coffee or a beer with somebody on e-mail or give them a hug" (Nie & Erbring, 2000, p. 19).

"Cyberpessimists" argue that there's a dark side to relying on mediated channels (for a review, see DeAndrea et al., 2010.) Some critics describe how the almost hypnotic attraction of an Internet connection discourages a sense of community (e.g., Putnam, 2000). Others claim that the "always on" nature of today's communication technology leads to more superficial relationships (Turkle, 2011). One study found that the mere presence of mobile

TABLE 1.1 Characteristics of Communication Channels

	SYNCHRONIZATION	CONTROL OVER MESSAGE	CONTROL OVER ATTENTION	TONE	LEVEL OF DETAIL IN MESSAGE
Face-to-Face	Synchronous	Low	High	Personal	Moderate
Telephone, Videoconferencing	Synchronous	Low	Moderate	Personal	Moderate
Voice Mail	Asynchronous	Moderate	Low	Moderate	Low
E-mail	Asynchronous	High	Low	Impersonal-Moderate	High
Text Messaging	Asynchronous, but potentially quick	High	Low	Impersonal-Moderate	Low
Hard Copy (e.g., handwritten or typed message)	Asynchronous	High	Low	Depends on writer's style	High

Adapted from Adler, R. B., Elmhorst, J., & Lucas, K. (2013). *Communicating at work: Strategies for success in business and the professions* (11th ed., p. 14). New York: McGraw-Hill.

devices can have a negative effect on closeness, connection, and conversation quality during face-to-face discussions of personal topics (Przybylski & Weinstein, 2013). That's why some groups begin business meetings or social events by depositing their cell phones at the door, so as not to disrupt their in-person interaction.

Despite these legitimate concerns, research also suggests that communicating and relating via social media can be rich and satisfying (Grieve et al., 2013; Walther & Ramirez, 2010). One survey revealed that social networking sites usually don't replace offline relationships as much as enhance and extend them (Kujath, 2011). Here are some research findings supporting that premise:

- Almost 60 percent of American teenagers report that their use of the Internet supports their relationships with their friends, and almost a third say that it helps them make new friends (Lenhart et al., 2010).
- People who frequent social networking sites report that they have more close friends and get more support from their friends than those who do not (Hampton et al., 2011).
- Facebook provides the opportunity to develop and maintain social connectedness, and that connectedness is associated with lower depression and anxiety and greater life satisfaction (Grieve et al., 2013).

- Couples who talk frequently via cell phone feel more loving, committed, and confident about their relationship (Jin & Peña, 2010).
- Participants who have both in-person and electronic contact with friends are less lonely than their counterparts who have fewer ways of keeping in touch (Baiocco et al., 2011).

There are several reasons why mediated channels can increase both the amount and quality of interpersonal communication (Barnes, 2003). For one thing, it makes communication easier. Busy schedules and long distances can make quality time in face-to-face contact difficult or impossible. The challenge of finding time is especially tough for people who are separated by long distances and multiple time zones (Dainton & Aylor, 2002). In relationships like this, the asynchronous nature of most social media provides a way to share information that otherwise would be difficult. And as you read earlier, lean messages can strip away some of the factors that complicate interpersonal communication. That's why Internet experts call social media tools "low-friction opportunities" to create, maintain, and rediscover social ties in our lives (Anderson, 2010).

Findings such as these help explain why Steve Jobs, the cofounder of Apple Computer, suggested that personal computers be renamed "*interpersonal* computers."

COMMUNICATING COMPETENTLY WITH SOCIAL MEDIA

Like face-to-face communication, mediated interaction can seem natural and almost effortless. But despite its apparent ease, there's potential for trouble unless you proceed mindfully. The following guidelines will help.

Be Careful What You Post

A quick scan of social networking home pages shows that many users post text and images about themselves that could prove embarrassing in some contexts: "Here I am just before my DUI arrest"; "This is me in Cancun on spring break." This is not the sort of information most people would be eager to show a prospective employer or certain family members.

As a cautionary tale about how your digital goofs can haunt you, consider the case of Kevin Colvin, a young intern at a Boston bank

MEDIA CLIP
Online but Disconnected:
The Social Network

In this character study, Facebook creator Mark Zuckerberg (Jesse Eisenberg) is portrayed as a genius at computer programming and meeting the needs of the marketplace. At the same time, he is a disaster in the domain of personal relationships.

Film critic Roger Ebert called Zuckerberg's character "a heat-seeking missile in search of his own goals." Zuckerberg insults and humiliates his girlfriend, Erica (Rooney Mara), and betrays his best friend, Eduardo Saverin (Andrew Garfield). He builds an empire but lives in an isolated world of his own creation, indifferent to the feelings of those around him.

The irony of Zuckerberg's successes and failures offers a parable for our times. Mastering communication technology is no guarantee of interpersonal competence. On the relational front, success must come the old-fashioned way. Meaningful relationships can't be reduced to bits, bytes, and dollars.

who e-mailed his boss saying "something came up at home" and he would need to miss a few days of work. A Facebook search by his boss revealed a photo showing Kevin's true location during the absence: an out-of-town Halloween party with the missing intern dressed in a fairy costume, complete with wings and wand. Besides seeing his pixie-like image plastered over the web, Kevin found that his indiscretion was not a brilliant career move. (To see the photo and read the boss's reaction, type the words "Kevin" and "cool wand" into your search engine.)

Some incautious posts can go beyond being simply amusing. One example is the practice of "sexting"—sharing explicit photos of one's self or others via mediated channels. One survey revealed that 10 percent of young adults between the ages of 14 and 24 have texted or e-mailed a nude or partially nude image of themselves to someone else, and 15 percent have received such pictures or videos of someone else they know (Lenhart, 2009; see also Lenhart & Duggan, 2014). Perhaps even more disturbing, 8 percent reported that they had received a nude or partially nude image of someone they knew from a third party (MTV, 2009). The impulsive message or post that seems harmless at the time can haunt you for a lifetime.

Be Considerate

The word "etiquette" calls to mind old-fashioned rules that have little to do with today's world. But whatever you call them, mostly unspoken rules of conduct still keep society running smoothly. We don't shove or cut in waiting lines. We return others' greetings, say "please" and "thanks," and (mostly) let others speak without cutting them off. By acting appropriately, we feel good about ourselves, and we're more effective in getting our needs met.

Communication by social media calls for its own rules and competencies (Tolman, 2011), which some refer to as "netiquette." Here are a few.

Respect Others' Need for Undivided Attention If you've been texting, IM-ing, and e-mailing since you could master a keypad, it might be hard to realize that some people are insulted when you divide your attention between your in-person conversational partner and distant contacts. As one observer put it, "While a quick log-on may seem, to the user, a harmless break, others in the room receive it as a silent dismissal. It announces: 'I'm not interested'" (Bauerlein, 2009).

In Chapter 7, we have plenty to say about the challenges of listening effectively when you are multitasking. Even if you think you can understand others while dealing with communication media, it's important to realize that they may perceive you as being rude.

Keep Your Tone Civil If you've ever posted a snide comment on a blog, shot back a nasty reply to a text or instant message, or forwarded an embarrassing e-mail, you know that it's easier to behave badly when the recipient of your message isn't right in front of you.

The tendency to transmit messages without considering their consequences is called **disinhibition,** and research shows it is more likely in mediated channels than in face-to-face contact (Hollenbaugh & Everett, 2013;

Lapidot-Lefler & Barak, 2012). Sometimes communicators take disinhibition to the extreme, blasting off angry—even vicious—e-mails, text messages, and blogs. The common term for these outbursts is flaming. In text-based forms of social media, flaming includes profanity, all capital letters, excessive exclamation points, and question marks (Turnage, 2007). Here is the account of one writer who was the target of an obscenity-filled e-mail:

> No one had ever said something like this to me before, and no one could have said this to me before: In any other medium, these words would be, literally, unspeakable. The guy couldn't have said this to me on the phone, because I would have hung up and not answered if the phone rang again, and he couldn't have said it to my face, because I wouldn't have let him finish. . . . I suppose the guy could have written me a nasty letter: He probably wouldn't have used the word "rectum," though, and he probably wouldn't have mailed the letter; he would have thought twice while he was addressing the envelope. But the nature of e-mail is that you don't think twice. You write and send. (Seabrook, 1994, p. 71)

In some online communities, flaming is part of the culture, and is a way to instruct or correct a member who has misstated facts or abused the group's rules. But in most contexts, it's hard to find a justification for flaming.

Flaming isn't the only type of mediated harassment. Ongoing "cyberbullying" has become a widespread phenomenon, often with dire consequences (Bauman, 2011; Holfeld & Grabe, 2012). More than 4 in 10 teens report being the target of online harassment—and the problem is international in scope (Huang & Chou, 2010). Recipients of cyberbullying often feel helpless and scared, to such a degree that they are eight times more likely to carry a weapon to school than other students. There are several reported cases in the United States in which a victim of cyberbullying committed suicide (Bauman et al., 2013; Ybarra & Mitchell, 2007), which is sobering in light of reports that 81 percent of cyberbullies admit their only reason for bullying is because "it's funny" (National Crime Prevention Council, 2007). See the Dark Side box in Chapter 11 for more discussion of this serious problem.

One way to behave better in asynchronous situations is to ask yourself a simple question before you send, post, or broadcast: Would you deliver the same message to the recipient in person? If your answer is no, then you might want to think before hitting the "enter" key.

Be Mindful of Bystanders If you spend even a little time in most public spaces, you're likely to encounter communicators whose use of technology interferes with others: restaurant patrons whose phone voices intrude on your conversation, pedestrians who are more focused on their handheld device than on avoiding others, or people in line who are trying to pay the cashier and talk on their cell phone at the same time. If you

"It keeps me from looking at my phone every two seconds."

aren't bothered by this sort of behavior, it can be hard to feel sympathetic with others who are offended by it. Nonetheless, this is another situation in which the "platinum rule" applies: Consider treating others the way they would like to be treated.

Balance Mediated and Face Time Being connected 24/7 can steal time from in-person communication. But research confirms what commonsense suggests: "Face time" is still important (Vitak et al., 2011).

Overuse of social media can range from slightly abnormal to borderline obsessive. For instance, online gaming—especially intensive role-playing games—can decrease the relational satisfaction of marriage partners (Ahlstrom et al., 2012). And as noted in the Dark Side box on p. 8, overuse of online communication (to the exclusion of the in-person variety) can lead to loneliness and other negative consequences (Kuss et al., 2013).

So what is the happy medium? There's no simple answer, but there are a couple of tests to keep in mind. If your loved ones hint—or directly tell you—that they would like more face time with you, it's probably wise to heed their request. And if you find that technological devices are subtracting from, rather than adding to, your interpersonal relationships, it might be time to monitor and limit your use of social media.

CHECK YOUR UNDERSTANDING

Objective 1.1 Recognize the needs that communication satisfies.

Communication is important for a variety of reasons. Besides satisfying practical needs, meaningful communication contributes to physical health, plays a major role in defining our identity, and forms the basis for our social relationships.

Q: Using a representative two-day period, identify the needs you try to satisfy by communicating. How might the results be better if your communication was more skillful?

Objective 1.2 Explain the relational, transactional nature of interpersonal communication.

Communication is a complex process. The transactional model presented in this chapter shows that meanings are determined by the people who exchange messages, not in the messages themselves. Interpersonal communicators usually send and receive messages simultaneously, particularly in face-to-face exchanges. Environment and noise affect the nature of interaction, as do the channels used to exchange messages.

Communication follows several principles. For instance, it is transactional, irreversible, and unrepeatable; and it can be intentional or unintentional. Messages also have both content and relational dimensions.

Communication in interpersonal relationships is distinguished by uniqueness, interdependence, disclosure, and intrinsic rewards. Interpersonal communication is best understood in contrast to impersonal communication.

To understand the communication process, it is important to recognize and avoid several common misconceptions. More communication is not always better. Sometimes total understanding isn't as important as we might think. Even at its best, communication is not a panacea that will solve every problem. Effective communication is not a natural ability. Whereas some people have greater aptitude at communicating, everyone can learn to interact with others more competently.

Q: Apply the transactional model to a situation that illustrates the qualities of interpersonal communication described on pages 15–17.

Objective 1.3   Identify characteristics of effective communication and competent communicators.

Communication competency is the ability to be both effective and appropriate. There is no single ideal way to communicate. Flexibility and adaptability are characteristics of competent communicators, as are skill at performing behaviors, involvement with others, empathy and perspective taking, cognitive complexity, and self-monitoring. The good news is, communication competency can be learned.

Q: Identify interpersonal situations in which you communicate competently and those in which

your competence is less than satisfactory. (Consider inviting people who know you well to help with this process.) Based on these observations, identify goals for improving your interpersonal communication skills.

Objective 1.4   Understand the advantages and drawbacks of various social media communication channels in relationship to face-to-face communication.

Social media differ from the face-to-face variety in several noteworthy ways: They are typically leaner, often asynchronous, and can be permanent. Social media do pose risks for relationships; but when used mindfully, they can enhance them. This chapter offers several guidelines for using social media with due caution and consideration.

Q: Evaluate the optimal level of social media use in your relationships. What are some ways you can increase your competence level when using social media?

KEY TERMS

- Asynchronous communication (27)
- Channel (12)
- Cognitive complexity (23)
- Communication (9)
- Communication apprehension (24)
- Communication competence (19)
- Content dimension (of a message) (14)

- Disinhibition (31)
- Environment (11)
- Feedback (10)
- Hyperpersonal communication (27)
- Leanness (26)
- Noise (external, physiological, and psychological) (12)
- Relational dimension (of a message) (15)
- Richness (26)

- Self-monitoring (23)
- Social media (24)
- Synchronous communication (27)
- Transactional (13)

ACTIVITIES

1. As you read in this chapter, communication satisfies a variety of physical, identity, and social needs. With a group of classmates, evaluate how well social media enable you to address those needs compared with face-to-face communication.

2. Select three important relationships in your life. These might include your relationships with people at work or school, or with friends and family.

For each relationship, rate on a scale ranging from 1 to 10 (with 1 = low and 10 = high) the degree to which the relationship is characterized by each of these four factors: *uniqueness, interdependence, self-disclosure,* and *intrinsic rewards.* Share your analysis with a classmate and discuss what these factors say about the interpersonal nature of your relationships.

3. How competent are you as a communicator? You can begin to answer this question by interviewing people who know you well: a family member, friend, or fellow worker, for example. Interview different people to determine if you are more competent in some relationships than others, or in some situations than others.

   a. Describe the characteristics of competent communicators outlined in this chapter. Be sure your interviewee understands each of them.

   b. Ask your interviewee to rate you on each of the observable qualities. (It won't be possible for others to evaluate internal characteristics, such as cognitive complexity and self-monitoring.) Be sure this evaluation reflects your communication in a variety of situations: It's likely you aren't uniformly competent—or incompetent—in all of them.

   c. If your rating is not high in one or more areas, discuss with your partner how you could raise it.

4. Knowing how you want to communicate isn't the same as being able to perform competently. The technique of behavior rehearsal provides a way to improve a particular communication skill before you use it in real life. Behavior rehearsal consists of four steps:

   a. Define your goal. Begin by identifying the way you want to behave.

   b. On your own or with the help of classmates, break the goal into the behaviors it involves. Most goals are made up of several verbal and nonverbal parts.

You may be able to identify these parts by thinking about them yourself, by observing others, by reading about them, or by asking others for advice.

   c. Practice each behavior before using it in real life. First, imagine yourself behaving more competently. Next, practice a new behavior by rehearsing it with others.

   d. Try out the behavior in real life. You can increase the odds of success if you follow two pieces of advice when trying out new communication behaviors: Work on only one subskill at a time, and start with easy situations. Don't expect yourself suddenly to behave flawlessly in the most challenging situations. Begin by practicing your new skills in situations in which you have a chance of success.

5. Construct a diary of the ways you use social media in a three-day period. For each instance when you use social media (e-mail, social networking website, phone, Twitter, etc.), describe

   a. The kind(s) of social media you use

   b. The nature of the communication (e.g., "Wrote on friend's Facebook wall," "Texted roommate to pick up dinner on the way home")

   c. The reason you chose that medium for that particular message

Share your findings with your classmates. Describe the types of media you use most often and why you chose them. Do you think some of your messages could have been more effective if you had used a different medium?

SCORING FOR ASSESSING YOUR COMMUNICATION (PAGE 26)

Add your responses to 1 through 6. The total is your "Social Integration and Emotional Connection" score—a measure of how social media are integrated into your daily life and the extent to which you have an emotional connection to your use of social media. The average college student scores about 18 on this instrument. Did you score higher or lower? As you consider your score, think about the role social media play in your relationships: Are you more interested in interacting with friends via social media than in person? If you are, what might you be missing? On the other hand, if social media are not a part of your daily life, what may you be missing out on? What's a "healthy" social integration of and emotional connection to social media?

chapter 2

Culture and Interpersonal Communication

CHAPTER OUTLINE

FEATURES

LEARNING OBJECTIVES

2.1 Understand the relationship between intercultural and interpersonal dimensions of communication.

2.2 Describe five key values that help shape a culture's communication norms.

2.3 Recognize the range of co-cultures in today's society and how co-cultural factors can affect interpersonal communication.

2.4 Explain the factors that shape a culture's verbal codes, nonverbal codes, and decoding of messages.

2.5 Identify the attitudes, knowledge, and skills required for intercultural communication competence.

MORE THAN A HALF-CENTURY AGO, Marshall McLuhan (1962) coined the metaphor of the world as a "global village" where members of every nation are connected by communication technology. Just like members of a traditional village, McLuhan suggested, the affairs and fates of the occupants of planet Earth are connected—for better or worse. This analysis has proven to be increasingly true. Demographic changes are transforming countries like the United States into microcosms of the global village. Immigration has made society more multicultural and multiethnic than ever before (see Figure 2.1).

Thanks to the growth in communication technology, even stay-at-homes have access to virtually the entire world, and commerce has changed in ways that would have been unimaginable just a generation ago. International telephone service is affordable and efficient. The Internet allows users around the world to share information with one another instantaneously at a cost no greater than exchanging computer messages with someone in the same town. Organizations span the globe, and their members form virtual teams that meet in cyberspace.

In this chapter, we explore how interpersonal communication operates in a networked world where members of different cultures interact.

CULTURE AND COMMUNICATION

Before going any further, we need to clarify two important concepts: *culture* and *intercultural communication*. We also need to look at what distinguishes intercultural communication from interpersonal communication.

CULTURE AND CO-CULTURE

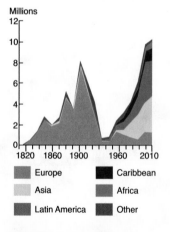

FIGURE 2.1 United States Immigration Patterns by Region of Origin

Source: Immigration Research Group, University of California, Riverside

Defining culture isn't an easy task, as scholars acknowledge (Faulkner et al., 2006; Jahoda, 2012). For our purposes, Larry Samovar and his colleagues (2007) offer a clear and comprehensive definition of **culture**: "the language, values, beliefs, traditions, and customs people share and learn."

This definition shows that culture is, to a great extent, a matter of *perception* and *definition*. When you identify yourself as a member of a culture, you must (a) recognize yourself and others as sharing certain characteristics and (b) see others who don't possess these characteristics as members of different categories. For example, eye color doesn't seem like a significant factor in distinguishing "us" from "them," whereas skin color plays a more important role, at least in some cases. It's not hard to imagine a society where the opposite were true (look up Jane Elliott's famous "blue-eye/brown-eye" experiment). Social scientists use the label **in-groups** to describe groups with which we identify and **out-groups** to describe those that we view as different (Caughron et al., 2013). Cultural membership contributes to every person's **social identity**—the part of the self-concept that is based on membership in groups. Your answer to the question "Who are you?" might include social categories such as your ethnicity and nationality.

FOCUS ON RESEARCH
Fitting In: Disabilities on the Job

People with physical disabilities represent about 15 percent of the U.S. population. Communication scholars Marsha Cohen and Susan Avanzino investigated how members of this co-culture manage the challenges of fitting into organizational cultures where they are in the minority. The researchers interviewed 24 people with a variety of physical disabilities and job positions, asking about their experiences with employers and coworkers.

The participants described several strategies for integrating into the culture of their organizations. One is *assimilation*—adapting and conforming to the dominant (nondisabled) group. This involves de-emphasizing differences and in some cases staying quiet about disabilities (one participant said, "The less you tell about your disability, the better off you are"). A different strategy, *accommodation*, involves acknowledging one's disability and asking for ways that it can be accommodated. It can also include educating others about disabilities and actively dispelling misperceptions. A few opted for *separation*, distancing themselves from nondisabled people and banding together only with others who had physical disabilities. This last approach was the least common and viewed as least productive.

Some of the study participants were more comfortable with accommodation, others with assimilation. But none of them wanted to be defined by their disabilities. The authors provided this summary (p. 300):

> With many voices and different backgrounds and experiences, the participants in this study are stating: "We are people first."

Cohen, M., & Avanzino, S. (2010). We are people first: Framing organizational assimilation experiences of the physically disabled using co-cultural theory. *Communication Studies, 61*, 272–303.

Social scientists use the term **co-culture** to describe the perception of membership in a group that is part of an encompassing culture (Herakova, 2012; Orbe & Spellers, 2005). Co-cultures in North American society include categories based on

- age (e.g., teens, senior citizens)
- race/ethnicity (e.g., African American, Latino)
- sexual orientation (e.g., lesbian, straight)
- nationality (e.g., immigrants from a particular country, expatriates)
- geographic region (e.g., Southerners, Midwesterners)
- physical disability (e.g., wheelchair users, persons who are deaf)
- religion (e.g., Church of Jesus Christ of Latter Day Saints, Muslim)
- activity (e.g., biker, gamer)

Members of co-cultures develop unique patterns of communication and connection. Deaf culture is a good example: The shared experiences of deafness can create strong bonds. Most notably, distinct languages build a shared worldview and solidarity. There are Deaf schools, Deaf competitions (e.g., Miss Deaf America), Deaf performing arts (including Deaf comedians), and other organizations that bring Deaf people together. Of course, the connection experienced by members of this co-culture can create challenges when communicating with those outside the group—for instance, between Deaf children and their hearing parents (Miller, 2010).

Regional co-cultures also have distinctive communication patterns. Researchers that have looked at differences associated with areas of the United States have uncovered significant state-by-state variations (Rentfrow, 2014). They found that

> The country broke down into three macro regions: New England and the Mid-Atlantic states, which the researchers termed "temperamental and uninhibited"; the South and Midwest, which were labeled "friendly and conventional"; and the West Coast, Rocky Mountains, and Sun Belt, described as "relaxed and creative." (Kluger & Wilson, 2013)

And true to an enduring stereotype, people from New York City are typically more assertive than those from the Upper Midwest (Sigler et al., 2008). Given these differences, it's easy to imagine how a first-year college student from Iowa might regard a new roommate from "The Big Apple" as pushy and unpredictable, and how the Northeasterner might view the Midwesterner as placid and unadventurous.

Membership in co-cultures can be a source of enrichment and pride. But there are often tensions between identifying with one group and fitting into the culture at large. For example, focus groups revealed that African American students in predominantly white universities struggled to be proud of their cultural heritage while also trying to adapt to the "whiteness of their schools" (Simmons et al., 2013). On one hand they wanted to share cultural insights with white students, but they were reluctant to call attention to themselves.

When a co-cultural group is stigmatized, being identified with it can be problematic. For instance, Patrice Buzzanell (1999) describes how members of underrepresented groups are disadvantaged in employment interviews, where the rules are established by the dominant culture. Studies of Jamaican children (Ferguson & Cramer, 2007) and Latino children (Golash-Boza & Darity, 2008) indicate that skin color influences self-identification and self-esteem. In other cases, co-cultures voluntarily embrace the chance to distinguish themselves from society at large—such as teens creating slang that is understood only by members of their in-group. Some scholars (e.g., Kimmel, 2008; Wood, 2013) have even characterized men and women as belonging to different co-cultures because their communication styles are so distinct. As you read this chapter, you will notice that many of the communication challenges that arise between members of different cultures also operate when people from different co-cultures interact.

INTERCULTURAL COMMUNICATION

Having defined culture, we can go on to define **intercultural communication** as the process that occurs when members of two or more cultures or co-cultures exchange messages in a manner that is influenced by their different cultural perceptions and symbol systems, both verbal and nonverbal (Samovar et al., 2007).

Because all of us belong to many groups (e.g., ethnic, economic, interest-based, age), you might be asking yourself whether there is any communication that *isn't* intercultural, or at least co-cultural. The answer to this question is "yes" for two reasons. First, even in an increasingly diverse world, there are still plenty of relationships in which people share a basic common background. Within co-cultural groups such as Irish marchers in a St. Patrick's Day parade, suburban-bred men who play poker on Fridays, and a college sorority or fraternity, members are likely to share fundamentally similar personal histories and, therefore, have similar norms, customs, and values. Second, even when people with different cultural backgrounds communicate, those differences may not be important. David may be a Jewish male whose ancestors came from Eastern Europe whereas Lisa is a third-generation Japanese person whose parents are practicing Christians, but they have created a life together that usually is more significant than their differences and that leaves them able to deal comfortably with those differences when they do arise.

Rather than classifying some exchanges as intercultural and others as free from cultural influences, it's more accurate to talk about *degrees* of cultural significance (King et al., 2013; Lustig & Koester, 2005). Encounters can fit along a spectrum of "interculturalness." At the "most intercultural" end are situations in which communicators have highly different backgrounds or beliefs. A traveler visiting a new country for the first time with little knowledge of local society is an obvious example. At the "least intercultural" end of the spectrum fall exchanges in which cultural differences are not significant. A student from Los Angeles who attends a small liberal arts college in the Midwest might find life there somewhat different, but the adjustment would be far less difficult than that for the international traveler. In between these extremes falls a whole range of encounters in which culture plays varying roles.

Note that intercultural communication (at least as we'll use that term here) doesn't always occur when people from different cultures interact. The cultural backgrounds, perceptions, and symbol systems of the participants must have a significant impact on the exchange before we can say that culture has made a difference. Social scientists use the term **salience** to describe how much weight we attach to a particular person or phenomenon. Consider a few examples where culture has little or no salience:

- A group of preschool children is playing together in a park. These 3-year-olds don't recognize the fact that their parents may come from different countries, or even that they don't speak the same language. At this point we wouldn't say that intercultural communication is taking place. Only when cultural factors become salient (diet, sharing, or parental discipline, for example) do the children begin to think of one another as different.
- Members of a school basketball team—some Asian, some black, some Latino, and some white—are intent on winning the league championship. During a game, cultural distinctions aren't salient. There's plenty of communication, but it isn't fundamentally intercultural. Away from their games, they might notice some fundamental differences in the way members of each group communicate.

- A husband and wife were raised in homes with different religious traditions. Most of the time their religious heritage makes little difference, and the partners view themselves as a unified couple. Every so often, however—perhaps during religious holidays or when meeting members of each other's family—the different backgrounds are more salient. At those times we can imagine the partners feeling quite different from each other—thinking of themselves as members of separate cultures.

INTERPERSONAL AND INTERCULTURAL COMMUNICATION

What is the relationship between intercultural communication and interpersonal relationships? William Gudykunst and Young Kim (2002; Gudykunst, 2005) suggest that interpersonal and intercultural factors combine to form a two-by-two matrix in which the importance of interpersonal communication forms one dimension and intercultural significance forms the second one (Figure 2.2). This model shows that some interpersonal transactions (e.g., a conversation between two siblings who have been raised in the same household) have virtually no intercultural elements. Other encounters (such as a traveler from Senegal trying to get directions from a Ukrainian taxi driver in New York City) are almost exclusively intercultural, without the personal dimensions that we have discussed throughout this book.

Still other exchanges—the most interesting ones for our purposes—contain elements of both intercultural and interpersonal communication. This range of encounters is broad in the global village: Business people from different backgrounds try to wrap up a deal; U.S. born and immigrant children learn to get along in school; health care educators seek effective ways to serve patients from around the world; neighbors from different racial or ethnic backgrounds look for ways to make their streets safer and cleaner; suburban-bred teachers seek common ground with inner-city students—the list seems almost endless.

FIGURE 2.2 Some Possible Interactions between Interpersonal and Intercultural Dimensions of Communication

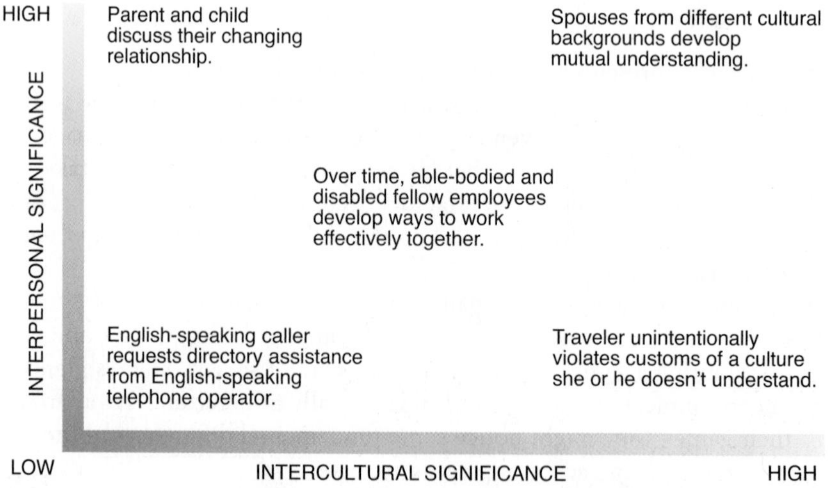

HIGH

Parent and child discuss their changing relationship.

Spouses from different cultural backgrounds develop mutual understanding.

INTERPERSONAL SIGNIFICANCE

Over time, able-bodied and disabled fellow employees develop ways to work effectively together.

English-speaking caller requests directory assistance from English-speaking telephone operator.

Traveler unintentionally violates customs of a culture she or he doesn't understand.

LOW   INTERCULTURAL SIGNIFICANCE   HIGH

INTERCULTURAL DIFFERENCES AS GENERALIZATIONS

In the following pages, we spell out a variety of ways communication varies from one culture to another. Although these variations can sometimes be significant, it's important to remember that cultural practices aren't *totally* different: People from varied backgrounds often share enough common ground to make relationships work. When all the physical and social attributes of human beings are added up, there are far more similarities than differences among the people of the world.

Moreover, there are sometimes greater differences *within* cultures than *between* them. Consider the matter of formality as an example: By most measures, U.S. culture is far more casual than many others. But Figure 2.3 shows that there may be more common ground between a formal American and a casual member of a formal culture than there is between two Americans with vastly differing levels of formality. Furthermore, within every culture, members display a wide range of communication styles. For instance, although most Asian cultures tend to be collectivistic, many members of those cultures would identify themselves as individualists. For these reasons, it's important to remember that generalizations—even when accurate and helpful—don't apply to every member of a group.

CULTURAL VALUES AND NORMS

Some cultural influences on communication are obvious. However, some far less visible values and norms can shape how members of cultures think and act (Amarasinghe, 2012). In this section, we look at five of these subtle yet vitally important values and norms that shape the way members of a culture communicate. Unless communicators are aware of these differences, they may see people from other cultures as unusual—or even offensive—without realizing that their apparently odd behavior comes from following a different set of beliefs and unwritten rules about the "proper" way to communicate.

HIGH VERSUS LOW CONTEXT

Anthropologist Edward Hall (1959) identified two distinct ways that members of various cultures deliver messages. A **low-context culture** uses language primarily to express thoughts, feelings, and ideas as directly as possible. To low-context communicators, the meaning of a statement lies in the words spoken. By contrast, a **high-context culture** relies heavily on subtle, often nonverbal cues to maintain social harmony. Rather than upsetting others by speaking directly, communicators in these societies learn to discover

FIGURE 2.3 **Differences and Similarities within and between Cultures**

Adapted from Trompenaars, F. (1994). *Riding the waves of culture.* New York: McGraw-Hill/Irwin, p. 28.

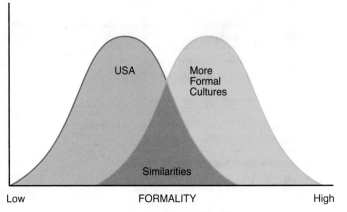

meaning from the context in which a message is delivered: the nonverbal behaviors of the speaker, the history of the relationship, and the general social rules that govern interaction between people.

There are many examples of how context and culture affect communication. People in high-context India tend to disclose less private information in online discussions than low-context Germans; they also use more emoticons, reflecting the higher importance of nonverbal communication in their culture (Pflug, 2011). A study in which expressions of appreciation were examined found that in the low-context culture of the United States, people rely about evenly on verbal and nonverbal methods of expressing themselves, whereas people in the high-context culture of China favor nonverbal over verbal ones (Bello et al., 2010). And as might be expected, low-context communicators use more competitive and dominating conflict styles, whereas high-context people are more obliging and accommodating (Croucher et al., 2012). Even websites designed for global audiences reflect differences attributable to whether the country is high or low context (Usunier & Roulin, 2010). For example, those from low-context-communication countries invite more contact and contain more relationship-related content than websites from high-context-communication countries. Table 2.1 summarizes some key differences in how people from low- and high-context cultures communicate.

Mainstream culture in the United States, Canada, Northern Europe, and Israel falls toward the low-context end of the scale. Longtime residents generally value straight-talk and grow impatient with "beating around the bush." By contrast, most Asian and Middle Eastern cultures fit the high-context pattern and can be offended by the bluntness of low-context communication styles.

In many Asian societies, for example, maintaining harmony is important, so communicators avoid speaking directly if that threatens another person's "face," or dignity. For this reason, communicators raised in Japanese or Korean cultures are less likely than Americans to offer a clear "no" to an undesirable request.

TABLE 2.1 High-Context and Low-Context Communication Styles

LOW-CONTEXT CULTURES (E.G., GERMANY, SCANDINAVIA, MOST ENGLISH-SPEAKING COUNTRIES)	HIGH-CONTEXT CULTURES (E.G., MOST SOUTHERN EUROPEAN, MIDDLE EASTERN, ASIAN, AND LATIN AMERICAN COUNTRIES)
Majority of information is carried in explicit verbal messages, with less focus on the situational context.	Important information is carried in contextual cues such as time, place, relationship, situation. Less reliance on explicit verbal messages.
Self-expression is valued. Communicators state opinions and desires directly and strive to persuade others to accept their own viewpoint.	Relational harmony is valued and maintained by the indirect expression of options. Communicators abstain from saying "no" directly.
Clear, eloquent speech is considered praiseworthy. Verbal fluency is admired.	Communicators talk "around" the point, allowing the others to fill in the missing pieces. Ambiguity and use of silence are admired.

To members of high-context cultures, communicators with a low-context style can appear overly talkative, lacking in subtlety, and redundant. On the other hand, to people from low-context backgrounds, high-context communicators often seem unexpressive or even dishonest. It is easy to see how the clash between directness and indirectness can aggravate problems between straight-talking, low-context Israelis and their Arab neighbors, whose high-context culture stresses smooth interaction. Israelis might view their Arab counterparts as evasive, while the Arabs might perceive the Israelis as insensitive and blunt.

INDIVIDUALISM VERSUS COLLECTIVISM

Some cultures value the individual, whereas others place greater emphasis on the group. Members of an **individualistic culture** view their primary responsibility as helping themselves, whereas communicators in **collectivistic cultures** feel loyalties and obligations to an in-group: one's extended family, community, or even the organization one works for (Triandis, 1995). Individualistic cultures also are characterized by self-reliance and competition, whereas members of a collectivistic culture are more attentive to and concerned with the opinions of significant others. The consequences of a culture's individualistic–collectivistic orientation are often so powerful that some scholars (e.g., Merkin & Ramadan, 2010; Nguyen et al., 2010) have labeled it as the most fundamental dimension of cultural differences. Table 2.2 summarizes some differences between individualistic and collectivistic cultures.

Members of individualistic cultures tend to view themselves in terms of what they *do*, whereas people in collectivistic cultures are more likely to define themselves in terms of group membership. For instance, members of several cultures were asked to answer the question "Who am I?" 20 times

TABLE 2.2 The Self in Individualistic and Collectivistic Cultures

INDIVIDUALISTIC CULTURES (E.G., USA, CANADA, UK)	COLLECTIVISTIC CULTURES (E.G., PAKISTAN, INDONESIA, ECUADOR)
Self is separate, unique individual; should be independent, self-sufficient.	People belong to extended families or in-groups; "we" or group orientation.
Individual should take care of himself or herself and immediate family.	Person should take care of extended family before self.
Many flexible group memberships; friendships based on shared interests and activities.	Emphasis is on belonging to a very few permanent in-groups, which have a strong influence over the person.
Reward is for individual achievement and initiative; individual decision making is encouraged; individual credit and blame are assigned.	Reward is for contribution to group goals and well-being; cooperation with in-group members; group decision making is valued; credit and blame are shared.
High value on autonomy, change, youth, individual security, equality.	High value on duty, order, tradition, age, group security, status, and hierarchy.

Adapted by Sandra Sudweeks from Triandis, H. C. (1990). Cross-cultural studies of individualism and collectivism. In J. Berman (Ed.), *Nebraska symposium on motivation* (pp. 41–133). Lincoln: University of Nebraska Press; and Hall, E. T. (1959). *Beyond culture*. New York: Doubleday.

The LEGO Movie illustrates the pros and cons of individualism and collectivism. Whereas the town folks value working together cooperatively (singing "everything is cool when you're part of a team"), Emmett (voiced by Chris Pratt) demonstrates the importance of unique and nonconformist thought and action.

(DeAngelis, 1992). North Americans were likely to respond by giving individual factors ("I am athletic"; "I am short"). By contrast, members of more collectivistic societies—Chinese, Filipinos, Japanese, and some South Americans, for example—answered in terms of their relationships with others ("I am a father"; "I am an employee of XYZ Corporation").

The difference between individualistic and collectivistic cultures also shows up in the level of comfort or anxiety their respective members feel when communicating. In societies where the need to conform is great, there is a higher degree of communication apprehension. For example, as a group, residents of China, Korea, and Japan exhibit a significantly higher degree of anxiety about speaking out in public than do members of individualistic cultures such as the United States and Australia (Berry, 2007; Klopf, 1984). It's important to realize that different levels of communication apprehension don't mean that shyness is a "problem" in some cultures. In fact, just the opposite is true: In these societies, reticence is valued. When the goal is to avoid being "the nail that sticks out," it's logical to feel nervous when you make yourself appear different by calling attention your way. A self-concept that includes "assertive" might make a Westerner feel proud, but in much of Asia it would more likely be cause for shame.

POWER DISTANCE

For members of democratic societies, the principle embodied in the U.S. Declaration of Independence that "all men [and women] are created equal" is so fundamental that we accept it without question. However, not all cultures share this belief. Some operate on the assumption that certain groups of people (an aristocracy or an economic class, for example) and some institutions (such as a church or the government) have the right to control the lives of individuals. Geert Hofstede (1984) coined the term **power distance** to describe the degree to which members of a society accept an unequal distribution of power.

Cultures with low power difference believe in minimizing distinctions between various social classes. Rich and poor, educated and uneducated groups may still exist, but there is a pervasive belief in low power difference cultures that one person is as good as another regardless of that person's station in life. Low power difference cultures also support the notion that challenging authority is acceptable—even desirable. Members aren't necessarily punished for raising questions about the status quo. According to Hofstede's research, U.S. and Canadian societies have relatively low power distance, although not the lowest in the world. Austria, Denmark, Israel, and New Zealand proved to be the most egalitarian countries. At the other end of the spectrum are countries with a high degree of power distance: Philippines, Mexico, Venezuela, India, and Singapore.

The degree of power distance in a culture is reflected in key relationships (Lustig & Koester, 1999; Santilli & Miller, 2011). Children who are raised in cultures with high power difference are expected to obey their parents and other authority figures to a degree that might astonish most children raised in the United States or Canada. Power automatically comes with age in many countries. For example, the Korean language has separate terms for *older brother, oldest brother, younger sister, youngest sister*, and so on. Parents in cultures with low power distance don't expect the same degree of unquestioning obedience. They are not surprised when children ask "Why?" when presented with a request or demand.

On-the-job communication is different in low- and high-power-distance societies (A. Cohen, 2007). In countries with higher degrees of power distance, employees have much less input into the way they perform their work. In fact, workers from these cultures are likely to feel apprehensive when given freedom to make their own decisions (Madlock, 2012) or when a more egalitarian boss asks for their opinion. The reverse is true when management from a culture with an egalitarian tradition tries to do business in a country whose workers are used to high power distance. They can be surprised to find that employees do not expect much say in decisions and do not feel unappreciated when they aren't consulted. They may regard dutiful, submissive, respectful employees as lacking initiative and creativity—traits that helped them gain promotions back home. Given these differences, it's easy to understand why multinational companies need to consider fundamental differences in communication values and behavior when they set up shop in a new country.

UNCERTAINTY AVOIDANCE

The desire to resolve uncertainty seems to be a trait shared by people around the world (Berger, 1988). Although uncertainty may be universal, cultures have different ways of coping with an unpredictable future. Hofstede (2001; Merkin, 2006) uses the term **uncertainty avoidance** to reflect the degree to which members of a culture feel threatened by ambiguous situations and how much they try to avoid them. He developed an uncertainty avoidance index (UAI) to measure differing degrees of uncertainty avoidance around the world. Residents of some countries (including Singapore, Great Britain, Denmark, Sweden, Hong Kong, and the United States) proved to be relatively unthreatened by change, whereas others (such as natives of Belgium, Greece, Japan, and Portugal) found new or ambiguous situations discomfiting.

A culture's degree of uncertainty avoidance is reflected in the way its members communicate. In countries that avoid uncertainty, deviant people and ideas are considered dangerous, and intolerance and ethnocentrism are high (Cargile & Bolkan, 2013; Samovar & Porter, 2004). People in these cultures are especially concerned with security, so they have a strong need for clearly defined rules and regulations. By contrast, people in a culture that is less threatened by the new and unexpected are more likely to tolerate—or even welcome—people who don't fit the norm.

When a mainstream North American who is relatively comfortable with change and novelty spends time with someone from a high UAI culture such as Japan, both communicators may find the other behaving in disconcerting ways. The North American is likely to view the Japanese as rigid and overly controlled, whereas the Japanese would probably regard the North American as undisciplined, overly tolerant, and generally lacking self-control. On the other hand, if the communicators understand how their cultural conditioning affects their style, then they are more likely to understand, and maybe even learn from, the other's different style.

ACHIEVEMENT VERSUS NURTURING

The term **achievement culture** describes societies that place a high value on material success and a focus on the task at hand, whereas **nurturing culture** is a descriptive term for cultures that regard the support of relationships as an especially important goal.

There are significant differences in how people from an achievement culture like the United States and those from a nurturing culture like the Netherlands voice their opinions (van den Bos et al., 2010). In achievement cultures—which emphasize outperforming others—those who see themselves as highly capable feel more empowered to voice their opinions and are satisfied when they can do so. By contrast, in nurturing cultures—which emphasize helping—those who see themselves as *less* capable feel valued as important group members and feel more satisfied when they have the opportunity to voice their opinions.

As you think about the cultural values described here, you may realize that they don't just arise between people from different countries. In today's increasingly multicultural society, people from different cultural backgrounds are likely to encounter one another "at home," in the country they share. Consider the United States and Canada in the new millennium: Native Americans; Latinos from the Caribbean, Mexico, and South America; Middle Easterners; and Asians from China, Japan, Korea, Vietnam, and other countries mingle with first-generation and longtime residents whose ancestors probably came from Europe and Africa. This is a cultural mixture that often seems less like a melting pot than a salad bowl in which the many "ingredients" retain much of their own identity.

CO-CULTURES AND COMMUNICATION

Much of how we view ourselves and how we relate to others grows from our cultural and co-cultural identity—the groups with which we identify. Where do you come from? What's your ethnicity? Your sexual orientation? Your age? Your socioeconomic status? These have become increasingly important factors in interpersonal communication in contemporary society.

In the following pages, we look at some—although by no means all—of the factors that help shape our cultural identity and hence the way we perceive and communicate with others.

ETHNICITY AND RACE

Race is a category originally created to explain differences between people whose ancestors originated in different regions of the world—Africa, Asia, Europe, and so on. Modern scientists acknowledge that although there are some genetic differences between people with different heritage, they mostly involve superficial qualities such as hair color and texture, skin color, and the size and shape of facial features. One analyst puts it this way:

> There is less to race than meets the eye. . . . The genes influencing skin color have nothing to do with the genes influencing hair form, eye shape, blood type, musical talent, athletic ability or forms of intelligence. Knowing someone's skin color doesn't necessarily tell you anything else about him or her. ("Ten Things," 2003)

There are several reasons why race has little use in explaining individual differences. Most obviously, racial features are often misinterpreted. A well-traveled friend of ours from Latin America says that she is often mistaken as Italian, Indian, Spanish, or Native American.

More important, there is more genetic variation within races than between them. For instance, some people with Asian ancestry are short, but others are tall. Some have sunny dispositions, and others are more dour. Some are terrific athletes, and others much less so. The same applies to people from every background. Even within a physically recognizable population, personal experience plays a far greater role than superficial characteristics like skin color in creating a person's communication style. As you will read in Chapter 4, stereotyping is usually a mistake—and yet it occurs far too frequently with issues of race.

Whereas race is a somewhat dated concept, **ethnicity** is used more commonly. Ethnicity refers to the degree to which a person identifies with a particular group, usually on the basis of nationality, culture, or some other unifying perspective (Samovar et al., 2013). For example, Irish Protestants and Catholics may appear virtually identical, but they identify themselves as distinct and different from one another in important ways. The same holds true for many Sunni and Shia Muslims as well as French- and English-speaking Canadians.

Even ethnicity can be problematic because it is usually simplistic to think of people as members of a single category. Consider U.S. president

Barack Obama. He is generally recognized as the country's first African American president despite the fact that his mother was white. Obama experienced a variety of cultures while living in Indonesia, Hawaii, California, New York, Chicago, and Washington, DC. A single term can't describe such a culturally complex background. Projections suggest this will become the norm rather than the exception in the United States in the coming years (Taylor, 2014).

Being identified as belonging to more than one group can be challenging. Consider someone like Heather Greenwood. In an article describing her experiences as a biracial person, Greenwood reports that strangers inquire how her children can have fair skin when she is dark. Others ask if she is the children's nanny or joke that the kids must have been "switched in the hospital" when they were born. The implication, Greenwood says, is that a legitimate family is either one color or another. She hears comments such as these nearly every day. "Each time is like a little paper cut, and you think, 'Well, that's not a big deal.' But imagine a lifetime of that. It hurts," she says (Saulny, 2011). It's important for intercultural communicators to avoid these kinds of assumptions and comments that can damage interpersonal relationships (Durovic, 2008).

Along with the challenges, multiple-group membership can sometimes be a bonus. Many people say they are more open-minded and respectful of others as a result of coming from culturally rich backgrounds (Ross, 1996). Some research suggests they are also more comfortable establishing relationships with a diverse array of people, which increases their options for friendships, romantic partners, and professional colleagues (Bonham & Shih, 2009).

DARK SIDE OF COMMUNICATION
ACCENTS AND STIGMAS

In the musical *My Fair Lady*, Professor Henry Higgins transforms Eliza Doolittle from a humble flower girl into a high-society woman by replacing her Cockney accent with an upper-crust British speaking style. Although the story (based on George Bernard Shaw's play *Pygmalion*) is fictional, the notion that we judge people by their accents is all too real.

Several decades of research show that judgments of attractiveness and status are strongly influenced by style of speech. In one study (Frumkin, 2007), jurors in the United States found testimony less believable when delivered by witnesses speaking with German, Mexican, or Middle Eastern accents. Not surprisingly, other research shows that speakers with nonnative accents feel stigmatized by the bias against them, often leading to a lower sense of belonging and more communication problems (Gluszek et al., 2011).

In another experiment (Bailey, 2003), researchers asked human resource professionals to rate the intelligence, initiative, and personality of job applicants after hearing a 45-second recording of their voices. The speakers with identifiable regional accents—Southern or New Jersey, for example—were recommended for lower-level jobs, whereas those with less pronounced speech styles were tagged for higher-level jobs that involved more public contact.

It's common knowledge that we shouldn't judge a book by its cover or people by superficial characteristics—but, unfortunately, we do so all the time. Remember when listening to people whose accent is different from yours to stay focused on what they're saying, not how they're saying it.

GENDER IDENTITY/ SEXUAL ORIENTATION

"NOBODY KNOWS I'M GAY." That ironic saying is emblazoned on thousands of t-shirts sold by former comedian Skyler Thomas, a champion of the

LGBTQ movement. *LGBTQ* stands for lesbian, gay, bisexual, transgender, and queer—a collection of adjectives that describes people with diverse gender identities and sexual orientations.

Thomas's shirt slogan points to a communication dilemma facing many LGBTQ individuals. On one hand, being open about their gender identity has advantages—including a sense of being authentic with others and belonging to a supportive co-culture. On the other hand, the disclosure can be risky. People may be shocked or judgmental. They may ridicule LGBTQ individuals, discriminate against them, or even attack them. On average, one in five hate crimes in the United States targets people on the basis of their sexual orientation (Federal Bureau of Investigation, 2012). We talk more about bullying and its antidotes in Chapter 11.

CNN host Anderson Cooper didn't tell the public he was gay for years because he considered it private information. He was also concerned it might put him and others in danger, and he thought he could do a better job as a journalist if he "blended in" (Sullivan, 2012). However, Cooper says his silence sometimes felt disingenuous. "I have given some the mistaken impression that I am trying to hide something," he says. He also believed he was missing an opportunity to dispel some of the fear and prejudice that surrounds the issue. "The tide of history only advances when people make themselves fully visible." We talk more about the relationship between self-concept, impression management, and self-disclosure in Chapter 3.

The social climate has become more receptive to LGBTQ individuals than in the past, at least in most of the developed world (Goldberg & Allen, 2013). As one report put it

MEDIA CLIP
A Blending of Cultures: *Modern Family*

The hit television show *Modern Family* isn't just about an extended clan's triumphs and trials. It also illustrates the challenges and rewards of merging several different cultures in a family unit.

As the title suggests, the diverse range of relationships in *Modern Family* would have been improbable in previous generations. The most traditional household includes cheerfully uncool dad Phil (Ty Burrell), overstressed mom Claire (Julie Bowen), and their three very different children. Claire's father, Jay (Ed O'Neill), is in a second marriage with Columbian wife Gloria (Sofia Vergara), who is half his age. They live with Manny (Rico Rodriguez), Gloria's son from a previous relationship. Claire's brother Mitchell (Jesse Tyler Ferguson) is married to Cameron (Eric Stonestreet), and they have an adopted Vietnamese daughter.

Straight and gay, foreign and native born, young and old—many different co-cultures are represented in this clan.

Most LGBT people who are now adults can recall feeling that they were "the only one" and fearing complete rejection by their families, friends, and associates should their identity become known. Yet today, in this era of GSAs [gay straight alliances] . . . openly gay politicians and civil unions; debates about same-sex marriage, gay adoption, and gays in the military; and a plethora of websites aimed specifically at LGBT youth, it is hard to imagine many youths who would believe they are alone in their feelings. (Russell & Bohan, 2005, p. 3)

Among those websites is ItGetsBetter.org, where people can post messages to encourage LGBTQ youth that any harassment they may be experiencing is not their fault and that people care about making it better. Since Dan Savage and Terry Miller launched the It Gets Better Project in 2010, people have posted more than 50,000 videos, which have been viewed more than 50 million times ("About the It Gets Better Project," 2013). Savage says it shows what can happen when communication technology and good intentions combine (Barth, 2013).

AGE/GENERATION

Imagine how odd it would seem to hear an 8-year-old or a senior citizen talking, dressing, or otherwise acting like a twentysomething. We tend to think of getting older as a purely physical process. But age-related communication reflects culture at least as much as biology. In many ways, we learn how to "do" various ages—how to dress, how to talk, and what not to say and do—in the same way we learn how to play other roles in our lives.

Relationships between older and younger people are shaped by cultural assumptions that change over time. At some points in history, older adults have been regarded as wise, accomplished, and even magic (Fitch, 1985). At others, they have been treated as "dead weight" and uncomfortable reminders of mortality and decline (Gergen & Gergen, 2010).

Today, for the most part, Western cultures honor youth, and attitudes about aging are more negative than positive. On balance, people over age 40 are still twice as likely as younger ones to be depicted in the media as unattractive, bored, and in declining health (Bailey, 2010). And people over age 60, especially women, are still underrepresented in the media. However, the data present a different story. Studies show that, overall, people in their 60s are just as happy as people in their 20s (Frijters & Beatoon, 2012).

Unfavorable attitudes about aging can show up in interpersonal relationships. Even though gray or thinning hair and wrinkles don't necessarily signify diminished capacity, they may be interpreted that way—with powerful consequences. People who believe older adults have trouble communicating are less likely to interact with them. When they do, they tend to use the mannerisms listed in Table 2.3, all examples of overaccomodation (Giles et al., 2002; Giles & Gasiorek, 2011). Even when these speech styles are well intentioned, they can have harmful effects. Older adults who are treated as less capable than their peers tend to perceive *themselves* as older and less capable (Lin et al., 2004). And challenging ageist treatment presents seniors with a dilemma: Speaking up can be taken as a sign of being cranky or bitter, reinforcing the stereotype that those seniors are curmudgeons (Harwood, 2007).

Communication challenges can arise when members of different generations work together. For example, millennials (born between 1980 and 2000) tend to have a much stronger need for affirming feedback than previous generations (Myers & Sadaghiani, 2010). Because of their strong desire for achievement, they want clear guidance on how to do a job correctly—but not be micromanaged when they do it. After finishing the task, they have an equally strong desire for praise. To a baby-boomer boss, that type of

TABLE 2.3 Patronizing Speech Directed at Seniors

ELEMENT	DEFINITION AND EXAMPLE
Simplified grammar	Use of short sentences without multiple clauses. "Here's your food. You can eat it. It is good."
Simplified vocabulary	Use of short words rather than longer equivalents. Saying *dog* instead of *Dalmatian*, or *big* instead of *enormous*.
Endearing terms	Calling someone "sweetie" or "love."
Increased volume, reduced rate	Talking LOUDER and s-l-o-w-e-r!
High and variable pitch	Using a slightly squeaky voice style, and exaggerating the pitch variation in speech (a "sing-song" type speech style).
Use of repetition	Saying things over and over again. Repeating. Redundancy. Over and over again. The same thing. Repeated. Again. And again . . .
Use of babyish terms	Using words like *doggie* or *choo-choo* instead of *dog* or *train*: "Oh look at the cute little doggie, isn't he a coochie-coochie-coo!"

Source: Harwood, J. (2007). *Understanding communication and aging: Developing knowledge and awareness*. Newbury Park, CA: Sage, p. 76.

guidance and feedback may feel more like a nuisance. In the boss's experience, "no news is good news," and not being told that you screwed up should be praise enough. Neither perspective is wrong. But when members of these co-cultures have different expectations, miscommunication can occur.

SOCIOECONOMIC STATUS

Social class can have a major impact on how people communicate. People in the United States typically identify themselves as belonging to the working class, middle class, or upper class; and they feel a sense of solidarity with people in the same social strata (Engen, 2004; Lucas, 2011). Social upbringing can have an effect on communication style. College professors often find that working-class college students who are raised not to challenge authority can have a difficult time speaking up, thinking critically, and arguing persuasively (Kim & Sax, 2009; Snell, 2013). The effects of social class continue into the workplace, where skills such as assertiveness and persuasiveness are career enhancers. People who come from working-class families and attain middle- or upper-class careers face special challenges. New speech and language, clothing, and nonverbal patterns often are necessary to gain acceptance (Kaufman, 2003). Many of these individuals also must cope with emotional ambivalences related to their career success (Lubrano, 2004; Lucas, 2011). Moving up the social ladder can create feelings of both pride and guilt; a sense of both finding and losing one's identity.

Even within the same family, educational level can create intercultural challenges. First-generation college (FGC) students feel the intercultural strain of "trying to live simultaneously in two vastly different worlds" of school and home (Lippincott & German, 2007; Orbe & Groscurth, 2004). Because no one in their family has attended college, FGC students often cope with

The film *Blue Jasmine* shows how socioeconomic status can create a cultural gap. Although they grew up together, the patrician Jasmine (Cate Blanchett) and her working-class sister Ginger (Sally Hawkins) occupy different worlds.

an unfamiliar environment by trying to assimilate—going out of their way to fit in on campus. In addition, some FGC students say they overcompensate by studying harder and getting more involved on campus than their non-FGC classmates, just to prove they belong in the college culture. At home, FGC students also engage in self-censorship but for different reasons. They are cautious when talking about college life for fear of threatening and alienating their families. Some even feel like "traitors" (Simmons et al., 2013). The only exception is that some feel a need to model their new educational status to younger family members so "they can see that it can be done."

CODES AND CULTURE

At this point, you probably have a healthy appreciation for the challenges that arise when people try to communicate interpersonally and interculturally. These challenges become even greater when the communicators use different verbal and nonverbal communication systems.

VERBAL CODES

Although there are remarkable similarities between the world's many languages (Lewis et al., 2013; Whaley, 1997), they also differ in important respects that affect the way their speakers communicate with one another and with speakers of other tongues. In the following sections, we outline some of those factors.

Language and Identity

If you live in a culture where everyone speaks the same tongue, then language will have little noticeable impact on how you view yourself and others. But when some members of a society speak the dominant language and others speak a minority one, or when that second language is not prestigious, the sense of being a member of an out-group is strong. At this point, the speaker of a nondominant language can react in one of two ways: either feel pressured to assimilate by speaking the "better" language or refuse to accommodate to the majority language and maintain loyalty to the ethnic tongue (Gann, 2004). The impact of language on the self-concept is powerful. On one hand, the feeling is likely to be "I'm not as good as speakers of the native language"; and on the other hand, the belief is "There's something unique and worth preserving in my language" (Bergman et al., 2008; Meissner, 2008).

Even the names a culture uses to identify its members reflect its values and shape the way its members relate to one another. When asked to identify themselves, individualistic Americans, Canadians, Australians, and Europeans would probably respond by giving their first name, surname, street, town, and country. Many Asians do it the other way around (Servaes, 1989;

● ORGANIZATIONS ARE CULTURES

@WORK

Organizations have cultures that can be just as distinctive as those of larger societies. **Organizational culture** reflects a relatively stable, shared set of rules about how to behave and set of values about what is important (Alvesson, 2011). In everyday language, culture is the insiders' view of "the way things are around here."

Not all the rules and values of an organization are written down. And some that are written down aren't actually followed. Perhaps the workday officially ends at 5 P.M., but you quickly notice that most people stay until at least 6:30. That says something about the culture. Or, even though it doesn't say so in the employee handbook, employees in some companies consider one another extended family, taking personal interest in the lives of coworkers. That's culture, too.

Because you're likely to spend as much time at work as you do in personal relationships, selecting the right organization is as important as choosing a best friend. Research shows that we are likely to enjoy our jobs and do them well if we believe that the organization's values reflect our own and are consistently and fairly applied (Hartnell et al., 2011). For example, some companies reward team members for offering great customer service without exception. On the other hand, a boss who talks about customer service but violates those principles cultivates a culture of cynicism and dissatisfaction.

Ask yourself these questions when considering whether a specific organization's culture is a good fit for you. (Notice how important communication is in each case.)

- How does the organization present itself online and on the phone? Is the tone welcoming and inviting?
- Are customers happy with the service and quality provided?
- Do members of the organization have the resources and authority to do a good job?
- Do employees have fun? Are they encouraged to be creative?
- Is there a spirit of cooperation or competition among team members?
- What criteria are used to evaluate employee performance?
- What happens during meetings? Is communication open or highly scripted?
- How often do people leave their jobs to work somewhere else?
- Do leaders make a point of listening, respecting, and collaborating with employees?
- Do people use their time productively, or are they bogged down with inefficient procedures or office politics?

Research suggests that communication—even seemingly unimportant small talk (Mak & Chui, 2013)—is the vehicle through which we both create and embody culture. At a personal and organizational level, effective, consistent, value-based communication is essential to success.

The TV series *Orange is the New Black* follows Piper Chapman (Taylor Schilling), whose privileged life changes when she is sentenced to federal prison for a crime committed years before. Piper has to adapt to the culture of prison—including its raw language codes—to survive.

Smith, 2011). If you ask Hindus for their identity, they will give you their caste and village and then their name. The Sanskrit formula for identifying oneself begins with lineage and goes on to state family and house, and ends with one's personal name (Bharti, 1985). The Japanese language has as many as 100 different ways to say *I*, depending on whether you want to be polite, casual, businesslike, or arrogant; to emphasize your family role, your social situation, age, or gender ("100 Ways to Say 'I' in Japanese," 2013).

Verbal Communication Styles

Using language is more than just a matter of choosing a particular group of words to convey an idea. Each language has its own unique style that distinguishes it from others. Matters such as the amount of formality or informality, precision or vagueness, and brevity or detail are major ingredients in speaking competently. When a communicator tries to use the verbal style from one culture in a different one, problems are likely to arise.

Gudykunst (2005) describes three important types of cultural differences in verbal style. One is *directness* or *indirectness*. We have already discussed how low-context cultures use language primarily to express thoughts, feelings, and ideas as clearly, directly, and logically as possible, whereas high-context cultures may speak less directly, using language to maintain social harmony.

Another way in which verbal styles can vary across cultures is in terms of whether they are *elaborate* or *succinct*. For instance, speakers of Arabic commonly use language that is much more rich and expressive than normally found in English. Strong assertions and exaggerations that would sound ridiculous in English are a common feature of Arabic. This contrast in linguistic style can lead to misunderstandings between people from different backgrounds.

Succinctness is most extreme in cultures where silence is valued. In many Native American cultures, for example, the favored way to handle ambiguous social situations is to remain quiet (Ferraro & Andreatta, 2012). When you contrast this silent style to the talkativeness that is common when people first meet in mainstream American cultures, it's easy to imagine how the first encounter between an Apache or Navajo and a European American might be uncomfortable for both people.

A third way that verbal styles differ from one culture to another involves *formality* and *informality*. One guidebook for British readers who want to understand how Americans communicate describes the openness and informality that characterizes U.S. culture:

> Visitors may be overwhelmed by the sheer exuberant friendliness of Americans, especially in the central and southern parts of the country. Sit next to an American on an airplane and he will immediately address you by your first name, ask "So—how do you like it in the States?," explain his recent divorce

in intimate detail, invite you home for dinner, offer to lend you money, and wrap you in a warm hug on parting. This does not necessarily mean he will remember your name the next day. Americans are friendly because they just can't help it; they like to be neighbourly and want to be liked. (Faul, 2008, p. 1)

The informal approach that characterizes communication in countries like the United States is quite different from the great concern for propriety in many parts of Asia and Africa (Bjørge, 2007). Formality isn't so much a matter of using correct grammar as of defining social relationships. For example, there are different degrees of formality for speaking with old friends, nonacquaintances whose background one knows, and complete strangers. One sign of being a learned person in Korea is the ability to use language that recognizes these relational distinctions. When you contrast these sorts of distinctions with the casual friendliness many North Americans use even when talking with complete strangers, it's easy to see how a Korean might view American communicators as boorish and how an American might see Koreans as stiff and unfriendly.

NONVERBAL CODES

Many elements of nonverbal communication are shared by all humans, regardless of culture (Matsumoto, 2006; Schiefenhövel, 1997). For instance, people of all cultures convey messages through facial expressions and gestures. Furthermore, some of these physical displays have the same meaning everywhere. Crying is a universal sign of unhappiness or pain, and smiles signal friendly intentions. (Of course, smiles and tears may be insincere and manipulative, but their overt meanings are similar and constant in every culture.)

Despite nonverbal similarities, the range of differences in nonverbal behavior is tremendous. On an obvious level, customs such as belching after a meal or appearing nude in public that might be appropriate in some parts of the world would be considered outrageous in others. Along with social customs like these, there are more subtle differences in competent communication. Consider the use of gestures such as the "OK" sign made by joining thumb and forefinger to form a circle. This gesture is a cheery affirmation to most Americans, but it has very different meanings in other parts of the world (Knapp & Hall, 2006; Matsumoto & Hwang, 2013). In France and Belgium, it means "you're worth zero"; in Japan, it means "money"; and in Greece and Turkey, it is an insulting or vulgar sexual invitation. Given this sort of cross-cultural ambiguity, it's easy to visualize how an innocent tourist from the United States could wind up in serious trouble overseas without understanding why.

Less obvious cross-cultural differences can damage relationships without the communicators ever recognizing exactly what has gone wrong (Beaulieu, 2004; Hall, 1959). For example, Anglo-Saxons use the largest zone of personal space, followed by Asians. People from the Mediterranean and Latinos use the closest distance. It is easy to visualize the awkward advance and retreat pattern that might occur when two diplomats or businesspeople from these cultures meet. The Middle Easterner would probably

keep moving forward to close the gap that feels so wide, while the North American would continually back away. Both would probably feel uncomfortable without knowing why.

Like distance, patterns of eye contact vary around the world. Americans learn to maintain eye contact during conversations and avoiding eye contact can be interpreted as insincerity or a sign of weakness. By contrast, in China a mutual gaze is only appropriate in close, interdependent relationships (Guo & Hu, 2013). In either case, deviations from the norm are likely to make a culturally uneducated listener uncomfortable. You'll read much more about cultural differences in nonverbal communication in Chapter 6.

TABLE 2.4 Culture Affects Attributions

BEHAVIOR	ATTRIBUTION
American: How long will it take you to finish the report? Greek: I do not know. How long should it take?	American: I asked him to participate. Greek: His behavior makes no sense. He is the boss. Why doesn't he tell me? American: He refuses to take responsibility. Greek: I asked him for an order.
American: You are in the best position to analyze time requirements. Greek: Ten days. American: Take fifteen. It is agreed you will do it in fifteen days? Greek: These are my orders. Fifteen days.	American: I press him to take responsibility for his own actions. Greek: What nonsense! I better give him an answer. American: He lacks the ability to estimate time; this estimate is totally inadequate. American: I offer a contract.
American: Where is the report? Greek: It will be ready tomorrow.	American: I am making sure he fulfills his contract. Greek: He is asking for the report. (Both understand that it is not ready.)
American: But we agreed that it would be ready today.	American: I must teach him to fulfill an agreement.
The Greek hands in his resignation. The American is surprised.	Greek: The stupid, incompetent boss! Not only did he give me wrong orders, but he does not appreciate that I did a thirty-day job in sixteen days. Greek: I can't work for such a man.

DECODING MESSAGES

As you'll see in Chapter 4, attribution is the process of making sense of another person's behavior. Attribution is an unavoidable part of communicating: We have to form some sort of interpretation of what others' words and actions mean. But most behavior is so ambiguous that it can be interpreted in several ways. Furthermore, the usual tendency is to stick to the first attribution one makes. It's easy to see how this quick, sloppy attribution process can lead to making faulty interpretations—especially when communicators are from different cultural backgrounds.

In Table 2.4, a supervisor from the United States invites a subordinate from Greece to get involved in making a decision (Triandis, 1975, pp. 42–43). Because U.S. culture ranks relatively low on power distance, the supervisor encourages input from the employee. In Greece, however, the distance between bosses and their subordinates is much greater. Therefore, the Greek employee wants and expects to be told what to do. After all, it's the boss's job to give orders. Table 2.4 shows how the differing cultural beliefs shape both figures' attributions of the other's messages.

DEVELOPING INTERCULTURAL COMMUNICATION COMPETENCE

What distinguishes competent and incompetent intercultural communicators? In the rest of this chapter, we focus on answering this question. But before we get to the answers, take a moment to complete the "Assessing Your Communication" quiz on page 61 to evaluate your intercultural communication competence.

To a great degree, interacting successfully with strangers calls for the same ingredients of general communicative competence outlined in Chapter 1. It's important to have a wide range of behaviors and to be skillful at choosing and performing the most appropriate ones in a given situation. A genuine concern for others plays an important role. Cognitive complexity and the ability to empathize also help, although empathizing with someone from another culture can be challenging (Cassels et al., 2010; DeTurk, 2001). Finally, self-monitoring is important because the need to make midcourse corrections in your approach is often necessary when dealing with people from other cultures.

But beyond these basic qualities, communication researchers have worked long and hard to identify qualities that are unique, or at least especially important, ingredients of intercultural communicative competence (Ang et al., 2007; Arasaratnam & Banerjee, 2011).

MOTIVATION AND ATTITUDE

The desire to communicate successfully with strangers is an important start. For example, people high in willingness to communicate with people from other cultures report a greater number of friends from different backgrounds than those who are less willing to reach out (Kassing, 1997;

Massengill & Nash, 2009). But desire alone isn't sufficient (Arasaratnam, 2006). Some other ways of thinking described here are essential when dealing with people from other backgrounds (Samovar et al., 2007).

TOLERANCE FOR AMBIGUITY

As noted earlier, one of the most important concerns facing communicators is their desire to reduce uncertainty about one another (Berger, 1988; Gibbs et al., 2011). When we encounter communicators from different cultures, the level of uncertainty is especially high. Consider the basic challenge of communicating in an unfamiliar language. Pico Iyer (1990, pp. 129–130) captures the ambiguity that arises from a lack of fluency when he describes his growing friendship with Sachiko, a Japanese woman he met in Kyoto:

> I was also beginning to realize how treacherous it was to venture into a foreign language if one could not measure the shadows of the words one used. When I had told her, in Asuka, "*Jennifer Beals ga suki-desu. Anata mo*" ("I like Jennifer Beals—and I like you"), I had been pleased to find a way of conveying affection, and yet, I thought, a perfect distance. But later I looked up suki and found that I had delivered an almost naked protestation of love. . . .
>
> Meanwhile, of course, nearly all her shadings were lost to me. . . . Once, when I had to leave her house ten minutes early, she said, "I very sad," and another time, when I simply called her up, she said, "I very happy"—and I began to think her unusually sensitive, or else prone to bold and violent extremes, when really she was reflecting nothing but the paucity of her English vocabulary. . . . Talking in a language not one's own was like walking on one leg; when two people did it together, it was like a three-legged waltz.

Competent intercultural communicators accept—even welcome—this kind of ambiguity. Iyer (1990, pp. 220–221) describes the way the mutual confusion he shared with Sachiko actually helped their relationship develop:

> Yet in the end, the fact that we were both speaking in this pared-down diction made us both, I felt, somewhat gentler, more courteous, and more vulnerable than we would have been otherwise, returning us to a state of innocence.

Without a tolerance for ambiguity, the mass of often confusing and sometimes downright incomprehensible messages that bombard intercultural sojourners would be impossible to manage. Some people seem to come equipped with this sort of tolerance, while others have to cultivate it. One way or the other, that ability to live with uncertainty is an essential ingredient of intercultural communication competence (Gudykunst, 1993).

OPEN-MINDEDNESS

Being comfortable with ambiguity is important, but without an open-minded attitude a communicator will have trouble interacting competently with people from different backgrounds. To understand open-mindedness, it's helpful to consider two traits that are incompatible with it. **Ethnocentrism** is an attitude that one's own culture is superior to others. An ethnocentric person thinks—either privately or openly—that anyone who does not belong to his or her in-group is somehow strange, wrong, or even inferior.

ASSESSING YOUR COMMUNICATION

What Is Your Intercultural Communication Competence?

Imagine yourself interacting with people from a wide variety of cultural groups, not just one or two. Record your first impression to each of the following statements using a scale ranging from 1 to 7, where 1 = strongly disagree and 7 = strongly agree. Consider inviting someone who knows you well to also rate you on each item.

_____ **1.** I am conscious of the cultural knowledge I use when interacting with people with different cultural backgrounds.

_____ **2.** I adjust my cultural knowledge as I interact with people from a culture that is unfamiliar to me.

_____ **3.** I check the accuracy of my cultural knowledge as I interact with people from different cultures.

_____ **4.** I know the rules (e.g., vocabulary, grammar) of other languages.

_____ **5.** I know the cultural values and religious beliefs of other cultures.

_____ **6.** I know the rules for expressing nonverbal behaviors in other cultures.

_____ **7.** I enjoy interacting with people from different cultures.

_____ **8.** I am confident that I can socialize with locals in a culture that is unfamiliar to me.

_____ **9.** I enjoy living in cultures that are unfamiliar to me.

_____ **10.** I change my verbal behavior (e.g., accent, tone) when a cross-cultural interaction requires it.

_____ **11.** I use pause and silence differently to suit different cross-cultural situations.

_____ **12.** I vary the rate of my speaking when a cross-cultural situation requires it.

_____ **13.** I change my nonverbal behavior when a cross-cultural situation requires it.

_____ **14.** I alter my facial expressions when a cross-cultural interaction requires it.

Adapted from Ang, S., Van Dyne, L., Koh, C., Ng, K., Templer, K. J., Tay, C., & Chandrasekar, N. (2007). Cultural intelligence: Its measurement and effects on cultural judgment and decision making, cultural adaptation and task performance. *Management and Organization Review, 3*, 335–371.

For scoring information, see page 66 at the end of the chapter.

Travel writer Rick Steves (n.d.) describes how an ethnocentric point of view can interfere with respect for other cultural practices:

> We [Americans] consider ourselves very clean, but when we take baths, we use the same water for soaking, cleaning, and rinsing. (We wouldn't wash our dishes that way.) The Japanese, who use clean water for every step of the bathing process, might find our ways strange or even disgusting. People in some cultures blow their nose right onto the street. They couldn't imagine doing that into a small cloth, called a hanky, and storing it in their pocket to be used again and again....
>
> Too often we judge the world in terms of "civilized" and "primitive." I was raised thinking the world was a pyramid with the US on top and everyone else was trying to get there. I was comparing people on their ability (or interest) in keeping up with us in material consumption, science, and technology....
>
> Over the years, I've found that if we measure cultures differently (maybe according to stress, loneliness, heart attack rates, hours spent in traffic jams, or family togetherness), the results stack up differently. It's best not to fall into the "rating game." All societies are complex and highly developed in their own way.

Ethnocentrism leads to an attitude of **prejudice**—an unfairly biased and intolerant attitude toward others who belong to an out-group. (Note that the root term in *prejudice* is "prejudge.") An important element of prejudice is stereotyping. Stereotypical prejudices include the obvious exaggerations that all women are emotional, all men are sex-crazed and insensitive goons, all older people are out of touch with reality, and all immigrants are welfare parasites. Stereotyping can even be a risk when it comes to knowledge of cultural characteristics such as individualism or collectivism. Not all members of a group are equally individualistic or collectivistic. For example, a close look at Americans of European and Latin descent showed differences within each group (Oetzel, 1998). Some Latinos were more independent than some European Americans, and vice versa. Open-mindedness is especially important in intercultural work teams (Matveev, 2004). We have more to say about stereotyping in Chapter 4.

KNOWLEDGE AND SKILL

Attitude alone isn't enough to guarantee success in intercultural encounters. Communicators need to possess enough knowledge of other cultures to know what approaches are appropriate. The ability to "shift gears" and adapt one's style to the norms of another culture or co-culture is an essential ingredient of communication competence (Ang et al., 2007; Self, 2009).

How can a communicator acquire the culture-specific information that leads to competence? One important element is what Stella Ting-Toomey (1999) and others label as *mindfulness*—awareness of one's own behavior and that of others. Communicators who lack this quality blunder through intercultural encounters *mindlessly*, oblivious of how their own behavior may confuse or offend others, and how behavior that they consider weird may be simply different.

Charles Berger (1979) suggests three uncertainty reduction strategies for moving toward a more mindful, skillful style of intercultural communication:

- *Passive observation* involves noticing what behaviors members of a different culture use and applying these insights to communicate in ways that are most effective.
- *Active strategies* include reading, watching films, and asking experts and members of the other culture how to behave as well as taking academic courses related to intercultural communication and diversity.
- *Self-disclosure* involves volunteering personal information to people from the other culture with whom you want to communicate. One type of self-disclosure is to confess your cultural ignorance: "This is very new to me. What's the right thing to do in this situation?" This approach is the riskiest of the three described here because some cultures may not value candor and self-disclosure as much as others. Nevertheless, most people are pleased when strangers attempt to learn the practices of their culture, and they are usually more than willing to offer information and assistance.

PATIENCE AND PERSEVERANCE

Becoming comfortable and competent in a new culture or co-culture may be ultimately rewarding, but the process isn't easy. After a "honeymoon" phase, it's typical to feel confused, disenchanted, lonesome, and homesick. To top it off, you may feel disappointed in yourself for not adapting as easily as you expected. This stage—which typically feels like a crisis—has acquired the labels *culture shock* or *adjustment shock*.

You wouldn't be the first person to be blindsided by culture shock. When Lynn Chih-Ning Chang (2011) came to the United States from Taiwan for graduate school, she cried every day on the way home from class. All her life, she had been taught that it was respectful and ladylike to sit quietly and listen, so she was shocked that American students spoke aloud without raising their hands, interrupted each other, addressed the teacher by first name, and ate food in the classroom. What's more, Chang's classmates answered so quickly that by the time she was ready to say something, they were already on a new topic. The same behavior that made her "a smart and patient lady in Taiwan," she says, made her seem like a "slow learner" in the United States.

MEDIA CLIP
Out of His Element:
An Idiot Abroad

Karl Pilkington has led a sheltered life. He's British through and through, and he hates leaving the familiar comforts of his homeland. His friends Ricky Gervais and Stephen Merchant decide it's their responsibility to broaden Karl's world. They send him to various locations across the globe so he can experience unfamiliar cultures. Merchant's motives are honorable: He believes travel will enrich his friend. Gervais is more devious, and he finds twisted pleasure in watching Karl flail and fail.

As the title suggests, Karl doesn't always conduct himself well as an intercultural communicator—perhaps because he lacks the proper motivation. Over time, however, he usually gains the necessary knowledge and skills to help him succeed (to Merchant's delight and Gervais's dismay). The show provides plenty of laughs, but it also raises this question for reflection: How would *you* do as an interpersonal communicator if you were thrust into similar situations? Empathic viewers will identify with and appreciate Karl's intercultural struggles and successes.

Communication theorist Young Yum Kim (2005) has studied cultural adaptation extensively. She says it's natural to feel a sense of push and pull between the familiar and the novel. Kim encourages sojourners to regard stress as a good sign. It means they have the potential to adapt and grow. With patience, the sense of crisis begins to wane and, and once again, there's energy and enthusiasm to learn more.

Communication can be a challenge while you're learning how to operate in new cultures, but it can also be a solution. Chang, the Taiwanese student adapting to life in America, learned this firsthand. At first, she says, she was reluctant to approach American students and they were reluctant to approach her. Gradually, she got up the courage to initiate conversations, and she found that her classmates were friendly and receptive. Eventually, she made friends, began to fit in, and successfully completed her degree.

The transition from culture shock to adaptation and growth is usually successful, but it isn't a smooth, linear process. Instead, people tend to take two steps forward and one step back and to repeat that patterns many times. Kim (2008) calls this a "draw back and leap" pattern. Above all, she says, if people are patient and they keep trying, the rewards are worth it.

FOCUS ON RESEARCH
The Relational Challenges of Studying Abroad

Studying abroad is a popular and growing opportunity in higher education. Many students report that their learning is enhanced by taking courses in other cultures. Communication scholar Elisabeth Gareis has found that interpersonal communication and relationships make a significant difference in the educational experiences of foreign students in the United States.

Gareis and her colleagues surveyed international students studying in the United States and learned that most of them make closer friendships with fellow foreign students than with their hosts. Those who created the greatest number of local friendships tended to score high on measures of "communicative adaptability." In other words, these students made an effort to mesh with the communication patterns of their host culture.

In a separate study, Gareis found that some U.S. hosts are more welcoming than others. In an interesting statement about regional co-cultures, international students reported more satisfying experiences in the U.S. South than in the Northeast and in rural than in metropolitan environments.

Taken together, these studies tell us something important that we should probably already know: For study-abroad relationships to work, it takes effort and investment from both the travelers and their hosts.

Gareis, E. (2012). Intercultural friendship: Effects of home and host region. *Journal of International and Intercultural Communication, 5,* 309–328.

Gareis, E., Merkin, R., & Goldman, J. (2011). Intercultural friendship: Linking communication variables and friendship success. *Journal of Intercultural Communication Research, 40,* 153–171.

CHECK YOUR UNDERSTANDING

Objective 2.1 Understand the relationship between intercultural and interpersonal dimensions of communication.

The growing diversity of American culture at home and the increased exposure to people from around the world make an understanding of intercultural communication essential. In a diverse society, interpersonal encounters are marked by degrees of cultural and co-cultural salience.

Q: What are the most salient intercultural differences you are likely to encounter in your interpersonal relationships?

Objective 2.2 Describe five key values that help shape a culture's communication norms.

When members of different cultures interact, their values can affect interaction in ways that may be felt but not understood. These values include an emphasis on high- or low-context communication, individualism or collectivism, high or low power distance, relatively more or less avoidance of uncertainty, and either achievement or nurturing.

Q: What key values characterize the culture in which you communicate most comfortably?

Q: What communication challenges arise when you communicate with people with different values?

Objective 2.3 Recognize the range of co-cultures in today's society and how co-cultural factors can affect interpersonal communication.

Within any society, people belong to a variety of co-cultures, each of which carries its own identity and operates with its own set of communication rules. Some co-cultures include ethnicity and race, gender identity and sexual orientation, age/generation, and socioeconomic status.

Q: What co-cultures do you belong to, and what rules govern communication within these groups? How do these rules differ for members of other co-cultures you are likely to encounter?

Q: How can you best manage your communication with members of other co-cultures?

Objective 2.4 Explain the factors that shape a culture's verbal codes, nonverbal codes, and decoding of messages.

The codes that are used by members of a culture are often the most recognizable factors that shape communication between people from different backgrounds. Verbal codes include language spoken and the worldview created by it, as well as verbal communication style. Nonverbal codes also differ significantly, as do the attributions that cultural conditioning generate.

Q: Describe a set of cultural values, norms, and codes different from yours that could result in different cultural communication patterns.

Objective 2.5 Identify the attitudes, knowledge, and skills required for intercultural communication competence.

Intercultural communicative competence involves five dimensions: motivation and attitude, tolerance for ambiguity, open-mindedness, knowledge and skill, and patience and perseverance.

Q: Explain how you can apply the guidelines for intercultural competence in this chapter when interacting with people of cultural backgrounds different from your own.

KEY TERMS

- Achievement culture (48)
- Co-culture (39)
- Collectivistic culture (45)
- Culture (38)
- Ethnicity (49)
- Ethnocentrism (60)
- High-context culture (43)

- Individualistic culture (45)
- In-group (38)
- Intercultural communication (40)
- Low-context culture (43)
- Nurturing culture (48)
- Organizational culture (55)

- Out-group (38)
- Power distance (46)
- Prejudice (62)
- Race (49)
- Salience (41)
- Social identity (38)
- Uncertainty avoidance (47)

ACTIVITIES

1. With a group of classmates, identify the co-cultures to which each of you belongs. What in-groups do you belong to? You can best answer this question by thinking about whom you regard as belonging to out-groups. Based on your observations, consider the criteria you use to define in- and out-groups. Do you rely on race? Ethnicity? Age? Lifestyle? How do your judgments about in- and out-group membership affect your communication with others?

2. With a partner, identify one of your important interpersonal relationships. Consider how that relationship might be different if you and your partner adopted values and norms that were opposite from the ones you already hold. For example, if your communication is low context, how would things be different if you shifted to a high-context style? If you are tolerant of uncertainty, what might happen if you avoided any surprises? Based on your answers, consider the advantages and disadvantages of the cultural values and norms you hold. Think about the pros and cons of cultures that have differing values and norms.

3. The At Work sidebar on p. 55 describes how organizations have the properties of a culture. Select a place of business where you have worked and describe in a few sentences its organizational culture. What rules, either explicit or implicit, guide the communication in that workplace? Describe how these cultural norms affect how you have interacted with supervisors, coworkers, and customers on that job.

4. Identify one culture with which you currently interact or could interact with in the future. Collect information on communication rules and norms in that culture through library/Internet research and personal interviews. Based on your findings, describe the steps you can take to communicate more effectively with the culture's members.

5. Use the criteria on pages 59–64 to evaluate your intercultural communication competence. If possible, invite someone from a different culture or co-culture to help with this assessment.

SCORING FOR ASSESSING YOUR COMMUNICATION (PAGE 61)

Add responses to items 4, 5, and 6. This is your cognitive cultural intelligence score.

Add responses to items 7, 8, and 9. This is your motivational cultural intelligence score.

Add responses to items 10, 11, 12, 13, and 14. This is your behavioral cultural intelligence score.

Metacognitive cultural intelligence refers to the mental processes individuals use, such as planning and monitoring, to understand cultures. Those with high metacognitive cultural intelligence—scores of 15 and higher—are consciously aware of others' cultural preferences before and during interactions, and question their assumptions and adjust accordingly.

Cognitive cultural intelligence refers to knowledge of the norms, practices, and conventions in different cultures. Those with high cognitive cultural intelligence—scores of 11 and higher—understand similarities and differences across cultures.

Motivational cultural intelligence refers to the capability to direct attention and energy toward learning about and functioning in situations characterized by cultural differences. Those with high motivational cultural intelligence—scores of 16 and higher—direct attention and energy toward cross-cultural situations and have confidence in their interaction effectiveness.

Behavioral cultural intelligence refers to the capability to exhibit appropriate verbal and nonverbal communication behaviors when interacting with people from different cultures. Those with high behavioral cultural intelligence—scores of 21 and higher—exhibit behaviors appropriate to the situation.

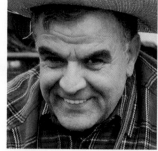

chapter 3

Interpersonal Communication and the Self

CHAPTER OUTLINE

LEARNING OBJECTIVES

3.1 Describe how the self-concept is subjective and is shaped by, and consequently affects, communication with others.

3.2 Explain how we manage impressions in person and online to enhance our presenting image.

3.3 Identify an optimal level of self-disclosure and non-disclosure in effective relationships.

WHO ARE YOU? Before reading on, take a few minutes to try a simple experiment. First, make a list of the 10 words or phrases that describe the most important features of who you are. Some of the items on your list may involve social roles: student, son or daughter, employee, and so on. Or you could define yourself through physical characteristics such as body type, height, skin color, or hair style. You may focus on your intellectual characteristics: smart, curious, inquisitive. Perhaps you can best define yourself in terms of moods, feelings, or attitudes: optimistic, critical, energetic. Or you could consider your social characteristics: outgoing, shy, defensive. You may see yourself in terms of belief systems: pacifist, Christian, vegetarian, libertarian. Maybe your work is an important part of who you are: barista, teacher, blogger. Finally, you could focus on particular skills (or lack of them): swimmer, artist, athlete. In any case, choose 10 words or phrases that best describe you and write them down.

Next, choose the one item from your list that is the most fundamental to who you are and copy it on another sheet of paper. Then pick the second most fundamental item and record it as number two on your new list. Continue ranking the 10 items until you have reorganized them all.

COMMUNICATION AND THE SELF-CONCEPT

The list you created in the exercise you just completed offers clues about your **self-concept**: the relatively stable set of perceptions you hold of yourself. One way to understand self-concept is to imagine a special mirror that not only reflects physical features but also allows you to view other aspects of yourself—emotional states, talents, likes, dislikes, values, roles, and so on. The reflection in that mirror would be your self-concept.

Any description of your self-concept that you constructed in this exercise is only a partial one. To make it complete, you'd have to keep adding items until your list ran into hundreds of words. Of course, not every dimension of your self-concept list is equally important. For example, the most significant part of one person's self-concept might consist of social roles, whereas for another it might be physical appearance, health, friendships, accomplishments, or skills.

Self-esteem is the part of the self-concept that involves evaluations of self-worth. A communicator's self-concept might include being quiet, argumentative, or serious. His or her self-esteem would be determined by how he or she feels about these qualities.

High or low self-esteem has a powerful effect on communication behavior, as Figure 3.1 shows. People who feel good about themselves have positive expectations about how they will communicate (Baldwin & Keelan, 1999). These feelings increase the chance that communication will be successful, and successes contribute to positive self-evaluations, which reinforce self-esteem. Of course, the same principle can work in a negative way

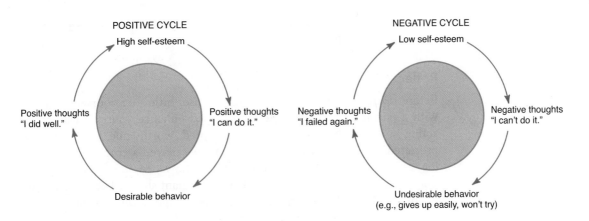

POSITIVE CYCLE

High self-esteem

Positive thoughts
"I did well."

Positive thoughts
"I can do it."

Desirable behavior

NEGATIVE CYCLE

Low self-esteem

Negative thoughts
"I failed again."

Negative thoughts
"I can't do it."

Undesirable behavior
(e.g., gives up easily, won't try)

FIGURE 3.1   **The Relationship between Self-Esteem and Communication Behavior**

Adapted from Johnson, H. M. (1998). *How do I love me?* (3rd ed.). Salem, WI: Sheffield, pp. 3, 5.

with communicators who have low self-esteem. One study found that people with low self-esteem don't fare well on social networking sites (Forest & Wood, 2012): They tend to post more negative information, and people are less likely to respond to downbeat messages. What could be a tool for connecting them with others ends up perpetuating their low self-regard.

Although high self-esteem has obvious benefits, it doesn't guarantee interpersonal success (Baumeister et al., 2003). People with high levels of self-esteem may *think* they make better impressions on others and have better friendships and romantic lives, but neither impartial observers nor objective tests verify these beliefs. It's easy to see how people with an inflated sense of self-worth could irritate others by coming across as condescending know-it-alls, especially when their self-worth is challenged (vanDellen et al., 2010; Vohs & Heatherton, 2004). Moreover, people with low self-esteem have the potential to change their self-appraisals. The point here is that positive self-evaluations can often be the starting point for positive communication with others.

HOW THE SELF-CONCEPT DEVELOPS

Researchers generally agree that self-concept does not exist at birth (Rochat, 2001). At about 6 or 7 months of age, infants begin to recognize "self" as distinct from surroundings. If you've ever watched children at this age, you've probably marveled at how they can stare with great fascination at their own foot or hand, almost as if these were strange objects belonging to someone else. Then the connection is made: "The foot is me," "The hand is me." These first revelations form the child's earliest concept of self.

As the child develops, this rudimentary sense of identity expands into a much more complete and sophisticated picture that resembles the self-concept of adults. This evolution is almost totally a product of social interaction (Schmidt, 2006; Weigert & Gecas, 2003). Two complementary theories describe how interaction with others shapes the way individuals view themselves: reflected appraisal and social comparison (Suls et al., 2002; Wallace & Tice, 2012).

Reflected Appraisal

Before reading on, try the following exercise: Either by yourself or aloud with a partner, recall someone who helped enhance your self-esteem by acting in a way that made you feel accepted, worthwhile, important, appreciated, or loved. This person needn't have played a crucial role in your life, as long as the role was positive. Often how people see themselves is shaped by many tiny nudges as well as a few giant shoves. For instance, you might recall a childhood neighbor who took a special interest in you, or a grandparent who never criticized or questioned your youthful foolishness.

After thinking about this supportive person, recall someone who acted in either a big or small way to diminish your self-esteem. For instance, you may have had a coach who criticized you in front of the team, or a teacher who said or implied that you wouldn't amount to much.

After thinking about these two types of people, you should begin to see that everyone's self-concept is to some degree a **reflected appraisal**: a mirroring of the judgments of those around a person. To the extent that you have received supportive messages, you have learned to appreciate and value yourself. To the degree that you have received critical signals, you are likely to feel less valuable, lovable, and capable (Jaret et al., 2005). Your self-concept can be seen, at least in part, as a reflection of the messages you've received throughout your life. The Focus on Research sidebar in this section describes how social media now play a role in this process for some.

Social scientists use the term **significant other** to describe a person whose evaluations are especially influential. Messages from parents, of course, are an early and important influence on the self-concept. Supportive parents are more likely to raise children with stable self-concepts and high self-esteem. By contrast, parents with low self-esteem and poor, negative, or deviant self-concepts tend to have unhappy children who view themselves in primarily negative ways (Salimi et al., 2005), communicate less effectively (Huang, 1999), and go on to have unsatisfying relationships (Vangelisti & Crumley, 1998). Along with family, the messages from many other significant others shape our self-concept (Hergovitch et al., 2002). A teacher from long ago, a special friend or relative, someone you dated, or even a barely known acquaintance whom you respected can all leave an imprint on how you view yourself—sometimes for better, sometimes for worse (Rill et al., 2009).

As we grow older, the power of messages from significant others remains. Some social scientists have coined the phrase "Michelangelo phenomenon" to describe the way significant others sculpt one another's self-concepts (Righetti et al., 2010; Rusbult et al., 2009). Romantic partners, people on the job, friends, and many others can speak and act in ways that have a profound effect on the way we view ourselves.

You might argue that not every part of your self-concept is shaped by others, that there are certain objective facts recognizable by self-observation alone. After all, nobody needs to tell you whether you are taller than others, speak with an accent, have curly hair, and so on. Indeed, some features of the self are immediately apparent. But the *significance* we attach to them—that is, the rank we assign them in the hierarchy of our list and the interpretation we give them—depends greatly on the opinions of others.

Social Comparison

So far, we have looked at the way others' messages shape one's self-concept and self-esteem. In addition to using these messages, we form our self-image by the process of **social comparison**: evaluating ourselves in terms of how we compare with others (Johnson & Stapel, 2010). We decide whether we are superior or inferior (which influences our self-esteem) and similar or different (which influences our self-concept) by comparing ourselves to what social scientists call **reference groups**—those people against whom we evaluate our own characteristics. You might feel ordinary or inferior in terms of talent, friendships, or attractiveness if you compare yourself with an inappropriate reference group (Pahl & Eiser, 2007). For instance, studies have shown that young women who regularly compare themselves with ultra-thin models develop negative appraisals of their own bodies, in some cases leading to eating disorders (Harrison & Hefner, 2006; Krcmar et al., 2008). Men, too, who compare themselves to media-idealized male physiques evaluate their bodies negatively (Cho & Lee, 2013; Strong, 2005). People also use others' online profiles as points of comparison, and they may feel less attractive, successful, and happy after doing so (Haferkamp & Krämer, 2010; Cho & Edge, 2012).

FOCUS ON RESEARCH
Mirror, Mirror on the Cyberwall

Reflected appraisal is a longstanding concept in the social sciences. Recently, scholars believe it has gained new dimensions because of technological advances (Wallace & Tice, 2012). They've coined the term *internet-mediated reflected appraisal* to describe how contemporary communicators draw conclusions about themselves by considering how others view them online.

Put more simply, you might decide who you think you are (in part) by looking at how you portray yourself on social networking sites. Researchers asked participants to spend time reviewing their own Facebook profiles and then measured the participants' self-esteem. They found that participants

felt better about themselves after looking at their Facebook pages. In essence, the participants viewed their well-crafted profiles and thought, "This is how others see me—and darn, I look pretty good!"

Of course, this raises questions about the validity of these self-appraisals. Facebook profiles are edited presentations that usually put a person's best foot forward. As we discuss later in this chapter, managing impressions via social media can lead to less-than-accurate portrayals and perceptions by the self and others. But at the very least, social networking sites can be a tool for helping people view themselves in the best light possible.

Gonzales, A. L., & Hancock, J. T. (2011). Mirror, mirror on my Facebook wall: Effects of exposure to Facebook on self-esteem. *Cyberpsychology, Behavior, and Social Networking, 41*, 79–83.

To some degree, we're in control of whom we choose for comparison. It's possible to seek out people with whom we compare favorably (Beer & Hughes, 2011). This technique may bring to mind a search for a community of idiots in which you would appear as a genius, but there are healthier ways of changing your standards for comparison. For instance, you might decide that it's foolish to constantly compare your athletic prowess with that of professionals or your looks with those of movie stars. Once you place yourself alongside a truly representative sample, your self-concept may become more realistic.

CHARACTERISTICS OF THE SELF-CONCEPT

Now that you have a better idea of how your self-concept has developed, we can take a closer look at some of its characteristics.

The Self-Concept Is Subjective

The way we view ourselves may be at odds with others' perceptions—and often with the observable facts. For instance, people are notoriously bad judges of their own communication skills. In one study, there was no relationship between the subjects' self-evaluations as interpersonal communicators, public speakers, or listeners and their observed ability to perform well in any of these areas (Carrell & Willmington, 1996). In another study (Myers, 1980), college students were asked to rank themselves on their ability to get along with others. Defying mathematical laws, all subjects—every last one of more than 800,000—put themselves in the top half of the population. A total of 60 percent rated themselves in the top 10 percent of the population, and an amazing 25 percent believed they were in the top 1 percent. These students had similarly lofty appraisals of their leadership and athletic abilities.

There are several reasons why some people have a level of self-esteem that others would regard as unrealistically favorable. First, a self-estimation might be based on obsolete information. Perhaps your jokes used to be well received, or your grades were high, or your work was superior, but now the facts have changed. Self-esteem might also be excessively favorable due to distorted feedback from others. A boss may claim to be an excellent manager because assistants pour on false praise to keep their jobs. A child's inflated ego may be based on the praise of doting parents. A third reason is that we may simply ignore negative qualities. One study found that online daters often have a "foggy mirror"—that is, they see themselves more positively than others do (Ellison et al., 2006). This leads to inflated self-descriptions that don't always match what an objective third party might say about them.

There are also times when we view ourselves more harshly than the facts warrant. We have all experienced a temporary case of the "uglies," convinced we look much worse than others say that we really appear. Research confirms what common sense suggests—people are more critical of themselves when they are experiencing these negative moods than when they are feeling more positive (Sturman & Mongrain, 2008) and may even feel they don't deserve good things to happen to them (Wood et al., 2009). Although everyone suffers occasional bouts of low self-esteem, some people suffer from long-term or even permanent states of excessive self-doubt and criticism (Gara et al., 1993). It's easy to understand how this chronic condition can influence the way these people approach and respond to others.

What are the reasons for such excessively negative self-evaluations? As with unrealistically high self-esteem, one source for an overabundance of self-put-downs is obsolete information. A string of past failures in school or with social relations can linger to haunt a communicator long after they have occurred. Similarly, we've known slender students who still think of themselves as fat, and clear-complexioned people who still behave as if they were acne ridden.

MEDIA CLIP
Overcoming a Negative Appraisal: *The Way Way Back*

"On a scale of 1 to 10, what do you think you are?" It's a self-appraisal question that shy, awkward Duncan (Liam James) would rather not answer. It's asked by Trent (Steve Carell), who is dating Duncan's mother and sees himself in a stepfather role. After a long hesitation, Duncan labels himself "a 6." Trent quickly responds, "I'd put you down as a 3"—and then he upbraids Duncan for his lack of initiative.

This opening appraisal sets the tone for *The Way Way Back*, as 14-year-old Duncan spends his summer in quest of more positive regard from others. He finally finds it from an unlikely source: fun-loving Owen (Sam Rockwell), who loosely manages a water park and is intent on enjoying life. Owen takes Duncan under his wing, and over time Duncan gains a sense of identity and purpose—due in large measure to Owen's affirming input.

The movie is cowritten by Jim Rash, who says the opening scene was taken verbatim from a conversation he had with his stepfather as a teen. This serves as a reminder that negative appraisals can leave a lasting impact—and that confirming communication from significant others like Owen can redeem and restore a damaged self-concept and low self-esteem.

Distorted feedback also can lead to low self-esteem. Feedback becomes distorted when we give it more power than it deserves, ignoring positive messages. Most of us can remember earning plenty of praise for a performance but obsessing instead about the one or two negative comments that were offered. Hanging on to hurtful things we've been told can distort our sense of self.

Along with obsolete information and distorted feedback, another cause for low self-esteem is the myth of perfection that is common in our society. From the time most of us learn to understand language, we are exposed to fairy-tale models who appear to be perfect at whatever they do. Unfortunately, many parents perpetuate the myth of perfection by refusing to admit that they are ever mistaken or unfair. Children, of course, accept this perfectionist façade for a long time, not being in a position to dispute the wisdom of such powerful beings. From the behavior of the adults around them comes the clear message: "A well-adjusted, successful person has no faults." We have a great deal to say about perfection and other irrational ideas, both later in this chapter and in Chapter 8.

A final reason people often sell themselves short is also connected to social expectations. Curiously, the perfectionist society to which we belong rewards those people who downplay the strengths we demand they possess (or pretend to possess). We term these people "modest" and find their behavior agreeable. On the other hand, we consider some of those who honestly appreciate their own strengths to be "braggarts" or "egotists," confusing them with the people who boast about accomplishments they do not possess (Miller et al., 1992). This convention leads most of us to talk freely about our shortcomings while downplaying our accomplishments. It's all right to proclaim that you're miserable if you have failed to do well on a project, but it's seen as boastful to express your pride at a job well done.

A Healthy Self-Concept Is Flexible

People change. Shy children might turn into outgoing adults. Moody teenagers can become upbeat professionals. People also change from context to context. You might be a relaxed conversationalist with people you know but at a loss for words with strangers. The self-concepts of most communicators react to these changes ("I'm patient at work," "I'm not patient at home"), and these changes affect self-esteem ("I'm not as good a person at home as I am in the office").

As we change in these and many other ways, our self-concept must also change to stay realistic. An accurate self-portrait today would not be exactly the same as the one we had a year ago, a few months ago, or even yesterday. This does not mean that you change radically from day to day. The fundamental characteristics of your personality will stay the same for years, perhaps for a lifetime. However, it is likely that in slow but important ways you are changing—physically, intellectually, emotionally, and spiritually.

The Self-Concept Resists Change

A realistic self-concept should reflect the way we change over time, but the tendency to resist revision of our self-perception is strong. Once a communicator fastens onto a self-concept, the tendency is to seek out people who confirm it. Numerous studies (e.g., Rehman et al., 2009; Stets & Cast, 2007) have shown that both college students and married couples with high self-esteem seek out partners who view them favorably, whereas those with low self-esteem are more inclined to interact with people who view them unfavorably. This tendency to seek information that conforms to an existing self-concept, labeled *cognitive conservatism*, appears to hold true for people in a variety of cultures (Church et al., 2012).

We are understandably reluctant to revise a favorable self-perception (DeMarree et al., 2011). If you were a thoughtful, romantic partner early in a relationship, it would be hard to admit that you might have become less considerate and attentive lately. Likewise, if you used to be a serious student, acknowledging that you have slacked off isn't easy.

Curiously, the tendency to cling to an outmoded self-perception holds even when the new image would be more favorable (DeMarree et al., 2010). We can recall scores of attractive, intelligent students who still view themselves as the gawky underachievers they were in the past. The tragedy of this sort of cognitive conservatism is obvious. People with unnecessarily negative self-esteem can become their own worst enemies, denying themselves the validation they deserve and the need to enjoy satisfying relationships.

Once the self-concept is firmly rooted, only a powerful force can change it. At least four requirements must be met for an appraisal to be regarded as important (Dehart et al., 2010):

- The person who offers a particular appraisal must be *someone we see as competent to offer it*. Parents satisfy this requirement extremely well because as young children, we perceive that our parents know so much about us—sometimes more than we know about ourselves.
- *The appraisal must be perceived as highly personal.* The more the other person seems to know about us and adapts what is being said to fit us, the more likely we are to accept judgments from this person.
- The appraisal must be *reasonable in light of what we believe about ourselves.* If an appraisal is similar to one we give ourselves, we will believe it; if it is somewhat dissimilar, we might accept it; but if it is completely dissimilar, we will probably reject it.
- Appraisals that are *consistent* and *numerous* are more persuasive than those that contradict usual appraisals or those that occur only once. As long as only a *few* students yawn in class, a teacher can safely disregard them as a reflection on his or her teaching ability. In like manner, you could safely disregard the occasional customer who doesn't like your service in light of the many who do. Of course, when you get a second or third similar appraisal in a short time, the evaluation becomes harder to ignore.

THE SELF-FULFILLING PROPHECY AND COMMUNICATION

Self-concept is such a powerful influence on the personality that it not only determines how you see yourself in the present but also can actually affect your future behavior and that of others. Such occurrences come about through a phenomenon called the self-fulfilling prophecy. A **self-fulfilling prophecy** occurs when a person's expectations of an event, and her or his subsequent behavior based on those expectations, make the outcome more likely to occur than would otherwise have been true (Watzlawick, 2005). A self-fulfilling prophecy involves four stages:

1. Holding an expectation (for yourself or for others)
2. Behaving in accordance with that expectation
3. The expectation coming to pass
4. Reinforcing the original expectation

Let's use a slightly exaggerated example to illustrate the concept. One morning you read your horoscope, which offers the following prediction: "Today you will meet the person of your dreams, and the two of you will live happily ever after." Assuming you believe in horoscopes, what will you do? You'll probably start making plans to go out on the town that night in search of your "dream person." You'll dress up, groom yourself well, and carefully evaluate every person you encounter. You'll also be attentive, charming, witty, polite, and gracious when you end up meeting your "dream candidate." As a result, that person is likely to be impressed and attracted to you—and lo and behold, the two of you end up living happily ever after. Your conclusion? That horoscope sure had it right!

On closer examination, the horoscope—which helped create the Stage 1 expectation—really wasn't the key to your success. Although it got the ball rolling, you would still be single if you had stayed home that evening. Stage 2—going out on the town and acting charming—was what led your "dream person" to be attracted to you, bringing about the positive results (Stage 3). While it's tempting to credit the horoscope for the outcome (Stage 4), it's important to realize that *you* were responsible for bringing the prediction to pass—hence the term *self-fulfilling* prophecy.

The horoscope story is fictional, but research shows that self-fulfilling prophecies operate in real-life situations. To see how, read on.

Types of Self-Fulfilling Prophecies

There are two types of self-fulfilling prophecies. Self-imposed prophecies occur when your own expectations influence your behavior. You've probably had the experience of waking up in a cross mood and saying to yourself, "This will be a bad day." Once you made such a decision, you may have acted in ways that made it come true. If you avoid the company of others because you expect they

"I don't sing because I am happy. I am happy because I sing."

had nothing to offer, your suspicions would have been confirmed—nothing exciting or new is likely to happen. On the other hand, if you approach the same day with the idea that it could be a good one, this expectation may well be met. Smile at people, and they're more likely to smile back. Enter a class determined to learn something, and you probably will—even if it's how not to instruct students! In these cases and other similar ones, your attitude has a great deal to do with what you see and how you behave.

Research has demonstrated the power of self-imposed prophecies. In one study, communicators who believed they were incompetent proved less likely than others to pursue rewarding relationships and more likely to sabotage their existing relationships than did people who were less critical of themselves (Kolligan, 1990). Research also suggests that communicators who feel anxious about giving speeches seem to create self-fulfilling prophecies about doing poorly, which causes them to perform less effectively (MacIntyre & Thivierge, 1995). On the other hand, students who perceive themselves as capable achieve more academically (Zimmerman, 1995).

A second category of self-fulfilling prophecies occurs when one person's expectations govern another's actions (Blank, 1993). The classic example was demonstrated by Robert Rosenthal and Lenore Jacobson (1968; Jussim et al., 2009) in a study they described in their book *Pygmalion in the Classroom*. The experimenters told teachers that 20 percent of the children in a certain elementary school showed unusual potential for intellectual growth. The names of the 20 percent were drawn by means of a table of random numbers—much as if they were drawn out of a hat. Eight months later these unusual or "magic" children showed significantly greater gains in IQ than did the remaining children, who had not been singled out for the teachers' attention. The change in the teachers' behavior toward these allegedly "special" children led to changes in their intellectual performance. Among other things, the teachers gave the "smart" students more time to

The film *Divergent* pictures a dystopian society where citizens are pigeonholed into categories that shape their adult lives—in essence, an other-imposed prophecy. Sixteen-year-old Tris Prior (Shailene Woodley) doesn't fit those categories, so she sets out to define herself on her own terms. In doing so, she demonstrates the power of self-fulfilling prophecies to help us become the kind of person we choose.

answer questions and provided more feedback to them. These children did better not because they were any more intelligent than their classmates, but because their teachers—significant others—communicated the expectation that they could.

Notice that it isn't just the observer's *belief* that creates a self-fulfilling prophecy for the person who is the target of the expectations. The observer must *communicate that belief* verbally or nonverbally for the prediction to have any effect. If parents have faith in their children but the kids aren't aware of that confidence, they won't be affected by their parents' expectations. If a boss has concerns about an employee's ability to do a job but keeps those worries to herself or himself, the subordinate won't be influenced. In this sense, the self-fulfilling prophecies imposed by one person on another are as much a communication phenomenon as a psychological one.

 PRESENTING THE SELF

So far, we've described how communication shapes the way communicators view themselves. We will now turn the tables and focus on the topic of **impression management**—the communication strategies people use to influence how others view them. In the following pages, you will see that many of our messages are aimed at creating desired impressions.

PUBLIC AND PRIVATE SELVES

To understand why impression management exists, we have to discuss the notion of self in more detail. So far, we have referred to the "self" as if each of us had only one identity. In truth, each of us possesses several selves, some private and others public (Fenigstein, 2009). These selves are often quite different.

The **perceived self** is the person you believe yourself to be in moments of honest self-examination. The perceived self may not be accurate in every respect. For example, you might think you are much more (or less) intelligent than an objective test would measure. Accurate or not, the perceived self is powerful because we believe it reflects who we are. You can call the perceived self "private" because you are unlikely to reveal all of it to another person. You can verify the private nature of the perceived self by thinking of elements of your self-perception that you would not disclose. For example, you might be reluctant to share some feelings about your appearance ("I think I'm rather unattractive"), your goals ("The most important thing to me is becoming rich"), or your motives ("I care more about myself than about others").

In contrast to the perceived self, the **presenting self** is a public image—the way we want to appear to others. In most cases the presenting self we seek to create is a socially approved image: diligent student, loving partner, conscientious worker, loyal friend, and so on. Sociologist Erving Goffman (1959, 1983) used the word **face** to describe this socially approved identity, and he coined the term **facework** to describe the verbal and nonverbal ways in which we act to maintain our own presenting image and the images of others. Goffman argued that each of us can be viewed as a kind of playwright who creates roles that we want others to believe, as well as the performer who acts out those roles. This "playwriting" starts early in life as children interact with their parents (Gerholm, 2011), and it continues into adulthood in both personal and professional settings.

Goffman (1983) suggested that each of us maintains face by putting on a *front* when we are around others whom we want to impress. In contrast, behavior in the *back region*—when we are alone—may be quite different. You can recognize the difference between front and backstage behavior by recalling a time when you observed a driver, alone in her or his car, behaving in ways that would never be acceptable in public. All of us engage in backstage ways of acting that we would never exhibit in front of others. Just recall how you behave in front of the bathroom mirror when the door is locked, and you will appreciate the difference between public and private behavior. If you knew someone was watching, would you behave differently?

CHARACTERISTICS OF IMPRESSION MANAGEMENT

Now that you have a sense of what impression management is, we can look at some characteristics of this process (Locher, 2010).

We Strive to Construct Multiple Identities

It is an oversimplification to suggest we use impression management strategies to create just one identity. In the course of even a single day, most people play a variety of roles: "respectful student," "joking friend," "kind neighbor," and "helpful worker," to suggest just a few. We even play a variety of roles around the same person. As you grew up, you almost certainly changed characters as you interacted with your parents. In one context you acted as the responsible adult ("You can trust me with the car!"), and at another time you were the helpless child ("I can't find my socks!"). At some times—perhaps on birthdays or holidays—you were a dedicated family member, and at other times you may have played the role of rebel. Likewise, in romantic relationships, we switch among many ways of behaving, depending on the context: friend, lover, business partner, scolding critic, apologetic child, and so on.

Each of us constructs multiple identities, many of which may be independent of each other, and some of which may even conflict with one another (Spears, 2001). For example, some student-athletes experience tension when the roles of student and athlete seem to have incompatible demands (Yopyk & Prentice, 2005). And for most of us, the top two impressions we seek are to be perceived as warm (friendly, trustworthy) and as competent (intelligent, skillful). Many, however, see these two impressions as a trade-off; you can't be both at the same time. Thus, people often "play dumb" when the goal is to be liked, and they become overly critical when the goal is to look smart (Holoien & Fiske, 2013). Balancing these two impressions is a skillful act.

It's tempting to regard some of your identities as more "real" than others, but it's more accurate to recognize that all of them are you in various roles. You may not enjoy brownnosing the boss or placating an angry customer, but that doesn't make those behaviors "not you." Instead, it means you're playing the role of "respectful employee" or "dedicated server" in ways that you (and perhaps society) deem appropriate. Communication researchers argue that differentiating between "fake" and "real" selves is counterproductive (Tracy & Trethewey, 2005). Instead, it's healthier to recognize that competent communicators are multifaceted people with a variety of roles and identities—all of which are "you."

Impression Management Is Collaborative

As we perform like actors trying to create a front, our "audience" is made up of other actors who are trying to create their own characters. Identity-related communication is a kind of improvisation in which our character reacts with others. Good-natured teasing only works if the other person appreciates your humor and responds well. (Imagine how your kidding would fall flat if somebody didn't get or enjoy the joking.) Likewise, being a successful romantic can succeed only if the object of your affections plays his or her part.

Impression Management Can Be Deliberate or Unconscious

There's no doubt that sometimes we are highly aware of managing our identities. Most job interviews and first dates are clear examples of deliberate impression management. But in other cases we unconsciously act in ways that are really small public performances. For example, experimental participants expressed facial disgust in reaction to eating sandwiches laced with a supersaturated solution of saltwater only when there was another person present; when they were alone, they made no faces on eating the same snack (Brightman et al., 1975). Another study showed that communicators engage in facial mimicry (such as smiling or looking sympathetic in response to another's message) only in face-to-face settings, when their expressions can be seen by the other person. When they are speaking over the phone and their reactions cannot be seen, they do not make the same expressions (Chovil, 1991). Studies such as these suggest that much of our behavior is aimed at sending messages to others—in other words, impression management.

Despite the claims of some theorists, it seems an exaggeration to suggest that *all* behavior is aimed at making impressions. Young children certainly aren't strategic communicators. A baby spontaneously laughs when pleased and cries when sad or uncomfortable, without any notion of creating an impression in others. Likewise, there are almost certainly times when we, as adults, act spontaneously. But when a significant other questions the presenting self we try to portray, the likelihood of acting to prop it up increases.

FACE-TO-FACE IMPRESSION MANAGEMENT

In face-to-face interaction, communicators can manage their front in three ways: manner, appearance, and setting. *Manner* consists of a communicator's words and nonverbal actions. In Chapters 5 and 6, we describe in detail how what you say and do creates impressions. Because you have to speak and act, the question isn't whether your manner sends a message; rather, it's whether these messages will be intentional.

A second dimension of impression management is *appearance*—the personal items people use to shape an image. Sometimes clothing is part of creating a professional image. A physician's white lab coat and a police officer's uniform set the wearer apart as someone special. In the business world, a tailored suit creates a very different impression than a rumpled outfit. Off the job, clothing is just as important. People dressed in upper-middle-class fashion have a very different experience shopping than those in lower-class fashion (Aliakbari & Abdollahi, 2013) We choose clothing

---

IMPRESSION MANAGEMENT IN THE WORKPLACE @WORK

Some advisors encourage workers to "Just be yourself" on the job. But there are times when disclosing certain information about your personal life can damage your chances for success (Connell, 2012; Fleming & Sturdy, 2009). This is especially true for people with "invisible stigmas"—traits that run the risk of being viewed unfavorably (Ragins, 2008).

Many parts of a worker's identity have the potential to be invisible stigmas: Religion (evangelical Christian, Muslim), sexual orientation (gay, lesbian, bisexual), health (bipolar, HIV positive). What counts as a stigma to some people (liberal, conservative) might be favored in another organization (Ragins & Singh, 2007).

As you consider how to manage your identity at work, take the following into account:

- *Proceed with caution.* In an ideal world, it would be safe to reveal ourselves without hesitation.

But in real life, total candor can have consequences, so it may be best to move slowly.

- *Assess the organization's culture.* If your workplace seems supportive of differences—and especially if it appears to welcome people like you—then revealing more of yourself may be safe.
- *Consider the consequences of not opening up.* Keeping an important part of your identity secret can also take an emotional toll (Pachankis, 2007). If staying quiet is truly necessary, you may be better off finding a more welcoming place to work.
- *Test the waters.* If you have a trusted colleague or manager, think about revealing yourself to that person and asking advice about whether and how to go further. But realize that secrets can be leaked, so be sure the person you approach can keep confidences.

MEDIA CLIP
The Promise and Perils of Online Relationships: *Catfish*

Twentysomething New York photographer Nev Schulman is flattered and intrigued when a bright 8-year-old Michigan girl named Abby begins sending him fan mail and paintings based on his work. Nev and Abby strike up a long-distance friendship via social media, and soon the artist is also exchanging messages with Abby's family and friends. The narrative becomes more intriguing when Nev falls into an online romance with Abby's older sister, Megan, even though the two haven't met in person.

Nev and his buddies impulsively take a road trip to Michigan to meet Megan and her family. Without spilling too many details, they discover that Megan isn't who or what they thought she was. In the process, everyone involved learns some hard lessons about impression management in mediated relationships.

The movie struck a chord with viewers and helped launch *Catfish: The TV Show*. Schulman plays host in the reality series and helps online romantic partners meet face-to-face for the first time—often with surprising results. Both the film and the show turned the word "catfish" into a pop culture verb (to be "catfished" means to be relationally duped, primarily by means of mediated communication). See the Dark Side box on page 86 to read Nev's tips on how not to be victimized by online deception.

that sends a message about ourselves: "I'm wealthy," "I'm stylish," "I'm sexy," "I'm athletic," and a host of other possible messages.

A final way to manage impressions is through the choice of *setting*—physical items we use to influence how others view us. In modern Western society, the car is a major part of impression management. This explains why many people lust after cars that are far more expensive and powerful than they really need. A sporty convertible or fancy imported sedan doesn't just get drivers from one place to another; it also makes statements about the kind of people they are. The physical setting we choose and the way we arrange it is another important way to manage impressions. What colors do you choose for the place you live? What artwork is on your walls? What music do you play? If possible, we choose a setting that we enjoy, but in many cases we create an environment that will present the desired front to others.

IMPRESSION MANAGEMENT IN SOCIAL MEDIA

The preceding examples involve face-to-face interaction, but impression management is just as pervasive and important in mediated communication. At first glance, social media seem to limit the potential for impression management. Texting and e-mail, for example, appear to lack the "richness" of other channels. They don't convey the tone of your voice, postures, gestures, or facial expressions. However, what is missing in mediated messages can actually be an advantage for communicators who want to manage the impressions they make (Hancock & Dunham, 2001). John Suler (2002, p. 455) put it this way:

One of the interesting things about the Internet is the opportunity it offers people to present themselves in a variety of different ways. You can alter your style of being just slightly or indulge in wild experiments with your identity by changing your age, history, personality, and physical appearance, even your gender. The username you choose, the details you do or don't indicate about yourself, the information presented on your personal web page, the persona or avatar you assume in an online community—all are important aspects of how people manage their identity in cyberspace.

E-mailers and texters can choose the desired level of clarity or ambiguity, seriousness or humor, logic or emotion in their messages. And as we discussed in Chapter 1, the asynchronicity of most electronic correspondence allows a sender to say difficult things without forcing the receiver to respond immediately, and it permits the receiver to ignore a message rather than give an unpleasant response. Options like these show that social media can serve as a tool for impression management at least as well as the face-to-face variety (Renner & Schütz, 2008; Tong & Walther, 2011b).

Like other forms of online communication, "broadcasting" on the Internet is also a tool for managing one's identity. Blogs, personal web pages, and profiles on social networking websites such as Facebook all provide opportunities for their creators to manage their identities (Mehdizadeh, 2010; Salimkhan et al., 2010). Consider how featuring or withholding the following kinds of information affects how others might regard your online profile: age, personal photo, educational or career accomplishments, sexual orientation, job title, personal interests, personal philosophy and religious beliefs, and organizations to which you belong (Doster, 2013).

Comments posted on social networking sites also create impressions. For instance, one study showed that Facebook users are more likely to express positive rather than negative emotions, and that they present better emotional well-being online than in real life (Qiu et al., 2012). As the Focus on Research sidebar on page 73 explains, that's why people feel better about themselves after reviewing their Facebook profiles—after all, they're looking at idealized versions of themselves (Toma & Hancock, 2013).

Viewing your online presence as a neutral third party can be a valuable impression management exercise. Enter your name in a search engine and see what pops up. You may decide it's time to engage in what researchers call "reputation management" (Madden & Smith, 2010). Perhaps you'll want to change privacy settings on your profiles, customize who can see certain updates, and delete unwanted information about yourself.

IMPRESSION MANAGEMENT AND HONESTY

At first, impression management might sound like an academic label for manipulation or phoniness. There certainly are situations where people misrepresent themselves to gain the trust of others (Rui & Stefanone, 2013; Whitty, 2007). A manipulative date who pretends to be affectionate to gain sexual favors is clearly unethical and deceitful. So are job applicants who lie about their academic records to get hired or salespeople who pretend to be dedicated to customer service when their real goal is to make a quick buck.

Deception in cyberspace is common—indeed, "it may be normative to distort reality online" (Zimbler & Feldman, 2011, p. 2492). In one survey, 27 percent of respondents had engaged in deceptive behaviors while online (Lenhart et al., 2001), and a diary study found that 22 to 25 percent of mediated interactions involve deception (George & Robb, 2008). A quarter of teens have pretended to be a different person online, and a third confess they have given false information about themselves while e-mailing, IMing, or game playing. Even the selection of an avatar can involve deception (Galanxhi & Nah, 2007). And a surprising number of people represent themselves as members of the opposite sex (Samp et al., 2003). Some of these deceptions are relatively harmless, but others have serious consequences (see the Dark Side box in this section).

Interviewees in one study (Toma et al., 2008) acknowledged the delicate task of balancing an ideal online identity against the "real" self behind their profile. Many admitted they sometimes fudged facts about themselves—using outdated photos or "forgetting" information about their age, for instance. But respondents were less tolerant when prospective dates posted inaccurate identities. For example, one date-seeker expressed resentment upon learning that a purported "hiker" hadn't hiked in years.

These examples raise important ethical questions about impression management. Is it okay to omit certain information in an online dating service in an attempt to put your best foot forward? In a job interview, is it legitimate to act more confident and reasonable than you really feel? Likewise, are you justified in acting attentive in a boring conversation

DARK SIDE OF COMMUNICATION
GETTING HOAXED ONLINE

Manti Te'o was a star linebacker at the University of Notre Dame, but his senior year will be remembered by many for the headlines he garnered off the field. Te'o tugged heartstrings by telling the media about the death of his beloved girlfriend. It turned out he had been duped. His relationship with his "girlfriend" was actually an elaborate online hoax that was orchestrated by a male acquaintance. In essence, Te'o fell in love with a woman who didn't exist.

When the story hit the press, people around the world began coming forward with tales of being relationally deceived in cyberspace. Nev Schulman of *Catfish* fame (see the Media Clip on p. 84) created a TV reality series about the topic. He and his co-host Max Joseph ("*Catfish* Stars," 2012) offer these tips on how not to plunge into the dark side of virtual romance:

- If it seems too good to be true, it probably is. Proceed with caution and make the other person earn your trust before telling too much about yourself.
- Get proof the other person exists. Ask for photos of the person holding something specific that you've requested.
- Use a webcam and communicate with the other person visually and in real time.
- Be yourself and know what you want. It's easy to get wrapped up in a fairy-tale version of love, but remember real life isn't a fairy tale or a movie. Love takes work.

out of courtesy to the other person? Is it sometimes wise to use false names and information on the Internet for your protection and security? Situations like these suggest that managing impressions doesn't necessarily make you a liar. In fact, it is almost impossible to imagine how we could communicate effectively without making decisions about which front to present in one situation or another.

Each of us has a repertoire of faces—a cast of characters—and part of being a competent communicator is choosing the best role for a situation. Imagine yourself in each of the following situations, and choose the most effective way you could act, considering the options:

- You offer to teach a friend a new skill, such as playing the guitar, operating a computer program, or sharpening up a tennis backhand. Your friend is making slow progress with the skill, and you find yourself growing impatient.
- You've been corresponding for several weeks with someone you met online, and the relationship is starting to turn romantic. You have a physical trait that you haven't mentioned.
- At work you face a belligerent customer. You don't believe that anyone has the right to treat you this way.

In each of these situations—and in countless others every day—you have a choice about how to act. It is an oversimplification to say that there is only one honest way to behave in each circumstance and that every other response would be insincere and dishonest. Instead, impression management involves deciding which face—which part of yourself—to reveal.

DISCLOSING THE SELF

What we choose to disclose about ourselves is an important component of impression management. So what constitutes self-disclosure? You might argue that aside from secrets, it's impossible *not* to make yourself known to others. After all, every time you open your mouth to speak, you're revealing your tastes, interests, desires, opinions, beliefs, or some other bit of information about yourself. In addition, in Chapter 6, we describe how each of us communicates nonverbally.

If every verbal and nonverbal behavior in which you engage is self-revealing, how can self-disclosure be distinguished from any other act of communication? Psychologist Paul Cozby (1973) offers an answer. He suggests that for a communication act to be considered self-disclosing, it must (1) contain personal information about the sender, (2) the sender must communicate this information verbally, and (3) another person must

be the target. Put differently, the subject of self-disclosing communication is the *self*, and information about the self is *purposefully communicated to another person*.

Although this definition is a start, it ignores the fact that some messages intentionally directed toward others are not especially revealing. For example, telling an acquaintance "I don't like clams" is quite different from announcing "I don't like you." Let's take a look at several factors that further distinguish self-disclosure from other types of communication.

Honesty

It almost goes without saying that true self-disclosure has to be honest. It's not revealing to say "I've never felt this way about anyone before" to every Saturday night date, or to preface every lie with the statement "Let me be honest. . . ."

As long as you are honest and accurate to the best of your knowledge, communication can qualify as an act of self-disclosure. On the other hand, painting an incomplete picture of yourself (telling only part of what's true) is not genuine disclosure. We talk more about the relationship between honesty and disclosure later in this chapter.

Depth

A self-disclosing statement is generally regarded as being personal—containing relatively "deep" rather than "surface" information. Of course, what is personal and intimate for one person may not be for another. You might feel comfortable admitting your spotty academic record, short temper, or fear of spiders to anyone who asks, whereas others would be embarrassed to do so. Even basic demographic information, such as age, can be extremely revealing for some people.

Availability of Information

Self-disclosing messages must contain information that the other person is not likely to know at the time or be able to obtain from another source. For example, describing your conviction for a drunk-driving accident might feel like an act of serious disclosure because the information concerns you, is offered intentionally, is honest and accurate, and is considered personal. However, if the other person could obtain that information elsewhere without much trouble—from a glance at the morning newspaper or from various gossips, for example—your communication would not be especially self-disclosing.

Context of Sharing

Sometimes the self-disclosing nature of a statement comes from the setting in which it is uttered. For instance, relatively innocuous information about family life seems more personal when a student shares it with the class (Myers, 1998), when an athlete tells it to her coach (Officer & Rosenfeld, 1985), or when it's shared online (Jiang et al., 2013; Lee et al., 2013).

We can summarize our definitional tour by saying that **self-disclosure** (1) has the self as subject, (2) is intentional, (3) is directed at another person,

(4) is honest, (5) is revealing, (6) contains information generally unavailable from other sources, and (7) gains much of its intimate nature from the context in which it is expressed.

Although many acts of communication may be self-revealing, this definition makes it clear that few of our statements may be classified as self-disclosure. Most conversations—even among friends—focus on everyday, mundane topics and disclose little or no personal information (Dindia et al., 1997). Even partners in intimate relationships don't talk about personal matters with a high degree of frequency (Alberts et al., 2005).

MODELS OF SELF-DISCLOSURE

Now that we've defined self-disclosure, let's take a look at two models that help us better understand how self-revelations operate in our relationships with others.

Degrees of Self-Disclosure: The Social Penetration Model

Social psychologists Irwin Altman and Dalmas Taylor (Taylor & Altman, 1987) describe two ways in which communication can be more or less disclosing. Their **social penetration model** is pictured in Figure 3.2. The first dimension of self-disclosure in this model involves the breadth of information volunteered—the range of subjects being discussed. For example, the breadth of disclosure in your relationship with a fellow worker will expand as you begin revealing information about your life away from the job as well as on-the-job details. The second dimension of disclosure is the depth of the information being volunteered—the shift from relatively impersonal messages to more personal ones.

Depending on the breadth and depth of information shared, a relationship can be defined as casual or intimate. In a casual relationship, the breadth

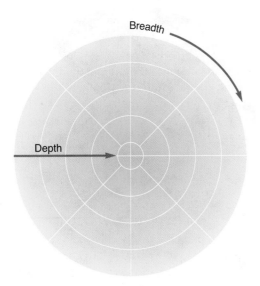

FIGURE 3.2 Social Penetration Model

may be great, but not the depth. A more intimate relationship is likely to have high depth in at least one area. The most intimate relationships are those in which disclosure is great in both breadth and depth. Altman and Taylor (1973) see the development of a relationship as a progression from the periphery of their model to its center, a process that typically occurs over time. Each of your personal relationships probably has a different combination of breadth of subjects and depth of revelation. Figure 3.3 pictures a student's self-disclosure in one relationship.

One way to classify the depth of disclosure is to look at the types of information that can be revealed. *Clichés* are ritualized, stock responses to social situations—virtually the opposite of self-disclosure: "How are you doing?" "Fine." Although hardly revealing, clichés can serve as a valuable kind of shorthand that makes it easy to keep the social wheels greased.

Another kind of message involves communicating *facts*. Not all factual statements qualify as self-disclosure. To qualify they must fit the criteria of being intentional, significant, and not otherwise known: "This isn't my first try at college. I dropped out a year ago with terrible grades." Disclosing personal facts like these often signals a desire to move a relationship to a deeper level of intimacy.

Opinions can be a kind of self-disclosure because they often reveal more about a person than facts alone do. Every time you offer a personal opinion (such as your political or religious beliefs, or an analysis of another person), you are giving others valuable information about yourself.

The fourth level of self-disclosure—and usually the most revealing one—involves the expression of *feelings*. At first glance, feelings might appear to be the same as opinions, but there's a big difference. "I don't think

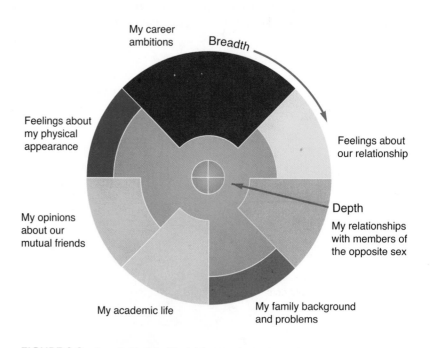

FIGURE 3.3 **Sample Model of Social Penetration**

you're telling me about what's on your mind" is an opinion. Notice how much more we learn about the speaker by looking at three different feelings that could accompany this statement: "I don't think you're telling me what's on your mind . . .

and I'm suspicious."
and I'm angry."
and I'm hurt."

Awareness of Self-Disclosure: The Johari Window Model

Another way to illustrate how self-disclosure operates in communication is to look at a model called the **Johari Window**, developed by Joseph Luft and Harry Ingham (Janas, 2001; Luft, 1969).

Imagine a frame that contains everything there is to know about you: your likes and dislikes, your goals, your secrets, your needs—everything. This frame could be divided into information you know about yourself and things you don't know. It could also be split into things others know about you and things they don't know. Figure 3.4 reflects these divisions.

Part 1 represents the information of which both you and the other person are aware. This part is your *open area*. Part 2 represents the *blind area*: information of which you are unaware but that the other person knows. You learn about information in the blind area primarily through feedback from others. Part 3 of the Johari Window represents your *hidden area*: information that you know but aren't willing to reveal to others. Items in this hidden area become public primarily through self-disclosure, which is the focus of this section. Part 4 of the Johari Window represents information that is *unknown* to both you and to others. At first the unknown area seems impossible to verify. After all, if neither you nor others know what it contains, how can you be sure it exists at all? We can deduce its existence because we are constantly discovering new things about ourselves. For example, it is not unusual to discover that you have an unrecognized talent, strength, or weakness. Items move from the unknown area into the open area when you share your insight, or into the hidden area, where it becomes a secret.

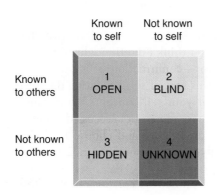

FIGURE 3.4   Johari Window

The relative size of each area in our personal Johari Windows changes from time to time according to our moods, the subject we are discussing, and our relationship with the other person. Despite these changes, a single Johari Window could represent most people's overall style of disclosure.

BENEFITS AND RISKS OF SELF-DISCLOSURE

By now it should be clear that neither all-out disclosure nor complete privacy is desirable. On one hand, self-disclosure is a key factor in relational development, and relationships suffer when people keep important information from one another (Erwin & Pressler, 2011; Mashek & Sherman, 2004). On the other hand, revealing deeply personal information can threaten the stability—or even the survival—of a relationship. Communication researchers use the term **privacy management** to describe the choices people make to reveal or conceal information about themselves (Bridge & Schrodt, 2013; Petronio, 2007). In the following pages, we outline both the benefits and risks of opening yourself to others.

Benefits of Disclosure

Modern culture, at least in the United States, places high value on self-disclosure (Marshall, 2008). The following are some reasons people disclose personal information.

Catharsis Sometimes you might disclose information in an effort to "get it off your chest." Catharsis can indeed relieve the burden of pent-up emotions (Pennebaker, 1997), whether face-to-face or online (Vilhauer, 2009)—but when it's the *only* goal of disclosure, the results of opening up may not be good. Later in this chapter, you'll read guidelines for disclosing that increase the odds that you can achieve catharsis in a way that helps, instead of harming, relationships.

Self-Clarification It is often possible to clarify your beliefs, opinions, thoughts, attitudes, and feelings by talking about them with another person. This sort of gaining insight by "talking the problem out" occurs in many psychotherapies, but it also goes on in other relationships ranging from good friends to interaction with bartenders or hairdressers.

Self-Validation If you disclose information with the hope of seeking the listener's agreement ("I think I did the right thing"), you are seeking validation of your behavior—confirmation of a belief you hold about yourself. On a deeper level, this sort of self-validating disclosure seeks confirmation of important parts of your self-concept. For instance, self-validation is an important part of the "coming out" process through which gay people recognize their sexual orientation and choose to disclose this knowledge in their personal, family, and social lives (Han, 2001; Savin-Williams, 2001).

Reciprocity A well-documented conclusion from research is that one person's act of self-disclosure increases the odds that the other person will reveal personal information (Dindia, 2000b, 2002; Sprecher et al., 2013). There is no guarantee that revealing personal information will trigger self-disclosures by others, but your own honesty can create a climate that makes the other person feel safer and perhaps even obligated to match your level of candor ("I've been bored with our relationship lately" might get a response of "Wow, me too!"). Reciprocity applies online as well as in person: The number of mediated friendships a person has may be predicted by the amount of perceived reciprocity (Detenber et al., 2008). Reciprocity doesn't always occur on a turn-by-turn basis: Telling a friend today about your job-related problems might help her feel comfortable opening up to you later about her family history, when the time is right for this sort of disclosure.

Impression Formation Sometimes we reveal personal information to make ourselves more attractive, and research shows that this strategy seems to work. One study revealed that both men's and women's attractiveness was associated with the amount of self-disclosure in conversations (Stiles et al., 1996). Consider a couple on their first date. It's not hard to imagine how one or both partners might share personal information to appear more sincere, interesting, sensitive, or curious about the other person. The same principle applies in other situations. A salesperson might say, "I'll be honest with you" primarily to show that she or he is on your side.

Relationship Maintenance and Enhancement Research demonstrates that we like people who disclose personal information to us. In fact, the relationship between self-disclosure and liking works in several directions: We like people who disclose personal information to us; we reveal more about ourselves to people we like; and we tend to like others more after we have disclosed to them (Dindia, 2000b; Sprecher et al., 2013).

Appropriate self-disclosure is positively related to marital satisfaction (Hess et al., 2007; Rosenfeld & Bowen, 1991). Disclosing spouses give their relationships higher evaluations and have more positive expectations than do partners who disclose less (MacNeil & Byers, 2009). And a number of studies have demonstrated that increased self-disclosure can improve troubled marriages (Laurenceau et al., 2005; Waring, 1981). With the guidance of a skilled counselor or therapist, partners can learn constructive ways to open up.

Moral Obligation Sometimes we disclose personal information out of a sense of moral obligation. People who are HIV-positive, for example, are often faced with the choice of whether they should tell their health care providers and their partner. One study (Agne et al., 2000) found that patients typically did disclose their HIV status to their health care provider because they felt it was the responsible thing to do for themselves (to help fight their illness) and to protect the provider. Another study (Derlega et al., 2000) found that people who are HIV-positive often see disclosing their status "as a duty" and as a way to educate the partner—as an obligation.

ASSESSING YOUR COMMUNICATION

Online and Offline Self-Disclosure

Assess your online and face-to-face self-disclosure by rating each of the following statements using a scale ranging from 1 to 7, with 1 = strongly disagree and 7 = strongly agree. Consider inviting others who know you well to assess your disclosure by responding to the same statements.

When communicating using an online social networking site . . .

_____   **1.** I make frequent posts about myself.

_____   **2.** Posts I make about myself are often long and detailed.

_____   **3.** In posts about myself I let others know openly about who I really am.

_____   **4.** My posts contain a lot of highly personal information about my thoughts, feelings, relationships, and activities.

When communicating face to face . . .

_____   **5.** I often talk about myself.

_____   **6.** I usually talk about myself for fairly long periods of time.

_____   **7.** When I talk about myself I let others know openly about who I really am.

_____   **8.** My talk about myself contains a lot of highly personal information about my thoughts, feelings, relationships, and activities.

Adapted from Bateman, P. J., Pike, J. C., & Butler, B. S. (2011). To disclose or not: Publicness in social networking sites. *Information Technology & People, 24*, 78–100.

For scoring information, see page 105 at the end of the chapter.

Risks of Self-Disclosure

Although the benefits of disclosing are certainly important, opening up can also involve risks that make the decision to disclose a difficult and sometimes painful one (Afifi & Caughlin, 2007; Nosko et al., 2010). The risks of self-disclosure fall into several categories (Greene et al., 2006; Rosenfeld, 2000).

Rejection In answering the question that forms the title of his book, *Why Am I Afraid to Tell You Who I Am?*, John Powell (1969) summed up the risks of disclosing: "I am afraid to tell you who I am because if I tell you who I am, you may not like who I am, and that's all I have." The fear of disapproval is powerful. Sometimes it is exaggerated and illogical, but there are real dangers in revealing personal information:

A: I'm starting to think of you as more than a friend. To tell the truth, I think I love you.

In the movie *Silver Linings Playbook*, troubled ex-teacher Pat (Bradley Cooper) almost drives away his love interest Tiffany (Jennifer Lawrence) by disclosing too much, too soon.

B: I think we should stop seeing one another.

Negative Impression Even if disclosure doesn't lead to total rejection, it can create a negative impression:

A: You know, I've never had a relationship with a woman that lasted more than a month.

B: Really? I wonder what that says about you.

Decrease in Relational Satisfaction Besides affecting others' opinions of you, disclosure can lead to a decrease in the satisfaction that comes from a relationship. Consider a scenario such as this where the incompatible wants and needs of each person become clear through disclosure:

A: Let's get together with Wes and Joanne on Saturday night.

B: To tell you the truth, I'm tired of seeing Wes and Joanne. I don't have much fun with them, and I think Wes is kind of a jerk.

A: But they're my best friends!

Loss of Influence Another risk of disclosure is a potential loss of influence in the relationship. Once you confess a secret weakness, your control over how the other person views you can be diminished:

A: I'm sorry I was so sarcastic. Sometimes I build myself up by putting you down.

B: Is that it? I'll never let you get away with that again!

Loss of Control Revealing something personal about yourself means losing control of the information. What might happen if the person tells others what you disclosed, people you prefer not know, or who you would like to tell yourself? One study (Venetis et al., 2012) found that even solemn pledges from others to maintain your secret are often not kept.

A: I never really liked Leslie. I agreed to go out because it meant a good meal in a nice restaurant.

B: Really? Leslie would sure like to know that!

Hurt the Other Person Even if revealing hidden information leaves you feeling better, it might hurt others—cause them to be upset, for example. It's probably easy to imagine yourself in a situation like this:

A: Well, since you asked, I have felt less attracted to you lately. I know you can't help it when your skin breaks out, but it is kind of a turnoff.

B: I know! I don't see how you can stand me at all!

GUIDELINES FOR SELF-DISCLOSURE

Self-disclosure is a special kind of sharing that is not appropriate for every situation. We now take a look at some guidelines that can help you recognize how to express yourself in a way that's rewarding for you and for the others involved (Derlega et al., 2011; Greene et al., 2006).

Is the Other Person Important to You?

There are several ways in which someone might be important. Perhaps you have an ongoing relationship deep enough so that sharing significant parts of yourself justifies keeping your present level of togetherness intact. Perhaps the person to whom you're considering disclosing is someone with whom you've previously related on a less personal level. Now you see a chance to grow closer, and disclosure may be the path toward developing that personal relationship.

Is the Risk of Disclosing Reasonable?

Most people intuitively calculate the potential benefits of disclosing against the risks of doing so (Affifi & Steuber, 2009; Vangelisti et al., 2001). Even if the probable benefits are great, opening yourself up to almost certain rejection may be asking for trouble. For instance, it might be foolhardy to share your important feelings with someone you know is likely to betray your confidences or ridicule them. On the other hand, knowing that your partner will respect the information makes the prospect of speaking out more reasonable. This is true in both personal and professional relationships. See the At Work sidebar on page 83 for a discussion of the potential risks of revealing personal information on the job.

Is the Self-Disclosure Appropriate?

Some people have trouble with what's popularly known as "TMI"—that is, sharing "too much information" (Alter & Oppenheimer, 2009). In general, it's wise not to divulge personal secrets with strangers, in classroom discussions, or on public Facebook postings, among other settings. Even students who appreciate self-disclosure from their teachers acknowledge that they

FOCUS ON RESEARCH
TMI in the Classroom

Many college instructors encourage participation during class sessions. Contributions from students can provide valuable insights and illustrations—but sometimes they can offer TMI (too much information). How and when do student disclosures cross the line from appropriate to inappropriate?

Communication researchers Brandi Frisby and Robert Sidelinger asked more than 200 college students to report on self-disclosures they had heard in their classes. While participants readily identified disclosures that helped the learning process (such as a student describing her heart condition in a physiology class), they also noted comments that crossed the line. In particular, participants objected to classroom self-disclosures that were too (a) frequent, (b) negative, (c) irrelevant to course materials, and (d) unexpected. (Take a moment and you can probably think of an example from each of these categories that you've encountered during a class.)

These findings offer helpful reminders of things we should follow intuitively, but often don't. If you're going to make disclosing comments in a college classroom—or in most public settings—it's best to engage in a bit of self-monitoring and make them brief, upbeat, and on-topic.

Frisby, B. N., & Sidelinger, R. J. (2013). Violating student expectations: Student disclosures and student reactions in the college classroom. *Communication Studies, 64,* 241–258.

don't want to hear too much, too often about their instructors' personal lives (Myers & Brann, 2009). Of course, it's also possible to *withhold* too much information—perhaps in a marital counseling session or at a doctor's appointment. The key is to recognize that there's a time and a place for engaging in, and refraining from, self-disclosure. (See the Focus on Research sidebar above.)

Is the Disclosure Reciprocated?

There's nothing quite as disconcerting as talking your heart out to someone, only to discover that the other person has yet to say anything to you that is half as revealing. You think to yourself, "What am I doing?" Unequal self-disclosure creates an unbalanced relationship, one with potential problems. This doesn't mean that you are obliged to match another person's revelations on a tit-for-tat basis. What's important is that there is an appropriate balance of disclosure for maintaining each party's investment in the relationship.

Will the Effect Be Constructive?

Self-disclosure can be a vicious tool if it's not used carefully. Every person has a psychological "beltline," and below that beltline are areas about which the person is extremely sensitive. It's important to consider the effects of your candor before opening up to others. Comments such as "I've always thought you were pretty unintelligent" or "Last year I made love to your best friend" may sometimes resolve old business and thus be constructive, but they also can be devastating—to the listener, to the relationship, and to your self-esteem.

ALTERNATIVES TO SELF-DISCLOSURE

Although self-disclosure plays an important role in interpersonal relationships, it isn't the only type of communication available. To understand why complete honesty isn't always an easy or ideal choice, consider some familiar dilemmas:

- You have grown increasingly annoyed with some habits of the person you live with. You fear that bringing up this topic could lead to an unpleasant conversation and maybe even damage the relationship.
- Your friend, who is headed out the door for an important job interview, says, "I know I'll never get this job! I'm really not qualified, and besides I look terrible." You agree with your friend's assessment.
- You've just been given a large, extremely ugly lamp as a gift by a relative who visits your home often. How would you respond to the question, "Where will you put it?"

Although honesty is desirable in principle, it often has risky, potentially unpleasant consequences. It's tempting to sidestep situations in which self-disclosure would be difficult, but examples like the ones you just read indicate that avoidance isn't always possible. Research and personal experience show that communicators—even those with the best intentions—aren't always completely honest when they find themselves in situations when honesty would be uncomfortable (Ennis et al., 2008; Scott, 2010). Four common alternatives to self-disclosure are silence, lying, equivocation, and hinting. Let's take a closer look at each one.

Silence

One alternative to self-disclosure is to keep your thoughts and feelings to yourself. As the cartoon on page 99 shows, there are many times when keeping information to yourself can seem like the best approach, both for you and the other person. One study showed that in the workplace, withholding information is often seen as a better alternative than lying or engaging in deception (Dunleavy et al., 2010).

You can get a sense of how much you rely on silence instead of disclosing by keeping a record of when you do and don't express your opinions. You're likely to find that withholding thoughts and feelings is a common approach for you.

Lying

A **lie** is a deliberate attempt to hide or misrepresent the truth. Lying to gain unfair advantage over an unknowing victim seems clearly wrong, but another kind of mistruth—the "benevolent lie"—isn't so easy to dismiss as completely unethical. **Benevolent lies** are defined (at least by the people who tell them) as not being malicious—and perhaps they are even helpful to the person to whom they are told. You can almost certainly recall times when you have been less than truthful to avoid hurting someone you care for.

Whether or not they are innocent, benevolent lies are certainly common. In several studies spanning four decades, a significant majority of

ZITS   **BY JERRY SCOTT AND JIM BORGMAN**

ZITS ©2004 Zits Partnership, Dist. By King Features

people surveyed acknowledged that even in their closest relationships, there were times when lying was justified (DePaulo et al., 2009; Knapp, 2006). Whereas many of the lies told to best friends and friends are benevolent, many of those told to acquaintances and strangers are self-serving (Ennis et al., 2008). Table 3.1 identifies various reasons for lying, adapted

TABLE 3.1 Some Reasons for Lying

REASON	EXAMPLE
Save face for others	"Don't worry—I'm sure nobody noticed that stain on your shirt."
Save face for self	"I wasn't looking at the files—I was accidentally in the wrong drawer."
Acquire resources	"Oh, *please* let me add this class. If I don't get in, I'll never graduate on time!"
Protect resources	"I'd like to lend you the money, but I'm short myself."
Initiate interaction	"Excuse me, I'm lost. Do you live around here?"
Be socially gracious	"No, I'm not bored—tell me more about your vacation."
Avoid conflict	"It's not a big deal. We can do it your way. Really."
Avoid interaction	"That sounds like fun, but I'm busy Saturday night."
Leave taking	"Oh, look what time it is! I've got to run!"
Present a competent image	"Sure I understand. No problem."
Increase social desirability	"Yeah, I've done a fair amount of skiing."
Exaggeration	"You think *this* is cold? Let me tell you about how cold it was on that trip. . . ."

from Agosta et al. (2013), Scott (2010), and other research cited in this section.

Not all lies are equally devastating. Feelings such as dismay and betrayal are greatest when the relationship is most intense, the importance of the subject is high, and when there was previous suspicion that the other person wasn't being completely honest. Of these three factors, the importance of the information lied about proved to be the key factor in provoking a relational crisis (McCornack & Levine, 1990). We may be able to cope with "misdemeanor" lying, but "felonies" are a grave threat—often leading to the end of a relationship.

The lesson here is clear: Lying about major parts of your relationship can have the gravest of consequences. If preserving a relationship is important to you, then honesty—at least about important matters—really does appear to be the best policy.

Equivocation

Lying isn't the only alternative to self-disclosure. When faced with difficult disclosure choices, communicators can—and often do—use **equivocation**: statements that are not literally false but cleverly avoid an unpleasant truth.

The value of equivocation becomes clear when you consider the alternatives. Consider the dilemma of what to say when you've been given an unwanted present—an ugly painting, for example—and the giver asks what you think of it. How can you respond? On one hand, you need to choose between telling the truth and lying. At the same time, you have a choice of whether to make your response clear or vague. Figure 3.5 displays these choices.

A study by Sandra Metts and her colleagues (1992) showed how equivocation can save face in difficult situations. Several hundred college students were asked how they would turn down unwanted sexual overtures from a person whose feelings were important to them: a close friend, a prospective date, or a dating partner. The majority of students chose a diplomatic reaction ("I just don't think I'm ready for this right now") as being more face-saving and comfortable than a direct statement such as "I just don't feel sexually attracted to you." The diplomatic reaction seemed sufficiently clear to get the message across but not so blunt as to embarrass or humiliate the other person. As Bavelas et al. (1990, p. 171) put it, "Equivocation is neither a false message nor a clear truth, but rather an alternative used precisely when both of these are to be avoided."

The underlying point of equivocal messages is usually understood by their recipients. Renee Edwards and Richard Bello (2001; Bello & Edwards, 2005) explored how receivers interpreted equivocal statements, such as a friend calling your speech "interesting" instead of saying "You messed up." Besides regarding the equivocal statements as more polite, the recipients had no trouble discerning the intended meaning—that the speech was poor, to use our example.

Given the advantages of equivocation, it's not surprising that most people usually will choose to equivocate rather than tell a lie. In a series of experiments, subjects chose between telling a face-saving lie, the truth, and

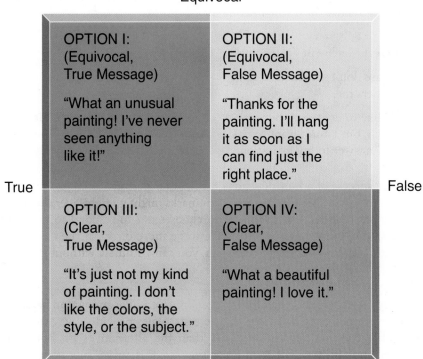

FIGURE 3.5   Dimensions of Truthfulness and Equivocation

equivocating (Bavelas et al., 1990). Only 6 percent chose the lie, and between 3 and 4 percent chose the hurtful truth. By contrast, over 90 percent chose the equivocal response. People may say they prefer truth-telling to equivocating, but given the choice, they usually finesse the truth (Robinson et al., 1998).

Hinting

Hints are more direct than equivocal statements. Whereas an equivocal message isn't necessarily aimed at changing another's behavior, a hint seeks to get the desired response from the other person. As Michael Motley (1992) suggests, some hints are designed to save the receiver from embarrassment:

Direct Statement	Face-Saving Hint
You're too overweight to be ordering dessert.	These desserts are terribly overpriced.
I'm too busy to continue with this conversation. I wish you would let me go.	I know you're busy; I'd better let you go.

Other hints are less concerned with protecting the receiver than with saving the sender from embarrassment:

Direct Statement	Face-Saving Hint
Please don't smoke here; it bothers me.	I'm pretty sure that smoking isn't permitted here.
I'd like to invite you out for lunch, but I don't want to risk a "no" answer to my invitation.	Gee, it's almost lunch time. Have you ever eaten at that new Italian restaurant around the corner?

The success of a hint depends on the other person's ability to pick up the unexpressed message. Your subtle remarks might go right over the head of an insensitive receiver, or one who chooses not to respond to them. If this happens, you still have the choice to be more direct. If the costs of a straightforward message seem too high, you can withdraw without risk.

The Ethics of Evasion

It's easy to see why people often choose hints, equivocations, and benevolent lies instead of self-disclosure. These strategies provide a way to manage difficult situations that is easier than the alternatives for both the speaker and the receiver of the message. In this sense, successful liars, equivocators, and hinters can be said to possess a certain kind of communicative competence. On the other hand, there *are* times when honesty is the right approach, even if it's painful. At times like these, evaders could be viewed as lacking either the competence or the integrity to handle a situation effectively.

Are hints, benevolent lies, and equivocations ethical alternatives to self-disclosure? Some of the examples in these pages suggest the answer is a qualified "yes." Many social scientists and philosophers agree. For example, researchers David Buller and Judee Burgoon (1994) argue that the morality of a speaker's motives for lying ought to be judged, not the deceptive act itself. Another approach is to consider whether the effects of a lie will be worth the deception. Ethicist Sissela Bok (1999) offers some circumstances where deception may be justified: doing good, avoiding harm, and protecting a larger truth. One example is when a patient asks, "How am I doing?" If a nurse perceives that telling the truth could be harmful, it would violate the obligation to "do good and avoid harm," and honesty would be less important than caring (Tuckett, 2005). Perhaps the right questions to ask, then, are whether an indirect message is truly in the interests of the receiver and whether this sort of evasion is the only effective way to behave. Bok suggests another way to check the justifiability of a lie: Imagine how others would respond if they knew what you were really thinking or feeling. Would they accept your reasons for not disclosing?

CHECK YOUR UNDERSTANDING

Objective 3.1 Describe how the self-concept is subjective and is shaped by, and consequently affects, communication with others.

The self-concept is a relatively stable set of perceptions individuals hold about themselves. It begins to develop soon after birth, being shaped by the appraisals of significant others and by social comparisons with reference groups. The self-concept is subjective and can vary substantially from the way a person is perceived by others. Although the self may evolve over time, the self-concept resists change.

A self-fulfilling prophecy occurs when a person's expectations of an event and subsequent behavior influence the event's outcome. One type of prophecy consists of predictions by others, whereas another category is self-imposed.

Q: Identify your own self-concept and identify the messages from others that have shaped it.

Q: Describe how self-fulfilling prophecies (both self-imposed and from others) affect the ways you communicate.

Objective 3.2 Explain how we manage impressions in person and online to enhance our presenting image.

Impression management consists of an individual's strategic communication designed to influence others' perceptions. It aims at presenting one or more faces to others, which may be different from private, spontaneous behavior that occurs outside of others' presence. Communicating through mediated channels can enhance a person's ability to manage impressions. Because each person has a variety of faces that she or he can reveal, choosing which one to present is a central concern of competent communicators.

Q: Describe the various identities you attempt to present to others and the strategies you use (in person and via mediated channels) to construct them.

Objective 3.3 Identify an optimal level of self-disclosure and nondisclosure in effective relationships.

Self-disclosure consists of honest, revealing messages about the self that are intentionally directed toward others. Disclosing communication contains information that is generally unavailable via other sources. The percentage of messages that are truly self-disclosing is relatively low. A number of factors govern whether a communicator will be judged as being a high- or low-level discloser.

Two models for describing self-disclosure are the social penetration model and the Johari Window model. The social penetration model describes two dimensions of self-disclosure: breadth and depth. The Johari Window illustrates the amount of information that an individual reveals to others, hides, is blind to, and is unaware of.

Communicators disclose personal information for a variety of reasons. There also are several reasons to choose not to self-disclose, some of which serve primarily the interests of the nondiscloser, and others of which are intended to benefit the target. When deciding whether to disclose, communicators should consider a variety of factors detailed in the chapter.

Four alternatives to revealing self-disclosures are silence, lies (both benevolent and self-serving), equivocations, and hints. These may be ethical alternatives to self-disclosure; however, whether they are or not depends on the speaker's motives and the effects of the deception.

Q: Use the social penetration model and Johari Window model to represent the level of disclosure involving an important topic in one of your important relationships.

Q: Compose responses to a situation that reflect varying degrees of candor and equivocation. Choose the response that seems most appropriate and effective for the situation.

KEY TERMS

- Benevolent lie (98)
- Equivocation (100)
- Face (81)
- Facework (81)
- Impression management (80)
- Johari Window (91)
- Lie (98)

- Perceived self (80)
- Presenting self (80)
- Privacy management (92)
- Reference groups (73)
- Reflected appraisal (72)
- Self-concept (70)
- Self-disclosure (88)

- Self-esteem (70)
- Self-fulfilling prophecy (78)
- Significant other (72)
- Social comparison (73)
- Social penetration model (89)

ACTIVITIES

1. With a group of classmates, compile a list of reference groups you use to define your self-concepts. You can recognize them by answering several questions:

   a. Select one area in which you compare yourselves to others. In what area is the comparison made? (For example, is the comparison based on wealth, intelligence, or social skill?)

   b. In the selected area, ask yourselves, "Which people am I better or worse than?"

   c. In the selected area, ask yourselves, "Which people am I the same as or different from?"

What is the effect of using these groups as a basis for judging yourselves? How might you view yourselves differently if you used other reference groups as a basis for comparison?

2. Share with your classmates two incidents in which self-fulfilling prophecies you have imposed on yourself have affected your communication. Explain how each of these predictions shaped your behavior, and describe how you might have behaved differently if you had made a different prediction. Next, describe two incidents in which you imposed self-fulfilling prophecies on others. What effect did your prediction have on these people's actions?

3. As a class, construct a gallery of public and private selves. Each student should fold a piece of paper to create two areas. On the top half, draw an image to reflect your private self, and write 10 words that describe the most important characteristics of the private self. (Don't put names on these papers—anonymity is important.) On the bottom half, draw an image that captures the public self you try to show the world, and write 10 words that describe important parts of that public image.

Once drawings are finished, display the images in a gallery that all class members can examine. What patterns emerge regarding the similarity or difference between public and private selves?

4. Recall three recent situations in which you used each of the following evasive approaches: benevolent lying, equivocating, and hinting. Write an anonymous written description of each situation on a separate sheet of paper. Submit the cases to a panel of "judges" (most likely fellow students) who will use the criteria of justifiable motives and desirable effects to evaluate the morality of this deception. Invite the "judges" to consider how they would feel if they knew someone used these evasive approaches with them.

5. Use the guidelines on pages 96–97 to develop one scenario in which you *might* reveal a self-disclosing message. Share a message of this type with a group of your classmates and discuss the risks and benefits of sharing the message.

SCORING FOR ASSESSING YOUR COMMUNICATION (PAGE 94)

Add responses to items 1 and 2. This is your *Amount of Online Disclosure* score: _____.

Add responses to items 3 and 4. This is your *Depth of Online Disclosure* score: _____.

Add responses to items 5 and 6. This is your *Amount of Face-to-Face Disclosure* score: _____.

Add responses to items 7 and 8. This is your *Depth of Face-to-Face Disclosure* score: _____.

Amount of Online Disclosure score: Scores above 6 indicate a willingness to disclose more than average when communicating via a social networking site.

Depth of Online Disclosure score: Scores above 5 indicate a willingness to disclose at higher levels of depth or intimacy than average when communicating via a social networking site.

Amount of Face-to-Face Disclosure score: Scores above 7 indicate a willingness to disclose more than average when communicating face to face.

Depth of Face-to-Face Disclosure score: Scores above 6 indicate a willingness to disclose more than average when communicating face to face.

chapter 4

Perceiving Others

LEARNING OBJECTIVES

4.1 Understand the subjective nature of perceiving interpersonal messages and relationships.

4.2 Identify the variety of influences on interpersonal perception.

4.3 Recognize how common tendencies in perception shape interpersonal communication.

4.4 Use perception checking and adjust attitudes to enhance empathy with communication partners.

"Look at it my way. . . ."
"Put yourself in my shoes. . . ."
"YOU DON'T UNDERSTAND ME!"

STATEMENTS LIKE THESE reflect one of the most common communication challenges. We can talk to (or at) one another until we're hoarse and exhausted, yet we still don't really understand one another. Research confirms this fact: Typical dyads can interpret and explain only 25–50 percent of each other's behavior accurately (Spitzberg, 1994), and spouses consistently overestimate the degree to which they agree with their partners (Fletcher & Kerr, 2010; Iafrate et al., 2012). Some communication scholars (e.g., Eisenberg & Goodall, 2001) have suggested complete understanding could lead to more disagreement and dissatisfaction, not smoother relationships. Nonetheless, failing to share each other's view of the world can leave us feeling isolated and frustrated, despairing that our words don't seem able to convey the depth and complexity of what we think and feel.

Just like the boxes in Figure 4.1, virtually every interpersonal situation can be seen from many points of view. Take a minute to study that figure. How many ways can you discover to view this image? If you only see one or two, keep looking. (You can see at least four ways of viewing the image by looking at Figure 4.2.) If making quick and accurate sense of simple drawings is a difficult task, imagine the challenge involved in trying to understand the perspectives of other human beings, who are far more complex and multidimensional.

In this chapter, we provide tools for communicating in the face of perceptual differences. We begin by explaining that reality is constructed through communication. Then we introduce some of the many reasons why

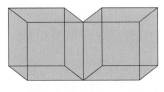

FIGURE 4.1 **Two Cubes Touching**

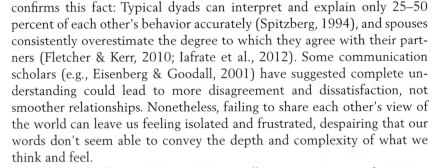

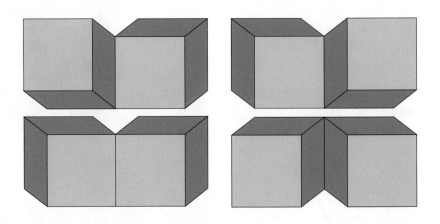

FIGURE 4.2 **Four Sets of Two Cubes Touching**

the world appears so different to each of us. After examining the perceptual factors that make understanding so difficult, we look at tools for bridging the perceptual gap.

THE PERCEPTION PROCESS

How do our perceptions affect our communication with others? We begin to answer these questions by taking a look at the way we make sense of the world.

REALITY IS CONSTRUCTED

Most social scientists agree that the world we know isn't "out there." Rather, we create our reality with others through communication (DeCapua, 2007; Kotchemidova, 2010). This may seem hard to accept until we recognize that there are two levels of reality, which have been labeled "first-order" and "second-order" (Nardone & Watzlawick, 2005; Watzlawick, 1984, 1990). **First-order realities** are physically observable qualities of a thing or situation. For example, the fact that your grandmother wrapped you in a big hug would be obvious to any observer. Likewise, there probably wouldn't be an argument about what word was uttered if a friend called you a "bonehead." By contrast, **second-order realities** involve our *attaching meaning* to first-order things or situations. Second-order realities don't reside in objects or events, but rather in our minds.

Life runs most smoothly when we share second-order realities:

First-order reality:	Your grandma gives you a hug.
Shared second-order reality:	It's appropriate for grandparents to hug their grandchildren.
First-order reality:	A job interviewer asks you how your day has been going.
Shared second-order reality:	This is a reasonable question for the situation.

ZITS ©2001 Zits Partnership, Dist. by King Features

Communication becomes more problematic when we have different second-order realities. For example:

First-order reality:	Your friend calls you a "bonehead."
Your second-order reality:	Your friend is being critical.
Friend's second-order reality:	The remark was an affectionate joke.
First-order reality:	A job interviewer asks whether you are married.
Your second-order reality:	The question has nothing to do with the job and is inappropriate.
Interviewer's second-order reality:	The interviewer is trying to make conversation.

Many communication problems can arise when we don't realize that our views of the world are personal constructions, not objective facts. In this chapter, we explore factors that cause us to experience and make sense of the world in different ways. Perhaps more important, we introduce you to some communication tools that can help bridge the gap between differing perceptions, and in so doing improve relationships.

STEPS IN THE PERCEPTION PROCESS

We attach meanings to our experiences in four steps: selection, organization, interpretation, and negotiation.

Selection

Because we're exposed to more input than we can possibly manage, the first step in perception is the **selection** of which data we will attend to. There are several factors that cause us to notice some messages and ignore others.

Stimuli that are *intense* often attract our attention. Something that is louder, larger, or brighter stands out. This explains why—other things being equal—we're more likely to remember extremely tall or short people and why someone who laughs or talks loudly at a party attracts more attention (not always favorable) than do more quiet guests.

Repetitious stimuli, repetitious stimuli, repetitious stimuli, repetitious stimuli, repetitious stimuli, repetitious stimuli also attract attention (Coon, 2009). Just as a quiet but steadily dripping faucet can come to dominate our awareness, people to whom we're frequently exposed become noticeable.

Attention is also frequently related to *contrast* or *change* in stimulation. Put differently, unchanging people or things become less noticeable. This principle offers an explanation (excuse?) for why we take consistently wonderful people for granted when we interact with them frequently. It's only when they stop being so wonderful or go away that we appreciate them.

Later in this chapter, we look at a variety of other factors—physiological, psychological, social, and cultural—that lead us to pay attention to certain people and events while ignoring others.

Organization

After selecting information from the environment, we must arrange it in some meaningful way to make sense of the world. We call this stage **organization**. The raw sense data we perceive can be organized in more than one way. (See Figure 4.2 for a visual example of this principle.) We do this by using *perceptual schema*, cognitive frameworks that allow us to give order to the information we have selected (Macrae & Bodenhausen, 2001).

We use four types of schema to classify others (Andersen, 1999; Freeman & Ambady, 2011). As you read about each category, think about how you use it to organize your perceptions.

Physical constructs classify people according to their appearance (e.g., beautiful or plain, heavy or thin, young or old).

Role constructs use social position (e.g., student, attorney, spouse).

Interaction constructs focus on social behavior (e.g., friendly, helpful, aloof, sarcastic).

Psychological constructs refer to internal states of mind and dispositions (e.g., confident, insecure, happy, neurotic).

Once we have selected an organizing scheme to classify people, we use it to make generalizations about members of the groups who fit our categories. For example, if you are especially aware of a person's sex, you might be alert to the differences between the way men and women behave or the way they are treated. You might even misremember or distort information that doesn't fit with your beliefs on the subject (Frawley, 2008). If religion plays an important part in your life, you might think of members of your faith differently than you do others. If ethnicity is an important issue for you, you probably tune into the differences between members of various ethnic groups. There's nothing wrong with generalizations about groups as long as they are accurate. In fact, it would be impossible to get through life without them. But faulty overgeneralizations can lead to problems of stereotyping, which you'll read about in a few pages.

Perceptual differences don't just involve the general categories we use to classify others. We also can organize specific communication transactions in different ways, and these differing organizational schemes can have a powerful effect on our relationships. Communication theorists have used the term **punctuation** to describe the determination of causes and effects in a series of interactions (Watzlawick et al., 1967). You can begin to understand how punctuation operates by visualizing a running quarrel between a husband and wife. The husband accuses the wife of being demanding, while she complains that he is withdrawing from her. Notice that the order in which each partner punctuates this cycle affects how the dispute looks. The husband begins by blaming the wife: "I withdraw because you're so demanding." The wife organizes the situation differently, starting with the husband: "I demand so much because you're withdrawing." These kinds of demand–withdraw arguments are common in intimate relationships (Reznik & Roloff, 2011; Schrodt et al., 2014). Once the cycle gets rolling, it is impossible to say which accusation is accurate, as Figure 4.3 indicates. The answer depends on how the sequence is punctuated.

FIGURE 4.3 The way a communication sequence is punctuated affects its perceived meaning. Which comes first, the demanding or the withdrawing?

Anyone who has seen two children argue about "who started it" can understand that haggling over causes and effects isn't likely to solve a conflict. In fact, assigning blame will probably make matters worse (Caughlin & Huston, 2002). Rather than argue about whose punctuation of an event is correct, it's far more productive to recognize that a dispute can look different to each person and then move on to the more important question of "What can we do to make things better?"

Interpretation

Once we have selected and organized our perceptions, we interpret them in a way that makes some sort of sense. **Interpretation**—attaching meaning to sense data—plays a role in virtually every interpersonal act. Is the person who smiles at you across a crowded room interested in romance or simply being polite? Is a friend's kidding a sign of affection or irritation? Should you take an invitation to "drop by any time" literally or not?

There are several factors that cause us to interpret a person's behavior in one way or another. *Relational satisfaction* is a powerful one: The behavior that seems positive when you are happy with a partner might seem completely different when the relationship isn't satisfying (Luo et al., 2010). For example, couples in unsatisfying relationships are more likely than satisfied partners to blame one another when things go wrong (Bradbury & Fincham, 1990; Diamond & Hicks, 2012). And the opposite also holds true: Partners in a satisfying relationship are likely to view each other more benevolently than accurately (Segrin et al., 2009).

Expectation is another factor that shapes our interpretations (Burgoon & Burgoon, 2001). If you go into a conversation expecting a hostile attitude, you're likely to hear a negative tone in the other person's voice—even if that tone isn't there (Hample et al., 2007). We talk more about how expectations affect perception later in this chapter.

A third factor that influences interpretations is *personal experience*. For instance, if you've been taken advantage of by landlords in the past, you might be skeptical about an apartment manager's assurances that careful housekeeping will ensure the refund of your cleaning deposit.

One's *personality* can also affect perception. A study found that people with cold (relative to warm) dispositions have difficulty interpreting and labeling the emotions of others (Moeller et al., 2012). The researchers suggest that this deficiency can contribute to poorer social relationships for those with cold personalities.

Assumptions about human behavior also influence interpretations. Do you assume people are lazy, dislike work, avoid responsibility, and must be coerced to do things—or do you believe people exercise self-direction and self-control, possess creativity, and seek responsibility? Imagine the differences in a boss who assumes workers fit the first description versus one who assumes they fit the second (Neuliep, 1996; Sager, 2008).

Note that the selection, organization, and interpretation phases of perception can occur in differing sequences. For example, a parent's or babysitter's past interpretations (such as "Jason is a troublemaker") can influence future selections (his behavior becomes especially noticeable) and the organization of events (when there's a fight, the assumption is that Jason started it). As with all communication, perception is an ongoing process in which it is hard to pin down beginnings and endings.

Negotiation

In Chapter 1 you read that meaning is created both *in* and *among* people. So far our discussion has focused on the inner components of perception—selection, organization, and interpretation—that take place in each individual's mind. Now we need to examine the part of our sense making that occurs *among* people. The process by which communicators influence each other's perceptions through communication is known as **negotiation**.

One way to explain negotiation is to view interpersonal communication as the exchange of stories. Scholars call the stories we use to describe our personal worlds **narratives** (Bromberg, 2012; Langellier & Peterson, 2006). Just as the boxes in Figure 4.1 on page 108 can be viewed in several ways, virtually every interpersonal situation can be described by more than one narrative. These narratives often differ in their casting of characters as "heroes" and "villains" (Aleman, 2005). For instance, consider a conflict between a boss and employee. If you ask the employee to describe the situation, she might depict the manager as a "heartless bean counter" while she sees herself as a worker who "always gets the job done." The manager's narrative might cast the roles quite differently: the "fair boss" versus the "clock watcher who wants to leave early." Similarly, children may say their parents are too controlling, while the parents talk about their children as irresponsible and naïve. Stepmothers and mothers-in-law who see themselves as "helpful" might be portrayed as "meddlesome" in the narratives of stepdaughters and daughters-in-law (Christian, 2005; Sandel, 2004).

FOCUS ON RESEARCH
Online Channels Affect Perception

You've been asked to come up with a list of tips for first-year college students. As you work on this task with an assigned stranger, that person says to you, "I bankrupted my checking account my freshman year." Later that person mentions, "My parents got divorced two years ago." How would you perceive those comments? Researchers at Cornell University believe your interpretation would be affected by whether the conversation took place in person or online.

Previous research has shown that people tend to engage in more self-disclosure via social media than they do face to face. This study focused on *perceptions* of such disclosures. Participants interpreted others' self-revelations as more personal and intimate when they read them online than when they heard them in person. They would then reciprocate, offering more of their own disclosures electronically than they would face to face.

The study lends support to the hyperpersonal nature of mediated communication discussed in Chapter 1. When cues are reduced and we see only typed words, we may read more into those comments than we would if they were delivered in person.

Jiang, L. C., Bazarova, N. N., & Hancock, J. T. (2013). From perception to behavior: Disclosure reciprocity and the intensification of intimacy in computer-mediated communication. *Communication Research, 40,* 125–143.

MEDIA CLIP
One Person, Many Narratives:
Stories We Tell

Diane Polley was an open book. And had secrets. She was a free spirit. And carried guilt. She lived life to the fullest. And died young.

The many facets of Diane Polley are the subject of *Stories We Tell*, a documentary created by her daughter Sarah. In the film, Sarah interviews a variety of family and friends in an attempt to tell her late mother's story. It's a tale with many twists and turns. What viewers quickly learn is that every narrative paints a distinct picture. Diane is a different person to different people, and each storyteller seems to believe that he or she knows the "real" Diane.

It's easy to think that once you've heard all the interviews, you know the whole story. However, as Sarah quickly acknowledges, she made choices on what she left in and took out of the movie—and that the "truth" about her mother is elusive. Her documentary is therefore just one more narrative about Diane Polley.

When our narratives clash with those of others, we can either hang on to our own point of view and refuse to consider anyone else's (usually not productive), or try to negotiate a narrative that creates at least some common ground. Shared narratives provide the best chance for smooth communication. For example, romantic partners who celebrate their successful struggles against relational obstacles are happier than those who don't have this shared appreciation (Flora & Segrin, 2000). Likewise, couples that agree about the important turning points in their relationships are more satisfied than those who have different views of which incidents were most important (Baxter & Pittman, 2001).

Shared narratives don't have to be accurate to be powerful (Martz et al., 1998). Couples who report being happily married after 50 or more years seem to collude in a relational narrative that doesn't always jibe with the facts (Miller et al., 2006). They agree that they rarely have conflict, although objective analysis reveals that they have had their share of disagreements and challenges. Without overtly deciding to do so, they choose to blame outside forces or unusual circumstances for problems, instead of attributing responsibility to one another. They offer the most charitable interpretations of one another's behavior, believing that their spouse acts with good intentions when things don't go well. They seem willing to forgive or even forget transgressions. And their narratives usually have happy endings (Frost, 2013). Examining this research, Judy Pearson (2000) asks the following:

Should we conclude that happy couples have a poor grip on reality? Perhaps they do, but is the reality of one's marriage better known by outside onlookers than by the players themselves? The conclusion is evident. One key to a long happy marriage is to tell yourself and others that you have one and then to behave as though you do! (p. 186)

🦋 INFLUENCES ON PERCEPTION

How we select, organize, interpret, and negotiate data about others is influenced by a variety of factors. Some of our perceptual judgments are affected by the information available, others by physiology, others by cultural and social factors, and still others by psychological factors.

ACCESS TO INFORMATION

We can only make sense of what we know, and none of us knows everything about even the closest people in our lives. When new information becomes available, perceptions of others change. If you see your instructor only when she's teaching in the classroom, your conclusions about her will be based solely on her behaviors in that role. You might change your perception if you observe her in the roles of rush-hour driver, concertgoer, or grocery shopper.

We often gain access to new information about others when their roles overlap. Consider how that might occur at an office party. A person's "office" and "party" roles are usually quite different—so at an off-site work celebration, you may see behaviors you hadn't expected. Similarly, when your sweetheart takes you home to meet the family, you might get to watch your partner playing a "spoiled son" or "princess daughter" role. If you've ever said, "I saw a whole new side of you tonight," chances are it's because you gained access to information you didn't have before.

Social media can provide new information that affects perceptions. That's why job hunters are encouraged to clean up their online profiles, being careful to manage the impressions they might make (Kluemper et al., 2012). It's also why children and parents sometimes don't want to be Facebook friends with each other (Child & Westermann, 2013), which we discuss further in Chapter 10. Some roles are best kept private—or at least played to a select audience.

PHYSIOLOGICAL INFLUENCES

Sometimes differing perspectives come from our physical environment and the ways that our bodies differ from others.

The Senses

The differences in how each of us sees, hears, tastes, touches, and smells stimuli can affect interpersonal relationships (Clark, 2000; Croy et al., 2013). Consider a few examples arising from physiological differences:

"Turn down that radio! It's going to make me go deaf."
"It's not too loud. If I turn it down, it will be impossible to hear it."

"It's freezing in here."
"Are you kidding? We'll suffocate if you turn up the heat!"

"Why don't you pass that truck? The highway is clear for half a mile."
"I can't see that far, and I'm not going to get us killed."

Age

We experience the world differently throughout our lifetimes. Besides the obvious physical changes, age also alters perspective. Consider, for instance, how you've viewed your parents through the years. When you were a child, you probably thought they were all-knowing and flawless. As a teen, you may have viewed them as old-fashioned and mean. In adulthood, many people begin to regard their parents as knowledgeable and perhaps even wise. Although your parents have probably changed a bit over time, it's likely that your *perception* of them has changed far more than they have. A tongue-in-cheek observation attributed to Mark Twain puts it this way: "When I was a boy of fourteen, my father was so ignorant I could hardly stand to have the old man around. But when I got to be twenty-one, I was astonished at how much he had learned in seven years."

Health and Fatigue

Recall the last time you came down with a cold, flu, or some other ailment. Health can have a strong impact on how you relate to others. It's good to realize that someone else may be behaving differently because of illness. In the same way, it's important to let others know when you feel ill so they can give you the understanding you need.

Likewise, fatigue can affect relationships. People who are sleep deprived, for example, perceive time intervals as longer than they really are (Miró et al., 2003). One study found that when married couples don't sleep well, they have more negative perceptions of each other the following day, leading to more interpersonal discord (Seidman, 2011). Toward that end, a good night's sleep is an invaluable asset for managing interpersonal conflict (Gordon & Chen, 2014).

Biological Cycles

Are you a "morning person" or a "night person"? Each of us has a daily cycle in which all sorts of changes constantly occur, including variations in body temperature, sexual drive, alertness, and tolerance to stress (Koukkari & Sothern, 2006) and to pain (Jankowski, 2013). These cycles can affect the way we relate to each other. For example, you are probably better off avoiding prickly topics in the morning with someone who is not a "morning person."

On the TV show *Girls*, Hannah (Lena Dunham) has obsessive–compulsive disorder and Jessa (Jemima Kirke) has borderline personality disorder and addiction issues. Their portrayals capture some neurobehavioral challenges that can affect interpersonal communication.

Hunger

Your own experience probably confirms that being hungry (and getting grumpy) or having overeaten (and getting tired) affects how we interact with others. For example, a study by Katherine Alaimo and her colleagues (2001) found that teenagers who reported that their family did not get enough food to eat were almost three times as likely to have been suspended from school, almost twice as likely to have difficulty getting along with others, and four times as likely to have no friends. Although the exact nature of the causes and effects in this study are hard to pin down, one thing is clear: Hunger can affect our perception and communication.

Neurobehavioral Challenges

Some differences in perception are rooted in neurology. For instance, people with ADHD (attention-deficit/hyperactivity disorder) are easily distracted from tasks and have difficulty delaying gratification (Goldstein, 2008; Tripp et al., 2007). It's easy to imagine how those with ADHD might find a long lecture boring and tedious, whereas others are fascinated by the same lecture (Von Briesen, 2007). People with bipolar disorder experience significant mood swings in which their perceptions of events, friends, family members, and even attempts at social support shift dramatically (Doherty & MacGeorge, 2013). The National Institute of Mental Health (2013) estimates that between 5 million and 7 million Americans are affected by these two disorders alone—and there are many other neurobehavioral conditions that influence people's perceptions.

PSYCHOLOGICAL INFLUENCES

Along with physiology, our psychological state also influences the way we perceive others.

Mood

Our emotional state strongly influences how we view people and events and therefore how we communicate (Avramova et al., 2010; Lount, 2010). An early experiment using hypnotism dramatically demonstrated the influence of mood on perception (Lebula & Lucas, 1945). Each subject was shown the same series of six pictures, each time having been put in a different mood. The descriptions of the pictures differed radically depending on the emotional state of the subject. For example, these are descriptions by one subject in various emotional states while describing a picture of children digging in a swampy area:

Happy mood: "It looks like fun, reminds me of summer. That's what life is for, working out in the open, really living—digging in the dirt, planting, watching things grow."

Anxious mood: "They're going to get hurt or cut. There should be someone older there who knows what to do in case of an accident. I wonder how deep the water is."

Critical mood: "Pretty horrible land. There ought to be something more useful for kids of that age to do instead of digging in that stuff. It's filthy and dirty and good for nothing."

Such evidence shows that our judgments often say more about our own emotional state than about the other people involved.

Although there's a strong relationship between mood and happiness, it's not clear which comes first: the perceptual outlook or the amount of relational satisfaction. There is some evidence that perception leads to satisfaction (Fletcher et al., 1987), and some that satisfaction drives positive perceptions (Luo et al., 2010). In other words, the attitude/expectation we bring to a situation shapes our level of happiness or unhappiness. Once started, this process can create a spiral. If you're happy about your relationship, you will be more likely to interpret your partner's behavior in a charitable way. This, in turn, can lead to greater happiness. Of course, the same process can work in the opposite direction. One study revealed that spouses who felt uncertain about the status of their marriage saw relational threats in conversations that seemed quite ordinary to outsiders (Knobloch et al., 2007).

One remedy to serious distortions—and unnecessary conflicts—is to monitor your own moods. If you're aware of being especially critical or sensitive, you can avoid overreacting to others (and you can warn others: "This isn't a good time for me to discuss this with you").

Self-Concept

Another factor that influences perception is self-concept (Hinde et al., 2001). For example, the recipient's self-concept has proven to be the single greatest factor in determining whether people who are being teased interpret the teaser's motives as being friendly or hostile and whether they respond with comfort or defensiveness (Alberts et al., 1996). Also, the extent to which people see themselves as funny is related to whether they perceive others as funny (Bosacki, 2013). Children who have a low opinion of themselves are more likely to see themselves as victims of bullying, both in their classrooms and online (Katzer et al., 2009; Kowalski & Limber, 2013). As discussed in Chapter 3, the way we think and feel about ourselves strongly influences how we interpret others' behavior.

SOCIAL INFLUENCES

Within a culture, our personal point of view plays a strong role in shaping perceptions. Social scientists have developed **standpoint theory** to describe how a person's position in a society shapes her or his view of society in general and of specific individuals (Litwin & Hallstein, 2007; Wood, 2005a). Standpoint theory is most often applied to the difference between the perspectives of privileged social groups and people who have less power, and to the perspectives of women and men (Dougherty, 2001). Unless one has been disadvantaged, it can be difficult to imagine how the world might look to someone who has been treated badly because of race, ethnicity, gender, biological sex, sexual orientation, or socioeconomic class. After some reflection, though, you probably can understand how being marginalized can make the world seem like a very different place.

We look now at how particular societal roles affect an individual's perception.

Sex and Gender Roles

Although people often use the terms *sex* and *gender* as if they're identical, there is an important difference (Katz-Wise & Hyde, 2014). *Sex* refers to biological characteristics of a male or female, whereas **gender** refers to the social and psychological dimensions of masculine and feminine behavior. Males and females can be more-or-less masculine, more-or-less feminine, or have both masculine *and* feminine characteristics. A person with relatively equal masculine and feminine characteristics is referred to as **androgynous**. In general, 80% of people see themselves as either sex typed (masculine male/feminine female) or androgynous (Choi et al., 2009).

A large body of research shows that men and women perceive the world differently, for reasons ranging from genes to neurology to hormones (Becker et al., 2007; Schroeder, 2010). For instance, one study found that women are better than men at reading emotion in facial expressions, which is consistent with research showing that women are generally more perceptive about interpreting others' nonverbal cues (Rennels & Cummings, 2013). However, the authors noted that these differences weren't in place at infancy, and it's hard to know whether nature or nurture was responsible for the development of this skill over time. Even cognitive researchers who focus on biological differences between men and women acknowledge that societal gender roles affect perception dramatically (Halpern, 2000).

Gender can sometimes influence perception more than biological sex does (Baglan, 1993). For instance, a study on perceptions of effective teacher behavior (Aylor, 2003) found that gender was superior to biological sex as a predictor. Masculine individuals, regardless of their biological sex, perceived good teaching as a teacher's use of communication to manage students' behavior (e.g., the teacher's being persuasive and managing conversations). Feminine individuals perceived good teaching as a teacher's

In the Oscar-winning drama *Dallas Buyers Club*, health challenges and a business partnership with the transgendered Rayon (Jared Leto) help transform Ron Woodroof (Matthew McConaughey) from a homophobic bigot to a less judgmental version of his former self.

"How is it gendered?"

use of communication to manage students' feelings (e.g., supporting students' egos and helping students realize their mistakes).

Occupational Roles

The kind of work we do also governs our view of the world. Imagine five people taking a walk through a park. One, a botanist, is fascinated by the variety of trees and plants. The zoologist is on the lookout for interesting animals. The third, a meteorologist, keeps an eye on the sky, noticing changes in the weather. The fourth, a psychologist, is totally unaware of the goings-on of nature, concentrating instead on the interaction among the people in the park. The fifth, a pickpocket, quickly takes advantage of the others' absorption to collect their wallets. There are two lessons in this little story: The first, of course, is to watch your wallet carefully. The second is that our occupational roles frequently govern our perceptions.

Perhaps the most dramatic illustration of how occupational roles shape perception occurred in the early 1970s. Stanford psychologist Philip Zimbardo (1971, 2007) recruited a group of well-educated, middle-class young men. He randomly chose 11 to serve as "guards" in a mock prison set up in the basement of Stanford's psychology building. He issued the guards uniforms, handcuffs, whistles, and billy clubs.

SEXUAL HARASSMENT AND PERCEPTION

@WORK

Almost 50 years after the U.S. Civil Rights Act prohibited it, sexual harassment in the workplace remains a problem. Complaints of unwanted sexual advances and a hostile work environment have cost employers almost $50 million annually in recent years (Equal Employment Opportunity Commission, 2010).

Scholars have tried to understand why complaints of harassment persist when the law clearly prohibits behavior that creates a "hostile work environment." They have discovered that although clear-cut examples of hostile sexism do exist, differing perceptions help explain many other incidents.

Not surprisingly, what constitutes harassment depends on one's sex (Ohse & Stockdale, 2008; Shechory Bitton & Shaul, 2013): Women are more likely than men to rate a behavior as hostile and/or offensive, regardless of whether the person harassed was female or male. Perhaps more surprisingly, younger people (both men and women) are less likely than older people to regard a scenario as sexual harassment.

Along with age and sex, cultural background helps shape perceptions of harassment (Fiedler & Blanco, 2006; Merkin, 2012). People from cultures with high power distance (see Chapter 2, pages 36–67) are less likely to perceive harassment than those from places with low power distance.

Findings like these may not excuse harassment, but they do help explain it. The less members of an organization understand one another's perceptions, the better the odds that unpleasant and unfortunate feelings of harassment will arise.

The remaining 10 participants became "prisoners" and were placed in rooms with metal bars, bucket toilets, and cots.

Zimbardo let the guards establish their own rules for the experiment: no talking during meals and rest periods and after lights out. They took head counts at 2:30 A.M. Troublemakers received short rations. Faced with these conditions, the prisoners began to resist. Some barricaded their doors with beds. Others went on hunger strikes. Several ripped off their identifying number tags. The guards reacted to the rebellion by clamping down hard on protesters. Some turned sadistic, physically and verbally abusing the prisoners. The experiment was scheduled to go on for two weeks, but after six days Zimbardo realized that what had started as a simulation had become too intense. Clearly the roles they had taken on led the guards and prisoners to perceive, and then treat, each other very differently.

You can probably think of ways in which jobs you've held have affected how you view others. If you've been in customer service, you're probably more patient and understanding with those in similar positions (although you could also be a bit more critical). And if you've ever been promoted to manager at your place of work, you know that it typically changes your perceptions of, and behavior toward, coworkers who are now under your supervision.

Relational Roles

Think back to the "Who am I?" list you made in Chapter 3. It's likely your list included roles you play in relation to others: daughter, roommate, spouse, friend, and so on. Roles like these don't just define who you are—they also affect your perception.

Take for example the role of parent. As most new mothers and fathers will attest, having a child alters the way they see the world. They might perceive their crying baby as a helpless soul in need of comfort, whereas nearby strangers have a less charitable appraisal. As the child grows, parents often pay more attention to the messages in the child's environment. One father we know said he never noticed how much football fans curse and swear until he took his 6-year-old to a game with him. In other words, his role as father affected what he paid attention to and how he interpreted it.

The roles involved in romantic love can also dramatically affect perception. These roles have many labels: partner, spouse, boyfriend/girlfriend, and so on. There are times when your affinity biases the way you perceive the object of your affection. You may see your sweetheart as more attractive than other people do and as more attractive than your previous partners, regardless of whether that's objectively accurate (Swami & Allum, 2012). As a result, perhaps you overlook some faults that others notice (Segrin et al., 2009). Your romantic role can also change the way you view others. One study found that when people are in love, they view other romantic candidates as less attractive than they normally would (Gonzaga et al., 2008).

Perhaps the most telltale sign of the effect of "love goggles" is when they come off. Many people have experienced breaking up with a romantic partner and wondering later, "What did I ever see in that person?" The answer—at least in part—is that you saw what your relational role led you to see.

CULTURAL INFLUENCES

Culture influences selection, organization, interpretation, and negotiation, and it exerts a powerful influence on the way we view others' communication. For example, when making judgments of emotion, Japanese tend to focus more on vocal cues, whereas Dutch tend to focus more on facial expressions (Tanaka et al., 2010). Even beliefs about the very value of talk differ from one culture to another (Dailey et al., 2005). Western cultures tend to view talk as desirable and use it for social purposes as well as to perform tasks. Silence has a negative value in these cultures. It is likely to be interpreted as lack of interest, unwillingness to communicate, hostility, anxiety, shyness, or a sign of interpersonal incompatibility. Westerners are uncomfortable with silence, which they find embarrassing and awkward.

On the other hand, Asian cultures tend to perceive talk quite differently. For thousands of years, Asian cultures have discouraged the expression of thoughts and feelings. Silence is valued, as Taoist sayings indicate: "In much talk there is great weariness," or "One who speaks does not know; one who knows does not speak." Unlike Westerners, who are uncomfortable with silence, Japanese and Chinese people believe that remaining quiet is the proper state when there is nothing to be said. To Asians, a talkative person is often considered a show-off or a fake.

It's easy to see how these different views of speech and silence can lead to communication problems when people from different cultures meet. Both the "talkative" Westerner and the "silent" Asian are behaving in ways they believe are proper, yet each may view the other with disapproval and mistrust. Only when they recognize the different standards of behavior can they adapt to one another, or at least understand and respect their differences.

The valuing of talk isn't the only way culture shapes perceptions. Author Anne Fadiman (1997) explains why Hmong immigrants from the mountains of Laos preferred their traditional shamanistic healers, called *txiv neeb*, to American doctors—and perceived their behaviors very differently:

> A *txiv neeb* might spend as much as eight hours in a sick person's home; doctors forced their patients, no matter how weak they were, to come to the hospital, and then might spend only twenty minutes at their bedsides. *Txiv neebs* were polite and never needed to ask questions; doctors asked about their sexual and excretory habits. *Txiv neebs* could render an immediate diagnosis; doctors often demanded samples of blood (or even urine or feces, which they liked to keep in little bottles), took X rays, and waited for days for the results to come back from the laboratory—and then, after all that, sometimes they were unable to identify the cause of the problem. *Txiv neebs* never undressed their patients; doctors asked patients to take off all their clothes, and sometimes dared to put their fingers inside women's vaginas. *Txiv neebs* knew that to treat the body without treating the soul was an act of patent folly; doctors never even mentioned the soul. (p. 33)

Perceptual differences don't just occur between residents of different countries. Within a single national culture, regional and ethnic co-cultures can create very different realities. In a fascinating series of studies, Peter Andersen and colleagues (1990) discovered that climate and geographic latitude were remarkably accurate predictors of communication predispositions. People living in southern latitudes of the United States were found to be less socially isolated, higher in self-esteem, more likely to touch others, and more likely to verbalize their thoughts and feelings than their northern counterparts. This sort of finding helps explain why communicators who travel from one part of a country to another find that their old patterns of communicating don't work as well in their new location. A Southerner whose relatively talkative, high-touch style seemed completely normal at home might be viewed as pushy and aggressive in a new, northern home.

Culture plays an important role in our ability to understand the perspectives of others (Amarasinghe, 2012; Croucher, 2013). Research shows that people raised in individualist cultures, which value independence, are often less adept at perspective taking than those from collectivist cultures, which value interdependence. In one study, Chinese and American players were paired together in a communication game that required the participants to take on the perspective of their partners (Wu & Keysar, 2007). In all measures, the collectivist Chinese had greater success in perspective taking than did their American counterparts. This isn't to suggest that one cultural orientation is better than the other; it only shows that culture shapes the way we perceive, understand, and empathize with others.

COMMON TENDENCIES IN PERCEPTION

By now it's obvious that many factors affect the way we interpret the world. Social scientists use the term **attribution** to describe the process of attaching meaning to behavior. We attribute meaning to both our own actions and to the actions of others, but we often use different yardsticks. Research has uncovered several perceptual tendencies that may lead to inaccurate attributions.

WE MAKE SNAP JUDGMENTS

Our ancestors often had to make quick judgments about whether strangers were likely to be dangerous, and there are still times when this ability can be a survival skill (Flora, 2004b). But there are many cases when judging others without enough knowledge or information can get us into trouble. In the most serious cases, innocent people are gunned down by shooters who make inaccurate snap decisions about "intruders" or "enemies." On a more personal level, most of us have felt badly misjudged by others who made unfavorable snap judgments about us. If you've ever been written off by a potential employer in the first few minutes of an interview, or have been unfairly rebuffed by someone you just met, then you know the feeling.

Despite the risks of rash decision making, in some circumstances people can make surprisingly good choices in the blink of an eye (Gladwell, 2004). The best snap judgments come from people whose decisions are based on expertise and experience. However, even nonexperts can be good at making some split-second decisions. For example, students who watched a silent,

FARCUS®
© LaughingStock Licensing Inc.

WAISGLASS/COULTHART

"There are two types of people in this world... those who generalize, and those who don't."

© Laughingstock Licensing Inc.

30-second video of a professor they never met and were asked to rate the teacher's effectiveness came up with ratings very similar to those of students who were in the professor's class for a semester (Ambady & Rosenthal, 1993). Similarly, in just a few minutes of interaction, many speed daters are able to use physically observable traits to determine whether a person they have just met will become a romantic partner (Kurzban & Weeden, 2005). And researchers have found that inferences about politicians based on snap judgments of their looks alone can be surprisingly accurate (Wänke et al., 2013).

Snap judgments become particularly problematic when they are based on **stereotyping**— exaggerated beliefs associated with a categorizing system. Stereotypes, which people automatically make on "primitive categories" such as race, sex, and age (Devos, 2014; Nelson, 2005), may be founded on a kernel of truth, but they go beyond the facts at hand and make claims that usually have no valid basis.

Three characteristics distinguish stereotypes from reasonable generalizations. The first involves *categorizing others on the basis of easily recognized but not necessarily significant characteristics*. For example, perhaps the first thing you notice about a person is his or her skin color—but that may not be nearly as significant as the person's intelligence or achievements. The second feature that characterizes stereotypes is *ascribing a set of characteristics to most or all members of a group*. For example, you might unfairly assume that all older people are doddering or that all men are insensitive to women's concerns (Hummert, 2011). Finally, stereotyping involves *applying the generalization to a particular person*. Once you believe all old people are geezers or all men are jerks, it's a short step to considering a particular senior citizen as senile or a particular man as a sexist pig.

By adulthood, we tend to engage in stereotyping frequently, effortlessly, and often unconsciously (Zenmore et al., 2000). Once we create and hold stereotypes, we seek out isolated behaviors that support our inaccurate beliefs in an attempt to be cognitively consistent. For example, men and women in conflict with each other often remember only behaviors of the opposite sex that fit their stereotypes (Allen, 1998). They then point to these behaviors—which might not be representative of how the other person typically behaves—as "evidence" to suit their stereotypical and inaccurate claims: "Look! There you go criticizing me again. Typical for a woman!"

One way to avoid the kinds of communication problems that come from excessive stereotyping is to "decategorize" others, giving yourself a chance to treat people as individuals instead of assuming that they possess the same characteristics as every other member of the group to which you assign them. As we discuss in Chapter 6, changing labels can aid the process of decategorizing. Instead of talking about white coworkers, gay friends, or foreign students, dropping the descriptors "white," "gay," and "foreign" might help you and others perceive people more neutrally.

WE CLING TO FIRST IMPRESSIONS

Snap judgments are significant because our initial impressions of others often carry more weight than the ones that follow. This is due in part to what social scientists call the **primacy effect**: Our tendency to pay more attention to, and to better recall, things that happen first in a sequence (Miller et al., 2004). You can probably recall first impressions you held of people who are now your close friends. With some it was "like at first sight." With others, your initial appraisal was negative and it took some time and effort for it to change. Either way, your first impressions played a significant role in the interactions that followed.

The term **halo effect** describes the tendency to form an overall positive impression of a person on the basis of one positive characteristic. Positive first impressions are often based on physical attractiveness, which can lead people to attribute all sorts of other virtues to the good-looking person (Lorenzo et al., 2010; van Leeuwen & Macrae, 2004). For example, employment interviewers rate mediocre but attractive job applicants higher than their less attractive candidates (Watkins & Johnston, 2000). Unfortunately, the opposite also holds true. The **horns effect** (also called the "devil" or "pitchfork" effect) occurs when a negative appraisal adversely influences the perceptions that follow (Koenig & Jaswal, 2011).

Once we form a first impression—whether it's positive or negative—we tend to seek out and organize our impressions to support that opinion. Psychologists use the term **confirmation bias** to describe this process. For example, experimental subjects asked more suspicious questions when they believed that a suspect had been cheating on a task (Hill et al., 2008). The same bias occurs in job interviews: once a potential employer forms a positive impression, the tendency is to ask questions that confirm the employer's image of the applicant (Dougherty et al., 1994; Powell et al., 2012). The interviewer might ask leading questions aimed at supporting her positive views ("What valuable lessons did you learn from that setback?"), interpret answers in a positive light ("Ah, taking time away from school to travel was a good idea!"), encourage the applicant ("Good point!"), and sell the company's virtues ("I think you would like working here"). Likewise, applicants who create a negative first impression are operating under a cloud that may be impossible to dispel.

A study of college roommates shows all these effects at work. Those roommates who had positive initial impressions of each other were likely to have positive subsequent interactions, manage their conflicts constructively, and continue living together (Marek et al., 2004). The opposite was also true: Roommates who got off to a bad start tended to spiral negatively. This reinforces the wisdom and importance of the old adage, "You never get a second chance to make a first impression."

WE JUDGE OURSELVES MORE CHARITABLY THAN WE DO OTHERS

Whereas we may evaluate others critically, we tend to judge ourselves more generously (Farah & Atoum, 2002; McClure et al., 2011). Social scientists use two theories to explain this phenomenon. The first is called the **fundamental attribution error**: the tendency to give more weight to personal qualities than to the situation when making attributions (McPherson & Young, 2004). For instance, if someone you know makes a hurtful comment, you're likely to chalk it up to flaws in her or his character (mean spirited) than to external factors (fatigue, peer pressure). We're more charitable when judging ourselves. This **self-serving bias** means that when we perform poorly, we usually blame external forces—and we credit ourselves rather than the situation when we behave well (Sedikides et al., 1998; Shepperd et al., 2008).

Consider a few examples of using different standards when making attributions of ourselves and others:

- When *they* botch a job, we think they weren't listening well; when *we* make the mistake, the problem was unclear directions.
- When *he* makes an overly critical comment, it's because he's insensitive; when *we* do, it's constructive criticism.
- When *she* uses profanity, it's because of a flaw in her character; when *we* swear, it's because the situation called for it (see Young, 2004).

Not surprisingly, self-serving bias is especially common in troubled relationships. In one study (Schütz, 1999), couples in conflict were more likely to blame their partner for the problem than to accept responsibility for their role in the problem. The researchers point out that these results came from couples dealing with ordinary relational challenges. They observe that self-serving bias is likely to be even stronger in troubled relationships. It's also easier to engage in self-serving bias in impersonal online relationships. A study showed that members of online teams, as opposed to in-person teams, were quicker to blame their partners when mistakes occurred (Walther & Bazarova, 2007). The researchers suggest that "unseen, unknown, and remote" teammates are easy scapegoats when something goes wrong.

When people are aware of both the positive and negative characteristics of another person, they tend to be more influenced by the undesirable traits (Baumeister et al., 2001; Kellermann, 1989). This attitude sometimes makes sense. If the negative quality clearly outweighs any positive ones, you would be foolish to ignore it. For example, a surgeon with shaky hands and a teacher who hates children would be unsuitable for their jobs, whatever their virtues. But much of the time it's a bad idea to pay excessive attention to negative qualities and overlook good ones.

WE ARE INFLUENCED BY OUR EXPECTATIONS

Suppose you took a class and were told in advance that the instructor is terrific. Would this affect the way you perceive the teacher? Research shows that it almost certainly would. In one study, students who read positive comments about instructors on a website viewed those teachers as more

FOCUS ON RESEARCH
Does Honesty Hurt? Receivers Say "Yes," Senders Say "No"

"All I want is the truth" is a familiar request—but how accurate is it when the truth hurts? Communication scholar Shuangyue Zhang explored this notion in a series of studies that examine honest but hurtful (HBH) messages in romantic relationships.

In one experiment, Zhang asked over 500 subjects to describe the impact of painfully honest messages. Lovers were much more likely to rate candid messages as hurtful when they were on the receiving end. When they were senders, they didn't even remember delivering many HBH messages to their partner. When confronted with these HBH messages, senders rated their own messages as more honest and constructive than did the partners on the receiving end.

Zhang's research confirms that we do often hurt the people we care most about—and that a self-serving bias prevents us from recognizing the effect of our words.

Zhang, S. (2009). Sender-recipient perspectives of honest but hurtful evaluative messages in romantic relationships. *Communication Reports, 22*, 89–101.

credible and attractive than did students who were not exposed to the same comments (Edwards et al., 2007; see also Edwards & Edwards, 2013).

Expectations don't always lead to more positive appraisals. There are times when we raise our expectations so high that we are disappointed with the events that occur. If you are told that someone you are about to meet is extremely attractive, you may create a picture in your mind of a professional model, only to be let down when the person doesn't live up to your unrealistic expectations. What if you had been told that the person isn't very good looking? In that case, you might have been pleasantly surprised by the person's appearance, and perhaps you would rate the person's attractiveness more positively. The point is, our expectations influence the way we see others, both positively and negatively—and may lead to self-fulfilling prophecies (DiPaola et al., 2010).

The knowledge that expectations influence our perceptions is important when making decisions about others. Many professions require that manuscripts submitted to journals be evaluated through "blind review"— that is, the person submitting the manuscript is not allowed to offer identifying information that might influence the evaluator's appraisal. Likewise, judges on the TV show *The Voice* keep their backs to contestants at first to help their evaluations from being swayed by information other than the performers' singing. In the same way, you can probably think of times when it would be wise to avoid advance information about another person so that you perceive the person as neutrally as possible.

WE ARE INFLUENCED BY THE OBVIOUS

Being influenced by what is most obvious is understandable. As you read earlier, we select stimuli from our environment that are noticeable—that is, intense, repetitious, unusual, or otherwise attention grabbing. The problem is that the most obvious factor is not necessarily the only cause—or the most significant one—of an event. For example

- When two children (or adults, for that matter) fight, it may be a mistake to blame the one who lashes out loudest. Perhaps the other one was at least equally responsible, teasing or refusing to cooperate.
- You might complain about an acquaintance whose malicious gossiping or arguing has become a bother, forgetting that by putting up with that kind of behavior you have been at least partially responsible.
- You might blame an unhappy work situation on the boss, overlooking other factors beyond her control, such as a change in the economy, the policy of higher management, or demands of customers or other workers.

These examples show that it is important to take time to gather all the facts before arriving at a conclusion.

WE ASSUME OTHERS ARE LIKE US

We commonly imagine that others possess the same attitudes and motives that we do (Human & Biesanz, 2011; Van Boven et al., 2012). The frequently mistaken assumption that others' views are similar to our own applies in a wide range of situations. For example

- You've heard a slightly raunchy joke that you found funny. You assume that it won't offend a friend. It does.
- You've been bothered by an instructor's tendency to get off the subject during lectures. If you were a professor, you'd want to know if you were creating problems for your students; so you decide that your instructor will probably be grateful for some constructive criticism. Unfortunately, you're wrong.
- You lost your temper with a friend a week ago and said some things you regret. In fact, if someone said those things to you, you would consider the relationship finished. Imagining that your friend feels the same way, you avoid making contact. In fact, your friend feels that he was partly responsible and has avoided you because he thinks you're the one who wants to end things.

These examples show that others don't always think or feel the way we do and that assuming similarities can lead to problems. Sometimes you can find out the other person's real position by asking directly, sometimes by checking with others, and sometimes by making an educated guess after you've thought the matter out. All these alternatives are better than simply assuming everyone would react the way you do. (We discuss the skill of perception checking in the following section.)

We don't always fall into the kind of perceptual tendencies described in this section. Sometimes, for instance, people *are* responsible for their misfortunes, or our problems *are not* our fault. Likewise, the most obvious interpretation of a situation may be the correct one. Nonetheless, a large amount of research has shown again and again that our perceptions of others are often distorted in the ways we have described. The moral, then, is clear: Don't assume your perceptions are accurate or unbiased.

SYNCHRONIZING OUR PERCEPTIONS

After reading this far, you can appreciate how out of synch our perceptions of one another can be. It's easy to understand how these mismatched perceptions can interfere with our communication. What we need, then, are tools to help others understand our perceptions and for us, in turn, to understand theirs. In the following section, we introduce two such tools.

PERCEPTION CHECKING

With the likelihood for perceptual errors so great, it's easy to see how a communicator can leap to the wrong conclusion and make inaccurate assumptions. Consider the defense-arousing potential of incorrect accusations such as these:

"Why are you mad at me?" (Who said I was?)
"What's the matter with you?" (Who said anything was the matter?)
"Come on now. Tell the truth." (Who said I was lying?)

Even if your interpretations are correct, these kinds of mind-reading statements are likely to generate defensiveness. The skill of **perception checking** provides a better way to review your assumptions and to share your interpretations (Hansen et al., 2002). A complete perception check has three parts:

1. A description of the behavior you noticed.
2. Two possible interpretations of the behavior.
3. A request for clarification about how to interpret the behavior.

Perception checks for the preceding three examples would look like this:

"When you stomped out of the room and slammed the door [behavior], I wasn't sure whether you were mad at me [first interpretation] or just in a hurry [second interpretation]. How did you feel? [request for clarification]"
"You haven't laughed much in the last couple of days [behavior]. It makes me wonder whether something's bothering you [first interpretation] or whether you're just being quiet [second interpretation]. What's up? [request for clarification]"
"You said you really liked the job I did [behavior], but there was something about your voice that made me think you may not like it [first interpretation]. Maybe it's just my imagination though [second interpretation]. How do you really feel? [request for clarification]"

Perception checking is a tool to help us understand others accurately instead of assuming that our first interpretation is correct. Because its goal is mutual understanding, perception checking is a cooperative approach to communication. Besides leading to more accurate perceptions, it signals an

DARK SIDE OF COMMUNICATION
DISTORTING PERCEPTION: THE GASLIGHT EFFECT

The gaslight effect (or "gaslighting") is a contemporary term for manipulating and controlling another person's perceptions. The term refers to the 1940s film classic *Gaslight*, in which a husband tries to convince his wife that she's insane by changing small elements in their environment—and then insisting she's wrong when she points out these changes.

Therapist Robin Stern has written extensively about the gaslight effect, identifying it as a form of mental abuse (2007). A less pathological form of gaslighting occurs when one person deceitfully tries to justify his or her behavior by blaming the other. "You never told me that," an accuser might say while knowing that the statement isn't true. Or more maliciously, "You expect me to be faithful when you're always coming on to other guys?" Shifting guilt to the innocent is a hallmark of gaslighting.

Victims of gaslighting tend to blame themselves, apologize, and offer excuses to others for their partner's behaviors. Depression and withdrawal often follow. It's hard to communicate freely when you've been led to believe you're always wrong.

Recognizing the symptoms of gaslighting is the first step in breaking the pattern. Another key is seeking out objective perspectives from trusted others. The perception-checking skills described in this section are useful tools in a healthy relationship. However, if you think you're being manipulated by a significant other, perception checking with people outside the relationship can help ensure that your perspective hasn't been distorted.

attitude of respect and concern for the other person, saying, in effect, "I know I'm not qualified to judge you without some help."

Sometimes an effective perception check won't need all of the parts listed in the preceding example to be effective:

"You haven't dropped by lately. Is anything the matter?" [single interpretation].

"I can't tell whether you're kidding me about being cheap or if you're serious [behavior combined with interpretations]. Are you mad at me?"

"Are you sure you don't mind driving? I can use a ride if it's no trouble, but I don't want to take you out of your way" [request for clarification comes first; no need to describe behavior].

The straightforward approach of perception checking has the best chance of working in what we identified in Chapter 2 as *low-context cultures*, ones in which members value candor and self-disclosure. The dominant cultures of North America and Western Europe fit into this category, and members of these groups are most likely to appreciate the kind of straight talking that perception checking embodies. On the other hand, members of *high-context cultures* (more common in Latin America and Asia) value social harmony over clarity. High-context communicators are more likely to regard candid approaches such as perception checking as potentially embarrassing, preferring instead less direct ways of understanding one another. Thus, a "let's get this straight" perception check might work well with a European American manager who was raised to value clarity, but it could be a serious mistake with a Mexican American or Asian American boss who has spent most of his or her life in a high-context culture.

Along with clarifying meaning, perception checking can sometimes be a face-saving way to raise an issue without directly threatening or attacking the other person. Consider these examples:

"Are you planning on doing those dishes later, or did you forget that it's your turn?"

"Am I boring you, or do you have something else on your mind?"

In the first case, you might have been quite confident that the other person had no intention of doing the dishes, and in the second that the other person was bored. Even so, a perception check is a less threatening way of pointing out their behavior than direct confrontation. Remember that one element of competent communication is the ability to choose the best option from a large repertoire, and perception checking can be a useful strategy at times.

BUILDING EMPATHY

Perception checking can help us decode messages more accurately, but it doesn't provide enough information for us to claim that we fully understand another person. For example, a professor who uses perception checking might learn that a student's reluctance to ask questions is due to confusion and not lack of interest. This information would be helpful, but imagine how much more effective the professor would be if she or he could get a sense of the confusion from the student's perspective. Likewise, parents whose perception checks reveal that their teenager's outlandish behavior grows from a desire to be accepted by others don't necessarily understand (or perhaps recall) what it feels like to crave that acceptance.

Empathy Defined

What we need, then, to understand others more completely is **empathy**—the ability to recreate another person's perspective, to experience the world from his or her point of view (Breithaupt, 2011; Geist, 2013). It is impossible to achieve total empathy, but with enough effort and skill, we can come closer to this goal (Krause, 2010; Long et al., 1999).

As we use the term here, empathy has three dimensions (Stiff et al., 1988; Watt, 2007). On one level, empathy involves *perspective taking*—the ability to take on the viewpoint of another person. This understanding requires a suspension of judgment so that for the moment you set aside your own opinions and take on those of the other person. Besides cognitive understanding, empathy also has an affective dimension—what social scientists term *emotional contagion*. In everyday language, emotional contagion means that we experience the same feelings that others have. We know their fear, joy, sadness, and so on. A third ingredient of empathy is a genuine *concern* for the welfare of the other person. Not only do we think and feel as others do, but we have a sincere interest in their well-being. Full empathy requires both intellectual understanding of the other person's position and an affective understanding of the other's feelings (Carré et al., 2013; Kerem et al., 2001).

It's easy to confuse empathy with sympathy, but the concepts are different. With sympathy, you view the other person's situation from your point of view. With empathy, you view it from the other person's perspective. Consider the difference between sympathizing and empathizing with a single parent or a homeless person. When you sympathize, your feelings

"How would you feel if the mouse did that to you?"

focus on the other person's confusion, joy, or pain. When you empathize, the experience becomes your own, at least for the moment. Note that empathy doesn't require you to agree with the other person. You can empathize with difficult relatives or rude strangers without endorsing their behavior.

There's a physiological basis for empathy. Brain scans reveal that neural firing patterns that register our own thoughts and feelings are in many cases identical to those that register thoughts and feelings about others (Lombardo et al., 2010). This explains empathy on the biochemical level: It's possible to feel others' experiences in the same way we feel our own.

Besides *imagining* how another person feels, another way to gain empathy is to *physically experience* the same reality. Because mind melds only occur in science fiction, simulations are the closest we can get to another person's reality. Several studies (Hogenboom, 2013) have found that spending even a short time in a virtual body of a different race can affect perception. Literally—or, at least, virtually—inhabiting the body of another provides the basis for the development of empathy, and with empathy comes a reduction in bias. Similarly, college students who took on avatars of elderly people and entered their virtual environment came away with new attitudes toward the aged (Yee & Bailenson, 2006).

There are many other ways to increase empathy. For example, one intriguing study suggests that a trip to the art museum can broaden children's worldviews and enhance their empathic imagination (Greene et al., 2014). A study of camera perspectives used to portray a victim of a social problem found that close-ups can increase empathy and intentions to help others (Cao, 2013). Things as simple as reading stories of people who are suffering (Carrera et al., 2013), sharing personal narratives (DasGupta & Charon, 2004), and interacting and communicating with wide varieties of people (Goleman, 2013) are other ways that help increase empathy.

Empathy and Ethics

The "golden rule" of treating others as we want to be treated points to the clear relationship between the ability to empathize and the ethical principles that enable society to function in a manner that we consider civilized (Howe, 2013; Rifkin, 2009). Martin Hoffman (1991) and Frans de Waal (2008, 2009) have cited research showing the link between empathy and ethical altruism. Bystanders who feel empathy for victims are more likely to intervene and offer help than those who are indifferent. On a larger scale, studies have revealed a relationship between feelings of empathy and the belief that resources should be allocated according to people's needs (Batson et al., 1995).

A look at criminal behavior also demonstrates the link between empathy and ethics. Typically, people who commit the most offensive crimes against others, such as rape and child abuse, are not inhibited by any sense of how their offenses affect the victims (Clements et al., 2007; Goleman, 1995). New treatments attempt to change behavior by instilling the ability to imagine how others are feeling (Day et al., 2010; Wade & Worthington, 2005). These programs have offenders read emotional descriptions of crimes similar to the ones they have committed and watch videotapes of victims describing what it was like to be assaulted. Offenders also write accounts of what their crimes must have felt like to the victim, read these stories to others in therapy groups, and even experience simulated reenactments of the crime in which they play the role of the victim. Through strategies such as these, therapists try to help offenders develop the ethical compass that makes it more difficult to be indifferent to causing pain in others.

Requirements for Empathy

Empathy may be valuable, but it isn't always easy to achieve (Ickes & Hodges, 2013). In fact, research shows that it's hardest to empathize with people who are radically different from us in age, sex, socioeconomic status, intelligence, and so forth (Goleman, 2013; Samovar et al., 2010). To make such perceptual leaps, you need to develop several skills and attitudes: open-mindedness, imagination, and commitment.

Perhaps the most important characteristic of an empathic person is the ability and disposition to be *open-minded*—to set aside for the moment your own beliefs, attitudes, and values and to consider those of the other person (Herfst et al., 2008; Nelson, 2009). Open-mindedness is especially difficult when the other person's position is radically different from your own. The temptation is to think (and sometimes say) "That's crazy!," "How can you believe that?," or "I'd do it this way. . . ." Being open-minded is often difficult because people confuse understanding another's position with accepting it. These are quite different matters. To understand why a friend disagrees with you, for example, doesn't mean you have to give up your position and accept theirs.

Being open-minded often isn't enough to allow empathy. You also need enough *imagination* to be able to picture another person's background and thoughts (Decety, 2005). A happily married or single person needs imagination to empathize with the problems of a friend considering divorce. A young person needs it to empathize with a parent facing retirement. A teacher needs it to understand the problems facing students, just as students can't be empathic without trying to imagine how their instructor feels.

MEDIA CLIP
Gaining and Using Empathy:
White Collar and *Undercover Boss*

Neal Caffrey (Matt Bomer) is known as a "white collar criminal." He's an art and securities thief, counterfeiter, and racketeer. When cornered by the FBI, he strikes a deal: In exchange for not going to prison, he'll use his expertise to help the feds catch con artists like himself.

The premise of *White Collar* is a reminder that to understand the way others see the world, it helps to have similar backgrounds. Neal is good at catching criminals because he knows how they think. This shared understanding can be helpful in many professions. It's no surprise, for instance, that counselors and therapists often have had challenging lives of their own, and thus they have empathy for their patients' experiences.

Another TV series, *Undercover Boss* (pictured here), shows a way to gain empathy for those from different walks of life. In the show, high-ranking company officials don disguises and take on the roles of "blue collar" employees in their organizations. Some of them rediscover what it was like when they were working their way up the occupational ladder. Others gain new empathy for a world they've never known.

Regardless of the color of one's collar, these shows demonstrate that empathy is a valuable asset in communicating with others.

Because empathizing is often difficult, a third necessary quality is *commitment*, a sincere desire to understand another person. Listening to unfamiliar, often confusing information takes time and isn't always fun. If you aim to be empathic, be willing to face the challenge.

By now, you can see the tremendous challenges that face us when we want to understand one another. Physiological distortion, psychological

ASSESSING YOUR COMMUNICATION

Your Empathy Quotient

Respond to each of the following statements using a scale ranging from 0 to 4, where 0 = never and 4 = always. Also have someone who knows you well fill out the instrument about you and compare notes afterward.

_____ **1.** When someone else is feeling excited, I tend to get excited too.

_____ **2.** Other people's misfortunes do not disturb me a great deal.

_____ **3.** It upsets me to see someone being treated disrespectfully.

_____ **4.** I remain unaffected when someone close to me is happy.

_____ **5.** I enjoy making other people feel better.

_____ **6.** I have tender, concerned feelings for people less fortunate than I am.

_____ **7.** When a friend starts to talk about his/her problems, I try to steer the conversation toward something else.

_____ **8.** I can tell when others are sad even when they do not say anything.

_____ **9.** I find that I am "in tune" with other people's moods.

_____ **10.** I do not feel sympathy for people who cause their own serious illnesses.

_____ **11.** I become irritated when someone cries.

_____ **12.** I am not really interested in how other people feel.

_____ **13.** I get a strong urge to help when I see someone who is upset.

_____ **14.** When I see someone being treated unfairly, I do not feel very much pity for them.

_____ **15.** I find it silly for people to cry out of happiness.

_____ **16.** When I see someone being taken advantage of, I feel a bit protective toward him/her.

Adapted from Spreng, R., McKinnon, M. C., Mar, R. A., & Levine, B. (2009). The Toronto Empathy Questionnaire: Scale development and initial validation of a factor-analytic solution to multiple empathy measures. *Journal of Personality Assessment, 91*, 62–71.

For scoring information, see page 137 at the end of the chapter.

interference, and social and cultural conditioning all insulate us from our fellow human beings. But the news isn't all bad: With a combination of determination and skill, we can do a better job of spanning the gap that separates us and, as a result, enjoy more satisfying interpersonal relationships.

CHECK YOUR UNDERSTANDING

Objective 4.1 Understand the subjective nature of perceiving interpersonal messages and relationships.

The reality we perceive is constructed through communication with others. First-order realities involve things and events that are tangible; second-order realities are the meanings we assign to those things and events. Interpersonal perception involves four phases: selection, organization, interpretation, and negotiation.

Q: Recall an important exchange in which you viewed matters differently than your relational partner. Describe how you selected, organized, and interpreted the other person's behavior and how your partner perceived the exchange differently. How successful were you in negotiating a shared perception of what happened?

Objective 4.2 Identify the variety of influences on interpersonal perception.

A number of influences can affect how we perceive others' behavior. Physiological factors include our senses, age, health and fatigue, biological cycles, hunger, and neurobehavioral challenges. Psychological factors such as mood and self-concept also have a strong influence on how we regard others. In addition, social influences such as sex and gender roles, occupational roles, and relational roles play an important part in the way we view those with whom we interact. Finally, cultural influences shape how we recognize and make sense of others' words and actions.

Q: Identify instances in which the physiological, psychological, and social influences described in

this chapter shaped your perceptions and consequently your interpersonal communication.

Objective 4.3 Recognize how common tendencies in perception shape interpersonal communication.

Our perceptions are often affected by common perceptual tendencies. We tend to make snap judgments and cling to first impressions, even if they are mistaken. We are more likely to blame others than ourselves for misfortunes. We are influenced by our expectations. We also are influenced by obvious stimuli, even if they are not the most important factors. Finally, we assume others are similar to us.

Q: Describe a case in which the perceptual tendencies described in this chapter shaped your perceptions and consequently your communication. How might the incident have turned out differently if you had not succumbed to these perceptual errors?

Objective 4.4 Use perception checking and adjust attitudes to enhance empathy with communication partners.

One way to coordinate our interpretations with others is through perception checking. Instead of jumping to conclusions, communicators who check their perceptions describe the behavior they noticed, offer two equally plausible interpretations, and ask for clarification from their partner.

Empathy is the ability to experience the world from another person's perspective. There are three dimensions to empathy: perspective taking, emotional involvement, and concern for the other person. Requirements for empathy include openmindedness, imagination, and commitment.

Q: Construct a perception-checking statement you could use to clarify your understanding in an important relationship. How might using this approach affect the relationship if you presented it using the empathy-enhancing attitudes described in this chapter?

KEY TERMS

- Androgynous (119)
- Attribution (123)
- Confirmation bias (125)
- Empathy (131)
- First-order realities (109)
- Fundamental attribution error (126)
- Gender (119)

- Halo effect (125)
- Horns effect (125)
- Interpretation (112)
- Narratives (113)
- Negotiation (113)
- Organization (111)
- Perception checking (129)
- Primacy effect (125)

- Punctuation (111)
- Second-order realities (109)
- Selection (110)
- Self-serving bias (126)
- Standpoint theory (118)
- Stereotyping (124)

ACTIVITIES

1. Complete the following sentences:

a. Women . . . _____

_____

b. Men . . . _____

_____

c. Latinos . . . _____

_____

d. European Americans . . . _____

_____

e. African Americans . . . _____

_____

f. Older people . . . _____

_____

Now share your observations with a classmate and discuss the degree to which each of your responses was a stereotype and/or a generalization. How could your answers to these questions change the way you perceive and respond to people in these groups? Discuss with your classmate ways in which your communication is affected by stereotyping.

2. You can get a better appreciation of the importance of punctuation by using the format pictured in Figure 4.3 (p. XX) to diagram the following situations:

a. A father and daughter are growing more and more distant. The daughter withdraws because she interprets her father's coolness as rejection. The father views his daughter's aloofness as a rebuff and withdraws further.

b. The relationship between two friends is becoming strained. One jokes to lighten up the tension, and the other becomes more tense.

c. A couple is on the verge of breaking up. One partner frequently asks the other to show more affection. The other withdraws physical contact.

Explain how each of these situations could be punctuated differently by each participant. Next, use the same procedure to identify how an event from your experience could be punctuated in at least two different ways. Describe the consequences of failing to recognize the plausibility of each of these punctuation schemes.

3. In a group, have each member choose one of the following situations, and describe how it could be perceived differently by each person. Be sure to include the steps of selection, organization, and interpretation. What might their narratives sound like as they negotiate their perceptions? List any relevant physiological, psychological, social, and cultural influences, as well as suggesting how the communicators' self-concepts might have affected their perceptions.

a. A customer complains to a salesperson about poor service in a busy store.

b. A parent and teenager argue about the proper time for returning home after a Saturday night date.

c. A quiet student feels pressured when called on by an instructor to speak up in class.

d. A woman and a man argue about whether to increase balance in the workplace by making special efforts to hire employees from underrepresented groups.

4. Improve your perception-checking ability by developing complete perception-checking statements for each of the following situations. Be sure your statements include a description of the behavior, two equally plausible interpretations, and a request for verification.

a. You made what you thought was an excellent suggestion to your boss. He or she said, "I'll get back to you about that right away." It's been 3 weeks, and you haven't received a response yet.

b. You haven't received the usual weekly phone call from your family in over a month. Last time you spoke, you had an argument about where to spend the holidays.

After you've created your perception-checking statements, share them with some friends or family members and see how they would respond if they were the recipients.

5. You can develop your empathy skills by putting yourself in the shoes of someone with whom you have an interpersonal relationship. With that person's help, describe *in the first person* how the other person views an issue that is important to him or her. In other words, try as much as possible to become that person and see things from his or her perspective. Your partner will be the best judge of your ability to make this perceptual jump, so use his or her feedback to modify your account. After completing the exercise, describe how your attempt changed the way you might relate to the other person.

SCORING FOR ASSESSING YOUR COMMUNICATION (PAGE 134)

Before summing your responses to the 16 items, reverse the scores for the negatively worded items: 2, 4, 7, 10, 11, 12, 14, and 15. That is, for these items, 0 = 4, 1 = 3, 2 = 2, 3 = 1, and 4 = 0. After reversing the scores for the noted items, sum all your responses to determine your total empathy score. In several studies, females scored slightly higher than males. For females, on average, the sum was 47; for males, the sum was 44.

The 16 items capture the most commonly measured aspect of empathy, "an emotional process or an accurate affective insight into the feeling state of another" (Spreng et al., 2009, p. 62).

chapter 5

Language

LEARNING OBJECTIVES

5.1 Understand the symbolic, rule-based, subjective, culture-bound nature of language.

5.2 Recognize the impact, both positive and negative, of language in interpersonal relationships.

5.3 Describe the influence gender has on language use in interpersonal relationships.

5.4 Identify ways in which online language usage is different from the in-person variety.

STANFORD UNIVERSITY professor Lera Boroditsky (2009) often begins her undergraduate lectures by asking students which cognitive faculty they would least want to lose. Most choose vision; a few pick hearing. Almost no one mentions language.

Boroditsky suggests that this is an oversight. After all, she reasons, people who lack the ability to see or hear can still have rich and satisfying lives. "But what would your life be like if you had never learned a language?" she wonders. "Could you still have friends, get an education, hold a job, start a family? Language is so fundamental to our experience, so deeply a part of being human, that it's hard to imagine life without it" (p. 116).

Language is arguably the most essential component of human communication. In this chapter, we explore the relationship between words and ideas. We describe some important characteristics of language and show how these characteristics affect our day-to-day communication. We outline several types of troublesome language and show how to replace them with more effective kinds of speech. Finally, we look at how gender and online communication influence the way we use language.

THE NATURE OF LANGUAGE

We begin our survey by looking at some features that characterize all languages. These features explain both why language is such a useful tool and why it can be so troublesome.

LANGUAGE IS SYMBOLIC

Words are arbitrary symbols that have no meaning in themselves. For example, the word *five* is a kind of code that represents the number of fingers on your hand only because we agree that it does. As Bateson and Jackson (1964) point out, "There is nothing particularly five-like in the number 'five'" (p. 271). To a speaker of French, the symbol *cinq* would convey the same meaning; to a computer, the same value would be represented by the electronically coded symbol *0101*.

Even sign language, as "spoken" by most deaf people, is symbolic in nature and not the pantomime it might seem (Sandler, 2013; Tolar et al., 2008). Because this form of communication is symbolic and not literal, there are hundreds of different sign languages used around the world that have evolved independently, whenever significant numbers of deaf people have come in contact (Meir et al., 2010). These distinct languages include American Sign Language, Mexican Sign Language, British Sign Language, French Sign Language, Danish Sign Language, Chinese Sign Language, and Australian Aboriginal and Mayan sign languages—and communicating across different sign languages can be as difficult as it is across different spoken languages (Quinto-Pozos, 2008).

LANGUAGE IS RULE-GOVERNED

The only reason symbol-laden languages work at all is that people agree on how to use them. The linguistic agreements that make communication possible can be codified in rules. Languages contain several types of rules that continuously evolve (Garner, 2014). **Phonological rules** govern how sounds are combined to form words. For instance, the words *champagne, double,* and *occasion* have the same meaning in French and English, but are pronounced differently because the languages have different phonological rules.

Whereas phonological rules determine how spoken language sounds, **syntactic rules** govern the way symbols can be arranged. Notice that the following statements contain the same words, but the shift in syntax creates quite different meanings:

Whiskey makes you sick when you're well.
Whiskey, when you're sick, makes you well.

Although most of us aren't able to describe the syntactic rules that govern our language (Hsu & Chater, 2010; Parisse, 2005), it's easy to recognize their existence when they are violated. A humorous example is the way the character Yoda speaks in the *Star Wars* movies. Phrases such as "the dark side are they" or "your father he is" often elicit a chuckle because they bend syntactical norms. Sometimes, however, apparently ungrammatical speech is simply following a different set of syntactic rules, reflecting regional or co-cultural dialects. Linguists believe it is crucial to view such dialects as *different* rather than *deficient* forms of English (Wolfram & Schilling-Estes, 2005).

Semantic rules also govern our use of language. Whereas syntax deals with structure, semantics governs the meaning of statements. Semantic rules are what make it possible for us to agree that "bikes" are for riding and "books" are for reading, and they help us know whom we will encounter when we use restrooms marked "men" and "women." Without

MEDIA CLIP
Sign Language and Culture: *See What I'm Saying*

Several entertainers who are deaf are spotlighted in the documentary *See What I'm Saying.* Some of them navigate quite effectively within and outside the deaf community. For instance, Bob Hiltermann is a drummer in the world's only deaf rock band, Beethoven's Nightmare. The movie shows him producing the largest show in the band's 30-year history.

But other artists in the film have mixed success. CJ Jones is a famous comic in deaf circles, but he has difficulty attracting an audience to the first international sign language theater festival in Los Angeles. And hard-of-hearing singer TL Forsberg, for whom signing is not her native language, feels caught between the deaf and hearing communities while producing her first musical CD, "Not Deaf Enough."

The movie is best viewed through the lens of intercultural communication. Like any other language, sign language empowers those who share in its culture. When deaf and "signing impaired" cultures overlap, it requires communicators to embrace the principles of intercultural competence discussed in Chapter 2.

semantic rules, communication would be impossible: Each of us would use symbols in unique ways, unintelligible to others.

Semantic rules help us understand the meaning of individual words, but they often don't explain how language operates in everyday life. Consider the statement "Let's get together tomorrow." The semantic meaning of the words in this sentence is clear enough, yet the statement could be taken in several ways. It could be a request ("I hope we can get together"), a polite command ("I want to see you"), or an empty cliché ("I don't really mean it"). We learn to distinguish the accurate meanings of such speech acts through **pragmatic rules** that tell us what uses and interpretations of a message are appropriate in a given context.

When pragmatic rules are understood by all players in the language game, smooth communication is possible. For example, one rule specifies that the relationship between communicators plays a large role in determining the meaning of a statement. Our example, "I want to see you," is likely to mean one thing when uttered by your boss and another entirely when it comes from your lover. Likewise, the setting in which the statement is made plays a role. Saying "I want to see you" will probably have a different meaning at the office than the same words uttered at a cocktail party—although the nonverbal behaviors that accompany a statement help us decode its meaning.

People in individual relationships create their own sets of pragmatic rules. Consider the use of humor: The teasing and jokes you exchange with gusto with one friend might be considered tasteless or offensive in another relationship. For instance, imagine an e-mail message typed in CAPITAL LETTERS and filled with CURSE WORDS, INSULTS, NAME-CALLING, and EXCLAMATION MARKS!!! How would you interpret such a message? An outside observer might consider this an example of "flaming" and be appalled, when in fact the message might be a fun-loving case of "verbal jousting" between buddies (O'Sullivan & Flanagin, 2003). If you have a good friend whom you call by a less-than-tasteful nickname as a term of endearment, then you understand the concept. Keep in mind, however, that those who aren't privy to your relationship's pragmatic rules are likely to misunderstand you, so you'll want to be wise about when and where to use these personal codes.

The *coordinated management of meaning* (CMM) theory describes some types of pragmatic rules that operate in everyday conversations. It suggests that we use rules at several levels to create our own messages and interpret others' statements, both in person and online (Moore & Mattson-Lauters, 2009; Pearce, 2005). Table 5.1 uses a CMM framework to illustrate how two people might wind up confused because they are using different rules at several levels. In situations such as this, it's important to make sure that the other person's use of language matches yours before jumping to conclusions about the meaning of his or her statements (Dougherty et al., 2009). The skill of perception checking described in Chapter 4 can be a useful tool at times like these.

LANGUAGE IS SUBJECTIVE

If the rules of language were more precise and if everyone followed them, we would suffer from fewer misunderstandings. You have an hour-long argument about "feminism" only to discover that you were using the term in different ways and that you really were in basic agreement. You tease a friend in what you mean to be a playful manner, but he takes you seriously and is offended.

These problems occur because people attach different meanings to the same message. Ogden and Richards (1923) illustrated this point in their well-known "triangle of meaning" (see Figure 5.1).

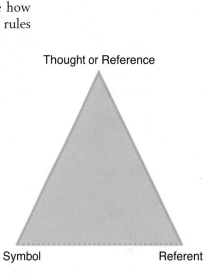

FIGURE 5.1 **Ogden and Richards' Triangle of Meaning**

TABLE 5.1 Pragmatic Rules Govern the Use and Meaning of a Statement

Notice how the same message ("You look great today") takes on a different meaning depending on which of a variety of rules are used to formulate and interpret it.

	BOSS	EMPLOYEE
Content Actual words	"You look great today."	
Speech Act The intent of the statement	To compliment the employee	Unknown
Relational Contract The perceived relationship between communicators	Boss who treats employees like family members	Subordinate, dependent on boss's approval for advancement
Episode Situation in which the interaction occurs	Casual conversation	Possible come-on?
Life Script Self-concept of each communicator	Someone who pays attention to employees in a friendly way	Someone who wants to impress the boss with talent rather than looks
Cultural Archetype Cultural norms that shape a member's perceptions and actions	Middle-class American	Working-class American

Adapted from Pearce, W. B., & Cronen, V. (1980). *Communication, action, and meaning.* New York: Praeger. Used by permission.

This model shows that there is only an indirect relationship—indicated by a broken line—between a word and the thing or idea it represents.

The Ogden and Richards model is oversimplified in that not all words refer to physical "things" or referents. For instance, some referents are abstract ideas (such as *love*), whereas others (such as *angry* or *exciting*) aren't even nouns. Despite these shortcomings, the triangle of meaning is useful because it clearly demonstrates an important principle: *Meanings are in people, not words.* Hence, an important task facing communicators is to establish a common understanding of the words they use to exchange messages. In this sense, communication—at least the effective kind—requires us to negotiate the meaning of our language (Leung & Lewkowicz, 2013). This brings us back to a familiar theme: Meaning is both *in* and *among* people. Language is a function of individuals who give each word unique meaning as well as cultures that create and share meaning collectively.

LANGUAGE AND WORLDVIEW

For more than 150 years, theorists have put forth the notion of **linguistic relativity**—that a language both reflects and shapes the worldview of those who use it (Deutscher, 2010; Everett, 2013). For instance, bilingual speakers seem to think differently when they change languages (Cook & Bassetti, 2011; Giles & Franklyn-Stokes, 1989). In one study, French Americans were asked to interpret a series of pictures. When they spoke in French, their descriptions were far more romantic and emotional than when they used English to describe the same kind of images. In Israel, both Muslim and Jewish students saw bigger distinctions between their group and "outsiders" when using their native language than when they spoke in English, a neutral tongue. Examples such as these show the power of language to shape cultural identity—sometimes for better and sometimes for worse.

The best-known declaration of linguistic relativity is the **Sapir–Whorf hypothesis**, credited to Benjamin Whorf, an amateur linguist, and anthropologist Edward Sapir (Tohidian, 2009; Whorf, 1956). Following Sapir's theoretical work, Whorf found that the language spoken by Hopi Native Americans represented a view of reality that is dramatically different from most tongues. For example, the Hopi language makes no distinction between nouns and verbs. Therefore, the people who speak it describe the entire world as being constantly in process. Whereas English speakers use nouns to characterize people or objects as being fixed or constant, the Hopi language represents them more as verbs, constantly changing. In this sense, English represents the world rather like a collection of snapshots, whereas Hopi reflects a worldview that is more like a motion picture.

Some languages contain terms that have no English equivalents (Rheingold, 1988; Wire, 2010). For example, consider a few words in other languages that have no simple translation in English:

- *Nemawashi* (Japanese): the process of informally feeling out the opinions of all the people involved with an issue before making a decision
- *Lagniappe* (French/Creole): an extra gift given in a transaction that wasn't expected by the terms of a contract

- *Lao* (Mandarin): respectful term used for older people, showing their importance in the family and in society
- *Dharma* (Sanskrit): each person's unique, ideal path in life and the knowledge of how to find it

It's possible to imagine concepts like these without having specific words to describe them, but linguistic relativity suggests that the terms do shape the thinking and actions of people who use them. Thus, speakers of a language that includes the notion of *lao* would probably be more inclined to treat their older members respectfully, and those who are familiar with *lagniappe* might be more generous.

"You'll have to phrase it another way. They have no word for 'fetch.'"

Research by Jennifer Prewitt-Freilino and her colleagues (2012) provides evidence that language reflects and shapes reality. Their study focused on the relationship between gendered language and gender equality in 111 countries. They compared countries with *gendered language* (nouns are assigned a feminine, masculine, or neutral gender, as in Spain, Israel, and Belgium), *genderless language* (nouns have no gender, as in Cambodia, Iran, and South Africa), and *natural language* (most nouns have no grammatical marking of gender, as in the United States, Sweden, and Barbados). Findings showed that countries using gendered languages have less gender equality, especially in terms of women's economic participation. In addition, women have greater access to political empowerment in countries that speak natural gender languages.

The effects of language on a speaker's thoughts and feelings can also be seen in a study conducted at the University of Bristol (Bowers & Pleydell-Pearce, 2011). Researchers asked participants to speak aloud words in three categories: swear words, euphemisms for swear words (such as saying "the F-word" instead of the actual term), and neutral words. When saying swear words, participants had much stronger physiological stress responses than when they used euphemistic or neutral terms. The researchers regard this as an example of linguistic relativity. Taboo words can evoke strong neurological responses, even when they are uttered without any desire to offend. This shows that the language we use has an impact on our brains—sometimes in ways we don't even realize.

THE IMPACT OF LANGUAGE

As linguistic relativity suggests, language can have a strong influence on our perceptions and how we regard one another. In this section, we examine some of the many ways language can impact our lives.

NAMING AND IDENTITY

"What's in a name?" Juliet asked rhetorically. If Romeo had been a social scientist, he would have answered, "A great deal." Research has demonstrated

FOCUS ON RESEARCH
The Negative Consequences of Fat Talk

A premise of linguistic relativity is that our words don't just *reflect* how we see the world; they also *affect* how we see it. The language we use shapes our perception of things, others, and ourselves.

Communication researcher Analisa Arroyo found this principle at work in her study of "fat talk." People who regularly put concerns about their weight into words ("I'm so fat"; "My butt is huge") reinforce a poor body image. Arroyo identified three particular signs that fat talk is doing harm: (1) when it's used routinely and compulsively; (2) when it involves constant comparisons with others; and (3) when it includes guilt words such as "should" and "ought"

("I really should drop some weight"). As discussed in Chapter 3, a steady diet of negative self-appraisals and social comparison can turn into a destructive cycle of thoughts, words, and behaviors.

In an interesting twist, there seems to be no harm in *listening* to fat talk. Says Arroyo, "It is the act of engaging in fat talk, rather than passively being exposed to it, that has these negative effects." She suggests that people struggling with this problem should establish "fat talk free" weeks with their friends. Arroyo also believes that replacing "I should" with "I will" or "I can" when talking about weight reduction can help people move in the right direction.

Arroyo, A. (2013). "I'm so fat!" The negative outcomes of fat talk. *Communication Currents, 7,* 1–2.

Arroyo, A., & Harwood, J. (2012). Exploring the causes and consequences of fat talk. *Journal of Applied Communication Research, 40,* 167–187.

that names are more than just a simple means of identification: They shape the way others think of us, the way we view ourselves, and the way we act (Lieberson, 2000).

For more than a century, researchers have studied the impact of rare and unusual names on the people who bear them (Christenfeld & Larsen, 2008). Early studies claimed that people with non-normative names suffered everything from psychological and emotional disturbance to failure in college. Later studies show that people often have negative appraisals not only of unusual names, but also of unusual name spellings (e.g., Mehrabian, 2001). In one study, for example, people with unusual names were judged least likely to be hired (Cotton et al., 2008). Of course, what makes a name (and its spelling) unusual changes with time. In 1900, the 20 most popular names for baby girls in the United States included Bertha, Mildred, and Ethel. By 2012, the top 20 names included Madison, Mia, and Sophia—names that would have been highly unusual a century earlier (Social Security Administration, 2013).

Some people regard unique names as distinctive rather than unusual. You can probably think of four or five unique names—of celebrities, sports stars, or even personal friends—that make the person easily recognizable and memorable. In one study, a poem signed with an unusual name was assessed as more creative than when signed by a more common name (Lebuda & Karwowski, 2013). Sometimes the choice of unique names is connected with cultural identity. For example, in some parts of the United States, nearly a third of African American girls born in the 1990s were given distinctively black names that belonged to no one else in the state (Dinwiddie-Boyd,

1994). Researchers suggest that distinctive names like these are a symbol of solidarity with the African American community. Conversely, choosing a less distinctive name can be a way of integrating the baby into the majority culture.

AFFILIATION

Language can be a way of building and demonstrating solidarity with others, and an impressive body of research has demonstrated that communicators who want to show affiliation with one another can adapt their speech in a variety of ways, including their choice of vocabulary, rate of talking, number and placement of pauses, and level of politeness (Giles et al., 2010). In one study, the likelihood of mutual romantic interest increased when conversation partners' use of pronouns, articles, conjunctions, prepositions, and negations matched (Ireland et al., 2011). The same study revealed that when couples used similar language styles while instant messaging, the chances of their relationship continuing increased by almost 50 percent. The researchers speculate that unconscious language-style matching relates to how much each is paying attention to what the other says.

Close friends and lovers often develop a set of special terms that serve as a way of signifying their relationship (Bell & Healey, 1992; Dunleavy & Booth-Butterfield, 2009). Using the same vocabulary serves to set these people apart from others, reminding themselves and the rest of the world of their relationship. The same process works among members of larger groups, ranging from street gangs to military personnel. Communication researchers call the process of adapting one's speech style to match that of others with whom the communicator wants to identify **convergence** (Giles & Ogay, 2006). This mirroring of others' linguistic patterns usually develops over time, but one study found that it can emerge quickly between strangers communicating online (Riordan et al., 2013).

When two or more people feel equally positive about one another, their linguistic convergence will be mutual. But when communicators want or need approval, they often adapt their speech to accommodate the other person's style, trying to say the "right thing" or speak in a way that will help them fit in. We see this process when employees who seek advancement start to speak more like their superiors and managers converge toward their bosses. One study (Baruch & Jenkins, 2006) even showed that adopting the swearing patterns of bosses and coworkers can help people feel connected on the job. (See the At Work sidebar in this section for a discussion of this topic.)

The principle of speech accommodation works in reverse, too. Communicators who want to set themselves apart from others adopt the strategy of

SWEARING ON THE JOB

@WORK

Swearing serves a variety of communication functions (Jay & Janschewitz, 2008). It's a way to express emotions and to let others know how strongly you feel. It can be part of a compliment ("that was #$&@ing terrific!") or the worst of insults. Swearing can offend and alienate, but it can also build solidarity and be a term of endearment.

Communication researchers Danette Johnson and Nicole Lewis (2010) investigated the effects of swearing in work settings. Not surprisingly, they found that the more formal the situation, the more negative the appraisal. The chosen swear word also made a difference: "F-bombs" were rated as more inappropriate than other less-volatile terms. When hearers were caught by surprise by a speaker's swearing, they were likely to deem the person as incompetent—unless they were *pleasantly* surprised (Johnson, 2012).

Despite these findings, Stanford University professor Robert Sutton (2010) notes that choosing *not* to swear can actually violate the norms of some organizations. Moreover, he maintains that swearing on rare occasions can be effective for the shock value. (The fact that Sutton authored a book called *The No Asshole Rule* suggests he practices what he preaches.)

But even Sutton adds a cautionary note about swearing on the job: "If you are not sure, don't do it." The rules of interpersonal competence apply: Analyze and adapt to your audience, and engage in self-monitoring. And when in doubt, err on the side of restraint.

divergence, speaking in a way that emphasizes their differences. For example, members of an ethnic group, even though fluent in the dominant language, might use their own dialect as a way of showing solidarity with one another—a sort of "we're proud of our heritage" strategy. The same can occur across age lines, such as teens who adopt the slang of subcultures other than their own to show divergence with adults (Reyes, 2005). Of course, communicators need to be careful about when—and when not—to converge their language with others. For example, using ethnic or racial epithets when you're not a member of that in-group may be inappropriate and even offensive. One of the pragmatic goals of divergence is the creation of norms about who has the "right" to use certain words and who does not.

POWER AND POLITENESS

Communication researchers have identified a number of language patterns that communicate more or less power (Bradac & Street, 1990; Hosman & Siltanen, 2006). Notice the difference between these two statements from an employee to a manager:

> Excuse me, sir. I hate to say this, but I . . . uh . . . I guess I won't be able to finish the project on time. I had a personal emergency and . . . well . . . it was just impossible to finish it by today. I'll have it to you first thing on Monday, okay?

> I won't be able to finish the project on time. I had a personal emergency and it was impossible to finish it by today. I will have it to you first thing on Monday.

The first statement is an example of what has been called **powerless language**: tentative and indirect word choices, with hedges and hesitations

("Excuse me, sir"; "I guess"; "okay?"). The second is labeled **powerful language**: direct and forceful word choices, with declarations and assertions ("I won't"; "I will"). Studies have shown that speakers who use powerful speech are rated as more competent, dynamic, and attractive than speakers who sound powerless (Ng & Bradac, 1993; Reid & Ng, 1999). In addition, when it comes to employment interview outcomes, a powerful speech style results in more positive attributions of competence and employability than a powerless one (Parton et al., 2002).

A *disclaimer* is a type of powerless speech that attempts to distance a speaker from remarks that might be unwelcome. For example, you might preface a critical message by saying "I don't mean to sound judgmental, but . . ." and then go on to express your disapproval. One study showed that disclaimers actually *increase* negative judgments (El-Alayli et al., 2008). For instance, the phrase "I don't mean to sound arrogant . . ." followed by a high-handed comment led subjects to regard the speaker as *more* arrogant. Disclaimers involving other negative qualities such as laziness and selfishness produced similar results. It seems that disclaimers backfire because they sensitize listeners to look for—and find—precisely the qualities that the speaker is trying to disavow.

Some scholars question the label "powerless" because tentative and indirect speech styles can sometimes achieve goals better than more assertive approaches (Lee & Pinker, 2010). For example, less forceful approaches can be attempts at **politeness**: communicating in ways that save face for both senders and receivers. Politeness is valued in some cultures more than others (Dunn, 2013). In Japan, saving face for others is an important goal, so communicators there tend to speak in ambiguous terms and use hedge words and qualifiers. In most Japanese sentences, the verb comes at the end of the sentence so the "action" part of the statement can be postponed. Traditional Mexican culture, with its strong emphasis on cooperation, also uses hedging to smooth over interpersonal relationships. By not taking a firm stand with their speech mannerisms, Mexicans believe they will not make others feel ill at ease.

Even in highly assertive cultures, simply counting the number of powerful or powerless statements won't always reveal who has the most control in a relationship. Social rules often mask the real distribution of power. A boss who wants to be pleasant might say to a secretary, "Would you mind getting this file?" In truth, both boss and secretary know this is an order and not a request, but the questioning form makes the medicine less bitter. Sociolinguist Deborah Tannen (1994) describes how politeness can be a face-saving way of delivering an order:

> I hear myself giving instructions to my assistants without actually issuing orders: "Maybe it would be a good idea to . . .;" "It would be great if you could . . ." all the while knowing that I expect them to do what I've asked right away. . . . This rarely creates problems, though, because the people who work for me know that there is only one reason I mention tasks—because I want them done. I *like* giving instructions in this way; it appeals to my sense of what it means to be a good person . . . taking others' feelings into account. (p. 101)

As the proceeding quotation suggests, high-status speakers—especially higher-status women, according to Tannen—often realize that politeness is

In the TV comedy *Parks and Recreation*, Leslie Knope (Amy Poehler) often uses politeness to get her needs met while protecting the dignity of others. By contrast, Ron Swanson (Nick Offerman) relies on his brusque personality and what little position of power he possesses to accomplish his goals.

an effective way to get their needs met while protecting the dignity of the less-powerful person. The importance of achieving both content and relational goals helps explain why a mixture of powerful and polite speech is usually most effective (Geddes, 1992). The key involves adapting your style to your conversational partner (Loyd et al., 2010). If the other person is likely to perceive politeness as weakness, it may be necessary to shift to a more powerful speaking style. Conversely, if the person sees powerful speech as rude and insensitive, it might be best to use a more polite approach (Fandrich & Beck, 2012). As always, competent communication requires flexibility and adaptability.

SEXISM AND RACISM

Sexist language "includes words, phrases, and expressions that unnecessarily differentiate between females and males *or* exclude, trivialize, or diminish" either sex (Parks & Roberton, 2000, p. 415). This type of speech can affect the self-concepts of women and men, which is why one author (Lillian, 2007) argues that it is a form of hate speech.

Suzanne Romaine (1999) offers several examples of how linguistic terms can subtly stereotype men and women. To say that a woman *mothered* her children focuses on her nurturing behavior, but to say that a man *fathered* a child talks only about his biological role. We are familiar with

ASSESSING YOUR COMMUNICATION

Sexist Language

SECTION I:

For each of the following statements, rate your agreement or disagreement on a scale ranging from 1 to 5, where 1 = strongly disagree and 5 = strongly agree.

_____ 1. Women who think that being called a "chairman" is sexist are misinterpreting the word "chairman."

_____ 2. Worrying about sexist language is a trivial activity.

_____ 3. If the original meaning of the word "he" was "person," we should continue to use "he" to refer to both males and females today.

_____ 4. The elimination of sexist language is an important goal.

_____ 5. Sexist language is related to sexist treatment of people in society.

_____ 6. When teachers talk about the history of the United States, they should change expressions, such as "our forefathers" to expressions that include women.

_____ 7. Teachers who require students to use nonsexist language are unfairly forcing their political views on their students.

SECTION II:

For each of the following situations, rate your willingness on a scale ranging from 1 to 5, where 1 = very unwilling and 5 = very willing.

_____ 8. When you are referring to a married woman, how willing are you to use the title "Ms. Smith" rather than "Mrs. Smith"?

_____ 9. How willing are you to use the word "server" rather than "waiter" or "waitress"?

_____ 10. How willing are you to use the expression "husband and wife" rather than "man and wife"?

_____ 11. How willing are you to use the title "flight attendant" instead of "steward" or "stewardess"?

This self-assessment contains 11 of the 21 items on the Inventory of Attitudes Toward Sexist/Nonsexist Language-General, developed by Parks and Roberton (2000).

For scoring information, see page 169 at the end of the chapter.

terms such as *working mother*, but there is no term *working father* because we assume (perhaps inaccurately) that men are the breadwinners.

Beyond just stereotyping, sexist language can stigmatize women. For example, the term *unmarried mother* is common, but we do not talk about *unmarried fathers* because for many people there is no stigma attached to this status for men. Whereas there are over 200 English words for promiscuous women, there are only 20 for men (Piercey, 2000). Perhaps that's why "attitude towards women" is a significant predictor of attitudes regarding nonsexist language (Parks & Roberton, 2008). Education and perspective taking are also positively related to mindsets about inclusive language.

There are at least two ways to eliminate sexist language (Lei, 2006; Rakow, 1992). The first circumvents the problem altogether by eliminating sex-specific terms or substituting neutral terms. For example, using the plural *they* eliminates the necessity for *he, she, she and he,* or *he and she*. When no sex reference is appropriate, you can substitute neutral terms. For example, *mankind* may be replaced with *humanity, human beings, human race,* and *people; man-made* may be replaced with *artificial, manufactured,* and *synthetic; manpower* may be replaced with *labor, workers,* and *workforce;* and *manhood* may be replaced with *adulthood*. In the same way, *Congressmen* and *Congresswomen* are *members of Congress; firemen* and *firewomen* are *firefighters; chairmen* and *chairwomen* are *presiding officers, leaders,* and *chairs; foremen* and *forewomen* are *supervisors; policemen* and *policewomen* are both *police officers;* and *stewardesses* and *stewards* are both *flight attendants*. Of course, some terms refer to things that could not possibly have a sex—so, for example, a *manhole* is a *sewer lid*.

The second method for eliminating sexism is to mark sex clearly—to heighten awareness of whether the reference is to a female or a male. For example, rather than substitute "chairperson" for "chairman," use the terms chairman and chairwoman to specify whether the person is a man or a woman. (Note, also, that there is nothing sacred about putting he before she; in fact, putting *she, her,* and *hers* after *he, him,* and *his,* without changing the order, continues to imply that males are the more important sex and should come first.)

Whereas sexist language usually defines the world as made up of superior men and inferior women, **racist language** reflects a worldview that classifies members of one racial group as superior and others as inferior (Asante, 2002). Not all language that might have racist overtones is deliberate. For example, the connotations of many words favor whites over people of color, as noted by Aaron Smith-McLallen and his colleagues (2006):

> In the United States and many other cultures, the color white often carries more positive connotations than the color black.... Terms such as "Black Monday," "Black Plague," "black cats," and the "black market" all have negative connotations, and literature, television, and movies have traditionally portrayed heroes in white and villains in black. The empirical work of John E. Williams and others throughout the 1960s demonstrated that these positive and negative associations with the colors black and white, independent of any explicit connection to race, were evident among white and black children as young as 3 years old ... as well as among adults. (pp. 47–48)

An obvious step toward eliminating racist language is to make sure your communication is free of offensive labels and slurs—even those "innocent" uses of racist language that are not meant to be taken seriously but are used to maintain relationship solidarity (Guerin, 2003). Some troublesome language will be easy to identify, whereas other problematic speech will be more subtle. For instance, you may be unaware of using racial and ethnic modifiers when describing others, such as "black professor" or "Pakistani merchant" (or modifiers identifying sex, such as "female doctor" or "male secretary"). Modifiers such as these usually aren't necessary, and they can be subtle indicators of racism/sexism. If you wouldn't typically use the phrases "white professor," "European American merchant," "male doctor," or "female secretary," then modifiers that identify race and sex might be indicators of attitudes and language that need to be changed.

PRECISION AND VAGUENESS

Most people assume that the goal of language is to make our ideas clear to one another. When clarity *is* the goal, we need language skills to make our ideas understandable to others. Sometimes, however, we want to be less than perfectly clear. In the following pages, we point out some cases where vagueness serves useful purposes as well as cases where perfect understanding is the goal.

Ambiguous Language

Ambiguous language consists of words and phrases that have more than one commonly accepted definition. Some ambiguous language is amusing, as the following newspaper headlines illustrate:

Police Begin Campaign to Run Down Jaywalkers
Teacher Strikes Idle Kids
20-Year Friendship Ends at the Altar

DARK SIDE OF COMMU[NICATION]
THE INCIVILITY OF H[ATE]

Sooner or later, you're bound to hear the s[omeone] disparage an ethnic group or perhaps a religio[n]. The insult could be sexist or focus on sexual orientation. Whatever the subject, the result is hate speech. This kind of speech politicizes social differences and portrays out-groups in negative and dehumanizing terms (Waltman & Haas, 2011). Hate speech was a problem before the Internet existed, but it has exploded on hate group websites (McNamee et al., 2010).

In many countries, hate speech is a crime. In the United States, even the vilest insults are protected by the First Amendment to the Constitution, as long as they don't incite immediate violence. (Private institutions such as employers or schools can constitutionally impose their own codes of conduct.)

Johns Hopkins University professor P. M. Forni (2010) argues that just because hateful language is legal doesn't make it right. He has dedicated his career to encouraging civility. He documents the physical and emotional toll that uncivil exchanges take on both the attacker and target. On a larger scale, Forni maintains that "vigorous civility is necessary for the survival of society as we know it."

To rephrase a well-known children's taunt, "Sticks and stones may break my bones, but words can *surely* hurt me." The next time you hear—or are tempted to use— hateful words, consider the toll they take on interpersonal relationships and a quest toward a more civil society.

Many misunderstandings that arise from ambiguity are trivial. We recall eating dinner at a Mexican restaurant and ordering a "tostada with beans." Instead of being served a beef tostada with beans on the side, we were surprised to see the waiter bring us a plate containing a tostada *filled* with beans. Other misunderstandings involving ambiguous messages can be more serious. A nurse gave one of her patients a scare when she told him that he "wouldn't be needing" his robe, books, and shaving materials anymore. The patient became quiet and moody. When the nurse inquired about the odd behavior, she discovered that the poor man had interpreted her statement to mean he was going to die soon. In fact, the nurse meant he would be going home shortly.

It's difficult to catch and clarify every instance of ambiguous language. For this reason, the responsibility for interpreting statements accurately rests in large part with the receiver. Feedback of one sort or another—for example, paraphrasing and questioning—can help clear up misunderstandings: "You say you love me, but you want to see other people. In my book, 'love' is exclusive. What about you?"

Abstraction

Abstractions are convenient ways of generalizing about similarities between several objects, people, ideas, or events. Figure 5.2 is an **abstraction ladder** that shows how to describe the same phenomenon at various levels of abstraction.

We use higher-level abstractions all the time. For instance, rather than saying "Thanks for washing the dishes," "Thanks for vacuuming the rug," and "Thanks for making the bed," it's easier to say "Thanks for cleaning up." In such everyday situations, abstractions are a useful kind of verbal shorthand.

High-level abstractions can help communicators find face-saving ways to avoid confrontations and embarrassment (Eisenberg, 1984; Eisenberg & Witten, 1987). If a friend apologizes for arriving late for a date, you can choose to brush off the incident instead of making it an issue by saying "Don't worry. It wasn't the end of the world"—a true statement, but less specific than saying "To tell you the truth, I was mad at the time, but I've cooled off now." If your boss asks your opinion of a new idea that you think is weaker than your own approach but you don't want to disagree, you could respond with a higher-level abstraction by saying "I never thought of it that way."

Although vagueness does have its uses, highly abstract language can cause several types of problems. At the most basic level, the vagueness of some abstract language makes it hard to understand the meaning of a message. Telling the hairstylist "not too short" or "more casual" might produce the look you want, or it might lead to an unpleasant surprise. Overly abstract language can also lead to stereotyping if, for instance, someone who has had one bad experience blames an entire group: "Marriage counselors are worthless"; "New Yorkers are all rude"; or "Men are no good." Overly abstract expressions such as these can cause people to think in generalities, ignoring uniqueness.

You might assume that abstract statements will soften the blow of all critical messages, but research suggests that isn't always the case. People who use vague language to describe others' negative actions are rated as less likeable than those who use concrete language (Douglas & Sutton, 2010). It seems a person describing another's negative behavior in abstract terms is assumed to have a hidden agenda. By contrast, using abstract language to describe the positive behaviors of others results in a more favorable impression of the describer.

Overly abstract language can also lead to problems of a more serious nature. For instance, accusations of sexual assault can arise because one person claims to have said "no" when the other person insists no such refusal was ever conveyed. In response to this sort of disagreement, specific rules of sexual conduct have become more common in work and educational settings. Perhaps the best-known code of this type is the one developed at Antioch College (2006) in Ohio. The policy uses low-level abstractions to minimize the chances of anyone claiming confusion about a partner's willingness. For example, the code states

FIGURE 5.2   **Abstraction Ladder**

A boss gives feedback to an employee about career advancement at various levels of specificity.

- If sexual contact and/or conduct is not mutually and simultaneously initiated, then the person who initiates sexual contact/conduct is responsible for getting verbal consent of the other individual(s) involved.
- Verbal consent [for sexual activity] should be obtained with each new level of physical and/or sexual behavior. . . . Asking "Do you want to have sex with me?" is not enough. The request for consent must be specific to each act.
- If someone has initially consented but then stops consenting during a sexual interaction, she/he should communicate withdrawal of consent verbally (example: saying "no" or "stop") and/or through physical resistance (example: pushing away). The other individual(s) must stop immediately.

Some critics have ridiculed rules like these as being unrealistic. Whatever their weaknesses, however, the Antioch code illustrates how low-level abstractions can reduce the chances of a serious misunderstanding. Specific language may not be desirable or necessary in many situations, but in an era when misinterpretations can lead to accusations of physical assault, it does seem to have a useful place.

You can make your language—and your thinking—less abstract and more clear by learning to make *behavioral descriptions* of your problems, goals, appreciations, complaints, and requests. We use the word *behavioral* because such descriptions move down the abstraction ladder to describe the specific, observable objects and actions we're thinking about. Table 5.2 shows how behavioral descriptions are much more clear and effective than vague, abstract statements.

Euphemism

Euphemisms (from a Greek word meaning "to use words of good omen") are innocuous terms substituted for blunt ones. A euphemism avoids a direct, literal reference to an event (such as "She died"), substituting terms describing its consequences ("She's no longer with us"); related events ("She took

TABLE 5.2 Abstract and Behavioral Descriptions

	ABSTRACT DESCRIPTION	BEHAVIORAL DESCRIPTION			REMARKS
		WHO IS INVOLVED	IN WHAT CIRCUMSTANCES	SPECIFIC BEHAVIORS	
Problem	I'm no good at meeting strangers.	People I'd like to date	At parties and in school	I think, "They'd never want to date me." Also, I don't originate conversations.	Behavioral description more clearly identifies thoughts and behaviors to change.
Goal	I'd like to be more assertive.	Telephone and door-to-door solicitors	When I don't want the product or can't afford it	Instead of apologizing, I want to keep saying "I'm not interested" until they go away.	Behavioral description clearly outlines how to act; abstract description doesn't.
Appreciation	"You've been a great boss."	(no clarification necessary)	When I've needed to change my schedule because of school exams or assignments	"You've been so willing to rearrange my work schedule."	Give both abstract and behavioral descriptions for best results.
Complaint	"I don't like some of the instructors around here."	Professors A and B	In class, when students ask questions the professors think are stupid	They either answer in a sarcastic voice (you might demonstrate) or accuse us of not studying hard enough.	If talking to A or B, use only behavioral descriptions. With others, use both abstract and behavioral descriptions.
Request	"Quit bothering me!"	You and your friends, X and Y	When I'm studying for exams	"Instead of asking me again and again to party with you, I wish you'd accept that I need to study tonight."	Behavioral description will reduce defensiveness and make it clear that you don't always want to be left alone.

her last breath"); metaphors ("She jumped the last hurdle"); or other, more abstract associations (McGlone et al., 2006). Euphemisms are typically used to soften the impact of information that might be unpleasant, both for one-self as well as for the other person (McCallum & McGlone, 2011). It's easy to imagine how a relational breakup might be easier to handle with the explanation, "I'm not ready for commitment" than with "I want to date other people." We tend to use euphemisms more when talking with people of higher status, probably as a way to avoid offending them (Makin, 2004). When choosing how to broach difficult subjects, the challenge is to be as kind as possible without sacrificing either your integrity or the clarity of your message.

Relative Language

Relative language gains meaning by comparison. For example, do you attend a large or a small school? This depends on what you compare it to. Alongside a campus such as Ohio State University, with more than 60,000 students, your school may look small; but compared with a smaller institution, it may seem quite large. Relative words such as fast and slow, smart and stupid, short and long are clearly defined only through comparison.

Using relative terms without explaining them can lead to communication problems. Have you ever responded to someone's question about the weather by saying it was warm only to find out the person thought it was cold? Have you followed a friend's advice and gone to a "cheap" restaurant, only to find that it was twice as expensive as you expected? Have classes you heard were "easy" turned out to be hard? The problem in each case resulted from failing to link the relative word to a more measurable term.

One way to make words more measurable is to turn them into numbers. Health care practitioners have learned that patients often use vague wording when describing their pain: "It hurts a little"; "I'm pretty sore." The use of a numeric pain scale can give a more precise response—and lead to a better diagnosis (Prentice, 2005). When patients are asked to rank their pain from 1 to 10, with 10 being the most severe pain they've ever experienced, the number 7 is much more concrete and specific than "It aches a bit." The same technique can be used when asking people to relate anything from the movies they've seen to their job satisfaction.

Static Evaluation

"Jose is a nervous guy." "Tiara is short-tempered." "You can always count on Wes." Descriptions or evaluations that use the word *is* contain a **static evaluation**—the usually mistaken assumption that people or things are consistent and unchanging. Instead of labeling Jose as permanently and completely nervous, it would probably be more accurate to outline the situations in which he behaves nervously: "Jose acts nervously until you get to know him." The same goes for Tiara, Wes, and the rest of us: We are so much more than the way static, everyday language describes us.

Edward Sagarian (1976) writes about an unconscious language habit that imposes a static view of others. Why is it, he asks, that we say, "He has a cold" but say, "He is a convict" or a genius, a slow learner, or any other set of

MEDIA CLIP
Hiding Behind Language: *The Help*

Eugenia "Skeeter" Phelen (Emma Stone) is determined to become a writer in 1960s Mississippi. She returns home from college to find that most of her friends are married socialites—part of a Southern status quo in which blacks serve whites in low-paying, labor-intensive domestic jobs.

Abstract language and euphemisms play a role in reinforcing the social order. Black maids are referred to as "the help," but they do far more than simply assist their employers. They are responsible for all the housekeeping and childrearing in the white homes. This frees up the socialites to play cards and create laws such as "The Home Help Sanitation Initiative." The white women try to pass off this act as a benefit for their hired hands, but it's just a means to sanction their unfounded prejudices about blacks being unclean and disease ridden.

Skeeter isn't immune to using deceptive language. She writes a household advice column under the pseudonym "Miss Myrna" even though she doesn't know the first thing about cooking and cleaning. She gets her tips from Aibileen Clark (Viola Davis), her friend's maid. Over time, Skeeter decides she has far more important writing to do. She interviews Aibileen and a host of other maids and pens a book about their experiences in a segregated world. Skeeter's forthright depiction of events enacts a well-known phrase from the 1960s: Telling it like it is.

behaviors that are also not necessarily permanent? Sagarian argues that such linguistic labeling leads us to typecast others and in some cases forces them to perpetuate behaviors that could be changed.

General semanticist Alfred Korzybski (1933; see Bhasker, 2013) suggested the linguistic device of *dating* to reduce static evaluation. He proposed adding a subscript whenever appropriate to show the transitory nature of a referent. For example, a teacher might write the following as an evaluation of a student: "Susan$_{May\ 12}$ had difficulty cooperating with her classmates." Although the actual device of subscripting is awkward in writing and impractical in conversation, the idea it represents can still be used. Instead of saying "I'm shy," a more accurate statement might be "I haven't approached any new people since I moved here." The first statement implies that your shyness is an unchangeable trait, rather like your height, whereas the second one suggests that you are capable of changing.

THE LANGUAGE OF RESPONSIBILITY

Besides providing a way to make the content of a message clear or obscure, language reflects the speaker's willingness to take responsibility for her or his beliefs, feelings, and actions. This acceptance or rejection of responsibility says a great deal about the speaker, and it can shape the tone of a relationship. To see how, read on.

"It" Statements

Notice the difference between the sentences of each set:

"It bothers me when you're late."
"I'm worried when you're late."

"It's a bad idea."
"I don't think that's a good idea."

"It's a problem."
"It's a problem for me."

As their name implies, **"it" statements** replace the personal pronouns *I* and *me* with the less immediate construction *it's*. By contrast, **"I" language** clearly identifies the speaker as the source of a message. Communicators who use "it" statements avoid responsibility for ownership of a message, instead attributing it to some unidentified body. This habit isn't just imprecise; it's an unconscious way for someone to avoid taking a position. An extension of "it" statement evasion involves avoiding pronouns altogether. Carol Tavris and Elliot Aronson (2007) note how people can dodge responsibility by using the passive voice in phrases such as "mistakes were made" rather than "I made mistakes." Such language rarely helps interpersonal relationships.

"But" Statements

Statements that take the form "X-but-Y" can be quite confusing. A closer look at the **"but" statement** explains why. *But* has the effect of canceling the thought that precedes it:

"You're really a great person, but I think we ought to stop seeing each other."
"You've done good work for us, but we're going to have to let you go."
"This paper has some good ideas, but I'm giving it a grade of *D* because it's late."

"Buts" *can* be a face-saving strategy worth using at times. When the goal is to be absolutely clear, however, the most responsible approach will deliver the central idea without the distractions that can come with "but" statements. Breaking statements such as the preceding ones into two sentences and explaining each one as necessary lets you acknowledge both parts of the statement without contradicting yourself.

"I," "You," and "We" Language

We've already seen that "I" language is a way of accepting responsibility for a message. **"You" language** is quite different. Like other forms of evaluative language, it expresses a judgment of the other person. Positive judgments ("You did a great job!") rarely cause problems, but notice how each of the following critical "you" statements implies that the subject of the complaint is doing something wrong:

"You left this place a mess!"
"You didn't keep your promise!"
"You're really crude sometimes!"

It's easy to see why "you" language can arouse defensiveness. A "you" statement implies that the speaker is qualified to judge the target—not an idea that most listeners are willing to accept, even when the evaluation is correct. "I" language provides a more accurate and less provocative way to express a complaint (Simmons et al., 2005). "I" language shows that the speaker takes responsibility for the accusation by describing his or her reaction to the other's behavior without making any judgments about its worth. Communicators who use these kinds of I-messages engage in **assertiveness**—clearly expressing their thoughts, feelings, and wants (Alberti & Emmons, 2008).

Assertive messages are composed of three different "I" statements. One describes the other person's behavior; one describes your feelings; and one describes the consequences the other's behavior has for you. Here are some examples of complete assertive messages:

"I get embarrassed [your feeling] when you talk about my poor grades in front of our friends [the behavior you observed]. I'm afraid they'll think I'm stupid [the possible consequence]."

"When you didn't pick me up on time this morning [behavior], I was late for class and wound up getting chewed out by the professor [consequences]. That's why I got so angry [feeling]."

"I haven't been very affectionate [consequence] because you've hardly spent any time with me in the past few weeks [behavior]. I'm confused [feeling] about how you feel about me."

When the chances of being misunderstood or getting a defensive reaction are high, it's a good idea to include all three elements in your assertive message. In some cases, however, only one or two of them will get the job done:

"I went to a lot of trouble fixing this dinner, and now it's cold. Of course I'm annoyed!" (The behavior is obvious.)

"I'm worried because you haven't called me." ("Worried" is both a feeling and a consequence in this statement.)

Even the best-constructed and best-delivered "I"-message won't always receive a nondefensive response (Bippus & Young, 2005). As Thomas Gordon (1970) points out, "nobody welcomes hearing that his behavior is causing someone a problem, no matter how the message is phrased" (p. 145). Furthermore, "I" language in large doses can start to sound egotistical (Proctor, 1989). Research shows that self-absorbed people, also known as "conversational narcissists," can be identified by their constant use of first-person singular pronouns (Vangelisti et al., 1990; Zimmermann et al., 2013). For this reason, "I" language works best in moderation.

One way to avoid overuse of "I" language is to consider the pronoun *we*. **"We" language** implies that the issue is the concern and responsibility of both the speaker and receiver of a message. Consider a few examples:

"We have a problem. We can't seem to talk about money without fighting."

"We aren't doing a very good job of keeping the apartment clean, are we?"

"We need to talk to your parents about whether we'll visit them for the holidays."

It's easy to see how "we" language can help build a constructive climate. It suggests a kind of "we're in this together" orientation, a component of what is known as *verbal immediacy* (Turman, 2008). In one study (Fitzsimons & Kay, 2004), strangers who were required to use "we" instead of "you and I" in their interactions felt closer to one another after doing so. Couples who use "we" language are more satisfied and manage conflict better than those who rely more heavily on "I" and "you" pronouns (Seider et al., 2009). On the other hand, using the pronoun "we" can be presumptuous and even demanding because you are speaking for the other person as well as for yourself (Rentscher et al., 2013). It's easy to imagine someone responding to the statement "*We* have a problem . . ." by saying "Maybe *you* have a problem, but don't tell me *I* do!"

As Table 5.3 summarizes, all three pronouns—*I, you*, and *we*—have their advantages and disadvantages. Given this fact, what advice can we give about the most effective pronouns to use in interpersonal communication? A study by Russell Proctor and James Wilcox (1993) offers an answer. The researchers found that "I"/"we" combinations (for example, "I think that we . . ." or "I would like to see us . . .") were strongly endorsed by college students, particularly for confrontational conversations in romantic relationships (cf. Gustafsson Sendén et al., 2014). Richard Slatcher and his associates (2008) came to a similar conclusion: There is value in both "I" and "we" messages in relational communication, as these pronouns demonstrate both autonomy and connection (see Chapter 9 for a discussion of these relational dialectics).

Because too much of any pronoun comes across as inappropriate, combining pronouns is generally a good idea—and it suggests you're able to see things from multiple perspectives (Pennebaker, 2011). If your "I" language reflects your position without being overly self-absorbed, your "you" language shows concern for others without judging them, and your "we" language includes others without speaking for them, you will probably come as close as possible to the ideal mix of pronouns.

TABLE 5.3 Pronoun Uses and Their Effects

PRONOUN	PROS	CONS	RECOMMENDATION
"I" Language	• Takes responsibility for personal thoughts, feelings, and wants. • Less defense provoking than evaluative "you" language.	• Can be perceived as egotistical, narcissistic, and self-absorbed.	• Use descriptive "I" messages in conflicts when the other person does not perceive a problem. • Combine "I" with "we" language in conversations.
"We" Language	• Signals inclusion, immediacy, cohesiveness, and commitment.	• Can speak improperly for others.	• Use in group settings to enhance sense of unity. • Avoid when expressing personal thoughts, feelings, and wants. • Combine with "I" language, particularly in personal conversations.
"You" Language	• Signals other-orientation, particularly when the topic is positive.	• Can sound evaluative and judgmental, particularly during confrontations.	• Use "I" language during confrontations. • Use "you" language when praising or including others.

Evaluative Language

Evaluative language (sometimes also called *"emotive language"*) seems to describe something but really announces the speaker's attitude toward it (Defour, 2008; Harding, 2007). If you approve of a friend's roundabout approach to a difficult subject, you might call her "tactful"; if you don't like it, you might accuse her of "beating around the bush." Whether the approach is good or bad is more a matter of opinion than of fact, although this difference is obscured by evaluative language.

You can appreciate how evaluative words are really editorial statements when you consider these examples:

If You Approve, Say	If You Disapprove, Say
thrifty	cheap
traditional	old-fashioned
extrovert	loudmouth
cautious	coward
progressive	radical
information	propaganda
eccentric	crazy

GENDER AND LANGUAGE

So far we have discussed language usage as if it were identical for both women and men. Are there differences between male and female language use? If so, how important are they?

EXTENT OF GENDER DIFFERENCES

Given the obvious physical differences between the sexes and the differences in how men and women are regarded in most societies, it's not surprising that the general public has been captivated by the topic of gender differences in language use. Some people believe that men and women communicate in significantly different ways, whereas others find far more similarities than differences. We outline two approaches that represent two different sides in the gender and language debate.

Approach 1: Significant Differences

In 1992, John Gray argued that men and women are so fundamentally different that they might as well have come from separate planets. In his best-selling book *Men Are from Mars, Women Are from Venus*, he claimed that

> Men and women differ in all areas of their lives. Not only do men and women communicate differently but they think, feel, perceive, react, respond, love,

need, and appreciate differently. They almost seem to be from different planets, speaking different languages and needing different nourishment. (p. 5)

Gray's work is based largely on anecdotes and conjecture and lacks scholarly support. However, social scientists have acknowledged that there are some significant differences in the way men and women behave socially (Palomares, 2008; Wood, 2013). This has led some scholars to describe males and females as members of distinct cultures, with their differences arising primarily from socialization rather than biology. The best known advocate of this "two-culture" theory is sociolinguist Deborah Tannen (1990, 1994, 2001). She suggests that men and women grow up learning different rules about how to speak and act.

In support of the two-culture hypothesis, communication researcher Anthony Mulac (2006) reports that men are more likely than women to speak in sentence fragments ("Nice photo."). Men typically talk about themselves with "I" references ("I have a lot of meetings") and use judgmental language. They are also more likely to make directive statements. By contrast, Mulac finds that female speech is more tentative, elaborate, and emotional. For instance, women's sentences are typically longer than men's. Women also make more reference to feelings and use intensive adverbs ("He's *really* interested") that paint a more complete verbal picture than the characteristically terse masculine style. In addition, female speech is often less assertive. It contains more statements of uncertainty ("It seems to be . . ."), hedges ("We're *kind of* set in our ways."), and tag questions ("Do you think so?"). Some theorists have argued that such differences cause women's speech to be less powerful, but more inclusive, than men's.

Approach 2: Minor Differences

Despite the differences in the way men and women speak, the link between sex and language use isn't as clear-cut as it might seem—and even where differences exist, the question is whether they amount to much. One analysis of over 1,200 research studies found that only 1 percent of variance in communication behavior resulted from sex differences (Canary & Hause, 1993). An analysis of 30 studies looking at power differences in women's and men's speech found that differences were small and, for the most part, not important (Timmerman, 2002). Another meta-analysis involving more than 3,000 participants found that women were only slightly more likely than men to use tentative speech (Leaper & Robnett, 2011). Finally, three separate sets of analyses (Leaper & Ayres, 2007) looked for sex differences in adults' talkativeness, affiliative speech, and assertive speech—and found negligible differences for all three language constructs. In fact, contrary to the popular myth that women are more talkative than men, overall, men were more talkative (but mostly during dyadic rather than group interactions). In essence, these studies found that men's and women's speech is far more similar than different.

In light of the considerable similarities between the sexes and the relatively minor differences, communication researcher Kathryn Dindia (2006) suggests that the "men are from Mars, women are from Venus" claim should be replaced by the metaphor that "men are from North Dakota, women are from South Dakota."

ACCOUNTING FOR GENDER DIFFERENCES

By now you might be confused by what seem like contradictory views of how large and important the differences are between male and female speech. A substantial body of research helps reconcile some of the apparent contradictions by pointing out factors other than communicator sex that influence language use.

Occupation can trump gender as an influence on speaking style. As an example, male and female athletes communicate in similar ways (Sullivan, 2004). Male day care teachers' speech to their students resembles the language of female teachers more closely than it resembles the language of fathers at home (Gleason & Greif, 1983). Female farm operators, working in a male-dominated world, reproduce the masculinity that spells success for their male counterparts, swearing and talking "tough as nails" (Pilgeram, 2007). A close study of trial transcripts showed that the speaker's experience on the witness stand and occupation had more to do with language use than did biological sex (O'Barr, 1982; Waara & Shaw, 2006).

Another factor that trumps sex differences is *power*. For instance, in gay and lesbian relationships, the conversational styles of partners reflect power differences in the relationship (e.g., who is earning more money) more than the biological sex of the communicators (Steen & Schwartz, 1995). There are also few differences between the way men and women use powerful speech (specifically, threats) when they have the same amount of bargaining strength in a negotiation (Scudder & Andrews, 1995). Findings like this suggest that characteristically feminine speech has been less a function of gender or sex than of women's historically less powerful positions in some parts of the social world. In fact, differences in social status often show up more clearly in language than gender differences do (Pennebaker, 2011).

What then is the verdict on gender and language? The simple answer is yes, there are some differences between male and female language patterns. However, those distinctions may not be as significant as some claim—and they might occur for reasons other than the biological sex of the communicator. Language differences between the sexes are easier to spot and measure in online communication, as we discuss in the next section.

SOCIAL MEDIA AND LANGUAGE

The principles described so far in this chapter apply to language in face-to-face interaction as well as in mediated communication. However, researchers have begun to discover some unique dimensions of language as it is used in social media.

In this section, we focus on two topics covered throughout this book—impression management and gender—and describe how they show up in online language choices.

ONLINE LANGUAGE AND IMPRESSION MANAGEMENT

As we noted in Chapter 3, much of online communication is an exercise in impression management. For example, text message errors can make the sender look bad to some recipients (such as professors, bosses, and customers), so it's important to manage those impressions. One way to do so is by using a block signature indicating that a text message was typed on a mobile device (Carr & Stefaniak, 2012). Some texters' signatures point blank say, "This was written on my cell phone, so please excuse the likely errors." This in essence shifts the blame for the mistakes from the message sender to the device.

Dating websites are all about impression management (Tomlinson, 2013). Subscribers to online dating services not only can manipulate their photos and videos but also their verbal self-descriptions. One study found that less attractive participants make more linguistic and numeric embellishments than attractive candidates do (Toma & Hancock, 2010). Women are more likely to lie about their weight on dating sites, whereas men misrepresent their professions and income (Huestis, 2010). On a less intentional level, even a person's first name creates an online impression (Gebauer et al., 2012). A German study found that men named Alexander were 102 percent more likely to get visits on a dating site than those named Kevin. (Although Kevin is a popular name in the United States, it is so unpopular in German-speaking countries that its negative appraisal is dubbed "Kevinism.")

FOCUS ON RESEARCH
The Languages of Texting and Talking

Unlike spoken communication, text-based messages leave a record for social scientists to examine. Thomas Holtgraves used a software program known as the Linguistic Inquiry and Word Count (LIWC) to explore what the content and structure of text messages reveals about their college student authors.

In one study, Holtgraves found that texters' personalities are reflected in the language of their messages. For instance, extraverts use more personal pronouns when texting, particularly first-person singular pronouns (*I, me, my, mine*). As in face-to-face interaction, texters who measure high in neuroticism use more negative emotion words, and disagreeable people swear more when texting than do those who are more amiable.

Holtgraves and a colleague then compared language use between text messages and transcribed phone conversations. Not surprisingly, texting communicators use shorter words and simpler language. They also use more emotion words ("nice," "hurt," "hate"), sexual terms ("love," "horny"), and swear words than they do in phone conversations. This gives further credence to the notion that communicators feel free to disclose more in writing than they do when speaking.

Holtgraves, T. (2011). Text messaging, personality, and the social context. *Journal of Research in Personality, 45,* 92–99.

Holtgraves, T., & Paul, K. (2013). Texting versus talking: An exploration in telecommunication language. *Telematics and Informatics, 30,* 289–295.

Impression management isn't restricted to the search for romantic partners. Facebook friends also try to put their best feet forward with strategic language choices (Bazarova et al., 2012). They use more positive emotion words in their public status updates, projecting an upbeat persona. In private messages, Facebookers are more willing to let their guard down and share negative feelings. Also, you can probably gauge how much two people like each other by the warmth of their language with each other on their Facebook walls. This suggests that Facebook wall messages are written with a larger audience in mind (the underlying message being, "This is my close friend, and I want everyone reading to know it").

Although e-mail has become a less popular means of online communication, it's still a mainstay in the business world. Executives acknowledge that they attempt to manage impressions in the way they craft their e-mails (Caron et al., 2013). For instance, their professional messages are less formal when written on smartphones than on office computers. Those sent from mobile devices often begin without a salutation and go straight into business talk. When written from an office computer, they tend to start with a greeting and first name ("Hello, Mary"). E-mail closings follow a similar pattern. Executives say this isn't an accident—when communicating by smartphone, they want to give the impression that they are busy and "don't have time to be friendly." Most of them use their mobile device's tagline ("Sent from my iPhone") to indicate the medium they used.

ONLINE LANGUAGE AND GENDER

Research shows that men and women have different written language styles (Pennebaker, 2011), which shows up in online communication. For instance, men tend to use more large words, nouns, and swear words than women do. On the other hand, women use more personal pronouns, verbs, and hedge phrases ("I think"). Of course, word count doesn't tell the whole story. For instance, whereas women and men use the word "we" about equally, they do so in different ways. Closer scrutiny suggests that women are more likely to use what's known as the "warm we" ("We have so much fun together"), and men are more inclined toward the "distant we" ("We need to do something about this."). It's also worth noting that computers aren't foolproof: They can correctly identify the sex of an author about 72 percent of the time (50 percent is chance). In other words, although there are indeed gender tendencies in language usage, they aren't absolute.

Data gathered from social networking sites show even greater distinctions. In one study, researchers analyzed more than 15 million Facebook status updates from approximately 75,000 volunteers over a 34-month period (Schwartz et al., 2013). There were marked differences in male and female language use (and also between people of different ages and personalities). Women used more emotion words ("excited"; "wonderful") and first-person singular pronouns, and they made more references to the people in their lives. Men made more object references ("game"; "government"; "Xbox") and swore far more often—a finding that seems to hold true across every study conducted about male and female word use.

It appears that people are intuitively aware of gender differences in online language. For instance, one study found that online communicators adopt different writing styles depending on their online gender identities (Palomares & Lee, 2010). Participants were given randomly selected gendered avatars—some matching their biological sex, some not. Communicators who were assigned feminine avatars expressed more emotion, made more apologies, and used more tentative language than did those with masculine avatars. In other words, participants adapted their language to match linguistic gender stereotypes.

Online language differences between the sexes are more pronounced among adolescents. A study looked at the word choices of teenage boys and girls in chat rooms (Kapidzic & Herring, 2011). The boys were more active and assertive, initiating interaction and making proposals, whereas the girls were more reactive ("wow"; "omg"; "lmao"). The boys were also more flirtatious and sexual ("any hotties wanna chat?"). The researchers noted that these accentuated differences were probably due to the age of the participants and that some of the distinctions would likely recede in adulthood.

It's important to remember that despite the relative anonymity you might feel at a computer keyboard or behind a smartphone, the words you use online say a lot about you. They reflect who you are and how you feel about others. And keep in mind that online messages can be recorded and saved. They can leave lasting reminders of your affinity for others, or they might come back to haunt you. As is true of face-to-face interaction, choose and use your words carefully.

CHECK YOUR UNDERSTANDING

Q: Describe how a recent, important communicative exchange from your life illustrates the symbolic, rule-based, subjective, culture-bound nature of language.

Objective 5.1 Understand the symbolic, rule-based, subjective, culture-bound nature of language.

Language is both a marvelous communication tool and the source of many interpersonal problems. Every language is a collection of symbols governed by a variety of rules. Because of its symbolic nature, language is not a precise vehicle: Meanings rest in people, not in words themselves. Finally, the very language we speak can shape our worldview.

Objective 5.2 Recognize the impact, both positive and negative, of language in interpersonal relationships.

Language both reflects and shapes the perceptions of its users. For example, names that people are given can influence their identity and the way they are viewed by others. Language also reflects the level of affiliation communicators have with each other. And language patterns reflect and shape a speaker's perceived power. Finally, language can reflect and influence sexist and racist attitudes.

When used carelessly, language can lead to a variety of interpersonal problems. The level of precision or vagueness of messages can affect a receiver's understanding of them. Both precise messages and vague, evasive messages have their uses in interpersonal relationships; and a competent communicator has the ability to choose the optimal level of precision for the situation at hand. Competent communicators also know how to use "I," "you," and "we" statements to accept the optimal level of responsibility and relational harmony. Using emotive terms can lead to unnecessary disharmony in interpersonal relationships.

Q: Analyze your language use over two days to identify both how it facilitates relationships and how it creates interpersonal problems.

Objective 5.3 Describe the influence gender has on language use in interpersonal relationships.

The relationship between gender and language is a complex one. Although some writers in the popular press have argued that men and women are radically different and thus speak different languages, this position isn't supported by scholarship. A growing body of research suggests that what differences do exist are relatively minor in light of the similarities between the sexes. Many of the language differences that first appear to be sex-related may actually be due to other factors such as occupation and interpersonal power.

Q: Identify similarities and differences in male and female language use, and provide explanations for such differences.

Objective 5.4 Identify ways in which online language usage is different from the in-person variety.

Language use in social media has some distinct features. Word choice is an important component of online impression management. Gender differences are also more pronounced (or at least more measurable) when written via social media.

Q: Analyze your social media messages to see whether they reflect the identity you wish to project.

KEY TERMS

- Abstraction ladder (154)
- Ambiguous language (153)
- Assertiveness (159)
- "But" statement (159)
- Convergence (147)
- Divergence (148)
- Euphemism (156)
- Evaluative language (162)
- "I" language (158)

- "It" statement (158)
- Linguistic relativity (144)
- Phonological rules (141)
- Politeness (149)
- Powerful language (149)
- Powerless language (148)
- Pragmatic rules (142)
- Racist language (152)
- Relative language (157)

- Sapir–Whorf hypothesis (144)
- Semantic rules (141)
- Sexist language (150)
- Static evaluation (157)
- Syntactic rules (141)
- "We" language (160)
- "You" language (159)

ACTIVITIES

1. Working with a group of classmates, describe one syntactic, one semantic, and one pragmatic rule for each situation:

   a. Asking an acquaintance out for a first date.

   b. Declining an invitation to a party.

   c. Responding to a stranger who has just said "excuse me" after bumping into you in a crowd.

2. The information about the impact of language on pages 145–162 shows how the words a communicator chooses can shape others' perceptions. Create

and present to your class two scenarios for each type of linguistic influence in the following list. The first should describe how the type of influence could be used constructively, and the second should describe an unethical application of this knowledge.

   a. Naming and identity

   b. Affiliation

   c. Power

   d. Sexism and racism

3. Translate the following into behavioral language and share with your classmates to get their feedback.

   a. An abstract goal for improving your interpersonal communication (for example, "Be more assertive" or "Stop being so sarcastic").

   b. A complaint you have about another person (for instance, that he or she is "selfish" or "insensitive").

In both cases, describe the person or people involved, the circumstances in which the communication will take place, and the precise behaviors involved. What difference will using the behavioral descriptions be likely to make in your relationships?

4. With a group of classmates, practice rephrasing each of the following "you" statements in "I" and/or "we" language:

   "You're not telling me the truth!"

   "You only think of yourself!"

   "Don't be so touchy!"

   "You don't understand a word I'm saying!"

Now think of three "you" statements you could make to people in your life. Transform each of these statements into "I" and "we" language, and rehearse them with a classmate.

5. Some authors believe that differences between male and female communication are so great that they can be characterized as "men are from Mars, women are from Venus." Other researchers believe the differences aren't nearly so dramatic and would describe them as "men are from North Dakota, women are from South Dakota." Which approach seems more accurate to you? Offer experiences from your life to support your point of view.

6. Do you communicate differently online or by text than in person? Does your social media language differ depending on the medium you use? Monitor your communication over three days and see if you "talk" distinctly in text messages, social networking posts, tweets, and blog entries compared with face-to-face communication. Are there some words you're more prone to use on Facebook, for example, than in person?

SCORING FOR ASSESSING YOUR COMMUNICATION (PAGE 151)

Add your responses to the 11 statements, making sure to reverse-score statements 1, 2, and 3 (if you indicated 5, change it to 1; change 4 to 2; change 2 to 4; and change 1 to 5). Scores can range from 11 to 55. Scores that are 38 or higher reflect a supportive attitude toward nonsexist language; scores between 11 and 27 reflect a negative attitude toward nonsexist language; and scores between 28 and 37 reflect a neutral attitude.

chapter

Nonverbal Communication

 CHAPTER OUTLINE

LEARNING OBJECTIVES

6.1 Define nonverbal communication.

6.2 Recognize the distinguishing characteristics of nonverbal communication.

6.3 Identify and offer examples of the various functions that nonverbal communication can serve.

6.4 Understand and describe how meaning is communicated through particular nonverbal cues.

People don't always say what they mean . . . but their body gestures and movements tell the truth!

Will he ask you out? Is she encouraging you?

Know what is really happening by understanding the secret language of body signals. You can:

Improve your sex life . . .

Pick up your social life . . .

Better your business life . . .

Read Body Language *so that you can penetrate the personal secrets, both of intimates and total strangers . . .*

Does her body say that she's easy?

Do his eyes say that he's interested in you?

Do her facial expressions say that she's a manipulator?

Does the way he's standing say that he's a player?

ALMOST EVERY pharmacy, supermarket, and airport book rack has its share of "body language" paperbacks with claims such as these. Popular seminars and YouTube videos make similar assertions. They promise that you can learn secrets that will change you from a fumbling social failure into a self-assured mind reader who can uncover a person's deepest secrets at a glance.

Before "talkies," films relied primarily on nonverbal cues (and the occasional subtitle) to convey messages. Today the acting in silent films seems overdone, but it offers a clear illustration of how emotions can be communicated nonverbally.

Observations like these are almost always exaggerations or fabrications. Don't misunderstand: There *is* a scientific body of knowledge about nonverbal communication, and it *has* provided many fascinating and valuable clues to human behavior. That's what this chapter is about. It's unlikely the next few pages will turn you instantly into a rich, sexy, charming communication superstar, but don't go away. Even without glamorous promises, a quick look at some facts about nonverbal communication shows that it's an important and valuable field to study—and that nonverbal skills are worth acquiring (Riggio, 2006).

NONVERBAL COMMUNICATION DEFINED

If *non* means "not" and *verbal* means "with words," then it seems logical that *nonverbal communication* would involve "communication without words." This definition is an oversimplification, however, because it fails to distinguish between *vocal* communication (by mouth) and *verbal* communication (with words). Some nonverbal messages have a vocal element. For example, the words "I love you" have different meanings depending on the way they are spoken. Furthermore, some nonspoken forms of communication,

including sign languages used in the deaf community, are actually linguistic and not really nonverbal in the sense most social scientists use the term. Therefore, a better definition of **nonverbal communication** is "messages expressed by nonlinguistic means."

These nonlinguistic messages are important because what we *do* often conveys more meaning than what we *say*. Psychologist Albert Mehrabian (1972) claimed that 93 percent of the emotional impact of a message comes from a nonverbal source, whereas only a paltry 7 percent is verbal. Anthropologist Ray Birdwhistell (1970) described a 65–35 percent split between actions and words, respectively. Although social scientists have disputed these figures and the relative importance of verbal versus nonverbal cues (e.g., Lapakko, 1997; Nagel et al., 2012), the point remains: Nonverbal communication contributes a great deal to shaping perceptions.

You might ask how nonverbal communication can be so powerful. At first glance, it seems as if meanings come from words. To answer this question, recall a time when you observed speakers of an unfamiliar language communicating. Although you couldn't understand the words being spoken, there were likely plenty of clues that gave you an idea of what was going on in the exchange. By tuning into their facial expressions, postures, gestures, vocal tones, and other behaviors you probably made assumptions about the way the communicators felt about one another at the moment and got some ideas about the nature of their relationship. Researchers (summarized in Knapp & Hall, 2010) have found that subjects who hear content-free speech—ordinary speech that has been electronically manipulated so that the words are unintelligible—can consistently recognize the emotion being expressed as well as identify its strength.

CHARACTERISTICS OF NONVERBAL COMMUNICATION

The many types of nonverbal communication share some characteristics. As Table 6.1 shows, these characteristics are quite different from verbal, linguistic means of communication. We now take a look at five characteristics of nonverbal communication.

ALL BEHAVIOR HAS COMMUNICATIVE VALUE

Some theorists suggest that *all* nonverbal behavior communicates information. They argue that it is impossible *not* to communicate. You can understand the impossibility of noncommunication by considering what you would do if someone told you not to communicate any messages at all. Even if you closed your eyes or left the room, these behaviors would communicate messages that mean you're avoiding contact. One study (DePaulo, 1992) took just this approach. When communicators were told not to express nonverbal clues, others viewed them as dull, withdrawn, uneasy, aloof, and deceptive.

The impossibility of not communicating is significant because it means that each of us is a kind of transmitter that cannot be shut off. No matter

TABLE 6.1 Some Differences between Verbal and Nonverbal Communication

VERBAL COMMUNICATION	NONVERBAL COMMUNICATION
• Mostly voluntary and conscious	• Often unconscious
• Usually content oriented	• Usually relational
• Can be clear or vague	• Inherently ambiguous
• Primarily shaped by culture	• Rooted in biology
• Discontinuous/intermittent	• Continuous
• Single channel (words only)	• Multichanneled

what we do, we send out messages that say something about ourselves and our relationships with others. If, for instance, others were observing you now, what nonverbal clues would they get about how you're feeling? Are you sitting forward or reclining back? Is your posture tense or relaxed? Are your eyes wide open, or do they keep closing? What does your facial expression communicate now? Can you make your face expressionless? Don't people with expressionless faces communicate something to you? Even uncontrollable behaviors can convey a message. You may not intend to show that you're embarrassed, but your blushing can still be a giveaway. Of course, not all behaviors (intentional or not) will be interpreted correctly: Your trembling hands might be taken as a sign of nervousness when you're really just shivering from the cold. But whether or not your behavior is intentional, and whether or not it is interpreted accurately, all nonverbal behavior has the potential to create messages.

Although nonverbal behavior reveals information, reviews of research show we aren't always conscious of what we and others communicate nonverbally (Byron, 2008; Lakin, 2006). In one study, less than a quarter of experimental participants who had been instructed to show increased or

decreased liking of a partner could describe the nonverbal behaviors they used (Palmer & Simmons, 1995). In addition, simply because communicators express themselves nonverbally doesn't mean that others will notice all of the available unspoken messages.

NONVERBAL COMMUNICATION IS PRIMARILY RELATIONAL

Some nonverbal messages serve practical functions. For example, a police officer directs the flow of traffic, or a team of street surveyors uses hand motions to coordinate their work. But nonverbal communication also serves in a far more common (and more interesting) series of *social* functions.

Nonverbal communication allows us to demonstrate the kind of relationships we have—or want to have—with others (Burgoon & Le Poire, 1999; Myers et al., 2011). You can appreciate this fact by thinking about the wide range of ways you could behave when greeting another person. You could wave, shake hands, nod, smile, clap the other person on the back, give a hug, or avoid all contact. Each one of these behaviors sends a message about the nature of your relationship with the other person.

Nonverbal messages perform another valuable social function: They convey emotions that we may be unwilling or unable to express, or ones we may not even be aware of. In fact, nonverbal communication is much better suited to expressing attitudes and feelings than it is ideas. You can prove this for yourself by imagining how you could express each item on the following list nonverbally:

1. "I'm tired."
2. "I'm in favor of capital punishment."
3. "I'm attracted to another person in the group."
4. "I think prayer in the schools should be allowed."
5. "I'm angry at someone in this room."

This experience shows that, short of charades, ideas (such as statements 2 and 4) don't lend themselves to nonverbal expressions nearly as well as attitudes and feelings (statements 1, 3, and 5). This explains why it's possible to understand the attitudes or feelings of others by reading nonverbal cues, even if you aren't able to understand the subject of their communication.

NONVERBAL COMMUNICATION IS AMBIGUOUS

In Chapter 5, we pointed out how some language can be ambiguous. (For example, the statement, "That nose piercing really makes you stand out," could be a compliment or a criticism; and the vague statement, "I'm almost done," could mean you have to wait a few minutes or an hour.) Most nonverbal behavior has the potential to be even more ambiguous than verbal statements such as these. To understand why, consider how you would interpret silence from your companion during an evening together. Think of all the possible meanings of this nonverbal behavior: warmth, anger, preoccupation, boredom, nervousness, thoughtfulness—the possibilities are many.

The ambiguity of nonverbal behavior was illustrated when one supermarket chain tried to emphasize its customer-friendly approach by instructing employees to smile and make eye contact with customers. Several clerks filed grievances when some customers mistook the service-with-a-smile approach as sexual come-ons. As this story suggests, nonverbal cues are much more ambiguous than verbal statements when it comes to expressing a willingness to become physically involved (La France, 2010; Lim & Roloff, 1999).

Because nonverbal behavior is so ambiguous, caution is wise when you are responding to nonverbal cues. Rather than jumping to conclusions about the meaning of a sigh, smile, slammed door, or yawn, it's far better to use the kind of perception-checking approach described in Chapter 4. "When you yawned, I thought I was boring you. But maybe you're just tired. What's going on?" The ability to consider more than one possible interpretation for nonverbal behavior illustrates the kind of cognitive complexity identified in Chapter 1 as an element of communication competence. Popular advice on the subject notwithstanding, it's usually not possible to read a person like a book.

NONVERBAL COMMUNICATION OCCURS IN MEDIATED MESSAGES

Given our coverage of social media and language in Chapter 5, it would be easy to think that all mediated communication is verbal—but that's not the case. Video calls obviously provide nonverbal information, as do photos on social networking sites; however, even text-based electronic communication has nonverbal features.

The most obvious way to represent nonverbal expressions in type is with *emoticons,* using keyboard characters such as the following (many programs now turn these keystroke combinations into graphic icons):

:-)	Basic smile
;-)	Wink and grin
:-(	Frown
:-@	Screaming, swearing, very angry
:-/ or :-\	Skeptical
:-O	Surprised, yelling, realization of an error

Emoticons can clarify the meaning that isn't evident from words alone (Derks et al., 2007; Lo, 2008). For example, see how each graphic below creates a different meaning for the same statement:

- You are driving me crazy

- You are driving me crazy

- You are driving me crazy

Similar to their in-person counterparts, emoticons are ambiguous and can communicate a variety of nonverbal messages (Dresner & Herring, 2010). A smiley face could mean "I'm really happy," "I'm only kidding," or "I

Zits: © 2013 Zits Partnership. Distributed by King Features Syndicate

just zinged you." The same is true of other online communication markers (Vandergriff, 2013). Exclamation marks (sometimes more than one!!!) can be used at the end of sentences, or even by themselves, to denote a variety of emotional states (see the cartoon above). Ellipses (…) at the end of a phrase can signal displeasure, thoughtfulness, or bemusement. They can also be turn-taking signals, similar to what might be conveyed nonverbally with your face or with pauses during in-person conversations. The same is true of "lexical surrogates" such as "hmmm" or "ooooh," with meanings ranging from delight to disapproval. Paralinguistic markers such as these are best understood within their communicative and relational contexts.

Not only does the content of a nonverbal message matter, but when it is sent matters as well (Ledbetter, 2008; Walther, 2009). If you've ever been upset by a friend who hasn't responded punctually to one of your texts, then you know the role that timeliness plays in mediated interpersonal communication. We talk more about the management of time later in this chapter, but here we note that it's a vital feature of online interaction. It's also a good example of the principle that you cannot *not* communicate. Communicators have expectations about when others should reply to their posts, e-mails, and text messages, and delays can be perceived negatively.

NONVERBAL COMMUNICATION IS INFLUENCED BY CULTURE AND GENDER

Cultures differ in their nonverbal languages as well as their verbal ones (Matsumoto, 2006). Fiorello LaGuardia, legendary mayor of New York from 1933 to 1945, was fluent in English, Italian, and Yiddish. Watching films of his campaign speeches with no sound, researchers found they could tell the language LaGuardia was speaking based solely on the changes in his nonverbal behavior (Birdwhistell, 1970).

Some nonverbal behaviors—called **emblems**—are culturally understood substitutes for verbal expressions (Matsumoto & Hwang, 2013). Nodding the head up and down is an accepted way of saying "yes" in most cultures. Likewise, a side-to-side head shake is a nonverbal way of saying "no"; and a shrug of the shoulders is commonly understood as meaning "I don't know" or "I'm not sure." Remember, however, that some emblems—such as the

FOCUS ON RESEARCH
It's About Time: The Costs of Delayed Online Responses

You receive an electronic message from someone in the business world—an e-mail from a potential employer, or a tweet from a customer. Are there consequences for not responding in timely fashion? You bet, according to research by Yoram Kalman.

Kalman and his colleagues assessed perceptions of delayed responses to computer-mediated messages. In one study, job candidates who were late in replying to managers' e-mails or who didn't respond at all lost credibility points (and presumably employment offers). In another study, participants engaged in online chats while solving a problem were regarded as less than trustworthy or even deceptive if they had long pauses while interacting. By not responding promptly, the communicators sabotaged themselves—whether they realized it or not.

In a busy life, it's easy to delay or forget to respond to incoming messages. Nevertheless, it's important to remember that the way you manage time—as measured by the promptness of your responses—is interpreted by the other person as making a statement about you.

Kalman, Y. M., & Rafaeli, S. (2011). Online pauses and silence: Chronemic expectancy violations in written computer-mediated communication. *Communication Research, 38,* 54–69.

Kalman, Y. M., Scissors, L. E., Gill, A. J., & Gergle, D. (2013). Online chronemics convey social information. *Computers in Human Behavior, 29,* 1260–1269.

thumbs-up gesture—vary from one culture to another. It means "Good job!" in the United States, the number 1 in Germany, and the number 5 in Japan. Most North Americans would say the hand gesture in the photo on this page means "Okay." But to a Buddhist it signifies acceptance of the world as it is, and in Greece and Turkey its meaning is vulgar.

Culture also affects how nonverbal cues are monitored. In Japan, for instance, people tend to look to the eyes for emotional cues, whereas Americans and Europeans focus on the mouth (Yuki et al., 2007). These differences can be seen in the text-based emoticons used in these cultures. American emoticons focus on mouth expressions, whereas Japanese emoticons feature the eyes (search in your web browser for "Western and Eastern emoticons" for examples).

Despite differences like these, some nonverbal behaviors are universal. Certain expressions have the same meanings around the world. For example, members of a preliterate, isolated tribe in West Africa identified the same behaviors reflecting pride as did Americans: a small smile, head tilted slightly back, expanded posture, and arms akimbo with hands on hips (Tracy & Robins, 2008). Smiles and laughter are universal signals of positive emotions, whereas sour expressions convey displeasure in most every culture. Charles Darwin believed that evolution was the cause of expressions like these, functioning as survival mechanisms that enabled early humans to convey emotions before the development of language. The innateness of some facial expressions becomes even clearer when we examine the behavior of children born deaf and blind (Eibl-Eibesfeldt, 1972; see also Bruce et al., 2007). Despite a lack of social learning, these children display a broad range of expressions. They smile, laugh, and cry in ways virtually identical to seeing and hearing infants.

Although some nonverbal expressions may be universal, the way they are used varies widely around the world (Matsumoto, 2006). In some cultures, overt demonstrations of feelings such as happiness or anger are discouraged. In other cultures, the same feelings are perfectly appropriate. Thus, a Japanese person might appear much more nonverbally controlled than an Italian person, when in fact their feelings might be identical. It's important to note that the *culture* in which people live is far more important than their *nationality* or *ethnicity*. For example, the facial expressions of Japanese nationals and Japanese Americans differ in ways that reflect their cultural backgrounds (Marsh et al., 2003).

Sex also influences nonverbal communication—and with rare exceptions, differences between sexes hold true across cultures (Knapp & Hall, 2010). In general, females are more nonverbally expressive than males, and they are better at interpreting others' nonverbal behavior. More specifically, research summarized by Judith Hall (2006b) shows that, compared to men, women

- Smile more
- Use more facial expression
- Use more (but less expansive) head, hand, and arm gestures
- Touch others more
- Stand closer to others
- Are more vocally expressive
- Make more eye contact

Despite these differences, men's and women's nonverbal communication patterns have a good deal in common (Dindia, 2006; Hall, 2006a). You can prove this by imagining what it would be like to use radically different nonverbal rules: standing only an inch away from others, sniffing strangers, or tapping people's foreheads to get their attention. Moreover, male–female nonverbal differences are less pronounced in conversations involving gay and lesbian participants (Knöfler & Imhof, 2007). Gender and culture certainly have an influence on nonverbal style, but the differences are often a matter of degree rather than kind.

FUNCTIONS OF NONVERBAL COMMUNICATION

Now that you understand what nonverbal communication is, we need to explore the functions it serves in relationships. As you'll read, nonverbal cues play several important roles in the way we relate with others.

CREATING AND MAINTAINING RELATIONSHIPS

As you will read in Chapter 9, communication is our primary means for beginning, maintaining, and ending relationships. Nonverbal behavior plays an important role during every relational stage.

Consider the importance of nonverbal communication at the beginning of a relationship. When we first meet another person, our initial goal is to reduce our uncertainty about her or him (Berger, 1987, 2011). We ask ourselves questions such as "Would I like to know this person better?" and "Is this person interested in me?" One of the first ways we answer these questions is by observing nonverbal cues, including facial expression, eye contact, posture, gesture, and tone of voice (Berger & Kellermann, 1994). This process occurs quite rapidly—often in a matter of seconds (Zebrowitz & Montepare, 2008).

At the same time we are sizing up others, we are providing nonverbal cues about our attitude toward them. We rarely share these thoughts and feelings overtly. Imagine how odd it would be to say or hear words such as "I'm friendly and relaxed" or "You look pretty interesting, but I won't pursue this unless you give me a sign that you're interested too." Messages like these are much more safely expressed via nonverbal channels. Of course, it's important to remember that nonverbal cues are ambiguous and that you may be misinterpreting them (Mehrabian, 2008). You might want to get an outside evaluation to check your perceptions ("Is it my imagination, or is she checking me out?").

Nonverbal cues are just as important in established, ongoing relationships in which they both create and signal the emotional climate. For example, nonverbal displays of affection—such as sitting close, holding hands, winks and gazes—are strongly connected to satisfaction and commitment in romantic relationships (Horan & Booth-Butterfield, 2010). In families, nonverbal cues offer a clear sign of relational satisfaction (Rogers, 2001) as well as who controls interaction and decision making (Aronsson & Cekaite, 2011; Brumark, 2010). On the job, supervisors who offer nonverbal cues of liking can increase subordinates' job motivation, job satisfaction, and affinity for their boss (Teven, 2010).

You can test the power of nonverbal behavior in relationships for yourself. First, observe the interaction of people in relationships without paying attention to their words. Watch couples or families in restaurants or other public places. Focus on fellow employees in the workplace. Observe professors and their students interacting in and outside of class. See how parents treat their children and vice versa. You are likely to see a multitude of cues that suggest the quality of each relationship. Chances are good that you could make educated guesses about whether the people you're watching are satisfied with each other—and whether their relationship is beginning, maintaining, or ending.

REGULATING INTERACTION

Nonverbal **regulators** are cues that help control verbal interaction. The best example of such regulation is the wide array of turn-taking signals in everyday conversation (Wiemann & Knapp, 2008). Three nonverbal signals that indicate a speaker has finished talking and is ready to yield to a listener are (1) changes in vocal intonation—a rising or falling in pitch at the end of a clause, (2) a drawl on the last syllable or the stressed syllable in a clause, and (3) a drop in vocal pitch or loudness when speaking a common expression such as "you know."

Eye contact is another way of regulating verbal communication (Bavelas et al., 2002). In conversations, the person listening typically looks more at the speaker than the reverse. When the speaker seeks a response, he or she signals by looking at the listener, creating a brief period of mutual gaze called a "gaze window." At this point, the listener is likely to respond with a nod, "uh-huh," or other reaction, after which the speaker looks away and continues speaking. Children and some people on the autism spectrum have not learned all the subtle signals of such turn taking. Through a rough series

ASSESSING YOUR COMMUNICATION

Nonverbal Immediacy Behaviors

Most communication researchers agree that *nonverbal immediacy*—the display of involvement signaled by physical closeness, eye contact, movement, and touch—is an important ingredient of communication competence. You can measure your immediacy by completing this self-assessment. Indicate the degree to which you believe each statement applies to you on a scale ranging from 1 to 5, where 1 = never and 5 = very often. Then ask someone who knows you well to complete the assessment, requesting that she or he be as honest as possible. When you're finished, compare notes on your conclusions.

_____ **1.** I use my hands and arms to gesture while talking to people.

_____ **2.** I use a monotone or dull voice while talking to people.

_____ **3.** I avoid eye contact while talking to people.

_____ **4.** I have a tense body position while talking to people.

_____ **5.** I am animated when I talk to people.

_____ **6.** I have a bland facial expression when I talk to people.

_____ **7.** I am stiff when I talk to people.

_____ **8.** I have a lot of vocal variety when I talk to people.

_____ **9.** I lean toward people when I talk to them.

_____ **10.** I maintain eye contact with people when I talk to them.

_____ **11.** I smile when I talk to people.

_____ **12.** I avoid touching people when I talk to them.

The 12 items are from the 26-item measure developed by Virginia Richmond and her colleagues.

Richmond, V. P., McCroskey, J. C., & Johnson, A. D. (2003). Development of the Nonverbal Immediacy Scale (NIS): Measures of self- and other-perceived nonverbal immediacy. *Communication Quarterly, 51*, 504–517.

For scoring information, see page 201 at the end of the chapter.

of trial and error, children finally learn how to "read" other people well enough to avoid interrupting.

INFLUENCING OTHERS

How we look, act, and sound can be more important in meeting our goals than the words we speak. The influence of nonverbal behavior comes in many forms. It can capture attention, show or increase liking, generate power, and boost credibility (Cesario & Higgins, 2008; Gifford, 2011). Sometimes deliberately and sometimes without thought, we use nonverbal behaviors in ways that get others to satisfy our wants and needs. For example, people are more willing to do our bidding when we look them directly in the eye (Segrin, 1993); wear high-status clothing (Bushman, 1988); use open body postures (Burgoon et al., 1990); touch them (Guéguen et al., 2010); and behave in a friendly, upbeat way (Kleman, 2008). That's why job seekers are coached to offer firm handshakes (Stewart et al., 2008) and smile often and genuinely (Krumhuber et al., 2009) to help influence employers to hire them.

CONCEALING/DECEIVING

We may value and honor the truth, but many of the messages we exchange are not completely truthful. Sometimes we keep silent, sometimes we hedge, and sometimes we downright lie. As you read in Chapter 3, not all deception is self-serving or malicious: Much of it is aimed at saving the "face" of the communicators involved. For example, you might pretend to have a good time at a family celebration or business event, even though you are bored senseless. In other cases, you might lie to save your own face and avoid embarrassment ("Of *course* I read the message you sent me!"). In situations such as these and many others, it's easy to see how nonverbal factors can make the face-saving deception either succeed or fail. When verbal and nonverbal messages conflict, we tend to believe the nonverbal. That's why most people monitor (and self-monitor) nonverbal cues—facial expression, eye contact, posture, vocal pitch and rate—when trying to detect or conceal deception.

Communication scholars Judee Burgoon and Tim Levine (2010) have studied deception detection for years. In their review of decades of research on the subject, they came up with what they call "Deception Detection 101"—three findings that have been supported time and again in studies. They are

- We are accurate in detecting deception only slightly more than half the time—in other words, only a shade better than what we could achieve with a coin flip.

- We overestimate our abilities to detect others' lies—in other words, we're not as good at catching deception as we think we are.
- We have a strong tendency to judge others' messages as truthful—in other words, we want to believe people wouldn't lie to us (which biases our ability to detect deceit).

These principles serve as a reminder that it's not easy to determine whether someone is lying—and nonverbal cues aren't dead giveaways. As one writer put it, "There is no unique telltale signal for a fib. Pinocchio's nose just doesn't exist, and that makes liars difficult to spot" (Lock, 2004, p. 72). Moreover, some popular prescriptions about liars' nonverbal behaviors simply aren't accurate (Guerrero & Floyd, 2006). For instance, conventional wisdom suggests that liars avert their gaze and fidget more than nonliars. Research, however, shows just the opposite: Liars often sustain *more* eye contact and fidget *less*, in part because they believe that to do otherwise might look deceitful (Mann et al., 2013). They also make more eye contact to help them determine if the other person believes the tales they're telling (Jundi et al., 2013).

Despite the challenges, there are some nonverbal clues that may reveal dishonest communication (Ekman, 2009). For example, deceivers typically make more speech errors than truth-tellers: stammers, stutters, hesitations, false starts, and so on. Vocal pitch often rises when people tell lies, and liars pause longer before offering answers than do truth-tellers (Sporer & Schwandt, 2007; Vrij et al., 2000). Perhaps most significantly—because it's a physiological reaction that's not easily controlled—liars' pupils tend to dilate because of the arousal associated with fib-telling (Vrij, 2006). That's why many professional poker players wear sunglasses to hide what their eyes might reveal.

Similar to pupil dilation, the face sometimes reveals a liar's true feelings in brief, unconscious displays. Researchers call these *microexpressions* because they happen so quickly (Yan et al., 2013). Without being aware, liars may leak how they genuinely feel through brief furrows of the brow, pursing of the lips, or crinkling around the eyes (Porter et al., 2012). Microexpressions are more likely

MEDIA CLIP
Trying to Spot Deception: *Scandal*

Olivia Pope's (Kerry Washington) job is to get people out of trouble—to help them avoid a scandal. Equal parts press agent and private investigator, Pope decides whether to take on clients by listening carefully to their stories. She looks them in the eye, monitors their voice, watches their body movements, processes their words—and then quickly determines if the clients are telling the truth. Pope proudly declares, "My gut tells me what I need to know," and she insists her instincts are never wrong. And she's usually right.

But not always. Pope is better at judging the deception of strangers than of those who are close to her. That's consistent with what research shows—people are more easily deceived by loved ones because they don't want to believe people they care for would lie to them. She's also less likely to spot a liar when she's not looking for one—when her "radar is down," so to speak.

It's entertaining to watch Pope size up a situation in seconds and determine who's lying and who's truth-telling. But it's important to remember that infallible instincts are more fiction than fact—and that despite her claims otherwise, Pope is still susceptible to being deceived.

to occur during what's known as "high-stakes" lying, such as when there are severe punishments for being caught (Ekman, 2009). Keep in mind that slow-motion recordings and trained professionals are often required to pick up these microexpressions.

The bottom line is that nonverbal cues offer important information for detecting deception, but most lies aren't detected through snap judgments of a facial expression or a shift in posture. Instead, people who suspect a lie tend to collect a variety of clues (including information from third parties and physical evidence) over a period of days, weeks, or even longer (Park et al., 2002). Jumping to conclusions based on limited information isn't wise communication, and it may lead to relational difficulties. Handle this material about deception detection with care and good judgment.

MANAGING IMPRESSIONS

In Chapter 3, we explained that one major goal of communicating is impression management: getting others to view us as we want to be seen. In many cases, nonverbal cues can be more important than verbal messages in creating impressions (DePaulo, 1992; Zuckerman et al., 1999), and a positive impression seems to be associated with consistency between our verbal and nonverbal behavior (Weisbuch et al., 2010). To appreciate how we manage impressions via nonverbal means, consider what happens when you meet strangers you would like to know better. Instead of projecting your image verbally ("Hi! I'm attractive, friendly, and easygoing"), you behave in ways that will present this identity. For example, you might dress fashionably, smile a lot, and perhaps try to strike a relaxed pose.

There are several ways of managing impressions nonverbally. Sandra Metts and Erica Grohskopf (2003) reviewed professional trade journal articles on constructing good impressions and found examples of each of the following categories (their examples are in parentheses in the following list):

- *Manner* refers to the way we act: how we deliberately stand and move, the way we control facial expressions, and the adjustments we make in our voice. ("Stand tall and walk proudly"; "When meeting others, make direct eye contact and use a firm but friendly handshake.")
- *Appearance* involves the way we dress, the artifacts we wear, hair, makeup, scents, and so on. ("Dress how you wish to be remembered: with assurance, some spark of originality, and in a way that makes you feel comfortable and confident.")
- *Setting* involves the physical items we surround ourselves with: personal belongings, vehicles, and even the place we live. ("Mat and frame awards and certificates and display them in your office.")

Outside of the business world, French psychologist Nicolas Guéguen and his colleagues (Guéguen et al., 2013) ran studies to see if small differences in setting could influence attraction. A male research confederate was asked to approach local women at a shopping center and ask for their phone numbers. When he made the request while holding a guitar case, he was successful far more times (31%) than when carrying nothing (14%) or a sports bag (9%). In another study, Guéguen (2013) had female research confederates lie face down on the beach, reading a book. Some had a (temporary) tattoo of a butterfly on their lower backs; some did not. Those bearing tattoos were approached by men for conversation more often, and more quickly, than were those without tattoos. The researchers suggest that in both studies, seemingly minor changes played major roles in nonverbal impression management.

TYPES OF NONVERBAL COMMUNICATION

So far, we've talked about the role nonverbal communication plays in our interpersonal relationships. Now it's time to look at the many types of nonverbal communication.

BODY MOVEMENT

A primary way we communicate nonverbally is through the physical movement of our bodies: our posture, gestures, eye contact, facial expressions, and so on. Social scientists use the term **kinesics** to describe the study of how people communicate through bodily movements. We break them down by category here, although these various features usually work in combination with each other.

Face and Eyes

The face and eyes are probably the most noticeable parts of the body. However, the nonverbal messages they send are not always the easiest to read. The face is a tremendously complicated channel of expression to interpret, for several reasons.

First, it's hard to describe the number and kind of expressions commonly produced by the face and eyes. For example, researchers have found that there are at least 8 distinguishable positions of the eyebrows and forehead, 8 more of the eyes and lids, and 10 for the lower face (Ekman, 2003). When you multiply this complexity by the number of emotions we experience, you can see why it would be almost impossible to compile a dictionary of facial expressions and their corresponding emotions.

The significance of the face in interpersonal communication can be seen in the many phrases that allude to it. We talk about "saving face," needing some "face time," maintaining a "poker face," and "facing our fears." That's because, according to Knapp and Hall (2010), the face may well be "the primary source of communicative information next to human speech" (p. 293).

A central component of facial expression is eye behavior. The study of how the eyes can communicate is known as **oculesics**. Gazes and glances are usually signals of the looker's interest. However, the *type* of interest can vary. Sometimes, as mentioned earlier, looking is a conversational turn-taking signal that says, "I'm finished talking. Now it's your turn." Gazing also is a good indicator of liking (Schotter et al., 2010). Sometimes, eye contact *reflects* liking that already exists, and at other times it actually creates or *increases* liking—hence the expression "making eyes." Thera-pists who maintain eye contact, combined with a forward lean, are perceived as more empathic and credible (Dowell & Berman, 2013). In other situations, eye contact indicates interest, but not attraction or approval, such as when a teacher glares at a rowdy student or a police officer "keeps an eye on" a suspect. Of course, the meaning of eye contact is influenced by culture. For instance, East Asian cultures tend to see the avoidance of eye contact as a sign of respect and excessive eye contact as unpleasant and even aggressive (Akechi et al., 2013).

In addition to influencing verbal responses, research by Stephen Davis and Jamie Kieffer (1998; see also Kleman, 2008) details at least one effect of eye contact on an important nonverbal behavior: tipping. They found that customers in both small towns and urban areas leave larger tips when their servers (whether male or female) maintain eye contact with them. The authors speculate that good eye contact makes the atmosphere of the restaurant friendlier and makes the customers feel as if they are dining at home. Research also suggests there's a relationship between eye *contact* (note that word) and touching (Knapp & Hall, 2010).

Posture

To appreciate the communicative value of body language, stop reading for a moment and notice how you're sitting. What does your position say nonverbally about how you feel? Are there any other people near you now? What messages do you get from their present posture? By paying attention to the postures of those around you, as well as to your own, you'll find another channel of nonverbal communication that reveals how people feel about themselves and others.

The English language indicates the deep links between posture and communication. English is full of expressions that tie emotional states with body postures:

"I won't take this lying down!"
"Stand on your own two feet."
"Take a load off your back."
"Don't be so uptight!"

Phrases such as these show an awareness of posture, even if it's often unconscious. The main reason we miss most posture messages is that they are usually subtle. It's seldom that people who feel weighed down by a problem hunch over dramatically. In interpreting posture, then, the key is to look for small changes that might be shadows of the way people feel.

Some body language *can* be dramatic. Research shows that expansive poses—hands on hips, feet propped on a desk, or hawk-like stances—are

FOCUS ON RESEARCH
Power Posing

It's no surprise that commanding postures reflect self-confidence. But a team of researchers from Columbia and Harvard universities has discovered that bold postures can actually make people feel more self-assured.

The researchers assigned participants to strike and maintain either high-power or low-power poses for two minutes. Lab tests showed that high-power posers experienced testosterone increases and lowered cortisol, both of which are linked to physiological empowerment. They also made bolder bets when given the chance to gamble after posing. A subsequent study found that people who struck power poses increased their tolerance for pain, and they were more authoritative in interactions with others.

The results suggest that a change in posture can actually improve confidence and performance in communication contexts that include job interviews, public speeches, standing up to a boss, and taking risks that can lead to success. The researchers believe people can "fake it 'til they make it" by practicing powerful poses prior to an event and letting their feelings and behaviors follow. (Note that researcher Amy Cuddy has an inspiring presentation about this research on TED.com.)

Bohns, V. K., & Wiltermuth, S. S. (2012). It hurts when I do this (or you do that): Posture and pain tolerance. *Journal of Experimental Social Psychology, 48,* 341–345.

Carney, D. R., Cuddy, A. J., & Yap, A. J. (2010). Power posing: Brief nonverbal displays affect neuroendocrine levels and risk tolerance. *Psychological Science, 21,* 1363–1368.

signs of power and status (Hall et al., 2005). The Focus on Research sidebar above ("Power Posing") describes how adopting these poses can actually alter how we feel about ourselves.

Gestures

Gestures are a fundamental element of communication—so fundamental, in fact, that people who have been blind from birth use them (Bruce et al., 2007). Gestures are sometimes intentional—for example, a cheery wave or thumbs-up. In other cases, however, our gestures are unconscious. Occasionally, an unconscious gesture will consist of an unambiguous emblem, such as a shrug that clearly means "I don't know." More often, however, there are several possible interpretations to gestures. A group of ambiguous gestures consists of what we usually call *fidgeting*—movements in which one part of the body grooms, massages, rubs, holds, pinches, picks, or otherwise manipulates another part. Social scientists call these behaviors **manipulators**. Social rules may discourage us from performing more manipulators in public, but people still do so without noticing.

Research reveals what common sense suggests—that an increased use of manipulators is often a sign of discomfort (Ekman & Friesen, 1974b). But not *all* fidgeting signals uneasiness. People also are likely to use manipulators when relaxed. When they let their guard down (either alone or with friends), they will be more likely to fiddle with an earlobe, twirl a strand of hair, or clean their fingernails.

The amount and type of gesturing a person uses can be a measure of power and status (Andersen, 1999). For example, people who gesture more are rated by observers as being in positions of control and power, whereas those who gesture less are judged by observers as being subordinate. Head bowing is generally perceived as a submissive gesture and head raising as a dominant gesture (Mignault & Chaudhuri, 2003). Head lowering occurs more often when speaking with a person of higher status than of equal status. For instance, a student nods down more when talking with a professor than with another student (Helweg-Larsen et al., 2004). And pointing is judged by observers as one indicator of power because it implies at least some ability to order other people around.

Gestures can produce a wide range of reactions in receivers. In many situations, the right kinds of gestures can increase persuasiveness (Maricchiolo et al., 2009). For example, increasing hand and arm movements, leaning forward, fidgeting less, and keeping limbs open all make a speaker more effective at influencing others. Even more interesting is the fact that persuasiveness increases when one person mirrors another's movements (Van Swol, 2003). This is logical considering that nonverbal mirroring is a common way to express similarity and affiliation with others (Kouzakova et al., 2010).

As with almost any nonverbal behavior, the context in which gestures occur makes all the difference in the results they produce. Animated movements that are well received in a cooperative social setting may seem like signals of aggression or attempts at domination in a more competitive setting. Fidgeting that might suggest deviousness in a bargaining session could be appropriate when you offer a nervous apology in a personal situation. In any case, trying to manufacture insincere, artificial gestures (or any other nonverbal behaviors) will probably backfire. A more useful goal is to recognize the behaviors you find yourself spontaneously delivering and to consider how they reflect the attitudes you already feel.

TOUCH

Social scientists use the term **haptics** to distinguish the study of touching. Research confirms the value of touch for infants (Feldman et al., 2010; Field, 2007). In particular, studies show the value of "kangaroo care" for premature babies (Feldman et al., 2014). This involves mothers holding their underdeveloped infants close to their skin for one hour a day over two weeks. Compared with babies kept exclusively in incubators, these infants had stronger physiological and cognitive development, slept better, and had lower stress levels. Moreover, the touch sessions increased the mothers' bonds with the babies and reduced their anxiety, showing that touch is important for both givers and receivers. The effects on the children in this study were still evident 10 years later.

Touch also plays a large part in how we respond to others. For instance, Guéguen and Fischer-Lokou (2002) conducted an experiment in which confederates asked passersby to look after a large and very excited dog for 10 minutes so the owner could go into a pharmacy where animals were prohibited. In half of the cases, the passerby was touched during the request. Results confirmed that touch has a large effect on compliance: When touched, 55 percent agreed with the request, whereas only 35 percent in the no-touch condition agreed.

● TOUCH AND CAREER SUCCESS

The old phrase "keeping in touch" takes on new meaning once you understand the relationship between haptics and career effectiveness.

Some of the most pronounced benefits of touching occur in medicine and the health and helping professions. For example, patients are more likely to take their medicines when physicians give a slight touch while prescribing (Guéguen & Vion, 2009). Touch between therapists and clients has the potential to encourage a variety of beneficial changes: more self-disclosure, client self-acceptance, and better client–therapist relationships (Driscoll et al., 1988). In addition, patients with dementia who were administered hand massages, along with intermittent gentle touches on the arm and shoulder, decreased their anxiety and dysfunctional behavior (Kim & Buschmann, 1999).

Touch can also enhance success in sales and marketing. Customers in stores who were briefly touched by a greeter spent more time shopping and bought more (Hornik, 1992). When an offer to try samples of a product is accompanied by a touch, customers are more likely to try the sample and buy the product (Smith et al., 1982).

Even athletes benefit from touch. One study of the National Basketball Association revealed that the touchiest teams had the most successful records, whereas the lowest scoring teams touched each other the least (Kraus et al., 2010).

It's important to note that too much contact can be annoying, harassing, and even downright creepy. But research confirms that *appropriate* professional contact can enhance your occupational success.

An additional power of touch is its on-the-job utility. Studies show that even fleeting touches on the hand or forearm can result in larger tips for restaurant servers (Crusco & Wetzel, 1984; Guéguen & Jacob, 2005). And a server who touches a patron's arm while suggesting a meal choice increases the probability of the patron's making the recommended choice (Guéguen et al., 2007). The effect extends to alcohol consumption: Both women and men in taverns, whether in same-sex or different-sex dyads, increase their alcohol consumption when touched (appropriately, of course) by the server (Kaufman & Mahoney, 1999). For other examples of the power of touch on the job, see the At Work sidebar in this section.

In the United States, touching is generally perceived as more appropriate for women than for men (Derlega et al., 1989; Jones, 1986). Men touch their male friends less than they touch their female friends and also less than women touch their female friends. Although women are generally more comfortable about touching than men, biological sex isn't the only factor that shapes contact. In general, the degree of touch comfort goes along with openness to expressing intimate feelings, an active interpersonal style, and satisfactory relationships (Fromme et al., 1989).

VOICE

Social scientists use the term **paralanguage** to describe the way a message is spoken. Vocal rate, pronunciation, pitch, tone, volume, and emphasis can give the same word or words many meanings. For example, note how many meanings come from a single sentence just by shifting the emphasis from one word to another:

This is a fantastic interpersonal communication book.
(Not just any book, but *this* one in particular.)

This *is* a fantastic interpersonal communication book.
(Without any doubt, this book is fantastic.)

This is a *fantastic* interpersonal communication book.
(This book is superior, exciting.)

This is a fantastic *interpersonal communication* book.
(The book is good as far as interpersonal communication goes; it may not
  be so great as literature or as drama.)

This is a fantastic interpersonal communication *book*.
(It's not a movie or music album; it's a book.)

There are many other ways we communicate paralinguistically—even through pauses. Consider two types of pauses that can lead to communication snags. The first is the *unintentional pause*—those times when people stop to collect their thoughts before deciding how best to continue their verbal message. It's no surprise that liars tend to have more unintentional pauses than truth-tellers, as they often make up stories on the fly (Guerrero & Floyd, 2006). When people pause at length after being asked a delicate question ("Did you like the gift I bought you?"), it might mean they're buying time to come up with a face-saving—and perhaps less-than-honest—response. A second type of pause is the *vocalized pause*. These range from **disfluencies** such as "um," "er," and "uh" to filler words such as "like," "okay," and "ya know." Vocalized pauses reduce a person's perceived credibility (Davis et al., 2006) and should thus be avoided—especially in job interviews (Latz, 2010).

The impact of paralinguistic cues is strong. For example, children are drawn more to playmates who, regardless of race, have similar speech styles than they are to students of the same race who speak differently (Kinzler et al., 2009). "Accent trumps race," as the authors put it. In addition, listeners pay more attention to paralanguage than to the content of the words when asked to determine a speaker's attitudes (Burns & Beier, 1973) and emotions (Rodero, 2011). Furthermore, when vocal factors contradict a verbal message (as when a speaker shouts "I am *not* angry!"), listeners tend to judge the speaker's intention from the paralanguage, not the words themselves (Mehrabian & Weiner, 1967). Toward that end, it's important to pay attention to the paralinguistic messages you're sending. When first-year medical students watched videos of themselves and rated their doctor–patient communication, some of the primary shortcomings they noticed had to do with their paralanguage—particularly tone, rate, volume, and disfluencies (Zick et al., 2007).

Sarcasm is one approach in which we use emphasis, tone of voice, and length of utterance to change a statement's meaning to the opposite of its verbal message (Rockwell, 2007b). Experience this reversal yourself with the following three statements. First, say them literally; and then say them sarcastically:

"You look terrific!"
"I really had a wonderful time on my blind date."
"There's nothing I like better than calves' brains on toast."

As with other nonverbal messages, people often ignore or misinterpret the vocal nuances of sarcasm. Members of certain groups—children, people with weak intellectual skills, poor listeners, people who have communication apprehension, and people with certain forms of brain damage—are more likely to misunderstand sarcastic messages than are others (Rockwell, 2007a; Shamay et al., 2002).

Young children in particular have difficulty making sense of mixed messages (Friend, 2003). In one study (Morton & Trehub, 2001), youngsters ages 4–8 years old were presented with a series of positive and negative statements. When positive statements (such as "Dad gave me a new bike for my birthday") were delivered in a sad tone of voice, the children gauged the speaker as happy because they paid attention to the words rather than the vocal cues. When negative statements were read in an upbeat tone, children interpreted the message as negative—again, relying more on the content than the paralanguage. There was a direct relationship between age and sensitivity to nonverbal cues, with the youngest children relying most heavily on the words spoken.

In addition to reinforcing or contradicting messages, some vocal factors influence the way a speaker is perceived by others (Castelan-Cargile & Bradac, 2001). For example, surgeons whose voices were regarded as dominating and indifferent were more likely to be sued for malpractice than those with a less threatening vocal style (Ambady et al., 2002). Faster rates of speech and louder voices are generally perceived as more persuasive and credible, although there's an upper limit to both (Knapp & Hall, 2010). Communicators with more attractive voices are rated more highly than those whose speech sounds less attractive (Zuckerman & Driver, 1989).

Just what makes a voice attractive can vary. As Figure 6.1 shows (Valentine & Saint Damian, 1988), culture can make a difference. Surveys indicate that there are both similarities and differences between what Mexicans and U.S. citizens view as the "ideal" voice. Second-language learners have a hard time learning to speak without a noticeable accent, even after years or decades of living in a new culture. And even when accented speech is perfectly understandable, it can create discriminatory attitudes for some listeners (Felps et al., 2009). (See the Dark Side box in Chapter 2 for more discussion of stigmas attached to accents.)

DISTANCE

Proxemics is the study of how communication is affected by the use, organization, and perception of space and distance. Each of us carries around a sort of invisible bubble of **personal space** wherever we go. We think of the area inside this bubble as our own—almost as much a part of us as our own bodies. Our personal bubbles vary in size according to the culture in which we were raised, the person we're with, and the situation. It's precisely the varying size of our personal space—the distance we put between ourselves and others—that gives a nonverbal clue to our feelings (Horan & Booth-Butterfield, 2013; Sommer, 2002).

D. Russell Crane (1987) and other researchers tested over 100 married couples, asking partners to walk toward one another and stop when they reached a "comfortable conversational distance." Then they gave each partner a battery of tests to measure their marital intimacy, desire for change, and potential for divorce. The researchers discovered that there was a strong relationship between distance and marital happiness. The average space between distressed couples was about 25 percent greater than that between satisfied partners. On average, the happy couples stood 11.4 inches apart, whereas the distance between unhappy spouses averaged 14.8 inches.

Preferred spaces are largely a matter of cultural norms (Beaulieu, 2004; Høgh-Olesen, 2008). For example, people living in hyperdense Hong Kong manage to live in crowded residential quarters that most North Americans would find intolerable (Chan, 1999). The influence of culture on proxemic behavior even extends to online communication. In avatar interactions, Asian dyads maintain larger distances than European dyads, consistent with what occurs in face-to-face interactions (Hasler & Friedman, 2012). Looking at the distances that North American communicators use in everyday interaction, Edward Hall (1969) found four, each of which reflects a different way we feel toward others at a given time. By "reading" which distance people select, we can get some insight into their feelings.

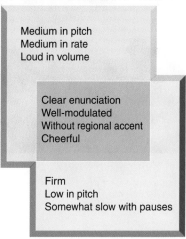

MEXICAN IDEAL SPEAKER'S VOICE

Medium in pitch
Medium in rate
Loud in volume

Clear enunciation
Well-modulated
Without regional accent
Cheerful

Firm
Low in pitch
Somewhat slow with pauses

U.S. IDEAL SPEAKER'S VOICE

FIGURE 6.1 A Comparison of the Ideal Speaker's Voice Types in Mexico and the United States

Intimate Distance

The first of Hall's zones begins with skin contact and ranges out to about 18 inches. We usually use **intimate distance** with people who are emotionally close to us, and then mostly in private situations—making love, caressing, comforting, protecting. By allowing people to move into our intimate distance, we let them enter our most personal space. When we allow them in voluntarily, it's usually a sign of trust: We've willingly lowered our defenses. On the other hand, when someone invades this most personal area without our consent, we usually feel threatened (especially when they're "in your face").

Personal Distance

The second spatial zone, **personal distance**, ranges from 18 inches at its closest point to 4 feet at its farthest. Its closer phase is the distance at which most couples stand in public. If someone thought to be sexually attractive stands this near one partner at a party, the other partner is likely to become alert. This "moving in" often is taken to mean that something more than casual conversation is taking place. The far range of personal distance runs from about 2.5 to 4 feet. It's the zone just beyond the other person's reach. As Hall puts it, at this distance we can keep someone "at arm's length." His choice of words suggests the type of communication that goes on at

this range: The contacts are still reasonably close, but they're much less personal than the ones that occur a foot or so closer.

Social Distance

The third zone is **social distance**. It ranges from 4 to about 12 feet out. Within this zone, the distance between communicators can have a powerful effect on how we regard and respond to others. For example, students are more satisfied with teachers who reduce (at appropriate levels, of course) the distance between themselves and their classes. They also are more satisfied with the course itself and are more likely to follow the teacher's instructions (Hackman & Walker, 1990). Likewise, medical patients are more satisfied with physicians who use close physical proximity to convey warmth and concern (Conlee et al., 1993; Grant et al., 2000). However, people with high social anxiety are likely to keep social distance at the far reaches to reduce their discomfort with strangers (Perry et al., 2013).

Public Distance

Public distance is Hall's term for the farthest zone, running outward from 12 feet. The closer range of public distance is the one that most teachers use in the classroom. In the farther reaches of public space—25 feet and beyond—two-way communication is almost impossible. In some cases it's necessary for speakers to use public distance to reach a large audience, but we can assume that anyone who chooses to use it when more closeness is possible is not interested in a dialogue.

When our spatial bubble is invaded, we experience stress; and we respond with *barrier behaviors*, strategies designed to create a barrier (or fix a broken one) between ourselves and other people (Evans & Wener, 2007; Kanaga & Flynn, 1981). Invade someone's personal space, and notice the reaction. At first the person is most likely simply to back away, probably without realizing what is happening. Next, your partner might attempt to put an object between you, such as a desk, a chair, or some books clutched to the chest, all in an effort to get some separation. Then the other person will probably decrease eye contact (the "elevator syndrome," in which we can crowd in and even touch one another so long as we avoid eye contact). Furthermore, your reluctant partner might sneeze, cough, scratch, and exhibit any variety of behaviors to discourage your antisocial behavior. In the end, if none of these behaviors achieves the desired goal of getting some space between the two of you, the other person might leave or "counterattack," gently at first ("Move back, will you?"), then more forcefully (probably with a shove).

TERRITORIALITY

Whereas personal space is the invisible bubble we carry around, the area that serves as an extension of our physical being, **territory**, remains stationary (Hidalgo & Hernandez, 2001). Robert Sommer (1969) watched students in a college library and found that there's a definite pattern for people who want to study alone. Although the library was uncrowded, students almost always chose corner seats at one of the empty rectangular tables. After each table was occupied by one reader, new readers would choose a seat on the opposite side and at the far end, thus keeping the maximum distance between themselves and the other readers. One of Sommer's associates tried violating these unspoken rules by sitting next to and across from other female readers when more distant seats were available. She found that the approached women reacted defensively, signaling their discomfort through shifts in posture, gesturing, or moving away.

Consider how you would react if someone took "your" seat in one of your classes. Even though the chair isn't your possession, you probably have some sense of ownership about it (Kaya & Burgess, 2007). How you respond to perceived violations depends on *who* enters and uses your territory (a friend is less threatening than a stranger), *why* they do so (a "mistake" is less important than a "planned attack"), and *what* territory is entered or used (you may care more about a territory over which you have exclusive rights, such as your bedroom, than about a territory in a public area, such as your seat in class).

TIME

Social scientists use the term **chronemics** to describe the study of how humans use and structure time. Our use of time can express both intentional and unintentional messages (Stephens et al., 2012). Social psychologist Robert Levine (1988) describes several ways that time can be used to communicate. For instance, in cultures such as those of the United States, Canada, and northern Europe, which value time highly (Kirkcaldy et al., 2001), waiting can be an indicator of status. "Important" people may be seen by appointment only, while it is acceptable to intrude without notice on those deemed less important. Consider how natural it is for a boss to drop into an employee's office unannounced, whereas the employee would never intrude in a similar fashion without an appointment. Similarly, it would be a serious mistake to show up late for a job interview, although the interviewer might keep you waiting.

The use of time depends greatly on culture. In some cultures, punctuality is critically important, whereas in others it is barely considered (Levine & Norenzayan, 1999; Levine et al., 2008). Punctual U.S. mainlanders often report welcoming the laid-back Hawaiian approach to time. One psychologist discovered the difference between North and South American attitudes when teaching at a university in Brazil (Levine, 1988). He found that some students arrived halfway through a 2-hour class and that most of them stayed put and kept asking questions when the class was scheduled to end. A half hour after the official end of the period, the professor finally closed off discussion because there was no indication that the students intended to leave. This flexibility of time is quite different from what is common in most North American colleges and universities!

Even within a culture, rules of time vary. Sometimes the differences are geographic. In New York City, the party invitation may say 9:00 P.M., but

DARK SIDE OF COMMUNICATION
THE INEQUALITY OF "LOOKISM"

What's the problem if attractive people get advantages in life? According to Rachel Gordon and her colleagues (2013), it's that "lookism" is a version of prejudice similar to racism, sexism, and classism. When people get preferential treatment based on their physical appearance, it does a disservice to everyone involved.

The researchers maintain that advantages for the attractive begin in childhood and pick up steam in adolescence. Young people who are rated as better looking get higher grades and are more likely to attain college degrees than their peers, setting the stage for better economic outcomes throughout adulthood. These outcomes include the following:

- Women gain an 8 percent wage bonus for above-average looks; they pay a 4 percent wage penalty for below-average appearance.
- For men, the attractiveness wage bonus is only 4 percent. However, the penalty for below-average looks is even higher than for women: a full 13 percent.

Deborah Rhode (2010) claims this bias for beauty is quite literally unjust, as less-than-attractive people get poorer treatment in the legal system. A starting point for change is raising awareness. It's important to realize that no one—not teachers, not clergy, not parents—is above giving preferential treatment to others on the basis of their beauty. When possible, students and job candidates should be evaluated through blind review to avoid partiality. And pay attention to how you treat people in your interactions, asking yourself the question, "Is this person's appearance affecting the way I communicate with him or her?" If you're honest, you might be surprised at how often the answer to that question is "Yes."

nobody would think of showing up before 10:30 P.M. In Salt Lake City, guests are expected to show up on time, or perhaps even a bit early. Even within the same geographic area, different groups establish their own rules about the use of time. Consider your own experience. In school, some instructors begin and end class punctually, whereas others are more casual. With some people, you feel comfortable talking for hours in person or on the phone; with others, time seems precious and not to be "wasted."

Time can be a marker not only of status and culture but also of relationships. Research shows that the amount of time spent with a relational partner sends important messages about valuing that person (Andersen et al., 2006). In one study analyzing 20 nonverbal behaviors, "spending time together" was the most powerful predictor of both relational satisfaction and perceived interpersonal understanding (Egland et al., 1997). And as we discuss in Chapter 10, spending "quality time" with a partner is one of love's languages.

PHYSICAL ATTRACTIVENESS

The importance of beauty has been emphasized in the arts for centuries. More recently, social scientists measured the degree to which physical attractiveness affects interaction between people (Lorenzo et al., 2010). Men and women whom others view as attractive are rated as being more sensitive, kind, strong, sociable, and interesting than their less fortunate brothers and sisters (Knapp & Hall, 2010). More than 200 managers in a *Newsweek* survey admitted that attractive people get preferential treatment both in hiring decisions and on the job (Bennett, 2010). And professors perceived to be "hot" are judged as having more expertise, and students are more motivated to learn from them and give them higher teaching evaluations (Liu et al., 2013). Occasionally beauty has a negative effect: Interviewers may turn down highly attractive candidates if they're perceived as threats (Agthe et al., 2011). On the whole, however, the interpersonal benefits of attractiveness far outweigh the downsides, as the Dark Side box on page 196 describes.

Fortunately, attractiveness is something we can control without having to call the plastic surgeon. If you aren't totally gorgeous or handsome, don't despair: Evidence suggests that, as we get to know more about people and like them, we start to regard them as better looking (Albada et al., 2002; Bazil, 1999). Moreover, we view others as beautiful or ugly not just on the basis of their "original equipment" but also on how they use that equipment. Posture, gestures, facial expressions, and other behaviors can increase the attractiveness of an otherwise unremarkable person. Finally, the way we dress can make a significant difference in the way others perceive us, as you'll now see.

CLOTHING

Besides protecting us from the elements, clothing is a means of nonverbal communication. It's a way for some to strategically hide "problem areas" and accentuate "assets" (Frith & Gleeson, 2008). One writer has suggested that clothing conveys at least 10 types of messages to others (Thourlby, 1978):

1. Economic level
2. Education level
3. Trustworthiness
4. Social position
5. Level of sophistication
6. Economic background
7. Social background
8. Educational background
9. Level of success
10. Moral character

We do make assumptions about people based on their style of clothing. For example, the way people are dressed affects judgments of their credibility. In one experiment, a man and a woman were stationed in a hallway so that anyone who wished to go by had to avoid them or pass between them. In one condition, the conversationalists wore "formal daytime dress"; in the other, they wore "casual attire." Passersby behaved differently toward the couple, depending on the style of clothing: They responded positively to the well-dressed couple and showed more annoyance when the same people were casually dressed (Fortenberry et al., 1978).

Attire makes a difference in the classroom too. College students' perceptions of their graduate teaching associate's (GTA) expertise decreases as the GTA's attire becomes more casual. On the other hand, GTAs who dress casually are seen as more interesting, extroverted, and sociable than those who dress more formally (Morris et al., 1996; Roach, 1997). Dressing up may be more important for men than for women when it comes to perceptions of status. Observers rely more on women's nonverbal behavior as cues to their social position, whereas men are rated more on their attire (Mast & Hall, 2004).

MEDIA CLIP
The Clothes (Help) Make the Man:
Crazy, Stupid, Love

Cal Weaver (Steve Carell) is a middle-aged man who is reeling because his wife has asked for a divorce. Jacob Palmer (Ryan Gosling) is a handsome young "player" who takes pity on Cal and decides to coach him on how to get back in the dating game.

Jacob's first stop? A trip to an upscale shopping mall, where he overhauls Cal's appearance. Shoes, shirts, suits, jeans, hair—nothing goes unchanged. When Cal emerges from the dressing room, he feels uncomfortable in his new attire. However, he gets a favorable review from an admiring woman, so he adopts the look and begins dating with renewed confidence.

It would be nice to think that a wardrobe change is all that's needed to enhance one's luck in romance. As the rest of the movie shows, it takes much more than new clothing to find "crazy, stupid, love." But for Cal Weaver, at least it's a start.

Judgments based on what a person wears, like other perceptions, need to be made carefully. For example, whereas many Americans believe a *hijab*—a "veil" or "head-scarf"—functions to oppress women, veiled women see their hijab as helping them define their Muslim identity, resist sexual objectification, and afford more respect (Droogsma, 2007). As the cartoon on the next page demonstrates, perception of attire is affected by a variety of cultural factors and values.

PHYSICAL ENVIRONMENT

We conclude our look at nonverbal communication by examining how physical settings, architecture, and interior design affect communication. As Barbara Brown and her colleagues remind us, "relationships are inseparable from their settings; they do not simply take place against a backdrop of homes and communities" (2006, p. 673).

Research confirms that an environment can shape the kind of interaction that takes place in it. For example, a study of 10 neighborhoods in Portland, Oregon, examined the sidewalks, presence of front porches, traffic-calming devices, bars on windows, and the presence of litter or graffiti. Levels of neighborliness among the residents increased as the number of positive physical-environment characteristics increased (Wilkerson et al., 2012). Inner-city adults and children who have access to landscaped public spaces interact in ways that are much more prosocial than do those who have to interact in more barren environments (Taylor et al., 1998). On the other hand, public housing residents living in relatively barren buildings reported more mental fatigue, aggression, and violence than did their counterparts in buildings with nearby grass and trees (Kuo & Sullivan, 2001a, 2001b).

Recall the different homes you've visited lately. Were some of them more inviting than others? Homes reflect their occupants. For example, partners seem to arrange furnishings to mirror their closeness. A higher number of jointly acquired objects reflect greater interpersonal affinity (Arriaga et al., 2004). In addition, how rooms are furnished influences how the people in them feel and interact. For example, students participating in a structured interview in a room with dim lighting were more relaxed, had a more favorable impression of the interviewer, and were more self-disclosing than those exposed to bright lighting (Miwa & Hanyu, 2006). Offices perceived as having a high creativity potential are furnished simply, have more plants, bright lighting conditions, windows, cooler colors, and a computer facility (Ceylan et al., 2008).

Students see professors who occupy well-decorated offices as being more credible than those occupying less attractive work areas (Teven & Comadena, 1996). Physicians have shaped environments to improve the quality of interaction with their patients. According to environmental psychologist Robert Sommer (1969), simply removing a doctor's desk made patients feel almost five times more at ease during office visits. Sommer also found that redesigning a convalescent ward of a hospital greatly increased the interaction between patients. In the old design, seats were placed shoulder to shoulder around the edges of the ward. By grouping the chairs around small tables so that patients faced each other at a comfortable distance, the amount of conversations doubled.

You might want to keep these concepts in mind the next time you get the opportunity to arrange furniture, purchase lighting, or redesign your living space. Your physical environment can affect your interpersonal communication.

CHECK YOUR UNDERSTANDING

Objective 6.1 Define nonverbal communication.

Nonverbal communication consists of messages expressed by nonlinguistic means. Often what we *do* conveys more meaning than what we *say*, and nonverbal communication shapes perceptions. By tuning into facial expressions, postures, gestures, vocal tones, and other behaviors, you can make assumptions about the way communicators feel about one another and get some sense about the nature of their relationship.

Q: In a public place, unobtrusively record field notes describing the nonverbal messages you observe. For each observation, record at least two assumptions about the significance of the behavior in question.

Objective 6.2 Recognize the distinguishing characteristics of nonverbal communication.

Nonverbal communication is pervasive; in fact, nonverbal messages are always available as a source of information about others. Most nonverbal behavior suggests messages about relational attitudes and feelings, in contrast to verbal statements, which are better suited to expressing ideas. Messages that are communicated nonverbally are usually more ambiguous than verbal communication. Contrary to what some might think, nonverbal cues also play a role in mediated communication. Nonverbal communication is also affected by culture and gender.

Q: Keep a one-day log of significant nonverbal communication (both face to face and mediated) in one of your important relationships. For each entry, note (a) whether the behavior was deliberate or unintentional; (b) the relational messages that seem to have been exchanged; (c) the degree of ambiguity about the meaning of the behavior; and (d) gender and cultural factors that may have shaped the nonverbal behavior.

Objective 6.3 Identify and offer examples of the various functions that nonverbal communication can serve.

Nonverbal communication serves many functions. It can help in the creating and maintaining of relationships. It also serves to regulate interaction and to influence others. In addition, nonverbal communication can be used to conceal or reveal deception. Finally, we use nonverbal cues to manage impressions with others.

Q: Using the log you created for Objective 6.2, note the functions of the nonverbal behavior in each entry.

Objective 6.4 Understand and describe how meaning is communicated through particular nonverbal cues.

Nonverbal messages can be communicated in a variety of ways: through body movement (including the face and eyes, gestures, and posture), touch, voice, distance, territory, time, physical appearance, clothing, and environment. Culture plays a significant role in determining the rules and meanings for each of these factors.

Q: Describe one significant incident in which you communicated nonverbally through each of the channels described in this chapter.

KEY TERMS

- Chronemics (195)
- Disfluencies (191)
- Emblems (178)
- Haptics (189)
- Intimate distance (193)
- Kinesics (186)

- Manipulators (188)
- Nonverbal communication (174)
- Oculesics (186)
- Paralanguage (190)
- Personal distance (193)
- Personal space (192)

- Proxemics (192)
- Public distance (194)
- Regulators (181)
- Social distance (194)
- Territory (194)

ACTIVITIES

1. Demonstrate for yourself that it is impossible to avoid communicating nonverbally by trying *not* to communicate with a friend or family member. (You be the judge of whether to tell the other person about this experiment beforehand.) See how long it takes for your partner to inquire about what is going on and to report on what he or she thinks you might be thinking and feeling.

2. Interview someone from a culture different from your own, and learn at least three ways in which nonverbal codes differ from the environment where you were raised. Together, develop a list of ways you could violate unstated but important rules about nonverbal behavior in your partner's culture in three of the following areas:

Eye contact	Voice
Posture	Touch
Gesture	Time

Facial expression	Clothing
Distance	Environmental design
Territory	Territory

Describe how failure to recognize different cultural codes could lead to misunderstandings, frustrations, and dissatisfaction. Discuss how awareness of cultural rules can be developed in an increasingly multicultural world.

3. Watch a television program or film, and identify examples of the following nonverbal functions:

Creating and maintaining relationships

Regulating interaction

Influencing others

Concealing or deceiving

Managing impressions

If time allows, show these examples to your classmates.

4. Learn more about the nonverbal messages you send by interviewing someone who knows you well: a friend, family member, or coworker. Ask your interview participant to describe how he or she knows when you are feeling each of the following emotions, even though you may not announce your feelings verbally:

> Anger or irritation
>
> Boredom or indifference
>
> Happiness
>
> Sadness
>
> Worry or anxiety

Which of these nonverbal behaviors do you display intentionally, and which are not conscious? Which functions do your nonverbal behaviors perform in the situations your partner described: creating/maintaining relationships, regulating interaction, influencing others, concealing/deceiving, and/or managing impressions?

5. Explore your territoriality by listing the spaces you feel you "own," such as your parking space, parts of the place you live, and seats in a particular classroom. Describe how you feel when your territory is invaded, and identify things you do to "mark" it.

Share your findings with a group of classmates and see if they have similar or different territoriality habits.

6. This activity requires you to observe how people use space in a particular setting and to note reactions to violations of spatial expectations. Select a supermarket, department store, college bookstore, or some other common setting in which people shop for things and then pay for them on a checkout line. Observe the interaction distances that seem usual between salesclerks and customers, between customers as they shop, and between customers in the checkout line.

a. What are the average distances between the people you observed?

b. How do people respond when one person comes too close to another or when one person touches another? How do people react to these violations of their space? How could they avoid violating each other's personal space?

c. Try to observe people from a culture other than your own in this store. Describe their use of spatial distance. If this is not possible in the store, think back to a foreign film or a film that contains interaction between North Americans and people of another culture, as well as people from that same culture.

SCORING FOR ASSESSING YOUR COMMUNICATION (PAGE 182)

Step 1. Reverse score items 2, 3, 4, 6, 7, and 12 (i.e., 5 = 1, 4 = 2, 3 = 3, 2 = 4, and 1 = 5).

Step 2. After reverse scoring the 6 items in step 1, sum the scores for all 12 items. This is your Nonverbal Immediacy Scale score.

Scores can range from 12 to 60. Men and women differed in their self-evaluations using this measure, with women perceiving themselves as engaging in more nonverbal immediacy behaviors than men. College-age women had an average score of 47, with most scores between 42 and 52. College-age men had an average score of 43, with most scores between 38 and 49.

chapter **7**

Listening

Receiving and Responding

LEARNING OBJECTIVES

7.1 Understand the nature of listening and the listening styles that interpersonal communicators use.

7.2 Recognize the challenges that can impede effective listening.

7.3 Identify the five components of the interpersonal listening process.

7.4 Effectively use a variety of reflective and directive listening responses.

TAKE A MOMENT to identify the worst listener you know. Maybe it's someone who interrupts when you're speaking, or whose attention seems to wander as you talk. Perhaps this person forgets important things you have said, steers the conversation back to himself or herself, or gives responses that reflect a lack of understanding. Now recall how you feel when you're conversing with this poor listener. Irritated? Frustrated? Discouraged?

Now think about how others view *you* as a listener. Which of these behaviors, so annoying in your conversational partners, do you engage in yourself?

In this chapter, you will learn just how important listening is in interpersonal communication. You will read about the many factors that make good listening difficult and find reasons for tackling those challenges. You will learn what really happens when listening takes place. Finally, you will read about a variety of listening responses that you can use to increase your own understanding, improve your relationships, and help others.

THE NATURE OF LISTENING

When it comes to the subject of listening, plenty of people have advice on how to do it better, such as "close your mouth and open your ears." Although such advice is a good start, simplistic prescriptions like these don't capture

---

● LISTENING ON THE JOB

@WORK

If you were asked to imagine the most talented communicators in the business world, it's likely that you would think about executives who are articulate, charismatic public figures. However, research shows that in the workplace, the ability to listen effectively is more important than public presentation skills.

Numerous studies (summarized in Flynn et al., 2008) find listening to be the most important communication skill for entry-level workers, subordinates, supervisors, and managers on several dimensions: job and career success, productivity, upward mobility, communication training, and organizational effectiveness. Senior executives, students, and employers, when asked what skills are most important on the job, identified listening more often than any other ability, including technical competence, computer knowledge, creativity, and administrative talent (Gabric & McFadden, 2001; Landrum & Harrold, 2003).

It's not surprising then that there's a connection between good listening and good leadership (Kluger & Zaidel, 2013).

Unfortunately, there's no connection between how well most communicators *think* they listen and how competent they really are in their ability to understand others. A study by Judi Brownell (1990) illustrates this point vividly. A group of managers in her study were asked to rate their listening skills. Astonishingly, not one of the managers described himself or herself as a "poor" or "very poor" listener, and 94 percent rated themselves as "good" or "very good." The favorable self-ratings contrasted sharply with the perceptions of the managers' subordinates, many of whom said their bosses' listening skills were weak.

Some poor listening is inevitable. However, the good news is that listening can be improved through instruction and training (Lane et al., 2000).

the complex nature of listening. We begin our exploration of this subject by describing the importance of listening in interpersonal communication.

THE IMPORTANCE OF LISTENING

How important is listening? If we use frequency as a measure, it ranks at the top of the list. Surveys (Barker et al., 1981; Emanuel et al., 2008) show that as much as 55 percent of college students' communication time is spent listening (see Figure 7.1). The business world yields similar numbers: Executives spend approximately 60 percent of their communication time listening (Brown, 1982; Steil, 1996). When working adults were asked to name the most common communication behavior they observed in their place of business, "listening" topped the list (Keyton et al., 2013). The At Work box on page 204 shows that workers not only listen a lot on the job but that listening skills are highly valued.

The business world is not the only setting in which listening is vital. When a group of adults was asked to rank various communication skills according to their importance, listening topped the family/social list as well as the career list (Brownell & Wolvin, 2010; Wolvin, 1984). In committed relationships, listening to personal information in everyday conversations is considered an important ingredient of satisfaction (Prager & Buhrmester, 1998). John Gentile (2004) argues that listening to one another's personal narratives (see Chapter 4) is fundamental to our humanity and sense of well-being. With this in mind, we turn our attention to defining this important skill.

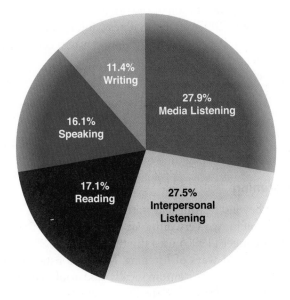

FIGURE 7.1   **Time Devoted to Communication Activities**

Emanuel, R., Adams, J., Baker, K., Daufin, E. K., Ellington, C., Fitts, E., Himsel, J., Holladay, L., & Okeowo, D. (2008). How college students spend their time communicating. *International Journal of Listening, 22,* 13–28.

"You're not listening to what you're hearing."

CartoonStock www.CartoonStock.com

LISTENING DEFINED

So far we have used the term "listening" as if it needs no explanation. Actually, there's more to this concept than you might suspect. We define **listening**—at least the interpersonal type—as the process of receiving and responding to others' messages.

Traditional approaches to listening focus on the reception of *spoken* messages. However, we've broadened the definition to include messages of all sorts because much of contemporary listening takes place through mediated channels, some of which involve the written word. Consider times you've said something like, "I was talking with a friend and she *said . . .*," and the conversation you recount actually took place via e-mail, text, or messaging. You'll read in Chapter 9 how social support can be offered in face-to-face communication but also through blogs, posts, tweets, and other social media mechanisms. We continue to focus on spoken messages in this chapter (beginning with our discussion of "hearing"), but recognize that "listening" in contemporary society involves more than meets the ear.

Hearing versus Listening

Listening and hearing aren't identical. **Hearing** is the process in which sound waves strike the eardrum and cause vibrations that are transmitted to the brain. Listening occurs when the brain reconstructs these electrochemical impulses into a representation of the original sound and then gives them meaning (Robinshaw, 2007). Barring illness, injury, or cotton plugs, you can't stop hearing. Your ears will pick up sound waves and transmit them to your brain whether you want them to or not.

Listening, however, isn't automatic. Many times we hear but do not listen. Sometimes we automatically and unconsciously block out irritating sounds, such as a neighbor's lawn mower or the roar of nearby traffic. We also stop listening when we find a subject unimportant or uninteresting. Boring stories, television commercials, and nagging complaints are common examples of messages we may tune out.

Mindless Listening

When we move beyond hearing and start to listen, researchers note that we process information in two very different ways (Burleson, 2011; Todorov et al., 2002). Ellen Langer (1990) uses the terms "mindless" and "mindful" to describe these different ways of listening. **Mindless listening** occurs when we react to others' messages automatically and routinely, without much mental investment. Words such as "superficial" and "cursory" describe mindless listening better than terms such as "ponder" and "contemplate."

Although the term *mindless* may sound negative, this sort of low-level information processing is a potentially valuable type of communication because it frees us to focus our minds on messages that require our careful attention (Burgoon et al., 2000). Given the number of messages to which we're exposed, it's impractical to listen carefully and thoughtfully 100 percent of the time. It's unrealistic to devote your attention to long-winded stories, idle chatter, or remarks you've heard many times before. The only realistic way to manage the onslaught of messages is to be "lazy" toward many of them (Griffin, 2006). In situations like these, we forgo careful analysis and fall back on the schemas—and sometimes the stereotypes—described in Chapter 4 to make sense of a message. If you stop right now and recall the messages you have heard today, it's likely that you processed most of them mindlessly.

Mindful Listening

By contrast, **mindful listening** involves giving careful and thoughtful attention and responses to the messages we receive. You tend to listen mindfully when a message is important to you, and also when someone you care about is speaking about a matter that is important to him or her. Think of how your ears perk up when someone starts talking about your favorite hobby, or how you tune in carefully when a close friend tells you about the loss of a loved one. In situations like these, you want to give the message-sender your complete and undivided attention (see Figure 7.2).

FIGURE 7.2   **The Chinese characters that make up the verb "to listen"**

Sometimes we respond mindlessly to information that deserves—and even demands—our mindful attention. Ellen Langer's (1990) determination to study mindfulness began when her grandmother complained about headaches coming from a "snake crawling around" beneath her skull. The doctors quickly diagnosed the problem as senility—after all, they reasoned, senility comes with old age and makes people talk nonsense. In fact, the grandmother had a brain tumor that eventually killed her. The event made a deep impression on Langer (p. 3):

> For years afterward I kept thinking about the doctors' reactions to my grandmother's complaints, and about our reactions to the doctors. They went through the motions of diagnosis, but were not open to what they were hearing. Mindsets about senility interfered. We did not question the doctors; mindsets about experts interfered.

Most of our daily decisions about whether to listen mindfully don't have life-and-death consequences, but the point should be clear: There are times when we need to listen consciously and carefully to what others are telling us. That kind of mindful listening is the focus of the remainder of this chapter.

LISTENING STYLES

Not everyone listens the same way nor has the same listening goals. Communication researchers have identified four listening styles—task oriented, relational, analytical, and critical—each of which has both strengths and weaknesses (Bodie et al., 2013).

Task-Oriented Listening

Task-oriented listening is most concerned with efficiency and accomplishing the job at hand. Task-oriented listeners see time as scarce and valuable, and they often grow irritated when they believe others are wasting it.

When deadlines and other pressures demand immediate action, task orientation can be beneficial. It's most appropriate when the primary focus is taking care of business: Such listeners encourage others to be organized and concise.

Despite its advantages, however, a task orientation may alienate others when it seems to ignore their feelings. Those people with a different temperament, or those who are from cultures where it is impolite to be clear and direct, may not appreciate a no-nonsense, task-oriented approach. Also, a focus on getting things done quickly may come at the expense of thoughtful deliberation and consideration. Finally, the emotional issues and concerns that are so important to many business and personal transactions may be minimized by task-oriented listeners.

Relational Listening

People who are primarily focused on **relational listening** are most concerned with building emotional closeness with others. They are typically extroverted, attentive, and friendly (Villaume & Bodie, 2007).

Relational listeners aim to understand how others feel, are aware of their emotions, and are highly responsive to those individuals. Relational listeners are usually nonjudgmental about what others have to say. They are more interested in understanding and supporting people than in evaluating or controlling them.

Despite its obvious strengths, a relational orientation does have its drawbacks. It's easy to become overly involved with others' feelings. Relational listeners may lose their detachment and ability to objectively assess the quality of information others give them in an effort to be congenial and supportive (Gearhart & Bodie, 2011). Less relationally oriented communicators may view them as overly expressive and even intrusive.

Analytical Listening

People who are most interested in **analytical listening** are concerned about attending to the full message before coming to judgment. They want to hear details and analyze an issue from a variety of perspectives. More than just enjoying complex information, these listeners have a tendency to engage in systematic thinking. Analytical listeners can be a big help when the goal is to assess the quality of ideas and when there is value in looking at issues from a wide range of perspectives. They are especially valuable when the issues at hand are complicated. However, their thorough approach can be time consuming and impractical when a deadline is fast-approaching.

Critical Listening

People whose default mode is **critical listening** have a strong desire to evaluate messages. They may or may not apply the tools of analytical listening; but

Your Listening Styles

Record your first impression to each of the following statements by indicating the degree to which you agree or disagree with them on a scale ranging from 1–7, where 1 = strongly disagree and 7= strongly agree.

Relational Listening

_____ **1.** When listening to others, it is important to understand the feelings of the speaker.

_____ **2.** I listen to understand the emotions and mood of the speaker.

_____ **3.** I listen primarily to build and maintain relationships with others.

_____ **4.** I enjoy listening to others because it allows me to connect with them.

Analytical Listening

_____ **5.** I tend to withhold judgment about another's ideas until I have heard everything they have to say.

_____ **6.** When listening to others, I consider all sides of the issue before responding.

_____ **7.** I fully listen to what a person has to say before forming any opinions.

_____ **8.** To be fair to others, I fully listen to what they have to say before making judgments.

Task Listening

_____ **9.** I get frustrated when people get off topic during a conversation.

_____ **10.** I prefer speakers who quickly get to the point.

_____ **11.** I find it difficult to listen to people who take too long to get their ideas across.

_____ **12.** When listening to others, I appreciate speakers who give brief, to-the-point presentations.

Critical Listening

_____ **13.** I often catch errors in other speakers' logic.

_____ **14.** I tend to naturally notice errors in what other speakers' say.

_____ **15.** I have a talent for catching inconsistencies in what a speaker says.

_____ **16.** When listening to others, I notice contradictions in what they say.

This measure presents 16 of the 24 items of the original instrument developed by Graham Bodie and his colleagues: Bodie, G. D., Worthington, D. L., & Gearhart, C. C. (2013). The Listening Styles Profile-Revised (LSP-R): A scale revision and evidence for validity. *Communication Quarterly, 61,* 72–90.

For scoring information, see page 233 at the end of the chapter.

in either case, they go beyond trying to understand the topic at hand and try to assess its quality. Not surprisingly, critical listeners tend to focus on the accuracy and consistency of a message. Critical listening can be especially helpful when the goal is to investigate a problem. However, people who are critical listeners can also frustrate others who may think that they nitpick everything others say.

Many people use more than one listening style, and the style may vary depending on the situation at hand. Whichever styles you use, it is important to recognize that you can control the way you listen. When your relationship with the speaker needs attention, adopt a relational approach. If investigation is called for, put on your analytical persona. And when there is a need for evaluation, become a critical listener. You can also become more effective by assessing and adapting to the listening preferences and styles of your conversational partners.

THE CHALLENGE OF LISTENING

By now you can see that mindful listening is important. Even with the best intentions, though, listening carefully is a challenge. Now we take a look at some of the obstacles we need to overcome when we want to listen carefully.

LISTENING IS NOT EASY

Listening is more difficult than many realize. Common barriers to listening include information overload, personal concerns, rapid thought, and noise.

Information Overload

The sheer amount of information most of us encounter every day makes it impossible to listen carefully to everything we hear. We're bombarded with messages not only in face-to-face interaction, but also from the Internet, the media, cell phones, and various other sources (Arsenault, 2007). Given this barrage of information, it's virtually impossible for us to keep our attention totally focused for long. As a result, we often choose—understandably and sometimes wisely—to listen mindlessly rather than mindfully.

Personal Concerns

A second reason we don't always listen carefully is that we're often wrapped up in personal concerns of more immediate importance to us than the messages others are sending (Golen, 1990; Nichols, 2009). It's hard to pay attention to someone else when you're anticipating an upcoming test or thinking about the wonderful time you had last night. When we still feel that we have to pay attention to others while our focus is elsewhere, listening becomes mindless at best and often a polite charade.

Rapid Thought

Careful listening is also difficult because our minds are so active. Although we're capable of understanding speech at rates up to 600 words per minute (Versfeld & Dreschler, 2002), the average person speaks much more slowly—between 100 and 140 words per minute. Therefore, we have a lot of "spare time" to spend with our minds while someone is talking. The temptation is to use this time in ways that don't relate to the speaker's ideas, such as thinking about personal interests, daydreaming, planning a rebuttal, and so on. The trick is to use this spare time to understand the speaker's ideas better rather than let your attention wander.

Noise

Finally, our physical and mental worlds often present distractions that make it hard for us to pay attention. The sounds of other conversations, traffic, and music, as well the kinds of psychological noise discussed in Chapter 1, all interfere with our ability to listen well. For example, research supports the commonsense suspicion that background noise, such as from a television set, reduces the ability of a communicator to understand messages (Armstrong et al., 1991; Jones et al., 2007). Also, fatigue or other forms of discomfort can distract us from paying attention to a speaker's remarks. For instance, consider how the efficiency of your listening decreases when you are seated in a crowded, hot, stuffy room full of moving people and other noises. In such circumstances, even the best intentions aren't enough to ensure cogent understanding.

ALL LISTENERS DO NOT RECEIVE THE SAME MESSAGE

When two or more people are listening to a speaker, we tend to assume that each hears and understands the same message. In fact, such uniform comprehension isn't the case. Recall our discussion of perception in Chapter 4 where we pointed out the many factors that cause each of us to perceive an event in a different manner. Physiological factors, social roles, cultural background, personal interests, and needs all shape and distort the raw data we hear into very different messages. It's no wonder that dyads typically achieve only 25–50 percent accuracy in interpreting or representing each other's behavior (Spitzberg, 1994). Our listening is always colored and limited by our unique, and fairly consistent, view of the world (Robins et al., 2004).

POOR LISTENING HABITS

Most people possess one or more habits that keep them from understanding others'

MEDIA CLIP
The Boss From Hell: *The Devil Wears Prada*

Miranda Priestly (Meryl Streep) is every employee's nightmare. She's a self-centered, domineering, hard-driven boss who treats the people who work for her like slaves.

Priestly exemplifies every poor listening habit. She attends only to things that matter to her ("The details of your incompetence do not interest me") and does so insensitively ("Bore someone else with your questions"). Pseudolistening, defensive listening, and stage hogging: She does them all. She also interrupts, rolls her eyes when she doesn't like what she's hearing, and walks out on her subordinates in mid-conversation.

Priestly may be a successful businesswoman, but she fails on many other counts—especially as a listener.

messages. As you read about the following poor listening behaviors, see which ones describe you.

Pseudolistening is only an imitation of the real thing. Pseudolisteners pretend to pay attention: They look you in the eye, and they may even nod and smile, but their minds are in another world.

When **stage hogging**, people are interested only in expressing their ideas and don't care about what anyone else has to say. These individuals allow you to speak from time to time, but only so they can catch their breath and use your remarks as a basis for their own babbling. Research on "conversational narcissism" (Vangelisti et al., 1990) shows that self-centered stage hogs ask questions, but not other-oriented, information-seeking ones. Rather, these conversational narcissists ask counterfeit questions to demonstrate their superiority and hold the floor (we talk more about counterfeit vs. sincere questions later in this chapter). Research by Lisa Leit (2009) found that conversational narcissism characterizes as many as three quarters of marriages, with potentially devastating outcomes such as spouses feeling invisible and dialogue that does not allow the spouses to adapt to one another.

With **selective listening**, people respond only to the parts of a speaker's remarks that interest them, rejecting everything else. Unless and until you bring up one of these pet subjects, you might as well be talking to a tree.

People **filling in gaps** like to think that what they remember makes a whole story. These people manufacture information so that when they re-tell what they listened to, they can give the impression they "got it all." The message that's left is actually a distorted (not merely incomplete) version of the real message.

The habit of **insulated listening** is almost the opposite of selective listening. Instead of looking for something, these listeners avoid it. Whenever a topic arises they'd rather not deal with, insulated listeners simply fail to hear or acknowledge it.

People who engage in **defensive listening** take innocent comments as personal attacks. It's fair to assume that many defensive listeners are suffering from shaky self-images, and they avoid facing this by projecting their own insecurities onto others.

A person who engages in **ambushing** will listen carefully to you but only because he or she is collecting information that will be used to attack what you have to say. Needless to say, using this kind of strategy will justifiably initiate defensiveness from the other person.

COMPONENTS OF LISTENING

By now, you can begin to see that there is more to listening than sitting quietly while another person speaks. In truth, listening—especially *mindful* listening—consists of five separate elements: hearing, attending, understanding, remembering, and responding.

HEARING

As we have already discussed, hearing is the physiological aspect of listening. It is the nonselective process of sound waves impinging on the ear.

Hearing is obviously vital to listening because it's the starting point of the process. It can be diminished by physiological disorders, background noise, or auditory fatigue, which is a temporary loss of hearing caused by continuous exposure to the same tone or loudness. People who spend an evening at a rock concert or hearing fireworks may experience auditory fatigue and, if they are exposed often enough, permanent hearing loss ("5.2 Million Young Americans," 2001). And what used to be perceived as a problem just for the elderly is now a serious concern for adolescents, due in large part to the use of earphones for portable devices (Shargorodsky et al., 2010). It's wise to heed the warnings of the Dark Side box on this page and protect your hearing—for your own sake as well as for the sake of your relationship partners.

ATTENDING

Whereas hearing is a physiological process, **attending** is a psychological one, and it is part of the process of selection that we described in Chapter 4. As discussed earlier in this chapter, it's especially hard to focus on messages—even

DARK SIDE OF COMMUNICATION
HEARING LOSS AND RELATIONAL STRESS

Over 36 million Americans of all ages have some form of impaired hearing. Hearing loss can be challenging for those who experience it, and research suggests it can also affect their relationships. One survey (Shafer, 2007) explored the feelings of adults who have spouses with hearing loss. Nearly two-thirds of the respondents said they feel annoyed when their partner can't hear them clearly. Almost a quarter said that beyond just being annoyed, they felt ignored, hurt, or sad. Many of the respondents believe their spouses are in denial about their condition, which makes the problem even more frustrating.

Once a hearing problem has been diagnosed, it's often possible to treat it. One study found that two-thirds of hearing-aid users said their relationship with a loved one improved after adopting the device (Hear the World, 2012). If you suspect that you or someone you know might have a hearing loss, it's wise to have a physician or audiologist perform an examination. The results may lead to more satisfying relationships.

important ones—when we are bombarded by information. Face-to-face messages come from friends, family, work, and school. Personal media—text messages, phone calls, e-mails, and instant messages—demand your attention. Along with these personal channels, we are awash in messages from the mass media. This deluge of communication has made the challenge of attending tougher than at any time in human history (Hansen, 2007; Ralph et al., 2013).

We would go crazy if we attended to everything we hear, so we filter out some messages and focus on others. Not surprisingly, we attend most carefully to messages when there's a payoff for doing so (Burleson, 2007). If you're planning to see a movie, you'll listen to a friend's description more carefully than you otherwise would. And when you want to get to know others better, you'll pay careful attention to almost anything they say in hopes of improving the relationship.

As you read in Chapter 6, skillful communicators attend to both speakers' words and their nonverbal cues. If you asked a friend "How's it going?," you can easily imagine two ways he or she could answer "Fine": One set of nonverbal behaviors (big smile, enthusiastic vocal tone) would reinforce the verbal statement, whereas another (downcast eyes, slumped posture,

dejected vocal tone) would contradict it. Some people are simply inattentive to nonverbal cues, but others suffer from a physiological syndrome called nonverbal learning disorder (Casey, 2012). Due to a processing deficit in the right hemisphere of the brain, people with this disorder have trouble making sense of many nonverbal cues. Whether due to insensitivity or physiology, it's easy to see how failing to attend to nonverbal cues is a listening deficit.

One way to attend better to important messages is to screen out distractions. Some companies now hold "laptopless" meetings, prohibiting computer use that might distract participants (Guynn, 2008). You may be familiar with other public forums—including some classrooms—where cell phone interruptions are discouraged (Froese et al., 2012). Although new technology has greatly increased our ability to communicate with others, it's important to be mindful of when it intrudes on attentive listening.

One final word on technology and attention: Phoning and driving are a dangerous combination (O'Connor et al., 2013). In one lab study (Just et al., 2008), experimental participants steered a vehicle along a curving virtual road, either undisturbed or while listening to sentences that they judged as true or false. Brain imaging revealed that mentally processing the spoken messages led to a decrease in driving accuracy. The findings show that language comprehension draws mental resources away from performance, even when the driver isn't holding a phone. The researchers note that talking with a passenger in a car isn't as distracting as a phone conversation because the passenger is more likely to be aware of the competing demands for the driver's attention. Nevertheless, the verdict seems clear: Good listening requires full concentration—and so does good driving.

UNDERSTANDING

Paying attention—even close attention—to a message doesn't guarantee that you'll understand what's being said. **Understanding** is composed of several elements. First, of course, you must be aware of the syntactic and grammatical rules of the language. But beyond this basic ability, understanding a message depends on several other factors. One is your knowledge about the source of the message. Such background will help you decide, for example, whether a friend's insulting remark is a joke or a serious attack. The context of a message also helps you understand what's being said. A yawning response to your comments would probably have a different meaning at midnight than at noon.

The ideal in interpersonal listening is both to understand and to be understood. Communication researchers use the term **listening fidelity** to describe the degree of congruence between what a listener understands and what the message sender was attempting to communicate (Powers &Witt, 2008). Fidelity doesn't mean agreement. You might listen carefully to a point your friend is making, understand her position quite clearly, and still disagree completely. But the act of understanding sends a positive relational message, even if the communicators don't see eye to eye on the content.

REMEMBERING

The ability to recall information once we've understood it, or **remembering**, is a function of several factors: the number of times the information is heard or repeated, how much information there is to store in the brain, and whether the information may be "rehearsed" or not.

Early research on listening revealed that people remember only about half of what they hear immediately after hearing it, even when they listen mindfully (Barker, 1971). Within 2 months, 50 percent of the originally remembered portion

"This requires both ears."

is forgotten, bringing what we remember down to about 25 percent of the original message. However, this loss doesn't take 2 months: People start forgetting immediately (within 8 hours, the 50 percent remembered drops to about 35 percent). Of course, these amounts vary from person to person and depend on the importance of the information being recalled (Cowan & AuBuchon, 2008).

Whatever the particular amounts we remember may be, given the abundance of information we process every day in person and through mediated channels, the residual message (what we remember) is a small fraction of what we hear. This can cause relational problems, as people often feel slighted when others—especially loved ones—don't remember things they've heard. "I told you this repeatedly and you still forgot?" is a familiar refrain in many interpersonal conflicts.

RESPONDING

All the steps we have discussed so far—hearing, attending, understanding, and remembering—are internal activities. A final part of the listening process involves **responding** to a message—giving observable feedback to the speaker (Bostrom, 1996; Reis & Clark, 2013). One study of 195 critical incidents in banking and medical settings showed that a major difference between effective and ineffective listening was the kind of feedback offered (Lewis & Reinsch, 1988). Good listeners showed that they were attentive by nonverbal behaviors such as keeping eye contact and reacting with appropriate facial expressions. Their verbal behavior—for example, answering questions and exchanging ideas—also demonstrated their attention. It's easy to imagine how other responses would signal less effective listening. A slumped posture, bored expression, and yawning send a clear message that you are not tuned in to the speaker.

Adding responsiveness to our listening model demonstrates a fact we discussed in Chapter 1: that communication is transactional in nature. Listening isn't just a passive activity. As listeners, we are active participants in

FOCUS ON RESEARCH
Feeling Understood and Appreciated

Imagine holding a friendly conversation with someone you just met. What kind of listening responses would you like to receive from your conversational partner? That's what a research team led by communication scholar Harry Weger wanted to find out.

The researchers recruited student confederates who had completed a course in interpersonal communication. These students were trained to respond in conversations with research participants in one of three different ways: (1) simple acknowledgements, such as "I see" or "Okay"; (2) "active listening," primarily involving questioning and paraphrasing;

or (3) advice, such as suggesting activities or making recommendations.

In postconversation surveys, participants said they felt most understood when confederates used active listening responses rather than the other two styles. In measures of communication satisfaction and social attractiveness, both active listening and advising were preferred to simple acknowledgments. What this suggests is that when it comes to feeling heard in conversations, people appreciate highly responsive listeners.

Weger, H., Bell, G. C., Minei, E. M., & Robinson, M. C. (2014). The relative effectiveness of active listening in initial interactions. *International Journal of Listening, 28,* 13–31.

a communication transaction. At the same time that we receive messages, we also send them.

TYPES OF LISTENING RESPONSES

Of the five components of listening described in the preceding section, it's responding that lets us know if others are truly tuned in to what we're saying (Bippus, 2001; Maisel et al., 2008). Think for a moment of someone you consider a good listener. Why did you choose that person? It's probably because of the way she or he behaves while you are speaking. Participants in one study said they expect listeners to be attentive, understanding, friendly, responsive, and able to maintain a conversational flow (Bodie et al., 2012). What behaviors mark those characteristics? Good listeners ask and answer questions, provide reflective and relevant feedback, offer their own perspective, and respond nonverbally by making eye contact, nodding their heads, and leaning forward. In other words, although listening begins as an internal mental process, others will determine whether and how you're listening by monitoring your responses.

As Figure 7.3 illustrates, listening responses range from reflective feedback that invites the speaker to talk without concern of evaluation, to more directive responses that evaluate the speaker's messages. We spend the remainder of the chapter looking at each of these response styles in detail.

SILENT LISTENING

There are times when the best response is to say nothing. This is certainly true when you don't want to encourage a speaker to keep talking. For

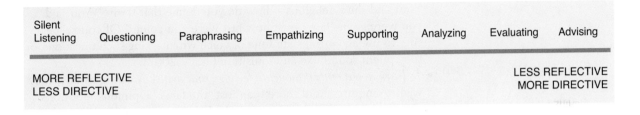

| Silent Listening | Questioning | Paraphrasing | Empathizing | Supporting | Analyzing | Evaluating | Advising |

MORE REFLECTIVE
LESS DIRECTIVE

LESS REFLECTIVE
MORE DIRECTIVE

FIGURE 7.3 Types of Listening Responses

instance, recall times when a boss or instructor droned on and on when you needed to leave for an appointment; or instances when a friend retold the story of a horrible date for what seemed like the 10th time. In situations like these, a verbal response would only encourage the speaker to continue—precisely the opposite reaction you would be seeking. The best response in these cases may be **silent listening**—staying attentive and nonverbally responsive without offering any verbal feedback.

Silent listening isn't just an avoidance strategy. It also can be the right approach when you are open to the other person's ideas but your interjections wouldn't be appropriate. If you are part of a large audience hearing a lecture, asking questions and offering comments would probably be disruptive. On a more interpersonal level, when a friend tells you a joke, butting in to ask for clarification ("There was a priest, a rabbi, and a *what?*") would probably spoil your friend's rhythm.

There are even times when silent listening can help others solve their problems (Cain, 2014). Sonia Johnson (1987; see also Smith, 2010) describes a powerful activity she calls "hearing into being." The process is simple: In brainstorming sessions, each participant has totally uninterrupted floor time. "When we are free to talk without threat of interruption, evaluation, and the pressure of time," notes Johnson, "we move quickly past known territory out into the frontiers of our thought" (p. 132). Johnson, who uses the technique in feminist seminars, reports that some women burst into tears when they first experience "hearing into being" because they are not used to being listened to so seriously and completely. Ask yourself, when was the last time you talked, uninterrupted, to an attentive partner for more than a few minutes? How would you like the chance to develop your ideas without pausing for another's comments? Silent listening is a response style that many of us could profit from using—and receiving—more often.

QUESTIONING

Regarded as "the most popular piece of language" (Goodman & Esterly, 1990), **questioning** occurs when the listener asks the speaker for additional information. There are several reasons to ask sincere, nondirective questions:

- *To clarify meanings.* By now you know that people who share words do not always share meanings. Good listeners don't assume they know what their partners mean; they ask for clarification with questions such as these: "What did you mean when you said he was being 'unfair'?"

"You said she's 'religious'—how do you define that term?" "You said you were going 'fast'—just how fast were you going?" Of course, be sure to use an appropriate tone of voice when asking such questions, or they might sound like an inquisition (Tracy, 2002).

- *To learn about others' thoughts, feelings, and wants.* A caring listener may want to inquire about more than just "the facts." Opinions, emotions, needs, and even hopes are buried inside many messages; with sensitivity, a sincere question can draw these out. "What do you think about the new plan?"; "How did you feel when you heard the news?"; and "Were you hoping for something different?" are examples of such probes. When inquiring about personal information, it is usually best to ask **open questions** that allow a variety of extended responses rather than **closed questions** that only allow a limited range of answers. For instance, "How did you feel?" is an open question that allows a variety of responses, whereas "Did you feel angry?" is a closed question that requires only a yes-or-no answer (and may direct respondents toward feelings they weren't experiencing).

- *To encourage elaboration.* People are sometimes hesitant to talk about themselves, or perhaps they aren't sure if others are interested. Remarks such as "Tell me more about that," "I'm not sure I understand," and "I'm following you" convey concern and involvement. Notice that none of these examples ends with a question mark. We can encourage elaboration simply by acknowledging that we are listening.

- *To encourage discovery.* People in the helping professions—clergy, counselors, therapists, and so on—often ask questions to prod their clients into discovering solutions for their problems (Watts et al., 2005). "Playing counselor" can be a risky game, but there are times when you can use questions to encourage others to explore their thoughts and feelings. "So, what do you see as your options?" may prompt an employee to come up with creative problem-solving alternatives. "What would be your ideal solution?" might help a friend get in touch with various wants and needs. Most important, encouraging discovery rather than dispensing advice indicates you have faith in others' ability to think for themselves. This may be the most important message that you can communicate as an effective listener.

- *To gather more facts and details.* Just because your conversational partner tells you something doesn't mean you understand the whole story. As long as your questions aren't intrusive (and you'll need to monitor others' nonverbal behavior to determine this), people often appreciate listeners who want to learn more. Questions such as "What did you do then?" and "What did she say after that?" can help a listener understand the big picture. One study found that teachers who ask questions in parent–teacher conversations before launching into problem solving are perceived as more effective communicators (Castro et al., 2013). It helps to know the facts prior to offering analysis and advice.

Not all questions are genuine requests for information. Whereas **sincere questions** are aimed at understanding others, **counterfeit questions** are really disguised attempts to send a message, not receive one. As such, they really fit better at the "more directive" end of the listening response continuum pictured in Figure 7.3 on page 217. It's also likely that they'll lead to a defensive communication climate, as discussed in Chapter 11.

Counterfeit questions come in several varieties:

- *Questions that trap the speaker.* When your friend says, "You didn't like that movie, did you?," you're being backed into a corner. It's clear that your friend disapproves, so the question leaves you with two choices: You can disagree and defend your position, or you can devalue your reaction by lying or equivocating—"I guess it wasn't the best." Consider how much easier it would be to respond to the sincere question, "What did you think of the movie?"

  Adding a tag question such as "Did you?" or "Isn't that right?" to the end of a question can be a tip-off that the asker is looking for agreement, not information. Although some listeners use these tag endings to confirm and facilitate understanding (Coates, 1986), our concern here is when tags are used to coerce agreement: "You said you'd call at five o'clock, but you forgot, didn't you?" Similarly, questions that begin with "Don't you" (such as "Don't you think she would make a good boss?") direct others toward a desired response. As a simple solution, changing "Don't you?" to "Do you?" makes the question less leading.

  Leading questions not only signal what the desired answer is, they also affect memory, especially in children. David Bjorklund and his colleagues (2000) showed children and adults a video of a theft and then interviewed them several days later, using both leading and neutral questions. Although the adults were unaffected by the type of question asked, the children who were asked leading questions had less accurate recall of the video than those who were asked free recall questions.

- *Questions that make statements.* "Are you *finally* off the phone?" is more of a statement than a question—a fact unlikely to be lost on the targeted person. Emphasizing certain words also can turn a question into a statement: "You lent money to *Tony?*" We also use questions to offer advice. The person who asks, "Are you going to stand up to him and give him what he deserves?" has clearly stated an opinion about what should be done.

- *Questions that carry hidden agendas.* "Are you busy Friday night?" is a dangerous question to answer. If you say "No," thinking the person has something fun in mind, you won't like hearing "Good, because I need some help moving my piano." Obviously, such questions are not designed to enhance understanding; they are setups for the proposal that follows. Other examples include "Will you do me a favor?" and "If I tell you what happened, will you promise not to get mad?" Because they are strategic rather than spontaneous, these questions are likely to provoke defensiveness (Gibb, 1961). Wise communicators answer questions that mask hidden agendas cautiously with responses such as "It depends" or "Let me hear what you have in mind before I answer."

- *Questions that seek "correct" answers.* Most of us have been victims of question-askers who only want to hear a particular response. "Which shoes do you think I should wear?" can be a sincere question—unless the asker has a predetermined preference. When this happens, the asker isn't interested in listening to contrary opinions, and "incorrect" responses get shot down. Some of these questions may venture into delicate territory. "Honey, do you think this looks bad?" is usually a request for a "correct" answer—and the listener must use good judgment to determine an appropriate response.

- *Questions based on unchecked assumptions.* "Why aren't you listening to me?" assumes the other person isn't paying attention. "What's the matter?" assumes that something is wrong. As we explained in Chapter 4, perception checking is a much better way of confirming assumptions. As you recall, a perception check offers a description of behavior and interpretations, followed by a sincere request for clarification: "When you keep looking at your phone, I think you're not listening to me, but maybe I'm wrong. Are you paying attention?"

No question is inherently sincere or counterfeit because the meaning and intent of any statement is shaped by its context. Moreover, a slight change in tone of voice or facial expression can turn a sincere question into a counterfeit one and vice versa. Consider how the questions "What are you doing?" or "When will you be finished?" could be asked in different ways, eliciting different responses.

It's also worth noting that counterfeit questions aren't all bad: They can be powerful tools for making a point. Lawyers use them to get confessions in the courtroom, and journalists ask them to uncover concealed information. Our point is that they usually get in the way of effective listening and relationship building—after all, most people don't like feeling trapped or "grilled" in a conversation.

Crime show franchises such as *CSI* and *Law & Order* are a fixture of television programming. Their main characters must listen carefully to do their jobs effectively. This involves asking probing questions, critically analyzing statements, and offering advice and judgments to their clients, colleagues, and coworkers.

PARAPHRASING

Paraphrasing is feedback that restates, in your own words, the message you thought the speaker sent. You may wonder, "Why would I want to restate what's already been said?" Consider this simple exchange:

"Let's make plans for next weekend."
"So you want to chat next week to make plans for Saturday?"
"No, I meant we should check our calendars now to see if we're free to
    go to the game on Sunday."

By paraphrasing, the listener learned that the speaker wanted to make plans now, not later—and that "weekend" meant Sunday, not Saturday. Note that the listener rephrased rather than repeated the message. In effective paraphrasing, you restate what you think the speaker has said in your own words as a way of checking the meaning you've assigned to the message. It's important that you paraphrase, not "parrot-phrase." If you simply repeat the speaker's comments verbatim, you'll sound foolish or hard of hearing—and just as important, you still might misunderstand what's been said.

Types of Paraphrasing Statements

Restating another person's message in a way that sounds natural can sometimes be a difficult skill to master. Here are three approaches to get you started:

1. Change the speaker's wording.

   Speaker: "Bilingual education is just another failed idea of bleeding-heart liberals."

   Paraphrase: "So, if I understand what you're saying, you're mad because you think bilingual ed sounds good, but it doesn't work?"

2. Offer an example of what you think the speaker is talking about.
   When the speaker makes an abstract statement, you may suggest a specific example or two to see if your understanding is accurate:

   Speaker: "Lee is such a jerk. I can't believe the way he acted last night."

   Paraphrase: "You thought those jokes were pretty offensive, huh?"

3. Reflect the underlying theme of the speaker's remarks.
   When you want to summarize the theme that seems to have run through another person's conversation, a complete or partial perception check is appropriate:

   Paraphrase: "You keep telling me to be careful. Sounds like you're worried something's going to happen to me. Am I right?"

There are several reasons why paraphrasing assists listening. First, as the preceding examples illustrate, paraphrasing allows you to find out if the message received is the message the sender intended. Second, paraphrasing often draws out further information from the speaker, much like questioning. (In fact, a good paraphrase often ends with a question such as, "Is that what you meant?") Third, paraphrasing is an ideal way to take the heat

" WOOF, WOOF, WOOF — BUT I'M PARAPHRASING. "

CartoonStock www.Cartoonstock.com

out of intense discussions. When conversations intensify, it is often because the people involved believe they aren't being heard. Rather than escalating the conflict, try paraphrasing what the other person says: "Okay, let me be sure I understand you. It sounds like you're concerned about. . . ." Paraphrasing usually short-circuits a defensive spiral because it assures the other person of your involvement and concern. When you take the time to restate and clarify a speaker's message, your commitment to mindful listening is hard to deny. For these and other reasons, we usually feel a sense of affinity for those who make the effort to paraphrase our messages (Weger et al., 2010).

There are two levels at which you can paraphrase messages. The first involves feedback of factual information; the second involves reflecting personal information.

Paraphrasing Factual Information

Summarizing facts, data, and details is important during personal or professional conversations. "We've agreed that we'll take another few days to think about our choices and make a decision on Tuesday—right?" might be an effective way to conclude a business lunch. A questioning tone should be used; a listener wants to be sure that meaning has been shared. Even personal topics are sometimes best handled on a factual level: "So your main problem is that our friends take up all the parking spaces in front of your place. Is that it?" Although this "neutral" response may be difficult when you are under attack, it helps to clarify facts before you offer your reaction. It is also a good idea to paraphrase instructions, directions, and decisions before acting on what you *think* has been said.

Paraphrasing Personal Information

Whereas restating factual information is relatively easy, it takes a sensitive ear to listen for others' thoughts, feelings, and wants. The "underlying message" is often the more important message, and effective listeners try to reflect what they hear at this level. Listening for thoughts, feelings, and wants addresses the cognitive (rational), affective (emotional), and behavioral (desired action) domains of human experience. Read the following statement as if a friend is talking to you, and listen for all three components in the message:

> Maria has hardly been home all week—she's been so busy with work. She rushes in just long enough to eat dinner, then she buries herself writing code until bedtime. Then she tells me today that she's going out Saturday with some friends from high school. I guess the honeymoon is over.

What is the speaker thinking, feeling, and wanting? Paraphrasing can help you find out: "Sounds like you're unhappy (feeling) because you think Maria is ignoring you (thought) and you want her to spend more time with you (want)." Recognize that you may not be accurate; the speaker might reply, "No, I really don't need to see her more often—I just want her to pay attention to me when she's around." Recognize also that you could identify an entirely different think-feel-want set: "So you're frustrated (feeling) because you'd like Maria to change (want), but you think it's hopeless because you have such different priorities (thought)." The fact that these examples offer distinct interpretations of the same message demonstrates the value of paraphrasing.

Your paraphrases don't have to be as long as the examples in the preceding paragraph. It's often a good idea to mix paraphrasing with other listening responses. In many cases, you'll want to reflect only one or two of the think-feel-want components. The key is giving feedback that is appropriate for the situation and offering it in a way that assists the listening process. Because paraphrasing is an unfamiliar way of responding, it may feel awkward at first. If you start by paraphrasing occasionally and then gradually increase the frequency of such responses, you can begin to see the benefits of this method.

EMPATHIZING

Empathizing is a response style listeners use when they want to show that they *identify* with a speaker. As discussed in Chapter 4, empathy involves perspective taking, emotional contagion, and genuine concern. When listeners put the attitude of empathy into verbal and nonverbal responses, they engage in empathizing. Sometimes these responses can be quite brief: "Uh-huh," "I see," "Wow!," "Ouch!," "Whew!," "My goodness." In other cases, empathizing is expressed in statements such as these:

"I can see that really hurts."
"I know how important that was to you."
"It's no fun to feel unappreciated."
"I can tell you're really excited about that."
"Wow, that must be rough."
"I think I've felt that way, too."
"Looks like that really made your day."
"This means a lot to you, doesn't it?"

Empathizing falls near the middle of the listening response continuum pictured in Figure 7.3. It is different from the more reflective responses at the left end of the spectrum, which attempt to gather information neutrally. It is also different from the more evaluative styles at the right end of the spectrum, which offer more direction than reflection. To understand how empathizing compares to other types of responses, consider these examples:

"So your boss isn't happy with your performance and you're thinking about finding a new job." (Paraphrasing)
"Ouch—I'll bet it hurt when your boss said you weren't doing a good job." (Empathizing)
"Hey, you'll land on your feet—your boss doesn't appreciate what a winner you are." (Supporting)

Notice that empathizing identifies with the speaker's emotions and perceptions more than paraphrasing does, yet offers less evaluation and agreement than supporting responses. In fact, it's possible to empathize with others while disagreeing with them. For instance, the response, "I can tell that this issue is important to you," legitimizes a speaker's feelings without assenting to that person's point of view (note that it could be said to either a friend or a foe at a business meeting). Empathizing is therefore an important skill not only for interacting with people with whom you agree but also for responding to those who see the world differently than you.

Perhaps a better way to explain empathizing is to describe what it *doesn't* sound like. Many listeners believe they are empathizing when, in fact, they are offering responses that are evaluative and directive—providing what has been called "cold comfort" (Burleson, 2003; Hample, 2006). Listeners are probably *not* empathizing when they display the following behaviors:

- *Denying others the right to their feelings.* Consider this common response to another person's problem: "Don't worry about it." Although the remark may be intended as a reassuring comment, the underlying message is that the speaker wants the person to feel differently. The irony is that the direction probably won't work—after all, it's unlikely that people can or will stop worrying just because you tell them to do so. Other examples of denying feelings are "It's nothing to get so upset about" and "That's a silly way to feel." Research shows that attempting to identify with others' emotions is more effective than denying their feelings and perspectives (Burleson & Samter, 1985, 1994).

- *Minimizing the significance of the situation.* Think about the times someone said to you, "Hey, it's only _____." You can probably fill in the blank a variety of ways: "a game," "words," "a test," "a party." How did you react? You probably thought the person who said it just didn't understand. To someone who has been the victim of verbal abuse, the hurtful message wasn't "just words"; to a child who didn't get an invitation, it wasn't "just a party" (see Burleson, 1984); to a student who has flunked an important exam, it wasn't "just a test" (see Burleson & Samter, 1985). When you minimize the significance of someone else's experience, you aren't empathizing. Instead, you are interpreting the event from your perspective and then passing judgment—rarely a helpful response.

- *Focus on yourself.* It can be tempting to talk at length about a similar experience you've encountered ("I know exactly how you feel. Something like that happened to me—let me tell you about it. . . ."). Although your intent might be to show empathy, research shows that such messages aren't perceived as helpful because they draw attention away from the distressed person (Burleson, 2008).

- *Raining on the speaker's parade.* Most of the preceding examples deal with difficult situations or messages about pain. However, empathizing involves identifying with others' joys as well as their sorrows. Many of us can recall coming home with exciting news, only to be told "A 5 percent raise? That isn't so great." "An *A minus*? Why didn't you get an *A*?" "Big deal—I got one of those years ago." Taking the wind out of someone's sails is the opposite of empathizing. Research shows that we don't get the full enjoyment out of good news until we share it with someone who responds empathically (Lambert et al., 2013; Reis et al., 2010).

Empathic listening is essentially an expression of affection, as it communicates validation and a sense of worth to the message-sender (Floyd, 2014). Research suggests that emotional intelligence is needed to offer these nonjudgmental, other-oriented responses (Pence & Vickery, 2012). Fortunately, research also indicates that the ability to offer such responses can be learned by both children and adults (Dexter, 2013). The exercises at the end of this chapter can offer you valuable practice in developing your skill as an empathic communicator.

SUPPORTING

So far, we have looked at listening responses that put a premium on being reflective and nonevaluative. However, there are times when other people want to hear more than a reflection of how *they* feel: They would like to know how *you* feel about *them*. **Supporting** responses reveal the listener's solidarity with the speaker's situation. Brant Burleson (2003) describes supporting as "expressions of care, concern, affection, and interest, especially during times of stress or upset" (p. 552). There are several types of supportive responses:

Agreement	"Yeah, that class was tough for me too." "You're right—the landlord is being unfair."
Offers to help	"I'm here if you need me." "Let me try to explain it to him."
Praise	"I don't care what the boss said: I think you did a great job!" "You're a terrific person! If she doesn't recognize it, that's her problem."
Reassurance	"The worst part seems to be over. It will probably get easier from here." "I know you'll do a great job."
Diversion	"Let's catch a movie and get your mind off this." "That reminds me of the time we. . . ."

Men and women differ in the way they act when the opportunity to support others arises. Women are more prone than men to give supportive responses when presented with another person's problem (Burleson et al., 2005; Hale et al., 1997) and are more skillful at composing and processing such messages (Burleson et al., 2009, 2011). In fact, women who *aren't* skillful at offering emotional support to their female friends run the risk of being shunned by their same-sex peers (Holmstrom et al., 2005). By contrast, men tend to respond to others' problems by offering advice or by diverting the topic (Derlega et al., 1994; Woodward et al., 1996). This may be due in part

MEDIA CLIP

Responding to Bad News: *50/50*

Twentysomething Adam Learner (Joseph Gordon-Levitt) is leading a good life in Seattle—until he is diagnosed with cancer. Once he hears the news, he seeks support from his mother (Anjelica Huston), girlfriend (Bryce Dallas Howard), best buddy (Seth Rogen), therapist (Anna Kendrick), and a cancer support group.

Sometimes the responses Adam receives are helpful, providing him with empathy and perspective. Other times, the reactions he gets frustrate him and leave him feeling emptier. For the most part, Adam just wants people to hear him out and assist him in making his own decisions. That's easier said than done for some of the characters in this film.

to societal norms that discourage men from offering sensitive emotional support (Burleson et al., 2005).

Although women and men may tend to offer different kinds of support, both sexes respond well to the same types of comforting messages. Both men and women feel most supported by messages that are highly personal and which are delivered with nonverbal immediacy such as touching and maintaining eye contact (Jones & Burleson, 2003). Moreover, both sexes appreciate the kind of social support we describe in Chapter 9.

Even the most sincere supportive efforts don't always help. Mourners suffering from the recent death of a loved one often report that a majority of the comments made to them are unhelpful (Davidowitz & Myrick, 1984; Glanz, 2007). Most of these statements are advice: "You've got to get out more" and "Don't question God's will." Another frequent response is an attempt to offer perspective, such as, "She's out of pain now" and "Time heals all wounds." A study of bereaved parents found that these kinds of clichés actually do more harm than good (Toller, 2011). People who are grieving don't appreciate being told how to feel or what they should do. Instead, bereaved parents said they would feel more supported by the silent listening approach described on page 217. One mother who lost a child offered this recommendation for people who want to help a grieving friend:

> Go and be with them. You don't have to say anything, just say, "I don't know how you feel, but I'm here." Go sit down and just be with that person. What I wouldn't have given to have somebody come and knock on the door and stop in. (Toller, 2011, p. 26)

As with the other helping styles, supporting can be beneficial, but only under certain conditions (Goldsmith & Fitch, 1997; Halone & Pecchioni, 2001):

- *Make sure your expression of support is sincere.* Phony agreement or encouragement is probably worse than no support at all because it adds the insult of your dishonesty to whatever pain the other person is already feeling.
- *Be sure the other person can accept your support.* Sometimes people are so upset that they aren't ready or able to hear anything positive. When you know a friend is going through a difficult time, it's important not

to be overly intrusive before that person is ready to talk and receive your support (Clark & Delia, 1997).

- *Focus on "here and now" rather than "then and there."* Although it's sometimes true that "You'll feel better tomorrow," it sometimes isn't (you can probably remember times when you felt worse the next day). More important, focusing on the future avoids supporting in the present. Even if the prediction that "10 years from now, you won't even remember her name" proves correct, it gives little comfort to someone experiencing heartbreak today.
- *Make sure you're ready for the consequences.* Talking about a difficult event may reduce distress for the speaker but increase distress for the listener (Lewis & Manusov, 2009). Recognize that supporting another person is a worthwhile but potentially taxing venture.

ANALYZING

In **analyzing** a situation, the listener offers an interpretation of a speaker's message ("I think what's really bothering you is . . ."; "She's doing it because . . ."; or "Maybe the problem started when he . . ."). Communicators who respond this way often use the analytical listening style described earlier in this chapter (page 208). Interpretations are often effective in helping people who have problems seeing alternative meanings of a situation— meanings they would have never thought of without your assistance. Sometimes an analysis helps clarify a confusing problem, providing an objective understanding of the situation. Research suggests that analytic listeners are able to hear the concerns of emotionally upset others without experiencing similar emotions, which can be an advantage in problem solving (Weaver & Kirtley, 1995).

In other cases, an analysis can create more problems than it solves. There are two reasons why: First, your interpretation may not be correct, in which case the problem holder may become even more confused by accepting it. Second, even if your analysis is accurate, sharing it with the problem holder might not be useful. There's a chance that it will arouse defensiveness (analysis implies being superior and in a position to evaluate). Besides, the problem holder may not be able to understand your view of the problem without working it out personally.

How can you know when it's helpful to offer an analysis? Here are some guidelines to follow:

- *Offer your interpretation in a tentative way rather than as absolute fact.* There's a big difference between saying "Maybe the reason is . . ." and insisting "This is the truth."
- *Your analysis ought to have a reasonable chance of being correct.* An inaccurate interpretation—especially one that sounds plausible—can leave a person more confused than before.
- *Make sure that the other person will be receptive to your analysis.* Even if you're completely accurate, your thoughts won't help if the problem holder isn't ready to consider them. Pay attention to the other person's verbal and nonverbal cues to see how your analysis is being received.

- *Be sure that your motive for offering an analysis is truly to help the other person.* It can be tempting to offer an analysis to show how brilliant you are or even to make the other person feel bad for not having thought of the right answer in the first place. Needless to say, an analysis offered under such conditions isn't helpful.

EVALUATING

An **evaluating** response appraises the sender's thoughts or behaviors in some way. The evaluation may be favorable ("That's a good idea" or "You're on the right track now") or unfavorable ("An attitude like that won't get you anywhere"). In either case, it implies that the person evaluating is in some way qualified to pass judgment on the speaker's thoughts or actions. Communicators who respond this way often approach situations with the critical listening style described earlier in this chapter (page 208).

In the film *American Hustle*, Sydney Prosser (Amy Adams) and Irving Rosenfeld (Christian Bale) are con artists whose victims are easy prey because they don't critically evaluate the swindlers' messages.

Sometimes negative evaluations are purely critical. How many times have you heard responses such as "Well, you asked for it!," or "I told you so!," or "You're just feeling sorry for yourself"? Although such comments can sometimes serve as a verbal slap that "knocks sense" into the problem holder, they usually make matters worse by arousing defensiveness in that person. After all, suggesting that someone is foolish or mistaken is an attack on the presenting image that most people would have a hard time ignoring or accepting.

Other times, negative evaluations are less critical. These involve what we usually call constructive criticism, which is intended to help the problem holder improve in the future. Friends give this sort of response about the choice of everything from clothing, to jobs, to friends. A common setting for constructive criticism is school, where instructors evaluate students' work to help them master concepts and skills. Even constructive criticism can arouse defensiveness because it may threaten the self-concept of the person at whom it is directed (see Chapter 11 for tips on creating supportive communication climates).

ADVISING

When approached with another's problem, the most common reaction is **advising** (Notarius & Herrick, 1988). We're all familiar with advising responses: "If you're so unhappy, you should just quit the job"; "Just tell him what you think"; "You should take some time off."

Even though advice might be just what a person needs, there are several reasons why it often isn't helpful. First, it may not offer the best suggestion about how to act. There's often a temptation to tell others how you would behave in their place, but it's important to realize that what's right for one person may not be right for another. Second, the position of "advice recipient" is a potentially unwelcome identity because it implies that the advice giver may be superior and that somehow the receiver is at fault (Shaw & Hepburn, 2013). Third, a related consequence of advising is that it often allows others to avoid responsibility for their decisions. A partner who follows a suggestion of yours that doesn't work out can always pin the blame on you. Finally, people often don't want advice: They may not be ready to accept it and instead may simply need to talk out their thoughts and feelings.

Studies on advice giving (summarized in MacGeorge et al., 2008) offer the following important considerations when trying to help others:

- *Is the advice needed?* If the person has already taken a course of action, giving advice after the fact ("I can't believe you got back together with him") is rarely appreciated.
- *Is the advice wanted?* People generally don't value unsolicited advice. It's usually best to ask if the speaker is interested in hearing your counsel. Remember that sometimes people just want a listening ear, not solutions to their problems.
- *Is the advice given in the right sequence?* Advice is more likely to be received after the listener first offers empathizing, paraphrasing, and questioning responses to understand the speaker and the situation better.
- *Is the advice coming from an expert?* If you want to offer advice about anything from car purchasing to relationship managing, it's important to have experience and success in those matters. If you *don't* have

FOCUS ON RESEARCH
Exchanging Advice Online

Once upon a time, if you wanted medical recommendations from someone other than a professional, you picked up the phone and called a friend or family member. Today, it's not uncommon to solicit advice from a virtual stranger—with *virtual* being the operative term.

Elizabeth Sillence categorized and analyzed advice exchanges in an online breast cancer support group site. Here are some of her observations:

- Nearly 40 percent of the posted messages involved advice seeking or giving—so it's clearly a site where people look for and extend counsel.
- Very few posters asked the community to tell them what they "should do." They typically requested "comments" rather than "advice."
- Recommendations were often couched within personal narratives, using a "here's what worked for me" format.
- Advice seekers tried to find people who were "in the same boat," preferring to hear from those whose situations matched their own.

These observations reinforce some important principles about communicating advice. People are more willing to listen to advice that's requested, especially when it comes from a credible, empathic source. When giving advice, it's best to offer it as openhanded information rather than as heavyhanded prescriptions.

Sillence, E. (2013). Giving and receiving peer advice in an online breast cancer support group. *Cyberpsychology, Behavior, and Social Networking, 16*, 480–485.

expertise, it's a good idea to offer the speaker supportive responses, then encourage the person to seek out expert counsel.

- *Is the advisor a close and trusted person?* Although sometimes we seek out advice from people we don't know well (perhaps because they have expertise), in most cases we value advice given within the context of a close and ongoing interpersonal relationship.
- *Is the advice offered in a sensitive, face-saving manner?* No one likes to feel bossed or belittled, even if the advice is good (Miczo & Burgoon, 2008). Remember that messages have both content and relational dimensions, and sometimes the unstated relational messages when giving advice ("I'm smarter than you"; "You're not bright enough to figure this out yourself") will keep people from hearing counsel.

WHICH STYLE TO USE?

By now, it should be clear that there are many ways to respond as a listener. You also can see that each style has advantages and disadvantages. This leads to the important question: Which style is best? There isn't a simple answer to this question. All response styles have the potential to help others accept their situation, feel better, and have a sense of control over their problems (Imhof, 2003; Weger et al., 2014).

As a rule of thumb, it's probably wise to begin with responses from the left and middle of the listening response continuum: silent listening, questioning, paraphrasing, empathizing, and supporting. Once you've gathered the facts and demonstrated your interest and concern, it's likely that the speaker will be more receptive to (and perhaps even ask for) your analyzing, evaluating, and advising responses.

You can boost the odds of choosing the best style in each situation by considering three factors. First, think about the *situation*, and match your response to the nature of the problem. People sometimes need your advice. In other cases, your encouragement and support will be most helpful; and in still other instances, your analysis or judgment may be truly useful. And, as you have seen, there are times when your questioning and paraphrasing can help others find their own answer.

Besides considering the situation, you also should think about the *other person* when deciding which approach to use. It's important to be sure that the other person is open to receiving *any* kind of help. Furthermore, you need to be confident that you will be regarded as someone whose support is valuable. The same response that would be accepted with gratitude when it comes from one communicator can be regarded as unhelpful when it's offered by the wrong person (Clark et al., 1998; Sullivan, 1996).

It's also important to match the type of response you offer with the style of the person to whom it is directed (Bippus, 2001). One study found that highly rational people tend to respond more positively to advice than do more emotional people (Feng & Lee, 2010). Many communicators are extremely defensive and aren't capable of receiving analysis or judgments without lashing out. Still others aren't equipped to think through problems clearly enough to profit from questioning and paraphrasing. Sophisticated listeners choose a style that fits the person.

Finally, think about *yourself* when deciding how to respond. Most of us reflexively use one or two styles. You may be best at listening quietly, posing a question, or paraphrasing from time to time. Or perhaps you are especially insightful and can offer a truly useful analysis of the problem. Of course, it's also possible to rely on a response style that is *unhelpful.* You may be overly judgmental or too eager to advise, even when your suggestions are invited or productive. As you think about how to respond to another's problems, consider your weaknesses as well as your strengths.

CHECK YOUR UNDERSTANDING

Objective 7.1 Understand the nature of listening and the listening styles that interpersonal communicators use.

Listening is both more frequent and less emphasized than speaking. Despite its relative invisibility, listening is at least as important as speaking. Research shows that good listening is vital for both personal and professional success.

Listening is the process of making sense of others' spoken messages. We listen to many messages mindlessly, but it's important to listen mindfully in a variety of situations. We also listen to others based on our personal styles and listening goals. Sometimes our listening is task oriented; other times it's more relational, analytical, or critical. Good listeners match their styles with the needs of the situation.

Q: Keep a diary of your listening behavior for a representative day. Identify your listening style(s) in each situation you record. Which styles did you use most and least often? How satisfied are you with this finding?

Objective 7.2 Recognize the challenges that can impede effective listening.

Most peoples' understanding of listening is based on poor listening habits and also on several misconceptions that communicators need to correct. Mindful listening is not easy; rather, it is a challenge that requires much effort and talent. Several barriers can

hamper effective listening: personal concerns, information overload, rapid thought, and both internal and external noise. Even careful listening does not mean that all listeners will receive the same message. A wide variety of factors discussed in this chapter can result in widely varying interpretations of even simple statements.

Q: For each entry in the diary from Objective 7.1, evaluate how effectively you listened. Which of the challenges described in this chapter interfered most with your listening? How can you better manage those challenges?

Objective 7.3 Identify the five components of the interpersonal listening process.

Listening consists of several components: hearing, attending to a message, understanding the statement, recalling the message after the passage of time, and responding to the speaker. Roadblocks to effective communication can occur at each stage of the process.

Q: Use the events in your diary to identify your strengths and weaknesses as a listener. Which components of the listening process do you manage well, and which are problematic? How can you address the problematic components?

Objective 7.4 Effectively use a variety of reflective and directive listening responses.

Listening responses are important because they let us know if others are truly tuned in to what we're ying. Listening responses can be placed on a continuum. More reflective/less directive responses include silent listening, questioning, paraphrasing, and empathizing. These put a premium on gathering information and showing interest and concern. Less reflective/more directive responses include supporting, analyzing, evaluating, and advising. These put a premium on offering input and direction. It is possible to use the "more reflective" listening responses to help people arrive at their own decisions without offering advice or evaluation. The most effective listeners use several styles, depending on the situation, the other person, and their own personal skills and motivation.

Q: Use your listening diary to identify your most and least frequent response styles. How satisfied are you with your findings? How can you respond more effectively?

KEY TERMS

- Advising (228)
- Ambushing (212)
- Analytical listening (208)
- Analyzing (227)
- Attending (213)
- Closed questions (218)
- Counterfeit questions (218)
- Critical listening (208)
- Defensive listening (212)
- Empathizing (223)
- Evaluating (228)

- Filling in gaps (212)
- Hearing (206)
- Insulated listening (212)
- Listening (206)
- Listening fidelity (214)
- Mindful listening (207)
- Mindless listening (206)
- Open questions (218)
- Paraphrasing (221)
- Pseudolistening (212)
- Questioning (217)

- Relational listening (208)
- Remembering (215)
- Responding (215)
- Selective listening (212)
- Silent listening (217)
- Sincere questions (218)
- Stage hogging (212)
- Supporting (225)
- Task-oriented listening (208)
- Understanding (214)

ACTIVITIES

1. With your classmates, develop a listening code of ethics. What responsibility do communicators have to listen as carefully and thoughtfully as possible to other speakers? Are there ever cases where the poor listening habits listed on pages 211–212 (for example, pseudolistening, stage hogging, and defensive listening) are justified? How would you feel if you knew that others weren't listening to you?

2. Explore the benefits of silent listening by using a "Talking Stick." Richard Hyde (1993) developed this exercise from the Native American tradition of "council." Gather a group of people in a circle, and designate a particular item as the talking stick. Participants will then pass the stick around the circle. Participants may speak

a. only when holding the stick;

b. for as long as they hold the stick; and

c. without interruption from anyone else in the circle.

When a member is through speaking, the stick passes to the left and the speaker surrendering the stick must wait until it has made its way around the circle before speaking again.

After each member of the group has had the chance to speak, discuss how this experience differs from more common approaches to listening. Decide how the desirable parts of this method could be introduced in everyday conversations.

3. Practice your ability to paraphrase by following these steps.

a. Choose a partner, and designate one of yourselves as A and the other as B. Find a subject on which you and your partner seem to disagree—a personal dispute, a philosophical or moral issue, or perhaps a matter of personal taste.

b. A begins by making a statement on the subject. B's job is to paraphrase the idea. In this step, B should only reiterate what he or she heard A say, without adding any judgment or interpretation. B's job here is simply to *understand* A—not to agree or disagree with A.

c. A responds by telling B whether the response was accurate and by making any necessary additions or corrections to clarify the message.

d. B then paraphrases the revised statement. This process should continue until A is sure that B understands him or her.

e. Now B and A reverse roles and repeat the procedure in steps a–d. Continue the conversation until both partners are satisfied that they have explained themselves fully and have been understood by the other person.

After the discussion has ended, consider how this process differed from typical conversations on controversial topics. Was there greater understanding here? Do the partners feel better about one another? Finally, ask yourself how your life might change if you used more paraphrasing in everyday conversations.

4. Explore the various types of listening responses by completing the following steps.

a. Join with two partners to form a trio. Designate members as A, B, and C.

b. A begins by sharing a current, real problem with B. The problem needn't be a major life crisis, but it should be a real one. B should respond in whatever way seems most helpful. C's job is to categorize each response by B as silent listening, questioning, paraphrasing, empathizing, supporting, analyzing, evaluating, or advising.

c. After a 4- to 5-minute discussion, C should summarize B's response styles. A then describes which of the styles were most helpful and which were not helpful.

d. Repeat the same process two more times, switching roles so that each person has been in all of the positions.

e. Based on their findings, the threesome should develop conclusions about what combination of response styles can be most helpful.

SCORING FOR ASSESSING YOUR COMMUNICATION (PAGE 209)

Add your responses to items 1–4. This is your Relational Listening score: _____. Undergraduate students had an average score of 22, with most scoring between 21 and 24.

Add your responses to items 5–8. This is your Analytical Listening score: _____. Undergraduate students had an average score of 19, with most scoring between 17 and 21.

Add your responses to items 9–12. This is your Task Listening score: _____. Undergraduate students had an average score of 20, with most scoring between 18 and 22.

Add your responses to items 13–16. This is your Critical Listening score: _____. Undergraduate students had an average score of 18, with most scoring between 16 and 20.

chapter 8

Emotions

CHAPTER OUTLINE

FEATURES

LEARNING OBJECTIVES

8.1 Explain how emotions are experienced and expressed.

8.2 Describe the various personal and social influences on emotional expression.

8.3 Understand how to express your emotions appropriately and effectively.

8.4 Distinguish between facilitative and debilitative emotions, and explain how reappraisal may be used to manage emotions effectively.

IMAGINE HOW different your life would be if you lost your ability to experience emotions. An emotionless world would be free of boredom, frustration, fear, and loneliness. But the cost of such a pain-free existence would be the loss of emotions such as joy, pride, excitement, and love. Few of us would be willing to make that sort of trade-off.

Daniel Goleman (1995) coined the term **emotional intelligence** to describe the ability to understand and manage one's own emotions and to be sensitive to others' feelings. Goleman maintains that cognitive IQ instruments are not the only way to measure one's talents and that success in the world depends in great part on one's "EQ"—emotional intelligence quota. In support of that claim, studies show that emotional intelligence is positively linked with self-esteem and life satisfaction (Carmeli et al., 2009; Singh & Woods, 2008), healthy conflict communication (Smith et al., 2008), empathic listening abilities (Pence & Vickery, 2012), and effective workplace interactions (Kidwell et al., 2011; Ybarra et al., 2011). Some employers even use emotional intelligence measures as part of their personnel selection process (Iliescu et al., 2012).

MEDIA CLIP
Intelligence of Another Variety:
The Big Bang Theory

Sheldon Cooper (Jim Parsons) is no dummy: He's a theoretical physicist who holds two doctorates. But although he may be book smart, Sheldon lacks emotional intelligence. He's short on empathy, social skills, and the ability to express his emotions effectively. He can also be blunt and sarcastic (punctuating his wisecracks with "bazinga!"). Whereas viewers may find Cooper's ineptitude amusing, it usually doesn't help his relationships with friends and coworkers.

Think of some of the other characters on *The Big Bang Theory* and you'll realize that emotional intelligence is best seen on a continuum—and some people have more of it than others. The good news is that emotional intelligence can grow, as Sheldon demonstrates. Over the course of several seasons, he begins picking up on emotional cues from others: very slowly.

Stop for a moment and identify someone you know who is emotionally intelligent. Perhaps it's a family member who is in touch with a wide range of feelings without being overwhelmed by them or a boss who makes wise and rational choices even under stress. Now think of a person who might be lacking emotional intelligence. Maybe it's a colleague who is uptight and dismissive about honest human feelings or a friend who blows up at the smallest inconvenience. And finally, assess your own emotional intelligence. How well do *you* understand and manage your emotions, and how sensitive are you to others' feelings? The Assessing Your Communication tool on page 252 can help you make that call.

Because emotions are such an important part of human communication, in this chapter we explore what feelings are, discuss the ways they are handled in contemporary society, and see how recognizing and expressing them can improve relationships. We also provide some guidelines that should give you a clearer idea of when and how to express your emotions constructively. Finally, we explore methods for coping with troublesome feelings and enhancing positive emotions.

WHAT ARE EMOTIONS?

Suppose an extraterrestrial visitor asked you to explain emotions. How would you answer? You might start by saying that emotions are things that we feel. But this doesn't say much, for in turn you would probably describe feelings as synonymous with emotions. Social scientists generally agree that there are several components to the phenomena we label as an emotion (Gentsch et al., 2014; Planalp et al., 2006).

PHYSIOLOGICAL CHANGES

When a person experiences strong emotions, many bodily changes occur (Chang et al., 2013; Rochman & Diamond, 2008). For example, the physical components of fear include an increased heartbeat, a rise in blood pressure, an increase in adrenaline secretions, an elevated blood sugar level, a slowing of digestion, and a dilation of pupils. Marriage researcher John Gottman notes that symptoms such as these also occur when couples engage in intense conflicts (Gottman & Silver, 1999). He calls the condition "flooding" and has found that it impedes effective problem solving.

Research supports the notion that individuals experience emotions not just in the mind, but throughout the body (Nummenmaa et al., 2014). Figure 8.1 shows that disgust may turn our stomachs, fear can result in tightening of the chest, and happiness makes us feel "warm all over." Physiological

FIGURE 8.1 Body Temperatures for Various Emotions

Nummenmaa, L., Glerean, E., Hari, R., & Hietanen, J. K. (2014). Bodily maps of emotions. *PNAS, 111,* 646–651.

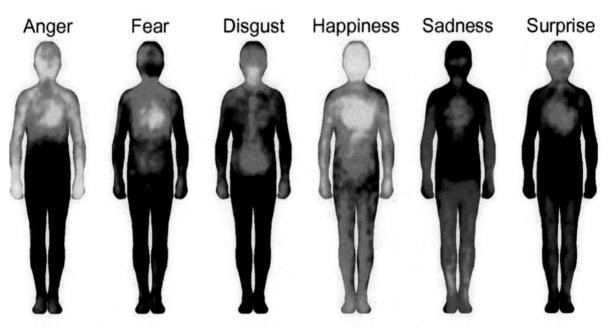

Anger Fear Disgust Happiness Sadness Surprise

sensations such as these can offer a significant clue to your emotions once you become aware of them.

NONVERBAL REACTIONS

Not all physical changes that accompany emotions are internal. Feelings are often apparent by observable changes to appearance, such as blushing or perspiring. Other changes involve behavior: a distinctive facial expression, posture, gestures, different vocal tone and rate, and so on. These reactions can often be noticed and interpreted by others. Subjects who watched short videos of basketball and table tennis players could determine from the players' nonverbal behavior alone whether the athletes were winning or losing, regardless of the subject's own experience with the sport (Furley & Schweizer, 2014).

Although it's reasonably easy to tell when someone is feeling a strong emotion, it's more difficult to be certain exactly what that emotion might be. A slumped posture and sigh may be a sign of sadness, or it may signal fatigue. Likewise, widened eyes might indicate excitement, or it may be an outward sign of fear. As you learned in Chapter 6, nonverbal behavior is usually ambiguous, and it's dangerous to assume that it can be "read" with much accuracy.

Although we usually think of nonverbal behavior as the reaction to an emotional state, there may be times when the reverse is true—when nonverbal behavior *causes* emotions. Research shows that people can actually create emotional states by altering their facial expressions. When volunteers in one study were coached to smile, they reported feeling better, and when they altered their expressions to look unhappy, they felt worse than before (Kleinke et al., 1998). Clenching your fists can help you feel stronger (Schubert & Koole, 2009) and so can adopting power poses (see Chapter 6, page 188). And "jumping for joy" is more than just an emotional reaction. Research suggests that the act of jumping up and down can actually trigger happiness (Shafir et al., 2013). As behavioral scientists like to say, it can be easier to act yourself into new ways of feeling than to feel yourself into new ways of acting.

There's also a connection between verbalizing emotions and nonverbal reactions. One study showed that participants who generated words associated with pride and disappointment experienced a change in posture (Oosterwijk et al., 2009). They unconsciously stood taller when talking about pride and slumped when using words for disappointment. The participants also experienced emotions associated with their words (e.g., feeling sad when speaking about disappointment). This reminds us that verbal and nonverbal expressions of emotion are often interconnected.

COGNITIVE INTERPRETATIONS

Although there may be instances when there is a direct connection between physical behavior and emotional states, in most situations, the mind plays an important role in determining how we feel (Genov, 2001). As noted earlier, some physiological components of fear are a racing heart, perspiration, tense muscles, and elevated blood pressure. Interestingly enough, these symptoms are similar to the physical changes that accompany excitement, joy, and other emotions. In other words, if we were to measure the physical condition of someone having a strong emotion, we would have a hard time knowing whether that person was trembling with fear or quivering with excitement. For example, Stephen Mallalieu and his colleagues (2003) found that some successful athletes experiencing precompetition stress labeled their feelings in positive emotional terms and interpreted their emotion as facilitating their work. The same holds true for emotion interpretation about public speaking: Telling yourself "I am excited" rather than "Calm down" will generally lead to a more successful performance (Brooks, 2013). As the old adage goes, you may not be able to get rid of butterflies in your stomach, but you can get them to fly in formation.

The recognition that the bodily components of most emotions are similar led some psychologists to conclude that the experience of fright, joy, or anger comes primarily from the labels—and the accompanying cognitive interpretations—we give to our physical symptoms (Kagan, 2007). Psychologist Philip Zimbardo (1977) offers a good example of this principle:

> I notice I'm perspiring while lecturing. From that I infer I am nervous. If it occurs often, I might even label myself a "nervous person." Once I have the label, the next question I must answer is "Why am I nervous?" Then I start to search for an appropriate explanation. I might notice some students leaving the room, or being inattentive. I am nervous because I'm not giving a good lecture. That makes me nervous. How do I know it's not good? Because I'm boring my audience. I am nervous because I am a boring lecturer and I want to be a good lecturer. I feel inadequate. Maybe I should open a delicatessen instead. Just then a student says, "It's hot in here, I'm perspiring and it makes it tough to concentrate on your lecture." Instantly, I'm no longer "nervous" or "boring." (p. 53)

Social scientists refer to this process as **reappraisal**—rethinking the meaning of emotionally charged events in ways that alter their emotional impact (Berger & Lee, 2011; Troy et al., 2013). Research shows that reappraisal is vastly superior to suppressing one's feelings: It often leads to lower stress and increased productivity (Moore et al., 2008; Wallace et al., 2009). Reappraisal has both psychological and physiological benefits (Denson et al., 2011; Hopp et al., 2011), regardless of a person's age or culture (Goodman & Southam-Gerow, 2010; Haga et al., 2009).

Reappraisal also has relational benefits. One study found that couples who regularly step back from their conflicts and reappraise them from a neutral perspective have higher levels of relational satisfaction (Finkel et al., 2013). In essence, these couples reduce the emotional impact of their disputes by looking at them rationally and dispassionately. (Use the key words "Finkel" and "marriage" to find a TEDˣ talk on this research.)

We walk you through the reappraisal process later in this chapter when we describe how to dispute your irrational beliefs.

VERBAL EXPRESSION

As you read in Chapter 6, nonverbal behavior is a powerful way of communicating emotion (Planalp, 1998). But sometimes words are necessary to express feelings. Saying "I'm really angry" is clearer and more helpful

Annoyed	Angry	Furious
Pensive	Sad	Grieving
Content	Happy	Ecstatic
Anxious	Afraid	Terrified
Liking	Loving	Adoring

FIGURE 8.2 **Intensity of Emotions**

than stomping out of the room, and "I'm feeling nervous" might help explain a pained expression on your face. Putting emotions into words can help you manage them more effectively (Lieberman et al., 2007), whereas leaving them unspoken can result in negative mental and even physiological effects (Eaker et al., 2007).

Some researchers believe there are several "basic" or "primary" emotions (Katzir & Eyal, 2013; Phillips & Slessor, 2011). However, there isn't much agreement among scholars about what those emotions are or about what makes them "basic" (Tracy & Randles, 2011). Moreover, emotions that are primary in one culture may not be primary in others; and some emotions may have no equivalent in other cultures (Ferrari & Koyama, 2002; Zhong et al., 2008). Despite this debate, most scholars acknowledge that *anger, joy, fear,* and *sadness* are common and typical human emotions.

We experience most emotions with different degrees of intensity—and we use specific emotion words to represent these differences. Figure 8.2 illustrates this point. To say you're "annoyed" when a friend breaks an important promise, for example, would probably be an understatement. In other cases, people chronically overstate the strength of their feelings. To them, everything is "wonderful" or "terrible." The problem with this sort of exaggeration is that when a truly intense emotion comes along, they have no words left to describe it adequately. If chocolate chip cookies from the local bakery are "fantastic," how does it feel to fall in love?

INFLUENCES ON EMOTIONAL EXPRESSION

Each of us is born with the disposition to reveal our emotions, at least nonverbally. But over time, a wide range of differences develops in emotional expression. In the next few pages, we look at some influences that shape how people communicate their feelings.

PERSONALITY

Science has established an increasingly clear relationship between personality and the way people experience and communicate emotions (Gross et al., 1998; McCroskey et al., 2004). For example, extroverted people report more positive emotions in everyday life than more introverted individuals (Lucas et al., 2008). Conversely, people with neurotic personalities—those with a tendency to worry, be anxious, and feel apprehensive—report more negative emotions than less neurotic individuals.

Although personality can be a powerful force, it doesn't have to govern your communication satisfaction. For instance, people who are shy by

FOCUS ON RESEARCH
Saying "I Love You": Different Cultures, Different Rules

It's been said that love is the universal language. To the contrary, Elisabeth Gareis and Richard Wilkins have found that saying "I love you" (or its equivalent in other languages) has very different meanings around the world.

In one study, the authors surveyed college students from a variety of countries and cultures. They found significant differences about when, where, how often, and with whom the phrase "I love you" is used. The investigation revealed that Americans say "I love you" more frequently and with more people than do members of most other cultures. By contrast, Middle Easterners in the survey believed that "I love you" should only be expressed between spouses. They warned that American men who use the phrase casually with Middle Eastern women might be misinterpreted as making a marriage proposal. Participants from several other cultures (e.g.,

Eastern Europe, India, Korea) also reported saying "I love you" sparingly, believing that the power of expressing their love would be diminished if used too often.

Interestingly, many participants for whom English is a second language said they were more likely to make declarations of love in English than in their native tongues. That matches what other researchers found in a study of Mandarin-English bilinguals. Participants in that study said it's easier to express emotions in English because of more relaxed social constraints in English-speaking contexts. They also had stronger physiological responses to saying "I love you" in English than in Mandarin.

This line of research shows that although love may be a universal emotion, the rules for *communicating* that sentiment vary greatly from culture to culture.

Caldwell-Harris, C. L., Tong, J., Lung, W., & Poo, S. (2011). Physiological reactivity to emotional phrases in Mandarin-English bilinguals. *International Journal of Bilingualism, 15,* 329–352.

Gareis, E., & Wilkins, R. (2011). Communicating love: A sociocultural perspective. In C. T. Salmon (Ed.), *Communication Yearbook* (Vol. 35, pp. 199–239). New York: Routledge.

nature can devise comfortable and effective strategies for reaching out, such as making contact with others online (Yen et al., 2012). Online relationships shouldn't be a way to avoid in-person communication (Ebeling-Witte et al., 2007), but they can be a rewarding way to gain confidence that will pay off in more satisfying face-to-face relationships.

CULTURE

Although people around the world experience the same emotions, the same events can generate quite different feelings in different cultures. The notion of eating snails might bring a smile of delight to some residents of France, although it would cause many North Americans to grimace in disgust. Culture also has an effect on how emotions are valued. One study (Tsai et al., 2006) found that Asian Americans and Hong Kong Chinese value "low arousal positive affect" such as being calm, relaxed, and peaceful. European Americans, by contrast, tend to value "high arousal positive affect" such as excitement, enthusiasm, and elation. More specifically, communication researcher Christina Kotchemidova (2010) notes that the United States is known internationally as a "culture of cheerfulness." She cites a Polish author who describes U.S. expressiveness this way: "Wow! Great! How nice! That's

"If I were a car, you could find the words."

fantastic! I had a terrific time! It was wonderful! Have a nice day! Americans. So damned cheerful" (p. 209).

Cultural background influences the way we interpret others' emotions as well as the way we express our own. In one experiment (Matsumoto, 1993), an ethnically varied group of students—European American, Latino American, African American, and Asian American—identified the type, intensity, and appropriateness of emotional expression in photos representing various social situations. Ethnicity led to considerable differences in the way subjects gauged others' emotional states. For example, African Americans perceived the emotions in the photos as the most intense, whereas Asian Americans perceived them as the least intense. Ethnicity also shaped ideas about appropriate rules for expressing one's own emotions. European Americans perceived the display of emotions as more appropriate than did the other groups; Asian Americans perceived their display as least appropriate. In a more recent study with American and Chinese subjects (using videos instead of photos), researchers found that positive expressions were rated as more intense when there was a cultural match between the expressor and the judge (Zhu et al., 2013). These findings remind us that, in a multicultural society, one element of communicative competence is the ability to understand our own cultural filters when judging others' emotion-related behaviors.

One of the most significant factors influencing emotional expression is the position of a culture on the individualism-collectivism spectrum (Halberstadt & Lozada, 2011; Kim-Prieto & Eid, 2004). Members of collectivistic cultures (such as Japan and India) prize harmony among members of their "in-group" and discourage expression of any negative emotions that might upset relationships among people who belong to it. By contrast, members of highly individualistic cultures, such as the United States and Canada, feel comfortable revealing their feelings to people with whom they are close. Individualists and collectivists also handle emotional expression with members of out-groups differently: Whereas individualists are quite frank about expressing negative emotions toward outsiders, collectivists are more likely to hide emotions such as disliking (Triandis, 1994). It's easy to see how differences in display rules can lead to communication problems. For example, individualistic North Americans might view collectivistic Asians as less than candid, whereas people raised in Asia could easily regard North Americans as overly demonstrative.

GENDER

Even within a culture, gender roles often shape the ways in which men and women experience and express their emotions (Lee et al., 2013; Wester et al., 2002). For example, research suggests that women are faster than men at recognizing emotions from facial cues (Hampson et al., 2006); are better at identifying multiple emotions (Hall & Matsumoto, 2004); are better at judging emotions from eye behavior alone (Kirkland et al., 2013); and are more physiologically attuned to emotions than men (Canli et al., 2002).

Research on emotional expression suggests that there is also some truth in the cultural stereotype of the inexpressive male and the more demonstrative female. On the whole, women seem more likely than men to verbally and nonverbally express a wide range of feelings (Burgoon & Bacue, 2003; Palomares, 2008). In fact, men are more likely to experience *alexithymia* (meaning "without words for emotions"), which can lead to relational challenges (Hesse et al., 2012). One study showed that fathers mask their emotions more than mothers do, which led their children to have more difficulty reading their fathers' emotional expressions (Dunsmore et al., 2009). When online, the same differences between male and female emotional expressiveness apply. For example, women are more likely to use emoticons to clarify their feelings (Brunet & Schmidt, 2010), whereas men are more likely to use emoticons sarcastically (Wolf, 2000). Women also express more affection on Facebook than do men (Mansson & Myers, 2011).

The point is, although men and women generally experience the same emotions, there are some significant differences in the ways they read and express them (Brody & Hall, 2008). These differences are due in large measure to social conventions, which we discuss now.

MEDIA CLIP
Social Rules and Emotions: *Mad Men*

In the 1960s, advertising was a glamour career and New York's Madison Avenue was the center of the action. The world was different in many ways. Many people smoked, even in elevators, and the two-martini lunch was commonplace. The executive suite was run by men. Casual sexual harassment, although no less distasteful than today, was often tolerated by the "girls" in the typing pool.

Relationships then evoked a wealth of emotions, but the rules for expressing those feelings were different. Women—whether at home or in the workplace—were expected to be deferential and positive. The ideal professional man was suave and unruffled. *Mad Men* makes it clear that social conventions masked a wealth of intense feelings about relationships. It also shows how important it seemed to avoid communicating about those feelings and the costs of doing so.

It's easy to feel smug when looking back at what seems like such dated social conventions—until you wonder what people a half-century from now will think of us.

SOCIAL CONVENTIONS AND ROLES

In mainstream U.S. society, the unwritten rules of communication discourage the direct expression of most emotions (Durik et al., 2006; Shimanoff, 1985). Count the number of genuine emotional expressions you hear over a 2- or 3-day period ("I'm angry"; "I feel embarrassed") and you'll discover that such expressions are rare. People are generally comfortable making statements of fact and often delight in expressing their opinions, but they rarely disclose how they feel.

Not surprisingly, the emotions that people do share directly are usually positive ("I'm happy to say . . ."; "I really enjoyed . . ."). Communicators are reluctant to send messages that embarrass or threaten the "face" of others (Shimanoff, 1988). Scholars offer detailed descriptions of the ways contemporary society discourages expressions of anger. When compared to past centuries, North Americans today strive to suppress this "unpleasant" emotion in almost every context, including child rearing, the workplace, and personal relationships (Kotchemidova, 2010). One study of married couples (Shimanoff, 1985) revealed that the partners shared complimentary feelings ("I love you") or face-saving ones ("I'm sorry I yelled at you"). They also willingly disclosed both positive and negative feelings about absent third parties ("I like Fred"; "I'm uncomfortable around Gloria"). On the other hand, the husbands and wives rarely verbalized face-threatening feelings ("I'm disappointed in you") or hostility ("I'm mad at you").

Researchers use the term **emotion labor** to describe situations in which managing and even suppressing emotions is both appropriate and necessary. Studies show that emotion labor is an important component of many if not most occupations (see the At Work box below for specific examples).

EMOTION LABOR ON THE JOB

@WORK

The rules for expressing emotions in the workplace are clearly different from those in personal life. In intimate relationships (at least in mainstream Western culture), it's often important to tell friends, family, and loved ones how you feel. In the workplace, however, it can be just as important to *conceal* emotions for the sake of clients, customers, coworkers, and supervisors—and also to protect your job.

Emotion labor—the process of managing and sometimes suppressing emotions—has been studied in a variety of occupational contexts. Here are a few examples:

- If firefighters don't mask their emotions of fear, disgust, and stress, it impedes their ability to help the people whose lives they are trying to save. Emotion-management training is therefore vital for new firefighters (Scott & Myers, 2005).
- Correctional officers at two minimum-security prisons described the challenge of needing to be "warm, nurturing, and respectful" to inmates while also being "suspicious, strong, and tough." The officers acknowledged that it's taxing to manage competing emotions and juggle conflicting demands (Tracy, 2005).

- Money is an emotion-laden topic, which means that financial planners often engage in emotion labor. Researchers concluded that "relationships and communication with clients may indeed be more central to the work of financial planners than portfolio performance reports and changes in estate tax laws" (Miller & Koesten, 2008, p. 23).

Whereas some of these occupations deal with life-and-death situations, emotion management is equally important in less intensive jobs (Eschenfelder, 2012; Sanders, 2013). For instance, most customer-service positions require working with people who may express their dissatisfaction in angry and inappropriate ways ("I hate this store—I'm never shopping here again!"). In situations such as these, it's usually unwise to "fight fire with fire," even if that's your natural impulse. Instead, competent on-the-job communicators can use the listening, defense-reducing, and conflict-management skills described in Chapters 7, 11, and 12.

It's not always easy to manage emotions, especially when you're feeling fearful, stressed, angry, or defensive. Nevertheless, doing the work of emotion labor is often vital for success on the job.

Just as a muscle withers away when it is unused, our capacity to recognize and act on certain emotions decreases without practice. It's hard to cry after spending most of one's life fulfilling the role society expects of a man (Cole & Spalding, 2009; Pollack, 1999). After years of denying anger, the ability to recognize that feeling takes real effort. And, for someone who has never acknowledged love for one's friends, accepting that emotion can be difficult indeed.

SOCIAL MEDIA

Communicators generally express more emotion online than they do in person (Derks et al., 2008). In some cases, that's good news. Those who have trouble sharing feelings face to face may find a freedom to do so behind the safety of a keyboard or touchscreen. Consider how it might be easier to type, rather than say, the words "I'm embarrassed" or "I love you."

Unfortunately, as discussed in Chapter 1, online disinhibition can also encourage emotional outbursts and tirades. This kind of venting can be hazardous to interpersonal relations, and it probably won't make you feel better (see the Focus on Research box on page 251).

Social media can also feed emotional responses. For instance, regularly checking a romantic partner's Facebook site may spur feelings of jealousy, resulting in relational dissatisfaction (Elphinston & Noller, 2011; Locatelli et al., 2012). The subtitle of one study asks this question: "Does Facebook Bring out the Green-Eyed Monster of Jealousy?" (Muise et al., 2009). The short answer is "yes, it can"—especially when the viewer is already suspicious, and more so for women than men (Muise et al., 2014). When keeping updated turns into an unhealthy surveillance of loved ones—or former loved ones (Marshall, 2012)—it can take an emotional toll. We have more to say about jealousy and rumination later in this chapter.

The bottom line is that both senders and receivers experience emotions more intensely online. It's wise to keep this in mind before hitting send on emotionally charged messages and before jumping to conclusions about ambiguous online information.

EMOTIONAL CONTAGION

Along with cultural rules, social roles, and social media, our emotions are also affected by the feelings of those around us through **emotional contagion**, the process by which emotions are transferred from one person to another (Dasborough et al., 2009; Hatfield et al., 1994). As Daniel Goleman (1995, p. 115) observes, "We catch feelings from one another as though they were some kind of social virus." There is evidence that students "catch" the mood of their teachers (Bakker, 2005), customers are affected by the emotions of employees who serve them (Jiangang et al., 2011), husbands and wives influence each other's feelings directly

Zombies like these in the TV show *The Walking Dead* are transformed from normal humans through a form of contagion. In everyday life, emotional contagion can transmit feelings with surprising rapidity.

(Randall et al., 2013), and that coworkers can affect each other's emotions—especially positive ones—with their online communication (Belkin, 2008).

Although people differ in the extent to which they're susceptible to emotional contagion (Lo Coco et al., 2014; Lundqvist, 2008), most of us recognize the degree to which emotions are "infectious." You can probably recall instances in which being around a calm person leaves you feeling more at peace, or when your previously sunny mood was spoiled by contact with a grouch. Researchers have demonstrated that this process can occur quickly and with little or no verbal communication. In one study (Sullins, 1991), two volunteers completed a survey that identified their moods. They spent two unsupervised minutes together, ostensibly waiting for the researcher to return to the room. At the end of that time, they completed another emotional survey. Time after time, the brief exposure resulted in the less expressive partner's moods coming to resemble the feelings of the more expressive one. If an expressive communicator can shape another person's feelings with so little input in such a short time, it's easy to understand how emotions can be even more "infectious" with prolonged contact (Du et al., 2011).

GUIDELINES FOR EXPRESSING EMOTIONS

A wide range of research supports the value of expressing emotions appropriately. Starting at a young age, the way parents talk to their children about emotions has a powerful effect on the children's development. John Gottman and his associates (1997) identified two distinct parenting styles: "emotion coaching" and "emotion dismissing." They show how the coaching approach gives children skills for communicating about feelings in later life that lead to much more satisfying relationships. In fact, children who grow up in families where parents dismiss emotions are at higher risk for behavior problems than those who are raised in families that practice emotion coaching (Lunkenheimer et al., 2007; Young, 2009).

At the most basic physiological level, people who know how to share their feelings appropriately are healthier than those who don't. Inexpressive people—those who avoid their feelings and impulses and deny distress—are more likely to get a host of ailments, including cancer, asthma, and heart disease (Consedine et al., 2002; Quartana & Burns, 2010). However, people who are overly expressive also suffer physiologically. When people lash out verbally, their blood pressure jumps an average of 20 points; and in some people, it increases by as much as 100 points (Mayne, 1999; Siegman & Snow, 1997). The key to health, then, is to learn how to express emotions *constructively*. In a few pages, you will find guidelines for this important communication skill.

Beyond the physiological benefits, another advantage of expressing emotions effectively is the chance of improving relationships (Calkins & Mackler, 2011; Graham et al., 2008). As we explain in Chapter 9, self-disclosure is one path (although not the only one) to intimacy. Even on the job, many managers and organizational researchers are contradicting generations of tradition by suggesting that constructively expressing emotions can lead to career success as well as helping workers feel better (O'Neill, 2009; Zapf & Holz, 2006). Of course, the rules for expressing emotions on the job are usually stricter than those in personal relationships—especially when it comes to the expression of anger (Brescoll & Uhlmann, 2008; Kramer & Hess, 2002).

Despite its benefits, expressing emotions effectively isn't a simple matter (Fussell, 2002). It's obvious that showing every feeling of boredom, fear, anger, or frustration would get you in trouble. Even the indiscriminate sharing of positive feelings—love, affection, and so on—isn't always wise. On the other hand, withholding emotions can be personally frustrating and can keep relationships from growing and prospering.

The suggestions that follow can help you decide when and how to express your emotions. Combined with the guidelines for self-disclosure in Chapter 3, they can improve the effectiveness of your emotional expression.

RECOGNIZE YOUR FEELINGS

Answering the question "How do you feel?" isn't as easy for some people as for others (Peper, 2000). Communication researchers Melanie Booth-Butterfield and Steven Booth-Butterfield (1998; see also Samter & Burleson, 2005) found that some people (whom they term "affectively oriented") are much more aware of their own emotional states and use information about those feelings when making important decisions. By contrast, people with a low affective orientation are usually unaware of their emotions and tend to regard feelings as useless, unimportant information. The researchers summarize studies showing a relationship between awareness of feelings and a wide range of valuable traits, including positive relationships between parents and children, the ability to comfort others, sensitivity to nonverbal cues, and even skillful use of humor. In other words, being aware of one's feelings is an important ingredient in skillful communication.

Beyond being *aware* of one's feelings, research shows that it's valuable to be able to specifically *identify* one's emotions. Lisa Barrett and her colleagues (2001) found that college students who could pinpoint the negative emotions they experienced (such as "nervous," "angry," "sad," "ashamed," and "guilty") also had the best strategies for managing those emotions. Studies like this led researchers (Grewal & Salovey, 2005) to conclude that the ability to distinguish and label emotions is a vital component of emotional intelligence.

As you read earlier in this chapter, there are a number of ways in which feelings become recognizable. Physiological changes can be a clear sign of your emotional state. Monitoring nonverbal behaviors is another excellent way to keep in touch with your feelings. You can also recognize your emotions by monitoring your thoughts as well as the verbal messages you send to others. It's not far from the verbal statement "I hate this!" to the realization that you're angry (or bored, nervous, or embarrassed).

CHOOSE THE BEST LANGUAGE

Most people suffer from impoverished emotional vocabularies. Ask them how they're feeling and the response will almost always include the same terms: *good* or *bad*, *terrible* or *great*, and so on. Take a moment now and see how many feelings you can write down. After you've done your best, look at Table 8.1 on page 249 and see which ones you've missed from this admittedly incomplete list.

Many communicators think they are expressing feelings when, in fact, their statements are emotionally counterfeit. For example, it sounds emotionally revealing to say "I feel like going to a show" or "I feel we've been seeing too much of each other." But in fact, neither of these statements has any emotional content. In the first sentence, the word *feel* really stands for an intention: "I *want* to go to a show." In the second sentence, the "feeling" is really a thought: "I *think* we've been seeing too much of each other." You can recognize the absence of emotion in each case by adding a genuine word of feeling to it. For instance, "I'm *bored* and I want to go to a show" or "I think we've been seeing too much of each other and I feel *confined*."

Relying on a small vocabulary of feelings is as limiting as using only a few terms to describe colors. To say that the ocean in all its moods, the sky as it varies from day to day, and the color of your true love's eyes are all "blue" only tells a fraction of the story. Likewise, it's overly broad to use a term such as *good* or *great* to describe how you feel in situations as different as earning a high grade, finishing a marathon, and hearing the words "I love you" from a special person.

There are several ways to express a feeling verbally:

- Through *single words*: "I'm angry" (or "excited," "depressed," "curious," and so on).
- By describing *what's happening to you metaphorically*: "My stomach is tied in knots"; "I'm on top of the world."
- By describing *what you'd like to do*: "I want to run away"; "I'd like to give you a hug."

Finally, you can improve emotional expression by making it clear that your feeling is centered on a specific set of circumstances rather than the whole relationship. Instead of saying "I resent you," say "I get resentful when you don't keep your promises." Rather than "I'm bored with you," say "I get bored when you talk about money."

Using specifics to express emotions may lead to desired results in other ways. Facebook's protocol for managing photos offers a good example. In earlier versions of the social networking site, people who were tagged in an unseemly photo could flag the image as offensive and hope the poster would remove it. In newer versions, a form pops up with a polite request to remove the photo and reasons such as "It's embarrassing," "It's inappropriate," and "It makes me sad." The results of this more expressive approach are dramatic: Including a message such as "it's embarrassing" makes it 83 percent more likely that the poster will respond or delete it (Hochman, 2013). Not only is the newer approach more polite, it's also more emotionally descriptive

TABLE 8.1 Descriptive Terms for Emotions

affectionate	foolish	preoccupied
afraid	forlorn	pressured
aggravated	frustrated	quiet
amazed	furious	regretful
ambivalent	glad	relieved
angry	glum	remorseful
annoyed	grateful	repulsed
anxious	guilty	resentful
apathetic	happy	restless
ashamed	hateful	sad
bashful	helpless	secure
bewildered	hopeful	sentimental
bored	hopeless	sexy
calm	horrible	shaky
comfortable	hurt	shocked
concerned	hyper	shy
confident	impatient	silly
confused	inhibited	smug
content	insecure	sorry
curious	irritable	stubborn
defensive	isolated	stupid
delighted	jealous	subdued
depressed	joyful	surprised
desperate	lazy	suspicious
detached	lonely	sympathetic
devastated	lovestruck	tense
disappointed	loving	terrified
disgusted	mad	tired
disturbed	mean	touchy
eager	melancholy	trapped
ecstatic	miserable	uneasy
edgy	mortified	unsure
elated	nervous	useless
embarrassed	overwhelmed	vulnerable
empty	passionate	wacky
enthusiastic	peaceful	warm
excited	pessimistic	weak
exhausted	playful	weary
exhilarated	pleased	worried
fidgety	possessive	zany

and accurate. Evaluating others' actions as "offensive" doesn't tell them (or you) how you feel. We talk more about the difference between evaluation and description in Chapter 11.

SHARE MULTIPLE FEELINGS

Many times the feeling you express isn't the only one you're experiencing. For example, you might often express your anger but overlook the confusion, disappointment, frustration, sadness, or embarrassment that preceded or accompanies it. To understand the importance of expressing multiple emotions, consider the following examples. For each one, ask yourself two questions: How would I feel? What feelings might I express?

- An out-of-town friend has promised to arrive at your house at six o'clock. When your guest hasn't arrived by nine o'clock, you are convinced that a terrible accident has occurred. Just as you pick up the phone to call the police and local hospitals, your friend breezes in the door with an offhand remark about getting a late start.
- A friend has posted a photo of you online, along with a positive message. On one hand, you're flattered by the display of affection. On the other hand, it's a picture that doesn't paint you in the best light. You wish the friend had asked first.

In situations such as these you would probably feel several emotions. Consider the case of the overdue friend. Your first reaction to his arrival would probably be relief—"Thank goodness, he's safe!" But you would also be likely to feel anger—"Why didn't he phone to tell me he'd be late?" The second example would probably leave you feeling pleased, embarrassed, and angry—all at the same time.

Despite it being commonplace to experience several emotions at the same time (Carofiglio et al., 2008), we often communicate only one feeling—usually, the most negative one. In both of the preceding examples you might show only your anger, leaving the other person with little idea of the full range of your feelings. Consider the different reaction you would get by describing *all* your emotions in these situations as well as others.

RECOGNIZE THE DIFFERENCE BETWEEN FEELING AND ACTING

Just because you feel a certain way doesn't mean you must always act on it. In fact, there is compelling evidence that people who act out angry feelings—even by hitting an inanimate punching bag—actually feel worse than those who experience anger without lashing out (Bushman et al., 1999; Lerner, 2005). More to the point of this book, researchers have discovered that people who deal with negative feelings by venting them indiscriminately have above-average levels of anxiety in their interpersonal relationships (Jerome & Liss, 2005). See the Focus on Research sidebar ("Online Ranting") for more on emotional venting.

Recognizing the difference between feeling and acting can liberate you from the fear that getting in touch with certain emotions will commit you to

FOCUS ON RESEARCH
Online Ranting: Helpful or Harmful?

You're ticked off and want to vent to someone. You go online to a "rant site" and let off some steam, typing out your fury in no uncertain terms. Will that help? Not much, according to recent studies.

Rant sites are Internet forums where posters write anonymously and without restraint, blasting away about social issues, personal relationships, or the lousy burger they had for lunch. The results can make for entertaining reading, which explains why the sites get so many hits.

In one study, rant-site regulars reported feeling calm and relaxed after posting. However, they also measured well above the norm on trait anger and its negative consequences (such as physical fighting), which suggests that venting doesn't assist their anger management. In a second study, random college volunteers were asked to post on rant sites. Afterward, those students registered increases in anger and decreases in happiness—the opposite of what the rant-site regulars reported.

It's worth noting that about a third of the ranters in the first study admitted they would prefer to talk with someone about their anger—and two-thirds appreciated the validation they felt when others commented on their posts. Although anonymous venting might offer brief catharsis, even rant-site regulars seem aware of the value of expressing their anger more interpersonally.

Martin, R. C., Coyier, K. R., VanSistine, L. M., & Schroeder, K. L. (2013). Anger on the Internet: The perceived value of rant-sites. *Cyberpsychology, Behavior, and Social Networking, 16,* 119–122.

a course of action. If, for instance, you think, "I'm so nervous about the interview that I want to cancel it and pretend that I'm sick," it becomes possible to explore why you feel so anxious and then work to remedy the problem. Pretending that nothing is the matter, on the other hand, will do nothing to diminish your anxiety, which can then block your chances for success.

ACCEPT RESPONSIBILITY FOR YOUR FEELINGS

People don't *make us* like or dislike them, and believing that they do denies the responsibility each of us has for our own emotions. It's important to make sure that your emotional expressions don't blame others for the way you feel (Bippus & Young, 2005; Oatley, 2010). The "I" language described in Chapter 5 makes it clear that you own your feelings. For example, instead of saying "You're making me angry," it's more accurate to say, "I'm feeling angry." Instead of "You hurt my feelings," a more responsible statement is, "I feel hurt when you do that."

CHOOSE THE BEST TIME AND PLACE TO EXPRESS YOUR FEELINGS

Often the first flush of a strong feeling is not the best time to speak out. If you're awakened by the racket caused by a noisy neighbor, storming over to complain might result in your saying things you'll regret later. In such a case, it's probably wiser to wait until you have thought out carefully how you might express your feelings in a way that would be most likely to be heard.

Even after you've waited for your initial emotion to subside, it's still important to choose the time that's best suited to the message. Being rushed or tired or disturbed by some other matter is probably a good reason for postponing the expression of your feeling. In the same manner, you ought to be sure that the recipient of your message is ready to hear you out before you begin. Sometimes that means checking the other person's mood before you start sharing emotions. In other cases, it's about calculating whether that person is ready to hear sentiments such as "I love you." But don't put off expressing emotions too long. It turns out that the old adage, "Never go to bed angry," has scientific validity (Hicks & Diamond, 2011). Interpersonal conflict between couples that's left unresolved overnight leads to poor sleep patterns, which can result in a variety of health problems.

There are also cases in which you may choose never to express your feelings. Even if you're dying to tell an instructor that her lectures leave

ASSESSING YOUR COMMUNICATION

Your Emotional Intelligence

To what extent is each of the following items true for you? Rate each one on a scale ranging from 1 to 5, where 1 = "very seldom true of me" and 5 = "very often true of me."

_____ **1.** It's hard for me to understand my feelings.

_____ **2.** I have trouble understanding how others feel.

_____ **3.** I don't fantasize or daydream.

_____ **4.** I find it hard to control my impulses.

_____ **5.** I have difficulty expressing my feelings.

_____ **6.** I'm good at understanding how others feel.

_____ **7.** When I'm in a difficult situation, I collect information.

_____ **8.** I tend to be impatient.

_____ **9.** It's hard for me to describe my feelings.

_____ **10.** I'm sensitive to others' feelings.

_____ **11.** I stop and think before solving problems.

_____ **12.** I find it hard to control my anxiety.

This assessment, based on adaptations of 12 of the 35 items of the original measure, is from Parker, J. A., Keefer, K. V., & Wood, L. M. (2011). Toward a brief multidimensional assessment of emotional intelligence: Psychometric properties of the Emotional Quotient Inventory–Short Form. *Psychological Assessment, 23,* 762–777.

For scoring information, see page 267 at the end of the chapter.

you bored to a stupor, you might decide it's best to answer her question "How's class going?" with an innocuous "Okay." And even though you may be irritated by the arrogance of a police officer stopping you for speeding, the smartest approach might be to keep your feelings to yourself. In cases in which you experience strong emotions but don't want to share them verbally (for whatever reason), writing out your feelings and thoughts has been shown to have mental, physical, and emotional benefits (Burton & King, 2008; Pennebaker, 2004). Putting your feelings into words—even if no one reads them—has therapeutic value (Wilson, 2011). This demonstrates once again the link between emotions and communication. The cognitive process of turning feelings into language helps manage the emotions. This can happen when talking with others or engaging in self-talk, as we describe later in this chapter.

MANAGING EMOTIONS

Not all emotions are beneficial. For instance, depression, terror, and irrational guilt do little to help you feel better or improve your relationships. Likewise, communication apprehension (as discussed in Chapter 1, page 24) can pose both personal and interpersonal challenges. In this section, we give you tools to minimize unproductive emotions and maximize helpful ones.

FACILITATIVE AND DEBILITATIVE EMOTIONS

It's important to distinguish **facilitative emotions**, which contribute to effective functioning, from **debilitative emotions**, which hinder or prevent effective performance. Positive emotions such as joy and love are obviously facilitative. Much of the time, "negative" emotions such as anger or fear are debilitative.

Sometimes, though, unpleasant emotions can be useful. The difference is often a matter of degree. For instance, a certain amount of anger or irritation can be constructive because it often stimulates a person to improve the unsatisfying conditions. Rage, on the other hand, usually makes matters worse. The same is true for fear. A little bit of nervousness before a job interview may boost you just enough to improve your performance (mellow athletes or actors usually don't do well), but a job candidate who is inordinately anxious isn't likely to impress potential employers (Ayres & Crosby, 1995). One big difference, then, between facilitative and debilitative emotions is their *intensity*.

A second characteristic of debilitative feelings is their extended *duration*. Feeling depressed for a while after the breakup of a relationship or the loss of a job is natural. Spending the rest of one's life grieving over the loss accomplishes nothing. In the same way, staying angry at someone for a wrong inflicted long ago can be just as punishing to the grudge holder as to the wrongdoer (Bushman et al., 2005). Social scientists call this **rumination**—recurrent thoughts not demanded by the immediate environment. For example, jealous lovers who dwell on imagined transgressions of their partners feel more distressed than necessary and act in counterproductive ways

In the TV show *Revenge,* Emily Thorne (Emily VanCamp) feels driven to settle scores with those she believes have wronged her. Most observers would agree that although Emily's grievances may be justified, her desire for retribution is debilitating.

toward their partners (Carson & Cupach, 2000). Likewise, teenage girls who ruminate about problems with their friends have an increased risk of suffering from anxiety and depression (Rose et al., 2007). And sometimes ruminating can be used to sustain anger in preparation for retaliation—not a healthy approach (Knobloch-Westerwick & Alter, 2006). The Dark Side box on page 262 describes the destructive relationship between jealousy and rumination.

THOUGHTS CAUSE FEELINGS

The goal, then, is to find a method for getting rid of debilitative feelings while remaining sensitive to the more facilitative emotions. Fortunately, such a method—termed a *rational-emotive* approach—does exist (Ellis & Ellis, 2014; Neenan & Dryden, 2006). This reappraisal method is based on the idea that the key to changing feelings is to change unproductive cognitive interpretations. Let's see how it works.

For most people, emotions seem to have a life of their own. People wish they could feel calm when approaching strangers, yet their voices quiver. They try to appear confident when asking for a raise, but their eyes twitch nervously. Many people would say that the strangers or the boss *makes* them feel nervous, just as they would say that a bee sting causes them to feel pain:

Activating Event	→	Consequence
bee sting	→	physical pain
meeting strangers	→	nervous feelings

When looking at emotions in this way, people may believe they have little control over how they feel. However, the causal relationship between activating events and emotional discomfort (or pleasure) isn't as great as it seems. Cognitive psychologists and therapists argue that it is not events, such as meeting strangers or being jilted by a lover, that cause people to feel poorly but rather the *beliefs they hold* about these events.

Consider this example to understand how thoughts cause feelings. Imagine you start receiving a string of angry, insulting messages from a friend. Under the circumstances, it's likely that you would feel hurt and upset. Now imagine that, after receiving the offensive messages, you learn that your friend had been hospitalized for mental illness. In this case, your reaction would probably be quite different. Most likely, you'd feel sadness and pity, and possibly embarrassment for ever imagining a good friend would turn against you so quickly and for no apparent reason.

In this story, the activating event—being called names—was the same in both cases, yet the emotional consequences were very different. The reason for different feelings has to do with the pattern of thinking in each case. In the first instance, you would most likely think that your friend was angry with you and that you must have done something terrible to deserve such a response. In the second case, you would probably assume that your friend had experienced some psychological difficulty, so you would probably feel sympathetic. This example illustrates that people's *interpretations* of events determine their feelings:

Activating Event	→	Thought or Belief	→	Consequences
being called names	→	"I've done something wrong."	→	hurt, upset
being called names	→	"My friend must be sick."	→	pity, sympathy

The same principle applies in more common situations. For example, the words "I love you" can be interpreted in a variety of ways. They could be taken at face value as a genuine expression of deep affection. They might also be decoded in a variety of other ways: for example, as an attempt at

manipulation; a sincere but mistaken declaration uttered in a moment of passion; or an attempt to make the recipient feel better. It's easy to imagine how different interpretations of a statement such as "I love you" can lead to different emotional reactions:

Event	→	Thought	→	Feeling
hearing "I love you"	→	"This is a genuine statement."	→	delight (perhaps)
hearing "I love you"	→	"She's (he's) just saying this to manipulate me."	→	anger

The key, then, to understanding and changing feelings lies in reappraising the event. This takes place through a form of intrapersonal communication professionals label **self-talk** (Kross et al., 2014; Vocate, 1994)—the nonvocal, internal monologue that is our process of thinking. To understand how self-talk works, pay attention to the part of you that, like a little voice, whispers in your ear. Take a moment now and listen to what the voice is saying.

Did you hear the voice? It was quite possibly saying "What little voice? I don't hear any voices!" This little voice talks to you almost constantly:

"Better pick up a loaf of bread on the way home."
"I wonder when he's going to stop talking."
"It sure is cold today!"
"Are there two or four cups in a quart?"

At work or at play, while reading the paper or brushing our teeth, we all tend to talk to ourselves. This thinking voice rarely stops. It may fall silent for a while when you're running, riding a bike, or meditating, but most of the time it rattles on. Let's look now at how that voice sometimes processes thoughts in ways that need reappraising.

IRRATIONAL THINKING AND DEBILITATIVE EMOTIONS

This process of self-talk is essential to understanding the debilitative feelings that interfere with effective communication (E. D. Cohen, 2007). Many debilitative feelings come from accepting a number of irrational thoughts—we call them *fallacies* here—that lead to illogical conclusions and, in turn, to debilitating feelings (Samar et al., 2013). We usually aren't aware of these thoughts, which makes them especially powerful.

The Fallacy of Perfection

People who accept the **fallacy of perfection** believe that a worthwhile communicator should be able to handle any situation with complete confidence and skill. Although such a standard of perfection can serve as a goal and a source of inspiration (rather like making a hole in one for a golfer), it's totally unrealistic to expect that you can reach or maintain this level of behavior. The truth is, people simply aren't perfect. Perhaps the myth of the perfect communicator comes from believing too strongly in novels, television, or

films. In these media, perfect characters are often depicted—the ideal mate or child, the totally controlled and gregarious host, the incredibly competent professional. Although these fabrications are certainly appealing, real people will inevitably come up short compared to them.

People who believe that it's desirable and possible to be a perfect communicator come to think that people won't appreciate them if they are imperfect. Admitting mistakes, saying "I don't know," or sharing feelings of uncertainty or discomfort thus seem to be social defects. Given the desire to be valued and appreciated, these people are tempted at least to try to *appear* perfect. They assemble a variety of social masks, hoping that if they can fool others into thinking that they are perfect, perhaps they'll find acceptance. The costs of such deception are high. If others ever detect that this veneer of confidence is false, then the person hiding behind it is considered a phony. Even if the facade goes undetected, the performance consumes a great deal of psychological energy and diminishes the rewards of approval.

Not only can subscribing to the myth of perfection keep others from liking you, but it also acts as a force to diminish self-esteem. How can you like yourself when you don't measure up to your own standards?

You become more liberated each time you comfortably accept the idea that you are not perfect. For example, like everyone else, you sometimes have a hard time expressing yourself. Like everyone else, you make mistakes from time to time, and there is no reason to hide it. You are honestly doing the best you can to realize your potential, to become the best person you can be.

The Fallacy of Approval

Another mistaken belief is based on the idea that it is vital—not just desirable—to obtain everyone's approval. Communicators who subscribe to the **fallacy of approval** go to incredible lengths to seek acceptance from others, even to the extent of sacrificing their own principles and happiness. Adherence to this irrational myth can lead to some ludicrous situations, such as feeling nervous because people you really don't like seem to disapprove of you or feeling apologetic when you are not at fault.

The myth of approval is irrational. It implies that some people are more respectable and more likable because they go out of their way to please others. Often, this implication simply isn't true. How respectable are people who have compromised important values simply to gain acceptance? Are people highly regarded when they repeatedly deny their own needs as a means of buying approval? In addition, striving for universal acceptance is irrational because it is simply not possible.

Don't misunderstand: Abandoning the fallacy of approval doesn't mean living a life of selfishness. It's still important to consider the needs of others. It's also pleasant—one might even say necessary—to strive for the respect of certain people. The point is that the price is too high if you must abandon your own needs and principles to gain this acceptance.

The Fallacy of Should

One huge source of unhappiness is the inability to distinguish between what *is* and what *should be*, or the **fallacy of should**. For instance, imagine a person who is full of complaints about the world:

"There should be no rain on weekends."
"People ought to live forever."
"Money should grow on trees."
"We should all be able to fly."

Beliefs such as these are obviously foolish. However pleasant such wishing may be, insisting that the unchangeable should be altered won't affect reality one bit. In each of these cases, the speaker *prefers* that people behave differently. Wishing that things were better is perfectly legitimate; and trying to change them is, of course, a good idea. However, it's unreasonable for people to insist that the world operate just as they want it to. Parents wish that their children were always considerate and neat. Teachers wish that their students were totally fascinated with their subjects and willing to study diligently. Consumers wish that inflation weren't such a problem. As the old saying goes, those wishes and a quarter (now you'd need much more) will get you a cup of coffee.

Becoming obsessed with shoulds yields three bad consequences. First, this preoccupation leads to unnecessary unhappiness. People who are constantly dreaming about the ideal are seldom satisfied with what they have. For instance, partners in a marriage who focus on the ways in which their mate could be more considerate, sexy, or intelligent may have a hard time appreciating the strengths that drew them together in the first place.

Second, the obsession keeps you from changing unsatisfying conditions. One employee, for example, constantly complains about the problems on the job: There should be better training, pay ought to be higher, the facilities should be upgraded, and so on. This person could be using the same energy to improve such conditions. Of course, not all problems have solutions, but when they do, complaining is rarely very productive. As one college manager puts it, "Rather than complain about the cards you are dealt, play the hand well."

Finally, this obsession tends to build a defensive climate in others. Imagine living around someone who insisted that people be more punctual, work harder, or refrain from using certain language. This kind of complaining is obviously irritating. It's much easier to be around people who comment without preaching.

Rather than demanding that people behave the way you wish they would and feeling overly disappointed when they don't, it can be more realistic to think to yourself, "I *wish* she (he) would behave the way I want—but if that doesn't happen, I can learn to live with it and be responsible for myself."

The Fallacy of Overgeneralization

The **fallacy of overgeneralization** occurs when a person bases a belief on a *limited amount of evidence.* Consider the following statements:

"I'm so stupid! I can't understand how to do my income tax."
"Some friend I am! I forgot my best friend's birthday."

In these cases, people have focused on a single shortcoming as if it represented everything. Sometimes people forget that despite their difficulties, they have solved tough problems; and although they can be forgetful, they're often caring and thoughtful.

A second, related category of overgeneralization occurs when we *exaggerate shortcomings:*

"You *never* listen to me."
"You're *always* late."
"I can't think of *anything.*"

On closer examination, such absolute statements are almost always false and usually lead to discouragement or anger. It's better to replace overgeneralizations with more accurate messages:

"You often don't listen to me."
"You've been late three times this week."
"I haven't had any ideas I like today."

The Fallacy of Causation

People who live their lives in accordance with the **fallacy of causation** believe they should do nothing that can hurt or in any way inconvenience others because it will cause undesirable feelings. For example, you might visit friends or family out of a sense of obligation rather than a genuine desire to see them because, you believe, not to visit them will hurt their feelings. Did you ever avoid objecting to behavior that you found troublesome because you didn't want to cause anger? You may, on occasion, have pretended to be attentive—even though you were running late for an appointment and in a rush—because you didn't want a person to feel embarrassed for "holding you up." Then there were the times when you substituted praise for more honest negative responses to avoid causing hurt.

A reluctance to speak out in such situations often results from assuming that one person can cause another's emotions—that others, for example, are responsible for your feeling disappointed, confused, or irritated; or that you are responsible for others feeling hurt, angry, or upset. Actually, this assumption is incorrect. We may *act* in provocative ways, but each person is responsible for the way he or she *reacts*.

To understand why each person is responsible for his or her own feelings, consider how strange it sounds to suggest that people *make* you fall in love with them. Such a statement simply doesn't make sense. It would be more correct to say that people first act in one way or another; then you may or may not fall in love as a result of these actions.

In the same way, it's not accurate to say that people *make* you angry, upset, or even happy. Behavior that upsets or pleases one person might not bring any reaction from another. If you doubt this fact, think about people you know who respond differently to the same behaviors that you find so bothersome. (You may scream "Idiot!" when you're driving and someone switches lanes in front of you without signaling, whereas the person with you in the car may not even notice or may notice but not care.) The contrast between others' reactions and yours shows that responses are determined more by our own temperament and thinking than by others' behavior.

One way to avoid the debilitative feelings that often accompany the fallacy of causation is to use responsible language, as discussed in Chapter 5. Instead of saying "He makes me so angry," reframe it as your reaction to the other person's behavior: "I don't like when he talks about me behind my back." Instead of saying, "I *had to* visit my parents this weekend; they gave me no option," take responsibility for your choices: "I decided to visit my parents this weekend, but I may choose differently next time." Taking ownership for your actions and reactions can often lead to a sense of empowerment.

The Fallacy of Helplessness

The **fallacy of helplessness** suggests that forces beyond our control determine satisfaction in life. People with this outlook continually see themselves as victims:

"There's no way a woman can get ahead in this society. It's a man's world, and the best thing I can do is to accept it."

"I was born with a shy personality. I'd like to be more outgoing, but there's nothing I can do about that."

"I can't tell my boss that she is putting too many demands on me. If I did, I might lose my job."

The error in such statements becomes apparent once a person realizes that few paths are completely closed. In fact, most "can't" statements may be more correctly restated in one of two ways.

The first is to say that you *won't* act in a certain way, that you choose not to do so. For instance, you may choose not to stand up for your rights or to follow unwanted requests, but it is usually inaccurate to claim that some outside force keeps you from doing so. The other way to rephrase a "can't" is to say that you *don't know how* to do something. Examples of such a situation include not knowing how to complain in a way that reduces defensiveness, or not being aware of how to conduct a conversation. Many difficulties a person claims can't be solved do have solutions: The task is to discover those solutions and to work diligently at applying them.

When viewed in this light, many "can'ts" are really rationalizations to justify an unwillingness to change. Research supports the dangers of helpless thinking. Lonely people, for example, tend to attribute their poor interpersonal relationships to uncontrollable causes (Marangoni & Ickes, 1989; Riggio & Kwong, 2009). "It's beyond my control," they think. Lonely people are more negative than nonlonely ones about ever finding a mate. Also, they expect their relational partners to reject them. Notice the self-fulfilling prophecy in this attitude: Believing that your relational prospects are dim can lead you to act in ways that make you an unattractive prospect. Once you persuade yourself that there's no hope, it's easy to give up trying. On the other hand, acknowledging that there is a way to change—even though it may be difficult—puts the responsibility for the predicament on your shoulders. Knowing that you can move closer to your goals makes it difficult to complain about the present. You *can* become a better communicator.

The Fallacy of Catastrophic Expectations

Some fearful people operate on the assumption that if something bad can happen, it probably will. This is the **fallacy of catastrophic expectations**—a position similar to Murphy's Law. These statements are typical of such an attitude:

"If I invite them to the party, they probably won't want to come."
"If I speak up to try to resolve a conflict, things will probably get worse."
"If I apply for the job I want, I probably won't be hired."
"If I tell them how I really feel, they'll probably just laugh at me."

Once you start imagining terrible consequences, a self-fulfilling prophecy can begin to build. One study revealed that people who believed that their romantic partners would not change for the better were likely to behave in ways that contributed to the breakup of the relationship (Metts & Cupach, 1990). And people who have a "pessimism bias" often perceive threats in their relationships that are not apparent to outsiders, leading to relational dissatisfaction (Knobloch et al., 2007).

Although it's easy to understand the personal benefits of reducing debilitative emotions, it's important to remember the *interpersonal* reasons for doing so. Simply put, relationships function better when the people involved manage their emotions (English et al., 2013; Knobloch & Metts, 2013). This obviously doesn't mean stifling feelings—quite the contrary. Emotion management involves self-awareness, emotional intelligence, and the kind of reappraisal we're about to discuss. Communicators who manage their emotions are able to express them in productive ways with their partners, and that helps maintain relationships. With that in mind, we look at how to reduce debilitative emotions that are generally counterproductive to personal and interpersonal health.

DARK SIDE OF COMMUNICATION
JEALOUSY AND RUMINATION: AN UNHEALTHY COMBINATION

A *little* bit of jealousy can be a good thing in a romantic relationship. It shows that you care about your partner and have a strong sense of commitment. But there's a reason jealousy is called "the green-eyed monster." In large doses, it can eat away at you emotionally and destroy your relationships.

Researchers suggest that rumination is what turns jealousy dark (Bevan, 2011; Elphinston et al., 2013). Brooding about past failures and imagining future transgressions feeds the monster—and leads to further rumination. Left to fester long enough, jealousy can result in destructive behaviors such as surveillance and stalking, as well as verbal and physical aggression.

Assuming your jealousy is unfounded, you might want to reappraise any underlying irrational beliefs. Positive self-talk ("I know my sweetheart loves me"; "I won't let the past dictate my future") can be an antidote to rumination. If the negative emotions don't subside, communication researchers recommend civil discussions (Bevan, 2008). The perception-checking method described in Chapter 4 may be useful: "I noticed you were talking a long time with that person at the party. Was it just a casual chat, or should I be concerned?" Of course, if you and your romantic partner are having these conversations on a regular basis, it may be a sign of larger relational problems.

MINIMIZING DEBILITATIVE EMOTIONS

How can you overcome irrational thinking? Social scientists have developed a simple yet effective approach (E. D. Cohen, 2007; Ellis & Dryden, 2007). When practiced conscientiously, it can help you cut down on the self-defeating thinking that leads to many debilitative emotions.

Monitor Your Emotional Reactions

The first step is to recognize when you're having debilitative emotions. (Of course, it's also nice to be aware of pleasant feelings when they occur!) As we suggested earlier, one way to notice feelings is through physical stimuli: butterflies in the stomach, racing heart, hot flashes, and so on. Although such reactions might be symptoms of food poisoning, more often they reflect a strong emotion. You also can recognize certain ways of behaving that suggest your feelings: stomping instead of walking normally, being unusually quiet, and speaking in a sarcastic tone of voice are some examples.

It may seem strange to suggest that it's necessary to look for emotions—they ought to be immediately apparent. However, the fact is that we often suffer from debilitative feelings for some time without noticing them. For example, at the end of a trying day, you've probably caught yourself frowning and realized that you've been wearing that face for some time without knowing it.

Remember the two key characteristics of debilitating emotions—intensity (they are *too* intense) and duration (they last *too* long)—and use them to guide your assessment.

Note the Activating Event

Once you're aware of how you're feeling, the next step is to figure out what activating event triggered your response. Sometimes it is obvious. If your sweetheart keeps calling you by the name of a former lover, you're likely to become upset. Research shows that dating couples can develop "social allergies" to each other, becoming hypersensitive about their partner's annoying behaviors (Cunningham et al., 2005). In these cases, it's easy to identify what triggers a given response. In other cases, however, the activating event isn't so apparent.

Sometimes there isn't a single activating event but rather a series of small incidents that finally build toward a critical mass and trigger a debilitative feeling. This sort of thing happens when someone teases you over and over about the same thing, or when you suffer a series of small disappointments.

The best way to begin tracking down activating events is to notice the circumstances in which you have debilitative feelings. Perhaps they occur when you're around *specific people*. For example, you may feel tense or angry every time you encounter a person with whom you have struggled in the past. Until those issues are dealt with, feelings about past events can trigger debilitative emotions, even in apparently innocuous situations.

In other cases, you might discover that being around certain *types of individuals* triggers debilitative emotions. For instance, you might become nervous around people who seem more intelligent or self-confident than you are. In other cases, certain *settings* can stimulate unpleasant emotions: parties, work, school. Sometimes the *topic of conversation* is the factor that sets you off, whether politics, religion, sex, or some other subject.

Record Your Self-Talk

This is the point at which you analyze the thoughts that are the link between the activating event and your feelings. If you're serious about getting rid of debilitative emotions, it's important to actually write down your self-talk when first learning to use this method. Putting your thoughts on paper will help you see whether they make any sense.

Monitoring your self-talk might be difficult at first. This is a new skill, and any new activity seems awkward. If you persevere, however, you'll find you will be able to identify the thoughts that lead to your debilitative feelings. Once you get in the habit of recognizing this internal monologue, you'll be able to identify your thoughts quickly and easily.

Dispute Your Irrational Beliefs

Now is the time to engage in the reappraisal process mentioned earlier in this chapter (page 239). Use the discussion of irrational fallacies on pages 256–262 to find out which of your internal statements are based on mistaken thinking. You can do this most effectively by following three steps. First, decide whether each belief you've recorded is rational or irrational. Next, explain why the belief does or doesn't make sense. Finally, if the belief is irrational, write down an alternative way of thinking that is more sensible and that can leave you feeling better when faced with the same activating event in the future.

After reading about this method for dealing with unpleasant emotions, some readers have objections:

"This rational-emotive approach sounds like nothing more than trying to talk yourself out of feeling bad." This accusation is totally correct. After all, because we talk ourselves into feeling bad, what's wrong with talking ourselves out of bad feelings, especially when they are based on irrational thoughts?

"The kind of disputing we just read sounds phony and unnatural. I don't talk to myself in sentences and paragraphs." There's no need to dispute your irrational beliefs in any special literary style. You can be just as colloquial as you want. The important thing is to clearly understand what thoughts led you into your debilitative feeling so you can clearly reappraise them. When the technique is new to you, it's a good idea to write or talk out your thoughts to make them clear. After you've had some practice, you'll be able to do these steps in a quicker, less formal way.

"This approach is too cold and impersonal. It seems to aim at turning people into calculating, emotionless machines." This is simply not true. A rational thinker can still dream, hope, and love: There's nothing necessarily irrational about feelings like these. Put another way, communicators can use both their heads and their hearts when making decisions (Fetterman & Robinson, 2013). We discuss accentuating positive emotions in the following section.

"This technique promises too much. There's no chance I could rid myself of all unpleasant feelings, however nice that might be." We can answer this by assuring you that rational-emotive thinking probably won't totally solve your emotional problems. What it can do is reduce their number, intensity, and duration. This method is not the answer to all your problems, but it can make a significant difference—which is not a bad accomplishment.

MAXIMIZING FACILITATIVE EMOTIONS

Reducing debilitative emotions is only part of the emotional health equation. Contemporary scholars maintain that fostering positive emotions is just as important as minimizing negative ones. Whether it's called "learned optimism" (Seligman, 2006) or "positivity" (Fredrickson, 2009), the approach is similar to what we've outlined in this section. If thoughts cause feelings, then positive thoughts can cause positive feelings. Ruminating on the good rather than the bad in life can enhance one's emotional, relational, and even physical health (Peterson, 2006; Rius-Ottenheim et al., 2013).

It's unrealistic to think that you'll have a positive emotional response to every event. The key, according to researcher Barbara Fredrickson (2009), is to leave plenty of room to enjoy and savor positive emotional experiences. And even though you can't dictate all the events of your life, you have the power to reappraise them. Clichés such as "look on the bright side" and "have an attitude of gratitude" may not be comforting when delivered by others, but they can serve as helpful self-reminders. You can regard challenging situations as growth opportunities. You can focus on what you gained rather than what you lost. You can choose compassion over contempt. The difference between "That really hurt me" and "I found out how strong and capable I really am" is often a matter of mindset—and positive emotions follow positive appraisals.

Many people find it easier to focus on their negative emotional experiences. It often takes mindful effort to pay attention to and express pleasurable feelings in close relationships. Here are 10 emotions that Frederickson's research identifies as basic to positivity: *joy, gratitude, serenity, interest, hope, pride, amusement, inspiration, awe,* and *love.* How many have you experienced recently? How often do you express these emotions to people who matter? Is it possible that you felt but can't recall them? Identifying and then talking or writing about your positive emotional experiences can lead to greater personal and interpersonal satisfaction.

CHECK YOUR UNDERSTANDING

Objective 8.1 Explain how emotions are experienced and expressed.

Emotionally intelligent people are generally more effective communicators. Emotions have several dimensions. They are signaled by internal physiological changes, manifested by verbal and nonverbal reactions, and defined in most cases by cognitive interpretations.

> **Q:** Over the course of this week, keep a journal recording your emotional responses to interactions in an important relationship. In particular, pay attention to how those responses begin internally and then are expressed externally.

Objective 8.2 Describe the various personal and social influences on emotional expression.

There are several reasons why people do not verbalize many of the emotions they feel. Certain personality types respond to emotions more negatively than others. Some cultures encourage while others discourage the expression of emotions. Biological sex and gender roles also shape the way people experience and express emotions. Many social roles and rules discourage the expression of some feelings, particularly negative ones. Some people express emotions so rarely that they lose the ability to recognize when they are feeling them. Social media may also increase the intensity of emotions for both message senders and receivers. Finally, exposure to others' emotions can shape the way we feel ourselves through the process of emotional contagion.

Q: Nature versus nurture: Analyze the various factors that influence whether and how you express your emotions. To what extent do you think your responses are primarily based on your personality (i.e., nature)? What social and environmental factors (i.e., nurture) shape the way you do or don't express emotions? Give examples to illustrate your analysis.

Objective 8.3 Understand how to express your emotions appropriately and effectively.

Because total expression of feelings is not appropriate for adults, several guidelines help define when and how to share emotions effectively. Self-awareness, clear language, and expression of multiple feelings are important, as is the ability to recognize the difference between feeling and acting. Willingness to accept responsibility for feelings instead of blaming them on others leads to better reactions. Choosing the proper time and place to share feelings is also important.

Q: Assess how effectively you express your emotions. Are you able to identify your feelings and put them into words? How appropriately do you share them with others? How could you apply the guidelines in this chapter to express your emotions more effectively and appropriately?

Objective 8.4 Distinguish between facilitative and debilitative emotions, and explain how reappraisal may be used to manage emotions effectively.

Whereas some emotions are facilitative, meaning they contribute to effective functioning, other debilitative feelings inhibit effective performance. Many of these debilitative emotions are caused by various types of irrational thinking. It is often possible to communicate more confidently and effectively by identifying troublesome emotions, identifying the activating event and self-talk that triggered them, and reappraising any irrational thoughts with a more logical analysis of the situation. It's also important to identify and enjoy facilitative emotions.

Q: Consider the last time you experienced a debilitative emotion associated with an interpersonal relationship. How well were you able to manage it? How might the methods in this chapter help you process emotions such as this one in the future?

KEY TERMS

- Debilitative emotions (253)
- Emotional contagion (245)
- Emotional intelligence (236)
- Emotion labor (244)
- Facilitative emotions (253)
- Fallacy of approval (258)

- Fallacy of catastrophic expectations (261)
- Fallacy of causation (259)
- Fallacy of helplessness (260)
- Fallacy of overgeneralization (259)

- Fallacy of perfection (256)
- Fallacy of should (258)
- Reappraisal (239)
- Rumination (253)
- Self-talk (256)

ACTIVITIES

1. The Assessing Your Communication exercise on page 252 gives you a general sense of your emotional intelligence. Have two or three people who are close to you offer their appraisal using the assessment. Do their evaluations match yours? If not, what do you think explains the difference? What are some ways you might improve your emotional intelligence?

2. Choose an important emotion you experience in one of your relationships. This relationship needn't be highly personal. You might, for example, focus on an employer, a professor, or a neighbor. Use the guidelines on pages 246–253 to determine whether and how you might express this emotion. Ask someone you know to give you feedback on the choice you made.

3. Explore whether you subscribe to the fallacy of helplessness by completing the following lists. Describe two important (to you) communication-related difficulties you have for each of the following: communicating with family members, people at school or at work, strangers, and friends. Use the following format for each difficulty:

I can't _____

because _____.

Now read the list aloud to a classmate, but with a slight difference. For each "can't," substitute the word "won't." Note which statements are actually "won'ts." Tell your classmate if you feel differently about this statement when you change the wording.

Read the list to your classmate again, only this time substitute "I don't know how to" for your original "can't." Rewrite any statements that are truly "don't know hows," and decide what you could do to learn the skill that you presently lack. Tell your classmate if you feel differently about this statement when you change the wording.

Based on your experience, decide whether you subscribe to the fallacy of helplessness, and what you could do to eliminate this sort of debilitative thinking.

4. Choose an important situation in which you experience debilitative emotions that interfere with your ability to communicate effectively. With the help of a partner or class group, use the four steps on pages 262–264 to reappraise the rationality of your beliefs. Report on how the rational-emotive approach affects your communication in this important situation.

5. For one week, keep a daily journal in which you identify all the positive emotions you experience in your relationships. In particular, watch for these 10 emotions: *joy, gratitude, serenity, interest, hope, pride, amusement, inspiration, awe,* and *love.*

At the end of the week, reflect on whether your journaling helped you notice and remember positive emotions you might otherwise have missed or forgotten. What strategies can you develop to help you experience and express positive emotions more often?

SCORING FOR ASSESSING YOUR COMMUNICATION (PAGE 252)

Reverse-score items 1, 2, 4, 5, 8, 9, and 12 (i.e., 5 = 1, 4 = 2, 3 = 3, 2 = 4, and 1 = 5).

Add items 1, 5, and 9. This is your score on the intrapersonal dimension of Emotional Intelligence: _____. The average score for young adult men on this dimension is about 10, with most scores between 8 and 12; for young adult women, the average was about 11, with most scores between 9 and 13.

Add items 2, 6, and 10. This is your score on the interpersonal dimension of Emotional Intelligence: _____. The average score for young adult men on this dimension is about 12, with most scores between 10 and 14; for young adult women, the average was about 13, with most scores between 11 and 15.

Add items 3, 7, and 11. This is your score on the adaptability dimension of Emotional Intelligence: _____. The average score for young adult women and men on this dimension is about 12, with most scores between 10 and 14.

Add items 4, 8, and 12. This is your score on the stress management dimension of Emotional Intelligence: _____. The average score for young adult women and men on this dimension is about 9, with most scores between 7 and 11.

chapter 9

Dynamics of Interpersonal Relationships

CHAPTER OUTLINE

FEATURES

LEARNING OBJECTIVES

9.1 Understand the various reasons for entering into interpersonal relationships.

9.2 Recognize the stages and dialectical tensions typically experienced in interpersonal relationships.

9.3 Identify specific skills communicators can use to maintain and improve their interpersonal relationships.

"I'm looking for a meaningful relationship."
"Our relationship has changed lately."
"The relationship is good for both of us."
"This relationship isn't working."

RELATIONSHIP IS one of those words that people use all the time but have trouble defining. Even scholars who have devoted their careers to studying relationships don't agree on what the term means (Guerrero et al., 2007). Their definitions include words such as "closeness," "influence," "commitment," and "intimacy"—but coming up with a single definition can be (as the old adage goes) like nailing Jell-O to a wall.

In this chapter, we explore some of the dynamics that characterize interpersonal relationships and the communication that occurs within them. After reading it, you will see that relationships aren't fixed or unchanging. Rather, they can, and often do, change over time. In other words, a relationship is less a *thing* than a *process*. We look at why we form relationships, the dynamics of those relationships, and how to manage them. We then extend our discussion in Chapter 10 by focusing on close relationships with friends, family, and romantic partners.

WHY WE FORM RELATIONSHIPS

Why do we form relationships with some people and not with others? Sometimes we have no choice: Children can't select their parents, and most workers aren't able to choose their colleagues. In many other cases, however, we seek out some people and actively avoid others.

Social scientists have collected an impressive body of research on interpersonal attraction (e.g., Finkel & Baumeister, 2010; Graziano & Bruce, 2008). The following are some of the factors they have identified that influence our choice of relational partners.

APPEARANCE

Most people claim that we should judge others on the basis of how they act, not how they look. However, the reality is quite the opposite (Mehrabian & Blum, 2003; Swami & Furnham, 2008). Appearance is especially important in the initial stages of a relationship. In one early study, a group of over 700 men and women were matched as blind dates for a social event. After the party was over, they were asked whether they would like to date their partners again. The result? The more physically attractive the person (as judged in advance by independent raters), the more likely he or she was seen as desirable. Other factors—social skills and intelligence, for example—didn't seem to affect the decision (Walster et al., 1966).

In a more contemporary example, physical appearance seems to be the primary basis for attraction for speed daters (Luo & Zhang, 2009), and online daters routinely enhance their photographs and information about their height and weight to appear more attractive to potential suitors (Toma & Hancock, 2010). These first impressions can influence secondary ones. For instance, when attractive photos accompany online profiles, raters appraise the profile text more positively (Brand et al., 2012). Online profile owners are also rated as more attractive when they have pictures of physically attractive friends on their sites (Antheunis & Schouten, 2011; Jaschinski & Kommers, 2012). The opposite is also true: Attractive faces are seen as less attractive when in the middle of unattractive or average faces (Rodway et al., 2013).

Even if your appearance isn't beautiful by societal standards, consider these facts: First, after initial impressions have passed, ordinary-looking people with pleasing personalities are likely to be judged as attractive (Berscheid & Walster, 1978; Lewandowski et al., 2007); and perceived beauty can be influenced by traits such as liking, respect, familiarity, and social interaction (Albada et al., 2002; Singh et al. 2009). Second, physical factors become less important as a relationship progresses. In fact, as romantic relationships develop, partners create "positive illusions," viewing one another as more physically attractive over time (Barelds et al., 2011). As one observer put it, "Attractive features may open doors, but apparently, it takes more than physical beauty to keep them open" (Hamachek, 1982, p. 59).

"Before the Internet, I just assumed I was the only one, and kept more or less to myself."

SIMILARITY

It's comforting to know someone who seems to like the same things you like, appears to have similar values, and may even be of the same race, economic class, or educational standing. The basis for this sort of relationship, commonly known as the *similarity thesis*, is the most frequently discussed and strongly supported determinant of relationship formation (Montoya & Horton, 2013; Reid et al., 2013). For example, one study found that similar values about politics and religion are the best predictors of mate choice—significantly more than attraction to physical appearance or personality traits (Alford et al., 2011).

Similarity plays an important role in initial attraction. People are more likely to accept a Facebook friend request from a stranger who is perceived to be similar (Martin et al., 2013). The word "perceived" is important in the preceding sentence. Research shows that speed daters are more attracted to similarities they *believe* they have ("We *seem* to have a lot in common") than to actual similarities (Tidwell et al., 2013). This demonstrates that attraction based on similarities is a subjective process. In fact, research suggests

Partners in the TV crime drama *True Detective* couldn't be more different. Martin Hart (Woody Harrelson) is a jovial family man, and Rustin Cohle (Matthew McConaughey) is a loner with a troubled past. Despite—or perhaps because of—their differences, the two detectives make a winning team.

that deciding you like someone often leads to perceptions of similarity rather than the other way around (Sprecher, 2014).

There are several reasons why similarity is a strong foundation for relationships. First, similarities can be validating. The fact that another person shares your beliefs, tastes, and values is a form of ego support. One study described the lengths to which "implicit egotism" may unconsciously affect perceptions of attractiveness (Jones et al., 2004). Results showed that people are disproportionately likely to marry others whose first or last names resemble their own, and they're also attracted to those with similar birthdays and even sports jersey numbers (see also Simonsohn, 2011).

Second, when someone is similar to you, you can make fairly accurate predictions—whether the person will want to eat at the Mexican restaurant or hear the concert you're so excited about. This ability to make confident predictions reduces uncertainty and anxiety (Duck & Barnes, 1992; Montoya & Horton, 2013).

There's a third explanation for the similarity thesis. It may be that when we learn that other people are similar to us, we assume they'll probably like us, so we in turn like them. The self-fulfilling prophecy creeps into the picture again.

Similarity turns from attraction to dislike when we encounter people who are like us in many ways but who behave in a strange or socially offensive manner (Taylor & Mette, 1971). For instance, you have probably disliked people others have said were "just like you" but who talked too much, were complainers, or had some other unappealing characteristic. In fact, there is a tendency to have stronger dislike for similar but offensive people than for those who are offensive but different. One likely reason is that such people threaten our self-esteem, causing us to fear that we may be as unappealing as they are. In such circumstances, the reaction is often to put as much distance as possible between ourselves and this threat to our ideal self-image.

COMPLEMENTARITY

The old saying "opposites attract" seems to contradict the principle of similarity we just described. In truth, though, both are valid. Differences strengthen a relationship when they are *complementary*—when each partner's characteristics satisfy the other's needs. Research suggests that attraction to partners who have complementary temperaments might be rooted in biology (Fisher, 2007). In addition, some studies show that couples are more likely to be attracted to each other when one partner is dominant and the other passive (Swami & Furnham, 2008). Relationships also work well when the partners agree that one will exercise control in certain areas ("You make the final decisions about money") and the other will take the lead in different ones ("I'll decide how we ought to decorate the place"). Strains occur when control issues are disputed. One study shows that "spendthrifts and tightwads" are often attracted to each other, but their differences in financial management lead to significant conflict over the course of a relationship (Rick et al., 2011).

Studies that have examined successful and unsuccessful couples over a 20-year period show the interaction between similarities and differences (Klohnen & Luo, 2003). When partners are radically different, the dissimilar qualities that at first appear intriguing later become cause for relational breakups (Amodio & Showers, 2005; Felmlee, 2001). Partners in successful marriages were similar enough to satisfy each other physically and mentally, but were different enough to meet each other's needs and keep the relationship interesting. Successful couples find ways to keep a balance between their similarities and differences while adjusting to the changes that occur over the years (Shiota & Levenson, 2007).

REWARDS

Some relationships are based on an economic model called *exchange theory* (Stafford, 2008; Thibaut & Kelley, 1959). This approach suggests that we often seek out people who can give us rewards that are greater than or equal to the costs we encounter in dealing with them. Social exchange theorists define rewards as any outcomes we desire. They may be tangible (a nice place to live, a high paying job) or intangible (prestige, emotional support, companionship). Costs are undesirable outcomes: unpleasant work, emotional pain, and so on. A simple formula captures the social exchange explanation for why we form and maintain relationships:

Rewards – Costs = Outcome

According to social exchange theorists, we use this formula (often unconsciously) to calculate whether a relationship is a "good deal" or "not worth the effort," based on whether the outcome is positive or negative.

At its most blatant level, an exchange approach seems cold and calculating, but in some types of relationships it seems quite appropriate. A healthy business relationship is based on how well the parties help one another, and some friendships are based on an informal kind of barter: "I don't mind listening to the ups and downs of your love life because you rescue me when the house needs repairs." Even close relationships have an element of exchange. Friends and lovers often tolerate each other's quirks because the comfort and enjoyment they get make the less-than-pleasant times worth accepting. However, when one partner feels "underbenefited," it often leads to relational disruption or termination (DeMaris, 2007).

Costs and rewards don't exist in isolation: We define them by comparing a certain situation with alternatives. For example, consider a hypothetical woman, Gloria, who is struggling to decide whether to remain in a relationship with Raymond, her longtime boyfriend. Raymond loves Gloria, but he's not perfect: He has a hair-trigger temper, and he has become verbally abusive from time to time. Also, Gloria knows that Raymond was unfaithful to her at least once. In deciding whether to stay with Raymond, Gloria will use two standards.

The first standard is her **comparison level (CL)**—her minimum standard of what behavior is acceptable. If Gloria believes that relational partners have an obligation to be faithful and treat one another respectfully at all times, then Raymond's behavior will fall below her comparison level. This will be especially true if Gloria has had positive romantic relationships in the past (Merolla et al., 2004). On the other hand, if Gloria adopts a "nobody's perfect" standard, she is more likely to view Raymond's behavior as meeting or exceeding her comparison level.

Gloria also will rate Raymond according to her **comparison level of alternatives (CL_{alt})**. This standard refers to a comparison between the rewards she receives in her present situation and those she could expect to receive in others (Overall & Sibley, 2008). If, for example, Gloria doesn't want to be alone and she thinks, "If I don't have Raymond I won't have anyone," then her CL_{alt} would be lower than her present situation; but if she is confident that she could find a kinder partner, her CL_{alt} would be higher than the status quo.

DARK SIDE OF COMMUNICATION
THE ANGUISH OF ABUSIVE RELATIONSHIPS

"We always hurt the ones we love" is a sad maxim with an even darker side. The unfortunate truth is that when interpersonal abuse occurs, it often happens within close relationships—particularly familial or romantic ones. Abuse can be mental, emotional, verbal, sexual, or physical, and it can leave scars that remain long after the relationship is over.

Many abusive relationships don't end when they should. Why do people stay in them? Social exchange theory offers an explanation (Rusbult & Martz, 1995). Abused partners often believe that a bad relationship is better than no relationship at all. They may also have trouble seeing viable relational alternatives. Perspective gets lost and rationalizations get made—and the pain goes on. Research supports this: One study found that people in abusive dating relationships underestimate how unhappy they really are and overestimate how unhappy they would be if the relationship were to end (Arriaga et al., 2013).

Professional help is vital for pulling free from an abusive relationship (*www.healthyplace.com/abuse* offers information and resources). Experts recommend the following:

- *Don't keep abuse a secret.* At the very least, tell a trusted friend or family member what's happening to you—and then ask that person to help you get help.
- *Watch for patterns.* Abuse often happens in cycles. If you're in the upside of a cycle and all is calm, it can be easy to ignore or overlook a previous violation. But if the abuse returns, it probably won't be the last time.
- *Resist self-blame.* Abused people often believe they are at fault for what happened to them, and that somehow they "had it coming." Remember—*no one deserves abuse.*

Research suggests that when a sense of connection is lacking in a romantic relationship, the draw of intimacy from romantic alternatives becomes particularly strong (Spielmann et al., 2012).

Social exchange theorists suggest that communicators unconsciously use this calculus to decide whether to form and stay in relationships. At first this information seems to offer little comfort to communicators who are in unsatisfying relationships, such as when the partner's behavior is below the CL and there are no foreseeable alternatives (CL_{alt}). But there are other choices than being stuck in situations where the costs outweigh the rewards. First, you might make sure that you are judging your present relationship against a realistic comparison level. Expecting a situation to be perfect can be a recipe for unhappiness. (Recall the discussion of the "fallacy of shoulds" in Chapter 8.) If you decide that your present situation truly falls below your comparison level, you might explore whether there are other alternatives you haven't considered. And finally, the skills introduced throughout this book may help you negotiate a better relationship with the other person (assuming the relationship isn't abusive—see the Dark Side box on page 274).

COMPETENCY

We like to be around talented people, probably because we hope their skills and abilities will rub off on us. On the other hand, we are uncomfortable around those who are too competent—perhaps because we look bad by comparison. And we're attracted most to competence in others when it's accompanied by a warm rather than cool personality (Fiske et al., 2007).

Elliot Aronson and his associates demonstrated how competence and imperfection combine to affect attraction by having subjects evaluate recordings of candidates for a quiz program (summarized in Aronson, 2008). One was a "perfect" candidate who answered almost all the questions correctly and modestly admitted that he was an honor student, athlete, and college yearbook editor. The "average" candidate answered fewer questions correctly, had average grades, was a less successful athlete, and was a low-level member of the yearbook staff. Toward the end of half the recordings, the candidates committed a blunder, spilling coffee all over themselves. The remaining half of the recordings contained no such blunder. These, then, were the four experimental conditions: (1) a person with superior ability who blundered; (2) a person with superior ability who did not blunder; (3) an average person who blundered; and (4) an average person who did not blunder. The students who rated the attractiveness of these four types of people revealed an interesting and important principle of interpersonal attraction. The most attractive person was the superior candidate who blundered. Aronson's conclusion was that we like competence—but we also like people who are somewhat flawed because they remind us of ourselves.

PROXIMITY

As common sense suggests, we are likely to develop relationships with people with whom we interact frequently (Flora, 2004a). In many cases, proximity leads to liking. For instance, we're more likely to develop friendships with

MEDIA CLIP
Entertaining Relationships:
TV Reality Shows

Beginning with *The Real World* in the 1990s, many so-called reality shows have allowed viewers to watch people create, maintain, and end interpersonal relationships in televised episodes. Some of these programs (such as *The Bachelor/Bachelorette*) are matchmaking contests in which participants select relational partners. Physical attractiveness plays an important role in initial attraction in these shows, but increased proximity and disclosure allow participants to assess the costs and rewards of an ongoing relationship with their selected partners.

Other reality shows (such as the long-running *Big Brother* and *Survivor*) pit participants against each other, with each person vying not to be voted off the show by fellow contestants. In many cases, alliances form between contestants based on similarities (women vs. men; older participants vs. younger ones) and proximity (allied teammates spend more time with each other and often—but not always—grow to like each other). Competence is also a factor in that participants are attracted to those who perform well in the shows' survival contests. And complementarity plays a role when contestants' differing talents create "odd bedfellow" partnerships.

Although reality shows don't match most people's real worlds, the interpersonal relationships that develop on these programs often mirror what happens in everyday life.

close neighbors—whether near where we live or in adjacent seats in our classrooms (Back et al., 2008)—than with distant ones. Chances are also good that we'll choose a mate with whom we cross paths often. Proximity even has a role in social media, where messaging or chatting can create virtual proximity (Baker, 2008). As one researcher notes, when it comes to social networking sites, cultural proximity outweighs geographic proximity (Rohn, 2014). Facts like these are understandable when we consider that proximity allows us to get more information about other people and benefit from a relationship with them. Also, people in close proximity may be more similar to us—for example, if we live in the same neighborhood, odds are we share the same socioeconomic status.

Familiarity, on the other hand, can breed contempt. Evidence to support this fact comes from police blotters as well as university laboratories. Thieves frequently prey on nearby victims, even though the risk of being recognized is greater. Most aggravated assaults occur within the family or among close neighbors. The same principle holds in more routine contexts: You are likely to develop strong personal feelings, either positive or negative, toward others you encounter frequently.

DISCLOSURE

In Chapter 3, we describe how telling others important information about yourself can help build liking, both in person (Dindia, 2002; Sprecher et al., 2013) and through social media (Ledbetter et al., 2011). Sometimes the basis of this attraction comes from learning about ways we are similar, either in experiences ("I broke off an engagement myself") or in attitudes ("I feel nervous with strangers, too"). Self-disclosure also increases liking because it indicates regard. Sharing private information is a form of respect and trust—a kind of liking that we've already seen increases attractiveness.

Not all disclosure leads to liking. Research shows that the key to satisfying self-disclosure is reciprocity: getting back an amount and kind of information equivalent to that which you reveal (Dindia,

2000a). A second important ingredient in successful self-disclosure is timing. It's probably unwise to talk about your sexual insecurities with a new acquaintance or express your pet peeves to a friend at your birthday party. This is particularly true on Facebook: Disclosures made privately are perceived as more appropriate and intimate than those made publicly; also, disclosures made publicly reduce liking for the discloser (Bazarova, 2012). Finally, for the sake of self-protection, it's important to reveal personal information only when you are sure the other person is trustworthy (Shirley et al., 2007).

RELATIONAL DYNAMICS AND COMMUNICATION

Even the most stable relationships vary from day to day and over longer periods of time. Communication scholars have attempted to describe and explain how communication creates and reflects the changing dynamics of relational interaction. In this section, we discuss two different characterizations of relational development and interaction.

DEVELOPMENTAL MODELS OF INTERPERSONAL RELATIONSHIPS

One of the best-known models of relational stages was developed by Mark Knapp (Knapp et al., 2014; see also Dunleavy & Booth-Butterfield, 2009; Mongeau & Henningsen, 2008), who broke the waxing and waning of relationships into 10 steps that involve coming together and coming apart. Other researchers have suggested that any model of relational communication ought to contain a third area—**relational maintenance**—aimed at keeping relationships operating smoothly and satisfactorily (we'll discuss relational maintenance in more detail later in this chapter). Figure 9.1 shows how Knapp's 10 stages fit into this three-part view of relational communication. We now explore each stage in detail.

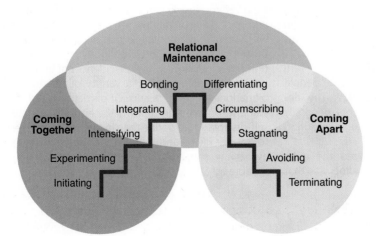

FIGURE 9.1 **Stages of Relationship Development**

Adapted from Knapp, M. L., Vangelisti, A. L., & Caughlin, J. P. (2014). *Interpersonal communication in human relationships* (7th ed.). Boston: Pearson Education.

Initiating

The goals in the **initiating** stage are to show that you are interested in making contact and to demonstrate that you are a person worth talking to (Sprecher et al., 2008). Communication during this stage is usually brief, and it generally follows conventional formulas: handshakes, remarks about innocuous subjects such as the weather, and friendly expressions. Such behavior may seem superficial and meaningless, but it is a way of signaling that you're interested in building some kind of relationship with the other person. It allows us to say, without saying, "I'm a friendly person, and I'd like to get to know you."

Initiating relationships—especially romantic ones—can be particularly difficult for people who are shy. Social media can make it easier for reticent people to strike up a relationship (Baker & Oswald, 2010; Sheeks & Birchmeier, 2007). One study of an online dating service found that participants who identified themselves as shy expressed a greater appreciation for the system's anonymous, nonthreatening environment than did nonshy users (Scharlott & Christ, 1995). The researchers found that many shy users employed the online service specifically to help them overcome their inhibitions about initiating relationships in face-to-face settings. The Focus on Research box below describes how this once novel approach to dating has become commonplace—and successful.

Keep in mind that initiating is the opening stage of *all* relationships, not just romantic ones. Friendships start here (Johnson et al., 2004), and so do business partnerships. In fact, some have compared employment interviews to first dates because they have similar properties (Sobel, 2009).

FOCUS ON RESEARCH
Online Dating: Many Happy Returns

Once upon a time, online dating services were viewed as last-ditch options for the romantically challenged. Skeptics questioned how well a computer could match people together, and whether relationships started online could be successful in person. Research by John Cacioppo and his colleagues may put those concerns to rest.

The scope of the study was huge. A survey firm collected responses from more than 19,000 people who married between 2005 and 2012. The demographic makeup of the respondents generally matched that of the U.S. married population during that period.

Cacioppo's research team analyzed the data, and perhaps their most surprising finding was that one-third of the respondents said their marital relationship began online. Although "online" included social networking sites, e-mail, chat rooms, and other such venues, nearly half of these initial online meetings took place on dating websites. When compared with marital relationships that began in person, those that started online had slightly higher satisfaction rates and slightly lower incidences of breakups.

The researchers offer a variety of possible explanations for these results. Of particular interest to students of communication is the notion that daters self-disclose more online than in person, which leads to greater liking and expectation matching. Whatever the reason, it seems clear that meeting online is a viable way to initiate a romantic relationship.

Cacioppo, J. T., Cacioppo, S., Gonzaga, G. C., Ogburn, E. L., & VanderWeele, T. J. (2013). Marital satisfaction and break-ups differ across on-line and off-line meeting venues. *PNAS, 110,* 10135–10140.

As you read about the stages that follow, consider how the communication involved could be true of landing a job, connecting with a roommate, or joining an organization—as well as forming a romantic relationship.

Experimenting

After making contact with a new person, we generally begin the search for common ground. This search usually starts with the basics: "Where are you from? What's your major?" From there we look for other similarities: "You're a runner too? How many miles do you run a week?"

It usually doesn't take long for communicators who are interested in one another to move from initiating to **experimenting**. The hallmark of experimenting is small talk. We tolerate the ordeal of small talk because it serves several functions. First, it is a useful way to find out what interests we share with the other person. It also provides a way to "audition" the other person—to help us decide whether a relationship is worth pursuing. In addition, small talk is a safe way to ease into a relationship. You haven't risked much as you decide whether to proceed further.

Scholars have noted, and your experience probably confirms, that the Internet and social networking sites are changing the nature of this stage of relational development for many. As Katrina Shonbeck (2011) points out, information gathering that used to occur over a gradual period of self-disclosure can be done quickly:

> By perusing someone's social networking profile, I can, more often than not, learn many of the same things I'd learn from them during the first couple of dates without the other person being present. From what they disclose on the general information page, I can learn their relationship statuses, political preferences, favorite hobbies, music, books, and movies. By looking through their pictures and their wall, I can get a pretty good sense of the kinds of people they like to hang out with, what they like to do on weekends, their personal styles. (p. 398)

College students in one study said this stage in romantic relationships used to involve securing a person's phone number; now it often involves a Facebook friend request (Fox et al., 2013). Once access is given, communicators can look over each other's site, allowing them to "chug" rather than "sip" information about the other person. Photos and mutual friends are important factors in deciding whether to continue developing a relationship. And of course, gathering this information online is less face-threatening and involves no stammering, blushing, or awkward pauses.

Of course, not all relational experiments are successful. You can probably remember an evening spent with a new friend or a first date in which you knew things were going nowhere before an hour had passed. Bowing out of such situations requires a measure of diplomacy and tact—but research shows it's easier to do so in online dating than in face-to-face encounters (Tong & Walther, 2011).

Intensifying

When a relationship begins **intensifying**, the kind of qualitatively interpersonal relationship defined in Chapter 1 starts to develop. In friendships, intensifying often includes spending more time together, participating in shared activities, hanging out with mutual friends, or taking trips together (Johnson et al., 2004). Dating couples use a wide range of strategies to communicate that their relationship is intensifying (Levine et al., 2006; Tolhuizen, 1989). About a quarter of the time they express their feelings directly to discuss the state of the relationship, such as saying "I love you" (Brantley et al., 2002). More often they use less direct methods of communication, perhaps as a way to protect their face: doing favors for the partner, giving tokens of affection, hinting and flirting, expressing feelings nonverbally, getting to know the partner's friends and family, and trying to look more physically attractive (Richmond et al., 1987).

The intensifying stage is usually a time of relational excitement and even euphoria. In friendships, it's about enthusiasm for having a new "BFF." For romantic partners, it's often filled with starstruck gazes, goose bumps, and daydreaming. As a result, it's a stage that's regularly depicted in movies and romance novels—after all, we love to watch lovers in love (Johnson & Holmes, 2009). The problem, of course, is that the stage doesn't last forever. Sometimes romantic partners who stop feeling goose bumps begin to question whether they're still in love, and friends begin to discover one another's flaws. Although it's possible that the relationship isn't as good as it seems, it's equally likely that it has simply moved on to a different stage—such as integrating.

Integrating

As the relationship strengthens, the individuals enter an **integrating** stage. They begin to take on an identity as a social unit. Invitations begin to come addressed to a couple. Social circles merge. The partners share each other's commitments: "Sure, we'll spend Thanksgiving with your family." Common property may begin to be designated—our apartment, our car, our song (Baxter, 1987). Partners create their own personal idioms (Dunleavy & Booth-Butterfield, 2009) and forms of play (Baxter, 1992). They develop routines and rituals that reinforce their identity as a couple—jogging together, eating at a favorite restaurant, expressing physical affection, and worshipping together (Afifi & Johnson, 1999; Bosson et al., 2006). As these examples illustrate, the stage of integrating is a time when we give up some characteristics of our former selves and become enmeshed with another person (Slotter & Gardner, 2009).

As we become more integrated with others, our sense of obligation to them grows (Korchmaros & Kenny, 2006; Roloff et al., 1988). We feel obliged to provide a variety of resources, such as class notes and money, whether the other person asks for them or not. When intimates do make requests of one another, they are relatively straightforward. Gone are the elaborate explanations, inducements, and apologies. In short, partners in an integrated relationship expect more from one another than they do in less intimate associations.

In contemporary relationships, integrating may include going "Facebook Official" (FBO) by declaring publicly that the couple is "in a relationship" (Fox et al., 2013). Of course, problems arise when one partner wants to be

FBO and the other doesn't (Papp et al., 2012). And the meaning of FBO can be different for each partner. One study found that in heterosexual relationships, women tend to perceive FBO declarations as involving more intensity and commitment than men do (Fox & Warber, 2013). As a result, women may connect FBO status with the rights and restrictions normally associated with bonding—a stage we look at now.

Bonding

During the **bonding** stage, partners make symbolic public gestures to show the world that their relationship exists and that a commitment has been made (Foster, 2008; Sandberg et al., 2012). These can include engagement or marriage, sharing a residence, a public ceremony, or a written or verbal pledge. The key is that bonding is the culmination of a developed relationship—the "officializing" of a couple's integration.

Relationships don't have to be romantic to achieve bonding. Consider, for instance, authors contracting to write a book together or a student being initiated into a sorority. As Lillian Rubin (1985) notes, in some cultures there are rituals for friends to mark their bonded status through a public commitment:

> Some Western cultures have rituals to mark the progress of a friendship and to give it public legitimacy and form. In Germany, for example, there's a small ceremony called *Duzen,* the name itself signifying the transformation in the relationship. The ritual calls for the two friends, each holding a glass of wine or beer, to entwine arms, thus bringing each other physically close, and to drink up after making a promise of eternal brotherhood with the word *Bruderschaft.* When it's over, the friends will have passed from a relationship that requires the formal *Sie* mode of address to the familiar *du.*

Bonding usually marks an important turning point in relationships. Up to now the relationship may have developed at a steady pace: Experimenting gradually moved into intensifying and then into integrating. Now, however, there is a spurt of commitment. The public display and declaration of exclusivity make this a critical period in the relationship.

Differentiating

So far, we have been looking at the growth of relationships. Although some reach a plateau of development, going on successfully for as long as a lifetime, others pass through several stages of decline and dissolution. Even in the most committed relationships, partners often find themselves needing to reestablish their individual identities in a stage Knapp calls **differentiating**. This transition often shows up in a couple's pronoun usage. Instead of talking about "our" weekend plans, differentiating conversations focus on what "I" want to do. Relational issues that were once agreed on (such as "You'll be the breadwinner and I'll manage the home") now become points of contention: "Why am *I* stuck at home when I have better career potential

MEDIA CLIP
Stages They're Going Through: (500) Days of Summer

"You should know upfront, this is not a love story" intones the narrator ominously at the outset of *(500) Days of Summer*. Indeed, this is not a typical romantic comedy. The story of Tom (Joseph Gordon-Levitt) and Summer (Zooey Deschanel) is told by reviewing various days, nonchronologically, in their tumultuous relationship.

Relational stages play an important role for this couple. Tom believes their romance has long-term potential, and he wants them to move toward what Knapp would label as integrating and bonding. Summer, on the other hand, seems content to stay at the stages of experimenting and intensifying. When Tom pushes for more commitment, Summer engages in behaviors typical of relational deterioration: differentiating, circumscribing, and avoiding.

The movie illustrates that relational stages are often a matter of perception. The people involved might not agree on the stage they are—or want to be—in.

than *you?*" The root of the term *differentiating* is the word *different*, suggesting that change plays an important role in this stage.

Differentiation also can be positive, for people need to be individuals as well as part of a relationship. Think, for instance, of young adults who want to forge their own unique lives and identity, even while maintaining their relationships with their families of origin (Skowron et al., 2009). The same can hold true for international couples who want to stay connected to their cultural values as well to each other (Kim et al., 2012). As Figure 9.1 on page 277 shows, differentiating is often a part of normal relational maintenance in which partners manage the inevitable challenges that come their way. The key to successful differentiation is maintaining commitment to a relationship while creating the space for being individuals as well (we describe this later in the chapter as the connection-autonomy dialectic).

Circumscribing

In the **circumscribing** stage, partners reduce the scope of their contact with each other. The word "circumscribe" comes from the Latin meaning "to draw circles around." Distinctions that emerged in the differentiating stage become more clearly marked and labeled: "my friends" and "your friends"; "my bank account" and "your bank account"; "my room" and "your room." Such distinctions can be markers of a healthy balance between individual and relational identity. They become a problem, however, when there are clearly more areas of separation than integration in a relationship, or when the areas of separation seriously limit interaction, such as taking a personal vacation expressly to put space between you and your partner.

Stagnating

If circumscribing continues, the relationship begins to stagnate. Members behave toward each other in old, familiar ways without much feeling. No growth occurs; relational boredom sets in (Harasymchuk & Fehr, 2013). The **stagnating** relationship is a hollow shell of its former self. We see stagnation in many workers who have lost enthusiasm for their job yet continue to go through the motions for years. The same sad event occurs for some couples who unenthusiastically have the same conversations, see the same people, and follow the same routines without any sense of joy or novelty.

Avoiding

When stagnation becomes too unpleasant, people in a relationship begin to create distance between each other by **avoiding**. Sometimes they do it under the guise of excuses ("I've been sick lately and can't see you") and sometimes directly ("Please don't call me; I don't want to see you now"). In either case, by this point the handwriting is on the wall about the relationship's future.

Research by Jon Hess (2000, 2003) reveals that there are several ways we gain distance. One way is *expressing detachment*, such as avoiding the other person altogether, or zoning out. A second way is *avoiding involvement*, such as leaving the room, ignoring the person's questions, steering clear of touching, and being superficially polite. *Showing antagonism* is a third technique, which includes behaving in a hostile way and treating the other person as a lesser person. A fourth strategy is to *mentally dissociate* from the other person, such as thinking about the other person as less capable, or as unimportant. A vicious cycle gets started when avoiding the other person: the more one person avoids the other, the greater the odds the other will reciprocate. And the more topics they both avoid, the less satisfactory is the relationship (Sargent, 2002).

Terminating

Not all relationships end: Many partnerships, friendships, and marriages last for a lifetime once they're established. But many do deteriorate and reach the final stage of **terminating**. The process of terminating has its own distinguishable pattern (Battaglia et al., 1998; Conlan, 2008). Characteristics of this stage include summary dialogues of where the relationship has gone and the desire to dissociate. The relationship may end with a cordial dinner, a note left on the kitchen table, a phone call, a text, or a legal document stating the dissolution. Depending on each person's feelings, this terminating stage can be quite short and amicable, or it may be bitterly drawn out over time.

How do the individuals deal with each other after a romantic relationship has ended? The best predictor of whether the individuals will become friends after the relationship is terminated is whether they were friends before their romantic involvement (Metts et al., 1989). The way the couple splits up also makes a difference. It's no surprise to find that positive communication during a breakup—for example, expressions of no regrets for time spent together and other attempts to minimize hard feelings—leads to more friendships. Ongoing friendship is less likely when communication during termination is negative and involves manipulation or complaining to third parties.

Scholars have begun to investigate the role technology can play in relational termination. One survey of 1,000 cell phone users found that 45 percent had used their mobile device to end a relationship, usually by text (Mychalcewycz, 2009). Obviously, breaking up this way runs the risk of wounding and infuriating the person being dumped ("She didn't even have the guts to tell me to my face") and lessens the likelihood of postrelationship goodwill. A different study found that those on the receiving end of a breakup via technology tended to have high levels of attachment anxiety—which

might explain why their partners didn't want to deliver the news in person (Weisskirch & Delevi, 2013). Once a romantic relationship is over, it may be wise to take a break from being Facebook friends with an ex-partner. Checking up on your former sweetheart may reduce some uncertainty (Tong, 2013), but surveillance of an ex's Facebook page is associated with greater distress over the breakup, more negative feelings, and lower personal growth (Marshall, 2012).

Terminating a relationship is, for many people, a learning experience. Ty Tashiro and Patricia Frazier (2003) asked college students who recently had a romantic relationship breakup to describe the positive things they learned that might help them in future romantic relationships. Responses fell into four categories: "person positives," such as gaining self-confidence and that it's all right to cry; "other positives," such as learning more about what is desired in a partner; "relational positives," such as how to communicate better and how not to jump into a relationship too quickly; and "environment positives," such as learning to rely more on friends and how to better balance relationships and school work. And scholars note that although gaining *closure* might be an ideal for relational termination, finding *meaning* might be a more attainable and healthy goal (Boss & Carnes, 2012; Roets & Soetens, 2010).

Limits of Developmental Models

Although Knapp's model offers insights into relational stages, it doesn't describe the ebb and flow of communication in every relationship. The model suggests that a relationship exhibits only the most dominant traits of just one of the 10 stages at any given time, but in reality elements of other stages are usually present. For example, two lovers deep in the throes of integrating may still do their share of experimenting ("Wow, I never knew that about you!") and have differentiating disagreements ("I think it's more important for us to be close to our parents than you do"). Likewise, family members who spend most of their energy avoiding each other may have an occasional good spell in which their former closeness briefly intensifies. Relationships can experience features of "coming together" and "coming apart" at the same time, as exemplified by relational dialectics.

DIALECTICAL PERSPECTIVES ON RELATIONAL DYNAMICS

Not all theorists agree that relational stages are the best way to explain interaction in relationships. Some suggest that communicators grapple with the same kinds of challenges whether a relationship is brand new or has lasted decades. Their focus, then, is on the ongoing maintenance of relationships. They argue that communicators seek important but apparently incompatible goals. The struggle to achieve these goals creates **dialectical tensions**: conflicts that arise when two opposing or incompatible forces exist simultaneously.

Communication scholars including Leslie Baxter (2011; Baxter & Braithwaite, 2008) and William Rawlins (1992) have identified several dialectical forces that make successful communication challenging. Table 9.1 summarizes three that we experience both *internally* within the relationship and *externally* as we and our relational partners face other people whose desires clash with our own.

Integration versus Separation

No one is an island. Recognizing this fact, we seek out involvement with others. But, at the same time, we are unwilling to sacrifice our entire identity to even the most satisfying relationship. The conflicting desires for connection and independence are embodied in the **integration-separation dialectic**. This set of apparently contradictory needs creates communication challenges that can show up both within a relationship and when relational partners face the world.

Internally, the struggle shows up in the **connection-autonomy dialectic**. We want to be close to others, but at the same time we seek independence (Frost & Forrester, 2013). Sociolinguist Deborah Tannen (1986) captures the insoluble integration-separation dialectic nicely by evoking the image of two porcupines trying to get through a cold winter:

> They huddle together for warmth, but their sharp quills prick each other, so they pull away. But then they get cold. They have to keep adjusting their closeness and distance to keep from freezing and from getting pricked by their fellow porcupines—the source of both comfort and pain.
>
> We need to get close to each other to have a sense of community, to feel we're not alone in the world. But we need to keep our distance from each other to preserve our independence, so others don't impose on or engulf us. This duality reflects the human condition. We are individual and social creatures. We need other people to survive, but we want to survive as individuals.

Baxter (1994) describes the consequences for relational partners who can't successfully manage the conflicting needs for connection and autonomy. Some of the most common reasons for relational breakups involve failure of partners to satisfy one another's needs for connection: "We barely spent any time together"; "My partner wasn't committed to the relationship"; "We had different needs." But other relational complaints involve excessive demands for connection: "I was feeling trapped"; "I needed freedom" (Hui et al., 2013).

TABLE 9.1 Dialectical Tensions

	DIALECTIC OF INTEGRATION-SEPARATION	DIALECTIC OF STABILITY-CHANGE	DIALECTIC OF EXPRESSION-PRIVACY
Internal Manifestations	Connection-Autonomy	Predictability-Novelty	Openness-Closedness
External Manifestations	Inclusion-Seclusion	Conventionality-Uniqueness	Revelation-Concealment

From Baxter, L. A. (1994). A dialogic approach to relationship maintenance. In D. J. Canary & L. Stafford (Eds.), *Communication and relational maintenance* (p. 240). San Diego, CA: Academic Press.

Perhaps not surprisingly, research suggests that in heterosexual romantic relationships, men often want more autonomy and women typically want more connection and commitment (Buunk, 2005; Feeney, 1999).

Romantic couples report that the autonomy-connection dialectic is one of the most significant factors affecting their relationships (Erbert, 2000; Pawlowski, 1998). The Focus on Research sidebar below ("Tethered by Cell Phones") describes how something as seemingly trivial as cell phone use can create dialectical tensions for couples. Research also shows that managing connection and autonomy is as important during divorce as it is at the beginning of a marriage (Pam & Pearson, 1998). Separating partners seek ways to salvage and reconcile the unbreakable bonds of their personal history (including finances, children, and friends) with their new independence.

Parents and children must deal constantly with the conflicting tugs of connection and autonomy. These struggles don't end when children grow up and leave home. Parents experience the mixed feelings of relief at their new freedom and longings to stay connected to their adult children. Likewise, grown children typically feel excitement at being on their own and yet miss the bonds that had been taken for granted since the beginning of their lives (Blacker, 1999; Fulmer, 1999). We discuss these family dialectics further in Chapter 10.

It's important to emphasize that autonomy-connection tensions aren't necessarily a sign of a troubled relationship. Look again at Figure 9.1 on page 277. In that model, you'll see that Integrating and Bonding (connection), as

FOCUS ON RESEARCH
Tethered by Cell Phones: A Connection-Autonomy Dilemma

Your sweetheart just texted you . . . for the third time this evening . . . for the tenth time today. It's nice to stay connected, but not when you're out with friends and want to focus on them.

For many, mobile devices mean that communicators are always available—perhaps when they don't want to be. Researchers surveyed individuals in romantic relationships and found that cell phone use is indeed a conflict issue for many couples. Typical tensions include frequency of contact (too much or too little) and timing of texts and calls. Some of those surveyed said they created rules about cell phone use with their significant others, with varying degrees of success and satisfaction. Interestingly, many respondents said, "We have no rules" about phone use and indicated they didn't want or need them.

The researchers acknowledged some methodological concerns. First, individuals rather than couples participated in the studies. It's possible, therefore, that those surveyed didn't adequately represent how their partners feel about cell phone use. Second, female participants outnumbered males more than 2 to 1. Given previous research showing that young men see cell phone access as a potential threat to their relational autonomy (Henderson et al., 2002), it's possible that the tension is even greater than this study suggests.

Duran, R. L., Kelly, L., & Rotaru, T. (2011). Mobile phones in romantic relationships and the dialectic of autonomy versus connection. *Communication Quarterly, 59,* 19–36.

Miller-Ott, A. E., Kelly, L., & Duran, R. L. (2012). The effects of cell phone usage rules on satisfaction in romantic relationships. *Communication Quarterly, 60,* 17–34.

well as Differentiating and Circumscribing (autonomy), fall in the circle labeled *Relational Maintenance*. Although descriptors such as "struggles" and "conflicts" can make dialectical tensions sound negative, it's best to see them as normal and manageable factors in maintaining healthy relationships.

The tension between integration and separation also operates externally, when people within a relationship struggle to meet the competing needs of the **inclusion-seclusion dialectic**. They struggle to reconcile a desire for involvement with the "outside world" with the desire to live their own lives, free of what can feel like interference from others. For example, when the end of a busy week comes, does a couple accept the invitation to a party (and sacrifice the chance to spend quality time with one another), or do they decline the invitation (and risk losing contact with valued friends)? Does a close-knit nuclear family choose to take a much anticipated vacation together (disappointing their relatives), or do they attend a family reunion (losing precious time to enjoy one another without any distractions)? How does a just-married couple negotiate time demands with newly acquired in-laws when inclusion-seclusions tensions typically run high (Prentice, 2009)?

Stability versus Change

Stability is an important need in relationships, but too much of it can lead to feelings of staleness. The **stability-change dialectic** operates both between partners and when they face others outside the relationship. Within a relationship, the **predictability-novelty dialectic** captures another set of tensions. Although nobody wants a completely unpredictable relational partner ("You're not the person I married!"), humorist Dave Barry (1990, p. 47) exaggerates only slightly when he talks about the boredom that can come when marriage partners know each other too well:

> After a decade or so of marriage, you know *everything* about your spouse, every habit and opinion and twitch and tic and minor skin growth. You could write a seventeen-pound book solely about the way your spouse eats. This kind of intimate knowledge can be very handy in certain situations—such as when you're on a TV quiz show where the object is to identify your spouse from the sound of his or her chewing—but it tends to lower the passion level of a relationship.

At an external level, the **conventionality-uniqueness dialectic** captures the challenges that people in a relationship face when trying to meet others' expectations as well as their own. On one hand, stable patterns of behavior do emerge that enable others to make useful judgments such as "happy family" or "dependable organization." But those blanket characterizations can stifle people in relationships who may sometimes want to break away from the expectations others hold of them. For example, playing the conventional role of "happy family" or "perfect couple" during a time of conflict can be a burden when the couple feels the need to behave in less stereotypical ways.

Expression versus Privacy

Disclosure is one characteristic of interpersonal relationships. Yet, along with the drive for intimacy, we have an equally important need to maintain some space between ourselves and others. These sometimes conflicting drives create the **expression-privacy dialectic**.

The internal struggle between expression and privacy shows up in the **openness-closedness dialectic**. What do you do in an intimate relationship when a person you care about asks an important question that you don't want to answer? "Do you think I'm attractive?" "Are you having a good time?" "What's my problem?" Your commitment to the relationship may compel you toward honesty, but your concern for the other person's feelings and a desire for privacy may lead you to be less than completely honest. Many people claim, "There are no secrets between my best friend and me," or "I tell my sweetheart everything," but that's likely an overstatement. Wise communicators make choices about what they will and won't share with loved ones—sometimes (but not always) for the other person's sake.

The same conflicts between openness and privacy operate externally in the **revelation-concealment dialectic**. If you and a longtime fellow worker haven't been getting along, do you answer the boss's question, "How's it going?" honestly, or do you keep your disagreement to yourselves? If your family has had a run of bad (or good) financial luck and a friend asks to borrow (or lend) money, do you share your situation or keep quiet? If you're part of a same-sex couple, but you're not sure your relationship will be endorsed by others, when and how do you go "public" with that information (Suter et al., 2006; Suter et al., 2008)? All of these questions speak to tensions related to concealing versus revealing. These challenges have increased as social media make privacy boundaries more difficult to manage (Debatin et al., 2009). We take a closer look at privacy management in Chapter 10.

Strategies for Managing Dialectical Tensions

Managing the dialectical tensions outlined thus far presents communication challenges (Duran et al., 2011; Prentice & Kramer, 2006). There are at least eight ways these challenges can be managed (Baxter & Braithwaite, 2006b).

- *Denial* In the strategy of denial, communicators respond to one end of the dialectical spectrum and ignore the other. For example, a couple caught between the conflicting desires for stability and novelty might find their struggle for change too difficult to manage and choose to follow predictable, if unexciting patterns of relating to one another.
- *Disorientation* In this mode, communicators feel so overwhelmed and helpless that they are unable to confront their problems. In the face of dialectical tensions, they might fight, freeze, or even leave the relationship. A couple who discovers soon after the honeymoon that living a "happily ever after" conflict-free life is impossible might become so terrified that they would come to view their marriage as a mistake.
- *Alternation* Communicators who use this strategy choose one end of the dialectical spectrum at some times and the other end on different occasions. Friends, for example, might manage the connection-autonomy dialectic by alternating between times when they spend a large amount of time together and other periods when they live independent lives.
- *Segmentation* Partners who use this tactic compartmentalize different areas of their relationship. For example, a couple might manage the openness-closedness dialectic by sharing almost all their feelings about

mutual friends with one another but keeping certain parts of their past romantic histories private.

- *Balance* Communicators who try to balance dialectical tensions recognize that both forces are legitimate and try to manage them through compromise. As we point out in Chapter 12, compromise is inherently a situation in which everybody loses at least a little of what he or she wants. A couple caught between the conflicting desires for predictability and novelty might seek balance by compromising with a lifestyle that is neither as predictable as one wants nor as surprise filled as the other seeks—not an ideal outcome.

- *Integration* With this approach, communicators simultaneously accept opposing forces without trying to diminish them. Barbara Montgomery (1993) describes a couple who accept both the needs for predictability and novelty by devising a "predictably novel" approach: Once a week they would do something together that they had never done before. Similarly, Dawn Braithwaite and her colleagues (1998) found that stepfamilies often manage the tension between the "old family" and the "new family" by adapting and blending their family rituals.

- *Recalibration* Communicators can respond to dialectical challenges by reframing them so that the apparent contradiction disappears. Consider how a couple who felt hurt by one another's unwillingness to share parts of their past might redefine the secrets as creating an attractive aura of mystery instead of being a problem to be solved. Rather than thinking "We're keeping secrets about our past," the partners might think "Those secrets make things a little mysterious and exciting." The desire for privacy would still remain, but it would no longer compete with a need for openness about every aspect of the past.

- *Reaffirmation* This approach acknowledges that dialectical tensions will never disappear. Instead of trying to make them go away, reaffirming communicators accept—or even embrace—the challenges they present. The metaphorical view of relational life as a kind of roller coaster reflects this orientation, and communicators who use reaffirmation view dialectical tensions as part of the ride.

Generally speaking, integration, recalibration, and reaffirmation are seen as the most productive for managing dialectical tensions; and researchers suggest it's wise to make use of multiple strategies (Baxter & Montgomery, 1996). For example, broken-up couples report having used denial, alternation, and segmentation less than successfully, and they tended to rely on only one strategy rather than using the variety at their disposal (Sahlstein & Dun, 2008). Because dialectical tensions are a part of life, choosing how to communicate about them can make a tremendous difference in the quality of your relationships.

COMMUNICATING ABOUT RELATIONSHIPS

By now it is clear that relationships are complex, dynamic, and important. In this section, we look at ways to improve relational communication. We start by revisiting an important principle of interpersonal communication discussed in Chapter 1: Every message has a *content* and a *relational* dimension.

CONTENT AND RELATIONAL MESSAGES

The most obvious component of most messages is their content—the subject being discussed. The content of statements such as "It's your turn to do the dishes" or "I'm busy Saturday night" is obvious. In addition, however, every message—both verbal and nonverbal—also has a second, relational dimension, which makes statements about how the communicators feel toward one another (Knobloch & Solomon, 2003; Watzlawick et al., 1967). These relational messages deal with one or more social needs: intimacy, affinity, respect, and control. Consider the examples we just mentioned:

- Imagine two ways of saying "It's your turn to do the dishes"—one that is demanding and another that is matter-of-fact. Notice how the different nonverbal messages make statements about how the sender views control in this part of the relationship. The demanding tone says, in effect, "I have a right to tell you what to do around the house"; whereas the matter-of-fact one suggests, "I'm just reminding you of something you might have overlooked."
- You can easily imagine two ways to deliver the statement "I'm busy Saturday night," one with little affection and the other with much liking.

Like these messages, every statement we make goes beyond discussing the subject at hand and says something about the way the speaker feels about the recipient and their relationship. You can prove this fact by listening for the relational messages implicit in your own statements to others and theirs to you.

Most of the time we are unaware of the relational messages that bombard us every day. Sometimes these messages don't capture our awareness because they match our belief about the amount of control, liking, or intimacy that is appropriate in a relationship. For example, you probably won't be offended if your boss tells you to drop everything and tackle a certain job because you agree that supervisors have the right to direct employees. However, if your boss delivered the order in a condescending, sarcastic, or abusive tone of voice, you would probably be offended. Your complaint wouldn't be with the order itself but with the way it was delivered. "I may work for this company," you might think, "but I'm not a slave or an idiot. I deserve to be treated like a human being."

Exactly how are relational messages communicated? As the boss-employee example suggests, they are usually expressed nonverbally. To test this fact for yourself, imagine how you could act while saying "Can you help

me for a minute?" in a way that communicates each of the
following relationships:

superiority	aloofness
helplessness	sexual desire
friendliness	irritation

"She's texting me, but I think she's also subtexting me."

Although nonverbal behaviors are a good source of relational messages, remember that they are ambiguous. The
sharp tone you take as a personal insult might be due to
fatigue, and the interruption you take as an attempt to ignore your ideas might be a sign of pressure that has nothing to do with you. Before you jump to conclusions about
relational clues, it is a good idea to verify the accuracy of
your interpretation with the other person: "When you cut
me off, it seemed like you were angry with me. Were you?"

Not all relational messages are nonverbal. Social scientists use the
term **metacommunication** to describe messages that refer to other messages (Craig, 2005; Weder, 2008). In other words, metacommunication is
communication about communication. Whenever we discuss a relationship
with others, we are metacommunicating: "I wish we could stop arguing so
much," or "I appreciate how honest you've been with me."

Despite its importance, overt metacommunication isn't a common feature of most relationships (Fogel & Branco, 1997; Wilmot, 1995). In fact,
there seems to be an aversion to it, even among many intimates (Bisson
& Levine, 2009; Zhang & Stafford, 2008). When 90 people were asked to
identify the taboo subjects in their personal relationships, the most frequent
topics involved metacommunication (Baxter & Wilmot, 1985). For example,
people were reluctant to discuss the state of their current relationships and
the norms ("rules") that governed their lives together. Nevertheless, there are
times when it becomes necessary to talk about what is going on between you
and the other person. And research shows that metacommunication can play
a vital role in relational maintenance and repair (Becker et al., 2008).

MAINTAINING AND SUPPORTING RELATIONSHIPS

Just as gardens need tending, cars need tune-ups, and bodies need exercise,
relationships need ongoing maintenance to keep them successful and satisfying (Lydon & Quinn, 2013). And when the chips are down, we count on
our interpersonal relationships to offer the support we need (Lakey, 2013).

Relational Maintenance

As noted earlier, relational maintenance can be defined as communication
that keeps relationships running smoothly and satisfactorily. What kinds of
communication help maintain relationships? Researchers have identified
five strategies that couples use to keep their interaction satisfying (Myers &
Goodboy, 2013; Ogolsky & Bowers, 2013).

- *Positivity.* Keeping the relational climate polite and upbeat and also
  avoiding criticism.

- *Openness*. Talking directly about the nature of the relationship and disclosing your personal needs and concerns. This includes *metacommunicating*.
- *Assurances*. Letting the other person know—both verbally and nonverbally—that he or she matters to you and that you are committed to the relationship.
- *Social networks*. Being invested in each other's friends, family, and loved ones.
- *Sharing tasks*. Helping one another take care of life's chores and obligations.

These maintenance strategies aren't just for romantic relationships. One study analyzed college students' e-mail to see which maintenance approaches they used (Johnson et al., 2008). With family and friends, two strategies were used most: openness ("Things have been a little crazy for me lately") and social networks ("How are you and Sam? Hopefully good"). With romantic partners, however, assurances ("This is just a little e-mail to say I love you") were the most-used maintenance devices.

Social media can play an important role in maintaining relationships (Ledbetter, 2010). Social networking sites such as Facebook, Twitter, and Instagram give communicators the chance to keep up with each other through status updates (Craig & Wright, 2012; Dainton, 2013). Of course, there's the risk that constant updates will leave little to talk about in person, as the cartoon on this page wryly suggests. Phone calls and e-mails can help too, with phoning being particularly valuable for more intimate topics (Utz, 2007). One study found that women use social media for relational maintenance more often than men do, regardless of the type of relationship maintained (Houser et al., 2012). This is consistent with research showing that women expect and receive more maintenance communication with their female friends than men do with males (Hall et al., 2011).

Social media can be especially useful for meeting the challenges of long-distance relationships. These relationships are increasingly common, and they can be as stable as, or even more so than, geographically close relationships (Merolla, 2010; Stafford, 2005). This is true not only for romantic and family relationships, but also for friendships (Johnson, Becker, et al., 2009). The key is a commitment to relational maintenance. In one study, female college students said that openness and mutual problem solving are vital maintenance strategies in long-distance dating relationships (McGuire & Kinnery, 2010). In another study, both men and women reported that openness (self-disclosure) was the most important factor for maintaining their long-distance friendships (Johnson, Haigh, et al., 2009). They conceded that sharing tasks and practical help may be less viable options in long-distance relationships ("I'd help if I could, but I'm a thousand miles away"). We talk more about relational maintenance strategies for close relationships in Chapter 10.

Jeroen Vanstiphout—www.kartoen.be

Social Support

Whereas relational maintenance is about keeping a relationship thriving, **social support** is about helping others during challenging times by providing emotional, informational, or instrumental resources (MacGeorge et al., 2011). Social support has been consistently linked to mental and physical health (Lakey, 2013) and can be offered in a variety of ways:

- Emotional support: Few things are more helpful during times of stress, hurt, or grief than a loved one who listens with empathy and responds in caring ways (Reis & Clark, 2013). Chapter 7 (pages 225–227) describes what supporting does and doesn't sound like when responding to others' emotional needs. It's important to keep your message *person centered* (High & Dillard, 2012)—that is, focused on the emotions of the speaker ("this must be difficult for you") rather than minimizing those feelings ("it's not the end of the world") or diverting attention ("tomorrow is a new day").
- Informational support: The people in our lives can be helpful information sources. They can give us recommendations for shopping, advice about relationships, or observations about our blind spots. Of course, keep in mind that advice is most likely to be regarded as supportive when it's wanted and requested by the person in need.
- Instrumental support: Sometimes support is best given by rolling up your sleeves and doing a task or favor to show that you care (Semmer et al., 2008). This can be as simple as a ride to the airport or as involved as caregiving during illness. We count on loved ones to offer assistance in times of need, and instrumental support is a primary marker of a meaningful friendship ("a friend in need is a friend indeed").

It's worth noting that social support can also be found online, often from people whom you may never meet in person (Rains & Keating, 2011). In fact, approximately 20 percent of Internet users go online to find others with similar health problems (Fox, 2011). When asked why, a common response is that they feel more comfortable talking with like-minded people with whom they have few formal ties—particularly when the health issues are embarrassing or stigma laden. As an example, there are blogs that offer social support for people who are morbidly obese (Sanford, 2010). These sites become interactive communities where people with similar conditions share their struggles and offer each other affirming feedback. One blogger put it this way: "When I have a bad week on the scale, all I have to do is write up an entry and post it on the blog. My readers are always full of good advice, comments and support" (Sanford, 2010, p. 577).

REPAIRING DAMAGED RELATIONSHIPS

Sooner or later, even the most satisfying and stable relationships hit a bumpy patch. Some problems arise from outside forces: work, finances, competing relationships, and so on. At other times, problems arise from differences and disagreements within the relationship. In Chapter 11, we offer guidelines for dealing with these sorts of challenges. A third type of relational problem

● SOCIAL CAPITAL AND CAREER ADVANCEMENT @WORK

The old saying, "It isn't what you know, it's *who* you know," is at least somewhat true. *Social capital*, in part, refers to the potential benefits that come from belonging to one or more social networks. An impressive body of research confirms that robust personal networks can pay off in your career (Krebs, 2008).

People with high social capital are more likely to find good jobs quickly and be promoted early. They receive more positive performance evaluations from their bosses and earn larger bonuses. Social capital doesn't just benefit individuals. Group members who have rich and diverse personal networks enhance the performance of their teams, helping them generate more creative solutions and reach their goals more rapidly.

Along with contacts that you make and maintain through face-to-face and phone contact, online social networks can be a powerful tool for building and using social capital (Ellison et al., 2007). Business-oriented resources such as LinkedIn can be helpful, as can "friends" on more general sites such as Facebook (Aubrey & Rill, 2013). Within large organizations, company "intranets" can provide a way for employees to keep in touch.

Whatever their nature, social networks can go beyond their obvious value as sources of friendship, providing you with the resources that can make a critical difference in your career success.

comes from **relational transgressions**, when one partner violates the explicit or implicit terms of the relationship, letting the other one down in some important way.

Types of Relational Transgressions

Table 9.2 lists some types of relational transgressions. Violations such as these fall into different categories (Emmers-Sommer, 2003; Guerrero & Bachman. 2008), which we now describe.

Minor versus Significant Some of the items listed in Table 9.2 aren't inherently transgressions, and in small doses they can actually aid relationships. For instance, a *little* distance can make the heart grow fonder, a *little* jealousy can be a sign of affection, and a *little* anger can start the process of resolving a gripe. In large and regular doses, however, these acts become serious transgressions that can damage personal relationships. When transgression severity is perceived as high, and the perceiver's communication competence is low, rumination increases and relational closeness decreases (Robbins & Merrill, 2014).

Social versus Relational Some transgressions violate *social rules* shared by society at large. For example, almost everyone would agree that ridiculing or humiliating a friend or family member in public is a violation of a fundamental social rule regarding saving others' face. Other rules are *relational* in nature—unique norms constructed by the people involved. For instance, some families have a rule stating, "If I'm going to be more than a little bit late, I'll let you know so that you don't worry." Once such a rule exists, failure to honor it feels like a violation, even though outsiders might not view it as such.

TABLE 9.2 Some Types of Relational Transgressions

Lack of Commitment
Failure to honor important obligations (e.g., financial, emotional, task related)
Self-serving dishonesty
Unfaithfulness

Distance
Physical separation (beyond what is necessary)
Psychological separation (avoidance, ignoring)

Disrespect
Criticism (especially in front of third parties)

Problematic Emotions
Jealousy
Unjustified suspicion
Rage

Aggression
Verbal hostility
Physical violence

Deliberate versus Unintentional Some transgressions are unintentional. You might reveal something about a friend's past without realizing that this disclosure would be embarrassing. Other violations, though, are intentional. In a fit of anger, you might purposely lash out with a cruel comment, knowing that it will hurt the other person's feelings.

One-time versus Incremental The most obvious transgressions occur in a single episode: an act of betrayal, a verbal assault, or walking out in anger. But more subtle transgressions can occur over time. Consider emotional withdrawal: People have times when they retreat into themselves, and we usually give one another the space to do just that. But if the withdrawal slowly becomes pervasive, it becomes a violation of the fundamental rule in most relationships that partners should be available to one another.

Strategies for Relational Repair

Research confirms the commonsense notion that a first step to repairing a transgression is to talk about the violation (Brandau-Brown & Ragsdale, 2008; Dindia & Baxter, 1987). Stating the negative outcomes of the transgression or making an explicit demand for an apology are both associated with more positive relational outcomes than a spontaneous apology (Peyton & Goei, 2013). In Chapter 5, we offer tips for sending clear, assertive "I-messages" when you believe you've been wronged ("I was really embarrassed when you yelled at me in front of everybody last night"), whether describing the outcomes of the transgression or asking for an apology.

In other cases, you might be responsible for the transgression and want to raise it for discussion: "What did I do that you found so hurtful?" "Why was my behavior a problem for you?" Asking questions such as these—and listening nondefensively to the answers—can be an enormous challenge. In Chapter 7, we offer guidelines for listening; and in Chapter 11, we provide tips about how to manage criticism.

Not surprisingly, some transgressions are harder to repair than others. One study of dating partners found that sexual infidelity and breaking up with the partner were the two least forgivable offenses (Bachman & Guerrero, 2006). The seriousness of the transgression and the relative strength of the relationship prior to the offense are the two most significant factors in whether forgiveness will be granted (Guerrero & Bachman, 2010).

For the best chance of repairing a seriously damaged relationship, an apology needs to be offered. *The Last Lecture* author Randy Pausch (2008) notes, "If you have done something wrong in your dealings with another person, it's as if there's an infection in your relationship. A good apology is like an antibiotic, a bad apology is like rubbing salt in the wound" (p. 161). As the cartoon above illustrates, some apologies are less than sincere. An ideal apology contains these three elements (Kelley & Waldron, 2005; Villadsen, 2008):

- An explicit admission that the transgression was wrong: "I acted like a selfish jerk."
- A genuine acknowledgment of regret: "I'm really sorry. I feel awful for letting you down."
- Some type of compensation: "No matter what happens, I'll never do anything like that again."

An apology will be convincing only if the speaker's nonverbal behaviors match what is said (Hannawa, 2014). Even then, it may be unrealistic to expect immediate forgiveness. Sometimes, especially with severe transgressions, expressions of regret and promises of new behavior will only be accepted conditionally, with a need for them to be demonstrated over time before the aggrieved party regards them as genuine (Merolla, 2008).

Given the challenges and possible humiliation involved in apologizing, is it worth the effort? Research suggests yes. Participants in one study consistently reported that they had more remorse over apologies they *didn't* offer than about those they did (Exline et al., 2007).

Forgiving Transgressions

Many people think of forgiveness as a topic for theologians and philosophers. However, social scientists have found that forgiving others has both personal and relational benefits (Antonuccio & Jackson, 2009; McCullough et al., 2009). On a personal level, forgiveness has been shown to reduce emotional distress and aggression (Eaton & Struthers, 2006; Orcutt, 2006) as well as to improve cardiovascular functioning (Hannon et al., 2012; Lawler et al., 2003). Interpersonally, extending forgiveness to lovers, friends, and family can often help restore damaged relationships (Fincham & Beach, 2013; Waldron & Kelley, 2005). Moreover, most research shows that transgressors who have been forgiven are usually less likely to repeat their offenses than those who have not received forgiveness (Wallace et al., 2008; Whited et al., 2010).

Even when a sincere apology is offered, forgiving others can be difficult. Research shows that one way to improve your ability to forgive is to recall times when you have mistreated or hurt others in the past—in other words, to remember that you, too, have wronged others and needed their forgiveness (Exline et al., 2008; Takaku et al., 2001). Given that it's in our own best interest to be forgiving, we would do well to remember these words from Richard Walters (1984), who saw forgiveness as a choice requiring courage and continuous acts of will: "When we have been hurt we have two alternatives: be destroyed by resentment, or forgive. Resentment is death; forgiving leads to healing and life" (p. 366).

ASSESSING YOUR COMMUNICATION

Forgiveness-Granting Strategies

Presented here is a list of behaviors a person might use to respond to someone seeking forgiveness. To what extent do you use each strategy? Rate each one on a scale ranging from 0 to 7, where 0 = never use and 7= use extensively.

_____ **1.** I touch my partner in a way that communicates forgiveness.

_____ **2.** I say I would forgive my partner if the offense never happened again.

_____ **3.** I tell my partner it was no big deal.

_____ **4.** I initiate discussion about the offense.

_____ **5.** I put what happened aside so that we can resume our relationship.

_____ **6.** The expression on my face says, "I forgive you."

_____ **7.** I say I would forgive my partner only if things changed.

_____ **8.** I tell my partner not to worry about it.

_____ **9.** I discuss the offense with my partner.

_____ **10.** I don't say anything but just do my best to restore our relationship.

_____ **11.** I tell my partner, "I forgive you."

_____ **12.** I am direct in telling my partner I forgive her or him.

Adapted from Waldron, V. R., & Kelley, D. L (2005). Forgiving communication as a response to relational transgressions. *Journal of Social and Personal Relationships, 22,* 723–742.

Guerrero, L. K., & Bachman, G. F. (2010). Forgiveness and forgiving communication in dating relationships: An expectancy-investment explanation. *Journal of Social & Personal Relationships, 27,* 801–823.

For scoring information, see page 299 at the end of the chapter.

CHECK YOUR UNDERSTANDING

Objective 9.1　Understand the various reasons for entering into interpersonal relationships.

There are several explanations for why we form relationships with some people and not with others. These explanations include appearance (physical attractiveness), similarity, complementarity, rewards, competency, proximity, and disclosure.

Q: Which of the factors listed in this chapter best describe the bases of your most important interpersonal relationships?

Objective 9.2　Recognize the stages and dialectical tensions typically experienced in interpersonal relationships.

Some theorists argue that interpersonal relationships may go through as many as 10 stages of growth and deterioration, including initiating, experimenting, intensifying, integrating, bonding, differentiating, circumscribing, stagnating, avoiding, and terminating. They suggest that communication may reflect more than one stage at a given time, although one stage will generally be dominant.

Other models describe the dynamics of interpersonal communication in terms of dialectical tensions: mutually opposing, incompatible desires that can never be completely resolved. These dialectical tensions include integration-separation, stability-change, and expression-privacy.

Q: Trace the stages through which an important close relationship has passed. What is the current stage of this relationship? In what direction is the relationship headed? Then, describe the relational dialectics that shape communication in your most important relationships. Which strategies are most effective for dealing with these tensions?

Objective 9.3　Identify specific skills communicators can use to maintain and improve their interpersonal relationships.

Relational messages sometimes are expressed overtly via verbal metacommunication; however, more frequently they are conveyed nonverbally.

Interpersonal relationships require maintenance to stay healthy. Relational partners should use positive and open communication that includes assurances and demonstrates commitment and that the relationship matters. Partners should invest in each other's social networks and share tasks. Interpersonal communicators should also offer social support in their relationships through the exchange of emotional, informational, and instrumental resources.

Some relationships become damaged over time; others are hurt by relational transgressions. There are several strategies for repairing damaged relationships, with apologies and forgiveness being particularly important.

Q: To what extent does your most important close relationship exhibit the kinds of positive and open communication described here and in this chapter? Identify transgressions you have made in this relationship. Consider (or ask the other person) whether it's necessary to repair your transgression. How could you put the strategies described in this chapter into action?

KEY TERMS

- Avoiding (283)
- Bonding (286)
- Circumscribing (282)
- Comparison level (CL) (274)
- Comparison level of alternatives (CL$_{alt}$) (274)
- Connection-autonomy dialectic (285)

- Conventionality-uniqueness dialectic (287)
- Dialectical tensions (284)
- Differentiating (281)
- Experimenting (279)
- Expression-privacy dialectic (287)
- Inclusion-seclusion dialectic (287)

- Initiating (287)
- Integrating (280)
- Integration-separation dialectic (285)
- Intensifying (279)
- Metacommunication (291)
- Openness-closedness dialectic (288)
- Predictability-novelty dialectic (287)

- Relational maintenance (277)
- Relational transgressions (294)
- Revelation-concealment dialectic (288)
- Social support (293)
- Stability-change dialectic (287)
- Stagnating (282)
- Terminating (283)

ACTIVITIES

1. Conduct a survey on interpersonal relationships. Ask your respondents the most important reasons they have formed, and continue to maintain, close interpersonal relationships, using the categories on pages 270–277. Report your findings to your class. Together, compile an aggregate ranking of the reasons.

2. With a group of classmates, share the dialectical tensions that operate in your close personal relationships. Discuss the strategies you and your classmates use to deal with these tensions, focusing on the way those strategies are expressed via communication.

Finally, discuss how well each strategy helps promote a healthy and satisfying relationship.

3. Identify an important relational dimension (positive or troublesome) in a current or past close relationship. Describe to your classmates how you did express, or could have expressed, your thoughts and feelings via metacommunication.

4. Along with your classmates, write (anonymously) a relational transgression that you have committed. Describe how you did communicate, or how you could have communicated, in an attempt to repair the relationship.

SCORING FOR ASSESSING YOUR COMMUNICATION (PAGE 297)

Add your responses to items 1 and 6:   Nonverbal display of forgiveness (the average score for undergraduate students is between 5 and 6)

Add your responses to items 2 and 7:   Conditional forgiveness (the average score is approximately 5)

Add your responses to items 3 and 8:   Minimize the consequences of the transgression (the average score is between 4 and 5)

Add your responses to items 4 and 9:   Discussion of the offense (the average score is approximately 6)

Add your responses to items 5 and 10:   Benevolent forgiveness (the average score is between 5 and 6)

Add your responses to items 11 and 12:   Explicit, direct forgiveness (the average score is approximately 6)

Your scores should give you an indication of which strategies you use most frequently and how you may compare to other students.

chapter 10

Communication in Close Relationships

Friends, Family, and Romantic Partners

CHAPTER OUTLINE

FEATURES

LEARNING OBJECTIVES

10.1 Explain the ways intimacy can be expressed in close relationships.

10.2 Identify the different types of friendship and the role communication plays in maintaining them.

10.3 Describe how communication creates and sustains relationships within families.

10.4 Describe the ways in which love is expressed in romantic relationships.

WHAT RELATIONSHIPS ARE most important to you? When researchers posed this question to several hundred college students, the answers were varied (Berscheid et al., 1989). Roughly half (47 percent) identified a romantic partner. About a third (36 percent) chose a friendship. Most of the rest (14 percent) cited a family member. These meaningful relationships aren't just nice to have—they're vital. Christopher Peterson (2006) summarizes research showing that close relationships "may be the *single most important* source of life satisfaction and emotional well-being, across different ages and cultures" (p. 261).

In Chapter 1, we looked at factors that make some relationships more interpersonal than others: uniqueness, interdependence, self-disclosure, and intrinsic rewards. In this chapter, we look at how these factors operate in the three contexts that most of us regard as central to our lives: friendships, families, and romantic partnerships. The information here builds on concepts you learned in earlier chapters (particularly Chapter 9), but the focus here is on unique characteristics that shape communication in each type of relationship. We'll begin by exploring the concept of intimacy—a thread that runs through all close relationships.

INTIMACY IN CLOSE RELATIONSHIPS

What does it mean to have a close interpersonal relationship? Scholars have coined the term *inclusion-of-other-in-the-self* (IOS) to describe the key element of interpersonal connection. In a close relationship, "the other's resources, perspectives, and identities are experienced, to some extent, as one's own" (Aron et al., 2013, p. 90). In other words, as you become close with another person, that person in a sense becomes a part of you.

Your own experience probably supports the principle of IOS. Recall times when you've joked that you and your best friend are "sharing a brain," or when you've heard a parent's voice in the back of your mind, or when wedding vows describe "the two becoming one." Andrew Ledbetter (2013) notes the important role communication plays in the IOS process. Factors such as verbal affection, shared tasks, both informal and deep talks, and even humor help create and maintain a sense of integration with a relational partner. Becoming enmeshed with another person changes who you are—often for better, sometimes for worse, but always in significant ways (Mattingly et al., 2014).

Another term for relational closeness is **intimacy** (Laurenceau & Kleinman, 2006; Lippert & Prager, 2001). Whereas intimacy is often linked to romantic relationships, it's actually a broader concept. Robert Sternberg (2004), whose triangular model we look at later in this chapter, describes intimacy as feelings of closeness, bondedness, and connectedness; and he notes that it is often experienced with family and friends as well as in romantic relationships (see also Hughes, 2009; H. D. Johnson, 2012). We take a closer look at how intimacy operates in close relationships.

DIMENSIONS OF INTIMACY

Relational intimacy comes in many forms. One type is *emotional*: sharing important information and feelings. In Chapters 3 and 8, we described these kinds of self-disclosures in detail. Sometimes emotional intimacy comes from talking about feelings, such as acknowledging when you're hurt and embarrassed or saying "I love you." In other cases, emotional intimacy develops as a result of topics that are discussed—personal information, secrets, or delicate subjects. One such subject can be money, which has led some self-help authors to use the term *financial intimacy* to describe how couples need to be open, honest, and in sync on this important topic (Price, 2012; Timmons, 2009).

Another form of intimacy is *physical*. Even before birth, a baby experiences a kind of physical closeness with his or her mother that will never happen again: "Floating in a warm fluid, curling inside a total embrace, swaying to the undulations of the moving body and hearing the beat of the pulsing heart" (Morris, 1973, p. 7). As they grow up, fortunate children are continually nourished by physical intimacy: being rocked, fed, hugged, and held. As we grow older, the opportunities for physical intimacy are less regular but still possible and important. Some physical intimacy is sexual, but this category also can include affectionate hugs, kisses, and even struggles (Rosenfeld & Ribner, 2011). Companions who have endured physical challenges together—for example, in athletics or during emergencies—form a bond that can last a lifetime.

In other cases, intimacy comes from *intellectual* sharing (Cowan & Mills, 2004; Schaefer & Olson, 1981). Not every exchange of ideas counts as intimacy, of course. Talking about next week's midterm with your professor or classmates isn't likely to forge strong relational bonds. But when you engage another person in an exchange of important ideas, a kind of closeness develops that can be powerful and exciting.

Shared activities can provide a fourth way to emotional closeness (Williams & Russell, 2013; Wood & Inman, 1993). Not all shared activities lead to intimacy. You might work with a colleague for years without feeling any sort of emotional connection. But some shared experiences—struggling together against obstacles or living together as housemates are good examples—can create strong bonds. Play is one valuable form of shared activity. Leslie Baxter (1992) found that both same-sex friendships and opposite-sex romantic relationships were characterized by several forms of play. Partners invented private codes, teased one another, and played games such as arm wrestling.

The amount and type of intimacy can vary from one relationship to another (Hoffman, 2010; Speicher, 1999). Some intimate relationships exhibit all four qualities: emotional disclosure, physical intimacy, intellectual exchanges, and shared activities. Other intimate relationships exhibit only one or two. Of course, some relationships aren't intimate in any way. Acquaintance, roommate, and coworker relationships may never become intimate. In some cases, even family members develop smooth but relatively impersonal relationships.

Despite the fact that no relationship is *always* intimate, living without *any* sort of intimacy is hardly desirable. For example, people who fear intimacy in dating relationships anticipate less satisfaction in a long-term relationship and report feeling more distant from even longtime dating partners. A great deal of evidence supports the conclusion that fear of intimacy can cause major problems in both creating relationships and sustaining them (Greenberg & Goldman, 2008; Vangelisti & Beck, 2007).

GENDER AND INTIMACY

If emotional closeness is used as the standard for intimacy, most social scientists regard women as more concerned with and better than men at developing and maintaining intimate relationships (Impett & Peplau, 2006). Research shows that women (taken as a group, of course) are generally more interested than men in achieving emotional intimacy (Eldridge & Christensen, 2002; Hoffman, 2010), more willing to make emotional commitments (Rusbult & Van Lange, 1996), and more willing to share their most personal thoughts and feelings (Dindia & Allen, 1992; Walton & Rice, 2013).

© King Features Syndicate (Sally Forth cartoon)

Men are more likely than women to experience a condition called *alexithymia* (meaning "without words for emotions"), a finding that researchers attribute to traditional masculine socialization (Frye-Cox & Hesse, 2013; Karakis & Levant, 2012). This difficulty in identifying and talking about emotions is associated with lower relational and communication satisfaction and heightened fear of intimacy.

But as noted earlier, emotional expression isn't the *only* way to develop close relationships (Floyd, 1996; Zorn & Gregory, 2005). Whereas women place a somewhat higher value on talking about personal matters as a measure of intimacy, men are more likely to create and express closeness by doing things together—often in groups rather than in one-on-one interactions (Baumeister, 2005). Of course, it's important not to assume that all men who value shared activities are reluctant to share feelings, or that doing things together isn't important to women. Recent scholarship offers convincing evidence that, in many respects, the meaning of intimacy is more similar than different for men and women (Gaia, 2013; Goldsmith & Fulfs, 1999).

Whatever differences do exist between male and female styles of intimacy help explain some of the stresses and misunderstandings that can arise between the sexes. For example, a woman who looks for emotional disclosure as a measure of affection may overlook an inexpressive man's efforts to show he cares by doing favors or spending time with her. Fixing a leaky faucet or taking a hike may look like ways to avoid getting close, but to the man who proposes them, they may be measures of affection and bids for intimacy. Likewise, differing ideas about the timing and meaning of sex can lead to misunderstandings. Whereas many women think of sex as a way to *express* an intimacy that has already developed, men are more likely to see it as a way to *create* that intimacy (Reissman, 1990). In this sense, the man who encourages sex early in a relationship or after a fight may not be a lecher: He may view the shared activity as a way to build closeness. By contrast, the woman who views personal talk as the pathway to intimacy may resist the idea of physical closeness before the emotional side of the relationship has been discussed.

As with all research looking at women's and men's communication, it's important to realize that no generalization applies to every person. Furthermore, stereotypes are changing. For example, an analysis of prime-time television sitcoms revealed that male characters who disclose personal information generally receive favorable responses from other characters (Good et al., 2002). In addition, researchers Mark Morman and Kory Floyd (2002) note that a cultural shift is occurring in the United States in which fathers are becoming more affectionate with their sons than they were in previous generations—although some of that affection is still expressed through shared activities.

CULTURE AND INTIMACY

Historically, the notions of public and private behavior have changed dramatically (Adamopoulos, 1991; Gadlin, 1977). What would be considered intimate behavior today was quite public at times in the past. For example, in 16th-century Germany, the new husband and wife were expected to

MEDIA CLIP
Intimacy in the Digital Age: *Her*

In the not-too-distant future, Theodore Twombly (Joaquin Phoenix) lives alone in a high-rise apartment, wounded on the heels of a failed marriage. He spends his days in a cubicle at BeautifulHandwrittenLetters.com writing warm, sensitive messages for other people.

Theodore's life changes when he buys an artificially intelligent operating system who calls herself Samantha (voiced by the disembodied Scarlett Johansson). With a beguiling personality and insights more keen than those of most humans, Samantha draws Theodore out of his self-imposed shell and helps him find joy in everyday life. Before long they grow to love one another. As in every relationship, the couple struggles to meet their differing needs.

Unlike most flesh-and-blood partners, Theodore and Samantha build their relationship entirely through speech. Their only tools are their words and voices. That's enough to achieve a level of intimacy most couples would relish.

It's easy to view this romance as a warning about the dangers of our digital era. Whether or not technology can indeed satisfy our interpersonal needs, the movie *Her* demonstrates that emotional connection is what humans crave, and that they'll go to great lengths to find it.

consummate their marriage on a bed carried by witnesses who would validate the marriage! Conversely, in England as well as in colonial America, the customary level of communication between spouses was once rather formal—not much different from the way acquaintances or neighbors spoke to one another.

Contemporary notions of intimacy vary from one culture to another (Adams et al., 2004; Marshall, 2008, 2010). In one study, researchers asked residents of Great Britain, Japan, Hong Kong, and Italy to describe their use of 33 rules that regulated interaction in social relationships (Argyle & Henderson, 1985). The rules governed a wide range of communication behaviors: everything from the use of humor, to handshaking, to the management of money. The results showed that the greatest differences between Asian and European cultures involved the rules for dealing with intimacy, including showing emotions, expressing affection in public, engaging in sexual activity, and respecting privacy. (See the Focus on Research box in Chapter 8, page 241, for a description of how the expression "I love you" is interpreted across cultures.)

Although some of these distinctions continue to hold true, cultural differences in intimacy are becoming less prominent as the world becomes more connected through the media, travel, and technology. For instance, romance and passionate love were once seen as particularly "American" concepts of intimacy. However, recent evidence shows that men and women in a variety of cultures—individualist and collectivist, urban and rural, rich and poverty stricken—may be every bit as romantic as Americans (Hatfield & Rapson, 2006). These studies suggest that the large differences that once existed between Western and Eastern cultures may be fast disappearing.

SOCIAL MEDIA AND INTIMACY

A few decades ago, it would have been hard to conceive that the words *computer* and *intimacy* could be positively linked. Computers were viewed as impersonal machines that couldn't transmit important features of human communication, such as facial expression, tone of voice, and touch. Phones were used only for vocal messages, and social networking sites didn't exist.

However, as we have described in previous chapters, researchers now know that communication through social media can be just as personal as face-to-face (FtF) interaction. In fact, studies show that relational intimacy may develop more quickly through mediated channels than in FtF communication (Finkel et al., 2012; Hian et al., 2004).

Your own experience probably supports these claims. The relative anonymity of chat rooms, blogs, and online dating services fosters a freedom of expression that might not occur in FtF meetings (Ben-Ze'ev, 2003; Wildermuth & Vogl-Bauer, 2007), giving relationships a chance to get started. In addition, e-mailing, text messaging, and communicating via social networking sites offer more constant contact with loved ones than might otherwise be possible (Boase et al., 2006). And the potential for developing and maintaining close friendships through online channels is captured well by one user's comment (which has a fun double meaning): "I've never clicked this much with anyone in my life" (Henderson & Gilding, 2004; see also Brody, 2013).

In each of the sections that follow, we look at how social media affects—both positively and negatively—relationships with friends, family, and romantic partners.

COMMUNICATION IN FRIENDSHIPS

Type the word "friendship" into a web browser along with one of these phrases: "in songs," "in movies," "in TV shows." You'll see that popular culture is filled with references to friends and friendship. In fact, you can probably think of several artistic tributes to friendship on your own without searching online. We depict and celebrate these special relationships because they are central to what it means to be human.

But what exactly is a friend? Scholars have offered many definitions of friendships (e.g., Bell, 1991; Bukowski et al., 2009; Fehr, 2000). Most of them include the notions that a **friendship** is a voluntary relationship that provides social support. Most important for our purposes, friendships are created, managed, and maintained through communication (Johnson, Becker, et al., 2009; McEwan & Guerrero, 2010). Different types of friendships involve different levels of communication, as we explore now.

TYPES OF FRIENDSHIPS

Before reading further, identify three friends from distinct parts of your life—perhaps an old neighborhood pal, someone from work, and your BFF ("best friend forever"). Keep these three friends in mind as you read each of the following sets of dimensions. These categories will help you see that all friendships are not the same, and that communication patterns vary depending on the type of friendship.

Short versus Long Term

Friends come in and out of our lives for a variety of reasons. Some friendships last for years or even a lifetime, while others fade or end because of life changes (such as finishing high school, moving to a new location, or switching jobs). Although modern technologies have decreased the likelihood that a friendship will end because of a long-distance move (Utz, 2007), some falter or fail without face-to-face contact. Another reason some friendships may be short term is due to a change in values (Solomon & Knafo, 2007). Perhaps you once had a group of friends with whom you enjoyed parties and nightlife, but as you grew out of that phase of your life, the mutual attraction waned. Take a moment to consider the three friends you identified earlier and where they fall on a short-term versus long-term continuum (you can do the same comparison for each of the following categories).

Task versus Maintenance Oriented

Sometimes we choose friends because of shared activities: teammates in a softball league, coworkers, or fellow movie buffs. These types of friendships are considered task oriented if they primarily revolve around certain activities. On the other hand, maintenance-oriented friendships are grounded in mutual liking and social support, independent of shared activities. Of course these categories overlap: Some friendships are based in both joint activities and emotional support.

Low versus High Disclosure

How much do you tell your friends about yourself? No doubt your level of disclosure differs from friend to friend. Some know only general information about you, whereas others are privy to your most personal secrets. The Social Penetration Model in Chapter 3 (pages 89–91) can help you explore the breadth and depth of your disclosure with various friends.

Low versus High Obligation

There are some friends for whom we would do just about anything—no request is too big. We feel a lower sense of obligation to other friends, both in terms of what we would do for them and how quickly we would do it. Our closest friends usually get fast responses when they ask for a favor, give us a call, or even post on our Facebook wall (see the Focus on Research on page 314).

Infrequent versus Frequent Contact

You probably keep in close touch with some friends. Perhaps you work out, travel, or socialize together, or you Skype daily. Other friendships have less frequent contact—maybe an occasional phone call or e-message. Of course, infrequent contact doesn't always correlate with levels of disclosure or obligation. Many close friends may see each other only once a year, but they pick right back up in terms of the breadth and depth of their shared information.

After reading this far, you can begin to see how the nature of communication can vary from one friendship to another. Furthermore, communication *within* a friendship can also change over time. Impersonal friendships can have sudden bursts of disclosure. The amount of communication can swing from more to less frequent. Low-obligation friendships can evolve into stronger commitments, and vice versa. In a few pages you'll read about types of communication that are common in virtually all good friendships. But for now, it's important to recognize that variety is a good thing.

FRIENDSHIPS, GENDER, AND COMMUNICATION

Not all friendships are created equal. Along with the differences described in the preceding pages, gender plays a role in how we communicate with friends.

Same-Sex Friendships

Recall the first friend you ever had. If you're like most people, that person was probably the same sex as you. Many of the first close relationships outside the family are with same-sex friends (Bukowski et al., 1996), and many adults maintain intimate same-sex friendships. In the popular vernacular, women often identify a female "BFF," and close but nonsexual friendships between men are sometimes referred to as "bromances" (Alberti, 2013; Demir et al., 2013).

In adolescence and adulthood, communication within same-sex friendships differs for men and women, even if the primary goal—support—is the same for both (Chao & Wang, 2013). As noted earlier in this chapter, men often experience intimacy by doing things together rather than through emotional disclosure. In one study on friendship (Greif, 2009), men indicated they valued shared activities more than women did, whereas women valued "being understood" more than men. These differences were more dramatic in an earlier study (Swain, 1989) in which more than 75 percent of the men surveyed said that their most meaningful experiences with friends came from doing things together. Through shared activities, male friends "grew on one another," developed feelings of interdependence, showed appreciation for one another, and demonstrated mutual liking. Findings from both studies indicate that for men, more than women, closeness grows from activities that don't always depend heavily on disclosure: A friend is a person who does things *for* you and *with* you.

Women tend to disclose personal information more than men, both in face-to-face relationships (Dindia & Allen, 1992; Rubin, 1983) and online (Bond, 2009). Whereas both men and women value friends who provide emotional support, women are generally more skilled at doing so and are more likely to seek out female friends when they need this type of support (Holmstrom, 2009). Activity 1 on page 334 will help you discover whether this research matches your own experience. Even without keeping records, you may be aware that the topics you talk and write about differ depending on the sex of the friend with whom you're communicating. Research suggests that sex differences like these seem to be stronger for friendships among heterosexuals than among homosexuals (de Vries and Megathlin, 2009).

Cross-Sex Friendships

Cross-sex friendships offer a wealth of benefits (Sapadin, 1988; Werking, 1997). They give us a chance to see how the "other half" lives, and they offer a welcome contrast to the kinds of interaction that characterize

CAN WOMEN BE COWORKERS AND FRIENDS?

The studies cited in these pages suggest that female friendships are sometimes closer and more open than male friendships or cross-sex friendships. Nonetheless, a body of research suggests that on-the-job friendships between women can be problematic.

In one survey of over 1,000 nurses, three out of four reported being undermined by another woman in the workplace (Briles, 1999). Another study conducted for the American Management Association found that 95% of the female participants felt that other women had disrupted their careers at some point (Heim & Murphy, 2001).

This isn't to suggest that men don't sabotage others in the workplace—but they may not have the same assumptions about friendships on the job. Some scholars argue that high expectations play a role in women's feelings of being undermined in the workplace (Litwin & Hallstein, 2007). If the expectation is that female colleagues should become friends, then any behavior to the contrary may feel like betrayal. Clarifying expectations about how to handle friendships in the workplace can lead to less confusing, more satisfying relationships.

Juggling the potentially conflicting demands of friendship and professionalism can be challenging for anyone. For women, it appears, the task contains another level of complexity.

communication with friends of the same sex (Holmstrom, 2009). For men, this often means a greater chance to share emotions and focus on relationships. For women, it can be a chance to lighten up and enjoy banter without emotional baggage. These friendships also give heterosexual singles access to a broader network of potential romantic partners (Hand & Furman, 2009).

Cross-sex friendships—at least for heterosexuals—present some challenges that don't exist among all-male or all-female companionships (Malachowski & Dillow, 2011; O'Meara, 1989). The most obvious is the potential for sexual attraction (Halatsis & Christakis, 2009; Schmitt et al., 2012). One study (Bleske-Rechek et al., 2012) found that romantic attraction between such friends is common—and problematic. Most participants who reported attraction to a cross-sex friend acknowledged that it negatively affected their current romantic relationship. Although it's possible to have romance-free, cross-sex friendships, defining that sort of relationship can take effort. Some evidence suggests that cross-sex friends communicate more online to keep the relationship platonic (Ledbetter et al., 2011). And some cross-sex friends don't keep things strictly platonic, as we discuss in the "friends with benefits" section that follows.

When it comes to the potential for romance, heterosexual cross-sex friendships fit into one of four categories (Guerrero & Chavez, 2005; we can assume the same holds true for same-sex friendships among gay men and lesbians):

- *Mutual Romance*—both partners want the friendship to turn romantic
- *Strictly Platonic*—neither partner wants the friendship to turn romantic
- *Desires Romance*—one partner wants romance but fears the friend does not

In the film *No Strings Attached*, life-long friends Emma (Natalie Portman) and Adam (Ashton Kutcher) try to have a physical relationship with no emotional overtones. They discover this isn't nearly as easy as they imagined.

- *Rejects Romance*—one partner does not want romance but thinks the friend does

Not surprisingly, the last two types of relationships are the most complicated. Guerrero and Chavez found that the less interested partner in these situations used strategies to communicate "no go" messages: less routine contact and activity, less flirtation, and more talk about outside romance (see also Weger & Emmett, 2009).

Friends with Benefits

Somewhere between friendship and romance is a *friends with benefits* (FWB) relationship—a popular term for friendships that include sexual activity. These relationships have become increasingly common and come in many varieties (Mongeau et al., 2013). Most participants claim it's an opportunity for sex with "no strings attached," although there are usually more "strings" than partners want to acknowledge. Some FWB relationships transition into romances (Owen & Fincham, 2012); others are transitioning *out* of romances; still others serve as "placeholders" until better options come along (Jonason, 2013).

Men and women are equally likely to be in FWB relationships. Some surveys suggest that both appreciate the chance to take care of physical needs without the challenges of emotional commitment (Green & Morman, 2011). Despite this similarity, there are gender differences in the way FWB relationships turn out. Although the majority of men describe their relationships as primarily sexual, women are much more likely to become emotionally involved. From findings such as these, observers have commented that women are typically more focused on being "friends," whereas men are more likely to be interested in the "benefits" (Lehmiller et al., 2011).

You might think that FWB partners would regularly discuss the status of their relationship, but research shows that they routinely avoid explicit communication about this important topic (Bisson & Levine, 2009). In comparison with traditional romantic couples, FWB partners also communicate less about sex and are less sexually satisfied (Lehmiller et al., 2014). They do, however, practice safe sex more often and are more willing to talk about the sexual experiences they've had outside their relationship. The communicative complexities of these relationships lead researchers to note a paradox: "FWB relationships are often problematic for the same reasons that they are attractive" (Bisson & Levine, 2009, p. 66).

Gender Considerations

Biological sex isn't the only factor to consider when we examine different sorts of friendships. Another important consideration is *sex role* (see Chapter 4, page 119). For instance, a friendship between a masculine male and a feminine female might have very different properties than a friendship between a masculine female and a feminine male—even though these are both technically cross-sex relationships (Holmstrom, 2009).

Sexual orientation is another factor that can shape friendships. Most obviously, for gay men and lesbians the potential for sexual attraction shifts from opposite- to same-sex relationships. But physical attraction aside, sexual orientation can still play a significant role in friendships (Galupo & Gonzalez, 2013). For example, many heterosexual women report that they value their friendships with gay men because (a) they often share interests, (b) the potential for romantic complications is small or nonexistent (Hopcke & Rafaty, 2001), and (c) the women feel more attractive (Bartlett et al., 2009).

FRIENDSHIP AND SOCIAL MEDIA

IRL (in real life) it's not hard to tell who counts as a friend. The Internet, however, has made friendship more complicated (Amichai-Hamburger et al., 2013). Consider Facebook, where a "friend" could be someone you met once at a party or on vacation, a former classmate or neighbor whom you haven't seen in years, someone you met online but have never known in person, or even a person who accepted your friend request simply to boost the size of his or her friends list.

Despite all the possibilities, research shows that social networking sites are used primarily to maintain current friendships or to revive old ones, rather than to build new relationships (Anderson et al., 2012). For example, the highest proportion of Facebook connections is between high school classmates (Ellison et al., 2007). Contrary to some reports, teens typically use social networking sites to connect with known others, not strangers (Reich et al., 2012).

Perhaps the most intriguing scholarship about friendship and social media has to do with the number of friends one has on social networking sites. A survey by the Pew Research Center found that the typical online adult has more than 200 Facebook friends (Smith, 2014). Younger adults (ages 18–29) have larger Facebook networks, with 27 percent having more than 500 friends. Research shows that if you have too few Facebook friends, others may regard you (perhaps unfairly) as not very social or friendly (Tong et al., 2008). On the other hand, if you have too many online friends, people might perceive those relationships as less than genuine.

Research is mixed about the connection between number of Facebook friends and well-being. Some scholars suggest "the more the better," finding positive correlations with factors such as perceived social support, reduced stress, and even physical health (Nabi et al., 2013). Other studies are less positive, finding that large collections of Facebook friends yield diminishing returns and might be compensation for low self-esteem (Kim & Lee, 2011; Lee et al., 2012). One thing seems clear: No matter the size of one's online social network, only a small percentage of those friendships qualify as *close* (Bryant & Marmo, 2012).

Social networking sites aren't the only media for communicating with friends. Phoning, texting, e-mailing, and even blogging are means for keeping up friendships. As noted in Chapter 9 (pages 291–293), these media can help friends maintain their relationship and provide a measure of social support. But the closest of friends realize that no matter how much they stay in touch with each other electronically, there's no substitute for a night on the town together, a stimulating in-person conversation, or a good hug.

Everyday People Cartoons by Cathy Thorne

COMMUNICATION IN SUCCESSFUL FRIENDSHIPS

Friendships come with a set of expectations about how to communicate. We rarely discuss these assumptions, and we often become aware of them only when they aren't met. Communication scholars have found that **expectancy violations**—instances when others don't behave as we assume they should—are the source of many relational problems (Cohen, 2010; Hall et al., 2011). The following guidelines, culled from several studies (Argyle & Henderson, 1984; Baxter et. al., 2001; Hall, 2012), offer prescriptions on what most people expect from their friends. Although these guidelines are validated by research, they may seem like common sense. Nonetheless, it's likely you can judge the success of your friendships at least in part by seeing how closely you follow them.

Share Joys and Sorrows

When you have bad news, you want to tell friends who will offer comfort and support. When a friend has good news, you want to hear about it and celebrate. When sharing sorrows and joys with friends, it's often important how quickly and in what order the news is delivered. The closer the friendship, the higher the expectation for sharing soon. Phrases such as "How come you got a new job and I'm the last to find out?" suggest a violation has occurred.

FOCUS ON RESEARCH
Rules for Facebook Friendships

Communication researchers Erin Bryant and Jennifer Marmo are familiar with the research and prescriptions noted in this section, but they wanted to know if Facebook has its own set of friendship rules. They ran focus groups and surveys with hundreds of college students to identify friendship rules specific to Facebook. Here are the five most important rules, according to the research participants:

- "I should expect a response from this person if I post on his/her profile."
- "I should not say anything disrespectful about this person on Facebook."

- "I should consider how a post might negatively impact this person's relationships."
- "If I post something that this person deletes, I should not repost it."
- "I should communicate with this person outside of Facebook."

Most of these rules are related to interpersonal communication and align with principles of face-to-face interaction (e.g., responsiveness, impression management, face-saving). The participants also indicated that, in general, the closer the friendship, the more important it is to abide by these rules.

Bryant, E. M., & Marmo, J. (2012). The rules of Facebook friendship: A two-stage examination of interaction rules in close, casual, and acquaintance friendships. *Journal of Social and Personal Relationships, 29,* 1013–1035.

Provide a Listening Ear

As you'll read in Chapter 11, listening is an important type of confirming message. Paying attention—even when you aren't especially interested—is one way to show that you care about your friend. In Chapter 7, we describe a variety of responses you can offer to a friend to demonstrate that you're listening and understanding.

Maintain Confidences

Betraying a confidence can injure, or even end, a friendship (Petronio, 2002). When you share personal information with a friend, you expect that person to be discreet about what you said—especially when the information could damage your reputation or other relationships.

Lend a Helping Hand

The old saying "A friend in need is a friend indeed" is supported by studies showing that providing assistance is one of the most tangible markers of a friendship (MacGeorge et al., 2004; Semmer et al., 2008). Need a ride to the airport, some help on moving day, or a quick loan until payday? These are the kinds of things we expect from friends.

Stand Up for Each Other

A loyal friend "has your back"—both when you're present and when you're not. Few things are more endearing than a friend who defends your rights, honor, and reputation.

Honor Pledges and Commitments

"You can count on me" and "I'll be there for you" are common friendship sentiments (Galupo & Gonzalez, 2013). These pledges, however, need to be backed up with actions. Whether it's showing up on time, attending a scheduled event, or fulfilling an agreement about a shared task, it's vital for friends to live up to their promises and obligations.

Treat Each Other with Respect

Sometimes we say the most hurtful things to people we care about the most (Vangelisti & Crumley, 1998; Zhang & Stafford, 2009). It's easy for banter in a friendship to slip into teasing that hurts and comments that sting. Good friends monitor their words and actions, making sure to communicate in ways that affirm the other person's dignity.

Have a Balanced Exchange

Social exchange theory (page 273) tells us that the rewards of a relationship need to outweigh the costs. This is as true in friendships as it is in other close relationships (Haselton & Galperin, 2013). College students in one study identified "Don't take more than you give" as an important friendship rule (Baxter et al., 2001).

Value Both Connection and Autonomy

In Chapter 9, we describe how all interpersonal relationships struggle with competing needs for both closeness and independence. In essence, we have a need to spend time with our friends and to spend time away from them. Allow your friends space to develop their own identity and nurture other relationships—and also the freedom to make choices that might not match your own.

Apologize and Forgive

Sooner or later friends are bound to make the kinds of "relational transgressions" described in Chapter 9 (pages 294–295). As you read there, a good apology has several components, including *sincerely* expressing remorse, admitting wrongdoing, promising to behave better, and requesting forgiveness. When you're the one who has been wronged, granting forgiveness can help repair the friendship and leave you feeling better than holding a grudge (Bernstein, 2010; Merolla, 2008).

COMMUNICATION IN THE FAMILY

A few generations ago, "What is a family?" was an easy question to answer for most people. Common notions of a family in the Western world typically stressed shared residence, reproduction or adoption of children by different-sexed adults, and a "socially approved sexual relationship" (Murdock, 1965, p. 1). A more recent study of college students found that their definitions of family contained many of these same elements (Baxter et al., 2009).

"I guess we'd be considered a family. We're living together, we love each other, and we haven't eaten the children yet."

However, social scientists, lawyers, judges, theologians, and the public at large have grappled with much broader definitions as they ponder questions such as who the parents are when there is an egg or sperm donor, the rights of adoptive parents and adopted children, and whether homosexual couples can adopt a child.

After reviewing a century's worth of definitions, Kathleen Galvin and her colleagues (2012) define family broadly enough to include many types of relationships. According to them, a **family** is a system with two or more interdependent people who have a common history and a present reality and who expect to influence each other in the future. With this broader definition in mind, communication scholars contend that families are defined primarily through their interaction rather than through biological relationship or kinship systems.

CREATING THE FAMILY THROUGH COMMUNICATION

Families are based on, formed, and maintained through communication (Noller & Fitzpatrick, 1993; Schrodt, 2009). It's through communication that family members create mental models of family life, and through communication those models endure over time and across generations (Vangelisti, 2004). In the following sections, we describe several ways that communication shapes and constitutes the family.

Family Narratives

In Chapter 4 (pages 113–114), we explained how shared narratives provide a story line that keeps relationships operating harmoniously. Narratives are especially important in families, as they serve a variety of functions that include reinforcing shared goals, teaching moral values, and stressing family concerns (Galvin et al., 2012). Families narrate their best and worst life experiences and pass them down from generation to generation (Kiser et al., 2010).

Family stories often have meaning that goes beyond the incident being recounted. Some might reflect beliefs about work ("I walked up the hill both ways, in the snow, barefoot"), family identity (e.g., stories related to immigrating to the United States), and warnings ("You don't want to end up like so-and-so, do you?"). Narratives may reflect a family's view of how members relate to one another: "We help each other a lot," or "We are proud of our heritage." Others reflect values about how to operate in the world: "It's impossible to be successful without a good education," or "It's our responsibility to help others less fortunate than ourselves." Even dysfunctional families can be united by a shared narrative: "What a hopeless bunch! We can never get along." One study showed that families who regularly engage in positive storytelling (focusing on achievements and using "we" language) have high levels of family functioning and satisfaction (Kellas, 2005).

Communication Rituals and Rules

Rituals are another way family is created through communication (Baxter & Braithwaite, 2006a). Some rituals center on celebrations: special family meals, certain types of gifts, the post-Thanksgiving touch football game, and so on. Other rituals are part of everyday life: good-natured teasing about family members' quirks, or saying "I love you" at the end of every phone conversation.

Rituals aren't the only way that families create their own communication systems. As unique cultures, families also have their own rules about a variety of communication practices. Some communication rules are explicit: "If you're going to be more than a half hour late, phone home." Other rules aren't ever discussed, but they are just as important: "If Mom slams the door after coming home from work, wait until she's had time to relax before speaking to her." Some rules govern communication within the family (Caughlin & Petronio, 2004; Guerrero & Afifi, 1995). How far is it okay to push challenges of parental decisions? What kinds of language are allowed and forbidden? How much kidding and teasing are acceptable? Are there any forbidden topics?

Research by Leslie Baxter and Chitra Akkoor (2011) showed that some topics of conversation are allowed and encouraged, whereas others are discouraged, if not off limits, in most families. For example, both parents and children agreed that conversations about friendships and everyday matters were fine. On the other hand, topics related to sex, drinking, money, and how teens were doing academically fell into the second group.

Stepfamilies often have their own unique rules. Tamara Golish (2000) interviewed 115 adolescents and young adults in stepfamilies to learn about topics they tend to avoid with their parents and stepparents. Stepchildren

The TV show *The Fosters* illustrates the changing nature of families in today's society. A same-sex couple raises one partner's biological son from a previous marriage, a pair of adopted twins, and two foster children.

reported more topic avoidance with their stepparents than with their parents. In particular, stepchildren say they often avoid "deep conversations" or talking about money and family issues with their stepparents. One factor affecting the comfort level in stepfamily communication is the type of parenting style used by the stepparents. Stepchildren feel more dissatisfied and avoid more topics with stepparents who are highly authoritarian (i.e., demanding and rigid). Interestingly, stepchildren also say they are dissatisfied with highly permissive stepparents.

Other rules—often explicit—govern communicating with people outside the family. Parents may tell a young child, "It's okay to talk with people you know, but don't talk to strangers when we're not around." Families may also have rules about Internet use (Papadakis, 2003). For example, parents can restrict the areas that can be visited online, as well as when (such as after homework is done) and how long children may be online.

PATTERNS OF FAMILY COMMUNICATION

Whatever form families take, the communication that occurs within them shares some important characteristics, which we examine now.

Families as Communication Systems

Every family has its own unique ways of communicating. Despite these differences, all families are **systems** whose members interact with one another to form a whole. Families, like all systems, possess a number of characteristics that shape the way members communicate (Galvin et al., 2012; Lerner et al., 2002).

Family Members Are Interdependent If you touch one piece of a mobile, all the other parts will move in response. In the same way, one family member's feelings and behaviors affect all the other members. If, for example, one family member leaves home to marry, or a parent loses a job, or feuding siblings stop talking to one another, the system is no longer the same. Each event is a reaction to the family's history, and each event shapes future interaction.

A Family Is More Than the Sum of Its Parts Even if you knew each member separately, you still wouldn't understand the family system until you saw the members interact. When those members are together, new ways of communicating emerge. For instance, you may have known friends who turned into very different people when they became a couple. Maybe they became better as individuals—more confident, clever, and happy. Or perhaps they became more aggressive and defensive. Likewise, the nature of a couple's relationship is likely to change when a child arrives, and that family's interaction will change again with the arrival of each subsequent baby.

Families Have Systems within the Larger System Like boxes within boxes, families have subsystems (systems within the family). For example, a traditional family of four can have six communication subsystems with two people: mother and father, mother and son, mother and daughter, father and son, father and daughter, and daughter and son. If you add three-person subsystems to these six (e.g., mother, father, and daughter), the number of combinations is even greater. The nuclear family itself is a subsystem of larger suprasystems (systems of which the family is a part) that include aunts and uncles, cousins, grandparents, in-laws, and so on.

A recent study illustrates the systemic nature of family interaction (Galovan et al., 2013). Spouses reported higher marital quality when they were equally responsible for family tasks. Which shared task best predicted marital satisfaction? Responsibility for child rearing. In other words, if parents want to improve their relationship with each other, one way to do so is to be more invested in the care of their children. A change in one part of the family system (parent–child interaction) affects other parts of the system (spouse–spouse interaction).

Conversation and Conformity in the Family

Ascan Koerner and Mary Ann Fitzpatrick (2002, 2006a; see also Koerner & Schrodt, 2014) have identified two categories of rules about communication in the family: conversation and conformity. **Conversation orientation** involves the degree to which families favor an open climate of discussion of a wide array of topics. Families with a high conversation orientation interact freely, frequently, and spontaneously, without many limitations regarding topic or time spent interacting. They believe that this interaction is important in order to have an enjoyable and rewarding family life. Conversation-oriented families communicate with their children for relationally oriented motives, such as affection, pleasure, and relaxation (Barbato et al., 2003). Their conflict is characterized by integrating and compromising strategies (Sherman & Dumlao, 2008). On the other hand, members of families with a low conversation orientation interact less, and there is less exchange of private thoughts. It's no surprise that families with a strong conversation orientation regard communication as rewarding (Avtgis, 1999), and that children who grow up in conversation-oriented families have a greater number of interpersonal skills in their later relationships (Koesten, 2004).

Conformity orientation refers to the degree to which family communication stresses uniformity of attitudes, values, and beliefs. High-conformity families seek harmony, interdependence, and obedience. They are often hierarchical, with a clear sense that some members have more authority than others—so it's not surprising that conflict in these families is characterized by avoiding and obliging strategies (Sherman & Dumlao, 2008). Conformity-oriented families communicate with their children for personal-influence motives (control and escape) and to show affection (Barbato et al., 2003). By contrast, communication in families with a low conformity orientation is characterized by individuality, independence, and equality.

Conversation and conformity orientations can combine in four ways, as shown in Figure 10.1. Each of these modes reflects a different **family communication pattern**: consensual, pluralistic, protective, or laissez-faire. To understand these combinations, imagine four different families. In each, a 15-year-old daughter wants to get a very visible and irreverent tattoo that concerns the parents. Now imagine how communication surrounding this

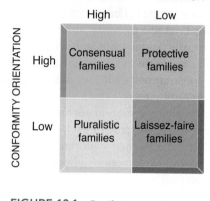

FIGURE 10.1 **Family Communication Patterns**

issue would differ depending on the various combinations of conversation and conformity orientations.

Families high in both conversation orientation and conformity orientation are *consensual:* Communication in these families reflects the tension between the pressure to agree and preserve the hierarchy, and an interest in open communication and exploration. In a consensual family, the daughter would feel comfortable making her case for the tattoo, and the parents would be willing to hear the daughter out. Ultimately the decision would rest with the mother and father.

Families high in conversation orientation and low in conformity orientation are *pluralistic:* Communication in these families is open and unrestrained, with all family members' contributions evaluated on their own merits. It's easy to visualize an ongoing family discussion about whether the tattoo is a good idea. Older and younger siblings—and maybe even other relatives—would weigh in with their perspectives. In the best of worlds, a decision would emerge from these discussions.

Families low in conversation orientation and high in conformity orientation are *protective:* Communication in these families emphasizes obedience to authority and the reluctance to share thoughts and feelings. In a protective family, there would be little if any discussion about the tattoo. The parents would decide, and their word would be final.

Families low in both conversation orientation and conformity orientation are *laissez-faire:* Communication in these families reflects family members' lack of involvement with each other, the fact that they are emotionally divorced, and that decision making is individual. In this type of family, the parents would have little to say about their daughter's desire to get a tattoo. With this issue—and most others—their response would be "Whatever" (if she even brought it up for discussion).

Which of these four patterns best represents your family? Which would you *like* to be true of your family? You can use the Assessing Your Communication instrument on page 321 to help determine your family's communication pattern. As you complete the assessment, keep in mind that family members may disagree on how their family is classified (Baxter & Pederson, 2013), so it may be interesting to have each member of your family complete the assessment.

A growing body of research suggests that some communication patterns are more productive and satisfying than others (Schrodt et al., 2008). For example, young adults from consensual and pluralistic families are more

ASSESSING YOUR COMMUNICATION

Your Family's Communication Pattern

Presented here is a list of statements that describe family communication. With your family in mind, rate your agreement with each statement on a scale ranging from 1 to 5, where 1 = strongly disagree and 5 = strongly agree.

Conversation Orientation

_____ **1.** In our family we often talk about controversial topics like politics and religion.

_____ **2.** My parents often ask my opinion when the family is talking about something.

_____ **3.** I can tell my parents almost anything.

_____ **4.** In our family we often talk about our feelings and emotions.

_____ **5.** My parents and I often have long, relaxed conversations about nothing in particular.

_____ **6.** In our family, we often talk about our plans and hopes for the future.

Conformity Orientation

_____ **7.** In our home, my parents usually have the last word.

_____ **8.** My parents sometimes become irritated with my views if different from theirs.

_____ **9.** If my parents don't approve of it, they don't want to know about it.

_____ **10.** When I am at home, I am expected to obey my parents' rules.

_____ **11.** My parents often say things like "You'll know better when you grow up."

_____ **12.** My parents often say things like "You should give in on arguments rather than risk making people mad."

Adapted from Koroshnia, M. M., & Latifian, M. M. (2008). An investigation on validity and reliability of Revised Family Communication Patterns instrument. *Journal of Family Research, 3,* 855–875.

Fife, E. M., Leigh Nelson, C. C., & Messersmith, A. S. (2014). The influence of family communication patterns on religious orientation among college students. *Journal of Family Communication, 14,* 72–84.

For scoring information, see page 335 at the end of the chapter.

confident listeners and more intellectually flexible than those from protective and laissez-faire backgrounds (Ledbetter & Schrodt, 2008). Offspring from pluralistic families are less verbally aggressive than those from any other type (Schrodt & Carr, 2012). By contrast, a protective approach by parents leads to more secrecy by children and lower satisfaction for all members of a family (Ledbetter & Vik, 2012). Fathers tend to be confrontational and pressuring during conflicts in high-conformity families, but they're conciliatory and analytic in pluralistic ones (Sillars et al., 2014). In other words, open communication and shared decision making produce better results than do power plays and refusal to have open dialogue.

EFFECTIVE COMMUNICATION IN FAMILIES

It's one thing to identify a family's communication pattern; it's another to improve it. In this section, we look at ways for families to better manage their communication.

Manage the Connection-Autonomy Dialectic

As you read in Chapter 9 (pages 284–289), dialectical tensions arise in relationships when two opposing or incompatible forces exist simultaneously. The connection-autonomy dialectic is particularly challenging for families and their communication.

As children grow into adolescents, the "leave me alone" orientation becomes apparent. Teenagers who used to happily spend time with their parents now may groan at the thought of a family vacation, or even the notion of sitting down at the dinner table each evening. They spend more time alone or with friends. Often, answering the question "Who am I?" requires challenging family rules and beliefs, establishing powerful nonfamily relationships, and weakening family bonds. But through conflict, hopefully, an answer emerges; then, the adolescent can turn around and reestablish good relationships with family members.

Families who are most successful at negotiating this difficult period tend to be those with high flexibility who, for example, can change how they discipline and how they determine family roles. Adolescents are most likely to be healthy and well-adjusted when rules and roles can be discussed adult-to-adult with their parents, when they can explore alternative identities without excessive criticism, when their caring family relationships do not give way to conflict and abuse, and when they are encouraged to take responsibility for their lives. "The quality of the communication between parents and adolescents is a critical feature of all these tasks" (Noller, 1995, p. 106).

In the United States, it is common for children to move out of the family home—to be "launched"—when they are in their late teens or early 20s. Communication between parents and offspring changes as the family adjusts to the dramatic alteration in family life. During this stage, young adults need to consider how to stay connected to the family: for example, how often to call home, whether to go home during vacations, and how to maintain open lines of communication with both parents—perhaps through social networking sites (Stephenson-Abetz & Holman, 2012). Studies of "emerging adults" show that their postlaunch communication patterns usually reflect how they conversed with their parents before they left home. In other words, young adults from conversation-oriented families tend to be more open with their parents about everything from credit card use (Thorson & Horstman, 2014) to more intimate matters (Ledbetter & Vik, 2012).

When a child moves out, dynamics change among the family members still at home. For example, the parents need to renegotiate their "coupleness," and both the parents and the remaining children need to negotiate who takes on the roles previously filled by the launched family member. (For example, if the launched member helped resolve conflicts among other people in the family, how will that happen now?)

Finally, communication between elderly parents and their adult children provides its own set of challenges. In many families, interaction comes full circle, as the children now provide for their parents while simultaneously meeting the obligations of their jobs and their own immediate families (Kees et al., 2007; Merrill, 1997). Daughters who take care of elderly family members report being more satisfied when there is plenty of autonomy in their relationship with the loved ones they care for (Semlak & Pearson, 2011). When there's too much connection, caretakers can lose their sense of freedom and identity.

Strive for Closeness While Respecting Boundaries

In Chapter 9, we described the conflicting needs we all have for both integration and separation in our relationships as well as for both expression and privacy. Nowhere are these opposing drives stronger than in families. We all know the importance of keeping close ties with our kin, although too much cohesion can be a problem. When cohesion is too high, a family may be **enmeshed**, that is, suffer from too much consensus, too little independence, and a very high demand for loyalty—all of which may feel stifling. At the other extreme, of course, members of families with too little cohesion may be **disengaged**—disconnected, with limited attachment or commitment to one another (Olson, 2000).

Families cope with these dialectical tensions by creating **boundaries**—limits on family members' actions. Communication researchers have devoted a good deal of attention to the importance of boundary management in interpersonal and family relationships (Petronio, 2000) under the umbrella of *communication privacy management theory* (Petronio, 2013). The most obvious boundaries are physical (e.g., don't enter a bedroom without knocking if the door is closed; stay out of the garage when Dad is tinkering with the car). Other boundaries involve conversational topics. In some families, discussion of politics or religion is off limits. In others, expression of certain emotions is restricted. Sex is one of the most-avoided topics with parents and stepparents (Golish & Caughlin, 2002). Money is also a delicate subject in many families. Adult children who care for their elderly parents report that boundaries about finances often remain "thick," even when caretakers need access to their parents' financial accounts (Plander, 2013).

In addition to governing what to talk about, boundaries can also dictate how topics are handled. In some families it is fine to persist if the first overture to discussion is rebuffed ("Come on, what's on your mind?"). In

MEDIA CLIP
Mismanaging Family Boundaries:
Our Idiot Brother

If you've ever said (or thought) during a family conversation, "I'm going to stay out of this" or "What's said here stays here," then you understand boundary management. Unfortunately, Ned Rochlin (Paul Rudd) does not.

Easygoing and not-so-bright Ned is told a lot of personal information by his sisters and their romantic partners, perhaps because he's so innocent and accepting. Unfortunately, he naively shares this information with anyone and everyone, which leads to a variety of problems and conflicts. It's not that Ned is malicious or a gossip; he just doesn't think through the consequences of his disclosures.

In typical Hollywood form, these slipped secrets ultimately help his sisters reevaluate their relationships, and they end up appreciating his indiscrete disclosures. In real life, it's likely they wouldn't be so happy with his loose lips—and they would probably learn not to trust him with important personal information.

other families, privacy rules discourage this kind of persistence. Although the particulars may differ, every family has communication boundaries—and newcomers would be wise to learn and heed those boundaries (consider the many television shows and movies that poke fun at in-laws violating each other's family rules).

Social networking sites—particularly Facebook—provide new challenges for family privacy management. Decisions to send or accept a friend request, unfriend, or block family members are essentially boundary issues. Facebook also has privacy settings that can limit access for particular friends. Studies show that adolescents engage in more self-disclosure but use fewer privacy settings than adults do (Christofides et al., 2012), which is why many of them are reluctant to accept a parent's friend request. Adolescents who agree to share online social networks with their parents report stronger relational bonds (Coyne et al., 2014). Conversely, those who deny parents access tend to have higher levels of aggression and delinquency and lower levels of connectedness. Although the cause–effect relationship isn't clear, it appears that sharing portions of a social network with one's parents is associated with a variety of positive outcomes for adolescents.

As teens transition into adulthood, they become less concerned about Facebook privacy with their parents (Child & Westermann, 2013). Young adults who become Facebook friends with their parents are more likely to be female and to come from families with a high conversation orientation (Ball et al., 2013). Those from lower conversation orientations are more likely to adjust their privacy settings once they add their parents as friends. Regardless of age or orientation, it's important for family members to communicate social networking expectations. This might include negotiating rules such as "Don't post pictures of me from my childhood" or "If you have something personal to say, please do it through private messaging."

Healthy family boundaries allow for relational communication without infringement on privacy and freedom. Sometimes these boundaries need to be openly negotiated. At other times they are established through trial and error. In either case, healthy boundaries allow us to balance the opposing and equally important needs for connection and autonomy, for openness and closedness.

Encourage Confirming Messages

In Chapter 11, we describe the importance of confirming messages—ones that show in one way or another that we value the other person. Confirming messages from parents help satisfy a great many of their children's needs, such as the need for nurturance and respect. Kathleen Ellis (2002) looked at the different ways mothers and fathers communicate valuing and support to their children. She found that two highly confirming behaviors parents offer are (1) telling their children that they are unique and valuable as human beings and (2) genuinely listening to their children when being told something of importance. Two highly disconfirming behaviors are (1) belittling their children and (2) making statements that communicate that their ideas don't count: "Nobody asked for your opinion," or "What do you know about this anyway?"

Confirming messages are just as important for older children as for young ones. One study found a strong relationship between the amount of confirmation adolescents feel and the openness they exhibit in communication with their parents (Dailey, 2006). College students are more likely to reveal their risky behavior to their family members when they think the response is likely to be confirming (Aldeis & Afifi, 2013).

Siblings can also be a source of confirming messages. Research shows that sibling relationships can offer vital support throughout our lives (Goetting, 1986; Rittenour et al., 2007), and thus it's important to maintain them through behaviors such as sharing tasks, expressing positivity, and offering assurances (Myers, 2003). Another way older siblings can nurture their relationships is by talking about their family: reminiscing about their childhood, crazy family events, and wild relatives. Sharing these stories holds the siblings together, as well as helps them clarify family events and validate their feelings and life choices (McGoldrick et al., 1999).

COMMUNICATION IN ROMANTIC RELATIONSHIPS

In Chapter 1 (page 6), we cite numerous studies showing that interpersonal relationships are good for one's mental, emotional, and physical health. A review by Timothy Loving and Richard Slatcher (2013) is even more specific, describing the connection between *romantic* unions and well-being. In short, people in loving romantic relationships live longer, happier, healthier lives. Unfortunately, the ending of a romantic partnership—or being in a distressed intimate relationship—is linked to illness, depression, and even death rates.

In a study of more than 2,200 participants recruited by couples' therapists and counselors, "communication" was rated the most important competency for ensuring success in romantic relationships—more than sex and romantic passion or any other factor (Epstein et al., 2013). In this section, we focus on communication in romantic relationships, which we broadly define as longer-term, loving connections between partners. These relationships can include couples who are dating exclusively, partners who live together, and spouses who have been married for years. The crucial issue is whether the people involved identify themselves as being romantically connected.

CHARACTERISTICS OF ROMANTIC RELATIONSHIPS

"Are we 'just friends' or something more?" It's not unusual for couples to ask questions such as this to determine if they're moving into a romantic relationship. Although the lines of demarcation aren't always clear, in this section we look at three characteristics that typify most romantic relationships: love, commitment, and affection. As you'll see, these concepts overlap (for instance, commitment and affection are components of love in one of the models we use). We break them into three categories here as a way to focus on the research about each of these related topics.

Love

More than two millennia ago, Aristotle maintained that "Love is composed of a single soul inhabiting two bodies." His mentor Plato was a bit more cynical: "Love is a serious mental disease." Philosophers and artists through the years have waxed eloquently about love, with mixed conclusions about its joys and sorrows.

Social scientists have studied love as well, recognizing that it's a force that draws most people into romantic relationships. Researcher Beverly Fehr (2013) puts it this way:

> Love plays a powerful role in people's lives, determining how satisfied they are in a relationship, how committed they are to it, and, at least in premarital relationships, whether or not the relationship continues. (p. 228)

If you ask a dozen scholars for a definition of love, you'll get a dozen different responses. For our purposes, we turn to the work of Robert Sternberg (2004) and his well-known **triangular theory of love**. He maintains that love has three components:

Intimacy: This is the closeness and connectedness one feels in a relationship. We already discussed how intimacy can be found and expressed in all the relational contexts described in this chapter. Using temperature as an analogy, Sternberg regards intimacy as the "warm" component of love.

Passion: This involves physical attraction and emotional arousal, often including sexuality. This is the "hot" component of love.

Commitment: This is the rational side of love, involving decisions to maintain a relationship over time (more on this later). This is love's "cool" component.

Figure 10.2 depicts these three components as corners of a triangle and identifies seven possible combinations resulting from their intersection. It's easy to imagine the communication patterns that accompany each form of love represented in the model. For instance, couples experiencing *romantic*

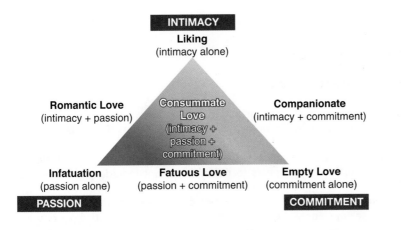

FIGURE 10.2   Components of Sternberg's Triangular Theory of Love

love might exchange highly emotional messages ("I adore you" in a clutched embrace), with many displays of affection. *Companionate love* would be more verbally and nonverbally subdued, with phrases such as "I enjoy your company" more typical. And *empty love* would be a shell of a relationship, void of most if not all affectionate messages. We talk more about the communication of affection later in this section.

As the Focus on Research box on page 328 notes, it's healthy for loving couples to have both companionate and romantic affection for each other. Sternberg acknowledges that *consummate love*—the combination of intimacy, passion, and commitment—is an ideal that's rare to achieve and challenging to maintain. Typically, love's components wax and wane over the course of a relationship. There can be rushes of passion on occasion; at other times, love is more a cool decision than a warm feeling. Maturity is also a factor in the experience of love. For instance, adolescents don't identify with the triangle components as well as adults do (Sumter et al., 2013). As couples age, they tend to value commitment more than the other components, although long-term partners experience more passion and intimacy than some stereotypes suggest (Acevedo & Aron, 2009).

If you consider romantic partnerships you've been in or observed, you can probably think of examples of all the types of love depicted in the triangular model. You can also likely see how the factors ebb and flow over time. Similar to the models of relational stages and dialectics described in Chapter 9, it's healthy to regard love as a dynamic and changing process rather than a static property.

Commitment

How important is the role of commitment in romantic relationships? Sentiments such as the following suggest an answer: "I'm looking for a committed relationship." "I'm just not ready for commitment." "I'm committed to making this relationship work."

Relational commitment involves a promise—sometimes implied and sometimes explicit—to remain in a relationship and to make that

FOCUS ON RESEARCH
Friends or Lovers? What about Both?

It's typical to think of friends and lovers as discrete categories (indeed, we cover them in separate sections in this chapter). But Laura VanderDrift and her colleagues maintain that "romantic relationships are, at their core, friendships." They conducted studies to investigate the role of friendship in loving relationships.

The researchers surveyed college students in nonmarital romantic partnerships. Those who highly valued the friendship component of their relationship had stronger scores on qualities such as love, sexual gratification, and romantic commitment. Four months later, those qualities had increased for the "friendly lovers," and those couples were less likely to have broken up. In other words, friendship appears to be an important ingredient of successful romances.

These findings support a familiar maxim: It's good for romantic partners to both love *and* like each other.

VanderDrift, L. E., Wilson, J. E., and Agnew, C. R. (2013). On the benefits of valuing being friends for nonmarital romantic partners. *Journal of Social and Personal Relationships, 30,* 115–131.

relationship successful. Commitment is both formed and reinforced through communication. Table 10.1 spells out commitment indicators in romantic relationships. Research shows that couples who regularly communicate their commitment have more positive feelings about their relationship and experience less relational uncertainty (Weigel et al., 2011).

As Table 10.1 indicates, words alone aren't a surefire measure of true commitment. Deeds are also important. Simply saying "You can count on me" doesn't guarantee loyalty. But without language, commitment may not be clear. For this reason, ceremonies formalizing relationships are an important way to recognize and cement commitment (see Chapter 9's discussion of "bonding" on page 281).

A cultural note about commitment: It's a decidedly Western approach to view commitment as a culmination of romantic love (as the familiar chant

TABLE 10.1 Major Indicators of Commitment in a Romantic Relationship

- Providing affection
- Providing support
- Maintaining integrity
- Sharing companionship
- Making an effort to communicate regularly
- Showing respect
- Creating a relational future
- Creating a positive relational atmosphere
- Working on relationship problems together
- Reassuring one's commitment

Source: Weigel, D. J. (2008). Mutuality and the communication of commitment in romantic relationships. *Southern Communication Journal, 73,* 24–41.

goes, "First comes love, then comes marriage"). Many of the world's marriages are arranged, and their axiom is "first comes marriage, then comes love." In a study of satisfied couples in arranged marriages, "commitment" was identified as the most important factor that helped their love flourish over time (Epstein et al., 2013). The second most important factor was "communication," with a strong emphasis on self-disclosure as a means to learn to love one's mate. Regardless of the order, there is a strong relationship between commitment and communication in successful romantic relationships.

Affection

Expressions of affection—both verbal and nonverbal—are typical in romantic relationships. These can range from holding hands to saying "I love you" to sexual activity. Romantic affection is often communicated privately; sometimes it's expressed publicly. In fact, the phrase "public displays of affection" has its own acronym (PDA) and social rules (deOliveira et al., 2013; Vaquera & Kao, 2005).

Communicating affection is beneficial for romantic partners in a variety of ways. In one study (Floyd et al., 2009), married and cohabiting couples were asked to increase their amount of romantic kissing over a six-week period. In comparison with a control group, the frequent kissers experienced improvements not only in their stress levels and relational satisfaction, but also in their cholesterol counts (you probably want to know how to sign up for studies like these). Other research shows similar physiological benefits of expressing affection verbally, both in person and in writing (Floyd & Riforgiate, 2008). In terms of relational benefits, received affection works like a bank account—when a loved one has made plenty of deposits, the partner is more willing to overlook a transgression than when the affection account is depleted (Horan, 2012).

There can be discrepancies between feelings and expressions of affection. Perhaps you can recall times when you said "Love ya" at the end of a phone call, despite not feeling very charitable toward your partner. Maybe you gave your partner a hug or a kiss in the midst of a disagreement, even though it didn't match your emotional state. Communication researchers call these acts of "deceptive affection" and say they're common in romantic relationships (Horan & Booth-Butterfield, 2013). Rather than being negative, deceptions of this sort can be a normal part of relational maintenance and support. And of course, while you're busy "deceiving" your partner with these words and behaviors, you might just be convincing yourself. Research shows that engaging in romantic actions, such as gazing into a lover's eyes, sitting at intimate distances, or sharing personal secrets, can often lead to romantic feelings rather than the other way around (Epstein, 2010).

Sexual activity is an important means of expressing and receiving affection in most romantic relationships. One research review notes that the strongest and most reliable predictor of sexual satisfaction is relational satisfaction (Diamond, 2013). In other words, sex is best enjoyed as part of a healthy romantic relationship. Communication also plays an important role: There is a strong correlation between a couple's communication skills and their sexual satisfaction (Byers, 2011). And contrary to some media depictions of passionate sex occurring in wordless vacuums, research shows that sexual activity is more satisfying when accompanied by direct verbal communication ("Here's how I feel"; "This is what I want"), both before and after the encounter (Theiss & Solomon, 2007). When those conversations are uncomfortable, satisfied lovers often use face-saving communication and even humor to express themselves (Miller-Ott & Linder, 2013).

EFFECTIVE COMMUNICATION IN ROMANTIC RELATIONSHIPS

In the preceding section, we identify some ways to improve communication in romantic relationships, such as conversing about commitment and displaying affection. We look now at two more ways to enhance romantic interaction.

Learning Love Languages

"If you love me, please listen."
"If you love me, say so."
"If you love me, show me."

The underlying message in statements such as these is, "Here is what love means to me." Author Gary Chapman (2010) contends that each person has a particular notion of what counts as love. He calls these **love languages** and suggests that we get into trouble when we fail to recognize that our way of expressing love may not match our partner's.

Chapman identifies five love languages in romantic relationships, and research offers support for their being related to effective relational maintenance (Egbert & Polk, 2006). Although they're not technically "languages," the term is used to suggest that these five categories are means of communication. They are

- *Words of affirmation:* These include compliments, words of praise, verbal support, written notes or letters, or other ways of saying that a person is valued and appreciated. People who use this love language are easily hurt by insults or ridicule, or when their efforts aren't verbally acknowledged.
- *Quality time:* This is about being present and available for your partner and giving that person your complete, undivided attention for a significant period of time. Being inattentive or distracted takes the "quality" out of time spent together.
- *Gifts:* People who measure love in terms of gifts believe "it's the thought that counts." A gift needn't be expensive to be meaningful. The best ones are the type that the recipient will appreciate. To gift-oriented partners, neglecting to honor an important event is a transgression.
- *Acts of service:* Taking out the trash, filling the car with gas, doing laundry—the list of chores that can be acts of service is endless. Similar to gifts, the key to service is knowing which acts would be most appreciated by your partner. (Hint: it's probably the chore that your partner hates most.)

- *Physical touch:* Although this might include sexual activity, meaningful touch can also include other expressions of affection: an arm around the shoulder, a held hand, a brush of the cheek, or a neck rub.

Partners understandably but mistakenly can assume that the love language they prefer is also the one the other will appreciate. For example, if your primary love language is "gifts," then you probably expect presents from loved ones on special occasions—and perhaps even on ordinary ones. You're also likely to give gifts regularly and assume that they'll be received appreciatively.

As you can imagine, the assumption that your partner speaks the same love language as you can be a setup for disappointment. Chapman (2010) says this is often the case in marriages:

> We tend to speak our primary love language, and we become confused when our spouse does not understand what we are communicating. We are expressing our love, but the message does not come through because we are speaking what, to them, is a foreign language. (p. 15)

Most people learn love languages in their family of origin. To a degree then, we're imprinted with ways to give and receive affection from an early age (Davis & Haynes, 2012). The good news is that we can learn to communicate love in different ways, especially with help from our romantic partners. Take a look at the types of love languages in the preceding list and see if you can identify your primary style. You can then ask your partner to do the same and compare notes.

© Dan Piraro, distributed by King Features Syndicate (Bizarro cartoon)

Managing Social Media

As we note in Chapter 9 (page 278), it's no longer unusual for romantic relationships to begin online (see also Smith & Duggan, 2013). But even couples who initiate their romance in person need to manage their use of social media. A recent study found that 27% of online adults in romantic partnerships say the Internet has had an impact on their relationships (Lenhart & Duggan, 2014). Not all of that impact is positive. About a quarter of cell phone owners in the study said the phone distracts their romantic partners when they are alone together (the percentage is even higher for young adults, ages 18 to 29).

Communication via mediated channels such as texting, instant messaging, and social media websites can be an ingredient of relational maintenance (Tong & Walther, 2011b). In fact, some scholars suggest that interaction via social media is *more* effective than face-to-face interaction in improving the quality of a relationship (Walther & Ramirez, 2010). One reason text-based electronic channels are so effective is that lovers can

DARK SIDE OF COMMUNICATION

VIRTUALLY UNFAITHFUL: EMOTIONAL INFIDELITY ONLINE

Infidelity has been a fact of life as long as romance has existed. In the digital age, some people are "virtually unfaithful," engaging in romantic relationships online while already in a face-to-face relationship with someone else. Researchers have begun to study whether mediated infidelity is as damaging as the in-person variety. Here are some of their findings:

- A majority of university students in one study—both men and women—believed that infidelity in an online relationship is just as much of a betrayal as cheating in person (Whitty, 2005). In another study (Henline et al., 2007), both men and women regarded emotional infidelity as *more* distressing than cheating sexually.
- In heterosexual relationships, women generally regard online unfaithfulness as a more serious relational transgression than men do (Dijkstra et al., 2013; Docan-Morgan & Docan, 2007).
- Family therapists view Internet infidelity as a significant issue in contemporary romantic relationships (Cravens et al., 2013). They note that partners who are cheated on often need clinical treatment for trauma (Schneider et al., 2012).

Research such as this provides a warning about the dangers of online romance. Making emotional connections with someone in cyberspace—even if there's no physical involvement—can jeopardize committed face-to-face relationships.

craft their messages until they convey just the right expression of affection and immediacy (Walther, 2007). Also, edited messages allow communicators to perceive and present idealized versions of themselves, free of poor manners, stumbling speech, and other bad habits (Jiang & Hancock, 2013; Rabby & Walther, 2003). Of course, partners need to negotiate what constitutes acceptable online behavior—their "netiquette"—for maintaining their intimacy (Helsper & Whitty, 2010).

One indicator of romantic commitment is "making an effort to communicate regularly" (see Table 10.1). An easy way to do this is through calling and texting. One study shows a positive relationship between mobile device use and feelings of commitment and love in romantic relationships (Jin & Pena, 2010; see also Lenhart & Duggan, 2014). Keep in mind, however, that it's possible to have too much of good thing. The Focus on Research box in the previous chapter (page 286) describes the connection-autonomy dilemma of communicating via cell phones. There's a difference between regular contact with loved ones and keeping anxious tabs on them (Weisskirch, 2012). And although expressing affection via texting can enhance a romantic relationship, it's not a good medium for addressing serious issues (Coyne et al., 2011; Schade et al., 2013).

A couple's use of social networking sites both reflects and affects how the partners feel about each other. Individuals who post profile pictures that include their partners report being more satisfied with their relationships than those who post solo photos (Saslow et al., 2013). Moreover, on days when people feel more satisfied in their relationship, they're more likely to share relationship-related information online. But there's a downside to the use of these sites. For instance, one study found a negative relationship between relational intimacy and involvement in online social networking (Hand et al., 2013). Closely monitoring others on Facebook can be relationally intrusive and provoke jealousy (Elphinston & Noller, 2011), particularly for those with low self-esteem (Utz & Beukeboom, 2011). Some even blame Facebook for relational cheating, breakups, and divorce (Clayton et al., 2013). Although holding social media responsible for a relationship's demise may be extreme, it's important to recognize that online affairs are as serious as the in-person variety, as the Dark Side box on page 332 describes.

This returns us to a familiar maxim in this book: all things in moderation. When overused and abused, social media can negatively impact a romantic relationship. When employed with care and awareness, these tools can help maintain and strengthen loving partnerships.

CHECK YOUR UNDERSTANDING

Objective 10.1   Explain the ways intimacy can be expressed in close relationships.

Friendships, families, and romantic partnerships are three of the most important contexts of interpersonal communication. Close relationships in these contexts afford us an opportunity to achieve various forms of intimacy: emotional, physical, intellectual, and shared activities. Intimacy is influenced by gender and culture and can even take place through communication via social media.

> **Q:** Identify the types and extent of intimacy in your closest friendship, family, and romantic relationships (present or past). How satisfied are you with your findings? Could you take any steps to better achieve the ideal amount of intimacy in each of these relationships?

Objective 10.2   Identify the different types of friendship and the role communication plays in maintaining them.

Several factors determine friendship types, such as length of the relationship; task/maintenance orientation; and degrees of disclosure, obligation, and contact. Sex and gender affect the way friends communicate with each other. Successful friendships

follow a number of guidelines that help avoid expectancy violations.

> **Q:** Use the characteristics on pages 313–315 to describe the nature of communication in two of your relationships—one same sex and one cross sex. How satisfied are you with the quality of communication in each of these friendships? Could you make any changes to improve your satisfaction level?

Objective 10.3   Describe how communication creates and sustains relationships within families.

Contemporary families have a variety of traditional and nontraditional arrangements. These arrangements are formed through the communication of narratives, rituals, and rules. Over time, families develop into systems, as members interact with one another to form a whole.

Effective communication in families requires that members establish and maintain a moderate level of cohesion, and they do this by establishing appropriate boundaries. In addition, functional families are adaptable, managing change without too much rigidity or acquiescence. Members of healthy families encourage each other with confirming messages and strive for win-win solutions to their conflicts.

> **Q:** What narratives, rituals, and rules shape communication in your family? What communication patterns characterize your family system? Would any

changes in communication patterns and practices lead to a more cohesive, healthy system?

Objective 10.4 Describe the ways in which love is expressed in romantic relationships.

Most romantic relationships are typified by three components: love, commitment, and affection. Partners who want to improve their communication can learn each other's love languages and use social media in ways that enhance their relationship.

Q: In a romantic relationship you know well, describe the communication of love, commitment, and affection. Which love languages are most resonant for each person, and how well does each partner communicate in those languages? How does communication—both face-to-face and mediated—shape the quality of the relationship?

KEY TERMS

- Boundaries (323)
- Conformity orientation (319)
- Conversation orientation (319)
- Disengaged family (323)
- Enmeshed family (323)
- Expectancy violation (313)
- Family (316)
- Family communication patterns (319)
- Friendship (307)
- Intimacy (302)
- Love languages (330)
- Relational commitment (327)
- System (318)
- Triangular theory of love (326)

ACTIVITIES

1. With a group of classmates, analyze how gender affects communication in friendships. Each group member should begin by keeping a log of communication in two relationships: one same sex, and the other opposite sex. For each incident in your log, record both the subject being discussed (e.g., school, finances) and the nature of the interaction (e.g., emotional expression, personal information, shared activities). Compare your findings and identify the patterns that characterize same- and cross-sex friendships.

2. Gain a better understanding of the role narratives play in a family's interaction. Identify the ongoing narratives in either your current family or your family of origin. Explain:

   a. The narrative

   b. When and how it is retold

   c. The way this narrative portrays your family

   d. The function the narrative serves

Compare narratives with your classmates. What themes emerge? What do your findings say about the power of narratives to shape family relationships?

3. In your romantic relationships, which of the components of love—intimacy, passion, or commitment—is most important to you, and why? Which is least important? Conduct a survey of friends and family to learn their rankings of these three components in their relationships. Discuss your findings with a group of classmates and note any patterns that emerge.

4. With a group of classmates, describe a romantic relationship that embodies the best practices outlined in this chapter. Also describe relationships that suffer due to the lack of each of these best practices. What lessons can you learn from this exercise to make communication in your own romantic relationship more rewarding?

SCORING FOR ASSESSING YOUR COMMUNICATION (PAGE 321)

Add your responses to items 1 through 6. This is your perception of your family's conversation orientation: _____. The score can range from 6 to 30; using 18 as the midpoint, scores of 18 and above are high, and 17 and below are low.

Add your responses to items 7 through 12. This is your perception of your family's conformity orientation: _____. The score can range from 6 to 30; using 18 as the midpoint, scores of 18 and above are high, and 17 and below are low.

Low conversation orientation + low conformity orientation = family is classified as laissez-faire.

Low conversation orientation + high conformity orientation = family is classified as protective.

High conversation orientation + low conformity orientation = family is classified as pluralistic.

High conversation orientation + high conformity orientation = family is classified as consensual.

chapter 11

Communication Climate

LEARNING OBJECTIVES

11.1 Explain the nature of communication climates.
11.2 Describe how communication climates develop.
11.3 Recognize the factors that create defensive and supportive communication climates.
11.4 Identify the communication skills that create invitational climates.

HOW WOULD YOU describe your most important relationships? Fair and warm? Stormy? Hot? Cold? Just as physical locations have characteristic weather patterns, interpersonal relationships have unique climates, too. You can't measure the interpersonal climate by looking at a thermometer or glancing at the sky, but it's there nonetheless. Every relationship has a feeling, a pervasive mood that colors the goings-on of the participants.

WHAT IS COMMUNICATION CLIMATE?

The term **communication climate** refers to the social tone of a relationship. A climate doesn't involve specific activities as much as the way people feel about each other as they carry out those activities. For example, consider two interpersonal communication classes. Both meet for the same length of time and follow the same syllabus. It's easy to imagine how one of these classes might be a friendly, comfortable place to learn, whereas the other could be cold and tense—even hostile. It's not the course content that differs—it's the way the people in the class feel about and treat each other (Johnson, 2009), even if the learning takes place online (Zhang et al., 2012).

Just as every classroom has a unique climate, so does every relationship. Romances, friendships, and families—just like neighborhoods, cities, and countries—can be defined by their social tone. Another obvious context for observing a climate's impact is the workplace, which may explain why the topic is so widely studied (Sopow, 2008; Yurtsever & de Rivera, 2010). Think for a moment: Have you ever held a job where backbiting, criticism, and suspicion were the norm? Or have you been lucky enough to work where the atmosphere was positive, encouraging, and supportive? If you've experienced both, you know what a difference climate makes. Other studies (e.g., Anderson et al., 2004; Bartels et al., 2008) reinforce the fact that employees have a higher level of commitment at jobs in which they experience a positive communication climate (Bartels et al., 2008).

Like their meteorological counterparts, communication climates are shared by everyone involved. It's rare to find one person describing a relationship as open and positive while another characterizes it as cold and hostile. Also, just like the weather, communication climates can change over time. A relationship can be overcast at one time and sunny at another. Carrying the analogy to its conclusion, we should say that communication climate forecasting is not a perfect science. Unlike the weather, however, people can change their communication climates—and that's why it's important to understand them. We look at several climate issues in this chapter: how communication climates develop, how and why we respond defensively in certain climates, and what can be done to create positive climates and transform negative ones.

HOW COMMUNICATION CLIMATES DEVELOP

How do some types of communication create a positive climate whereas others have the opposite effect? Essentially, communication climate is determined by the degree to which people see themselves as *valued*. Communicators who perceive others as liking, appreciating, and respecting them react positively; whereas those who feel unimportant or abused react negatively. Communication scholars use the term **confirming communication** to describe messages that convey valuing (Dailey, 2010). In one form or another, confirming messages say "you exist," "you matter," and "you're important." By contrast, **disconfirming communication** signals a lack of regard (Betts & Hinsz, 2013). In one form or another, disconfirming messages say, "I don't care about you," "I don't like you," and "You're not important to me."

As we have stressed throughout this book, every message has a relational dimension along with its content. This means that we send and receive confirming and disconfirming messages whenever we communicate. It isn't what we communicate about that shapes a relational climate as much as how we speak and act toward one another. Choosing not to speak to someone can also communicate disconfirmation. For example, one way employees nudge unwanted coworkers to quit their jobs is to avoid interaction with them, creating a chilly communication climate (Cox, 1999).

It's hard to overstate the importance of confirming messages and the impact of disconfirming ones. Children who lack confirmation suffer a broad range of emotional and behavioral problems (Osterman, 2001), whereas those who feel confirmed have more open communication with their parents, higher self-esteem, and lower levels of stress (Dailey, 2009, 2010; Schrodt et al., 2006). In the classroom, confirming communication by teachers has been shown to enhance student learning and participation while reducing negative behaviors (Goodboy & Myers, 2008; Schrodt et al., 2009). A confirming climate is also important in marriage, where it is the best predictor of marital satisfaction (Veroff et al., 1998; Weger, 2005). Marriage researcher John Gottman (2003) says that as long as couples have five times as many positive interactions—touching, smiling, paying compliments, laughing, kind words, and so forth—as negative ones, they are likely to have happy and successful relationships.

The interpretation of a message as confirming or disconfirming is subjective. Consider, for example, times when you took a comment that might have sounded unsupportive to an outsider ("You're such a nerd!") as a sign of affection within the context of your personal relationship. Likewise, a comment that the sender might have meant to be helpful ("I'm telling you this for your own good . . .") could easily be regarded as a disconfirming attack.

LEVELS OF MESSAGE CONFIRMATION

Figure 11.1 shows the range of confirming, disagreeing, and disconfirming messages, which are described in the following pages.

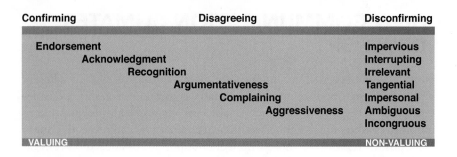

FIGURE 11.1 Confirmation-Disconfirmation Continuum

Confirming Messages

There's no guarantee that others will regard even your best attempts at confirming messages the way you intend them, but research shows that three increasingly positive types of messages have the best chance of being perceived as confirming (Cissna & Sieberg, 2006).

Recognition The most fundamental act of confirmation is to recognize the other person. Recognition seems easy and obvious, yet there are many times when we do not respond to others on this basic level. Failure to call or visit a friend is a common example. So is failure to respond to an e-mail or text message. Likewise, avoiding eye contact can send a negative message. Consider what it's like when a store clerk or bank teller fails to nonverbally acknowledge that you're waiting for service. Of course, this lack of recognition may simply be an oversight. The clerk may be attending to other business, or the pressures of work and school may prevent you from staying in touch with your friend. Nonetheless, if the other person *perceives* you as avoiding contact, the message has the effect of being disconfirming.

Acknowledgment Acknowledging the ideas and feelings of others is a stronger form of confirmation than simple recognition. Listening is probably the most common form of acknowledgment. Attending and responding to another person's words is one measure of your interest. Not surprisingly, employees give high marks to managers who solicit their opinions—even when the managers don't accept every suggestion (Allen, 1995). As you read in Chapter 7, reflecting the speaker's thoughts and feelings can be a powerful way to offer support when others have problems. As Simone Weil notes, "Attention is the rarest and purest form of generosity" (Saltz, 2012).

Endorsement Whereas acknowledgment communicates you are interested in another person, endorsement means that you agree with her or him or otherwise find her or him important. It's easy to see why endorsement is the strongest type of confirming message because it communicates the highest form of valuing. The most obvious form of endorsement is agreeing ("You're right about that"), but it isn't necessary to agree completely with other people to endorse their message. You can probably find something in the message that you endorse. "I can see why you were so angry," you

@WORK

● TAKE THIS JOB AND LOVE IT

"Please describe your best workplace experience." Pamela Lutgen-Sandvik and her associates (2011) posed that question to 835 U.S. employees in an on-line survey. Some responded with a single phrase. Others wrote extended paragraphs. The researchers analyzed the comments in hopes of learning what creates an ideal workplace environment.

The two most frequently cited categories of positive on-the-job experiences had to do with *recognition* and *relationships*. Recognition can be as simple as a private word of praise or as significant as a public award. Being recognized helps workers "feel interper-

sonally significant, needed, unique, and particularly successful" (p. 12). Meaningful workplace relationships include coworker friendships and feeling like part of an organizational family. Social events (such as birthday celebrations or out-of-office gatherings) are typical in companies where members feel a strong sense of affinity and belonging.

These findings show that interpersonal communication plays a central role in positive organizational experiences. Professional achievements and financial rewards are important, but they are valued much more within an affirming workplace environment.

might reply to a friend, even if you don't approve of his or her outburst. Of course, direct praise ("Great job!") is a strong form of endorsement, one you can use surprisingly often once you look for opportunities to compliment others (Berg & DeJong, 2005). Nonverbal endorsement also can enhance the quality of a relational climate (Dailey, 2008). For example, simple acts such as maintaining eye contact and nodding while someone speaks can confirm the value of a speaker's idea. On a more intimate level, hugs and embraces can sometimes communicate endorsement in ways that words cannot.

Disagreeing Messages

Between confirming and disconfirming lies a type of message that isn't always easy to categorize. A **disagreeing message** essentially says, "You're wrong." In its most constructive form, disagreement includes two of the confirming components we just discussed: recognition and acknowledgment. At its worst, a brutal disagreeing message can so devastate another person that the benefits of recognition and acknowledgment are lost. Because there are better and worse ways to disagree with others, disagreeing messages need to be put on a positive-to-negative scale. We do just that in this section as we discuss three types of disagreement: argumentativeness, complaining, and aggressiveness.

Argumentativeness Normally when we call a person "argumentative," we're making an unfavorable evaluation. However, the ability to create and deliver a sound argument is something we admire in lawyers, talk-show participants, and debaters. Taking a positive approach to the term, communication researchers define **argumentativeness** as presenting and defending positions on issues while attacking positions taken by others (Infante

MEDIA CLIP
The Cost of Unbridled Aggressiveness: *Bully*

The lives of bullied children are tragic, but their stories often go untold. The documentary *Bully* takes a close-up look at five families whose worlds are rocked by aggression and abuse at the hands of childhood peers. Sadly, two of the film's subjects committed suicide, and their heartbreaking stories are told retrospectively by loved ones who wish they could have done more to protect the victims.

Some of the adults depicted in this documentary take naïve approaches to bullying, believing that aggressive behavior is simply a matter of "kids being kids." But others clearly understand that vicious words, taunts, and threats are more than just "sticks and stones"—and that bullying hurts everyone involved, not just the victimized child.

& Rancer, 1996). Rather than being a negative trait, argumentativeness—at least in the United States—is sometimes associated with a number of positive attributes, such as enhanced self-concept (Rancer et al., 1992), leadership emergence (Limon & LaFrance, 2005), and communicative competence (Hsu, 2010). In the classroom, research shows a positive relationship between students' perceptions of their instructor as argumentative (not aggressive) and their motivation, learning, and satisfaction (Myers, 2002).

The key for maintaining a positive climate while arguing a point is the *way* you present your ideas. It is crucial to attack issues, not people. In addition, a sound argument is better received when it's delivered in a supportive, affirming manner (Infante & Gorden, 1989). The supportive kinds of messages outlined on pages 350–356 show how it is possible to argue in a respectful, constructive way.

Complaining When communicators aren't prepared to argue but still want to register dissatisfaction, they often complain. As is true of all disagreeing messages, some ways of **complaining** are better than others. Jess Alberts (1988, 1990) found that satisfied couples tend to offer behavioral complaints ("You always throw your socks on the floor"), whereas unsatisfied couples make more complaints aimed at personal characteristics ("You're a slob"). Personal complaints are more likely to result in an escalated conflict episode (Alberts & Driscoll, 1992). The reason should be obvious—complaints about personal characteristics attack a more fundamental part of the presenting self. Talking about socks deals with a habit that can be changed; calling someone a slob is a character assault that is unlikely to be forgotten when the conflict is over.

Marriage researcher John Gottman (2000) has found that complaining is not a sign of a troubled relationship—in fact, it's usually healthy for spouses to get their concerns out in the open. Elizabeth Hall and her colleagues (2013) agree: "Complaining [is] a relationship constructing tool, one which both lubricates and encourages bonding and increased intimacy within romantic relationships" (p. 59). However, when couples' communication is filled with disrespectful criticism (as opposed to mere complaining), it is often a symptom of a marriage headed for divorce. We talk more about this in Chapter 12.

Aggressiveness The most destructive way to disagree with another person is through aggressiveness. Dominic Infante and his associates (1992) define verbal **aggressiveness** as the tendency to "attack the self-concepts of other people in order to inflict psychological pain" (p. 116). Unlike argumentativeness, aggressiveness demeans the worth of others. Name calling, put-downs, sarcasm, taunting, yelling, badgering—and even some types of humor (Bishop et al., 2012)—all are methods of "winning" disagreements at others' expense.

It's no surprise that aggressiveness has been found to have a variety of serious consequences (Rancer & Avtgis, 2006). Research shows it is associated with physical violence in marriages (Infante et al., 1989), juvenile delinquency (Atkin et al., 2002; Straus & Field, 2003), lower self-esteem (Rill et al., 2009), depression (Lawrence et al., 2009), a negative climate in the workplace (Keashly & Neuman, 2009), lower organizational commitment (Houghton, 2001; Madlock & Kennedy-Lightsey, 2010), occupational burnout (Avtgis & Rancer, 2008), and a negative climate in the classroom (Myers & Rocca, 2001; Thomas et al., 2011). As one example of aggression's effect on communication, Scott Myers and his colleagues (2007) found that students who perceive their instructor as verbally aggressive are less likely to ask questions, interact in the classroom, or seek out-of-class communication.

It's possible to send clear, firm messages that are assertive (standing up for yourself) rather than aggressive (putting others down). For instructions on creating assertive "I" statements, refer to Chapter 5. For details on win-win versus win-lose approaches to conflict management, see Chapter 12.

Disconfirming Messages

Disconfirming messages are subtler than disagreeing ones but potentially more damaging. Disconfirming communication implicitly says, "You don't exist; you are not valued." You can assess the level of confirmation and disconfirmation in one of your friendships by completing the Assessing Your Communication quiz on page 346.

Disconfirming messages, unfortunately, are part of everyday life. Although an occasional disconfirming message may not injure a relationship, a pattern of them usually indicates a negative communication climate. Sieberg and Larson (1971; see also Cissna & Sieberg, 2006) found it was easiest to identify disconfirming communication by observing *responses* to others' messages. They noted seven types of disconfirming responses, listed here.

Impervious Response An **impervious response** fails to acknowledge the other person's communicative attempt, either verbally or nonverbally. Impervious responses are especially common when adults and children communicate. Parents often become enraged when they are ignored by their children; likewise, children feel diminished when adults pay no attention to their questions, comments, or requests. Impervious responses also bother students, who, when ignored, report feeling that their self-esteem is being threatened (Sommer et al., 2001). On a less deliberate level, people who tune out others while texting may communicate imperviousness.

Interrupting Response As its name implies, an **interrupting response** occurs when one person begins to speak before the other is through making a point.

Customer: I'm looking for an outfit I can wear on a trip I'm . . .

Salesperson: I've got just the thing. It's part wool and part polyester, so it won't wrinkle at all.

C: Actually, wrinkling isn't that important. I want something that will work as a business outfit and . . .

S: We have a terrific blazer that you can dress up or down, depending on the accessories you choose.

C: That's not what I was going to say. I want something that I can wear as a business outfit, but it ought to be on the informal side. I'm going to . . .

S: Say no more. I know just what you want.

C: Never mind. I think I'll look in some other stores.

Irrelevant Response It is disconfirming to respond with an **irrelevant response**, making comments totally unrelated to what the other person was just saying.

A: What a day! I thought it would never end. First the car overheated and I had to call a tow truck, and then my computer broke down at work.

B: Listen, we have to talk about a present for Ann's birthday. The party is on Saturday, and I only have tomorrow to shop for it.

A: I'm really beat. You won't believe what the boss did. Like I said, my computer was down, and in the middle of that mess he decided he absolutely had to have the sales figures for the last 6 months.

B: I just don't know what to get Ann. She's been so generous to us, and I can't think of anything she needs.

A: Why don't you listen to me? I beat my brains out all day and you don't give a damn.

B: And you don't care about me!

In the cult comedy film *Office Space*, the bumbling character Milton (Stephen Root) is downsized in an extreme act of disconfirmation. He is not fired, but his desk is moved to a basement storage area where he languishes, unpaid and ignored.

Tangential Response Unlike the three behaviors just discussed, a **tangential response** does acknowledge the other person's communication. However, the acknowledgment is used to steer the conversation in a new direction. Tangents can come in two forms. One is the "tangential shift," which is an abrupt change in conversation. For example, a young boy runs into the house excited, showing his mother the rock he found. She says, "Wash your hands;

that rock is dirty." In a "tangential drift" the speaker makes a token connection with what the other person is saying and then moves the conversation in another direction entirely. In the same scenario, the mother might look at the rock, say "Hmmm, nice rock," and then immediately add, "Go wash your hands before dinner."

Impersonal In an **impersonal response**, the speaker conducts a monologue filled with detached, intellectualized, and generalized statements. The speaker never really interacts with the other on a personal level:

Employee: I've been having some personal problems lately, and I'd like to take off early a couple of afternoons to clear them up.

Boss: Ah, yes. We all have personal problems. It seems to be a sign of the times.

"Go ask your search engine."

Ambiguous Response An **ambiguous response** contains a message with more than one meaning. The words are highly abstract or have meanings private to the speaker alone:

A: I'd like to get together with you soon. How about Tuesday?

B: Uh, maybe so. Anyhow, see you later.

C: Are you mad at me?

D: I feel the same about you as I always do.

Incongruous Response An **incongruous response** contains two messages that seem to deny or contradict each other, one at the verbal level and the other at the nonverbal level.

He: Darling, I love you!

She: I love you too. (*giggles*)

Teacher: Did you enjoy the class?

Student: Yes. (*yawns*)

DEFENSIVENESS

It's no surprise that disconfirming and disagreeing messages can pollute a communication climate. Perhaps the most predictable reaction to a hostile or indifferent message is defensiveness.

The word *defensiveness* suggests protecting yourself from attack, but what kind of attack? Seldom when you become defensive is a physical threat involved. If you're not threatened by bodily injury, what *are* you guarding against? To answer this question, we need to talk more about notions of **presenting self** and **face**, both of which we introduced in Chapter 3. Recall that the presenting self consists of the physical traits, personality

ASSESSING YOUR COMMUNICATION

Confirming and Disconfirming Communication

With a particular friendship in mind, respond to each of the statements below using a scale ranging from 1 to 5, where 1 = strongly disagree, and 5 = strongly agree.

PART I

_____ **1.** My friend pays attention to me when I am talking.

_____ **2.** My friend usually listens carefully to what I have to say.

_____ **3.** When we talk, my friend does his/her part to keep the conversation going.

_____ **4.** I feel as though I am usually able to say everything I want to say without being judged.

_____ **5.** My friend makes eye contact while we talk.

_____ **6.** My friend usually accepts my point of view as accurate.

_____ **7.** My friend often acts interested in what I have to say.

PART II

_____ **1.** My friend teases me in a way that hurts my feelings.

_____ **2.** When I bring up something that upsets me, my friend tells me that I shouldn't complain about it.

_____ **3.** My friend often tells me that my feelings or thoughts are wrong.

_____ **4.** My friend ignores me when I try to talk to him/her about something important.

_____ **5.** My friend often changes the subject to something he/she wants to discuss.

_____ **6.** My friend often seems uninvolved in our conversations.

_____ **7.** My friend often takes over the conversation and does not allow me to do much of the talking.

_____ **8.** My friend often interrupts me.

_____ **9.** My friend blames me when we have a disagreement about something.

_____ **10.** My friend often makes jokes at my expense.

Adapted from Bloch, A. S., & Weger, H. W., Jr. (2012 May). *Associations among friendship satisfaction, self-verification, self-enhancement, and friends' communication skill.* Paper presented at the annual meeting of the International Communication Association, Phoenix, AZ.

For scoring information, see page 365 at the end of the chapter.

characteristics, attitudes, aptitudes, and all the other parts of the image you want to present to the world. Actually, it is a mistake to talk about a single face: We try to project different selves to different people. For instance, you might try to impress a potential employer with your seriousness but want your friends to see you as a joker.

When others are willing to accept and acknowledge important parts of our presenting image, there is no need to feel defensive. On the other hand, when others confront us with **face-threatening acts**—messages that we perceive as challenging the image we want to project—we are likely to resist what they say. **Defensiveness**, then, is the process of protecting our presenting self, our face. Although responding defensively to a face-threatening attack may seem logical, over time, defensiveness erodes relationship stability (Lannin et al., 2013).

You can understand how defensiveness operates by imagining what might happen if an important part of your presenting self were attacked. For instance, suppose an instructor criticized you in front of the class for making a mistake. Or consider how you would feel if a friend called you self-centered or your boss labeled you as lazy. You would probably feel threatened if these attacks were untrue. But your own experience will probably show that you sometimes respond defensively even when you know that others' criticism is justified. For instance, you have probably responded defensively at times when you *did* make a mistake, act selfishly, or cut corners in your work (Zhang & Stafford, 2008). In fact, we often feel most defensive when criticism is right on target (Becker et al., 2008; Stamp et al., 1992). Later in this chapter, we discuss how to respond nondefensively in such situations.

The topics that trigger defensiveness vary. Sometimes sensitive topics are personal. You might feel a strong need to protect your image of athletic

FOCUS ON RESEARCH
Saving Face While Delivering Constructive Criticism

It's never easy being the bearer of bad tidings. However, providing negative feedback is a "necessary evil" of being a supervisor, according to Catherine Kingsley Westerman and David Westerman. They conducted a study to learn how best to offer critical appraisals while saving face for both the boss and the employee.

Not surprisingly, research participants said that bad news from a supervisor was easier to take when it was offered with face-saving statements such as, "What was expected of you may not have been clear"; and "You're on the right track and your work

has potential." Phrases such as these also led to more positive perceptions of the bosses who delivered them. In other words, critical appraisals couched with supportive comments helped save face for both parties.

The researchers also found that face-saving criticism is better received in face-to-face interaction than through e-mail. It appears that when delivering tough news, a supervisor would do well to have a variety of verbal and nonverbal cues available—and that the "personal" approach is best.

Kingsley Westerman, C. Y., & Westerman, D. (2010). Supervisor impression management: Message content and channel effects on impressions. *Communication Studies, 61,* 585–601.

skill or intelligence, whereas another person might be more concerned with appearing fashionable or funny. Some research suggests that defense-provoking topics can vary by sex. In one study, men interpreted messages about mental or physical errors (such as misfiling a file or tripping on a carpet) more defensively than women did. Men and women got equally defensive over messages about their clothes and hair, but women got more defensive over messages regarding weight (Futch & Edwards, 1999). And professional women report a variety of face-threatening interactions in the workplace, particularly with men in traditionally male occupations (Irizarry, 2004).

Who offers the potentially defense-arousing remark or criticism also matters. Matthew Hornsey and his colleagues (2002) conducted three experiments examining group members' responses to criticism from in-group (other Australians) and out-group (people from another country) members. They found that in-group criticisms were tolerated surprisingly well, whereas out-group criticisms were met with defensiveness—probably because in-group criticisms are seen as more legitimate and more constructive.

So far, we have talked about defensiveness as if it is only the responsibility of the person who feels threatened. If this were the case, then the prescription would be simple: Grow a thick skin, admit your flaws, and stop trying to manage impressions. This approach isn't just unrealistic—it also ignores the role played by those who send face-threatening messages. In fact, competent communicators protect others' face needs as well as their own. Skilled instructors carefully protect their students' presenting faces, especially when offering constructive criticism (Trees et al., 2009). This facework leads to less defensive responses from their students. Similarly, wise students craft their e-mails politely when making requests of their teachers, showing them appropriate respect (Bolkan & Holmgren, 2012). Findings like this make it clear that defensiveness is *interactive:* all communicators contribute to the climate of a relationship.

As a practical example of these concepts, communication researcher Sarah Tracy (2002) analyzed emergency

DARK SIDE OF COMMUNICATION
CYBERBULLYING: INFLICTING PAIN ONLINE

The documentary *Bully* (see page 342) describes the impact of peer aggression on victims in schools and neighborhoods. Sadly, online communication has given tormenters new avenues to inflict wounds on their prey. What makes cyberbullying different from the face-to-face variety is that it's done through written taunts and threats sent via social network posts, text messages, blogs, and e-mail. This demonstrates the power of words to do great harm when misused.

Because cyberbullying is a relatively recent phenomenon, researchers are busy compiling data about the

call-center interactions to understand better how and why these conversations sometimes turn into contentious struggles. Tracy concluded that callers become defensive when they perceive call-takers' questions to be face threatening, and she offered suggestions for making the climate more supportive. For instance, changing "Tell me if . . ." to "Can you tell me if . . ." adds only two words—but those words soften the inquiry and make it more of a request than a demand. Changes like this take very little extra time, and they have the potential to keep the climate supportive rather than defensive—and in 911 calls, that's a small investment that can save a life.

CLIMATE PATTERNS

Once a communication climate is formed, whether positive or negative, it can take on a life of its own. In one study of married couples, each spouse's response in conflict situations was found to be similar to the other's (Burggraf & Sillars, 1987). Conciliatory statements (e.g., supporting, accepting responsibility, agreeing) were likely to be followed by conciliatory responses. Confrontive acts (e.g., criticism, hostile questions, faultfinding) were likely to trigger an aggressive response. The same pattern held for other kinds of messages: Avoidance led to avoidance, analysis evoked analysis, and so on. This reciprocal pattern can be represented as a **spiral** (Wilmot, 1987).

process and its outcomes (Cassidy et al., 2013; Roberto et al., 2014). Here are a few of their findings:

- Although middle school is the peak period for cyberbullying, it can start as early as grade school and continue into the college years and beyond.
- More than a third of contemporary students report being cyberbullied during their school careers.
- Cyberbullying has been linked to a variety of negative consequences including poor academic performance, depression, withdrawal, psychosomatic pain, drug and alcohol abuse, and even suicide.

A key to stopping cyberbullying is blowing the whistle on the perpetrators. Unfortunately, most adolescents are unwilling to do so for reasons ranging from fear of reprisal to fear of losing their social media privileges. They are far more likely to tell their friends than adults about online harassment, so many school programs encourage peer-led support and intervention.

Cyberbullying will remain a problem as long as it stays a secret. If you're being bullied online, keep copies of the harassing messages—and then contact an appropriate teacher, administrator, or supervisor. Most schools and companies have policies that can help provide protection. And if you know someone who is being victimized—especially if it's a young person—be receptive and help arrange professional intervention. Open communication is vital to bringing cyberbullying out of the shadows.

For more information on this important topic, go to StopBullying.gov

Fortunately, spirals can also work in a positive direction. One confirming behavior can lead to a similar response from the other person, which in turn leads to further confirmation by the first person. When a negative spiral gets out of hand, however, the partners might agree to back off from their disconfirming behavior. "Hold on," one might say, "this is getting us nowhere." At this point there may be a cooling-off period, or the partners might work together more constructively to solve their problem (Becker et al., 2008). This ability to "rebound" from negative spirals and turn them in a positive direction is a hallmark of successful relationships (Gottman & Levenson, 1999). However, if the partners pass "the point of no return" and continue spiraling downward, the relationship may end.

CREATING SUPPORTIVE CLIMATES

Even the most positive message isn't guaranteed to create a positive climate. A comment of praise can be interpreted as sarcasm; an innocent smile can be perceived as a sneer; an offer to help can be seen as condescension. Because human communication is so complex, there aren't any foolproof words, phrases, or formulas for creating positive climates. Nonetheless, research suggests that there *are* strategies that can increase the odds of expressing yourself in ways that lead to positive relational climates—even when the message you're delivering is a tough one.

Several decades ago, psychologist Jack Gibb published a helpful study (1961; see also 2008) that isolated six types of defense-arousing communication and six contrasting behaviors that seem to reduce the level of threat and defensiveness. These "Gibb categories" are listed in Table 11.1. Gibb's findings have commonsense appeal and multiple applications. As a result, they've played an important part in communication textbooks, training seminars, journals, and research studies (e.g., Becker et al., 2008; Forward et al., 2011). We use them here to discuss how positive climates can be created by sending supportive rather than defense-provoking messages.

EVALUATION VERSUS DESCRIPTION

The first type of defense-arousing message Gibb identified is **evaluation**. An evaluative message judges the other person, usually in a negative way. For instance, consider this message: "You don't care about me!" Evaluative messages such as this possess several characteristics that make them so face threatening. They judge what the other person is feeling rather than describing the speaker's thoughts, feelings, and wants. They don't explain how the speaker arrived at his or her conclusion, and they lack specifics. Furthermore, they're often phrased in the kind of defense-arousing "you" language described in Chapter 5. It's easy to understand why evaluative statements often trigger a defensive spiral.

Do the climate-threatening properties of evaluative messages mean that it's impossible to register a legitimate complaint?: No. They simply mean that

TABLE 11.1 The Gibb Categories of Defense-Provoking and Supportive Behaviors

DEFENSE-PROVOKING BEHAVIORS	SUPPORTIVE BEHAVIORS
1. Evaluation	1. Description
2. Control	2. Problem Orientation
3. Strategy	3. Spontaneity
4. Neutrality	4. Empathy
5. Superiority	5. Equality
6. Certainty	6. Provisionalism

you must be alert to more constructive ways to do so. **Description** is a way to offer your thoughts, feelings, and wants without judging the listener. Descriptive messages make documented observations that are specific and concrete. As we mentioned earlier when discussing complaining, description focuses on behavior that can be changed rather than on personal characteristics that cannot. In addition, descriptive messages often use "I" language, which tends to provoke less defensiveness than "you" language (Heydenberk & Heydenberk, 2007; Proctor & Wilcox, 1993). Contrast the evaluative "You don't care about me" with this more descriptive message: "I'm sorry that we don't spend as much time together as we did during the summer. When we don't talk during the week, I sometimes feel unimportant. Maybe we could try to text each other once a day—that would mean a lot to me."

Let's look at more examples of the difference between evaluative and descriptive messages:

Evaluation	Description
You're not making any sense.	I don't understand the point you're trying to make.
You're inconsiderate.	I would appreciate it if you'd let me know when you're running late—I was worried.
That's an ugly tablecloth.	I'm not crazy about big blue stripes: I like something more subtle.

Note several characteristics of these descriptive messages. First, their focus is on the speaker's thoughts, feelings, and wants, with little or no judgment of the other person. Second, the messages address specific behaviors rather than making sweeping character generalizations. The messages also provide information about how the speaker arrived at these conclusions. Finally—and perhaps most important—notice that each of the descriptive statements is just as honest as its evaluative counterpart. Once you have learned to speak descriptively, you can be as direct and straightforward as ever while avoiding personal attacks that can poison a climate.

CONTROL VERSUS PROBLEM ORIENTATION

A second defense-provoking message involves some attempt to control another person. **Controlling communication** occurs when a sender seems to be imposing a solution on the receiver with little regard for that person's needs or interests. The object of control can involve almost anything: where to eat dinner, how to spend a large sum of money, or whether to remain in a relationship. Whether done with words, gestures, or tone of voice, or through some other channel; whether control is accomplished through status, insistence on obscure or irrelevant rules, or physical power: The controller generates hostility. The unspoken message such behavior communicates is "I know what's best for you, and if you do as I say, we'll get along."

In **problem orientation**, however, communicators focus on finding a solution that satisfies both their own needs and those of the others involved.

The goal here isn't to "win" at the expense of your partner but to work out some arrangement in which everybody feels like a winner. (In Chapter 12, we have a great deal to say about "win-win" problem solving as a way to find problem-oriented solutions.) Problem orientation is often typified by "we" language (see Chapter 5), which suggests the speaker is making decisions *with* rather than *for* other people (Seider et al., 2009). University chairpersons found to be most effective by members of their departments were best characterized as using few control communications and adopting a problem orientation (Czech & Forward, 2010).

Here are some examples of how some controlling versus problem-oriented messages might sound:

Controlling	Problem Oriented
Get off your phone—now! I need to talk to you.	I really need to talk soon. Can you take a break?
There's only one way to handle this problem . . .	Looks like we have a problem. Let's work out a solution we can both live with.
Either you start working harder, or you're fired!	The production in your department hasn't been as high as I'd hoped. Any ideas on what we could do?

STRATEGY VERSUS SPONTANEITY

Gibb uses the word **strategy** to characterize defense-arousing messages in which speakers hide their ulterior motives. The terms *dishonesty* and *manipulation* reflect the nature of strategy. Even if the intentions that motivate strategic communication are honorable, the victim of deception who discovers the attempt to deceive is likely to feel offended at being played for a sucker (Tsang, 2006).

As we discussed in Chapter 7, counterfeit questions are a form of strategic communication because they try to trap others into desired responses. Many sales techniques are strategic, for they give customers limited information and then make it difficult to say no. This is not to say that all sales techniques are wrong or unethical, but most strategic ones aren't well suited for interpersonal relationships. If you've ever gotten defensive when you thought a friend was doing a "sales job" on you, you understand the concept.

Spontaneity is the behavior that contrasts with strategy. Spontaneity simply means being honest with others rather than manipulating them. What it doesn't mean is blurting out what you're thinking as soon as an idea comes to you (see the Focus on Research sidebar on page 354). Gibb was after setting aside hidden agendas that others both sense and resist. You can probably recall times when someone asked you a question and you suspiciously responded with "Hmmm . . . why do you want to know?" Your defensive antennae were up because you detected an underlying strategy.

If the person had told you up front why he or she was asking the question, then your defenses probably would have been lowered. That's what we mean by spontaneity. Here are some examples:

Strategy	Spontaneity
What are you doing Friday after work?	I have a piano I need to move Friday after work. Can you give me a hand?
Have you ever considered another line of work?	I'm concerned about your job performance over the last year; let's set up a time to talk about it.
Ali and Kasey go out to dinner every week.	I'd like to go out for dinner more often.

This is a good place to pause and talk about larger issues regarding the Gibb model. First, Gibb's emphasis on being direct is better suited for a low-context culture such as that of the United States, which values straight-talk, than for high-context cultures. Second, there are ways in which each of the communication approaches Gibb labels as "supportive" can be used to exploit others and, therefore, violate the spirit of positive climate building. For instance, consider spontaneity. Although it sounds paradoxical at first, spontaneity can be a strategy, too. Sometimes you'll see people using honesty in a calculating way, being just frank enough to win someone's trust or sympathy. This "leveling" is probably the most defense-arousing strategy of all because once you've learned someone is using frankness as a manipulation, there's almost no chance you'll ever trust that person again.

NEUTRALITY VERSUS EMPATHY

Gibb used the term **neutrality** to describe a fourth behavior that arouses defensiveness. Probably a better word would be *indifference*. For example, 911 emergency telephone dispatchers are taught to be neutral to calm down the caller, but they shouldn't communicate indifference or a lack of caring (Shuler & Sypher, 2000). Using Gibb's terminology, a neutral attitude is disconfirming because it communicates a lack of concern for the welfare of another and implies that the other person isn't very important to you. The poor effects of neutrality become apparent when you consider the hostility that most people have for the large, impersonal organizations with which they have to deal: "They think of me as a number instead of a person"; "I felt as if I were being handled by computers and not human beings." These common statements reflect reactions to being treated in an indifferent, neutral way.

The behavior that contrasts with neutrality is **empathy**. Gibb found that empathy helps rid communication of the quality of indifference. When people show that they care for the feelings of another, there's little chance that the person's self-concept will be threatened. Empathy means accepting another's feelings, putting yourself in another's place. This doesn't mean you need to agree with that person. By simply letting someone know about your care and respect, you'll be acting in a supportive way. We addressed the

FOCUS ON RESEARCH
A Blurt Can Hurt

When Gibb's model recommends "spontaneity" as a way of creating a supportive climate, it doesn't mean indiscriminately saying whatever you're thinking and feeling. That would be what Dale Hample and his colleagues call *blurting*—and their research shows that these kinds of impulsive disclosures are usually detrimental to interpersonal communication.

The researchers asked participants to write about blurting episodes, loosely described as speaking without thinking. The participants also completed a battery of scales to help the researchers determine the attributes of a chronic blurter. Interestingly, *all* of the participants' blurting episodes were about negative or regrettable comments they made. Although it's possible that people can blurt good news or positive appraisals, that's not what the respondents

thought of when they recalled themselves speaking before thinking.

Not surprisingly, blurting was associated with a variety of less-than-positive traits. Blurters tend to be high in verbal aggressiveness, psychoticism, and neuroticism; they rate low in empathy and perspective taking. They are also relatively unconcerned about the harm their comments might do to others and to their relationships.

Think back to the description of communication competence in Chapter 1 and you'll realize that blurting is at odds with most of the principles outlined there. Although it's hard to determine whether blurting is due to a lack of will or skill, one thing seems clear: There is interpersonal value in pausing to think before speaking your mind.

Hample, D., Richards, A. S., & Skubisz, C. (2013). Blurting. *Communication Monographs, 80,* 503–532.

concept of empathy in Chapter 4 and the skill of empathizing in Chapter 7; let's see what empathic messages look like when contrasted with neutral ones:

Neutrality	Empathy
This is what happens when you don't plan properly.	Ouch—looks like this didn't turn out the way you expected.
Sometimes things just don't work out. That's the way it goes.	I know you put a lot of time and effort into this project.
Don't get too excited— Everybody gets promoted sooner or later.	I'll bet you're pretty excited about the promotion.

SUPERIORITY VERSUS EQUALITY

A fifth behavior creating a defensive climate involves **superiority**. A body of research describes how patronizing messages irritate receivers ranging from young students to senior citizens (Draper, 2005; Harwood et al., 1997). Any message that suggests "I'm better than you" is likely to arouse feelings of defensiveness in the recipients. Research confirms what most of us know from experience: We dislike people who communicate superiority, especially when it involves an explicit comparison with others (Hoorens et al., 2012).

Many times in our lives we communicate with people who possess less talent or knowledge than we do, but it isn't necessary to convey an attitude of superiority in these situations. Gibb found ample evidence that many who have superior skills and talents are capable of projecting feelings of **equality** rather than superiority. Such people communicate that although they may have greater talent in certain areas, they see other human beings as having just as much worth as themselves.

Charles and Elizabeth Beck (1996) observe that equality is put to the test when a person doesn't have superior skills yet is in a position of authority. Supervisors sometimes have less expertise in certain areas than their subordinates but believe it would be beneath them to admit it. Think for a moment: You've probably been in situations where you knew more about the subject than the person in charge—be it a boss, a teacher, a parent, or a salesperson—yet this person acted as if he or she knew more. Did you feel defensive? No doubt. Did that person feel defensive? Probably. You both were challenging each other's presenting self, so the climate most likely became hostile. A truly secure person can treat others with equality even when there are obvious differences in knowledge, talent, and status. Doing so creates a positive climate in which ideas are evaluated not on the basis of who contributed them, but rather on the merit of the ideas themselves.

What does equality sound like? Here are some examples:

Superiority	Equality
When you get to be in my position someday, *then* you'll understand.	I'd like to hear how the issue looks to you. Then I can tell you how it looks to me.
No, not that way! Let me show you how to do it right.	What if you tried it this way?
You really believe *that*?	Here's another way to think about it . . .

CERTAINTY VERSUS PROVISIONALISM

Have you ever run into people who are positive they're right, who know that theirs is the only or proper way of doing something, who insist that they have all the facts and need no additional information? If you have, you've met individuals who project the defense-arousing behavior Gibb calls **certainty**.

Communicators who regard their own opinions with certainty while disregarding the ideas of others demonstrate a lack of regard for others. It's likely the receiver will take the certainty as a personal affront and react defensively.

PEARLS BEFORE SWINE © 2012 Stephan Pastis.
Reprinted by permission of Universal UClick
for UFS

In contrast to dogmatic certainty is **provisionalism**, in which people may have strong opinions but are willing to acknowledge that they don't have a corner on the truth and will change their stand if another position seems more reasonable. Provisionalism often surfaces in a person's word choice. Whereas people with certainty regularly use the terms *can't, never, always, must,* and *have to,* those with provisionalism use *perhaps, maybe, possibly, might,* and *could.* It's not that provisional people are spineless; they simply recognize that discussion is aided by open-minded messages. Katt and Collins (2009; 2013) found that when teachers use provisional language, it helps motivate students. For instance, students responded more favorably to the critique "Your introduction could have been developed more thoroughly" than to the starker "The introduction was not well developed."

Let's look at some examples:

Certainty	Provisionalism
That will *never* work!	My guess is that you'll run into problems with that approach.
You'll hate that class! Stay away from it!	I didn't like that class very much; I'm not sure you would, either.
You won't get anywhere without a college education: Mark my words.	I think it's important to get that degree. I found it was hard to land an interview until I had one.

You've probably noticed a good deal of overlap among the various Gibb components—overlap confirmed by researchers (Forward et al., 2011). For instance, look at the final example under "Provisionalism." The statement is likely to create a positive climate not only because it is provisional rather than certain, but also because it is descriptive rather than evaluative, problem oriented rather than controlling, and equal rather than superior. You may also have noticed a tone underlying all of the supportive examples: *respect.* By valuing and confirming others—even if you disagree with them— you create a respectful climate that helps enhance a positive communication climate, both now and in future interactions.

INVITATIONAL COMMUNICATION

It would be easy to see the prescriptions in this chapter as a fail-proof set of communication techniques: Just say some predetermined words in a particular way and your interpersonal problems will be solved. But of course you know (and we authors know) it doesn't work that way.

To become a truly competent communicator involves more than adopting particular phrases and methods. It requires an interpersonal philosophy that undergirds what you say and do. Communication scholars Sonja Foss and Cindy Griffin (1995; see also Modesti, 2012) have identified such an approach. Their study began in the field of rhetoric, which is traditionally associated with persuading others to change their minds and behaviors. Foss and Griffin offer an alternative view they call *invitational rhetoric*. Here is a description:

> Invitational rhetoric can be viewed as a communication exchange in which participants create an environment where growth and change can occur but where changing others is neither the ultimate goal nor the criterion for success in the interaction. (Bone et al., 2008, p. 436)

Invitational communication is an approach that welcomes others to see your point of view and to freely share their own. In an invitational climate, communicators offer ideas without coercion; they listen to ideas with an open mind; they exchange ideas without pressure. It doesn't mean they don't critically appraise the messages they hear. They also don't waffle about things they believe in. What it means is they endeavor to create a supportive climate based on *value, safety*, and *freedom*, leading to a greater *civility* in their communication (Bone et al., 2008).

Earlier in this chapter, we talked about valuing as the key component of confirming communication. To describe how safety and freedom tie into invitational communication and civility, it might be easier to describe what *incivility* looks like. Here's a brief review of some Dark Side topics in this book that illustrate uncivil, non-invitational communication:

- Getting hoaxed (page 86), whether in person or online, turns one's world upside down. There's nothing safe and free about being duped.
- The Gaslight Effect (page 130) imposes one person's perception on another's in an attempt to manipulate and control.
- Hate speech (page 153) denigrates others' value and worth, using language that demeans and destroys.
- Cyberbullying (page 348) communicates to its victims, "You have no value, and you're never safe."
- The silent treatment (page 375) disconfirms others, treating them as if they don't exist.

In contrast to these uncivil approaches, many of the skills described in this book—perception checking, responsible language, responsive listening—are rooted in an invitational approach to interpersonal communication. Building on their foundation, we look briefly at two more ways to put this invitational philosophy into action: using the language of choice and responding nondefensively to criticism.

THE LANGUAGE OF CHOICE

In Chapter 5, we explain the relationship between pronouns such as *I*, *we*, and *you* and the language of responsibility. The words that follow these pronouns are also important ingredients in responsible communication (Glasser & Glasser, 1999; Zeman, 2010). Read the following statements and consider how you feel about them (assume they involve activities you'd rather not do):

"I *have to* talk to my neighbor about the barking dog."
"I *should* be nicer to my roommate."
"I *ought to* be more assertive."
"I *can't* take this anymore."
"I had *no choice*—I *had to* tell her."

It's likely that you read those lines in a somber tone of voice and that you were left with a sense of heaviness and pressure. Consider how those same phrases might conjure a different feeling if worded this way (with possible reasons in parentheses):

"I'm going to talk to my neighbor about the barking dog" (I want to settle this problem).
"I will start being nicer to my roommate" (I want a more pleasant relationship).
"I'm determined to be more assertive" (I want to be a more effective communicator).
"I'm not going to take this anymore" (I want change).
"I decided to tell her" (I wanted her to know).

Notice how this list describes *choices* instead of *obligations*. The wording focuses on decisions made (e.g., will, going to), not grudging acquiescence (e.g., should, have to). You probably found the second list more motivating than the first, and research supports this notion. When participants in one study said "I *don't* eat unhealthy snacks" (suggesting personal choice) instead of "I *can't* eat unhealthy snacks" (suggesting external constraint), they had greater willpower and changes in their eating habits (Patrick & Hagtvedt, 2012). The researchers call this "empowered refusal" and maintain that word choice plays a significant role in the process. In the language of invitational communication, empowering words identify your *freedom* to make choices. In essence, you're inviting yourself to take charge of your decisions.

Consider then what it's like to offer that same freedom to others:

"You should"	becomes	"I'm going to" (and you can join me if you want)
"You have to"	becomes	"You're welcome to"
"We can't"	becomes	"I don't want to" (do you?)
"You make me . . ."	becomes	"I like (or don't like) when you . . ."

This last option ties into the fallacy of causation discussed in Chapter 8. Phrases such as "makes me," "drives me," and "forces me" are rarely accurate—and they can be personally and interpersonally constricting (Zeman, 2010). "My job drove me to drink" doesn't empower change (after all, it's the job's fault). "If you do that again, I'll be forced to punish you" blames others for your choices (and assigns guilt). "You make me mad" suggests my anger is your responsibility (instead of my emotional reaction). In an invitational approach, each party is responsible for his or her actions, reactions, and decisions. Communicators describe their choices with words such as "will," "want to," "going to," "choose to," "like to," "hope to"—as well as those words' opposite choices (won't, don't want to, not going to, etc.).

As mentioned earlier, there's nothing magical about these words—they simply reflect an invitational attitude. In essence they say, "Here is what's going on inside me; tell me what's going on inside you." They are also best understood as part of an exchange. Consider how phrases such as these demonstrate value, safety, and freedom for both parties in a dialogue:

"I hold a different opinion, but I understand why that's important to you."
"I have some thoughts on the matter—would you like to hear them?"
"I welcome your input" (I may or may not use it, but I value what you have to say).
"Here is something I feel strongly about" (it's okay if you don't).

This final statement illustrates an important point. Invitational communicators not only extend freedom to others, but they exercise it themselves. It's fine to let people know what you think, feel, and want, and to have values, beliefs, and convictions that guide your choices. The key is communicating those ideas responsibly rather than aggressively. Recognize that your perspective might not be shared by others, so offer it in a way that invites rather than imposes.

RESPONDING NONDEFENSIVELY TO CRITICISM

The world would be a happier place if everyone communicated invitationally. But sometimes when we invite others to offer their point of view, they criticize and attack. In those situations, it can be challenging to remain civil. How can you respond nondefensively when faced with criticism? Here we look at two such methods: seeking more information and agreeing with the critic. Despite their apparent simplicity, they have proven to be among the most valuable skills communicators can learn.

Seek More Information

The response of seeking more information makes good sense when you realize that it's foolish to respond to a critical attack until you understand what the other person has said (Gold & Castillo, 2010). Even comments that on first consideration appear to be totally unjustified or foolish often prove to contain at least a grain of truth and sometimes much more.

One way to seek more information is to *ask for specifics*. Often the vague attack of a critic is virtually useless, even if you sincerely want to change. Abstract accusations such as "you're being unfair" or "you never help out" can be difficult to understand. In such cases, it is a good idea to request

MEDIA CLIP
Everyone's a Critic: Performance
Contests on TV

Performance contests such as *American Idol* and *The Voice* have become a staple of television, both in the United States and around the world. These shows require contestants to put their talent on the line before a panel of judges who publicly critique their skills. Receiving criticism is always a challenge, but particularly so when a huge audience is watching.

Judges typically render their verdict in several ways. Some are blunt and judgmental ("That was awful!"). Others are broad and vague ("That didn't work"). The most helpful criticisms focus on specific behaviors and suggestions for change ("Be careful not to rush"; "Your last line was flat"; "You do better with ballads").

On the receiving end, performers don't always respond well to suggestions. Many quickly defend themselves ("I thought I did just fine") or shift the blame ("I didn't choose the song"). Others follow principles described in this chapter, such as seeking more information or agreeing with the critic, hoping to improve their next performance.

Performance contests are designed for entertainment, not education—but from a communication perspective, they offer valuable lessons about giving and receiving criticism.

more specific information from the senders, inviting them to explain their position more clearly. "What do I *do* that's unfair?" is an important question to ask before you can judge whether the accusation is correct. "When haven't I helped out?" you might ask before agreeing with or disputing the accusation. Remember that it's important to ask these kinds of questions in a tone of voice that suggests you genuinely want to learn more about the other person's perception.

Sometimes your critics won't be able to define precisely the behavior they find offensive—or they may be reluctant to tell you. In instances such as these, you can often learn more clearly what is bothering your critic by *guessing at the specifics* of a complaint. Like the technique of asking for specifics, guessing must be done with goodwill if it's to produce satisfying results. You need to convey to the critic that for both of your sakes you're truly interested in finding out what is the matter. Here are some typical questions you might hear from someone guessing about the details of another's criticism:

"So you object to the language I used in writing the paper. Was my language too formal?"

"Okay, I understand that you think the outfit looks funny. What is it that's so bad? Is it the color? Does it have something to do with the fit? The design?"

"When you say that I'm not doing my share around the house, do you mean that I haven't been helping enough with the cleaning?"

Another strategy is to draw out confused or reluctant speakers by *paraphrasing* their thoughts and feelings, using the reflective listening skills described in Chapter 7. By clarifying or amplifying what you understand critics to be saying, you may learn more about their objections (Homburg & Fürst, 2007). A brief dialogue between a disgruntled customer and a store manager who is an invitational listener might sound like this:

Customer: The way you people run this store is disgusting! I just want to tell you that I'll never shop here again.

Manager: *(reflecting the customer's feeling)* It seems that you're quite upset. Can you tell me the problem?

C: Your salespeople never help a customer find anything around here.

M: So you didn't get enough help locating the items you were looking for, is that it?

C: I spent 20 minutes looking around in here before I even talked to a clerk.

M: So what you're saying is that the clerks seemed to be ignoring the customers?

C: No. They were all busy with other people. It just seems to me that you ought to have enough help around to handle the crowds that come in at this hour.

M: I understand now. What frustrated you the most was the fact that we didn't have enough staff to serve you promptly.

C: That's right. I have no complaint with the service I get once I'm waited on, and I've always thought you had a good selection here. It's just that I'm too busy to wait so long for help.

M: Well, I'm glad you brought this to my attention. We certainly don't want loyal customers going away mad. I'll try to see that it doesn't happen again.

Agree with the Critic

Another method for responding invitationally to criticism is to agree with the critic. But, you protest, how can I honestly agree with comments I don't believe are true? The following pages will answer this question by showing how you can acknowledge and accept the other person's point of view and still maintain your position.

One way to agree with the critic is to *agree with the truth*. For instance, you agree with the truth when another person's criticism is factually correct:

"You're right; I am angry."
"I suppose I was just being defensive."
"Now that you mention it, I did get pretty sarcastic."

Agreeing with the truth seems quite sensible when you realize that certain matters are indisputable. If you agree to be somewhere at 4:00 P.M. and don't show up until 5:00, you are late, no matter how good your explanation for tardiness is. If you've broken a borrowed object, run out of gas, or failed to finish a job you started, there's no point in denying the fact. In the same way, if you're honest, you will have to agree with many interpretations of your behavior, even when they're not flattering. You do get angry, act foolishly, fail to listen, and behave inconsiderately. Once you acknowledge this, your communication can become more invitational—as this teacher-student dialogue demonstrates:

Teacher: Look at this paper! It's only two pages long, and it contains 12 misspelled words. I'm afraid you have a real problem with your writing.

Student: You know, you're right. I know I don't spell well at all.

T: I don't know what's happening in the lower grades. They just don't seem to be turning out people who can write a simple, declarative sentence.

S: You're not the first person I've heard say that.

T: I should think you'd be upset by the fact that after so much time in English composition classes you haven't mastered the basics of spelling.

S: You're right. It does bother me.

Notice that in agreeing with the teacher's comments the student did not in any way demean herself. Even though there might have been extenuating circumstances to account for her lack of skill, the student didn't find it necessary to justify her errors because she wasn't saddled with the burden of pretending to be perfect. By simply agreeing with the facts, she was able to maintain her dignity and avoid an unproductive argument.

Another way to agree with the critic is to *agree in principle*. Criticism often comes in the form of abstract ideals against which you're unfavorably compared:

"I wish you wouldn't spend so much time on your work. Relaxation is important too, you know."
"You shouldn't expect so much from your kids. Nobody's perfect."
"What do you mean, you're not voting? The government will get better only when people like you take more of an interest in it."
"You mean you're still upset by that remark? You ought to learn how to take a joke better."

In cases such as these, you can accept the principle on which the criticism is based and still behave as you have been. After all, some rules do allow occasional exceptions, and people often are inconsistent. Consider how you might sincerely agree with the preceding criticisms without necessarily changing your behavior:

"You're right. I am working hard now. It probably is unhealthy, but finishing the job is worth the extra strain to me."
"I guess my expectations for the kids are awfully high, and I don't want to drive them crazy. I hope I'm not making a mistake."
"You're right: If everybody stopped voting, the system would fall apart."
"Maybe I *would* be happier if I could take a joke in stride. I'm not ready to do that, though, at least not for jokes like that one."

What about times when there seems to be no basis whatsoever for agreeing with your critics? You've listened carefully and asked questions to make sure you understand the objections, but the more you listen, the more positive you are that they are totally out of line. In these cases, you can at least *agree with the critic's perception*. Such responses tell critics that you're acknowledging the reasonableness of their perceptions, even though you don't agree or wish to change your behavior. This lets you avoid debates over who is right and who is wrong, which can turn an exchange of ideas into an argument. Notice the difference in the following two scenes.

Disputing the perception defensively:

A: I don't see how you can stand to be around Josh. The guy is so crude that he gives me the creeps.

B: What do you mean, crude? He's a really nice guy. I think you're just touchy.

A: Touchy! If it's touchy to be offended by disgusting behavior, then I'm guilty.

B: You're not guilty about anything. It's just that you're too sensitive when people kid around.

A: Too sensitive, huh? I don't know what's happened to you. You used to have such good judgment about people. . . .

Agreeing with the perception:

A: I don't see how you can stand to be around Josh. The guy is so crude that he gives me the creeps.

B: Well, I enjoy being around him, but I guess I can see how his jokes would be offensive to some people.

A: You're damn right! I don't see how you can put up with him.

B: Yeah. I guess if you didn't appreciate his humor, you wouldn't want to have much to do with him.

All these responses to criticism may appear to buy peace at the cost of denying your feelings. However, as you can see by now, counterattacking usually makes matters worse. The invitational responses you have just learned won't solve problems or settle disputes by themselves. Nevertheless, they *will* make a constructive dialogue possible, setting the stage for a productive solution. How to achieve productive solutions is the topic of Chapter 12.

CHECK YOUR UNDERSTANDING

Objective 11.1 Explain the nature of communication climates.

Communication climate refers to the social tone of a relationship. The most influential factor in shaping a communication climate is the degree to which the people involved see themselves as being valued and confirmed. Messages have differing levels of confirmation. We can categorize them as confirming, disagreeing, or disconfirming.

Q: Using weather terminology, how would you describe the communication climate in one of your important relationships?

Objective 11.2 Describe how communication climates develop.

Confirming messages, which communicate "you exist and are valued," may involve endorsement or acknowledgment; at minimum, they involve recognition. Disagreeing messages, which communicate "you are wrong," use argumentativeness, complaining, or aggressiveness. Disconfirming messages, which communicate "you do not exist and are not valued," include responses that are impervious, interrupting, irrelevant, tangential, impersonal, ambiguous, or incongruous. Over time, all of these messages form climate patterns that often take the shape of positive or negative spirals.

Q: Identify representative confirming, disagreeing, and/or disconfirming messages that create and maintain the climate you identified in section 11.1. Describe how these messages have created positive or negative spirals.

Objective 11.3 Recognize the factors that create defensive and supportive communication climates.

Defensiveness is at the core of most negative spirals. Defensiveness occurs when individuals perceive that their presenting self is being attacked by face-threatening acts.

We get particularly defensive about flaws that we don't want to admit and those that touch on sensitive areas. Both the attacker and the person attacked are responsible for creating defensiveness because competent communicators protect others' face needs as well as their own.

Jack Gibb suggested a variety of ways to create a positive and nondefensive communication climate. These include being descriptive rather than evaluative, problem oriented rather than controlling, spontaneous rather than strategic, empathic rather than neutral, equal rather than superior, and provisional rather than certain.

Q: Recall an incident in which both you and the other communicator became defensive. Which parts of your face needs were you and the other person protecting? Which of Gibb's categories triggered defensive responses?

Objective 11.4 Identify the communication skills that create invitational climates.

Communicators can help create an invitational climate by using the language of choice. This involves describing decisions and options ("I'm going to"; "Do you want to?") rather than obligations and imposition ("I have to"; "You should").

When faced with criticism, there are two alternatives to responding defensively: seeking additional information from the critic and agreeing with some aspect of the criticism. When performed sincerely, these approaches can transform an actual or potentially negative climate into a more positive one.

Q: Using the scenario you identified in section 11.3, consider how the language of choice might have created a more invitational climate, and how nondefensive responses might have transformed the negative climate.

KEY TERMS

- Aggressiveness (343)
- Ambiguous response (345)
- Argumentativeness (341)
- Certainty (355)
- Communication climate (338)
- Complaining (342)
- Confirming communication (339)
- Controlling communication (351)

- Defensiveness (347)
- Description (351)
- Disagreeing message (341)
- Disconfirming communication (339)
- Empathy (353)
- Equality (355)
- Evaluation (350)
- Face (345)
- Face-threatening acts (347)

- Impersonal response (345)
- Impervious response (343)
- Incongruous response (345)
- Interrupting response (344)
- Invitational communication (357)
- Irrelevant response (344)
- Neutrality (353)
- Presenting self (345)
- Problem orientation (351)

- Provisionalism (356)
- Spiral (349)
- Spontaneity (352)
- Strategy (352)
- Superiority (354)
- Tangential response (344)

ACTIVITIES

1. Mental health experts generally find it is better to have others disagree with you than ignore you. With a partner or group of classmates, recall specific examples from personal experiences to illustrate this point. For these situations, devise ways of disagreeing without being disconfirming.

2. Gibb argues that spontaneous rather than strategic communication reduces defensiveness. However, in some situations a strategic approach may hold the promise of a better climate than a completely honest message. Consider situations such as these:

   a. You don't find your partner very attractive. He or she asks, "What's the matter?"

   b. You intend to quit your job because you hate your boss, but you don't want to offend him or her. How do you explain the reasons for your departure?

   c. You are tutoring a high school student in reading or math. The student is sincere and a hard worker but is perhaps the most dull-witted person you have ever met. What do you say when the teenager asks, "How am I doing?"

3. In a group, construct sets of contrasting statements—one using the language of obligation, and the other restating the issue using the language of choice (see page 358–359). Describe the difference each type of statement makes, both in terms of adjusting your attitude as a speaker and the receiver's likely reaction.

4. With a partner, practice your skill at responding nondefensively to critical attacks by following these steps:

   a. Identify five criticisms you are likely to encounter from others in your day-to-day communication. If you have trouble thinking of criticisms, invite one or more people who know you well to supply some real, sincere gripes.

   b. For each criticism, write one or more nondefensive responses using the alternatives on pages 359–363. Be sure your responses are sincere and that you can offer them without counterattacking your critic.

   c. Practice your responses by having your partner play the role of your critics or by approaching your critics directly and inviting them to share their gripes with you.

SCORING FOR ASSESSING YOUR COMMUNICATION (PAGE 346)

Add your responses to the 7 items in Part I. This is your *confirmation* score: _____. The average score for college students was 29, with a possible range from 7 to 35. Higher scores represent greater confirmation.

Add your responses to the 10 items in Part II. This is your *disconfirmation* score: _____. The average score for college students was 20 (the original instrument has 17 items for this part), with a possible range from 10 to 50. Higher scores represent greater disconfirmation.

Note that confirmation and disconfirmation are independent. Although a friendship relationship is usually high in confirmation and low in disconfirmation, it may be high or low in either or both.

chapter **12**

Managing Conflict

LEARNING OBJECTIVES

12.1 Understand the nature of conflict and its attributes.

12.2 Explain five styles of handling conflict and how they are communicated.

12.3 Recognize various communication patterns in relational conflicts.

12.4 Describe how gender and culture affect communication during conflict.

12.5 Understand how the conflict management process can ideally resolve interpersonal conflicts.

Once upon a time, there was a world without conflicts. The leaders of each nation recognized the need for cooperation and met regularly to solve any potential problems. They never disagreed on matters needing attention or on ways to handle these matters, and so there were never any international tensions, and of course there was no war.

Within each nation things ran just as smoothly. The citizens always agreed on who their leaders should be, so elections were always unanimous. There was no social friction among various groups. Age, race, and educational differences did exist, but each group respected the others, and all got along harmoniously.

Human relationships were always perfect. Strangers were always kind and friendly to each other. Neighbors were considerate of each other's needs. Friendships were always mutual, and no disagreements ever spoiled people's enjoyment of one another. Once people fell in love—and everyone did—they stayed happy. Partners liked everything about each other and were able to fully satisfy each other's needs. Children and parents agreed on every aspect of family life and never were critical or hostile toward each other. Each day was better than the one before.

Of course, everybody lived happily ever after.

THIS STORY IS OBVIOUSLY a fairy tale. Regardless of what we may wish for or dream about, a conflict-free world just doesn't exist. Even the best communicators, the luckiest people, are bound to wind up in situations where their needs don't match the needs of others. Money, time, power, sex, humor, aesthetic taste, and a thousand other issues arise and keep us from living in a state of perpetual agreement.

For many people, the inevitability of conflict is a depressing fact. They think that the existence of ongoing conflict means that there's little chance for happy relationships with others. Effective communicators know differently. They realize that although it's impossible to *eliminate* conflict, there are ways to *manage* it effectively. The skillful management of conflict can open the door to healthier, stronger, and more satisfying relationships, as well as to increased mental and physical health (Canary, 2003; Laursen & Pursell, 2009).

WHAT IS CONFLICT?

Stop reading for a moment and make a list of as many different conflicts as you can think of that you've experienced personally. The list will probably show you that conflict takes many forms. Sometimes there's angry shouting, as when parents yell at their children. In other cases, conflicts involve restrained discussion, as in labor–management negotiations or court trials. Sometimes conflicts are carried on through hostile silence, as in the

In the film *Neighbors*, a fraternity moves in next door to new parents Mac and Kelly Radner (Seth Rogen and Rose Byrne). Despite the professed best intentions of frat leader Teddy (Zac Efron) and the Radners, conflicts are inevitable (and amusing).

unspoken feuds of angry couples. Finally, conflicts may wind up in physical fighting between friends, enemies, or even total strangers.

Whatever forms they may take, all interpersonal conflicts share certain features. William Wilmot and Joyce Hocker (2013) provide a thorough definition of conflict. They state that **conflict** is an expressed struggle between at least two interdependent parties who perceive incompatible goals, scarce resources, and interference from the other party in achieving their goals. The various parts of this definition can help you gain a better understanding of how conflict operates in everyday life.

EXPRESSED STRUGGLE

For conflict to exist, all the people involved must know that some disagreement exists. You may be upset for months because a neighbor's loud music keeps you awake at night, but no conflict exists until the neighbor learns about your problem. An expressed struggle doesn't have to be verbal. You can show your displeasure with someone without saying a word. A dirty look, the silent treatment, and avoiding the other person are all ways of expressing yourself. One way or another, both people must know that a problem exists before it fits our definition of conflict.

PERCEIVED INCOMPATIBLE GOALS

All conflicts look as if one person's gain would be another's loss. For instance, consider the neighbor whose music keeps you awake at night. It appears that someone has to lose: if the neighbor turns down the music, then he loses the enjoyment of hearing it at full volume; but if the neighbor keeps the volume up, then you're still awake and unhappy.

The goals in this situation really aren't completely incompatible—solutions do exist that allow both people to get what they want. For instance, you could achieve peace and quiet by closing your windows or

MEDIA CLIP
High-Stakes Conflict:
The Hunger Games

In this dystopian tale, a malevolent government puts adolescents in a forested arena where spectators watch them fight one another to the death. These "games" possess all of the features of conflict noted in this chapter: an expressed struggle (for survival), incompatible goals (one contestant's win means death for the others), scarce resources (weapons, food, and water), and interdependence (the contestants' fates are linked).

Katniss Everdeen (Jennifer Lawrence) refuses to accept the win-lose structure of the game. She forms alliances with other participants and ultimately emerges with what most would regard as the best possible win-win solution.

getting the neighbor to close hers. You might use a pair of earplugs, or perhaps the neighbor could get a set of earphones, which would allow the music to play at full volume without bothering anyone. If any of these solutions prove workable, then the conflict disappears.

Unfortunately, people often fail to see mutually satisfying answers to their problems. As long as they *perceive* their goals to be mutually exclusive, the conflict is real, albeit unnecessary.

PERCEIVED SCARCE RESOURCES

Conflicts also exist when people believe there isn't enough of something to go around: affection, money, space, and so on. Time is often a scarce commodity. Many people struggle to meet the competing demands of school, work, family, and friends. "If there were only more hours in a day" is a common refrain, and making time for the people in your life—and for yourself—is a constant source of conflict.

INTERDEPENDENCE

However antagonistic they might feel, the people in a conflict are dependent on each other. The welfare and satisfaction of one depends on the actions of another. If this were not true, then there would be no need for conflict, even in the face of scarce resources and incompatible goals. In fact, many conflicts remain unresolved because the people fail to understand their interdependence. One of the first steps toward resolving a conflict is to take the attitude that "we're all in this together."

INEVITABILITY

Conflicts are bound to happen, even in the best relationships. Common sources of conflict among college roommates include access to each other's personal items and food, how clean/messy the rooms are, who can use what furniture, and how involved they should be in each other's personal lives (Ocana & Hindman, 2004). Some roommate conflicts become "episodic" in nature and continue off and on for a long time (Reznik & Roloff, 2011). Conflicts with friends also are typical, with an average of one or two disagreements a day (Burk et al., 2009). Among families, conflict can be even more frequent, whether the topic is money, being on time, who does what chores, how to handle relatives, or how to balance work and family obligations (Huffman et al., 2013).

Because it is impossible to avoid conflicts, the challenge is to handle them effectively when they do arise. Decades of research show that people in both happy and unhappy relationships have conflicts, but that they perceive them and manage them in very different ways (Simon et al., 2008; Wilmot & Hocker, 2013). Unhappy couples argue in ways cataloged in this book as destructive. They are more concerned with defending themselves than with being problem oriented. They fail to listen carefully to one another, have little or no empathy for their partners, use evaluative "you" language, and ignore each other's relational messages.

Many satisfied couples handle their conflicts more effectively. They recognize disagreements as healthy and know that conflicts need to be faced (Ridley et al., 2001; Segrin et al., 2009). Although they may argue vigorously, they use skills such as perception checking to find out what the other person is thinking; and they let the other person know that they understand the other side of the dispute. These people are willing to admit their mistakes, a habit that contributes to a harmonious relationship and also helps solve the problem at hand. With this in mind, we take a closer look at what makes some conflicts more functional than others.

CONFLICT STYLES

Most people have "default" styles of handling conflict—characteristic approaches they take when their needs appear incompatible with what others want. Although our habitual styles work sometimes, they may not work at all in other situations. What styles do you typically use to deal with conflict? Find out by thinking about how two hypothetical characters—Chris and Pat—manage a problem.

Chris and Pat have been roommates for several years. Chris is a soccer fan and loves watching games with his friends at every opportunity. Their apartment has a big-screen TV (owned by Chris) in the living room, and it has become a regular gathering spot for viewing. Pat doesn't mind watching an occasional game, but he's annoyed by what seems like endless TV (and endless houseguests). Chris thinks he ought to be able to watch his TV whenever he wants, with whomever he wants. Here are five ways they could handle their conflict, representing five different conflict styles:

- *Avoidance.* Chris and Pat don't discuss the issue again—the prospect of fighting is too unpleasant. Chris has tried to cut back on watching with friends but feels cheated. Pat keeps quiet, but when game time rolls around, his feelings of displeasure are obvious.
- *Accommodation.* Pat gives in, saying "Go ahead and watch all the soccer you want. After all, it's your TV. I'll just go in the bedroom and listen to music." Pat hopes Chris and the other fans will take the hint and scale back their viewing. Alternatively, Chris could accommodate by agreeing not to watch soccer at home anymore.
- *Competition.* Chris tries to persuade Pat that watching more soccer will lead to a better understanding of the game, and that Pat will want to watch it more as a result. Pat tries to convince Chris that spending so

much time watching TV isn't healthy. Both try to get the other person to give up and give in.

- *Compromise.* The roommates agree to split the difference. Chris gets to watch any and every game at home as long the friends don't come over. Chris gets soccer; Pat gets relative peace and quiet. Of course, Chris misses his friends and Pat must still endure hours of Chris's TV viewing.
- *Collaboration.* Chris and Pat brainstorm and discover other alternatives. For example, they decide that the fans could watch some games together at a local sports bar. They also realize that if each of Chris's friends could pitch in a modest sum, one of the friends could buy a large-screen TV where they could watch some games (and avoid the sports bar costs). Pat also suggests that he and Chris could watch some non-sports TV together.

These approaches represent the five styles depicted in Figure 12.1, each of which is described in the following paragraphs.

AVOIDANCE (LOSE-LOSE)

Avoidance occurs when people ignore or stay away from conflict. It can be physical (steering clear of a friend after having an argument) or conversational (changing the topic, joking, or denying that a problem exists).

Avoidance generally reflects a pessimistic attitude about conflict. Avoiders usually believe it's easier to put up with the status quo than to face the problem head-on and try to solve it. In the case of Chris and Pat, avoidance means that rather than having another fight, both of them will suffer in silence. Their case illustrates how avoidance often produces lose-lose results.

Although avoiding important issues can keep the peace temporarily, it typically leads to unsatisfying relationships (Afifi et al., 2009; Wang et al.,

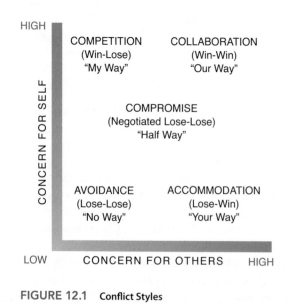

FIGURE 12.1   Conflict Styles

2012). Partners of "self-silencers" report more frustration and discomfort when dealing with the avoiding partner than with those who face conflict more constructively (Harper & Welsh, 2007). Chronic misunderstandings, resentments, and disappointments pile up and contaminate the emotional climate. For this reason, we can say that avoiders have a low concern both for their own needs and for the interests of the other person, who is also likely to suffer from unaddressed issues (see Figure 12.1).

Despite its obvious shortcomings, avoidance isn't always a bad idea (Caughlin & Arr, 2004; Oduro-Frimpong, 2007). You might choose to avoid certain topics or situations if the risk of speaking up is too great, such as getting fired from a job you can't afford to lose, being humiliated in public, or even suffering physical harm. You might also avoid a conflict if the relationship it involves isn't worth the effort. Even in close relationships, though, avoidance has its logic. If the issue is temporary or minor, you might let it pass. These reasons help explain why the communication of many happily married couples is characterized by "selectively ignoring" the other person's minor flaws (Segrin et al., 2009). This doesn't mean that a key to successful relationships is avoiding *all* conflicts. Instead, it suggests that it's smart to save energy for the truly important ones.

ACCOMMODATION (LOSE-WIN)

Accommodation occurs when we allow others to have their own way rather than asserting our own point of view. Figure 12.1 depicts accommodators as having low concern for themselves and high concern for others, resulting in lose-win, "we'll do it your way," outcomes. In our hypothetical scenario, Pat accommodates to Chris by letting Chris watch soccer with his friends. It's a kind gesture by Pat, but he probably wishes Chris would be equally gracious. Chris could also accommodate by not watching soccer on their home TV anymore.

The motivation of an accommodator plays a significant role in this style's effectiveness. If accommodation is a genuine act of kindness, generosity, or love, then chances are good that it will enhance the relationship. Most people appreciate those who "take one for the team," "treat others as they want to be treated," or "lose the battle to win the war." However, people are far less appreciative of those who habitually use this style to play the role of "martyr, bitter complainer, whiner, or saboteur" (Wilmot & Hocker, 2013).

We should pause here to mention the important role that culture plays in perceptions of conflict styles. People from high-context, collectivistic backgrounds (such as many Asian cultures) are likely to regard avoidance and accommodation as face-saving and noble ways to handle conflict (Oetzel & Ting-Toomey, 2003; Ohbuchi & Atsumi, 2010). In low-context, individualistic cultures (such as that of the United States), avoidance and accommodation are often viewed less positively. For instance, think of the many unflattering terms that North Americans use for people who give up or give in during conflicts ("pushover," "weakling," "doormat," "spineless"). As you will read later in this chapter, collectivistic cultures use positive words and phrases to describe such people. The point here is that all conflict

"It's not enough that we succeed. Cats must also fail."

styles have merit in certain situations, and that culture plays a significant role in determining how each style is valued.

COMPETITION (WIN-LOSE)

The flip side of accommodation is **competition**, a win-lose approach to conflict that involves high concern for self and low concern for others. As Figure 12.1 shows, competition seeks to resolve conflicts "my way." When Chris and Pat make their cases about soccer and TV viewing, trying to get each other to concede, they are using a competitive approach.

Many North Americans default to a competitive approach because it's ingrained in their culture, as Laura Tracy (1991) observes:

> Whether we like it or not, we live in a competitive society. Our economy is competitive by design, and as a nation, we see in competition a challenge to develop our resources and ourselves. (p. 4)

Just as competition can develop an economy, it can sometimes develop a relationship. Susan Messman and Rebecca Mikesell (2000) found that some men and women in dating relationships used competition to enrich their interaction. For example, some found satisfaction by competing in play (who's the better racquetball or Scrabble player?), in achievement (who gets the better job offer or the higher grade?), and in altruism (who's more romantic or does the most charity work?). These satisfied couples developed a shared narrative (see Chapter 4) that defined competition as a measure of regard, quite different from conflict that signaled a lack of appreciation and respect. Of course, it's easy to see how these arrangements could backfire if one partner became a gloating winner or a sore loser. It's also easy to see how feeling like you've been defeated can leave you wanting to get even, creating a downward competitive spiral that degrades to a lose-lose outcome (Olson & Braithwaite, 2004; Singleton & Vacca, 2007).

If you believe your way is the best one, you may feel justified in trying to control the situation, but it's likely that the other person won't view your bid for control so charitably (Gross et al., 2004). The dark side of competition is that it often breeds aggression (Warren et al., 2005). Sometimes aggression is obvious, but at other times it can be more subtle. To understand how, read on.

Passive Aggression

Passive aggression occurs when a communicator expresses dissatisfaction in a disguised manner (Brandt, 2013). In the case of Pat and Chris, perhaps Pat runs the vacuum cleaner loudly during the soccer matches—or Chris makes sarcastic jokes about Pat not liking sports. Passive aggression can take the form of "crazymaking" (Bach & Wyden, 1983)—tactics designed to punish another person without direct confrontation. Crazymaking takes its name from the effect such behavior usually has on its target.

There are a number of crazymaking ways to deal with conflict. One is through guilt: "Never mind. I'll do all the work myself [sigh]. Go ahead and have a good time. Don't worry about me [sigh]." Another crazymaker is when someone agrees with you to your face but has a different agenda behind your back—such as the teenager who says he'll clean his room and then doesn't do so as a means of getting back at the parent who grounded him. Some passive aggression is nonverbal: a roll of the eyes, a pained expression, or a disdainful laugh can get a message across. If the target of these messages asks about them, the passive aggressor can always deny the conflict exists. Even humor—especially sarcasm ("Gee, I can't *wait* to spend the weekend with your folks")—can be used as passive aggression (Bowes & Katz, 2011). And sometimes saying nothing is a crazymaker weapon, as the Dark Side box on this page describes.

Direct Aggression

A directly aggressive communicator lashes out to attack the source of displeasure. Dominic Infante (1987) identified nine types of **direct aggression:** character attacks, competence attacks, physical appearance attacks, maledictions (wishing the other bad fortune), teasing, ridicule, threats, swearing, and nonverbal emblems (e.g., fist shaking, arm waving). Like all types of relational communication, direct aggression has both verbal and nonverbal dimensions. In the case of Chris and Pat, the conflict might turn into an ugly shouting match, with denigrating comments about how only an "idiot" would or wouldn't like sports, watching TV, or having friends over.

The results of direct aggression can have a severe impact on the target. There is a significant connection between verbal aggression and physical aggression (Atkin et al., 2002; Roberto et al., 2007). Even if the attacks never lead to blows, the psychological effects can be harmful, or even devastating. Recipients can feel embarrassed, inadequate, humiliated, hopeless, desperate, or depressed. These results can lead to decreased effectiveness

DARK SIDE OF COMMUNICATION
WHEN SILENCE ISN'T GOLDEN

"Silence is golden," says the well-known maxim. There certainly are times when keeping resentments to yourself can be a smart approach. But the "silent treatment"—purposely acting aloof and nonresponsive when unhappy—is anything but golden. It's a form of passive aggression that's used as a weapon in interpersonal conflicts.

Why would anyone continue to use the silent treatment when a relational partner asks, "Is anything wrong?" Communication researchers Courtney Wright and Michael Roloff (2009) explored this conundrum. They found a link between relational commitment and the silent treatment. Romantic partners with low levels of commitment use the treatment far more than do people who are strongly invested in their relationship. Partners with high levels of commitment would admit to being upset if asked about a relational problem. These findings led Wright and Roloff to conclude that the silent treatment is a sign of a relationship that's in trouble.

If you're staying quiet during conflict because you don't want to say something you'll regret later, that's fine (in these cases, you might want to explain your silence). But if you're strategically punishing loved ones by not talking to them, recognize that you're probably harming yourself as well as the other person—and you're likely damaging the relationship as well.

in personal relationships (Muñoz-Rivas et al., 2007), on the job (Madlock & Kennedy-Lightsey, 2010), in the classroom (Martin et al., 2010), and in families (Doss et al., 2008). In Chapter 11, we describe how aggressiveness can be a lethal communication weapon, both in person and online.

COMPROMISE (NEGOTIATED LOSE-LOSE)

A **compromise** gives both people at least some of what they want, although both sacrifice part of their goals. People usually settle for a compromise when it seems that partial satisfaction is the best they can hope for. In the case of Pat and Chris, they strike a "halfway" deal by letting Chris watch all the soccer he wants as long as he doesn't invite friends to join him. Unlike avoidance, in which both people lose because they don't address their problem, compromisers actually negotiate a lose-lose solution.

Although a compromise may be better than losing everything, this approach hardly seems to deserve the positive image it often has. In his valuable book on conflict resolution, Albert Filley (1975) makes an interesting observation about our attitudes toward this method. Why is it, he asks, that if someone says, "I will compromise my values," we view the action unfavorably, yet we talk admiringly about people in a conflict who compromise to reach a solution? Although compromise may be the best obtainable result in some conflicts, it's important to realize that both people in a dispute can often work together to find much better solutions. In such cases, compromise is a negative word.

Most of us are surrounded by the results of bad compromises. Consider a common example: the conflict between one person's desire to smoke cigarettes and another's need for clean air. The win-lose outcomes on this issue are obvious: Either the smoker abstains or the nonsmoker gets polluted lungs—neither option a very satisfying one. But a compromise in which the smoker gets to enjoy only a rare cigarette or must retreat outdoors and in which the nonsmoker still must inhale some fumes or feel unaccommodating is hardly better. Both sides have lost a considerable amount of both comfort and goodwill. Of course, the costs involved in other compromises are even greater. For example, if a divorced couple haggles over custody in a

way that leaves them bitter and emotionally scars their children, it's hard to say that anybody has won no matter what the outcome.

Some compromises do leave everyone satisfied. You and the seller of a used car might settle on a price that is between what the seller was asking and what you wanted to pay. Although neither of you got everything you wanted, the outcome would still leave both of you satisfied. Likewise, you and your companion might agree to see a movie that is the second choice for both of you to spend an evening together. As long as everyone is at least somewhat satisfied with an outcome, compromise can be an effective way to resolve conflicts. Catherine Sanderson and Kim Karetsky (2002) found that college students with a strong focus on intimacy goals were likely to engage in open discussion and compromise, show concern for their partner, and seek social support—and importantly, they were likely to successfully resolve the conflict. When compromises are satisfying and successful, it might be more accurate to categorize them as the final style we discuss: collaboration.

COLLABORATION (WIN-WIN)

Collaboration seeks win-win solutions to conflict. It involves a high degree of concern for both self and others, with the goal of solving problems not "my way" or "your way" but "our way." In the best case, collaborating can lead to a *win-win* outcome, where each person gets what she or he wants (Bannink, 2010).

As noted in the scenario, the brainstorming by Chris and Pat yields several collaborative options: Chris watching soccer with his friends at a sports bar, the friends buying a new TV, and/or Chris and Pat watching non-sports programs together. Perhaps you can think of other options as well. The key to true collaboration is whether Pat and Chris are happy with their decision and its outcomes.

In **win-win problem solving**, the goal is to find a solution that satisfies the needs of everyone involved. Not only do the partners avoid trying to win at each other's expense, but there's also a belief that working together can provide a solution in which all reach their goals without needing to compromise.

A few examples show how collaboration can lead to win-win outcomes:

- A boss and his employees get into a conflict over scheduling. The employees often want to shift the hours they're scheduled to work so that they can accommodate personal needs, whereas the boss needs to be sure that the operation is fully staffed at all times. After some discussion they arrive at a solution that satisfies everyone: The boss works up a monthly master schedule indicating the hours during which each employee is responsible for being on the job. Employees are free to trade hours among themselves, as long as the operation is fully staffed at all times.

- A conflict about testing arises in a college class. Due to sickness and other reasons, some students need to take exams on a makeup basis. The instructor doesn't want to give these students any advantage over their peers and also doesn't want to go through the task of creating a brand-new test for just a few people. After working on the problem together, the instructor and students arrive at a win-win solution. The instructor will hand out a list of 20 possible exam questions in advance of the test day. At examination time, 5 of these questions are randomly drawn for the class to answer. Students who take makeup exams will draw from the same pool of questions at the time of their test. In this way, makeup students are taking a fresh test without the instructor having to create a new exam.

- A newly married husband and wife find themselves arguing frequently over their budget. The husband enjoys buying impractical items, whereas the wife fears that such purchases will ruin their carefully constructed budget. Their solution is to set aside a small amount of money each month for "fun" purchases. The amount is small enough to be affordable yet gives the husband a chance to indulge himself. The wife is satisfied with the arrangement because the luxury money is now a budget category by itself, which gives her the feeling that things are under control. The plan works so well that the couple continues to use it even after their income rises, by increasing the amount devoted to luxuries.

Although such solutions might seem obvious when you read them here, a moment's reflection will show you that such cooperative problem solving is all too rare. People faced with these types of conflicts often resort to such styles as avoiding, accommodating, or competing, and they wind up handling the issues in a manner that results in either a win-lose or lose-lose outcome. As we pointed out earlier, it's a shame to see one or both partners in a conflict come away unsatisfied when they could both get what they're seeking by communicating in a win-win manner. Later in this chapter, you'll learn a specific process for arriving at collaborative solutions to problems.

Of course, a win-win approach is not always possible or even always appropriate. Collaborative problem solving can be quite time consuming, and some conflict decisions need to be made quickly. Moreover, many conflicts are about relatively minor issues that don't call for a great deal of creativity and brainstorming. As you'll see in the following section, there certainly will be times when compromising is the most sensible approach. You will even encounter instances when pushing for your own solution is reasonable. Even more surprisingly, you will probably discover that there are times when it makes sense to willingly accept the loser's role. Much of the time, however, good intentions and creative thinking can lead to outcomes that satisfy everyone's needs.

WHICH STYLE TO USE?

Although collaborative problem solving might seem like the most attractive style, it's an oversimplification to imagine that there is a single best way to respond to conflicts (Gross & Guerrero, 2000). Generally speaking, win-win approaches are preferable to win-lose and lose-lose solutions. But we've already seen that there are times when avoidance, accommodation,

Your Method of Conflict Resolution

Think of a close relationship with someone you see regularly (e.g., a parent, sibling, roommate, close friend, spouse, partner, or lover). How do you usually respond to conflicts with this person? Indicate the degree to which you believe each of the following statements applies to you during these conflicts, using a scale ranging from 1 to 5, where 1 = never and 5 = very often.

_____ **1.** I am usually firm in pursuing my goals.

_____ **2.** I attempt to deal with all of the other person's and my concerns.

_____ **3.** I try to find a compromise solution.

_____ **4.** I try to avoid creating unpleasantness for myself.

_____ **5.** It's important to me that others are happy, even if it comes at my expense.

_____ **6.** I try to win my position.

_____ **7.** I consistently seek the other's help in working out a solution.

_____ **8.** I give up some points in exchange for others.

_____ **9.** I try to postpone dealing with the issue.

_____ **10.** I might try to soothe the other's feelings and preserve our relationship.

_____ **11.** I persistently try to get my points made.

_____ **12.** I try to integrate my concerns with the other person's concerns.

_____ **13.** I will let the other person have some of what she or he wants if she or he lets me have some of what I want.

_____ **14.** I sometimes avoid taking positions that would create controversy.

_____ **15.** I sometimes sacrifice my own wishes for the wishes of the other person.

_____ **16.** I try to show the other person the logic and benefits of my position.

_____ **17.** I tell the other person my ideas and ask for his or hers.

_____ **18.** I propose a middle ground.

_____ **19.** I try to do what is necessary to avoid tensions.

_____ **20.** I don't worry about my own concerns if satisfying them means damaging the relationship.

Adapted from the Thomas-Kilmann Conflict Mode Instrument: Thomas, K. W., & Kilmann, R. H. (2007). Thomas-Kilmann Conflict Mode Instrument. Mountain View, CA: Xicom, a subsidiary of CPP, Inc. (Original work published 1974)

Also see Thomas, K. W., & Kilmann, R. (1978). Comparison of four instruments measuring conflict behavior. *Psychological Report, 42,* 1139–1145.

For scoring information, see page 395 at the end of the chapter.

TABLE 12.1 When to Use Each Conflict Style

AVOIDANCE (LOSE-LOSE)	ACCOMMODATION (LOSE-WIN)	COMPETITION (WIN-LOSE)	COMPROMISE (NEGOTIATED LOSE-LOSE)	COLLABORATION (WIN-WIN)
When the issue is of little importance	When the issue is more important to the other person than it is to you	When the issue is not important enough to negotiate at length	When the issue is moderately important but not enough for a stalemate	When the issue is too important for a compromise
To cool down and gain perspective	When you discover you are wrong	When you are convinced that your position is right and necessary	When opponents are strongly committed to mutually exclusive goals	To merge insights with someone who has a different perspective on the problem
When the costs of confrontation outweigh the benefits	When the long-term cost of winning may not be worth the short-term gain	When there is not enough time to seek a win-win outcome	To achieve quick, temporary solutions to complex problems	To come up with creative and unique solutions to problems
	To build up credits for later conflicts	When the other person is not willing to seek a win-win outcome	As a backup mode when collaboration doesn't work	To develop a relationship by showing commitment to the concerns of both parties
	To let others learn by making their own mistakes	To protect yourself against a person who takes advantage of noncompetitive people		When a long-term relationship between you and the other person is important

Adapted from Wilmot, W. W., & Hocker, J. L. (2013). *Interpersonal conflict* (9th ed.). New York: McGraw-Hill.

competition, and compromise are appropriate. Table 12.1 suggests situations when it may be best to use a particular style.

A conflict style isn't necessarily a personality trait that carries across all situations. Wilmot and Hocker (2013) suggest that roughly 50 percent of the population change their style from one situation to another. As you learned in Chapter 1, this sort of behavioral flexibility is a characteristic of competent communicators. Several factors govern which style to use, including the situation, the other person, and your goals.

The Situation

When someone clearly has more power than you, accommodation may be the best approach. If the boss tells you to "fill that order *now!*," you probably ought to do it without comment. A more competitive response ("Why don't you ask Karen to do it? She has less work than I do.") might state your true feelings, but it could also cost you your job. Beyond power, other situational factors can shape your communication in a conflict. For example, you would probably try to set aside personal disagreements with siblings or parents when it's necessary to support one another during a family crisis.

The Other Person

Although win-win is a fine ideal, sometimes the other person isn't interested in (or good at) collaborating. You probably know communicators who are so competitive that they put winning on even minor issues ahead of the well-being of your relationship. In such cases, your efforts to collaborate may have a low chance of success.

Your Goals

When you want to solve a problem, it's generally good to be assertive (see Chapter 5 for information on creating assertive "I" messages). But there are other reasons for communicating in a conflict. Sometimes your overriding concern is to calm down an enraged or upset communicator. For example, tolerating an outburst from your crotchety and sick neighbor is probably better than standing up for yourself and triggering a stroke. Likewise, you might choose to sit quietly through the nagging of a family member at Thanksgiving dinner rather than make a scene. In other cases, your moral principles might compel an aggressive statement, even though it might not get you what you originally sought: "I've had enough of your racist jokes. I've tried to explain why they're so offensive, but you obviously haven't listened. I'm leaving!" Or your goal may be to be seen in a favorable way, in which case you may want to avoid being aggressive.

CONFLICT IN RELATIONAL SYSTEMS

So far, we have been describing individual conflict styles. Even though the style you choose in a conflict is important, your approach isn't the only factor that will determine how a conflict unfolds. In reality, conflict is *relational*: Its character is usually determined by the way the people involved interact (Kuttner, 2013; Williams-Baucom et al., 2010). For example, you might be determined to handle a conflict with your neighbors collaboratively, only to be driven to competition by their uncooperative nature or even to avoidance by their physical threats. Likewise, you might plan to hint to a professor that her apparent indifference bothers you but wind up discussing the matter in an open, assertive way in reaction to her constructive suggestion. Examples like these indicate that conflict isn't just a matter of individual choice. Rather, it depends on how the partners interact.

COMPLEMENTARY AND SYMMETRICAL CONFLICT

The conflict approaches of partners in interpersonal relationships—and impersonal ones, too—can be complementary or symmetrical. In **complementary conflict**, the partners use different but mutually reinforcing behaviors. As Table 12.2 illustrates, some complementary conflicts are destructive, whereas others are constructive. In **symmetrical conflict**, both people use the same tactics. Table 12.2 shows how the same conflict can unfold in very different ways, depending on whether the partners' communication is symmetrical or complementary.

TABLE 12.2 Complementary and Symmetrical Conflict

SITUATION	COMPLEMENTARY CONFLICT	SYMMETRICAL CONFLICT
Wife is upset because husband is spending little time at home.	Wife makes demands; husband withdraws, spending even less time at home. (Destructive complementarity)	Wife raises concern clearly and assertively, without aggression. Husband responds by explaining his concerns in the same manner. (Constructive symmetry)
Boss makes fun of employee in front of other workers.	Employee seeks out boss for private conversation, explaining why being the butt of public joking was embarrassing. Boss listens willingly. (Constructive complementarity)	Employee maliciously jokes about boss at company party. Boss continues to make fun of employee. (Destructive symmetry)
Parents are uncomfortable about teenager's new friends.	Parents express concerns. Teen dismisses them, saying "There's nothing to worry about." (Destructive complementarity)	Teen expresses concern that parents are being too protective. Parents and teen negotiate a mutually agreeable solution. (Constructive symmetry)

Research shows that a complementary "fight-flight" approach is common in many unhappy marriages. One partner—most commonly the wife—addresses the conflict directly, whereas the other—usually the husband—withdraws (Caughlin & Vangelisti, 2006). As discussed in Chapter 4, it's easy to see how this pattern can lead to a cycle of increasing hostility and isolation because each partner punctuates the conflict differently, blaming the other for making matters worse. "I withdraw because she's so critical," a husband might say. However, the wife wouldn't organize the sequence in the same way. "I criticize because he withdraws" would be her perception. Couples who use demand-withdraw patterns report being less than satisfied with their conflict discussions and that their negotiations rarely produce change (McGinn et al., 2009).

Complementary approaches aren't the only ones that can lead to problems. Some distressed relationships suffer from destructively symmetrical communication. If both partners treat one another with matching hostility, one threat and insult leads to another in an **escalatory spiral**. If the partners both withdraw from one another instead of facing their problems, a complementary **de-escalatory spiral** results, in which the satisfaction and vitality ebb from the relationship.

As Table 12.2 shows, however, both complementary and symmetrical behaviors can also be constructive. If the complementary behaviors are positive, then a positive spiral results, and the conflict stands a good chance of being resolved. This is the case in the second example in Table 12.2, when the boss is open to hearing the employee's concerns. Here, a complementary talk-listen pattern works well.

Constructive symmetry occurs when both people communicate assertively, listening to one another's concerns and working together to resolve them. Married couples who take this approach appraise their marriages more positively than any other type of couple does (Hanzal & Segrin, 2009; Ridley et al., 2001). The parent-teenager conflict in Table 12.2 has the potential for this sort of solution. With enough mutual respect and careful listening, both the parents and their teenager can understand one another's concerns and possibly find a way to give all three people what they want.

TOXIC CONFLICT: THE "FOUR HORSEMEN"

Some conflict approaches are so destructive that they are almost guaranteed to wreak havoc on relationships. These toxic forms of communication include what John Gottman has called the "Four Horsemen of the Apocalypse" (Gottman, 1994; see also Graber et al., 2011; Holman & Jarvis, 2003).

Gottman has gathered decades of data about newlywed couples and their communication patterns. By observing their interactions, he has been able to predict with high accuracy whether the newlyweds will end up divorcing. Here are the four destructive signs he looks for:

1. *Criticism:* These are attacks on a person's character. As you read in Chapters 5 and 11, there's a significant difference between legitimate complaints phrased in descriptive "I" language ("I wish you had been on time—we're going to be late to the movie") and critical character assaults stated as evaluative "you" messages ("You're so thoughtless—you never think of anyone but yourself").

2. *Defensiveness:* As we explained in Chapter 11, defensiveness is a reaction that aims to protect one's presenting self by denying responsibility ("You're crazy—I never do that") and counterattacking ("You're worse about that than I am"). Although some self-protection is understandable, problems arise when a person refuses to listen to or even acknowledge another's concerns.

3. *Contempt:* A contemptuous comment belittles and demeans. It can take the form of name-calling putdowns ("You're a real jerk") or sarcastic barbs ("Oh, *that* was brilliant"). Contempt can also be communicated nonverbally through dramatic eye rolls or disgusted sighs. (Try doing both of those at the same time and imagine how dismissing they can be).

4. *Stonewalling:* Stonewalling occurs when one person in a relationship withdraws from the interaction, shutting down dialogue—and any chance of resolving the problem in a mutually satisfactory way. It sends a disconfirming "you don't matter" message to the other person.

Here's a brief exchange illustrating how the "four horsemen" can lead to a destructive spiral of aggression:

"You overdrew our account again—can't you do *anything* right?" (Criticism)
"Hey, don't blame me—you're the one who spends most of the money." (Defensiveness)
"At least I have better math skills than a first-grader. Way to go, Einstein." (Contempt)
"Whatever" (said while walking out of the room). (Stonewalling)

It's easy to see how this kind of communication can be destructive in any relationship, not just a marriage. It's also easy to see how these kinds of comments can feed off each other and develop into destructive conflict rituals, as we discuss now.

CONFLICT RITUALS

When people have been in a relationship for some time, their communication often develops into **conflict rituals**—unacknowledged but very real repeating patterns of interlocking behavior (Wilmot & Hocker, 2013). Consider a few common rituals:

- A young child interrupts her parents, demanding to be included in their conversation. At first the parents tell the child to wait, but she whines and cries until the parents find it easier to listen than to ignore the fussing. This pattern reoccurs whenever the child has a demand the parents hesitate to fulfill.
- A couple fights. One partner leaves. The other accepts blame for the problem and begs forgiveness. The first partner returns, and a happy reunion takes place. Soon they fight again and the pattern repeats.
- One friend is unhappy with the other. The unhappy person withdraws until the other asks what's wrong. "Nothing," the first replies. The questioning persists until the problem is finally out in the open. The friends then solve the issue and continue happily until the next problem arises, when the pattern repeats itself.

FOCUS ON RESEARCH
Attachment, Conflict, and the Four Horsemen

Ever since Freud, psychologists have understood that who we are as adults is shaped by our earliest experiences. Attachment theorists believe that people who don't receive enough warmth, approval, and support as young children suffer a host of difficulties in their adult relationships. One set of challenges involves dealing with conflicts.

Communication scholars Craig Fowler and Megan Dillow wanted to know if people with anxious and avoidant attachment styles are likely to use Gottman's "Four Horsemen" (see page 383) during conflicts. More than 150 participants in long-term romantic relationships filled out surveys. Attachment was measured by responses to items such as "I worry about being abandoned" (anxious) and "I prefer not to be too close to romantic partners" (avoidant).

The participants also responded to questions about how they communicate during conflicts with their partners.

Subjects who had anxious feelings about attachment were prone to using all four of Gottman's horsemen—criticism, defensiveness, contempt, and stonewalling. Subjects whose backgrounds led them to avoid expressing their feelings were more likely to stonewall. Fowler and Dillow maintain that attachment styles generate self-fulfilling prophecies. Anxious and avoidant people expect the worst during conflicts, act in negative ways, and then reap what they feared. Professional therapy is strongly recommended for those with attachment disorders—for their own sake and the sake of their relationships.

Fowler, C., & Dillow, M. R. (2011). Attachment dimensions and the Four Horsemen of the Apocalypse. *Communication Research Reports, 28*, 16–26.

There's nothing inherently wrong with the interaction in many rituals (Olson, 2002). Consider the preceding examples. In the first, the child's whining may be the only way she can get the parents' attention. In the second, both partners might use the fighting as a way to blow off steam, and both might find that the joy of a reunion is worth the grief of the separation. The third ritual might work well when one friend is more assertive than the other.

Rituals can cause problems, though, when they become the *only* way relational partners handle their conflicts. As you learned in Chapter 1, competent communicators have a large repertoire of behaviors, and they are able to choose the most effective response for a given situation. Relying on one pattern to handle all conflicts is no more effective than using a screwdriver to handle every home repair or putting the same seasoning in every dish you cook: What works in one situation isn't likely to succeed in many others. Conflict rituals may be familiar and comfortable, but they aren't the best way to solve the variety of conflicts that are part of any relationship.

VARIABLES IN CONFLICT STYLES

By now you can see that every relational system is unique. The communication patterns in one family, business, or classroom are likely to be very different from any other. But along with the differences that arise in individual relationships, there are two powerful variables that affect the way people manage conflict: gender and culture. We now take a brief look at each of these factors and see how they affect the ways that conflict is managed.

GENDER

Some research suggests that men and women often approach conflicts differently (e.g., Archer, 2002; Gayle et al., 2002). Even in childhood, there is evidence that boys are (on average, of course) more likely to be aggressive, demanding, and competitive, whereas girls are more cooperative and accommodating. Studies of children from preschool to early adolescence have shown that boys try to get their way by ordering one another around: "Lie down." "Get off my steps." "Gimme your arm." By contrast, girls are

MEDIA CLIP
Love and Conflict: *Before Midnight*

This third installment of director Richard Linklater's movie trilogy continues to track the evolving relationship between Jesse (Ethan Hawke) and Céline (Julie Delpy). The romantic euphoria of their early years is now a memory, and the couple struggles with the challenges of raising children, juggling careers, and keeping their relationship alive.

While on a getaway in the Greek Isles, they spend much of the evening fighting. Céline's verbal jabs—and sometimes Jesse's—can be nasty. Of course, that's part of what makes the movie realistic. Céline and Jesse know how to push each other's buttons, but they also know when they've gone too far and need to be conciliatory. In the end, the film shows that loving couples can have passionate conflict and also passionate love.

more likely to make proposals for action that begin with the word *let's:* "Let's go find some." "Let's ask her if she has any bottles." "Let's move *these* out *first*" (Tannen, 1990; see also Noakes & Rinaldi, 2006). Whereas boys tell each other what role to take in pretend play ("Come on, be a doctor"), girls more commonly ask each other what role they want ("Will you be the patient for a few minutes?") or make a joint proposal ("We can both be doctors"). Furthermore, boys often make demands without offering an explanation ("I want to play on the Xbox right now"). In contrast, girls often give reasons for their suggestions ("We gotta clean 'em first 'cause they got germs").

Adolescent girls use aggression in conflicts, but their methods are usually more indirect than those of boys. Whereas teenage boys often engage in verbal showdowns or even physical fights, teenage girls typically use gossip, backbiting, and social exclusion (Hess & Hagen, 2006; Underwood, 2003). This is not to suggest that girls' aggression is any less destructive than boys'. The movie *Mean Girls* (based on Rosalind Wiseman's book *Queen Bees and Wannabes*, 2003) offers a vivid depiction of just how injurious these indirect assaults can be on the self-concepts and relationships of young women. Research suggests that these forms of female aggression continue into college and can occur online as well as in person (Miller-Ott & Kelly, 2013).

Gender differences in dealing with conflict often persist into adulthood. Esin Tezer and Ayhan Demir (2001) studied the conflict behaviors late adolescents use with same-sex and opposite-sex peers. They found that compared with females, males use more competing behaviors with same-sex peers and more avoiding behaviors with opposite-sex peers. On the other hand, regardless of culture or the sex of the person with whom they are interacting, females are more likely than males to compromise (Holt & De-Vore, 2005).

A survey of college students reinforced stereotypes about the influence of gender in conflicts (Collier, 1991). Regardless of their cultural background, female students described men as being concerned with power and more interested in content than in relational issues. Sentences used to describe male conflict styles included, "The most important thing to males in conflict is their egos"; "Men don't worry about feelings"; and "Men are more direct." In contrast, women were described as being more concerned with maintaining the relationship during a conflict. Sentences used to describe female conflict styles included, "Women are better listeners"; "Women try to solve problems without controlling the other person"; and "Females are more concerned with others' feelings."

In contrast with this extreme view, another body of research suggests that gender differences in handling conflict are rather small (Samter & Cupach, 1998; Woodin, 2011). As Woodin (2011) concluded, "men and women may be more similar than different in resolving conflict" (p. 332). People may *think* that there are greater differences in male and female ways of handling conflicts than actually exist (Allen, 1998). People who assume that men are aggressive and women accommodating may notice behavior that fits these stereotypes ("See how much he bosses her around? A typical

FOCUS ON RESEARCH
"We Have to Talk": Men and Women in Conflict

Imagine you're in a heterosexual dating relationship and get into a quarrel with your partner. One of you wants to drop the subject and move on. The other says, "No, we need to talk this out." Venture a guess: Who is likely the male in this episode, and who is the female?

Tamara Afifi and her colleagues asked 100 dating couples to hold a private conversation about a conflict issue in their relationship. Afterward, the researchers surveyed each partner about his or her relational communication and satisfaction, and they did so again a week later.

If you thought the "talk it out" person in the scenario was likely female, you're right. Women in the study wanted and expected open conversations about conflict. If they sensed their partners were being avoidant, they weren't happy. If they brooded about it for a week, their relational dissatisfaction grew. On the other hand, men didn't have the same expectations for openness during conflict. They also weren't bothered if they thought either partner was avoiding conflict.

These results reflect cultural "standards for openness," according to the researchers. It appears that American women often expect to talk things out during conflicts in ways that men do not. Men may avoid conflict to stay out of harm's way—but in doing so, they might create greater relational problems with the women they date.

Afifi, T. D., Joseph, A., & Aldeis, D. (2012). The "standards for openness hypothesis": Why women find (conflict) avoidance more dissatisfying than men. *Journal of Social and Personal Relationships, 29,* 102–125.

man!"). On the other hand, behavior that doesn't fit these preconceived ideas (accommodating men, pushy women) goes unnoticed.

What, then, can we conclude about the influence of gender on conflict? Research has demonstrated that there are some small but measurable differences by gender, but the individual style of each communicator is more important than gender in managing conflict.

CULTURE

People from most cultures prefer mutually beneficial resolutions to disagreements whenever possible (Cai & Fink, 2002). Nonetheless, the ways in which people communicate during conflicts vary from one culture to another (Croucher et al., 2012; Shearman et al., 2011). Cultures differ in their orientation toward disagreement (is it to be avoided or is it acceptable?), rapport management (how important is it to ensure relationship maintenance?), and the preserving of face (is it vital to preserve dignity for self and the other party?; Stadler, 2013).

As the following photo suggests, practices that are unremarkable in one culture may look odd to outsiders. As you read in Chapter 2, the kind of straight-talking, assertive approach that characterizes many low-context North American and Western European cultures is not the norm in other parts of the world. Assertiveness that might seem perfectly appropriate to a native of the United States or Canada would be rude and insensitive in many high-context Asian countries (Ma & Jaeger, 2010; Samovar et al., 2010).

Members of individualistic cultures often prefer competing as a conflict style, whereas members of collectivistic cultures prefer the styles of compromising and problem solving (Holt & DeVore, 2005; Lim, 2009).

Asian cultures tend to avoid confrontation, placing a premium on preserving and honoring the face of the other person. The Japanese notion of self-restraint is reflected in the important concept of *wa*, or harmony. This aversion to conflict is even manifested in the Japanese legal system. Estimates are that the Japanese have only one lawyer for every 4,000 people, whereas in the United States, a culture that values assertive behavior, there is one lawyer for every 275 people.

The same attitude toward conflict aversion prevails in China (which has approximately one lawyer for every 6,500 people), where one proverb states, "The first person to raise his voice loses the argument." Among Chinese college students (in both the People's Republic and Taiwan), the three most common methods of persuasion used are "hinting," "setting an example by one's own actions," and "strategically agreeing to whatever pleases others" (Ma & Chuang, 2001)—even if the consequences are negative (Zhang et al., 2011). However, young adults in China favor collaborative problem solving more than do their elders, who prefer accommodating styles (Zhang et al., 2005).

Within the United States, the ethnic background of communicators plays a role in their ideas about conflict (Orbe & Everett, 2006). When a group of Mexican American and European American college students were asked about their views regarding conflict, some important differences emerged (Collier, 1991). For example, European Americans seem more willing to accept conflict as a natural part of relationships, whereas Mexican Americans describe the short- and long-term dangers of disagreeing. European Americans' willingness to experience conflicts may be part of their individualistic, low-context communication style of speaking directly and avoiding uncertainty. It's not surprising that people from cultures that emphasize harmony among people with close relationships tend to handle conflicts in less direct ways. With differences like these, it's easy to imagine how two friends, lovers, or coworkers from different cultural backgrounds might have trouble finding a conflict style that is comfortable for both of them.

Despite these differences, it's important to realize that culture is only one of many factors that influence the way people think about conflict or how they behave when they disagree. Some research (e.g., Beatty & McCroskey, 1997; Horwitz et al., 2010) suggests that our approach to conflict may be part of our biological makeup. Emotional intelligence (see Chapter 8) also plays a role: People high in emotional intelligence tend to use a collaborating conflict style, whereas those low in emotional intelligence tend to use an accommodating style (Morrison, 2008). Furthermore, scholarship suggests a person's self-concept is more powerful than his or her culture in determining conflict style (Bechtoldt et al., 2010; Ting-Toomey et al., 2001). For example, African Americans, Asian Americans, European Americans, and Latin Americans who view themselves as mostly independent of others are likely to use a direct, solution-oriented conflict style, regardless of their cultural heritage. Those who see themselves as mostly interdependent are likely to use a style that avoids direct confrontation. And those who see themselves as both independent and interdependent are likely to have the widest variety of conflict behaviors on which to draw.

CONFLICT MANAGEMENT IN PRACTICE

The collaborative conflict management style described earlier in this chapter is a skill to be learned, and it pays off. In an 11-year longitudinal study following a hundred couples who had conflict skills training, Kurt Hahlweg and Diana Richter (2010) found that *it works* for couples willing to focus on improving their relationships.

Win-win problem solving can be enacted through a seven-step approach that is based on plans developed by Deborah Weider-Hatfield (1981) and Ellen Raider and her colleagues (2006). Notice how many of the skills that have been discussed throughout this book are incorporated in this process:

1. **Define your needs.** Begin by deciding what you want or need. Sometimes the answer is obvious, as in our earlier example of the neighbor whose loud music kept others awake. In other instances, however, the apparent problem masks a more fundamental one.

   Consider a scenario: Brook and Anat have been dating for several months and are now in an exclusive relationship. Brook calls or texts Anat frequently when they're apart. Anat rarely initiates contact with Brook and usually doesn't respond to messages. Each is annoyed with the other's behavior.

   At first, Anat thought the aggravation was due to being interrupted while trying to focus on school and work. More self-examination showed that the irritation centered on the relational message Brook's calls seemed to imply. Anat views the constant contact as a form of being monitored and perhaps as a sign that Brook didn't trust what Anat was doing when they weren't together.

   Because your needs won't always be clear, it's often necessary to think about a problem alone, before approaching the other person involved. Talking to a third person can sometimes help you sort out your thoughts. In either case, you should explore both the apparent content of your dissatisfaction and the relational issues that may lurk behind it.

2. **Share your needs with the other person.** Once you've defined your needs, it's time to share them with your partner. Two guidelines are important here: First, be sure to choose a time and place that is

suitable. Unloading on a tired or busy partner lowers the odds that your concerns will be well received. Likewise, be sure you are at your best: Don't bring an issue up when your anger may cause you to say things you'll later regret, when your discouragement blows the problem out of proportion, or when you're distracted by other business. Making a date to discuss the problem—such as after dinner or over a cup of coffee—often can boost the odds of a successful outcome.

The second guideline for sharing a problem is to use the descriptive "I" language outlined in Chapter 5. In the scenario introduced previously, Anat could offer this observation:

Brook, our relationship is very important to me, and I'm glad you want to keep in touch. I'm a bit concerned, however, about how often you call or text me. When I'm at school or work, or if I'm hanging out with my friends, I want to be able to focus on those activities. At times like that, your messages can seem like a distraction rather than a sign of affection. And I'll admit that I wonder *why* you're calling so often. Is there some sort of trust issue we need to discuss?

In a tense situation, it may not be easy to start sharing your needs. Raider et al. (2006) recommend beginning with what they call *ritual sharing*, which is preliminary, casual conversation. The goal is to build rapport and establish common ground and, perhaps, to pick up information.

3. **Listen to the other person's needs.** Once your own wants and needs are clear, it's time to find out what the other person wants and needs. (Now the listening skills described in Chapter 7 and the supportive behaviors described in Chapter 11 become most important.)

In our scenario, it's possible that Brook will have a defensive reaction to Anat's observation ("I can't believe you see my calls and texts as a *distraction*!"), but ideally the needs and concerns that drive the conversation will become clear. Brook might respond like this:

When I call and text you, it's my way of communicating that I'm thinking about you. When you don't respond, it hurts. I take it as a sign that you don't care about me as much as I care about you.

Now is a good time to engage in paraphrasing, both to make sure the other person has been heard and to draw out additional information. Anat might respond, "So you're saying that texts and calls are just a sign of care and concern, and they're not an attempt to monitor me?" This might allow Brook to explore the motives for messaging Anat. Brook might paraphrase Anat this way: "It sounds like you don't want to have contact with me when we're away from each other, and that you view my messages as an intrusion into your personal space." Anat can then clarify which parts of that interpretation are or are not accurate.

Recognize that this stage might take some time. Before moving to generating solutions, both people need to believe they have been heard and that all the content and relational issues of their conflict are on the table. This might include exploring how previous issues (or even previous relationships) are affecting how they're communicating with each other about this particular conflict.

● THIRD-PARTY DISPUTE RESOLUTION

@WORK

In a perfect world, people involved in disagreements would solve every problem themselves. But in real life, even the best intentions don't always lead to a satisfying conclusion. At times like these, a neutral third party can help—especially in workplace conflicts.

The list of business disputes in which a third party can help is long. It includes clashes between partners, contract disagreements, conflicts among team members, employee grievances, and consumer complaints. As these examples show, some conflicts occur between members of the same organization, whereas others involve an organization at odds with an outsider.

Third-party interventions can range from informal to legalistic. At the simple end of the spectrum, you and a colleague might ask a trusted coworker to help you work out a disagreement. In other cases, it may be useful to involve a trained mediator or facilitator who can help sort out issues and suggest solutions. In the most serious cases, parties may submit their grievances to an arbitrator or judge who will impose a decision. Whichever approach is used, it's important that a third party be neutral and unbiased to ensure a fair and effective outcome (Gent & Shannon, 2011). Whatever the form, third-party intervention can help bring closure to a dispute that would otherwise fester or explode.

4. **Generate possible solutions.** In the next step, you and your partner try to think of ways to satisfy both your needs. You can best do so by "brainstorming"—inventing as many potential solutions as you can. The key to success in brainstorming is to seek quantity without worrying about quality. Prohibit criticism of all ideas, no matter how outlandish they may sound. An idea that seems farfetched can sometimes lead to a more workable one. Another rule of brainstorming is that ideas aren't personal property. If one person makes a suggestion, the other should feel free to suggest another solution that builds on or modifies the original one. The original suggestion and its offshoots are all potential solutions that will be considered later. Once partners get over their possessiveness about ideas, the level of defensiveness drops, and both people can work together to find the best solution without worrying about whose idea it is. (The supportive and confirming behaviors discussed in Chapter 11 are particularly important during this step.)

Let's return to our scenario. Anat and Brook use brainstorming to generate solutions for their problem. The list includes eliminating, limiting, continuing, or increasing the number of calls Brook makes to Anat. Likewise, Anat could reduce or increase responses to Brook. The couple could decide that text messages are preferable to voice messages, or that one type of contact (call or text) needs to be answered and the other doesn't. Day calls might be okay but not evening calls, or vice versa. Perhaps Anat could initiate calls; maybe Brook could contact other friends instead when wanting to chat. They might also discuss larger issues about how much time they spend together in person or with their friends. It could even be an opportunity to discuss whether they want to slow down or speed up their relationship. Although some of these solutions are clearly unacceptable to both partners, they list all the ideas they can think of, preparing themselves for the next step in win-win problem solving.

5. **Evaluate the possible solutions and choose the best one.** The time to evaluate the solutions is after they all have been generated, after you feel you have exhausted all the possibilities. In this step, the possible solutions are reviewed for their ability to satisfy everyone's important goals. How does each solution stand up against the individual and mutual goals? Which solution satisfies the most goals? Partners need to work cooperatively in examining each solution and in finally selecting the best one—or perhaps some combination of ideas.

    Brook and Anat decide to limit texts and calls to two or three per day, and that Anat will initiate at least one of them. They also agree to briefly respond to the other's text messages when they're at social events, but not during school or work hours. Anat believes that fewer calls will communicate that Brook values autonomy and trusts their relationship. Brook thinks that messages Anat initiates or responds to will indicate that both are equally invested in the relationship.

6. **Implement the solution.** Now the time comes to try out the idea selected to see if it does, indeed, satisfy everyone's needs. How did it work out for Anat and Brook? They followed their new guidelines and for the most part were satisfied—but there were still some issues. If Brook contacts Anat simply to say, "I'll be home in 30 minutes," does that count as a call? Likewise, if Anat initiates a message but it's just about making arrangements, does that satisfy Brook?

    Sometimes solutions that seem good in theory don't work well in practice. Maybe Anat feels stifled by being "required" to place a call each day. Perhaps Brook doesn't like limits placed on spontaneous expressions of affection. That's why they need to be sure to engage in the final step of the problem-solving process—the follow-up.

7. **Follow up the solution.** To stop the process after selecting and implementing a particular solution assumes any solution is forever, that people remain constant, and that events never alter circumstances. Of course, this is not the case: As people and circumstances change, a particular solution may lose or increase its effectiveness. Regardless, a follow-up evaluation needs to take place.

    After you've tested your solution for a short time, it's a good idea to plan a meeting to talk about how things are going. You may find that you need to make some changes or even rethink the whole problem.

    Brook and Anat scheduled a date to talk about their solution two weeks later. Over dinner, they both reported feeling good about the new arrangements and realized that trust was indeed an issue for Brook. They agreed to differentiate between personal calls (which they would limit) and necessary calls to make arrangements as needed (which would have no constraints). Anat admitted that initiating calls was challenging and decided to turn off the phone during school and work hours. Brook asked Anat to send a quick text when open for contact. Anat saw that as a good way to remember to send a check-in message each day.

There are certainly other ways this conflict and its management might play out, but the key is that Brook and Anat need to be satisfied with their solution. What works for them might not work for other couples, but that's what makes communication unique to each relationship.

CHECK YOUR UNDERSTANDING

Objective 12.1 Understand the nature of conflict and its attributes.

Despite wishes and cultural myths to the contrary, conflict is a natural and unavoidable part of any relationship. Because conflict can't be escaped, the challenge is how to deal with it effectively so that it strengthens a relationship rather than weakens it. All conflicts possess the same characteristics: expressed struggle, perceived incompatible goals, perceived scarce resources, interdependence, and inevitability.

Q: Describe how the recurring conflicts in one of your important relationships embody the characteristics described in this section.

Objective 12.2 Explain five styles of handling conflict and how they are communicated.

Communicators can respond to conflicts in a variety of ways: avoidance, accommodation, competition, compromise, or collaboration. Each of these approaches can be justified in certain circumstances.

Q: Which of the five styles reflects your typical approach to conflicts? Which styles best describe those with whom you communicate? How

satisfying are the results of using these styles? Would other styles be more effective?

Objective 12.3 Recognize various communication patterns in relational conflicts.

The way a conflict is handled isn't always the choice of a single person because the communicators influence one another. In some relationships, partners engage in complementary conflict; whereas in others, the approach is more symmetrical. Some forms of communication during conflict are inherently toxic. These have been labeled the "Four Horsemen." In ongoing relationships, partners often develop conflict rituals—repeated patterns of interlocking behavior.

Q: Do your conflicts with relational partners tend to be more complementary or symmetrical? Are they more constructive or destructive? Do you or the other person ever resort to using any of the "Four Horsemen"? If so, what are the effects? What conflict rituals characterize your disputes? How beneficial are these rituals?

Objective 12.4 Describe how gender and culture affect communication during conflict.

Research shows that there are differences in how men and women typically approach conflict. Nonetheless, the individual style of each communicator is more important than biological sex in shaping the way he or she handles conflict. Cultural background also influences the way individuals handle conflict.

Q: To what extent do cultural and gender differences in managing conflict apply to communication in your important relationships? How can you take these differences into account to manage conflict most productively?

Objective 12.5 Understand how the conflict management process can ideally resolve interpersonal conflicts.

In most circumstances a collaborative, win-win outcome is the ideal, and it can be achieved by following the guidelines outlined in the last section of this chapter.

Q: Consider how the steps described on pages 389–393 could help you manage a conflict more productively. What parts prove most helpful? Which are most difficult?

KEY TERMS

- Accommodation (373)
- Avoidance (372)
- Collaboration (377)
- Competition (374)
- Complementary conflict (381)
- Compromise (376)
- Conflict (369)
- Conflict ritual (384)
- De-escalatory spiral (382)
- Direct aggression (375)
- Escalatory spiral (382)
- Passive aggression (374)
- Symmetrical conflict (381)
- Win-win problem solving (377)

ACTIVITIES

1. Interview someone who knows you well. Ask your informant which personal conflict styles (avoidance, accommodation, etc.) you use most often and the effect each of these styles has on your relationship with this person. Based on your findings, discuss whether different behavior might produce more productive results.

2. With a group of classmates, construct a hypothetical conflict scenario similar to the one between Chris and Pat (pages 371–372). Describe how the parties involved might approach the conflict using each of the following styles:

  a. Avoidance

  b. Accommodation

  c. Competition

  d. Compromise

  e. Collaboration

3. With a group of classmates, interview several people to answer the following questions:

  a. Is your relational style of handling conflict complementary or symmetrical? What are the consequences of this approach?

  b. What conflict rituals do you follow in this relationship? Are these rituals functional or dysfunctional? What might be better alternatives?

  c. Have you experienced any of Gottman's "Four Horsemen" during conflict? If so, which ones? What has been the result?

  d. Do gender and cultural background shape how you and your relational partners deal with conflict? If so, how?

4. As a class, construct a hypothetical conflict scenario similar to the one between Anat and Brook (page 389). Describe how the parties involved might engage in each step of the problem-solving process outlined on pages 389–393. Try to generate and select actual solutions to the problem.

SCORING FOR ASSESSING YOUR COMMUNICATION (PAGE 379)

Add your responses to items 1, 6, 11, and 16. This is your **competition** score.

Add your responses to items 2, 7, 12, and 17. This is your **collaboration** score.

Add your responses to items 3, 8, 13, and 18. This is your **compromise** score.

Add your responses to items 4, 9, 14, and 19. This is your **avoidance** score.

Add your responses to items 5, 10, 15, and 20. This is your **accommodation** score.

Scores on each dimension can range from 4 to 20, with higher scores indicating more of a preference for the particular conflict style. You may wish to complete the assessment several times, with different people or different conflicts in mind, to get a better sense of your preferred conflict styles.

Glossary

Abstraction ladder A range of more abstract to less abstract terms describing an event or object. p. 154

Accommodation A lose-win conflict style in which one person defers to the other. p. 373

Achievement culture A culture that places a high value on the achievement of material success and a focus on the task at hand. Also termed "masculine" culture. p. 48

Advising (response) A listening response in which the receiver offers suggestions about how the speaker should deal with a problem. p. 228

Aggressiveness Verbal attacks that demean others' self-concept and inflict psychological pain. p. 343

Ambiguous language Language consisting of words and phrases that have more than one commonly accepted definition. p. 153

Ambiguous response A response with more than one meaning, leaving the other person unsure of the responder's position. p. 345

Ambushing A style in which the receiver listens carefully to gather information to use in an attack on the speaker. p. 212

Analytical listening A style of listening that emphasizes hearing all details of a message and then assessing it from a variety of perspectives. p. 208

Analyzing (response) A listening response in which the listener offers an interpretation of a speaker's message. p. 227

Androgynous Possessing both masculine and feminine traits. p. 119

Argumentativeness Presenting and defending positions on issues while attacking positions taken by others. p. 341

Assertiveness Clearly and directly expressing one's thoughts, feelings, and wants to another person. p. 159

Asynchronous Communication that occurs when there is a time gap between when a message is sent and when it is received. p. 27

Attending A phase of the listening process in which the communicator focuses on a message, excluding other messages. p. 213

Attribution The process of attaching meaning to another person's behavior. p. 123

Avoidance A lose-lose conflict style in which people nonassertively ignore or stay away from conflict. p. 372

Avoiding A relational stage immediately prior to terminating in which the partners minimize contact with one another. p. 283

Benevolent lie A lie that is not considered malicious by the person who tells it. p. 98

Bonding A stage of relational development in which the partners make symbolic public gestures to show that their relationship exists. p. 286

Boundaries Limits that a family sets on its members' actions, such as what topics are permissible to discuss, how to discuss certain topics, and with whom family members may interact outside the family. p. 323

"But" statement A statement in which the second half cancels the meaning of the first, for example, "I'd like to help you, *but* I have to go or I'll miss my bus." p. 159

Certainty Dogmatically stating or implying that one's position is correct and others' ideas are not worth considering; likely to arouse defensiveness, according to Gibb. p. 355

Channel The medium through which a message passes from sender to receiver. p. 12

Chronemics The study of how people use and structure time. p. 195

Circumscribing A relational stage in which partners begin to reduce the scope of their contact and commitment to one another. p. 282

Closed questions Questions that limit the range of possible responses, such as questions that seek a yes-or-no answer. p. 218

Co-culture A group within an encompassing culture with a perceived identity. p. 39

Cognitive complexity The ability to construct a variety of frameworks for viewing an issue. p. 23

Collaboration A win-win conflict style in which both people get what they want. p. 377

Collectivistic culture A culture whose members feel loyalties and obligations to an in-group, such as an extended family, a community, and even a work organization. p. 45

Communication The use of messages to generate meanings. p. 9

Communication apprehension Feelings of anxiety that plague some people at the prospect of communicating in an unfamiliar or difficult context. p. 24

Communication climate The emotional tone of a relationship between two or more individuals. p. 338

Communication competence The ability to achieve one's goals in a manner that is personally acceptable and, ideally, acceptable to others. p. 19

Comparison level (CL) The minimum standard of what behavior is acceptable from a relationship partner. p. 274

Comparison level of alternatives (CL$_{alt}$) A comparison between the rewards one is receiving in a present situation and those one could expect to receive in others. p. 274

Competition A win-lose conflict style in which one person wins at the other person's expense. p. 374

Complaining A disagreeing message that directly or indirectly communicates dissatisfaction with another person. p. 342

Complementary conflict When partners in a conflict use different but mutually reinforcing behaviors. p. 381

Compromise A conflict style in which both people get only part of what they want because they sacrifice some of their goals. p. 376

Confirmation bias The tendency to seek out and organize data that supports already existing opinions. p. 125

Confirming communication A message that expresses caring or respect for another person; the person is valued by the speaker. p. 339

Conflict An expressed struggle between at least two interdependent people who perceive incompatible goals, scarce resources, and interference from the other person in achieving her or his goals. p. 369

Conflict ritual Repeating pattern of interlocking conflict behaviors. p. 384

Conformity orientation The degree to which family communication stresses uniformity of attitudes, values, and beliefs. p. 319

Connection-autonomy dialectic The tension between the need for integration and the need for independence in a relationship. p. 285

Content dimension The dimension of a message that communicates information about the subject being discussed. See *Relational dimension*. p. 14

Controlling communication According to Gibb, messages that attempt to impose some sort of outcome on another person, resulting in a defensive response. p. 351

Conventionality-uniqueness dialectic The tension between the need to behave in ways that conform to others' expectations and the need to assert one's individuality by behaving in ways that violate others' expectations. p. 287

Convergence The process of adapting one's speech style to match that of others with whom one wants to identify. See also *Divergence*. p. 147

Conversation orientation The degree to which families favor an open climate of discussion on a wide array of topics. p. 319

Counterfeit questions Questions that are disguised attempts to send a message rather than elicit information. p. 218

Critical listening A listening style that involves evaluating the content of a message. p. 208

Culture The language, values, beliefs, traditions, and customs people share and learn. p. 38

Debilitative emotions Emotions of high intensity and long duration that prevent a person from functioning effectively. p. 253

De-escalatory spiral A reciprocal communication pattern in which one person's nonthreatening behavior leads to reduced hostility by the other, with the level of hostility steadily decreasing. Opposite of *Escalatory spiral*. p. 382

Defensive listening A response style in which the receiver perceives a speaker's comments as an attack. p. 212

Defensiveness The attempt to protect a presenting image a person believes is being attacked. p. 347

Description Messages that describe a speaker's position without evaluating others. p. 351

Dialectical tensions Relational tensions that arise when two opposing or incompatible forces exist simultaneously. p. 284

Differentiating A relational stage in which the partners reestablish their individual identities after having bonded. p. 281

Direct aggression An expression of the sender's thoughts and/or feelings that attacks the position and dignity of the receiver. p. 375

Disagreeing message A message that essentially communicates to another person, "You are wrong," and includes argumentativeness, complaining, and aggressiveness. p. 341

Disconfirming communication A message that expresses a lack of caring or respect for another person; the person is not valued by the speaker. p. 339

Disengaged family Families with too little cohesion, in which members have limited attachment or commitment to one another. p. 323

Disfluencies Nonlinguistic verbalizations, for example, *um, er, uh.* p. 191

Disinhibition Expressing messages without considering the consequences of doing so. p. 31

Divergence Speaking in a way that emphasizes difference from others. See also *Convergence.* p. 148

Emblems Deliberate nonverbal behaviors with precise meanings, known to virtually all members of a cultural group. p. 178

Emotional contagion The process by which emotions are transferred from one person to another. p. 245

Emotional intelligence The ability to understand and manage one's own emotions and to be sensitive to others' feelings. p. 236

Emotion labor Managing and even suppressing emotions when it is both appropriate and necessary to do so. p. 244

Empathizing (response) A listening response that conveys identification with a speaker's perceptions and emotions. p. 223

Empathy The ability to project oneself into another person's point of view in an attempt to experience the other's thoughts and feelings. p. 131, 353

Enmeshed family Families with too much consensus, too little independence, and a very high demand for loyalty. p. 323

Environment Both the physical setting in which communication occurs and the personal perspectives of the people involved. p. 11

Equality A type of supportive communication described by Gibb, which suggests that the sender regards the receiver with respect. p. 355

Equivocation A statement that is not false but cleverly avoids an unpleasant truth. p. 100

Escalatory spiral A reciprocal communication pattern in which one person's attack leads to a counter-attack by the other, with the level of hostility steadily increasing. Opposite of *De-escalatory spiral.* p. 352

Ethnicity A person's identification with a social group on the basis of common national or cultural traditions. p. 49

Ethnocentrism An attitude that one's own culture is superior to that of others. p. 60

Euphemism A pleasant term substituted for a blunt one to soften the impact of unpleasant information. p. 156

Evaluating (response) A listening response that appraises a sender's thoughts or behaviors and implies that the person evaluating is qualified to pass judgment on the other. p. 228

Evaluation A message in which a sender judges a receiver in some way, usually resulting in a defensive response. p. 350

Evaluative language Language that conveys the sender's attitude rather than simply offering an objective description. p. 162

Expectancy violation An instance when others don't behave as we assume they should. p. 313

Experimenting An early stage in relational development, consisting of a search for common ground. If the experimentation is successful, the relationship progresses to intensifying. If not, it may go no further. p. 279

Expression-privacy dialectic The tension between the desire to be open and disclosive and the desire to be closed and private. p. 287

Face The image an individual wants to project to the world. See also *Presenting self.* p. 81, 345

Face-threatening acts Behavior by another that is perceived as attacking an individual's presenting image, or face. p. 347

Facework Actions people take to preserve their own and others' presenting images. p. 81

Facilitative emotions Emotions that contribute to effective functioning. p. 253

Fallacy of approval The irrational belief that it is vital to win the approval of virtually every person with whom a communicator interacts. p. 258

Fallacy of catastrophic expectations The irrational belief that the worst possible outcome will probably occur. p. 261

Fallacy of causation The irrational belief that emotions are caused by others and not by the person who has them. p. 259

Fallacy of helplessness The irrational belief that satisfaction in life is determined by forces beyond one's control. p. 260

Fallacy of overgeneralization Irrational beliefs in which (1) conclusions (usually negative) are based on limited evidence, or (2) communicators exaggerate their shortcomings. p. 259

Fallacy of perfection The irrational belief that a worthwhile communicator should be able to handle every situation with complete confidence and skill. p. 256

Fallacy of should The irrational belief that people should behave in the most desirable way, based on the inability to distinguish between what *is* and what *should be*. p. 258

Family A system with two or more interdependent people who have a common past history and a present reality and who expect to influence each other in the future. p. 316

Family communication patterns Typical interaction processes in a family, identified by these categories: consensual, pluralistic, protective, or laissez-faire. See also *Conversation orientation; Conformity orientation*. p. 319

Feedback A discernable response of a receiver to a sender's message. p. 10

Filling in gaps A listening habit that involves adding details never mentioned by a speaker to complete a message. p. 212

First-order realities The physically observable qualities of a thing or situation. p. 109

Friendship A voluntary interpersonal relationship that provides social support. p. 307

Fundamental attribution error The tendency to give more weight to personal qualities than to the situation when making attributions. p. 126

Gender Psychological sex-type. p. 119

Halo effect The tendency to form an overall positive impression of a person on the basis of one positive characteristic. See also *Horns effect*. p. 125

Haptics The study of touch in human communication. p. 189

Hearing The first stage in the listening process in which sound waves are received by a communicator. p. 206

High-context culture A culture that relies heavily on verbal and nonverbal cues to maintain social harmony. p. 43

Horns effect The tendency to form an overall negative impression of a person on the basis of one negative characteristic. See also *Halo effect*. p. 125

Hyperpersonal communication An acceleration of the discussion of personal topics and relational development. p. 27

"I" language Language that uses first-person singular pronouns to identify the source of the message and to take responsibility. See also *"You" language*. p. 158

Impersonal response A disconfirming response that is superficial or trite. p. 345

Impervious response A disconfirming response that ignores another person's attempt to communicate. p. 343

Impression management The communication strategies people use to influence how others view them. p. 80

Inclusion-seclusion dialectic The tension between a couple's desire for involvement with the "outside world" and their desire to live their own lives, free of what can feel like interference from others. p. 287

Incongruous response A disconfirming response in which two messages, one of which is usually nonverbal, contradict one another. p. 345

Individualistic culture A culture in which people view their primary responsibility as helping themselves. p. 45

In-group A group with which an individual identifies herself or himself. p. 38

Initiating The first stage in relational development in which the interactants express interest in one another. p. 278

Insulated listening A style in which the receiver ignores undesirable information. p. 212

Integrating A relational stage in which the interactants begin to take on a single identity. p. 280

Integration-separation dialectic The tension between the desire for connection with others and the desire for independence. p. 285

Intensifying A relational stage following experimenting in which the interactants move toward integration by increasing their amount of contact and the breadth and depth of their self-disclosure. p. 279

Intercultural communication Communication that occurs when members of two or more cultures or other groups exchange messages in a manner that is influenced by their different cultural perceptions and symbol systems. p. 40

Interpretation The process of attaching meaning to sense data. p. 112

Interrupting response A disconfirming response in which one communicator interrupts another. p. 344

Intimacy A state achieved via intellectual, emotional, and/or physical closeness as well as via shared activities. p. 302

Intimate distance One of Hall's four distance zones, ranging from skin contact to 18 inches. p. 193

Invitational communication An approach that welcomes others to see your point of view and to freely share their own. p. 357

Irrelevant response A disconfirming response in which one communicator's comments bear no relationship to the previous speaker's ideas. p. 344

"It" statements A statement in which "it" replaces the personal pronoun "I," making the statement less direct and more evasive. p. 158

Johari Window A model that describes the relationship between self-disclosure and self-awareness. p. 91

Kinesics The study of body movements. p. 186

Leanness A description of messages that carry less information due to a lack of nonverbal cues. See also *Richness*. p. 26

Lie A deliberate act of deception. p. 98

Linguistic relativity The notion that the language individuals use exerts a strong influence on their perceptions. p. 144

Listening The process of receiving and responding to others' messages. p. 206

Listening fidelity The degree of congruence between what a listener understands and what the message-sender was attempting to communicate. p. 214

Love languages Methods of expressing affection to a romantic partner, such as words of affirmation, quality time, gifts, acts of service, and physical touch. p. 330

Low-context culture A culture that uses language primarily to express thoughts, feelings, and ideas as clearly and logically as possible. p. 43

Manipulators Movements in which one part of the body grooms, massages, rubs, holds, fidgets with, pinches, picks, or otherwise manipulates another part. p. 188

Metacommunication Messages (usually relational) that refer to other messages; communication about communication. p. 291

Mindful listening Careful and thoughtful attention and responses to others' messages. p. 207

Mindless listening Reacting to others' messages automatically and routinely, without much mental involvement. p. 206

Narratives The stories we use to describe our personal worlds. p. 113

Negotiation The fourth stage of the perception process, in which communicators influence each other's perception through interaction. p. 113

Neutrality A defense-arousing behavior described by Gibb in which the sender expresses indifference toward a receiver. p. 353

Noise External, physiological, and psychological distractions that interfere with the accurate transmission and reception of a message. p. 12

Nonverbal communication Messages expressed by nonlinguistic means. p. 174

Nurturing culture A culture that regards the support of relationships as an especially important goal. Also termed "feminine" culture. p. 48

Oculesics The study of how the eyes can communicate. p. 186

Openness-closedness dialectic The tension between the desire to be honest and open and the desire for privacy. p. 288

Open questions Questions that allow for a variety of extended responses. p. 218

Organization The stage in the perception process that involves arranging data in a meaningful way. p. 111

Organizational culture A relatively stable, shared set of rules about how to behave and set of values about what is important in a given organization. p. 55

Out-group A group that an individual sees as different from herself or himself. p. 38

Paralanguage Nonlinguistic means of vocal expression, for example, rate, pitch, and tone. p. 190

Paraphrasing Restating a speaker's thoughts and feelings in the listener's own words. p. 221

Passive aggression An indirect expression of aggression, delivered in a way that allows the sender to maintain a facade of kindness. p. 374

Perceived self The person we believe ourselves to be in moments of candor. It may be identical with or different from the presenting and desired selves. p. 80

Perception checking A three-part method for verifying the accuracy of interpretations, including a description of the sense data, two possible interpretations, and a request for confirmation of the interpretations. p. 129

Personal distance One of Hall's four distance zones, ranging from 18 inches to 4 feet. p. 193

Personal space The distance we put between ourselves and others. p. 192

Phonological rules Rules governing the way in which sounds are pronounced in a language. p. 141

Politeness Communicating in ways that save face for both senders and receivers. p. 149

Power distance The degree to which members of a society accept the unequal distribution of power among members. p. 46

Powerful language Direct and forceful word choices, with declarations and assertions. p. 149

Powerless language Forms of speech that communicate to others a lack of power in the speaker: hedges, hesitations, intensifiers, and so on. p. 148

Pragmatic rules Rules that govern interpretation of language in terms of its social context. See also *Semantic rules; Syntactic rules.* p. 142

Predictability-novelty dialectic Within a relationship, the tension between the need for a predictable relational partner and one who is more spontaneous and less predictable. p. 287

Prejudice An unfairly biased and intolerant attitude toward others who belong to an out-group. p. 62

Presenting self The image a person presents to others. It may be identical with or different from the perceived and desired selves. p. 80, 345

Primacy effect The tendency to pay more attention to, and to better recall, things that happen first in a sequence. p. 125

Privacy management The choices people make to reveal or conceal information about themselves. p. 92

Problem orientation A supportive style of communication described by Gibb in which the communicators focus on working together to solve their problems instead of trying to impose their own solutions on one another. p. 351

Provisionalism A supportive style of communication described by Gibb in which a sender expresses open-mindedness to others' ideas and opinions. p. 356

Proxemics The study of how people use space. p. 192

Pseudolistening An imitation of true listening in which the receiver's mind is elsewhere. p. 212

Public distance One of Hall's four distance zones, extending outward from 12 feet. p. 194

Punctuation The process of determining the causal order of events. p. 111

Questioning (response) A listening response in which the receiver seeks additional information from the sender. p. 217

Race A social category originally created to explain differences between people whose ancestors originated in different regions of the world. p. 49

Racist language Language that classifies members of one racial group as superior and others as inferior. p. 152

Reappraisal Rethinking the meaning of emotionally charged events in ways that alter their emotional impact. p. 239

Reference groups Groups against which we compare ourselves, thereby influencing our self-concept and self-esteem. p. 73

Reflected appraisal The theory that a person's self-concept matches the way the person believes others regard him or her. p. 72

Regulators Nonverbal cues that help control verbal interaction. p. 181

Relational commitment A promise, explicit or implied, to remain in a relationship and to make that relationship successful. p. 327

Relational dimension The dimension of a message that expresses the social relationship between two or more individuals. See *Content dimension.* p. 15

Relational listening A listening style that is primarily concerned with emotionally connecting with others. p. 208

Relational maintenance Communication aimed at keeping relationships operating smoothly and satisfactorily (e.g., behaving in a positive way, being open, and assuring your partner that you're committed to the relationship). p. 277

Relational transgression A violation of the explicit or implicit terms of a relationship, letting the partner down in some important way. p. 294

Relative language Words that gain their meaning by comparison. p. 157

Remembering A phase of the listening process in which a message is recalled. p. 215

Responding A phase of the listening process in which feedback occurs, offering evidence that the message has been received. p. 215

Revelation-concealment dialectic The tension between a couple's desire to be open and honest with the "outside world" and their desire to keep things to themselves. p. 288

Richness The quantity of nonverbal cues that accompany spoken messages. See also *Leanness.* p. 26

Rumination Recurrent thoughts not demanded by the immediate environment. p. 253

Salience The significance attached to a particular person or phenomenon. p. 41

Sapir–Whorf hypothesis The best-known declaration of linguistic relativism, based on the work of Benjamin Whorf and Edward Sapir. p. 144

Second-order realities Perceptions that arise from attaching meaning to first-order things or situations. See *First-order realities.* p. 109

Selection A phase of the perception process in which a communicator attends to a stimulus from the environment. Also, a way communicators manage dialectical tensions by responding to one end of the dialectical spectrum and ignoring the other. p. 110

Selective listening A listening style in which the receiver responds only to messages that interest her or him. p. 212

Self-concept The relatively stable set of perceptions each individual holds of herself or himself. See also *Self-esteem*. p. 70

Self-disclosure The process of deliberately revealing information about oneself that is significant and that would not normally be known by others. p. 88

Self-esteem The part of the self-concept that involves evaluations of self-worth. See *Self-concept*. p. 70

Self-fulfilling prophecy The causal relationship that occurs when a person's expectations of an event and her or his subsequent behavior based on those expectations make the outcome more likely to occur than would otherwise have been true. p. 78

Self-monitoring The process of attending to one's behavior and using these observations to shape the way one behaves. p. 23

Self-serving bias The tendency to judge oneself in the most generous terms possible while being more critical of others. p. 126

Self-talk The nonvocal, internal monologue that is our process of thinking. p. 256

Semantic rules Rules that govern the meaning of language, as opposed to its structure. See *Syntactic rules; Pragmatic rules*. p. 141

Sexist language "Words, phrases, and expressions that unnecessarily differentiate between females and males or exclude, trivialize, or diminish" (Parks & Roberton, 2000, p. 415) either sex. p. 150

Significant other A person whose opinion is important enough to affect one's self-concept strongly. p. 72

Silent listening Staying attentive and nonverbally responsive without offering verbal feedback. p. 217

Sincere questions Genuine attempts to elicit information from others. p. 218

Social comparison Evaluating oneself in terms of or by comparison to others. p. 73

Social distance One of Hall's four distance zones, ranging from 4 to 12 feet. p. 194

Social identity The part of the self-concept that is based on membership in groups. p. 38

Social media Mediated communication channels used primarily for personal reasons including text messaging, twitter, e-mail, instant messaging, and social networking services. p. 24

Social penetration model A model that describes relationships in terms of their breadth and depth. p. 89

Social support Helping others during challenging times by providing emotional, informational, or instrumental resources. p. 293

Spiral A reciprocal communication pattern in which messages reinforce one another. See *Escalatory spiral; De-escalatory spiral*. p. 349

Spontaneity A supportive communication behavior described by Gibb in which the sender expresses a message without any attempt to manipulate the receiver. p. 352

Stability-change dialectic The tension between the desire to keep a relationship predictable and stable and the desire for novelty and change. p. 287

Stage hogging A listening style in which the receiver is more concerned with making his or her own point than in understanding the speaker. p. 212

Stagnating A relational stage characterized by declining enthusiasm and standardized forms of behavior. p. 282

Standpoint theory A body of scholarship that explores how one's position in a society shapes one's view of society in general and of specific individuals. p. 118

Static evaluation Treating people or objects as if they were unchanging. p. 157

Stereotyping Exaggerated beliefs associated with a categorizing system. p. 124

Strategy A defense-arousing style of communication described by Gibb in which a sender tries to manipulate or deceive a receiver. p. 352

Superiority A defense-arousing style of communication described by Gibb in which the sender states or implies that the receiver is inferior. p. 354

Supporting (response) A listening response in which the receiver reveals her or his solidarity with the speaker's situation. p. 225

Symmetrical conflict Partners in a conflict use the same tactics. p. 381

Synchronous communication Communication that occurs in real time. p. 27

Syntactic rules Rules that govern the ways symbols can be arranged, as opposed to the meanings of those symbols. See *Semantic rules; Pragmatic rules*. p. 141

System A group, such as a family, whose members interact with one another to form a whole. p. 318

Tangential response A disconfirming response that uses the speaker's remark as a starting point for a shift to a new topic. p. 344

Task-oriented listening A listening style that is primarily concerned with efficiency. p. 208

Terminating The conclusion of a relationship, characterized by the acknowledgment of one or both partners that the relationship is over. p. 283

Territory A stationary area claimed by a person or animal. p. 194

Transactional The dynamic process in which communicators create meaning together through interaction. p. 13

Triangular theory of love The notion that love is comprised of three interacting components: intimacy, passion, and commitment. p. 326

Uncertainty avoidance The tendency of a culture's members to feel threatened by ambiguous situations, and how much they try to avoid them. p. 47

Understanding A stage in the listening process in which the receiver attaches meaning to a message. p. 214

"We" language The use of first-person-plural pronouns to include others, either appropriately or inappropriately. Language implying that the issue being discussed is the concern and responsibility of both the speaker and the receiver of a message. See *"I" language; "You" language.* p. 160

Win-win problem solving An approach to conflict resolution in which people work together to satisfy all their goals. p. 377

"You" language A statement that expresses or implies a judgment of the other person. See *Evaluation; "I" language.* p. 159

References

100 ways to say "I" in Japanese. (2013, July 12). *Japanese Level Up*. Retrieved from http://japaneselevelup.com/100-ways-to-say-i-in-japanese/

5.2 million young Americans may have hearing problems. (2001, July 4). *The New York Times*, p. A11.

Aboud, F. E., & Mendelson, M. J. (1998). Determinants of friendship selection and quality: Developmental perspectives. In W. M. Bukowski & A. F. Newcomb (Eds.), *The company they keep: Friendship in childhood and adolescence* (pp. 87–112). New York, NY: Cambridge University Press.

About the It Gets Better Project. (2013). Retrieved from http://www.itgetsbetter.org/pages/about-it-gets-better-project/

Acevedo, B. P., & Aron, A. (2009). Does a long-term relationship kill romantic love? *Review of General Psychology, 13*, 59–65.

Adamopoulos, J. (1991). The emergence of interpersonal behavior: Diachronic and cross-cultural processes in the evolution of intimacy. In S. Ting-Toomey & F. Korzenny (Eds.), *Cross-cultural interpersonal communication* (pp. 155–170). Newbury Park, CA: Sage.

Adams, G., Anderson, S. L., & Adonu, J. K. (2004). The cultural grounding of closeness and intimacy. In D. Mashek & A. Aron (Eds.), *The handbook of closeness and intimacy* (pp. 321–339). Mahwah, NJ: Erlbaum.

Adler, R. B., Elmhorst, J., & Lucas, K. (2013). *Communicating at work: Strategies for success in business and the professions* (11th ed.). New York: McGraw-Hill.

Afifi, T. D., Joseph, A., & Aldeis, D. (2012). The "standards for openness hypothesis": Why women find (conflict) avoidance more dissatisfying than men. *Journal of Social and Personal Relationships, 29*, 102–125.

Afifi, T. D., McManus, T., Steuber, K., & Coho, A. (2009). Verbal avoidance and dissatisfaction in intimate conflict situations. *Human Communication Research, 35*, 357–383.

Afifi, T. D., & Steuber, K. (2009). The Revelation Risk Model (RRM): Factors that predict the revelation of secrets and the strategies used to reveal them. *Communication Monographs, 76*, 144–176.

Afifi, W. A., & Caughlin, J. P. (2007). A close look at revealing secrets and some consequences that follow. *Communication Research, 33*, 467–488.

Afifi, W. A., & Johnson, M. L. (1999). The use and interpretation of tie signs in a public setting: Relationship and sex differences. *Journal of Social and Personal Relationships, 16*, 9–38.

Afifi, W. A., & Metts, S. (1998). Characteristics and consequences of expectation violations in close relationships. *Journal of Social and Personal Relationships, 15*, 365–392.

Agne, R., Thompson, T. L., & Cusella, L. P. (2000). Stigma in the line of face: Self-disclosure of patients' HIV status to health care providers. *Journal of Applied Communication Research, 28*, 235–261.

Agosta, S., Pezzoli, P., & Sartori, G. (2013). How to detect deception in everyday life and the reasons underlying it. *Applied Cognitive Psychology, 27*, 256–262.

Agthe, M., Sporrle, M., & Maner, J. K. (2011). Does being attractive always help? Positive and negative effects of attractiveness on social decision making. *Personality and Social Psychology Bulletin, 37*, 1042–1054.

Ahlstrom, M., Lundberg, N., Zabriskie, R., Eggett, D., & Lindsay, G. (2012). Me, my spouse, and my avatar: The relationship between marital satisfaction and playing massively multiplayer online role-playing games (MMORPG's). *Journal of Leisure Research, 44*, 1–22.

Akechi, H., Senju, A., Uibo, H., Kikuchi, Y., Hasegawa, T., & Hietanen, J. K. (2013). Attention to eye contact in the West and East: Autonomic responses and evaluative ratings. *PLoS ONE, 8*, e59312.

Alaimo, K., Olson, C. M., & Frongillo, E. A. (2001). Food insufficiency and American school-aged children's cognitive, academic, and psychosocial development. *Pediatrics, 108*, 44–53.

Albada, K. F., Knapp, M. L., & Theune, K. E. (2002). Interaction appearance theory: Changing perceptions of physical attractiveness through social interaction. *Communication Theory, 12*, 8–40.

Alberti, J. (2013). I love you, man: Bromances and the construction of masculinity, and the continuing evolution of the romantic comedy. *Quarterly Review of Film and Video, 30*, 159–172.

Alberti, R. E., & Emmons, M. L. (2008). *Your perfect right: Assertiveness and equality in your life and relationships* (9th ed.). San Luis Obispo, CA: Impact.

Alberts, J. K. (1988). An analysis of couples' conversational complaints. *Communication Monographs, 55*, 184–197.

Alberts, J. K. (1990). Perceived effectiveness of couples' conversational complaints. *Communication Studies, 40*, 280–291.

Alberts, J. K., & Driscoll, G. (1992). Containment versus escalation: The trajectory of couples' conversational complaints. *Western Journal of Communication, 56,* 394–412.

Alberts, J. K., Kellar-Guenther, U., & Corman, S. R. (1996). That's not funny: Understanding recipients' responses to teasing. *Western Journal of Communication, 60,* 337–357.

Alberts, J. K., Yoshimura, C. G., Rabby, M., & Loschiavo, R. (2005). Mapping the topography of couples' daily conversation. *Journal of Social and Personal Relationships, 22,* 299–322.

Aldeis, D., & Afifi, T. D. (2013). College students' willingness to reveal risky behaviors: The influence of relationship and message type. *Journal of Family Communication, 13,* 92–113.

Aleman, M. W. (2005). Embracing and resisting romantic fantasies as the rhetorical vision on a SeniorNet discussion board. *Journal of Communication, 55,* 5–21.

Alford, J. R., Hatemi, P. K., Hibbing, J. R., Martin, N. G., & Eaves, L. J. (2011). The politics of mate choice. *The Journal of Politics, 73,* 362–379.

Aliakbari, M., & Abdolahi, K. (2013). Does it matter what we wear? A sociolinguistic study of clothing and human values. *International Journal of Linguistics, 5*(2), 34–45.

Allen, B. 1995). "Diversity" and organizational communication. *Journal of Applied Communication Research, 23,* 143–155.

Allen, M. (1998). Methodological considerations when examining a gendered world. In D. J. Canary & K. Dindia (Eds.), *Handbook of sex differences and similarities in communication* (pp. 427–444). Mahwah, NJ: Erlbaum.

Alter, A. L., & Oppenheimer, D. M. (2009). Suppressing secrecy through metacognitive ease: Cognitive fluency encourages self-disclosure. *Psychological Science, 20,* 1414–1420.

Altman, I., & Taylor, D. A. (1973). *Social penetration: The development of interpersonal relationships.* New York, NY: Holt, Rinehart & Winston.

Alvesson, M. (2011). Organizational culture: Meaning, discourse, and identity. In N. M. Ashkanasy, C. P. M. Wilderom, & M. F. Peterson (Eds.), *The handbook of organizational culture and climate* (2nd ed., pp. 11–28). Los Angeles, CA: Sage.

Amarasinghe, A. (2012). Understanding intercultural facework behaviours. *Journal of International Communication, 18,* 175–188.

Ambady, N., LaPlante, D., Nguyen, T., Rosenthal, R., Chaumeton, N., & Levinson, W. (2002). Surgeons' tone of voice: A clue to malpractice history. *Surgery, 132,* 5–9.

Ambady, N., & Rosenthal, R. (1993). Half a minute: Predicting teacher evaluations from thin slices of nonverbal behavior and physical attractiveness. *Journal of Personality and Social Psychology, 64,* 431–441.

American Management Association. (2012). *Critical skills survey.*

Amichai-Hamburger, Y., Kingsbury, M., & Scheider, B. H. (2013). Friendship: An old concept with a new meaning? *Computers in Human Behavior, 29,* 33–39.

Amodio, D. M., & Showers, C. J. (2005). "Similarity breeds liking" revisited: The moderating role of commitment. *Journal of Social and Personal Relationships, 22,* 817–836.

Andersen, P. A. (1999). *Nonverbal communication: Forms and functions.* Palo Alto, CA: Mayfield.

Andersen, P. A., Guerrero, L. K., & Jones, S. M. (2006). Nonverbal behavior in intimate interactions and intimate relationships. In V. Manusov & M. L. Patterson (Eds.), *The Sage handbook of nonverbal communication* (pp. 259–278). Thousand Oaks, CA: Sage.

Andersen, P. A., Lustig, M. W., & Andersen, J. F. (1990). Changes in latitude, changes in attitude: The relationship between climate and interpersonal communication predispositions. *Communication Quarterly, 38,* 291–311.

Anderson, B., Fagan, P., Woodnutt, T., & Chamorro-Premuzic, T. (2012). Facebook psychology: Popular questions answered by research. *Psychology of Popular Media Culture, 1,* 23–37.

Anderson, J. (July 2, 2010). *The future of social relations.* Pew Internet & American Life Project.

Anderson, R. A., Corazzini, K. N., & McDaniel, R. R., Jr. (2004). Complexity science and the dynamics of climate and communication: Reducing nursing home turnover. *Gerontologist, 44,* 378–388.

Ang, S., Van Dyne, L., Koh, C., Ng, K., Templer, K. J., Tay, C., & Chandrasekar, N. (2007). Cultural intelligence: Its measurement and effects on cultural judgment and decision making, cultural adaptation and task performance. *Management and Organization Review, 3,* 335–371.

Antheunis, M. L., & Schouten, A. P. (2011). The effects of other-generated and system-generated cues on adolescents' perceived attractiveness on social network sites. *Journal of Computer-Mediated Communication, 16,* 391–406.

Antioch College. (2006). *The Antioch College sexual offense prevention policy.*

Antonuccio, D., & Jackson, R. (2009). The science of forgiveness. In W. O'Donohue & S. R. Graybar (Eds.), *Handbook of contemporary psychotherapy: Toward an improved understanding of effective psychotherapy* (pp. 269–284). Thousand Oaks, CA: Sage.

Arasaratnam, L. A. (2006). Further testing of a new model of intercultural communication competence. *Communication Research Reports, 23*, 93–99.

Arasaratnam, L. A. (2007). Research in intercultural communication competence: Past perspectives and future directions. *Journal of International Communication, 13*(2), 66–73.

Arasaratnam, L. A., & Banerjee, S. C. (2011). Sensation seeking and intercultural communication competence: A model test. *International Journal of Intercultural Relations, 35*, 226–233.

Archer, J. (2002). Sex differences in physically aggressive acts between heterosexual partners: A meta-analytic review. *Aggression and Violent Behavior, 7*, 313–351.

Argyle, M., & Henderson, M. (1984). The rules of friendship. *Journal of Social and Personal Relationships, 1*, 211–237.

Argyle, M., & Henderson, M. (1985). The rules of relationships. In S. Duck & D. Perlman (Eds.), *Understanding personal relationships: An interdisciplinary approach* (pp. 63–84). Beverly Hills, CA: Sage.

Armstrong, G. B., Boiarsky, G. A., & Mares, M. L. (1991). Background television and reading performance. *Communication Monographs, 58*, 235–253.

Aron, A., Lewandowski, G. W., Mashek, D., & Aron, E. N. (2013). The self-expansion model of motivation and cognition in close relationships. In J. A. Simpson & L. Campbell (Eds.), *The Oxford handbook of close relationships* (pp. 90–115). New York, NY: Oxford University Press.

Aronson, E. (2008). *The social animal* (10th ed.). New York, NY: Worth.

Aronsson, K., & Cekaite, A. (2011). Activity contracts and directives in everyday family politics. *Discourse & Society, 22*, 137–154.

Arriaga, X. B., Capezza, N. M., Goodfriend, W., Ray, E. S., & Sands, K. J. (2013). Individual well-being and relationship maintenance at odds: The unexpected perils of maintaining a relationship with an aggressive partner. *Social Psychological and Personality Science, 4*, 676–684.

Arriaga, X. B., Goodfriend, W., & Lohmann, A. (2004). Beyond the individual: Concomitants of closeness in the social and physical environment. In D. J. Mashek & A. P. Aron (Eds.), *Handbook of closeness and intimacy* (pp. 287–303). Mahwah, NJ: Erlbaum.

Arroyo, A. (2013). "I'm so fat!" The negative outcomes of fat talk. *Communication Currents, 7*, 1–2.

Arroyo, A., & Harwood, J. (2012). Exploring the causes and consequences of fat talk. *Journal of Applied Communication Research, 40*, 167–187.

Arsenault, A. (2007, May). *Too much information?: Gate-keeping and information dissemination in a networked world.* Paper presented at the annual meeting of the International Communication Association, San Francisco.

Asante, M. K. (2002). Language and agency in the transformation of American identity. In W. F. Eadie & P. E. Nelson (Eds.), *The changing conversation in America: Lectures from the Smithsonian* (pp. 77–89). Thousand Oaks, CA: Sage.

Atkin, C. K., Smith, S. W., Roberto, A. J., Fediuk, T., & Wagner, T. (2002). Correlates of verbally aggressive communication in adolescents. *Journal of Applied Communication Research, 30*, 251–268.

Aubrey, J. S., & Rill, L. (2013). Investigating relations between Facebook use and social capital among college undergraduates. *Communication Quarterly, 61*, 479–496.

Avramova, Y. R., Stapel, D. A., & Lerouge, D. (2010). Mood and context-dependence: Positive mood increases and negative mood decreases the effects of context on perception. *Journal of Personality and Social Psychology, 99*, 203–214.

Avtgis, T. A. (1999). The relationship between unwillingness to communicate and family communication patterns. *Communication Research Reports, 16*, 333–338.

Avtgis, T. A., & Rancer, A. S. (2008). The relationship between trait verbal aggressiveness and teacher burnout syndrome in K-12 teachers. *Communication Research Reports, 25*, 86–89.

Aylor, B. (2003). The impact of sex, gender, and cognitive complexity on the perceived importance of teacher communication skills. *Communication Studies, 54*, 496–509.

Aylor, B., & Dainton, M. (2004). Biological sex and psychological gender as predictors of routine and strategic relational maintenance. *Sex Roles, 50*, 689–697.

Ayres, J., & Crosby, S. (1995). Two studies concerning the predictive validity of the personal report of communication apprehension in employment interviews. *Communication Research Reports, 12*, 145–151.

Ayres, J., & Hopf, T. (1993). *Coping with speech anxiety.* Norwood, NJ: Ablex.

Bach, G. R., & Wyden, P. (1983). *The intimate enemy: How to fight fair in love and marriage.* New York, NY: Avon Books.

Bachman, G. F., & Guerrero, L. K. (2006). Forgiveness, apology, and communicative responses to hurtful events. *Communication Reports, 19*, 45–56.

Back, M. D., Schmukle, S. C., & Egloff, B. (2008). Becoming friends by chance. *Psychological Science, 19*, 439–440.

Baglan, T. (1993). Relationship between psychological sex-type and interpersonal perception. *Florida Communication Journal, 21*(2), 22–28.

Baile, W. F., & Costantini, A. (2013). Communicating with cancer patients and their families. In T. N. Wise, M. Biondi, & A. Costantini (Eds.), *Psycho-oncology* (pp. 57–90). Arlington, VA: American Psychiatric Publishing.

Bailey, R. W. (2003). Ideologies, attitudes, and perceptions. *American Speech, 88*, 115–142.

Bailey, T. A. (2010). Ageism and media discourse: Newspaper framing of middle age. *Florida Communication Journal, 38*, 43–56.

Baiocco, R., Laghi, F., Schneider, B. H., Dalessio, M., Amichai-Hamburger, Y., Coplan, . . . Flament., M. (2011). Daily patterns of communication and contact between Italian early adolescents and their friends. *Cyberpsychology, Behavior, and Social Networking, 14*, 467–471. doi: 10.1089/cyber.2010.0208

Baker, A. J. (2008). Down the rabbit hole: The role of place in the initiation and development of online relationships. In A. Barak (Ed.), *Psychological aspects of cyberspace: Theory, research, applications* (pp. 163–184). New York, NY: Cambridge University Press.

Baker, L. R., & Oswald, D. L. (2010). Shyness and online social networking services. *Journal of Social & Personal Relationships, 27*, 873–889.

Bakker, A. B. (2005). Flow among music teachers and their students: The crossover of peak experiences. *Journal of Vocational Behavior, 66*, 26–44.

Baldwin, M. W., & Keelan, J. P. R. (1999). Interpersonal expectations as a function of self-esteem and sex. *Journal of Social and Personal Relationships, 16*, 822–833.

Ball, H., Wanzer, M. B., & Servoss, T. J. (2013). Parent-child communication on Facebook: Family communication patterns and young adults' decisions to "friend" parents. *Communication Quarterly, 61*, 615–629.

Bannink, F. (2010). *Handbook of solution-focused conflict management*. Cambridge, MA: Hogrefe Publishing.

Barbato, C. A., Graham, E. E., & Perse, E. M. (2003). Communicating in the family: An examination of the relationship of family communication climate and interpersonal communication motives. *Journal of Family Communication, 3*, 123–148.

Barelds, D. P. H., Dijkstra, P., Koudenburg, N., & Swami, V. (2011). An assessment of positive illusions of the physical attractiveness of romantic partners. *Journal of Social and Personal Relationships, 28*, 706–719.

Barge, J., & Little, M. (2008). A discursive approach to skillful activity. *Communication Theory, 18*, 505–534.

Barker, L. L. (1971). *Listening behavior*. Englewood Cliffs, NJ: Prentice-Hall.

Barker, L. L., Edwards, R., Gaines, C., Gladney, K., & Holley, F. (1981). An investigation of proportional time spent in various communication activities by college students. *Journal of Applied Communication Research, 8*, 101–109.

Barner, D., Inagaki, S., & Li, P. (2009). Language, thought, and real nouns. *Cognition, 111*, 329–344.

Barnes, S. B. (2003). *Computer-mediated communication: Human-to-human communication across the Internet*. Boston: Allyn & Bacon.

Barrett, L. F., Gross, J., Christensen, T., & Benvenuto, M. (2001). Knowing what you're feeling and knowing what to do about it: Mapping the relation between emotion differentiation and emotion regulation. *Cognition and Emotion, 15*, 713–724.

Barrick, M. R., Bradley, B. H., Kristof-Brown, A. L., & Colbert, A. E. (2007). The moderating role of top management team interdependence: Implications for real teams and working groups. *Academy of Management Journal, 50*, 544–557.

Barry, D. (1990). *Dave Barry turns 40*. New York, NY: Fawcett Columbine.

Bartels, J., Pruyn, A., De Jong, M., & Joustra, I. (2008). Multiple organizational identification levels and the impact of perceived external prestige and communication climate. *Journal of Organizational Behavior, 28*, 173–190.

Barth, K. (2013, January 14). Dan Savage: It gets better. *Take Part*. Retrieved from http://www.takepart.com/video/dan-savage-it-gets-better

Bartlett, N. H., Patterson, H. M., VanderLaan, D. P., & Vasey, P. L. (2009). The relation between women's body esteem and friendships with gay men. *Body Image, 6*, 235–241.

Baruch, Y., & Jenkins, S. (2006). Swearing at work and permissive leadership culture: When anti-social becomes social and incivility is acceptable. *Leadership & Organization Development Journal, 28*, 492–507.

Bateman, P. J., Pike, J. C., & Butler, B. S. (2011). To disclose or not: Publicness in social networking sites. *Information Technology & People, 24*, 78–100.

Bateson, G., & Jackson, D. D. (1964). Some varieties of pathogenic organization. *Disorders of Communication* [Research Publications: Association for Research in Nervous and Mental Disease], *42*, 270–283.

Batson, C. D., Batson, J. G., Todd, R. M., Brummett, B. H., Shaw, L. L., & Aldeguer, C. M. R. (1995). Empathy and the collective good: Caring for one of the others in a social dilemma. *Journal of Personality and Social Psychology, 68*, 619–631.

Battaglia, D. M., Richard, F. D., Datteri, D. L., & Lord, C. G. (1998). Breaking up is (relatively) easy to do:

A script for the dissolution of close relationships. *Journal of Social and Personal Relationships, 15,* 829–845.

Bauerlein, M. (2009, September 4). Why Gen-Y Johnny can't read nonverbal cues. *Wall Street Journal.* Retrieved from http://online.wsj.com/article/SB10001 42405297020386320457434849348320175 8.html

Bauman, S. (2011). *Cyberbullying: What counselors need to know.* Alexandria, VA: American Counseling Association.

Bauman, S., Toomey, R. B., & Walker, J. L. (2013). Associations among bullying, cyberbullying, and suicide in high school students. *Journal of Adolescence, 36,* 341–350.

Baumeister, R. F. (2005). *The cultural animal: Human nature, meaning, and social life.* New York, NY: Oxford University Press.

Baumeister, R. F., Bratslavsky, E., Finkenauer, C., & Vohs, K. D. (2001). Bad is stronger than good. *Review of General Psychology, 5,* 323–370.

Baumeister, R. F., Campbell, J. D., Krueger, J. I., & Vohs, K. D. (2003). Does high self-esteem cause better performance, interpersonal success, happiness, or healthier lifestyles? *Psychological Science in the Public Interest, 4,* 1–44.

Bavelas, J. B., Black, A., Chovil, N., & Mullett, J. (1990). *Equivocal communication.* Newbury Park, CA: Sage.

Bavelas, J. B., Coates, L., & Johnson, T. (2002). Listener responses as a collaborative process: The role of gaze. *Journal of Communication, 52,* 566–580.

Baxter, L. A. (1987). Symbols of relationship identity in relationship culture. *Journal of Social and Personal Relationships, 4,* 261–280.

Baxter, L. A. (1992). Forms and functions of intimate play in personal relationships. *Human Communication Research, 18,* 336–363.

Baxter, L. A. (1994). A dialogic approach to relationship maintenance. In D. J. Canary & L. Stafford (Eds.), *Communication and relational maintenance* (pp. 233–254). San Diego, CA: Academic Press.

Baxter, L. A. (2011). *Voicing relationships: A dialogical perspective.* Thousand Oaks, CA: Sage.

Baxter, L. A., & Akkoor, C. (2011). Topic expansiveness and family communication patterns. *Journal of Family Communication, 11,* 1–20.

Baxter, L. A., & Braithwaite, D. O. (2006a). Family rituals. In L. H. Turner & R. West (Eds.), *The family communication sourcebook* (pp. 259–280). Thousand Oaks, CA: Sage.

Baxter, L. A., & Braithwaite, D. O. (2006b). Social dialectics: The contradictions of relating. In B. Whaley & W. Samter (Eds.), *Explaining communication: Contemporary communication theories and exemplars* (pp. 305–324). Mahwah, NJ: Erlbaum.

Baxter, L. A., & Braithwaite, D. O. (2008). Relational dialectics theory. In L. A. Baxter & D. O. Braithwaite (Eds.), *Engaging theories in interpersonal communication: Multiple perspectives* (pp. 349–361). Thousand Oaks, CA: Sage.

Baxter, L. A., Dun, T., & Sahlstein, E. (2001). Rules for relating communicated among social network members. *Journal of Social and Personal Relationships, 18,* 173–200.

Baxter, L. A., Henauw, C., Huisman, D., Livesay, C., Norwood, K., Hua, S., . . . Young, B. (2009). Lay conceptions of "family": A replication and extension. *Journal of Family Communication, 9,* 170–189.

Baxter, L. A., & Montgomery, B. M. (1996). *Relating: Dialogues and dialectics.* New York, NY: Guilford Press.

Baxter, L. A., & Pederson, J. R. (2013). Perceived and ideal family communication patterns and family satisfaction for parents and their college-aged children. *Journal of Family Communication, 13,* 132–149.

Baxter, L. A., & Pittman, G. (2001). Communicatively remembering turning points of relational development in heterosexual romantic relationships. *Communication Reports, 14,* 1–17.

Baxter, L. A., & Wilmot, W. W. (1985). Taboo topics in close relationships. *Journal of Social and Personal Relationships, 2,* 253–269.

Bazarova, N. N. (2012). Public intimacy: Disclosure interpretation and social judgments on Facebook. *Journal of Communication, 62,* 815–832.

Bazarova, N. N., Taft, J. G., Choi, Y. H., & Cosley, D. (2012). Managing impressions and relationships on Facebook: Self-presentational and relational concerns revealed through the analysis of language style. *Journal of Language and Social Psychology, 32,* 121–141.

Bazil, L. G. D. (1999). The effects of social behavior on fourth- and fifth-grade girls' perceptions of physically attractive and unattractive peers. *Dissertation Abstracts International: Section B. Sciences and Engineering, 59*(8-B), 4533.

Beatty, M. J., & McCroskey, J. C. (1997). It's in our nature: Verbal aggressiveness as temperamental expression. *Communication Quarterly, 45,* 446–460.

Beaulieu, C. M. (2004). Intercultural study of personal space: A case study. *Journal of Applied Social Psychology, 34,* 794–805.

Bechtoldt, M. N., De Dreu, C. K. W., Nijstad, B. A., & Zapf, D. (2010). Self-concept clarity and the management of social conflict. *Journal of Personality, 78,* 539–574.

Beck, C. E., & Beck, E. A. (1996). The manager's open door and the communication climate. In K. M.

Galvin & P. Cooper (Eds.), *Making connections: Readings in relational communication* (pp. 286–290). Los Angeles, CA: Roxbury.

Becker, J. A. H., Ellevold, B., & Stamp, G. H. (2008) The creation of defensiveness in social interaction II: A model of defensive communication among romantic couples. *Communication Monographs, 75*, 86–110.

Becker, J. B., Berkley, K. J., Geary, N., Hampson, E., Herman, J. P., & Young, E. (2007). *Sex differences in the brain: From genes to behavior.* New York, NY: Oxford University Press.

Beer, J. S., & Hughes, B. L. (2011). Self-enhancement: A social neuroscience perspective. In M. D. Alicke & C. Sedikides (Eds.), *Handbook of self-enhancement and self-protection* (pp. 49–65). New York, NY: Guilford Press.

Belkin, L. Y. (2008). Emotional contagion in the electronic communication context in organizations. *Dissertation Abstracts International: Section A. Humanities and Social Sciences, 68*(9-A), 3940.

Bell, R. A. (1991). Gender, friendship, network density, and loneliness. *Journal of Social Behavior and Personality, 6*, 45–56.

Bell, R. A., & Healey, J. G. (1992). Idiomatic communication and interpersonal solidarity in friends' relational cultures. *Human Communication Research, 18*, 307–335.

Bello, R., & Edwards, R. (2005). Interpretations of messages: The influence of various forms of equivocation, face concerns, and sex differences. *Journal of Language and Social Psychology, 24*, 160–181.

Bello, R. S., Brandau-Brown, F. E., Zhang, S., & Ragsdale, J. D. (2010). Verbal and nonverbal methods for expressing appreciation in friendships and romantic relationships: A cross-cultural comparison. *International Journal of Intercultural Relations, 34*, 294–302.

Ben-Ze'ev, A. (2003). Privacy, emotional closeness, and openness in cyberspace. *Computers in Human Behavior, 19*, 451–467.

Benenson, J. F., Gordon, A. J., & Roy, R. (2000). Children's evaluative appraisals of competition in tetrads versus dyads. *Small Group Research, 31*, 635–652.

Bennehum, D. S. (2005, July). Daemon seed: Old emails never die. *Wired.* Retrieved from http://www.wired.com/wired/archive/7.05/email_pr.html

Bennett, J. (2010, July 19). The beauty advantage: How looks affect your work, your career, your life. *Newsweek.* Retrieved from http://www.newsweek.com/2010/07/19/the-beauty-advantage.html

Berg, I. K., & DeJong, P. (2005). Engagement through complimenting. *Journal of Family Psychotherapy, 16*, 51–56.

Berger, C. R. (1979). Beyond initial interactions: Uncertainty, understanding, and the development of interpersonal relationships. In H. Giles & R. St. Clair (Eds.), *Language and social psychology* (pp. 122–144). Oxford, England: Blackwell.

Berger, C. R. (1987). Communicating under uncertainty. In M. Roloff & G. Miller (Eds.), *Interpersonal processes: New directions in communication research* (pp. 39–62). Newbury Park, CA: Sage.

Berger, C. R. (1988). Uncertainty and information exchange in developing relationships. In S. Duck & D. F. Hay (Eds.), *Handbook of personal relationships: Theory, research and interventions* (pp. 239–255). New York, NY: Wiley.

Berger, C. R. (2011). From explanation to application. *Journal of Applied Communication Research, 39*, 214–222.

Berger, C. R., & Kellermann, K. (1994). Acquiring social information. In J. M. Wiemann & J. A. Daly (Eds.), *Communicating strategically* (pp. 1–31). Hillsdale, NJ: Erlbaum.

Berger, C. R., & Lee, K. J. (2011). Second thoughts, second feelings: Attenuating the impact of threatening narratives through rational reappraisal. *Communication Research, 38*, 3–26.

Bergman, M. E., Watrous-Rodriguez, K. M., & Chalkley, K. M. (2008). Identity and language: Contributions to and consequences of speaking Spanish in the workplace. *Hispanic Journal of Behavioral Sciences, 30*, 40–68.

Bernstein, E. (2010, October 18). I'm very, very, very sorry . . . really? We apologize more to strangers than family, and why women ask for forgiveness more than men. *Wall Street Journal*, pp. D1, D2.

Berry, S. (2007). Personal report of intercultural communication apprehension. In R. A. Reynolds, R. Woods, & J. D. Baker (Eds.), *Handbook of research on electronic surveys and measurements* (pp. 364–366). Hershey, PA: Idea Group Reference/IGI Global.

Berscheid, E., Schneider, M., & Omoto, A. M. (1989). Issues in studying close relationships: Conceptualizing and measuring closeness. In C. Hendrick (Ed.), *Close relationships* (pp. 63–91). Newbury Park, CA: Sage.

Berscheid, E., & Walster, E. H. (1978). *Interpersonal attraction* (2nd ed.). Reading, MA: Addison-Wesley.

Betts, K. R., & Hinsz, V. B. (2013). Group marginalization: Extending research on interpersonal rejection to small groups. *Personality & Social Psychology Review, 17*, 355–370.

Bevan, J. L. (2008). Experiencing and communicating romantic jealousy: Questioning the investment model. *Southern Communication Journal, 73*, 42–67.

Bevan, J. L. (2011). The consequence model of partner jealousy expression: Elaboration and refinement. *Western Journal of Communication, 75,* 523–540.

Bharti, A. (1985). The self in Hindu thought and action. In A. J. Marsella, G. DeVos, & F. L. K. Hsu (Eds.), *Culture and self: Asian and Western perspectives* (pp. 185–230). New York, NY: Tavistock.

Bhasker, G. (2013). General Semantics and effective communication. *ETC: A Review of General Semantics, 70,* 123–129.

Bippus, A. M. (2001). Recipients' criteria for evaluating the skillfulness of comforting communication and the outcomes of comforting interactions. *Communication Monographs, 68,* 301–313.

Bippus, A. M., & Young, S. L. (2005). Owning your emotions: Reactions to expressions of self- versus other-attributed positive and negative emotions. *Journal of Applied Communication Research, 33,* 26–45.

Birdwhistell, R. L. (1970). *Kinesics and context.* Philadelphia: University of Pennsylvania Press.

Bishop, S. C., Hill, P. S., & Yang, L. (2012). Use of aggressive humor: Aggressive humor style, verbal aggressiveness and social dominance orientation. *Ohio Communication Journal, 50,* 73–82.

Bisson, M. A., & Levine, T. R. (2009). Negotiating a friends with benefits relationship. *Archives of Sexual Behavior, 38,* 66–73.

Bjørge, A. K. (2007). Power distance in English lingua franca email communication. *International Journal of Applied Linguistics, 17,* 60–80.

Bjorklund, D. F., Cassel, W. S., Bjorklund, B. R., Brown, R. D., Park, C. L., & Ernst, K. (2000). Social demand characteristics in children's and adults' eyewitness memory and suggestibility: The effect of different interviewers on free recall and recognition. *Applied Cognitive Psychology, 14,* 421–433.

Blacker, L. (1999). The launching phase of the life cycle. In B. Carter & M. McGoldrick (Eds.), *The expanded family life cycle: Individual, family, and social perspectives* (3rd ed., pp. 287–306). Boston, MA: Allyn & Bacon.

Blank, P. D. (Ed.). (1993). *Interpersonal expectations: Theory, research, and applications.* Cambridge, England: Cambridge University Press.

Bleske-Rechek, A., Somers, E., Micke, C., Erickson, L., Matteson, L., Stocco, C., . . . Ritchie, L. (2012). Benefit or burden? Attraction in cross-sex friendship. *Journal of Social and Personal Relationships, 29,* 569–596.

Bloch, A. S., & Weger, H. W., Jr. (2012, May). *Associations among friendship satisfaction, self-verification, self-enhancement, and friends' communication skill.* Paper presented at the annual meeting of the International Communication Association, Phoenix, AZ.

Boase, J., Horrigan, J. B., Wellman, B., & Rainie, L. (2006). The strength of Internet ties. *Pew Internet & American Life Project.*

Bodie, G. D., St. Cyr, K., Pence, M., Rold, M., & Honeycutt, J. (2012). Listening competence in initial interactions I: Distinguishing between what listening is and what listeners do. *International Journal of Listening, 26,* 1–28.

Bodie, G. D., Worthington, D. L., & Gearhart, C. C. (2013). The Listening Styles Profile-Revised (LSP-R): A scale revision and evidence for validity. *Communication Quarterly, 61,* 72–90.

Bohns, V. K., & Wiltermuth, S. S. (2012). It hurts when I do this (or you do that): Posture and pain tolerance. *Journal of Experimental Social Psychology, 48,* 341–345.

Bok, S. (1999). *Lying: Moral choice in public and private life* (2nd ed.). New York, NY: Vintage.

Bolkan, S., & Holmgren, J. L. (2012). "You are such a great teacher and I hate to bother you but . . .": Instructors' perceptions of students and their use of email messages with varying politeness strategies. *Communication Education, 61,* 253–270.

Bonam, C. M., & Shih, M. (2009). Exploring multiracial individual's comfort with intimate interracial relationships. *Journal of Social Issues, 65,* 87–103.

Bond, B. J. (2009). He posted, she posted: Gender differences in self-disclosure on social network sites. *Rocky Mountain Communicator, 6*(2), 29–37.

Bone, J. E., Griffin, C. L., & Scholz, T.M.L. (2008). Beyond traditional conceptualizations of rhetoric: Invitational rhetoric and a move toward civility. *Western Journal of Communication, 72,* 434–462.

Booth-Butterfield, M., & Booth-Butterfield, S. (1998). Emotionality and affective orientation. In J. C. McCroskey, J. A. Daly, M. M. Martin, & M. J. Beatty (Eds.), *Communication and personality: Trait perspectives* (pp. 171–190). Cresskill, NJ: Hampton.

Boroditsky, L. (2009). How does our language shape the way we think? In M. Brockman (Ed.), *What's next?: Dispatches on the future of science* (pp. 116–129). New York, NY: Vintage.

Bosacki, S. L. (2013). A longitudinal study of children's theory of mind, self-concept, and perceptions of humor in self and other. *Social Behavior and Personality, 41,* 663–673.

Boss, P., & Carnes, D. (2012). The myth of closure. *Family Process, 51,* 456–469.

Bosson, J. K., Johnson, A. B., Niederhoffer, K., & Swann, W. B., Jr. (2006). Interpersonal chemistry through negativity: Bonding by sharing negative attitudes about others. *Personal Relationships, 13,* 135–150.

Bostrom, R. N. (1996). Aspects of listening behavior. In O. Hargie (Ed.), *Handbook of communication skills* (2nd ed., pp. 236–259). London, England: Routledge.

Bowers, J. S., & Pleydell-Pearce, C. W. (2011). Swearing, euphemisms, and linguistic relativity. *PLoS ONE, 6,* e22341.

Bowes, A., & Katz, A. (2011). When sarcasm stings. *Discourse Processes, 48,* 215–236.

Bradac, J. J., & Street, R. L. (1990). Powerful and powerless styles of talk: A theoretical analysis of language and impression formation. *Research on Language and Social Interaction, 23,* 195–242.

Bradbury, T. N., & Fincham, F. D. (1990). Attributions in marriage: Review and critique. *Psychological Bulletin, 107,* 3–33.

Braithwaite, D. O., Baxter, L. A., & Harper, A. M. (1998). The role of rituals in the management of the dialectical tension of "old" and "new" in blended families. *Communication Studies, 49,* 101–120.

Braithwaite, D. O., & Eckstein, N. (2003). Reconceptualizing supportive interactions: How persons with disabilities communicatively manage assistance. *Journal of Applied Communication Research, 31,* 1–26.

Brand, R., Bonatsos, A., D'Orazio, R., & DeShong, H. (2012) What is beautiful is good, even online: Correlations between photo attractiveness and text attractiveness in men's online dating profiles. *Computers in Human Behavior, 28,* 166–170.

Brandau-Brown, F. E., & Ragsdale, J. D. (2008). Personal, moral, and structural commitment and the repair of marital relationships. *Southern Communication Journal, 73,* 68–83.

Brandt, A. (2013). *8 keys to eliminating passive-aggressiveness.* New York, NY: W. W. Norton.

Brantley, A., Knox, D., & Zusman, M. E. (2002). When and why gender differences in saying "I love you" among college students. *College Student Journal, 36,* 614–615.

Breithaupt, F. (2011). How is it possible to have empathy? Four models. In P. Leverage, H. Mancing, R. Schweickert, & J. M. William (Eds.) *Theory of mind and literature* (pp. 273–288). West Lafayette, IN: Purdue University Press.

Brenner, J., & Smith, A. (August 5, 2013). *72% of online adults are social networking site users.* Pew Internet & American Life Project.

Brescoll, V. L., & Uhlmann, E. L. (2008). Can an angry woman get ahead? Status conferral, gender, and expression of emotion in the workplace. *Psychological Science, 19,* 268–275.

Bridge, M. C., & Schrodt, P. (2013). Privacy orientations as a function of family communication patterns. *Communication Reports, 26,* 1–12.

Brightman, V., Segal, A., Werther, P., & Steiner, J. (1975). Ethological study of facial expression in response to taste stimuli. *Journal of Dental Research, 54,* 141.

Briles, J. (1999), *Woman to woman 2000: Becoming sabotage savvy in the new millennium.* Far Hills, NJ: New Horizon Press.

Brody, L. R., & Hall, J. A. (2008). Gender and emotion in context. In M. Lewis, J. M. Haviland-Jones, & L. F. Barrett (Eds.), *Handbook of emotions* (3rd ed., pp. 395–408). New York, NY: Guilford.

Brody, N. (2013). Absence—and mediated communication—makes the heart grow fonder: Clarifying the predictors of satisfaction and commitment in long-distance friendships. *Communication Research Reports, 30,* 323–332.

Bromberg, J. B. (2012). Uses of conversational narrative: Exchanging personal experience in everyday life. *Narrative Inquiry, 22,* 165–172.

Brooks, A. W. (2013). Get excited: Reappraising pre-performance anxiety as excitement. *Journal of Experimental Psychology: General, 143,* 1144–1158.

Brown, B. B., Werner, C. M., & Altman, I. (2006). Relationships in home and community environments: A transactional and dialectic analysis. In A. L. Vangelisti & D. Perlman (Eds.), *The Cambridge handbook of personal relationships* (pp. 673–693). New York, NY: Cambridge University Press.

Brown, L. (1982). *Communicating facts and ideas in business.* Englewood Cliffs, NJ: Prentice-Hall.

Brown, R. F., Bylund, C. L., Gueguen, J. A., Diamond, C., Eddington, J., & Kissane, D. (2010). Developing patient-centered communication skills training for oncologists: Describing the content and efficacy of training. *Communication Education, 59,* 235–248.

Brownell, J. (1990). Perceptions of effective listeners: A management study. *Journal of Business Communication, 27,* 401–415.

Brownell, J., & Wolvin, A. (2010). *What every student should know about listening.* Upper Saddle River, NJ: Pearson.

Bruce, S. M, Mann, A., Jones, C., & Gavin, M. (2007). Gestures expressed by children who are congenitally deaf-blind: Topography, rate, and function. *Journal of Visual Impairment & Blindness, 101,* 637–652.

Brumark, Å. (2010). Behaviour regulation at the family dinner table. The use of and response to direct and indirect behaviour regulation in ten Swedish families. *Journal of Child Language, 37,* 1065–1088.

Brunet, P. M., & Schmidt, L. A. (2010). Sex differences in the expression and use of computer-mediated affective language: Does context matter? *Social Science Computer Review, 28,* 194–205.

Bryant, E. M., & Marmo, J. (2012). The rules of Facebook friendship: A two-stage examination of interaction rules in close, casual, and acquaintance friendships. *Journal of Social and Personal Relationships, 29,* 1013–1035.

Buck, R., & VanLear, C. A. (2002). Verbal and nonverbal communication: Distinguishing symbolic, spontaneous and pseudo-spontaneous nonverbal behavior. *Journal of Communication, 52,* 522–541.

Bukowski, W. M., Motzoi, C. C., & Meyer, F. (2009). Friendship as process, function, and outcome. In K. H. Rubin, W. M. Bukowski, & B. Laursen (Eds.), *Handbook of peer interactions, relationships, and groups* (pp. 217–231). New York, NY: Guilford Press.

Bukowski, W., Newcomb, A., & Hartup, W. (1996). *The company they keep: Friendship in childhood and adolescence.* Cambridge, England: Cambridge University Press.

Buller, D. B., & Burgoon, J. K. (1994). Deception: Strategic and nonstrategic communication. In J. A. Daly & J. M. Wiemann (Eds.), *Strategic interpersonal communication* (pp. 191–223). Hillsdale, NJ: Erlbaum.

Burggraf, C. S., & Sillars, A. L. (1987). A critical examination of sex differences in marital communication. *Communication Monographs, 54,* 276–294.

Burgoon, J. K., & Bacue, A. E. (2003). Nonverbal communication skills. In B. Burleson & J. O. Greene (Eds.), *Handbook of communication and social interaction skills* (pp. 179–219). Mahwah, NJ: Erlbaum.

Burgoon, J. K., Berger, C. R., & Waldron, V. R. (2000). Mindfulness and interpersonal communication. *Journal of Social Issues, 56,* 105–127.

Burgoon, J. K., Birk, T., & Pfau, M. (1990). Nonverbal behaviors, persuasion, and credibility. *Human Communication Research, 17,* 140–169.

Burgoon, J. K., & Burgoon, M. (2001). Expectancy theories. In W. P. Robinson & H. Giles (Eds.), *The new handbook of language and social psychology* (pp. 79–102). Sussex, England: Wiley.

Burgoon, J. K., & Le Poire, B. A. (1999). Nonverbal cues and interpersonal judgments: Participant and observer perceptions of intimacy, dominance, and composure. *Communication Monographs, 66,* 105–124.

Burgoon, J. K., & Levine, T. R. (2010). Advances in deception detection. In S. W. Smith & S. R. Wilson (Eds.), *New directions in interpersonal communication research* (pp. 201–220). Thousand Oaks, CA: Sage.

Burk, W. J., Denissen, J., Van Doorn, M. D., Branje, S. J. T., & Laursen, B. (2009). The vicissitudes of conflict measurement: Stability and reliability in the frequency of disagreements. *European Psychologist, 14,* 153–159.

Burleson, B. R. (1984). Comforting communication. In H. Sypher & J. Applegate (Eds.), *Communication by children and adults: Social cognitive and strategic processes* (pp. 63–104). Beverly Hills, CA: Sage.

Burleson, B. R. (2003). Emotional support skill. In J. O. Greene & B. R. Burleson (Eds.), *Handbook of communication and social interaction skills* (pp. 551–594). Mahwah, NJ: Erlbaum.

Burleson, B. R. (2007). Constructivism: A general theory of communication skill. In B. B. Whaley & W. Samter (Eds.), *Explaining communication: Contemporary theories and exemplars* (pp. 105–128). Mahwah, NJ: Erlbaum.

Burleson, B. R. (2008). What counts as effective emotional support? In M. T. Motley (Ed.), *Studies in applied interpersonal communication* (pp. 207–227). Thousand Oaks, CA: Sage.

Burleson, B. R. (2011). A constructivist approach to listening. *International Journal of Listening, 25,* 27–46.

Burleson, B. R., Hanasono, L., Bodie, G., Holmstrom, A., McCullough, J., Rack, J., & Rosier, J. (2011). Are gender differences in responses to supportive communication a matter of ability, motivation, or both? Reading patterns of situation effects through the lens of a dual-process theory. *Communication Quarterly, 59,* 37–60.

Burleson, B. R., Hanasono, L., Bodie, G., Holmstrom, A., Rack, J., Rosier, J., & McCullough, J. (2009). Explaining gender differences in responses to supportive messages: Two tests of a dual-process approach. *Sex Roles, 61,* 265–280.

Burleson, B. R., Holmstrom, A. J., & Gilstrap, C. M. (2005). "Guys can't say that to guys": Four experiments assessing the normative motivation account for deficiencies in the emotional support provided by men. *Communication Monographs, 72,* 468–501.

Burleson, B. R., & Samter, W. (1985). Individual differences in the perception of comforting messages: An exploratory investigation. *Central States Speech Journal, 36,* 39–50.

Burleson, B. R., & Samter, W. (1994). A social skills approach to relationship maintenance. In D. J. Canary & L. Stafford (Eds.), *Communication and relationship maintenance: How individual differences in communication skills affect the achievement of relationship functions* (pp. 61–90). San Diego, CA: Academic Press.

Burnard, P. (2003). Ordinary chat and therapeutic conversation: Phatic communication and mental health nursing. *Journal of Psychiatric and Mental Health Nursing, 10,* 678–682.

Burns, K. L., & Beier, E. G. (1973). Significance of vocal and visual channels for the decoding of emotional meaning. *Journal of Communication, 23,* 118–130.

Burton, C. M., & King, L. A. (2008). Effects of (very) brief writing on health: The two-minute miracle. *British Journal of Health Psychology, 13,* 9–14.

Bushman, B. J. (1988). The effects of apparel on compliance: A field experiment with a female authority figure. *Personality and Social Psychology Bulletin, 14,* 459–467.

Bushman, B. J., Baumeister, R. F., & Stack, A. D. (1999). Catharsis, aggression, and persuasive influence: Self-fulfilling or self-defeating prophecies? *Journal of Personality and Social Psychology, 76,* 367–376.

Bushman, B. J., Bonacci, A. M., Pedersen, W. C., Vasquez, E. A., & Miller, N. (2005). Chewing on it can chew you up: Effects of rumination on triggered displaced aggression. *Journal of Personality and Social Psychology, 88,* 969–983.

Buunk, A. P. (2005). How do people respond to others with high commitment or autonomy in their relationships? *Journal of Social and Personal Relationships, 22,* 653–672.

Buzzanell, P. M. (1999). Tensions and burdens in employment interviewing processes: Perspectives of non-dominant group members. *Journal of Business Communication, 36,* 143–162.

Byers, E. S. (2011). Beyond the birds and the bees and was it good for you?: Thirty years of research on sexual communication. *Canadian Psychology, 52,* 20–28.

Byron, K. (2008). Carrying too heavy a load? The communication and miscommunication of emotion by email. *Academy of Management Review, 33,* 309–327.

Cacioppo, J. T., Cacioppo, S., Gonzaga, G. C., Ogburn, E. L., & VanderWeele, T. J. (2013). Marital satisfaction and break-ups differ across on-line and off-line meeting venues. *PNAS, 110,* 10135–10140.

Cai, D. A., & Fink, E. L. (2002). Conflict style differences between individualists and collectivists. *Communication Monographs, 69,* 67–87.

Cain, D. J. (2014). Person-centered therapy process. In G. R. VandenBos, E. Meidenbauer, & J. Frank-McNeil (Eds.), *Psychotherapy theories and techniques: A reader* (pp. 261–269). Washington, DC: American Psychological Association.

Caldwell-Harris, C. L., Tong, J., Lung, W., & Poo, S. (2011). Physiological reactivity to emotional phrases in Mandarin-English bilinguals. *International Journal of Bilingualism, 15,* 329–352.

Calkins, S. D., & Mackler, J. S. (2011). Temperament, emotion regulation, and social development. In M. K. Underwood & L. H. Rosen (Eds.), *Social development: Relationships in infancy, childhood, and adolescence* (pp. 44–70). New York, NY: Guilford Press.

Canary, D. (2003). Managing interpersonal conflict: A model of events related to strategic choices. In J. O. Greene & B. R. Burleson (Eds.), *Handbook of communication and social interaction skills* (pp. 515–549). Mahwah, NJ: Erlbaum.

Canary, D. J., & Hause, K. (1993). Is there any reason to research sex differences in communication? *Communication Quarterly, 41,* 482–517.

Canary, D. J., & Wahba, J. (2006). Do women work harder than men at maintaining relationships? In K. Dindia & D. J. Canary (Eds.), *Sex differences and similarities in communication* (2nd ed., pp.359-377). Mahwah, NJ: Erlbaum.

Canli, T., Desmond, J. E., Zhao, Z., & Gabrieli, J. D. E. (2002). Sex differences in the neural basis of emotional memories. *Proceedings of the National Academy of Sciences, 10,* 10789–10794.

Cao, X. (2013). The effects of facial close-ups and viewers' sex on empathy and intentions to help people in need. *Mass Communication & Society, 16,* 161–178.

Caplan, S. E. (2003). Preference for online social interaction: A theory of problematic internet use and psychosocial well-being. *Communication Research, 30,* 625–648.

Cargile, A., & Bolkan, S. (2013). Mitigating inter- and intra-group ethnocentrism: Comparing the effects of culture knowledge, exposure, and uncertainty intolerance. *International Journal of Intercultural Relations, 37,* 345–353.

Carmeli, A., Yitzhak-Halevy, M., Weisberg, J. (2009). The relationship between emotional intelligence and psychological wellbeing. *Journal of Managerial Psychology, 24,* 66–78.

Carney, D. R., Cuddy, A. J., & Yap, A. J. (2010). Power posing: Brief nonverbal displays affect neuroendocrine levels and risk tolerance. *Psychological Science, 21,* 1363–1368.

Carofiglio, V., de Rosis, F., & Grassano, R. (2008). Dynamic models of multiple emotion activation. In L. Cañamero & R. Aylett (Eds.), *Animating expressive characters for social interaction* (pp. 123–141). Amsterdam, Netherlands: John Benjamins.

Caron, A. H., Hwang, J. M., & Brummans, B. (2013). Business writing on the go: How executives manage impressions through e-mail communication in everyday work life. *Corporate Communications: An International Journal, 18,* 8–25.

Carr, C. T., & Stefaniak, C. (2012). Sent from my iPhone: The medium and message as cues of sender professionalism in mobile telephony. *Journal of Applied Communication Research, 40,* 403–424.

Carré, A., Stefaniak, N., D'Ambrosio, F., Bensalah, L., & Besche-Richard, C. (2013). The Basic Empathy Scale in Adults (BES-A): Factor structure of a revised form. *Psychological Assessment, 25,* 679–691.

Carrell, L. J., & Willmington, S. C. (1996). A comparison of self-report and performance data in assessing speaking and listening competence. *Communication Reports, 9,* 185–191.

Carrera, P., Oceja, L., Caballero, A., Muñoz, D., López-Pérez, B., & Ambrona, T. (2013). I feel so sorry! Tapping the joint influence of empathy and personal distress on helping behavior. *Motivation and Emotion, 37*, 335–345.

Carroll, S., Hill, E., Yorgason, J. B., Larson, J. H., & Sandberg, J. G. (2013). Couple communication as a mediator between work–family conflict and marital satisfaction. *Contemporary Family Therapy: An International Journal, 35*, 530–545.

Carson, C. L., & Cupach, W. R. (2000). Fueling the flames of the green-eyed monster: The role of ruminative thought in reaction to romantic jealousy. *Western Journal of Communication, 64*, 308–329.

Casey, J. E. (2012). A model to guide the conceptualization, assessment, and diagnosis of nonverbal learning disorder. *Canadian Journal of School Psychology, 27*, 35–57.

Cassels, T. G., Chan, S., Chung, W., & Birch, S. J. (2010). The role of culture in affective empathy: Cultural and bicultural differences. *Journal of Cognition and Culture, 10*, 309–326.

Cassidy, W., Faucher, C., & Jackson, M. (2013). Cyberbullying among youth: A comprehensive review of current international research and its implications and application to policy and practice. *School Psychology International, 34*, 575–612.

Castelan-Cargile, A., & Bradac, J. J. (2001). Attitudes towards language: A review of speaker-evaluation research and a general process model. In W. B. Gudykunst (Ed.), *Communication yearbook 25* (pp. 347–382). Thousand Oaks, CA: Sage.

Castro, D. R., Cohen, A., Tohar, G., & Kluger, A. N. (2013). The role of active listening in teacher-parent relations and the moderating role of attachment style. *International Journal of Listening, 27*, 136–145.

"Catfish" stars Nev Schulman, Max Joseph's advice for online dating. (2012, November 30). Retrieved from abcnews.go.com/blogs/lifestyle/2012/11/catfish-star-nev-schulmans-advice-for-online-dating.

Caughlin, J. P., & Arr, T. D. (2004). When is topic avoidance unsatisfying? Examining moderators of the association between avoidance and dissatisfaction. *Human Communication Research, 30*, 479–513.

Caughlin, J. P., & Huston, T. L. (2002). A contextual analysis of the association between demand/withdraw and marital satisfaction. *Personal Relationships, 9*, 95–119.

Caughlin, J. P., & Petronio, S. (2004). Privacy in families. In A. L. Vangelisti (Ed.), *Handbook of family communication* (pp. 379–412). Mahwah, NJ: Erlbaum.

Caughlin, J. P., & Vangelisti, A. L. (2006). Conflict in dating and marital relationships. In J. G. Oetzel & S. Ting-Toomey (Eds.), *The Sage handbook of conflict communication* (pp. 129–158). Thousand Oaks, CA: Sage.

Caughron, J. J., Antes, A. L., Stenmark, C. K., Thiel, C. E., Wang, X., & Mumford, M. D. (2013). Competition and sensemaking in ethical situations. *Journal of Applied Social Psychology, 43*, 1491–1507.

Cesario, J., & Higgins, E. T. (2008). Making message recipients "feel right": How nonverbal cues can increase persuasion. *Psychological Science, 19*, 415–420.

Ceylan, C., Dul, J., & Aytac, S. (2008). Can the office environment stimulate a manager's creativity? *Human Factors and Ergonomics in Manufacturing, 18*, 589–602.

Chan, Y. K. (1999). Density, crowding, and factors intervening in their relationship: Evidence from a hyperdense metropolis. *Social Indicators Research, 48*, 103–124.

Chang, C., Chang, C., Zheng, J., & Chung, P. (2013). Physiological emotion analysis using support vector regression. *Neurocomputing: An International Journal, 122*, 79–87.

Chang, L. C.-N. (2011). My culture shock experience. *ETC: A Review of General Semantics, 68*, 403–405.

Chao, M., & Wang, S. (2013). The confirmation of the connotation of same-sex friendship quality and analysis of the gender differences among university students. *Bulletin of Educational Psychology, 44*, 829–852.

Chapman, G. (2010). *The 5 love languages*. Chicago, IL: Northfield.

Cherniss, G., Extein, M., Goleman, D., & Weissberg, R. P. (2006). Emotional Intelligence: What does the research really indicate? *Educational Psychologist, 41*, 239–245.

Child, J. T., & Westermann, D. A. (2013). Let's be Facebook friends: Exploring parental Facebook friend requests from a Communication Privacy Management (CPM) perspective. *Journal of Family Communication, 13*, 46–59.

Cho, A., & Lee, J. (2013). Body dissatisfaction levels and gender differences in attentional biases toward idealized bodies. *Body Image, 10*, 95–102.

Cho, H. G., & Edge, N. (2012). "They are happier and having better lives than I am": The impact of using Facebook on perceptions of others' lives. *Cyberpsychology, Behavior, & Social Networking, 15*, 117–121.

Choi, N., Fuqua, D. R., & Newman, J. L. (2009). Exploratory and confirmatory studies of the structure of the Bem Sex Role Inventory short form with two divergent samples. *Educational and Psychological Measurement, 69*, 696–705.

Chovil, N. (1991). Social determinants of facial displays. *Journal of Nonverbal Behavior, 15*, 141–154.

Christenfeld, N., & Larsen, B. (2008). The name game. *The Psychologist, 21,* 210–213.

Christian, A. (2005). Contesting the myth of the "wicked stepmother": Narrative analysis of an online stepfamily support group. *Western Journal of Communication, 69,* 27–48.

Christofides, E., Muise, A., & Desmarais, S. (2012). Hey mom, what's on your Facebook? Comparing Facebook disclosure and privacy in adolescents and adults. *Social Psychological and Personality Sciences, 3,* 48–54.

Church, A., Alvarez, J. M., Katigbak, M. S., Mastor, K. A., Cabrera, H. F., Tanaka-Matsumi, J., . . . Buchanan, A. L. (2012). Self-concept consistency and short-term stability in eight cultures. *Journal of Research in Personality, 46,* 556–570.

Cissna, K. N., & Sieburg, E. (2006). Patterns of interactional confirmation and disconfirmation. In J. Stewart (Ed.), *Bridges not walls* (9th ed., pp. 429–439). Boston, MA: McGraw-Hill.

Clark, A. (2000). *A theory of sentience.* New York, NY: Oxford University Press.

Clark, R. A., & Delia, J. G. (1997). Individuals' preferences for friends' approaches to providing support in distressing situations. *Communication Reports, 10,* 115–121.

Clark, R. A., Pierce, A. J., Finn, K., Hsu, K., Toosley, A., & Williams, L. (1998). The impact of alternative approaches to comforting, closeness of relationship, and gender on multiple measures of effectiveness. *Communication Studies, 49,* 224–239.

Clayton, R. B., Nagumey, A., & Smith, J. R. (2013). Cheating, breakup, and divorce: Is Facebook to blame? *CyberPsychology, Behavior & Social Networking, 16,* 717–720.

Clements, K., Holtzworth-Munroe, A., Schweinle, W., & Ickes, W. (2007). Empathic accuracy of intimate partners in violent versus nonviolent relationships. *Personal Relationships, 14,* 369–388.

Coates, J. (1986). *Women, men and language.* London, England: Longman.

Cohen, A. (2007). One nation, many cultures: A cross-cultural study of the relationship between personal cultural values and commitment in the workplace to in-role performance and organizational citizenship behavior. *Cross-Cultural Research: The Journal of Comparative Social Science, 41,* 273–300.

Cohen, E. D. (2007). *The new rational therapy: Thinking your way to serenity, success, and profound happiness.* Lanham, MD: Rowman & Littlefield.

Cohen, E. L. (2010). Expectancy violations in relationships with friends and media figures. *Communication Research Reports, 27,* 97–111.

Cohen, M., & Avanzino, S. (2010). We are people first: Framing organizational assimilation experiences of the physically disabled using co-cultural theory. *Communication Studies, 61,* 272–303.

Cole, J., & Spalding, H. (2009). *The invisible smile: Living without facial expression.* New York, NY: Oxford University Press.

Cole, S. W., Hawkley, L. C., Arevalo, J. M., Sung, C. Y., Rose, R. M., & Cacioppo, J. T. (2007). Social regulation of gene expression in human leukocytes. *Genome Biology, 8,* 189–201.

Collier, M. J. (1991). Conflict competence within African, Mexican, and Anglo American friendships. In S. Ting-Toomey & F. Korzenny (Eds.), *Cross-cultural interpersonal communication* (pp. 132–154). Newbury Park, CA: Sage.

Conlan, S. K. (2008). Romantic relationship termination. *Dissertation Abstracts International: Section B. The Sciences and Engineering, 68*(7-B), 4884.

Conlee, C., Olvera, J., & Vagim, N. (1993). The relationships among physician nonverbal immediacy and measures of patient satisfaction with physician care. *Communication Reports, 6,* 25–33.

Connell, C. (2012). Dangerous disclosures. *Sexuality Research & Social Policy: A Journal of the NSRC, 9,* 168–177.

Consedine, N. S., Magai, C., & Bonanno, G. A. (2002). Moderators of the emotion inhibition–health relationship: A review and research agenda. *Review of General Psychology, 6,* 204–228.

Cook, V., & Bassetti, B. (Eds.). (2011). *Language and bilingual cognition.* New York, NY: Psychology Press.

Coon, D. (2009). *Psychology: A modular approach to mind and behavior* (11th ed.). Boston, MA: Cengage.

Cotten, S. R., Anderson, W. A., & McCullough, B. M. (2013). Impact of internet use on loneliness and contact with others among older adults: Cross-sectional analysis. *Journal of Medical Internet Research, 15,* e39.

Cotton, J. L., O'Neill, B. S., & Griffin, A. (2008). The "name game": Affective and hiring reactions to first names. *Journal of Managerial Psychology, 23,* 18–39.

Cowan, G., & Mills, R. D. (2004). Personal inadequacy and intimacy predictors of men's hostility toward women. *Sex Roles, 51,* 67–78.

Cowan, N., & AuBuchon, A. M. (2008). Short-term memory loss over time without retroactive stimulus interference. *Psychonomic Bulletin & Review, 15,* 230–235.

Cox, S. A. (1999). Group communication and employee turnover: How coworkers encourage peers to voluntarily exit. *Southern Communication Journal, 64,* 181–192.

Coyne, S. M., Padilla-Walker, L. M., Day, R. D., Harper, J., & Stockdale, L. (2014). A friend request from dear old dad: Associations between parent-child social networking and adolescent outcomes. *Cyberpsychology, Behavior, and Social Networking, 17,* 8–13.

Coyne, S. M., Stockdale, L., Busby, D., Iverson, B., & Grant, D. M. (2011). "I luv u ☺!": A descriptive study of the media use of individuals in romantic relationships. *Family Relationships, 60,* 150–162.

Cozby, P. C. (1973). Self-disclosure: A literature review. *Psychological Bulletin, 79,* 73–91.

Craig, E., & Wright, B. (2012). Computer-mediated relational development and maintenance in Facebook. *Communication Research Reports, 29,* 119–129.

Craig, R. (2009, May). *Beyond the conduit metaphor: Multiple vocabularies in the rhetoric of communication.* Paper presented at the meeting of the International Communication Association, Chicago, IL.

Craig, R. T. (2005). How we talk about how we talk: Communication theory in the public interest. *Journal of Communication, 55,* 659–667.

Crane, D. R. (1987). Diagnosing relationships with spatial distance: An empirical test of a clinical principle. *Journal of Marital and Family Therapy, 13,* 307–310.

Cravens, J. D., Leckie, K. R., & Whiting, J. B. (2013). Facebook infidelity: When poking becomes problematic. *Contemporary Family Therapy, 35,* 74–90.

Croucher, S. (2013). The difference in verbal aggressiveness between the United States and Thailand. *Communication Research Reports, 30,* 264–269.

Croucher, S. M., Bruno, A., McGrath, P., Adams, C., McGahan, C., Suits, A., & Huckins, A. (2012). Conflict styles and high-low cultures: A cross-cultural extension. *Communication Research Reports, 29,* 64–73.

Croy, I., Bojanowski, V., & Hummel, T. (2013). Men without a sense of smell exhibit a strongly reduced number of sexual relationships, women exhibit reduced partnership security—A reanalysis of previously published data. *Biological Psychology, 92,* 292–294.

Crusco, A. H., & Wetzel, G. G. (1984). The Midas Touch: Effects of interpersonal touch on restaurant tipping. *Personality and Social Psychology Bulletin, 10,* 512–517.

Cunningham, M. R., Shamblen, S. R., Barbee, A. P., & Ault, L. K. (2005). Social allergies in romantic relationships: Behavioral repetition, emotional sensitization, and dissatisfaction in dating couples. *Personal Relationships, 12,* 273–295.

Czech, K., & Forward, G. L. (2010). Leader communication: Faculty perceptions of the department chair. *Communication Quarterly, 58,* 431–457.

Dailey, R. M. (2006). Confirmation in parent–adolescent relationships and adolescent openness: Toward extending confirmation theory. *Communication Monographs, 73,* 434–458.

Dailey, R. M. (2008). Assessing the contribution of nonverbal behaviors in displays of confirmation during parent-adolescent interactions: An actor-partner interdependence model. *Journal of Family Communication, 8,* 62–91.

Dailey, R. M. (2009). Confirmation from family members: Parent and sibling contributions to adolescent psychosocial adjustment. *Western Journal of Communication, 73,* 273–299.

Dailey, R. M. (2010). Testing components of confirmation: How acceptance and challenge from mothers, fathers, and siblings are related to adolescent self-concept. *Communication Monographs, 77,* 592–617.

Dailey, R. M., Giles, H., & Jansma, L. L. (2005). Language attitudes in an Anglo-Hispanic context: The role of the linguistic landscape. *Language & Communication, 25,* 27–38.

Dainton, M. (2013). Relationship maintenance on Facebook: Development of a measure, relationship to general maintenance, and relationship satisfaction. *College Student Journal, 47,* 112–121.

Dainton, M., & Aylor, B. (2002). Routine and strategic maintenance efforts: Behavioral patterns, variations associated with relational length, and the prediction of relational characteristics. *Communication Monographs, 69,* 52–66.

Darling, A. L., & Dannels, D. P. (2003). Practicing engineers talk about the importance of talk: A report on the role of oral communication in the workplace. *Communication Education, 52,* 1–16.

Dasborough, M. T., Ashkanasy, N. M., Tee, E. Y. J., & Tse, H. H. M. (2009). What goes around comes around: How meso-level negative emotional contagion can ultimately determine organizational attitudes toward leaders. *The Leadership Quarterly, 20,* 571–585.

DasGupta, S., & Charon, R. (2004). Personal illness narratives: Using reflective writing to teach empathy. *Academic Medicine, 79,* 351–356.

Davidowitz, M., & Myrick, R. (1984). Responding to the bereaved: An analysis of "helping" styles. *Death Education, 8,* 1–10.

Davis, K. L., & Haynes, M. T. (2012). With or without you: The absence of fathers and affection received from mothers as predictors of men's affection with their romantic partners. *Florida Communication Journal, 40,* 29–45.

Davis, M., Markus, K. A., & Walters, S. B. (2006). Judging the credibility of criminal suspect statements: Does mode of presentation matter? *Journal of Nonverbal Behavior, 30,* 181–198.

Davis, S. F., & Kieffer, J. C. (1998). Restaurant servers influence tipping behavior. *Psychological Reports, 83,* 223–226.

Day, A., Casey, S., & Gerace, A. (2010). Interventions to improve empathy awareness in sexual and violent offenders: Conceptual, empirical, and clinical issues. *Aggression and Violent Behavior, 15*, 201–208.

Day, D. V., Schleicher, D. J., Unckless, A. L., & Hiller, N. J. (2002). Self-monitoring personality at work: A meta-analytic investigation of construct validity. *Journal of Applied Psychology, 87*, 390–401.

DeAndrea, D. C., Tong, S. T., & Walther, J. B. (2010). Dark sides of computer-mediated communication. In W. R. Cupach & B. H. Spitzberg (Eds.), *The dark side of close relationships II* (pp. 95–118). New York, NY: Routledge.

DeAngelis, T. (1992, October). The "who am I" question wears a cloak of culture. *APA Monitor, 24*, 22–23.

Debatin, B., Lovejoy, J. P., Horn, A., & Hughes, B. N. (2009). Facebook and online privacy: Attitudes, behaviors, and unintended consequences. *Journal of Computer-Mediated Communication, 15*, 83–108.

DeCapua, A. (2007). The use of language to create realities: The example of Good Bye, Lenin! *Semiotica, 166*(1–4), 69–79.

Decety, J. (2005). Perspective taking as the royal avenue to empathy. In B. F. Malle & S. D. Hodges (Eds.), *Other minds: How humans bridge the divide between self and others* (pp. 143–157). New York, NY: Guilford Press.

Defour, T. (2008). The speaker's voice: A diachronic study on the use of well and now as pragmatic markers. *English Text Construction, 1*, 62–82.

Dehart, T., Pelham, B., Fiedorowicz, L., Carvallo, M., & Gabriel, S. (2010). Including others in the implicit self: Implicit evaluation of significant others. *Self and Identity, 10*, 127–135.

DeMaris, A. (2007). The role of relationship inequity in marital disruption. *Journal of Social and Personal Relationships, 24*, 177–195.

DeMarree, K. G., Morrison, K., Wheeler, S., & Petty, R. E. (2011). Self-ambivalence and resistance to subtle self-change attempts. *Personality and Social Psychology Bulletin, 37*, 674–686.

DeMarree, K. G., Petty, R. E., & Strunk, D. R. (2010). Self-esteem accessibility as attitude strength: On the durability and impactfulness of accessible self-esteem. *Personality and Social Psychology Bulletin, 36*, 628–641.

Demir, M. D., Simsek, O., & Procsal, A. (2013). I am so happy 'cause my best friend makes me feel unique: Friendship, personal sense of uniqueness and happiness. *Journal of Happiness Studies, 14*, 1201–1224.

Denson, T., Grisham, J., & Moulds, M. (2011). Cognitive reappraisal increases heart rate variability in response to an anger provocation. *Motivation & Emotion, 35*, 14–22.

deOliveira, J. M., Costa, C. G., & Nogueira, C. (2013). The workings of homonormativity: Lesbian, gay, bisexual, and queer discourses on discrimination and public displays of affections in Portugal. *Journal of Homosexuality, 60*, 1475–1493.

DePaulo, B. M. (1992). Nonverbal behavior and self-presentation. *Psychological Bulletin, 3*, 203–243.

DePaulo, B. M., Morris, W. L., & Sternglanz, R. W. (2009). When the truth hurts: Deception in the name of kindness. In A. L. Vangelisti (Ed.), *Feeling hurt in close relationships* (pp. 167–190). New York, NY: Cambridge University Press.

Derks, D., Bos, A. E. R., & von Grumbkow, J. (2007). Emoticons and social interaction on the Internet: The importance of social context. *Computers in Human Behavior, 23*, 842–849.

Derks, D., Fischer, A. H., & Bos, A. E. R. (2008). The role of emotion in computer-mediated communication: A review. *Computers in Human Behavior, 24*, 766–785.

Derlega, V. J., Anderson, S., Winstead, B. A., & Greene, K. (2011). Positive disclosure among college students: What do they talk about, to whom, and why? *The Journal of Positive Psychology, 6*, 119–130.

Derlega, V. J., Barbee, A. P., & Winstead, B. A. (1994). Friendship, gender, and social support: Laboratory studies of supportive interactions. In B. R. Burleson, T. L. Albrecht, & I. G. Sarson (Eds.), *Communication of social support: Message, interactions, relationships, and community* (pp. 136–151). Newbury Park, CA: Sage.

Derlega, V. J., Lewis, R. J., Harrison, S., Winstead, B. A., & Costanza, R. (1989). Gender differences in the initiation and attribution of tactile intimacy. *Journal of Nonverbal Behavior, 13*, 83–96.

Derlega, V. J., Winstead, B. A., & Folk-Barron, L. (2000). Reasons for and against disclosing HIV-seropositive test results to an intimate partner: A functional perspective. In S. Petronio (Ed.), *Balancing the secrets of private disclosures* (pp. 71–82). Mahwah, NJ: Erlbaum.

Detenber, B. H., Wijaya, M., & Go, Hui yi. (2008, May). *Blogging and online friendships: The role of self-disclosure and perceived reciprocity*. Paper presented at the Annual Meeting of the International Communication Association, Montreal, Quebec, Canada.

DeTurk, S. (2001). Intercultural empathy: Myth, competency, or possibility for alliance building? *Communication Education, 50*, 374–384.

Deutscher, G. (2010). *Through the language glass: Why the world looks different in other languages*. New York, NY: Metropolitan Books.

Devos, T. (2013). Stereotypes and intergroup attitudes. In F. L. Leong, L. Comas-Díaz, G. C. Nagayama Hall,

V. C. McLoyd, & J. E. Trimble (Eds.), *APA handbook of multicultural psychology, Vol. 1: Theory and research* (pp. 341–360). Washington, DC: American Psychological Association.

de Vries, B., & Megathlin, D. (2009). The meaning of friendships for gay men and lesbians in the second half of life. *Journal of GLBT Family Studies, 5*(1–2), 82–98.

de Waal, F. B. M. (2008). Putting the altruism back into altruism: The evolution of empathy. *Annual Review of Psychology, 59,* 279–300.

de Waal, F. B. M. (2009). *The age of empathy: Nature's lessons for a kinder society.* New York, NY: Random House.

Dexter, V. J. (2013). Research synthesis with meta-analysis of empathy training studies in helping professions. *Dissertation Abstracts International Section A, 73,* 10A(E).

Diamond, L. M. (2013). Sexuality in relationships. In J. A. Simpson & L. Campbell (Eds.), *The Oxford handbook of close relationships* (pp. 589–614). New York, NY: Oxford University Press.

Diamond, L. M., & Hicks, A. M. (2012). "It's the economy, honey!": Couples' blame attributions during the 2007–2009 economic crisis. *Personal Relationships, 19,* 586–600.

Dijkstra, P., Barelds, D. P., & Groothof, H. A. (2013). Jealousy in response to online and offline infidelity: The role of sex and sexual orientation. *Scandinavian Journal of Psychology, 54,* 328–336.

Dindia, K. (2000a). Self-disclosure research: Advances through meta-analysis. In M. A. Allen, R. W. Preiss, B. M. Gayle, & N. Burrell (Eds.), *Interpersonal communication research: Advances through meta-analysis* (pp. 169–186). Mahwah, NJ: Erlbaum.

Dindia, K. (2000b). Sex differences in self-disclosure, reciprocity of self-disclosure, and self-disclosure and liking: Three meta-analyses reviewed. In S. Petronio (Ed.), *Balancing the secrets of private disclosures* (pp. 21–35). Mahwah, NJ: Erlbaum.

Dindia, K. (2002). Self-disclosure research: Knowledge through meta-analysis. In M. Allen & R. W. Preiss (Eds.), *Interpersonal communication research: Advances through meta-analysis* (pp. 169–185). Mahwah, NJ: Erlbaum.

Dindia, K. (2006). Men are from North Dakota, women are from South Dakota. In K. Dindia & D. J. Canary (Eds.), *Sex differences and similarities in communication* (2nd ed., pp. 3–18). Mahwah, NJ: Erlbaum.

Dindia, K., & Allen, M. (1992). Sex differences in self-disclosure: A meta-analysis. *Psychological Bulletin, 112,* 106–124.

Dindia, K., & Baxter, L. A. (1987). Strategies for maintaining and repairing marital relationships. *Journal of Social and Personal Relationships, 4,* 143–158.

Dindia, K., Fitzpatrick, M. A., & Kenny, D. A. (1997). Self-disclosure in spouse and stranger dyads: A social relations analysis. *Human Communication Research, 23,* 388–412.

Dinwiddie-Boyd, E. (1994). *Proud heritage: 11,001 names for your African-American baby.* New York, NY: Harper Collins.

DiPaola, B. M., Roloff, M. E., & Peters, K. M. (2010). College students' expectations of conflict intensity: A self-fulfilling prophecy. *Communication Quarterly, 58,* 59–76.

Docan-Morgan, T., & Docan, C. A. (2007). Internet infidelity: Double standards and the differing views of women and men. *Communication Quarterly, 55,* 317–342.

Doherty, E. F., & MacGeorge, E. L. (2013). Perceptions of supportive behavior by young adults with bipolar disorder. *Qualitative Health Research, 23,* 361–374.

Doss, B. D., Mitchell, A. E., & De la Garza-Mercer, F. (2008). Marital distress. In M. Hersen & J. Rosqvist (Eds.), *Handbook of psychological assessment, case conceptualization, and treatment: Vol. 1. Adults* (pp. 563–589). Hoboken, NJ: Wiley.

Doster, L. (2013). Millennial teens design and redesign themselves in online social networks. *Journal of Consumer Behaviour, 12,* 267–279.

Dougherty, D. S. (2001). Sexual harassment as [dys]functional process: A feminist standpoint analysis. *Journal of Applied Communication Research, 29,* 372–402.

Dougherty, D. S., Kramer, M. W., Klatzke, S. R., & Rogers, T. K. K. (2009). Language convergence and meaning divergence: A meaning centered communication theory. *Communication Monographs, 76,* 20–46.

Dougherty, T., Turban, D., & Collander, J. (1994). Conforming first impressions in the employment interview. *Journal of Applied Psychology, 79,* 659–665.

Douglas, K. M., & Sutton, R. M. (2010). By their words ye shall know them: Language abstraction and the likeability of describers. *European Journal of Social Psychology, 40,* 366–374.

Dowell, N. M., & Berman, J. S. (2013). Therapist nonverbal behavior and perceptions of empathy, alliance, and treatment credibility. *Journal of Psychotherapy Integration, 23,* 158–165.

Draper, P. (2005). Patronizing speech to older patients: A literature review. *Reviews in Clinical Gerontology, 15,* 273–279.

Dresner, E., & Herring, S. C. (2010). Functions of the nonverbal in CMC: Emoticons and illocutionary force. *Communication Theory, 20,* 249–268.

Driscoll, M. S., Newman, D. L., & Seal, J. M. (1988). The effect of touch on the perception of counselors. *Counselor Education and Supervision, 27,* 344–354.

Droogsma, R. A. (2007). Redefining hijab: American Muslim women's standpoints on veiling. *Journal of Applied Communication Research, 35,* 294–319.

Du, J., Fan, X., & Feng, T. (2011). Multiple emotional contagions in service encounters. *Journal of the Academy of Marketing Science, 39,* 449–466.

Duck, S., & Barnes, M. K. (1992). Disagreeing about agreement: Reconciling differences about similarity. *Communication Monographs, 59,* 199–208.

Duck, S., & Pittman, G. (1994). Social and personal relationships. In M. L. Knapp & G. R. Miller (Eds.), *Handbook of interpersonal communication* (2nd ed., pp. 676–695). Newbury Park, CA: Sage.

Duggan, M. (2013, September 19). *Cell phone activities 2013.* Pew Internet & American Life Project. Retrieved from http://www.pewinternet.org /2013/09/19/cell-phone-activities-2013/

Dunleavy, K. N., & Booth-Butterfield, M. (2009). Idiomatic communication in the stages of coming together and falling apart. *Communication Quarterly, 57,* 416–432.

Dunleavy, K. N., Chory, R. M., & Goodboy, A. K. (2010). Responses to deception in the workplace: Perceptions of credibility, power, and trustworthiness. *Communication Studies, 61,* 239–255.

Dunleavy, K. N., & Martin, M. M. (2010). Instructors' and students' perspectives of student nagging: Frequency, appropriateness, and effectiveness. *Communication Research Reports, 27,* 310–319.

Dunn, C. D. (2013). Speaking politely, kindly, and beautifully: Ideologies of politeness in Japanese business etiquette training. *Multilingua, 32,* 225–245.

Dunsmore, J., Her, P., Halberstadt, A., & Perez-Rivera, M. (2009). Parents' beliefs about emotions and children's recognition of parents' emotions. *Journal of Nonverbal Behavior, 33,* 121–140.

Duran, R. L., Kelly, L., & Rotaru, T. (2011). Mobile phones in romantic relationships and the dialectic of autonomy versus connection. *Communication Quarterly, 59,* 19–36.

Durik, A. M., Hyde, J. S., Marks, A. C., Roy, A. L., Anaya, D., & Schultz, G. (2006). Ethnicity and gender stereotypes of emotion. *Sex Roles, 54,* 429–445.

Durovic, J. (2008). Intercultural communication and ethnic identity. *Journal of Intercultural Communication, 16,* 4.

Dwyer, K. K. (2000). The multidimensional model: Teaching students to self-manage high communication apprehension by self-selecting treatments. *Communication Education, 49,* 72–81.

Eaker, E. D., Sullivan, L. M., Kelly-Hayes, M., D'Agostino, R. B., & Benjamin, E. J. (2007). Marital status, marital strain and the risk of coronary heart disease or total mortality: The Framingham Offspring Study. *Psychosomatic Medicine, 69,* 509–513.

Eaton, J., & Struthers, C. W. (2006). The reduction of psychological aggression across varied interpersonal contexts through repentance and forgiveness. *Aggressive Behavior, 32,* 195–206.

Ebeling-Witte, S., Frank, M. L., & Lester, D. (2007). Shyness, Internet use, and personality. *CyberPsychology & Behavior, 10,* 713–716.

Edwards, A., & Edwards, C. (2013). Computer-mediated word-of-mouth communication: The influence of mixed reviews on student perceptions of instructors and courses. *Communication Education, 62,* 412–424.

Edwards, C., Edwards, A., Qingmei Q., & Wahl, S. T. (2007). The influence of computer-mediated word-of-mouth communication on student perceptions of instructors and attitudes toward learning course content. *Communication Education, 56,* 255–277.

Edwards, R., & Bello, R. (2001). Interpretations of messages: The influence of equivocation, face concerns, and ego involvement. *Human Communication Research, 27,* 597–691.

Egbert, N., & Polk, D. (2006). Speaking the language of relational maintenance: A validity test of Chapman's (1992) five love languages. *Communication Research Reports, 23,* 19–26.

Egland, K. I., Stelzner, M. A., Andersen, P. A., & Spitzberg, B. S. (1997). Perceived understanding, nonverbal communication, and relational satisfaction. In J. E. Aitken & L. J. Shedletsky (Eds.), *Intrapersonal communication processes* (pp. 386–396). Annandale, VA: Speech Communication Association.

Eibl-Eibesfeldt, I. (1972). Similarities and differences between cultures in expressive movements. In R. A. Hinde (Ed.), *Nonverbal communication* (pp. 297–314). Oxford, England: Cambridge University Press.

Eisenberg, E. M. (1984). Ambiguity as strategy in organizational communication. *Communication Monographs, 51,* 227–242.

Eisenberg, E. M., & Goodall, H., Jr. (2001). *Organizational communication* (3rd ed.). New York, NY: Bedfort/St. Martin's.

Eisenberg, E. M., & Witten, M. G. (1987). Reconsidering openness in organizational communication. *Academy of Management Review, 12,* 418–426.

Ekman, P. (2003). *Emotions revealed: Recognizing faces and feelings to improve communication and emotional life.* New York, NY: Holt.

Ekman, P. (2009). *Telling lies: Clues to deceit in the marketplace, politics, and marriage* (4th ed.). New York, NY: W. W. Norton.

Ekman, P., & Friesen, W. V. (1974b). Nonverbal behavior and psychopathology. In R. J. Friedman & M. N. Katz (Eds.), *The psychology of depression: Contemporary theory and research* (pp. 3–31). Washington, DC: Winston and Sons.

El-Alayli, A., Myers, C. J., Petersen, T. L., & Lystad, A. L. (2008). "I don't mean to sound arrogant, but . . ." The effects of using disclaimers on person perception. *Personality and Social Psychology Bulletin, 34,* 130–143.

Eldridge, K. A., & Christensen, A. (2002). Demand-withdraw communication during couple conflict: A review and analysis. In P. Noller & J. A. Feeney (Eds.), *Understanding marriage: Developments in the study of couple interaction* (pp. 289–322). New York, NY: Cambridge University Press.

Ellis, A., & Dryden, W. (2007). *The practice of Rational Emotive Behavior Therapy* (2nd ed.). New York, NY: Springer.

Ellis, A., & Ellis, D. (2014). Rational emotive behavior therapy. In G. R. VandenBos, E. Meidenbauer, & J. Frank-McNeil (Eds.), *Psychotherapy theories and techniques: A reader* (pp. 289–298). Washington, DC: American Psychological Association.

Ellis, K. (2002). Perceived parental confirmation: Development and validation of an instrument. *Southern Communication Journal, 67,* 319–334.

Ellison, N., Heino, R., & Gibbs, J. (2006). Managing impressions online: Self-presentation processes in the online dating environment. *Journal of Computer-Mediated Communication, 11,* 415–441.

Ellison, N. B., Steinfield, C., & Lampe, C. (2007). The benefits of Facebook "friends": Social capital and college students' use of online social network sites. *Journal of Computer-Mediated Communication, 12,* 1143–1168.

Elphinston, R. A., Feeney, J. A., Noller, P., Connor, J. P., & Fitzgerald, J. (2013). Romantic jealousy and relationship satisfaction: The costs of rumination. *Western Journal of Communication, 77,* 293–304.

Elphinston, R. A., & Noller, P. (2011). Time to face It! Facebook intrusion and the implications for romantic jealousy and relationship satisfaction. *Cyberpsychology, Behavior, and Social Networking, 14,* 631–635.

Emanuel, R., Adams, J., Baker, K., Daufin, E. K., Ellington, C., Fitts, E., . . . Okeowo, D. (2008). How college students spend their time communicating. *International Journal of Listening, 22,* 13–28.

Emmers-Sommer, T. M. (2003). When partners falter: Repair after a transgression. In D. J. Canary & M. Dainton (Eds.), *Maintaining relationships through communication* (pp. 185–205). Mahwah, NJ: Erlbaum.

Engen, D. (2004). Invisible identities: Notes on class and race. In Gonzalez, A., Houston, M., & Chen, V. (Eds.), *Our voices: Essays in culture, ethnicity and communication* (4th ed., pp. 250–255). Los Angeles, CA: Roxbury.

English, T., John, O. P., & Gross, J. J. (2013). Emotion regulation in close relationships. In J. A. Simpson & L. Campbell (Eds.), *The Oxford handbook of close relationships* (pp. 500–513). New York, NY: Oxford University Press.

Ennis, E., Vrij, A., & Chance, C. (2008). Individual differences and lying in everyday life. *Journal of Social and Personal Relationships, 25,* 105–118.

Epstein, R. (2010, January/February). How science can help you fall in love. *Scientific American Mind,* 26–33.

Epstein, R., Pandit, M., & Thakar, M. (2013). How love emerges in arranged marriage: Two cross-cultural studies. *Journal of Comparative Family Studies, 43,* 341–360.

Epstein, R., Warfel, R., Johnson, J., Smith, R., & McKinney, P. (2013). Which relationship skills count most? *Journal of Couple & Relationship Therapy, 12,* 297–313.

Equal Employment Opportunity Commission. (2010). *Sexual harassment charges EEOC & FEPAs combined: FY 1997–FY 2010.* Retrieved from http://www.eeoc.gov/eeoc/statistics/enforcement/sexual_harassment.cfm

Erbert, L. A. (2000). Conflict and dialectics: Perceptions of dialectical contradictions in marital conflict. *Journal of Social and Personal Relationships, 17,* 638–659.

Erwin, P. G., & Pressler, S. J. (2011). Love styles, shyness, and patterns of emotional self-disclosure. *Psychological Reports, 108,* 737–742.

Eschenfedler, B. (2012). Exploring the nature of nonprofit work through emotional labor. *Management Communication Quarterly, 26,* 173–178.

Evans, G. W., & Wener, R. E. (2007). Crowding and personal space invasion on the train: Please don't make me sit in the middle. *Journal of Environmental Psychology, 27,* 90–94.

Everett, C. (2013). *Linguistic relativity: Evidence across languages and cognitive domains.* Boston, MA: Walter de Gruyter.

Exline, J. J., Baumeister, R. F., & Zell, L. (2008). Not so innocent: Does seeing one's own capability for wrongdoing predict forgiveness? *Journal of Personality and Social Psychology, 94,* 495–515.

Exline, J. J., Deshea, L., & Holeman, V. T. (2007). Is apology worth the risk? Predictors, outcomes, and ways to avoid regret. *Journal of Social & Clinical Psychology, 26,* 479–504.

Fadiman, A. (1997). *The spirit catches you and you fall down*. New York, NY: Farrar, Straus & Giroux.

Fandrich, A. M., & Beck, S. J. (2012). Powerless language in health media: The influence of biological sex and magazine type on health language. *Communication Studies, 63*, 36–53.

Farah, A., & Atoum, A. (2002). Personality traits as self-evaluated and as judged by others. *Social Behavior and Personality, 30*, 149–156.

Faul, S. (2008). *Xenophobe's guide to the Americans*. London: Oval Books.

Faulkner, S. L., Baldwin, J. R., Lindsley, S. L., & Hecht, M. L. (2006). Layers of meaning: An analysis of definitions of culture. In J. R. Baldwin, S. L. Faulkner, M. L. Hecht, & S. L. Lindsley (Eds.), *Redefining culture: Perspectives across the disciplines* (pp. 27–52). Mahwah, NJ: Erlbaum.

Feaster, J. C. (2010). Expanding the impression management model of communication channels: An information control scale. *Journal of Computer-Mediated Communication, 16*, 115–138.

Federal Bureau of Investigation. (2012, December 10). *Hate crimes accounting: Annual report released*. Retrieved from http://www.fbi.gov/news/stories/2012/december/annual-hate-crimes-report-released/annual-hate-crimes-report-released

Feeney, J. A. (1999). Issues of closeness and distance in dating relationships: Effects of sex and attachment style. *Journal of Social and Personal Relationships, 16*, 571–590.

Fehr, B. (2000). Adult friendship. In S. Hendrick & C. Hendrick (Eds.), *Close relationships: A sourcebook* (pp. 71–82). Thousand Oaks, CA: Sage.

Fehr, B. (2013). The social psychology of love. In J. A. Simpson & L. Campbell (Eds.), *The Oxford handbook of close relationships* (pp. 201–233). New York, NY: Oxford University Press.

Feldman, R., Rosenthal, Z., & Eidelman, A. I. (2014). Maternal-preterm skin-to-skin contact enhances child physiologic organization and cognitive control across the first 10 years of life. *Biological Psychiatry, 75*, 56–64.

Feldman, R., Singer, M., & Zagoory, O. (2010). Touch attenuates infants' physiological reactivity to stress. *Developmental Science, 13*, 271–278.

Felmlee, D. H. (2001). From appealing to appalling: Disenchantment with a romantic partner. *Sociological Perspectives, 44*, 263–280.

Felps, D., Bortfeld, H., & Gutierrez-Osuna, R. (2009). Foreign accent conversion in computer assisted pronunciation training. *Speech Communication, 51*, 920–932.

Feng, B., & Lee, K. J. (2010). The influence of thinking styles on responses to supportive messages. *Communication Studies, 61*, 224–238.

Fenigstein, A. (2009). Private and public self-consciousness. In M. R. Leary & R. H. Hoyle (Eds.), *Handbook of individual differences in social behavior* (pp. 495–511). New York, NY: Guilford Press.

Ferguson, G. M., & Cramer, P. (2007). Self-esteem among Jamaican children: Exploring the impact of skin color and rural/urban residence. *Journal of Applied Developmental Psychology, 28*, 345–359.

Ferrari, M., & Koyama, E. (2002). Meta-emotions about anger and amae: A cross-cultural comparison. *Consciousness and Emotion, 3*, 197–211.

Ferraro, G., & Andreatta, S. (2012). *Cultural anthropology: An applied perspective* (9th ed.). Independence, KY: Cengage.

Fetterman, A. K., & Robinson, M. D. (2013). Do you use your head or follow your heart? Self-location predicts personality, emotion, decision making, and performance. *Journal of Personality and Social Psychology, 105*, 316–334.

Fiedler, A. M., & Blanco, R. I. (2006). The challenge of varying perceptions of sexual harassment: An international study. *Journal of Behavioral and Applied Management, 7*, 1274–1279.

Field, T. (2007). *The amazing infant: Touch research institute at the university of Miami school of medicine*. Oxford, England: Blackwell.

Fife, E. M., Leigh Nelson, C. C., & Messersmith, A. S. (2014). The influence of family communication patterns on religious orientation among college students. *Journal of Family Communication, 14*, 72–84.

Filley, A. C. (1975). *Interpersonal conflict resolution*. Glenview, IL: Scott, Foresman.

Fincham, F. D., & Beach, S. R. H. (2013). Gratitude and forgiveness in relationships. In J. A. Simpson & L. Campbell (Eds.), *The Oxford handbook of close relationships* (pp. 638–633). New York, NY: Oxford University Press.

Finkel, E. J., & Baumeister, R. F. (2010). Attraction and rejection. In R. F. Baumeister & E. J. Finkel (Eds.), *Advanced social psychology: The state of the science* (pp. 419–459). New York, NY: Oxford University Press.

Finkel, E. J., Eastwick, P. W., Karney, B. R., Reis, H. T., & Sprecher, S. (2012). Online dating: A critical analysis from the perspective of psychological science. *Psychological Science in the Public Interest, 13*, 3–66.

Finkel, E. J., Slotter, E. B., Luchies, L. B., Walton, G. M., & Gross, J. J. (2013). A brief intervention to promote conflict-reappraisal preserves marital quality over time. *Psychological Science, 24*, 1595–1601.

Fisher, H. (2007, May–June). The laws of chemistry. *Psychology Today, 40,* 76–81.

Fiske, S. T., Cuddy, A. J. C., & Glick, P. (2007). Universal dimensions of social cognition: Warmth and competence. *Trends in Cognitive Sciences, 11,* 77–83.

Fitch, V. (1985). The psychological tasks of old age. *Naropa Institute Journal of Psychology, 3,* 90–106.

Fitzpatrick, M. A., & Vangelisti, A. L. (2001). Communication, relationships, and health. In W. P. Robinson & H. Giles (Eds.), *The new handbook of language and social psychology* (2nd ed., pp. 505–530). New York, NY: Wiley.

Fitzsimons, G., & Kay, A. C. (2004). Language and interpersonal cognition: Causal effects of variations in pronoun usage on perceptions of closeness. *Personality and Social Psychology Bulletin, 30,* 547–557.

Fleming, P., & Sturdy, A. (2009). "Just be yourself!": Towards neo-normative control in organisations? *Employee Relations, 31,* 569–583.

Fletcher, G. J. O., Fincham, F. D., Cramer, L., & Heron, N. (1987). The role of attributions in the development of dating relationships. *Journal of Personality and Social Psychology, 53,* 481–489.

Fletcher, G. J. O., & Kerr, P. S. G. (2010). Through the eyes of love: Reality and illusion in intimate relationships. *Psychological Bulletin, 136,* 627–658.

Flora, C. (2005). Close quarters: Why we fall in love with the one nearby. *Psychology Today, 37,* 15–16.

Flora, J., & Segrin, C. (2000). Relationship development in dating couples: Implications for relational satisfaction and loneliness. *Journal of Social and Personal Relationships, 17,* 811–825.

Floyd, K. (1996). Communicating closeness among siblings: An application of the gendered closeness perspective. *Communication Research Reports, 13,* 27–34.

Floyd, K. (2014). Empathic listening as an expression of affection. *International Journal of Listening, 28,* 1–12.

Floyd, K., Boren, J. P., Hannawa, A. F., Hesse, C., McEwan, B., & Veksler, A. E. (2009). Kissing in marital and cohabiting relationships: Effects on blood lipids, stress, and relationship satisfaction. *Western Journal of Communication, 73,* 113–133.

Floyd, K., & Riforgiate, S. (2008). Affectionate communication received from spouses predicts stress hormone levels in healthy adults. *Communication Monographs, 75,* 351–368.

Flynn, J., Valikoski, T., & Grau, J. (2008). Listening in the business context: Reviewing the state of research. *International Journal of Listening, 22,* 141–151.

Fogel, A., & Branco, A. U. (1997). Metacommunication as a source of indeterminism in relationship development. In A. Fogel, M. C. D. P. Lyra, & J. Valsiner (Eds.), *Dynamics and indeterminism in developmental and social processes* (pp. 65–92). Hillsdale, NJ: Erlbaum.

Fogel, A., de Koeyer, I., Bellagamba, F., & Bell, H. (2002). The dialogical self in the first two years of life: Embarking on a journey of discovery. *Theory and Psychology, 12,* 191–205.

Forest, A. L., & Wood, J. V. (2012). When social networking is not working: Individuals with low self-esteem recognize but do not reap the benefits of self-disclosure on Facebook. *Psychological Science, 23,* 295–302.

Forni, P. M. (2010, July 23). Why civility is necessary for society's survival. *Dallasnews.com.* Retrieved from http://www.dallasnews.com/opinion/sunday -commentary/20100723-p.m.-forni-why-civility-is -necessary-for-society_s-survival.ece

Fortenberry, J. H., Maclean, J., Morris, P., & O'Connell, M. (1978). Mode of dress as a perceptual cue to deference. *Journal of Social Psychology, 104,* 131–139.

Fortney, S. D., Johnson, D. I., & Long, K. M. (2001). The impact of compulsive communicators on the self-perceived competence of classroom peers: An investigation and test of instructional strategies. *Communication Education, 50,* 357–373.

Forward, G. L., Czech, K., & Lee, C. M. (2011). Assessing Gibb's supportive and defensive communication climate: An examination of measurement and construct validity. *Communication Research Reports, 28,* 1–15.

Foss, S. K., & Griffin, C. L. (1995). Beyond persuasion: A proposal for an invitational rhetoric. *Communication Monographs, 62,* 2–18.

Foster, E. (2008). Commitment, communication, and contending with heteronormativity: An invitation to greater reflexivity in interpersonal research. *Southern Communication Journal, 73,* 84–101.

Fowler, C., & Dillow, M. R. (2011). Attachment dimensions and the Four Horsemen of the Apocalypse. *Communication Research Reports, 28,* 16–26.

Fox, J., & Warber, K. M. (2013). Romantic relationship development in the age of Facebook: An exploratory study of emerging adults' perceptions, motives, and behaviors. *Cyberpsychology, Behavior, and Social Networking, 16,* 3–7.

Fox, J., Warber, K. M., & Makstaller, D. C. (2013). The role of Facebook in romantic relationship development: An exploration of Knapp's relational stage model. *Journal of Social and Personal Relationships, 30,* 771–794.

Fox, S. (2011, February 28). *Peer-to-peer healthcare.* Washington, DC: Pew Internet & American Life Project.

Retrieved from http://www.pewinternet.org/files /old-media/Files/Reports/2011/Pew_P2P Healthcare_2011.pdf

Francis, L. E. (2003). Feeling good, feeling well: Identity, emotion, and health. In T. J. Owens & P. J. Burke (Eds.), *Advances in identity theory and research* (pp. 123–134). New York, NY: Kluwer Academic/Plenum Publishers.

Frawley, T. (2008). Gender schema and prejudicial recall: How children misremember, fabricate, and distort gendered picture book information. *Journal of Research in Childhood Education, 22,* 291–303.

Fredrickson, B. L. (2009). *Positivity.* New York, NY: Three Rivers.

Freeman, J. B., & Ambady, N. (2011). A dynamic interactive theory of person construal. *Psychological Review, 118,* 247–279.

Friend, M. (2003). What should I do? Behavior regulation by language and paralanguage in early childhood. *Journal of Cognition and Development, 4,* 161–183.

Frijters, P., & Beatoon, T. (2012). The mystery of the U-shaped relationship between happiness and age. *Journal of Economic Behavior & Organization, 82,* 525–542.

Frisby, B. N., & Sidelinger, R. J. (2013). Violating student expectations: Student disclosures and student reactions in the college classroom. *Communication Studies, 64,* 241–258.

Frith, H., & Gleeson, K. (2008). Dressing the body: The role of clothing in sustaining body pride and managing body distress. *Qualitative Research in Psychology, 5,* 249–264.

Froese, A. D., Carpenter, C. N., Inman, D. A., Schooley, J. R., Barnes, R. B., Brecht, P. W., & Chacon, J. D. (2012). Effects of classroom cell phone use on expected and actual learning. *College Student Journal, 46,* 323–332.

Fromme, D. K., Jaynes, W. E., Taylor, D. K., Hanold, E. G., Daniell, J., Rountree, J. R., & Fromme, M. (1989). Nonverbal behavior and attitudes toward touch. *Journal of Nonverbal Behavior, 13,* 3–14.

Frost, D. M. (2013). The narrative construction of intimacy and affect in relationship stories: Implications for relationship quality, stability, and mental health. *Journal of Social and Personal Relationships, 30,* 247–269.

Frost, D. M., & Forrester, C. (2013). Closeness discrepancies in romantic relationships: Implications for relational well-being, stability, and mental health. *Personality and Social Psychology Bulletin, 39,* 456–469.

Frumkin, L. (2007). Influences of accent and ethnic background on perceptions of eyewitness testimony. *Psychology, Crime & Law, 13,* 317–331.

Frye-Cox, N. E., & Hesse, C. R. (2013). Alexithymia and marital quality: The mediating roles of loneliness and intimate communication. *Journal of Family Psychology, 27,* 203–211.

Fulmer, R. (1999). Becoming an adult: Leaving home and staying connected. In B. Carter & M. McGoldrick (Eds.), *The expanded family life cycle: Individual, family, and social perspectives* (3rd ed., pp. 215–230). Boston, MA: Allyn & Bacon.

Furley, P., & Schweizer, G. (2014). The expression of victory and loss: Estimating who's leading or trailing from nonverbal cues in sports. *Journal of Nonverbal Behavior, 38,* 13–29.

Fussell, S. R. (Ed.). (2002). *The verbal communication of emotions: Interdisciplinary perspectives.* Mahwah, NJ: Erlbaum.

Futch, A., & Edwards, R. (1999). The effects of sense of humor, defensiveness, and gender on the interpretation of ambiguous messages. *Communication Quarterly, 47,* 80–97.

Gabric, D., & McFadden, K. L. (2001). Student and employer perceptions of desirable entry-level operations management skills. *Mid-American Journal of Business, 16,* 51–59.

Gadlin, H. (1977). Private lives and public order: A critical view of the history of intimate relations in the United States. In G. Levinger & H. L. Raush (Eds.), *Close relationships: Perspectives on the meaning of intimacy* (pp. 33–72). Amherst: University of Massachusetts Press.

Gaia, A. (2013). The role of gender stereotypes in the social acceptability of the expression of intimacy. *The Social Science Journal, 50,* 591–602.

Galanxhi, H., & Nah, F. F.-H. (2007). Deception in cyberspace: A comparison of text-only vs., avatar-supported medium. *International Journal of Human–Computer Studies, 65,* 770–783.

Galovan, A. M., Holmes, E. K., Schramm, D. G., & Lee, T. R. (2013, March 8). Father involvement, father-child relationship quality, and satisfaction with family work: Actor and partner influences on marital quality. *Journal of Family Issues.* doi: 10.1177/0192513X13479948

Galupo, M. P., & Gonzalez, K. A. (2013). Friendship values and cross-category friendships: Understanding adult friendship patterns across gender, sexual orientation, and race. *Sex Roles, 68,* 779–790.

Galvin, K. M., Bylund, C. L., & Brommel, B. J. (2007). *Family communication: Cohesion and change* (7th ed.). Boston: Allyn & Bacon.

Gann, R. (2004). Language, conflict and community: Linguistic accommodation in the urban US. *Changing English: Studies In Reading & Culture, 11,* 105–114.

Gara, M. A., Woolfolk, R. L., Cohen, B. D., Goldston, R. B., & Allen, L. A. (1993). Perception of self and other in major depression. *Journal of Abnormal Psychology, 102*, 93–100.

Gareis, E., & Wilkins, R. (2011). Communicating love: A sociocultural perspective. In C. T. Salmon (Ed.), *Communication Yearbook* (Vol. 35, pp. 199–239). New York, NY: Routledge.

Garner, M. (2014). Language rules and language ecology. *Language Sciences, 41*(Part A), 111–121.

Gayle, B. M., Preiss, R. W., & Allen, M. A. (2002). A meta-analytic interpretation of intimate and nonintimate interpersonal conflict. In M. Allen, R. W. Preiss, B. M. Gayle, & N. Burrell (Eds.), *Interpersonal communication research: Advances through meta-analysis* (pp. 345–368). Mahwah, NJ: Erlbaum.

Gearhart, C. G., & Bodie, G. D. (2011). Active-empathic listening as a general social skill: Evidence from bivariate and canonical correlations. *Communication Reports, 24*, 86–98.

Gebauer, J. E., Leary, M. R., & Neberich, W. (2012). Unfortunate first names: Effects of name-based relational devaluation and interpersonal neglect. *Social Psychological and Personality Science, 3*, 590–596.

Geddes, D. (1992). Sex-roles in management: The impact of varying power of speech style on union members' perception of satisfaction and effectiveness. *Journal of Psychology, 126*, 589–607.

Geist, R. A. (2013). How the empathic process heals: A microprocess perspective. *International Journal of Psychoanalytic Self Psychology, 8*, 265–281.

Genov, A. B. (2001). Autonomic and situational determinants of the subjective experience of emotion: An individual differences approach. *Dissertation Abstracts International: Section B. The Sciences and Engineering, 61*(9-B), 5043.

Gent, S. E., & Shannon, M. (2011). Bias and effectiveness of third-party conflict management mechanisms. *Conflict Management and Peace Science, 28*, 124–144.

Gentile, J. S. (2004). Telling the untold tales: Memory's caretaker. *Text and Performance Quarterly, 24*, 201–204.

Gentsch, K., Grandjean, D., & Scherer, K. R. (2014). Coherence explored between emotion components: Evidence from event-related potentials and facial electromyography. *Biological Psychology, 98*, 70–81.

George, J. F., & Robb, A. (2008). Deception and computer-mediated communication in daily life. *Communication Reports, 21*, 92–103.

Gergen, K. J. (1991). *The saturated self: Dilemmas of identity in contemporary life*. New York, NY: Basic Books.

Gergen, K. J., & Gergen, M. (2010). Positive aging: Resilience and reconstruction. In P. S. Fry & C. M. Keyes (Eds.), *New frontiers in resilient aging: Life-strengths and well-being in late life* (pp. 340–356). New York, NY: Cambridge University Press.

Gerholm, T. (2011). Children's development of facework practices—an emotional endeavor. *Journal of Pragmatics, 43*, 3099–3110.

Gibb, J. R. (1961). Defensive communication. *Journal of Communication, 11*(3), 141–148.

Gibb, J. R. (2008). Defensive communication. In C. D. Mortensen (Ed.), *Communication theory* (2nd ed., pp. 201–208). Piscataway, NJ: Transaction Publishers.

Gibbs, J. L., Ellison, N. B., & Lai, C.-H. (2011). First comes love, then comes Google: An investigation of uncertainty reduction strategies and self-disclosure in online dating. *Communication Research, 38*, 70–100.

Gifford, R. (2011). The role of nonverbal communication in interpersonal relations. In L. M. Horowitz & S. Strack (Eds.), *Handbook of interpersonal psychology: Theory, research, assessment, and therapeutic interventions* (pp. 171–190). Hoboken, NJ: John Wiley & Sons.

Giles, H., Ballard, D., & McCann, R. M. (2002). Perceptions of intergenerational communication across cultures: An Italian case. *Perceptual and Motor Skills, 95*, 583–591.

Giles, H., & Franklyn-Stokes, A. (1989). Communicator characteristics. In M. K. Asante & W. B. Gudykunst (Eds.), *Handbook of international and intercultural communication* (pp. 117–144). Newbury Park, CA: Sage.

Giles, H., & Gasiorek, J. (2011). Intergenerational communication practices. In K. Schaie & S. L. Willis (Eds.), *Handbook of the psychology of aging* (7th ed., pp. 233–247). San Diego, CA: Elsevier Academic Press.

Giles, H., Mulac, A., Bradac, J. J., & Johnson, P. (2010). Speech accommodation theory: The first decade and beyond. In M. L. Knapp & J. A. Daly (Eds.), *Interpersonal communication* (pp. 39–74). Thousand Oaks, CA: Sage.

Giles, H., & Ogay, T. (2006). Communication accommodation theory. In B. B. Whaley & W. Samter (Eds.), *Explaining communication: Contemporary theories and exemplars* (pp. 293–310). Mahwah, NJ: Erlbaum.

Gladwell, M. (2004). *Blink: The power of thinking without thinking*. Boston, MA: Little, Brown.

Glanz, B. A. (2007). *What can I do? Ideas to help those who have experienced loss*. Minneapolis, MN: Augsburg Fortress.

Glasser, W., & Glasser, C. (1999). *The language of choice theory*. New York, NY: HarperCollins.

Gleason, J. B., & Greif, E. B. (1983). Men's speech to young children. In B. Thorne, C. Kramarae, & N. Henley

(Eds.), *Language, gender, and society* (pp. 140–150). Rowley, MA: Newbury House.

Gluszek, A., Newheiser, A.-K., & Dovidio, J. F. (2011). Social psychological orientations and accent strength. *Journal of Language and Social Psychology, 30,* 28–45.

Goetting, A. (1986). The developmental tasks of siblingship over the life cycle. *Journal of Marriage and the Family, 48,* 703–714.

Goffman, E. (1959). *The presentation of self in everyday life.* Garden City, NY: Doubleday.

Goffman, E. (1983). The interaction order. *American Sociological Review, 48,* 1–17.

Golash-Boza, T., & Darity, W. (2008). Latino racial choices: The effects of skin colour and discrimination on Latinos' and Latinas' racial self-identifications. *Ethnic & Racial Studies, 31,* 899–934.

Gold, S. N., & Castillo, Y. (2010). Dealing with defenses and defensiveness in interviews. In D. L. Segal & M. Hersen (Eds.), *Diagnostic interviewing* (pp. 89–102). New York, NY: Springer.

Goldberg, A. E., & Allen, K. R. (2013). *LGBT-parent families: Innovations in research and implications for practice.* New York, NY: Springer Science + Business Media.

Goldschmidt, W. (1990). *The human career.* Cambridge, MA: Basil Blackman.

Goldsmith, D. J., & Fitch, K. (1997). The normative context of advice as social support. *Human Communication Research, 23,* 454–476.

Goldsmith, D. J., & Fulfs, P. A. (1999). "You just don't have the evidence": An analysis of claims and evidence in Deborah Tannen's *You just don't understand.* In M. E. Roloff (Ed.), *Communication yearbook, 22* (pp. 1–49). Thousand Oaks, CA: Sage.

Goldstein, S. (2008). Current literature in ADHD. *Journal of Attention Disorders, 11,* 614–616.

Goleman, D. (1995). *Emotional intelligence: Why it can matter more than I.Q.* New York, NY: Bantam.

Goleman, D. (2013, October 6). Rich people just care less. *New York Times,* p. SR12.

Golen, S. (1990). A factor analysis of barriers to effective listening. *Journal of Business Communication, 27,* 25–36.

Golish, T. D. (2000). Is openness always better? Exploring the role of topic avoidance, satisfaction, and parenting styles of stepparents. *Communication Quarterly, 48,* 137–158.

Golish, T. D., & Caughlin, J. P. (2002). "I'd rather not talk about it": Adolescents' and young adults' use of topic avoidance in stepfamilies. *Journal of Applied Communication Research, 30,* 78–106.

Gonzaga, G. G., Haselton, M. G., Smurda J., Davies, M., & Poore, J. C. (2008). Love, desire, and the suppression of thoughts of romantic alternatives. *Evolution and Human Behavior, 29,* 119–126.

Gonzales, A. L., & Hancock, J. T. (2011). Mirror, mirror on my Facebook wall: Effects of exposure to Facebook on self-esteem. *Cyberpsychology, Behavior, and Social Networking, 41,* 79–83.

Good, G. E., Porter, M. J., & Dillon, M. G. (2002). When men divulge: Men's self-disclosure on prime time situation comedies. *Sex Roles, 46,* 419–427.

Goodboy, A. K., & Myers, S. A. (2008). The effect of teacher confirmation on student communication and learning outcomes. *Communication Education, 57,* 153–179.

Goodman, G., & Esterly, G. (1990). Questions—The most popular piece of language. In J. Stewart (Ed.), *Bridges not walls* (5th ed., pp. 69–77). New York, NY: McGraw-Hill.

Goodman, K. L., & Southam-Gerow, M. A. (2010). The regulating role of negative emotions in children's coping with peer rejection. *Child Psychiatry & Human Development, 41,* 515–534.

Gordon, A. M., & Chen, S. (2014). The role of sleep in interpersonal conflict: Do sleepless nights mean worse fights? *Social Psychological and Personality Science, 5,* 168–175.

Gordon, R., Crosnoe, R., & Wang, X. (2013). Physical attractiveness and the accumulation of social and human capital in adolescence and young adulthood. *Monographs of the Society for Research in Child Development, 78,* 1–137.

Gordon, T. (1970). *P.E.T.: Parent effectiveness training.* New York, NY: Wyden.

Gottman, J. (1994). *Why marriages succeed or fail and how you can make yours last.* New York, NY: Simon & Schuster.

Gottman, J. (2000, September). Welcome to the love lab. *Psychology Today Online.* Retrieved from http://www.psychologytoday.com/articles/200009/welcome-the-love-lab

Gottman, J. (2003). Why marriages fail. In K. M. Galvin & P. J. Cooper (Eds.), *Making connections: Readings in relational communication* (pp. 258–266). Los Angeles, CA: Roxbury.

Gottman, J. M., Katz, L. F., & Hooven, C. (1997). *Meta-emotion: How families communicate emotionally.* Mahwah, NJ: Erlbaum.

Gottman, J. M., & Levenson, R. W. (1999). Rebound for marital conflict and divorce prediction. *Family Process, 38,* 287–292.

Gottman, J. M., & Silver, N. (1999). *The seven principles for making marriages work.* New York, NY: Three Rivers Press.

Graber, E. C., Laurenceau, J., Miga, E. Chango, J., & Coan, J. (2011). Conflict and love: Predicting newlywed marital outcomes from two interaction contexts. *Journal of Family Psychology, 25,* 541–550.

Graham, S. M., Huang, J. Y., Clark, M. S., & Helgeson, V. S. (2008). The positives of negative emotions: Willingness to express negative emotions promotes relationships. *Personality and Social Psychology Bulletin, 34,* 394–406.

Grant, C. H., III, Cissna, K. N., & Rosenfeld, L. B. (2000). Patients' perceptions of physicians' communication and outcomes of the accrual to trial process. *Health Communication, 12*(1), 23–39.

Gray, J. (1992). *Men are from Mars, women are from Venus: A practical guide for improving communication and getting what you want in your relationship.* New York, NY: HarperCollins.

Graziano, W. G., & Bruce, J. (2008). Attraction and the initiation of relationships: A review of the empirical literature. In S. Sprecher, A. Wenzel, & J. Harvey (Eds.), *Handbook of relationship initiation* (pp. 269–295). New York, NY: Psychology Press.

Green, K. J., & Morman, M. T. (2011). The perceived benefits of the friends with benefits relationship. *Human Communication, 14,* 327–346.

Greenberg, L. S., & Goldman, R. N. (2008). Fear in couples therapy. In L. S. Greenberg & R. N. Goldman (Eds.), *Emotion-focused couples therapy: The dynamics of emotion, love, and power* (pp. 283–313). Washington, DC: American Psychological Association.

Greene, J. P., Kisida, B., & Bowen, D. H. (2014). The educational value of field trips. *Education Next, 14,* 78–86.

Greene, K., Derlega, V. J., & Mathews, A. (2006). Self-disclosure in personal relationships. In A. Vangelisti & D. Perlman (Eds.), *The Cambridge handbook of personal relationships* (pp. 409–428). New York, NY: Cambridge University Press.

Grewal, D., & Salovey, P. (2005). Feeling smart: The science of emotional intelligence. *American Scientist, 93,* 330–339.

Grieve, R., Indian, M., Witteveen, K., Tolan, G., & Marrington, J. (2013). Face-to-face or Facebook: Can social connectedness be derived online? *Computers in Human Behavior, 29,* 604–609.

Griffin, E. A. (2006). *A first look at communication theory with conversations with communication theorists* (6th ed.). New York, NY: McGraw-Hill.

Gross, J. J., Sutton, S. K., & Ketelaar, T. V. (1998). Relations between affect and personality: Support for the affect-level and affective-reactivity views. *Personality and Social Psychology Bulletin, 24,* 279–288.

Gross, M. A., & Guerrero, L. K. (2000). Managing conflict appropriately and effectively: An application of the competence model to Rahim's organizational conflict styles. *International Journal of Conflict Management, 11,* 200–226.

Gross, M. A., Guerrero, L. K., & Alberts, J. K. (2004). Perceptions of conflict strategies and communication competence in task-oriented dyads. *Journal of Applied Communication Research, 32,* 249–270.

Gudykunst, W. B. (1993). Toward a theory of effective interpersonal and intergroup communication: An anxiety/uncertainty management (AUM) perspective. In J. Koester & R. L. Wiseman (Eds.), *Intercultural communication competence* (pp. 33–71). Thousand Oaks, CA: Sage.

Gudykunst, W. B. (2005). *Theorizing about intercultural communication.* Thousand Oaks, CA: Sage.

Gudykunst, W. B., & Kim, Y. Y. (2002). *Communicating with strangers: An approach to intercultural communication* (4th ed.). New York, NY: McGraw-Hill.

Guéguen, N. (2013). Effects of a tattoo on men's behavior and attitudes towards women: An experimental field study. *Archives of Sexual Behavior, 42,* 1517–1524.

Guéguen, N., & Fischer-Lokou, J. (2002). An evaluation of touch on a large request: A field setting. *Psychological Reports, 90,* 267–269.

Guéguen, N., & Jacob, C. (2005). The effect of touch on tipping: An evaluation in a French bar. *International Journal of Hospitality Management, 24,* 295–299.

Guéguen, N., Jacob, C., & Boulbry, G. (2007). The effect of touch on compliance with a restaurant's employee suggestion. *International Journal of Hospitality Management, 26,* 1019–1023.

Guéguen, N., Meineri, S., & Charles-Sire, V. (2010). Improving medication adherence by using practitioner nonverbal techniques: A field experiment on the effect of touch. *Journal of Behavioral Medicine, 33,* 466–473.

Guéguen, N., Meineri, S., & Fischer-Lokou, J. (2013). Men's music ability and attractiveness to women in a real-life courtship context. *Psychology of Music.* doi: 10.1177/0305735613482025

Guéguen, N., & Vion, M. (2009). The effect of a practitioner's touch on a patient's medication compliance. *Psychology, Health & Medicine, 14,* 689–694.

Guerin, B. (2003). Combating prejudice and racism: New interventions from a functional analysis of racist language. *Journal of Community and Applied Social Psychology, 13,* 29–45.

Guerrero, L. K., & Afifi, W. A. (1995). Some things are better left unsaid: Topic avoidance in family relationships. *Communication Quarterly, 43,* 276–296.

Guerrero, L. K., Anderson, P. A., & Afifi, W. A. (2007). *Close encounters: Communication in relationships* (2nd ed.). Thousand Oaks, CA: Sage.

Guerrero, L. K., & Bachman, G. (2008). Communication following relational transgressions in dating relationships: An investment-model explanation. *Southern Communication Journal, 73,* 4–23.

Guerrero, L. K., & Bachman, G. F. (2010). Forgiveness and forgiving communication in dating relationships: An expectancy-investment explanation. *Journal of Social and Personal Relationships, 27,* 801–823.

Guerrero, L. K., & Chavez, A. (2005). Relational maintenance in cross-sex friendships characterized by different types of romantic intent: An exploratory study. *Western Journal of Communication, 69,* 339–358.

Guerrero, L. K., & Floyd, K. (2006). *Nonverbal communication in close relationships.* Mahwah, NJ: Erlbaum.

Guo, M., & Hu, W. (2013). Teaching nonverbal differences in English class: Cross-cultural communicative approach. *Studies in Literature & Language, 7,* 60–64.

Gustafsson Sendén, M., Lindholm, T., & Sikström, S. (2014). Selection bias in choice of words: Evaluations of "I" and "we" differ between contexts, but "they" are always worse. *Journal of Language & Social Psychology, 33,* 49–67.

Guynn, J. (2008, March 31). Meetings going "topless." *Los Angeles Times.* Retrieved from http://www.latimes.com/business/la-fi-nolaptops31mar31,0,7194079.story

Hackman, M., & Walker, K. (1990). Instructional communication in the televised classroom: The effects of system design and teacher immediacy. *Communication Education, 39,* 196–206.

Haferkamp, N., & Krämer, N. C. (2010). Social comparison 2.0: Examining the effects of online profiles on social-networking sites. *Cyberpsychology, Behavior, and Social Networking, 14,* 309–314. doi:10.1089/cyber.2010.0120

Haga, S., Kraft, P., & Corby, E. (2009). Emotion regulation: Antecedents and well-being outcomes of cognitive reappraisal and expressive suppression in cross-cultural samples. *Journal of Happiness Studies, 10,* 271–291.

Hahlweg, K., & Richter, D. (2010). Prevention of marital instability and distress. Results of an 11-year longitudinal follow-up study. *Behaviour Research and Therapy, 48,* 377–383.

Halatsis, P., & Christakis, N. (2009). The challenge of sexual attraction within heterosexuals' cross-sex friendship. *Journal of Social and Personal Relationships, 26,* 919–937.

Halberstadt, A. G., & Lozada, F. T. (2011). Emotion development in infancy through the lens of culture. *Emotion Review, 3,* 158–168.

Hale, J. L., Tighe, M. R., & Mongeau, P. A. (1997). Effects of event type and sex on comforting messages. *Communication Research Reports, 14,* 214–220.

Hall, E., Travis, M., Anderson, S., & Henley, A. (2013). Complaining and Knapp's relationship stages: Gender differences in instrumental complaints. *Florida Communication Journal, 41,* 49–61.

Hall, E. T. (1959). *Beyond culture.* New York, NY: Doubleday.

Hall, E. T. (1969). *The hidden dimension.* Garden City, NY: Anchor.

Hall, J. A. (2006a). How big are nonverbal sex differences? The case of smiling and nonverbal sensitivity. In K. Dindia & D. J. Canary (Eds.), *Sex differences and similarities in communication* (2nd ed., pp. 55–81). Mahwah, NJ: Erlbaum.

Hall, J. A. (2006b). Women and men's nonverbal communication: Similarities, differences, stereotypes, and origins. In V. Manusov & M. L. Patterson (Eds.), *The Sage handbook of nonverbal communication* (pp. 201–218). Thousand Oaks, CA: Sage.

Hall, J. A. (2012). Friendship standards: The dimensions of ideal expectations. *Journal of Social and Personal Relationships, 29,* 884–907.

Hall, J. A., Coats, E. J., & Smith LeBeau, L. (2005). Nonverbal behavior and the vertical dimension of social relations: A meta-analysis. *Psychological Bulletin, 131,* 898–924.

Hall, J. A., Larson, K. A., & Watts, A. (2011). Satisfying friendship maintenance expectations: The role of friendship standards and biological sex. *Human Communication Research, 37,* 529–552.

Hall, J. A., & Matsumoto, D. (2004). Gender differences in judgments of multiple emotions from facial expressions. *Emotion, 4,* 201–206.

Halone, K. K., & Pecchioni, L. L. (2001). Relational listening: A grounded theoretical model. *Communication Reports, 14,* 59–65.

Halpern, D. F. (2000). *Sex differences in cognitive abilities* (3rd ed.). Mahwah, NJ: Lawrence Erlbaum.

Hamachek, D. E. (1982). *Encounters with others: Interpersonal relationships and you.* New York, NY: Holt, Rinehart & Winston.

Hample, D. (2006). Anti-comforting messages. In K. M. Galvin & P. J. Cooper (Eds.), *Making connections: Readings in relational communication* (4th ed., pp. 222–227). Los Angeles, CA: Roxbury.

Hample, D., Richards, A. S., & Skubisz, C. (2013). Blurting. *Communication Monographs, 80,* 503–532.

Hample, D., Warner, B., & Norton, H. (2007, November). *The effects of arguing expectations and predispositions on perceptions of argument quality and playfulness.* Paper presented at the annual meeting of the International Communication Association, San Francisco, CA.

Hampson, E., van Anders, S. M., & Mullin, L. I. (2006). A female advantage in the recognition of emotional facial expressions: Test of an evolutionary hypothesis. *Evolution and Human Behavior, 27*, 401–416.

Hampton, K., Goulet, L. S., Her, E. J., & Rainie, L. (2009, November 4). *Social isolation and new technology*. PewResearch Internet Project. Retrieved from http://www.pewinternet.org/2009/11/04/social -isolation-and-new-technology/

Hampton, K., Goulet, L. S., Rainie, L. & Purcell, K. (2011, June 16). *Social networking sites and our lives*. Pew Internet: Pew Internet & American Life Project.

Han, S. (2001). Gay identity disclosure to parents by Asian American gay men. *Dissertation Abstracts International: Section A. Humanities and Social Sciences, 62*(1-A), 329.

Hancock, J. T., & Dunham, P. J. (2001). Impression formation in computer-mediated communication revisited: An analysis of the breadth and intensity of impressions. *Communication Research, 28*, 325–347.

Hand, L., & Furman, W. (2009). Rewards and costs in adolescent other-sex friendships: Comparisons to same-sex friendships and romantic relationships. *Social Development, 18*, 270–287.

Hand, M. M., Thomas, D. B., Walter, C., Deemer, E. D., & Buyanjargal, M. (2013). Facebook and romantic relationships: Intimacy and couple satisfaction associated with online social network use. *Cyberpsychology, Behavior, and Social Networking, 16*, 8–13.

Hannawa, A. F. (2014). Disclosing medical errors to patients: Effects of nonverbal involvement. *Patient Education and Counseling, 94*, 310–313.

Hannon, P. A., Finkel, E. J., Kumashiro, M., & Rusbult, C. E. (2012). The soothing effects of forgiveness on victims' and perpetrators' blood pressure. *Personal Relationships, 19*, 279–289.

Hansen, F. C. B., Resnick, H., & Galea, J. (2002). Better listening: Paraphrasing and perception checking—A study of the effectiveness of a multimedia skills training program. *Journal of Technology in Human Services, 20*, 317–331.

Hansen, J. (2007). *24/7: How cell phones and the internet change the way we live, work, and play*. New York, NY: Praeger.

Hanzal, A., & Segrin, C. (2009). The role of conflict resolution styles in mediating the relationship between enduring vulnerabilities and marital quality. *Journal of Family Communication, 9*, 150–169.

Harasymchuk, C., & Fehr, B. (2013). A prototype analysis of relational boredom. *Journal of Social and Personal Relationships, 30*, 627–646.

Harding, J. R. (2007). Evaluative stance and counterfactuals in language and literature. *Language & Literature, 16*, 263–280.

Harper, M. S., & Welsh, D. P. (2007). Keeping quiet: Self-silencing and its association with relational and individual functioning among adolescent romantic couples. *Journal of Social & Personal Relationships, 24*, 99–116.

Harrison, K., & Hefner, V. (2006). Media exposure, current and future body ideals, and disordered eating among preadolescent girls: A longitudinal panel study. *Journal of Youth Adolescence, 35*, 153–163.

Hartnell, C. A., Ou, A., & Kinicki, A. (2011). Organizational culture and organizational effectiveness: A meta-analytic investigation of the competing values framework's theoretical suppositions. *Journal of Applied Psychology, 96*, 677–694.

Harwood, J. (2005). Social identity. In G. J. Shepherd, J. St. John, & T. Striphas (Eds.), *Communication as . . .: Perspectives on theory* (pp. 84–90). Thousand Oaks, CA: Sage.

Harwood, J. (2007). *Understanding communication and aging: Developing knowledge and awareness*. Newbury Park, CA: Sage.

Harwood, J., Bouchard, E., Giles, H., & Tyoski, S. (1997). Evaluations of patronizing speech and three response styles in a non-service-providing context. *Journal of Applied Communication Research, 25*, 170–195.

Haselton, M. G., & Galperin, A. (2013). Error management in relationships. In J. A. Simpson & L. Campbell (Eds.), *The Oxford handbook of close relationships* (pp. 234–254). New York, NY: Oxford University Press.

Hasler, B. S., & Friedman, D. A. (2012). Sociocultural conventions in avatar-mediated nonverbal communication: A cross-cultural analysis of virtual proxemics. *Journal of Intercultural Communication Research, 41*, 238–259.

Hatfield, E., Cacioppo, J. T., Rapson, R. L., & Oatley, K. (1994). *Emotional contagion*. Cambridge, England: Cambridge University Press.

Hatfield, E., & Rapson, R. L. (2006). Passionate love, sexual desire, and mate selection: Cross-cultural and historical perspectives. In P. Noller & J. A. Feeney (Eds.), *Close relationships: Functions, forms and processes* (pp. 227–243). Hove, England: Psychology Press/Taylor & Francis.

Hawken, L., Duran, R. L., & Kelly, L. (1991). The relationship of interpersonal communication variables to academic success and persistence in college. *Communication Quarterly, 39*, 297–308.

Hear the World. (2012, January). *Hearing is living: A study by Hear the World*. Hear the World Foundation.

Heard, H. E. (2007). The family structure trajectory and adolescent school performance: Differential effects by race and ethnicity. *Journal of Family Issues, 28,* 319–354.

Heim, P., & Murphy, S. A. (2001). *In the company of women: Indirect aggression among women: Why we hurt each other and how to stop*. New York, NY: Tarcher/Putnam.

Helsper, E. J., & Whitty, M. T. (2010). Netiquette within married couples: Agreement about acceptable online behavior and surveillance between partners. *Computers in Human Behavior, 26,* 916–926.

Helweg-Larsen, M., Cunningham, S. J., Carrico, A., & Pergram, A. M. (2004). To nod or not to nod: An observational study of nonverbal communication and status in female and male college students. *Psychology of Women Quarterly, 28,* 358–361.

Henderson, S., & Gilding, M. (2004). "I've never clicked this much with anyone in my life": Trust and hyperpersonal communication in online friendships. *New Media & Society, 6,* 487–506.

Henderson, S., Taylor, R., & Thompson, R. (2002). In touch: Young people, communication, and technologies. *Information, Communication, and Society, 5,* 494–512.

Henline, B. H., Lamke, L. K., & Howard, M. D. (2007). Exploring perceptions of online infidelity. *Personal Relationships, 14,* 113–128.

Herakova, L. L. (2012). Nursing masculinity: Male nurses' experiences through a co-cultural lens. *Howard Journal of Communications, 23,* 332–350.

Herfst, S. L., van Oudenhoven, J. P., & Timmerman, M. E. (2008). Intercultural effectiveness training in three western immigrant countries: A cross-cultural evaluation of critical incidents. *International Journal of Intercultural Relations, 32,* 67–80.

Hergovitch, A., Sirsch, U., & Felinger, M. (2002). Self-appraisals, actual appraisals and reflected appraisals of preadolescent children. *Social Behavior and Personality, 30,* 603–612.

Hess, J. A. (2000). Maintaining nonvoluntary relationships with disliked partners: An investigation into the use of distancing behaviors. *Human Communication Research, 26,* 458–488.

Hess, J. A. (2003). Measuring distance in personal relationships: The Relationship Distance Index. *Personal Relationships, 10,* 197–215.

Hess, J. A., Fannin, A. D., & Pollom, L. H. (2007). Creating closeness: Discerning and measuring strategies for fostering closer relationships. *Personal Relationships, 14,* 25–44.

Hess, N. H., & Hagen, E. H. (2006). Sex differences in indirect aggression: Psychological evidence from young adults. *Evolution and Human Behavior, 27,* 231–245.

Hesse, C., Rauscher, E. A., & Wenzel, K. A. (2012). Alexithymia and uncertainty management. *Communication Research Reports, 29,* 343–352.

Heydenberk, W., & Heydenberk, R. (2007). More than manners: Conflict resolution in primary level classrooms. *Early Childhood Education Journal, 35,* 119–126.

Hian, L. B., Chuan, S. L., Trevor, T. M. K., & Detenber, B. H. (2004). Getting to know you: Exploring the development of relational intimacy in computer-mediated communication. *Journal of Computer-Mediated Communication, 9*(3).

Hicks, A. M., & Diamond, L. M. (2011). Don't go to bed angry: Attachment, conflict, and affective and physiological reactivity. *Personal Relationships, 18,* 266–284.

Hidalgo, M. C., & Hernandez, B. (2001). Place attachment: Conceptual and empirical questions. *Journal of Environmental Psychology, 21,* 273–281.

High, A. C., & Dillard, J. P. (2012). A review and meta-analysis of person-centered messages and social support outcomes. *Communication Studies, 53,* 99–118.

Hill, C., Memon, A., & McGeorge, P. (2008). The role of confirmation bias in suspect interviews: A systematic evaluation. *Legal and Criminological Psychology, 13,* 357–371.

Hinde, R. A., Finkenauer, C., & Auhagen, A. E. (2001). Relationships and the self-concept. *Personal Relationships, 8,* 187–204.

Hochman, D. (2013, November 3). Mindfulness: Getting its share of attention. *The New York Times*, p. ST1.

Hoffman, L. (2010). Experiencing intimacy: Women's reports in same-sex and cross-sex relationships. *Dissertation Abstracts International: Section B. The Sciences and Engineering, 70*(9-B), 5895.

Hoffman, M. L. (1991). Empathy, social cognition, and moral action. In W. Kurtines & J. Gerwirtz (Eds.), *Moral behavior and development: Theory, research, and applications* (Vol. 1, pp. 275–301). Hillsdale, NJ: Erlbaum.

Hofstede, G. (1984). *Culture's consequences: International differences in work-related values*. Newbury Park, CA: Sage.

Hogenboom, M. (2013, November 27). *Can virtual reality be used to tackle racism?* BBC News: Science and Environment. Retrieved from http://www.bbc.com/news/science-environment-23709836

Høgh-Olesen, H. (2008). Human spatial behaviour: The spacing of people, objects, and animals in six cross-cultural samples. *Journal of Cognition and Culture, 8,* 245–280.

Holfeld, B., & Grabe, M. (2012). An examination of the history, prevalence, characteristics, and reporting of cyberbullying in the United States. In Q. Li, D. Cross, & P. K. Smith (Eds.), *Cyberbullying in the global playground: Research from international perspectives* (pp. 117–142). San Francisco, CA: Wiley-Blackwell.

Hollenbaugh, E. E., & Everett, M. K. (2013). The effects of anonymity on self-disclosure in blogs: An application of the online disinhibition effect. *Journal of Computer-Mediated Communication, 18,* 283–302.

Holman, T. B., & Jarvis, M. O. (2003). Hostile, volatile, avoiding, and validating couple-conflict types: An investigation of Gottman's couple-conflict types. *Personal Relationships, 10,* 267–282.

Holmstrom, A. J. (2009). Sex and gender similarities and differences in communication values in same-sex and cross-sex friendships. *Communication Quarterly, 57,* 224–238.

Holmstrom, A. J., Burleson, B., and Jones, S. (2005). Some consequences for helpers who deliver "cold comfort": Why it's worse for women than men to be inept when providing emotional support. *Sex Roles, 53,* 153–172.

Holoien, D. S., & Fiske, S. T. (2013). Compensation between warmth and competence in impression management. *Journal of Experimental Social Psychology, 49,* 33–41.

Holt, J. L., & DeVore, C. J. (2005). Culture, gender, organizational role, and styles of conflict resolution: A meta-analysis. *International Journal of Intercultural Relations, 29,* 165–196.

Holtgraves, T. (2011). Text messaging, personality, and the social context. *Journal of Research in Personality, 45,* 92–99.

Holtgraves, T., & Paul, K. (2013). Texting versus talking: An exploration in telecommunication language. *Telematics and Informatics, 30,* 289–295.

Holt-Lunstad, J., Smith T. B., & Layton, J. B. (2010). Social relationships and mortality risk: A meta-analytic review. *PLoS Med, 7*(7), e1000316. Retrieved from http://www.plosmedicine.org/article /info%3Adoi%2F10.1371%2Fjournal.pmed.1000316

Homburg, C., & Fürst, A. (2007). See no evil, hear no evil, speak no evil: A study of defensive organizational behavior towards customer complaints. *Journal of the Academy of Marketing Science, 35,* 523–536.

Hoorens, V., Pandelaere, M., Oldersma, F., & Sedikides, C. (2012). The hubris hypothesis: You can self-enhance, but you'd better not show it. *Journal of Personality, 80,* 1237–1274.

Hopcke, R. H., & Rafaty, L. (2001). *Straight women, gay men: Absolutely fabulous friendships.* Berkeley, CA: Wildcat Canyon Press.

Hopp, H., Troy, A. S., & Mauss, I. B. (2011). The unconscious pursuit of emotion regulation: Implications for psychological health. *Cognition & Emotion, 25,* 532–545.

Horan, S. M. (2012). Affection exchange theory and perceptions of relational transgressions. *Western Journal of Communication, 76,* 109–126.

Horan, S. M., & Booth-Butterfield, M. (2010). Investing in affection: An investigation of affection exchange theory and relational qualities. *Communication Quarterly, 58,* 394–413.

Horan, S. M., & Booth-Butterfield, M. (2013). Understanding the routine expression of deceptive affection in romantic relationships. *Communication Quarterly, 61,* 195–216.

Hornik, J. (1992). Effects of physical contact on customers' shopping time and behavior. *Marketing Letters, 3,* 49–55.

Hornsey, M. J., Oppes, T., & Svensson, A. (2002). "It's ok if we say it, but you can't": Responses to intergroup and intragroup criticism. *European Journal of Social Psychology, 32,* 293–307.

Horwitz, B. N., Neiderhiser, J. M., Ganiban, J. M., Spotts, E. L., Lichtenstein, P., & Reiss, D. (2010). Genetic and environmental influences on global family conflict. *Journal of Family Psychology, 24,* 217–220.

Hosman, L. A., & Siltanen, S. A. (2006). Powerful and powerless language forms: Their consequences for impression formation, attributions of control of self and control of others, cognitive responses, and message memory. *Journal of Language & Social Psychology, 25,* 33–46.

Houghton, T. J. (2001). A study of communication among supervisors: The influence of supervisor/supervisee verbal aggressiveness on communication climate and organizational commitment. *Dissertation Abstracts International: Section A. Humanities and Social Sciences, 61*(10-A), 3826.

Houser, M. L., Fleuriet, C., & Estrada, D. (2012). The cyber factor: An analysis of relational maintenance through the use of computer-mediated communication. *Communication Research Reports, 29,* 34–43.

Howe, D. (2013). *Empathy: What it is and why it matters.* New York, NY: Palgrave Macmillan.

Hsu, A. S., & Chater, N. (2010). The logical problem of language acquisition: A probabilistic perspective. *Cognitive Science, 34,* 972–1016.

Hsu, C.-F. (2010). Acculturation and communication traits: A study of cross-cultural adaptation among Chinese in America. *Communication Monographs, 77,* 414–425.

Huang, L. (1999). Family communication patterns and personality characteristics. *Communication Quarterly, 47,* 230–243.

Huang, Y.-Y., & Chou, C. (2010). An analysis of multiple factors of cyberbullying among junior high school students in Taiwan. *Computers in Human Behavior, 26*, 1581–1590.

Hubbard, A., Aune, K., & Lee, H. E. (2009, May). *Communication qualities, quantity, satisfaction, and talk impact in newly developing relationships: A longitudinal analysis.* Paper presented at the Annual Meeting of the International Communication Association, Chicago, IL.

Huestis, V. D. (2010). *Little white lies: Lies and deception in the virtual world of online dating.* Ann Arbor, MI: ProQuest LLC.

Huffman, A., Culbertson, S. S., Henning, J. B., & Goh, A. (2013). Work-family conflict across the lifespan. *Journal of Managerial Psychology, 28*, 761–780.

Hughes, D. (2009). The communication of emotions and the growth of autonomy and intimacy within family therapy. In D. Fosha, D. J. Siegel, & M. F. Solomon (Eds.), *The healing power of emotion: Affective neuroscience, development & clinical practice* (pp. 280–303). New York, NY: Norton.

Hui, C. M., Molden, D. C., & Finkel, E. J. (2013). Loving freedom: Concerns with promotion or prevention and the role of autonomy in relationship well-being. *Journal of Personality and Social Psychology, 105*, 61–85.

Hullman, G. A. (2007). Communicative Adaptability Scale: Evaluating its use as an "other-report" measure. *Communication Reports, 20*, 51–74.

Hullman, G. A., Planisek, A., McNally, J. S., & Rubin, R. B. (2010). Competence, personality, and self-efficacy: Relationships in an undergraduate interpersonal course. *Atlantic Journal of Communication, 18*, 36–49.

Human, L. J., & Biesanz, J. C. (2011). Through the looking glass clearly: Accuracy and assumed similarity in well-adjusted individuals' first impressions. *Journal of Personality and Social Psychology, 100*, 349–364.

Hummert, M. L. (2011). Age stereotypes and aging. In K. W. Schaie & S. L. Willis (Eds.), *Handbook of the psychology of aging* (7th ed., pp. 249–262). San Diego, CA: Elsevier Academic Press.

Hyde, R. B. (1993). Council: Using a talking stick to teach listening. *Communication Teacher, 7*, 1–2.

Hyvarinen, L., Tanskanen, P., Katajavuori, N., & Isotalus, P. (2010). A method for teaching communication in pharmacy in authentic work situations. *Communication Education, 59*, 124–145.

Iafrate, R., Bertoni, A., Donato, S., & Finkenauer, C. (2012). Perceived similarity and understanding in dyadic coping among young and mature couples. *Personal Relationships, 19*, 401–419.

Ickes, W., & Hodges, S. D. (2013). Empathic accuracy in close relationships. In J. A. Simpson & L. Campbell (Eds.), *The Oxford handbook of close relationships* (pp. 348–373). New York, NY: Oxford University Press.

Iliescu, D., Ilie, A., Ispas, D., & Ion, A. (2012). Emotional intelligence in personnel selection: Applicant reactions, criterion, and incremental validity. *International Journal of Selection and Assessment, 20*, 347–358.

Imhof, M. (2003). The social construction of the listener: Listening behavior across situations, perceived listening status, and cultures. *Communication Research Reports, 20*, 357–366.

Impett, E. A., & Peplau, L. A. (2006). "His" and "her" relationships? A review of the empirical evidence. In A. Vangelisti & D. Perlman (Eds.), *The Cambridge handbook of personal relationships* (pp. 273–292). New York, NY: Cambridge University Press.

Infante, D. A. (1987). Aggressiveness. In J. C. McCroskey & J. A. Daly (Eds.), *Personality and interpersonal communication* (pp. 157–192). Newbury Park, CA: Sage.

Infante, D. A., Chandler, T. A., & Rudd, J. E. (1989). Test of an argumentative skill deficiency model of interspousal violence. *Communication Monographs, 56*, 163–177.

Infante, D. A., & Gorden, W. I. (1989). Argumentativeness and affirming communicator style as predictors of satisfaction/dissatisfaction with subordinates. *Communication Quarterly, 37*, 81–90.

Infante, D. A., & Rancer, A. S. (1996). Argumentativeness and verbal aggressiveness: A review of recent theory and research. *Communication Yearbook, 19*, 320–351.

Infante, D. A., Riddle, B. L., Horvath, C. L., & Tumlin, S. A. (1992). Verbal aggressiveness: Messages and reasons. *Communication Quarterly, 40*, 116–126.

Ireland, M. E., Slatcher, R. B., Eastwick, P. W., Scissors, L. E., Finkel, E. J., & Pennebaker, J. W. (2011). Language style matching predicts relationship initiation and stability. *Psychological Science, 22*, 39–44.

Irizarry, C. A. (2004). Face and the female professional: A thematic analysis of face-threatening communication in the workplace. *Qualitative Research Reports in Communication, 5*, 15–21.

Iyer, P. (1990). *The lady and the monk: Four seasons in Kyoto.* New York, NY: Vintage.

Jackson, W. C. (1978, September 7). Lonely dean finishes "excrutiating" voyage. *Wisconsin State Journal.*

Janas, M. (2001). Getting a clear view. *Journal of Staff Development, 22*(2), 32–34.

Jankowski, K. S. (2013). Morning types are less sensitive to pain than evening types all day long. *European Journal of Pain, 17*, 1068–1073.

Jaret, C., Reitzes, D., & Shapkina, N. (2005). Reflected appraisals and self-esteem. *Sociological Perspectives, 48,* 403–419.

Jaschinski, C., & Kommers, P. (2012). Does beauty matter? The role of friends' attractiveness and gender on social attractiveness ratings of individuals on Facebook. *International Journal of Web Based Communities, 8,* 389–401.

Jay, T., & Janschewitz, K. (2008). The pragmatics of swearing. *Journal of Politeness Research: Language, Behavior, Culture, 4,* 267–288.

Jerome, E. M., & Liss, M. (2005). Relationships between sensory processing style, adult attachment, and coping. *Personality and Individual Differences, 38,* 1341–1352.

Jiang, L. C., Bazarova, N. N., & Hancock, J. T. (2011). The disclosure-intimacy link in computer-mediated communication: An attributional extension of the hyperpersonal model. *Human Communication Research, 37,* 58–77.

Jiang, L. C., Bazarova, N. N., & Hancock, J. T. (2013). From perception to behavior: Disclosure reciprocity and the intensification of intimacy in computer-mediated communication. *Communication Research, 40,* 125–143.

Jiang, L. C., & Hancock, J. T. (2013). Absence makes the communication grow fonder: Geographic separation, interpersonal media, and intimacy in dating relationships. *Journal of Communication, 63,* 556–577.

Jiangang, D., Xiucheng, F., & Tianjun, F. (2011). Multiple emotional contagions in service encounters. *Journal of the Academy of Marketing Science, 39,* 449–466.

Jin, B., & Peña, J. F. (2010). Mobile communication in romantic relationships: Mobile phone use, relational uncertainty, love, commitment, and attachment styles. *Communication Reports, 23,* 39–51.

Johnson, A. J., Becker, A. H., Craig, E. A., Gilchrist, E. S., & Haigh, M. M. (2009). Changes in friendship commitment: Comparing geographically close and long-distance young-adult friendships. *Communication Quarterly, 57,* 395–415.

Johnson, A. J., Haigh, M. M., Becker, J. A. H., Craig, E. A., & Wigley, S. (2008). College students' use of relational management strategies in email in long-distance and geographically close relationships. *Journal of Computer-Mediated Communication, 13,* 381–404.

Johnson, A. J., Haigh, M. M., Craig, E. A., & Becker, J. A. H. (2009). Relational closeness: Comparing undergraduate college students' geographically close and long-distance friendships. *Personal Relationships, 16,* 631–646.

Johnson, A. J., Wittenberg, E., Haigh, M., Wigley, S., Becker, J., Brown, K., & Craig, E. (2004). The process of relationship development and deterioration: Turning points in friendships that have terminated. *Communication Quarterly, 52,* 54–67.

Johnson, C. S., & Stapel, D. A. (2010). It depends on how you look at it: Being versus becoming mindsets determine responses to social comparisons. *British Journal of Social Psychology, 49,* 703–723.

Johnson, D. I. (2009). Connected classroom climate: A validity study. *Communication Research Reports, 26,* 146–157.

Johnson, D. I. (2012). Swearing by peers in the work setting: Expectancy violation valence, perceptions of message, and perceptions of speaker. *Communication Studies, 63,* 136–151.

Johnson, D. I., & Lewis, N. (2010). Perceptions of swearing in the work setting: An expectancy violations theory perspective. *Communication Reports, 23,* 106–118.

Johnson, H. D. (2012). Relationship duration moderation of identity status differences in emerging adults' same-sex friendship intimacy. *Journal of Adolescence, 35,* 1515–1525.

Johnson, K. R., & Holmes, B. M. (2009). Contradictory messages: A content analysis of Hollywood-produced romantic comedy feature films. *Communication Quarterly, 57,* 352–373.

Johnson, S. (1987). *Going out of our minds: The metaphysics of liberation.* Freedom, CA: Crossing.

Joint Commission on Accreditation of Healthcare. (2008). *Sentinel event statistics.* Oakbrook Terrace, IL: Author.

Joireman, J. (2004). Relationships between attributional complexity and empathy. *Individual Differences Research, 2,* 197–202.

Jonason, P. K. (2013). Four functions for four relationships: Consensus definitions of university students. *Archives of Sexual Behavior, 42,* 1407–1414.

Jones, C., Berry, L., & Stevens, C. (2007). Synthesized speech intelligibility and persuasion: Speech rate and non-native listeners. *Computer Speech & Language, 21,* 641–651.

Jones, J. T., Pelham, B. W., & Carvallo, M. (2004). How do I love thee? Let me count the Js: Implicit egotism and interpersonal attraction. *Journal of Personality and Social Psychology, 87,* 665–683.

Jones, S. E. (1986). Sex differences in touch behavior. *Western Journal of Speech Communication, 50,* 227–241.

Jones, S. M., & Burleson, B. R. (2003). Effects of helper and recipient sex on the experience and outcomes of comforting messages: An experimental investigation. *Sex Roles, 48,* 1–19.

Jundi, S. V., Mann, A., Hope, S., Hillman, L., Warmelink, J., & Lara Gahr, E. (2013). Who should I look at? Eye contact during collective interviewing as a cue to deceit. *Psychology, Crime & Law, 19,* 661–671.

Jussim, L., Robustelli, S. L., & Cain, T. R. (2009). Teacher expectations and self-fulfilling prophecies. In K. R. Wenzel & A. Wigfield (Eds.), *Handbook of motivation at school* (pp. 349–380). New York, NY: Routledge/Taylor & Francis Group.

Just, M. A., Keller, T. A., & Cynkar, J. A. (2008). A decrease in brain activation associated with driving when listening to someone speak. *Brain Research, 1205,* 70–80.

Kagan, J. (2007). *What is emotion? History, measures, and meanings.* New Haven, CT: Yale University Press.

Kahneman, D., Krueger, A. B., Schkade, D. A., Schwarz, N., & Stone, A. A. (2004). A daily measure. *Science, 306,* 1645.

Kalman, Y. M., & Rafaeli, S. (2011). Online pauses and silence: Chronemic expectancy violations in written computer-mediated communication. *Communication Research, 38,* 54–69.

Kalman, Y. M., Scissors, L. E., Gill, A. J., & Gergle, D. (2013). Online chronemics convey social information. *Computers in Human Behavior, 29,* 1260–1269.

Kanaga, K. R., & Flynn, M. (1981). The relationship between invasion of personal space and stress. *Human Relations, 34,* 239–248.

Kapidzic, S., & Herring, S. C. (2011). Gender, communication, and self-presentation in teen chatrooms revisited: Have patterns changed? *Journal of Computer-Mediated Communication, 17,* 39–59.

Karakis, E. N., & Levant, R. F. (2012). Is normative male alexithymia associated with relationship satisfaction, fear of intimacy and communication quality among men in relationships? *Journal of Men's Studies, 20,* 179–186.

Kassing, J. W. (1997). Development of the Intercultural Willingness to Communicate Scale. *Communication Research Reports, 14,* 399–407.

Katt, J., & Collins, S. (2009, November). *The effects of provisionalism and verbal immediacy in written student assessments on student motivation and affective learning.* Paper presented at the conference of the National Communication Association, Chicago, IL.

Katt, J. A., & Collins, S. J. (2013). The power of provisional/immediate language revisited: Adding student personality traits to the mix. *Communication Research Reports, 30,* 85–95.

Katz-Wise, S. L., & Hyde, J. S. (2014). Sexuality and gender: The interplay. In D. L. Tolman, L. M. Diamond, J. A. Bauermeister, W. H. George, J. G. Pfaus, & L. Ward (Eds.), *APA handbook of sexuality and psychology: Vol. 1. Person-based approaches* (pp. 29–62). Washington, DC: American Psychological Association.

Katzer, C., Fetchenhauer, D., & Belschak, F. (2009). Cyberbullying: Who are the victims?: A comparison of victimization in internet chatrooms and victimization in school. *Journal of Media Psychology: Theories, Methods, and Applications, 21,* 25–36.

Katzir, M., & Eyal, T. (2013). When stepping outside the self is not enough: A self-distanced perspective reduces the experience of basic but not of self-conscious emotions. *Journal of Experimental Social Psychology, 49,* 1089–1092.

Kaufman, D., & Mahoney, J. M. (1999). The effect of waitresses' touch on alcohol consumption in dyads. *Journal of Social Psychology, 139,* 261–267.

Kaufman, P. (2003). Learning to not labor: How working-class individuals construct middle-class identities. *Sociological Quarterly, 44,* 481–504.

Kaya, N., & Burgess, B. (2007). Territoriality: Seat preferences in different types of classroom arrangements. *Environment and Behavior, 39,* 859–876.

Keashly, L., & Neuman, J. H. (2009). Building a constructive communication climate: The Workplace Stress and Aggression Project. In P. Lutgen-Sandvik & B. D. Sypher (Eds.), *Destructive organizational communication: Processes, consequences, and constructive ways of organizing* (pp. 339–362). New York, NY: Routledge/Taylor & Francis Group.

Kees, N. L., Aberle, J. T., & Fruhauf, C. A. (2007). Aging parents and end-of-life decisions: Helping families negotiate difficult conversations. In D. Linville & K. M. Hertlein (Eds.), *The therapist's notebook for family health care: Homework, handouts, and activities for individuals, couples, and families coping with illness, loss, and disability* (pp. 211–216). New York, NY: Haworth Press.

Kellas, J. K. (2005). Family ties: Communicating identity through jointly told family stories. *Communication Monographs, 72,* 365–389.

Kellas, J. K., Willer, E. K., & Trees, A. R. (2013). Communicated perspective-taking during stories of marital stress: Spouses' perceptions of one another's perspective-taking behaviors. *Southern Communication Journal, 78,* 326–351.

Kellermann, K. (1989). The negativity effect in interaction: It's all in your point of view. *Human Communication Research, 16,* 147–183.

Kelley, D. L., & Waldron, V. R. (2005). An investigation of forgiveness-seeking communication and relational outcomes. *Communication Quarterly, 53,* 339–358.

Kerem, E., Fishman, N., & Josselson, R. (2001). The experience of empathy in everyday relationships: Cognitive and affective elements. *Journal of Social and Personal Relationships, 18,* 709–729.

Keyton, J., Caputo, J., Ford, E., Fu, R., Leibowitz, S. A., Liu, T., . . . Wu, C. (2013). Investigating verbal workplace communication behaviors. *Journal of Business Communication, 50*, 152–169.

Kidwell, B., Hardesty, D. M., Murtha, B. R., & Sheng, S. (2011). Emotional intelligence in marketing exchanges. *Journal of Marketing, 75*, 78–95.

Kim, E. J., & Buschmann, M. T. (1999). The effect of expressive physical touch on patients with dementia. *International Journal of Nursing Studies, 36*, 235–243.

Kim, H., Edwards, A. B., Sweeney, K. A., & Wetchler, J. L. (2012). The effects of differentiation and attachment on satisfaction and acculturation in Asian-White American international couple relationships: Assessment with Chinese, South Korean, and Japanese partners in relationships with white American partners in the United States. *American Journal of Family Therapy, 40*, 320–335.

Kim, J., LaRose, R., & Peng, W. (2009). Loneliness as the cause and effect of problematic internet use: The relationship between Internet use and psychological well-being. *CyberPsychology & Behavior, 12*, 451–455.

Kim, J., & Lee, J. R. (2011). The Facebook paths to happiness: Effects of the number of Facebook friends and self-presentation on subjective well-being. *Cyberpsychology, Behavior, and Social Networking, 14*, 359–364.

Kim, M. S., Shin, H. C., & Cai, D. (1998). Cultural influences on the preferred forms of requesting and re-requesting. *Communication Monographs, 65*, 47–66.

Kim, Y. K., & Sax, L. J. (2009). Student–faculty interaction in research universities: Differences by student gender, race, social class, and first-generation status. *Research in Higher Education, 50*, 437–459.

Kim, Y. Y. (2005). Adapting to a new culture: An integrative communication theory. In W. B. Gudykunst (Ed.), *Theorizing about intercultural communication* (pp. 375–400). Thousand Oaks, CA: Sage.

Kim, Y. Y. (2008). Intercultural personhood: Globalization and a way of being. *International Journal of Intercultural Relations, 32*, 359–368.

Kimmel, M. S. (2008) *The gendered society* (3rd ed.). New York, NY: Oxford University Press.

Kim-Prieto, C., & Eid, M. (2004). Norms for experiencing emotions in Sub-Saharan Africa. *Journal of Happiness Studies, 5*, 241–268.

King, P. M., Perez, R. J., & Shim, W. (2013). How college students experience intercultural learning: Key features and approaches. *Journal of Diversity in Higher Education, 6*, 69–83.

Kingsley Westerman, C. Y., & Westerman, D. (2010). Supervisor impression management: Message content and channel effects on impressions. *Communication Studies, 61*, 585–601.

Kinzler, K. D., Shutts, K., Dejesus, J., & Spelke, E. S. (2009). Accent trumps race in guiding children's social preferences. *Social Cognition, 27*, 623–634.

Kirchler, E. (1988). Marital happiness and interaction in everyday surroundings: A time-sample diary approach for couples. *Journal of Social and Personal Relationships, 5*, 375–382.

Kirkcaldy, B., Furnham, A., & Levine, R. (2001). Attitudinal and personality correlates of a nation's pace of life. *Journal of Managerial Psychology, 16*, 20–34.

Kirkland, R. A., Peterson, E., Baker, C. A., Miller, S., & Pulos, S. (2013). Meta-analysis reveals adult female superiority in "Reading the Mind in the Eyes" Test. *North American Journal of Psychology, 15*, 121–146.

Kiser, L. J., Baumgardner, B., & Dorado, J. (2010). Who are we, but for the stories we tell: Family stories and healing. *Psychological Trauma: Theory, Research, Practice, and Policy, 2*, 243–249.

Kleinke, C. L., Peterson, T. R., & Rutledge, T. R. (1998). Effects of self-generated facial expressions on mood. *Journal of Personality and Social Psychology, 74*, 272–279.

Kleman, E. E. (2008). "May I interest you in today's special?": A pilot study of restaurant servers' compliance-gaining strategies. *Rocky Mountain Communication Review, 5*(1), 32–42.

Klohnen, E. C., & Luo, S. (2003). Interpersonal attraction and personality: What is attractive—self similarity, ideal similarity, complementarity or attachment security? *Journal of Personality and Social Psychology, 85*, 709–722.

Klopf, D. (1984). Cross-cultural apprehension research: A summary of Pacific Basin studies. In J. Daly & J. McCroskey (Eds.), *Avoiding communication: Shyness, reticence, and communication apprehension* (pp. 157–169). Beverly Hills, CA: Sage.

Kluemper, D. H., Rosen, P. A., & Mossholder, K. W. (2012). Social networking websites, personality ratings, and the organizational context: More than meets the eye? *Journal of Applied Social Psychology, 42*, 1143–1172.

Kluger, A. N., & Zaidel, K. (2013). Are listeners perceived as leaders? *International Journal of Listening, 27*, 73–84.

Kluger, J., & Wilson, C. (2013, October 22). America's mood map: An interactive guide to the United States of attitude. *Time.* Retrieved from http://science.time.com/2013/10/22/the-united-states-of-attitude-an-interactive-guide-to-americas-moods/?hpt=hp_c2

Knapp, M. L. (2006). Lying and deception in close relationships. In A. Vangelisti & D. Perlman (Eds.), *The Cambridge handbook of personal relationships* (pp. 517–532). New York, NY: Cambridge University Press.

Knapp, M. L., & Hall, J. A. (2006). *Nonverbal communication in human interaction* (6th ed.). Belmont, CA: Wadsworth.

Knapp, M. L., & Hall, J. A. (2010). *Nonverbal communication in human interaction* (7th ed.). Boston: Cengage.

Knapp, M. L., Vangelisti, A. L., & Caughlin, J. P. (2014). *Interpersonal communication in human relationships* (7th ed.). Boston, MA: Pearson Education.

Knobloch, L. K., & Metts, S. (2013). Emotion in relationships. In J. A. Simpson & L. Campbell (Eds.), *The Oxford handbook of close relationships* (pp. 514–534). New York, NY: Oxford University Press.

Knobloch, L. K., Miller, L. E., Bond, B. J., & Mannone, S. E. (2007). Relational uncertainty and message processing in marriage. *Communication Monographs, 74,* 154–180.

Knobloch, L. K., & Solomon, D. H. (2003). Manifestations of relationship conception in conversation. *Human Communication Research, 29,* 482–515.

Knobloch-Westerwick, S., & Alter, S. (2006). Mood adjustment to social situations through mass media use: How men ruminate and women dissipate angry moods. *Human Communication Research, 32,* 58–73.

Knöfler, T., & Imhof, M. (2007). Does sexual orientation have an impact on nonverbal behavior in interpersonal communication? *Journal of Nonverbal Behavior, 31,* 189–204.

Koenig, M. A., & Jaswal, V. K. (2011). Characterizing children's expectations about expertise and incompetence: Halo or pitchfork effects? *Child Development, 82,* 1634–1647.

Koerner, A. F., & Fitzpatrick, M. A. (2002). Toward a theory of family communication. *Communication Theory, 12,* 70–91.

Koerner, A. F., & Fitzpatrick, M. A. (2006). Family communications patterns theory: A social cognitive approach. In D. O. Braithwaite & L. A. Baxter (Eds.), *Engaging theories in family communication: Multiple perspectives* (pp. 50–65). Thousand Oaks, CA: Sage.

Koerner, A. F., & Schrodt, P. (2014). An introduction to the special issue on family communication patterns. *Journal of Family Communication, 14,* 1–15.

Koesten, J. (2004). Family communication patterns, sex of subject, and communication competence. *Communication Monographs, 71,* 226–244.

Kolligan, J., Jr. (1990). Perceived fraudulence as a dimension of perceived incompetence. In R. J. Sternberg & J. Kolligan, Jr. (Eds.), *Competence considered* (pp. 261–285). New Haven, CT: Yale University Press.

Korchmaros, J. D., & Kenny, D. A. (2006). An evolutionary and close-relationship model of helping. *Journal of Social and Personal Relationships, 23,* 21–43.

Korn, C. J., Morreale, S. R., & Boileau, D. M. (2000). Defining the field: Revisiting the ACA 1995 definition of Communication Studies. *Journal of the Association for Communication Administration, 29,* 40–52.

Koroshnia, M. M., & Latifian, M. M. (2008). An investigation on validity and reliability of revised family communication patterns instrument. *Journal of Family Research, 3,* 855–875.

Korzybski, A. (1933). *Science and sanity.* Lancaster, PA: Science Press.

Kotchemidova, C. (2010). Emotion culture and cognitive constructions of reality. *Communication Quarterly, 58,* 207–234.

Koukkari, W. L., & Sothern, R. B. (2006). *Introducing biological rhythms: a primer on the temporal organization of life, with implications for health, society, reproduction and the natural environment.* New York, NY: Springer.

Kouzakova, M., van Baaren, R., & van Knippenberg, A. (2010). Lack of behavioral imitation in human interactions enhances salivary cortisol levels. *Hormones and Behavior, 57,* 421–426.

Kowalski, R. M., & Limber, S. P. (2013). Psychological, physical, and academic correlates of cyberbullying and traditional bullying. *Journal of Adolescent Health, 53*(1, Suppl.), S13–S20.

Kramer, M. W., & Hess, J. A. (2002). Communication rules for the display of emotions in organizational settings. *Management Communication Quarterly, 16,* 66–80.

Kraus, M. W., Huang, C., & Keltner, D. (2010). Tactile communication, cooperation, and performance: An ethological study of the NBA. *Emotion, 10,* 745–749.

Krause, R. (2010). An update on primary identification, introjection, and empathy. *International Forum of Psychoanalysis, 19,* 138–143.

Krcmar, M., Giles, S., & Helme, D. (2008). Understanding the process: How mediated and peer norms affect young women's body esteem. *Communication Quarterly, 56,* 111–130.

Krebs, V. (2008). Social capital: The key to success for the 21st century organization. *International Association for Human Resources Journal, 12,* 38–42.

Kross, E., Bruehlman-Senecal, E., Park, J., Burson, A., Dougherty, A., Shablack, H., . . . Ayduk, O. (2014). Self-talk as a regulatory mechanism: How you do it matters. *Journal of Personality and Social Psychology, 106*, 304–324.

Krumhuber, E., Manstead, A. S. R., Cosker, D., Marshall, D., & Rosin, P. L. (2009). Effects of dynamic attributes of smiles in human and synthetic faces: A simulated job interview setting. *Journal of Nonverbal Behavior, 33*, 1–15.

Kujath, C. L. (2011). Facebook and MySpace: Complement or substitute for face-to-face interaction? *Cyberpsychology, Behavior, and Social Networking, 14*, 75–78.

Kuo, F. E., & Sullivan, W. C. (2001a). Aggression and violence in the inner city: Effects of environment via mental fatigue. *Environment and Behavior, 33*, 543–571.

Kuo, F. E., & Sullivan, W. C. (2001b). Environment and crime in the inner city: Does vegetation reduce crime? *Environment and Behavior, 33*, 343–367.

Kurzban, R., & Weeden, J. (2005). HurryDate: Mate preferences in action. *Evolution and Human Behavior, 26*, 227–244.

Kuss, D. J., Rooij, A. J., Shorter, G. W., Griffiths, M. D., & van de Mheen, D. (2013). Internet addiction in adolescents: Prevalence and risk factors. *Computers in Human Behavior, 29*, 1987–1996.

Kuttner, R. (2013). From positionality to relationality: A Buddhist-oriented relational view of conflict escalation and its transformation. *Peace and Conflict Studies, 20*, 58–82.

La France, B. H. (2010). What verbal and nonverbal communication cues lead to sex?: An analysis of the traditional sexual script. *Communication Quarterly, 58*, 297–318.

Lakey, B. (2013). Social support processes in relationships. In J. A. Simpson & L. Campbell (Eds.), *The Oxford handbook of close relationships* (pp. 711–730). New York, NY: Oxford University Press.

Lakin, J. L. (2006). Automatic cognitive processes and nonverbal communication. In V. Manusov & M. L. Patterson (Eds.), *The Sage handbook of nonverbal communication* (pp. 59–77). Thousand Oaks, CA: Sage.

Lambert, N. M., Gwinn, A. M., Baumeister, R. F., Strachman, A., Washburn, I. J., Gable, S. L., & Fincham, F. D. (2013). A boost of positive affect: The perks of sharing positive experiences. *Journal of Social and Personal Relationships, 30*, 24–43.

Landrum, R. E., & Harrold, R. (2003). What employers want from psychology graduates. *Teaching of Psychology, 30*, 131–133.

Lane, K., Balleweg, B. J., Suler, J. R., Fernald, P. S., & Goldstein, G. S. (2000). Acquiring skills—Undergraduate students. In M. E. Ware & D. E. Johnson (Eds.), *Handbook of demonstrations and activities in the teaching of psychology: Vol. 3. Personality, abnormal, clinical-counseling, and social* (2nd ed., pp. 109–124). Mahwah, NJ: Erlbaum.

Langellier, K. M., & Peterson, E. E. (2006). Narrative performance theory: Telling stories, doing family. In D. O. Braithwaite, & L. A. Baxter (Eds.), *Engaging theories in family communication: Multiple perspectives* (pp. 99–114). Thousand Oaks, CA: Sage.

Langer, E. (1990). *Mindfulness*. Reading, MA: Addison-Wesley.

Lannin, D. G., Bittner, K. E., & Lorenz, F. O. (2013). Longitudinal effect of defensive denial on relationship instability. *Journal of Family Psychology, 27*, 968–977.

Lapakko, D. (1997). Three cheers for language: A closer examination of a widely cited study of nonverbal communication. *Communication Education, 46*, 63–67.

Lapidot-Lefler, N., & Barak, A. (2012). Effects of anonymity, invisibility, and lack of eye-contact on toxic online disinhibition. *Computers in Human Behavior, 28*, 434–443.

Latz, J. (2010, May 28). 4 steps to speak better in interviews. *The Ladders*. Retrieved from http://www.theladders .com/career-advice/4-steps-speak-better-interviews

Laurenceau, J.-P., Barrett, L. F., & Rovine, M. J. (2005). The Interpersonal Process Model of intimacy in marriage: A daily-diary and multilevel modeling approach. *Journal of Family Psychology, 19*, 314–323.

Laurenceau, J.-P., & Kleinman, B. M. (2006). Intimacy in personal relationships. In A. Vangelisti & D. Perlman (Eds.), *The Cambridge handbook of personal relationships* (pp. 637–656). New York, NY: Cambridge University Press.

Laursen, B., & Pursell, G. (2009). Conflict in peer relationships. In K. H. Rubin, W. M. Bukowski, & B. Laursen (Eds.), *Handbook of peer interactions, relationships, and groups* (pp. 267–286). New York, NY: Guilford Press.

Lawler, K. A., Younger, J. W., Piferi, R. L., Billington, E., Jobe, R., Edmondson, K., & Jones, W. H. (2003). A change of heart: Cardiovascular correlates of forgiveness in response to interpersonal conflict. *Journal of Behavioral Medicine, 26*, 373–393.

Lawrence, E., Yoon, J., Langer, A., & Ro, E. (2009). Is psychological aggression as detrimental as physical aggression? The independent effects of psychological aggression on depression and anxiety symptoms. *Violence and Victims, 24*, 20–35.

Leaper, C., & Ayres, M. M. (2007). A meta-analytic review of gender variations in adults' language use: Talkativeness, affiliative speech, and assertive speech. *Personality and Social Psychology Review, 11*, 328–363.

Leaper, C., & Robnett, R. D. (2011). Women are more likely than men to use tentative language, aren't they? A meta-analysis testing for gender differences and moderators. *Psychology of Women Quarterly, 35,* 129–142.

Lebuda, I., & Karwowski, M. (2013). Tell me your name and I'll tell you how creative your work is: Author's name and gender as factors influencing assessment of products' creativity in four different domains. *Creativity Research Journal, 25,* 137–142.

Lebula, C., & Lucas, C. (1945). The effects of attitudes on descriptions of pictures. *Journal of Experimental Psychology, 35,* 517–524.

Ledbetter, A. M. (2008). Chronemic cues and sex differences in relational e-mail: Perceiving immediacy and supportive message quality. *Social Science Computer Review, 26,* 466–482.

Ledbetter, A. M. (2010). Assessing the measurement invariance of relational maintenance behavior when face-to-face and online. *Communication Research Reports, 27,* 30–37.

Ledbetter, A. M. (2013). Relational maintenance and inclusion of the other in self: Measure development and dyadic test of a self-expansion theory approach. *Southern Communication Journal, 78,* 289–310.

Ledbetter, A. M., Mazer, J. P., DeGroot, J. M., & Meyer, K. R. (2011). Attitudes toward online social connection and self-disclosure as predictors of Facebook communication and relational closeness. *Communication Research, 38,* 27–53.

Ledbetter, A. M., & Schrodt, P. (2008). Family communication patterns and cognitive processing: Conversation and conformity orientations as predictors of informational reception apprehension. *Communication Studies, 59,* 388–401.

Ledbetter, A. M., & Vik, T.A. (2012). Parental invasive behaviors and emerging adults' privacy defenses: Instrument development and validation. *Journal of Family Communication, 12,* 227–247.

Lee, E., & Jang, J. (2013). Not so imaginary interpersonal contact with public figures on social network sites: How affiliative tendency moderates its effects. *Communication Research, 40,* 27–51.

Lee, J. J., & Pinker, S. (2010). Rationales for indirect speech: The theory of the strategic speaker. *Psychological Review, 117,* 785–807.

Lee, J. R., Moore, D. C., Park, E., & Park, S. G. (2012). Who wants to be "friend rich"? Social compensatory friending on Facebook and the moderating role of public self-consciousness. *Computers in Human Behavior, 28,* 1036–1043.

Lee, K., Noh, M., & Koo, D. (2013). Lonely people are no longer lonely on social networking sites: The mediating role of self-disclosure and social support. *Cyberpsychology, Behavior, and Social Networking, 16,* 413–418.

Lehmiller, J. J., VanderDrift, L. E., & Kelly, J. R. (2011). Sex differences in approaching friends with benefits relationships. *Journal of Sex Research, 48,* 275–284.

Lehmiller, J. J., VanderDrift, L. E., & Kelly, J. R. (2014). Sexual communication, satisfaction, and condom use behavior in friends with benefits and romantic partners. *Journal of Sex Research, 51,* 74–85.

Lei, X. (2006). Sexism in language. *Journal of Language and Linguistics, 5*(1), 87–94.

Leit, L. (2009). Conversational narcissism in marriage: Effects on partner mental health and marital quality over the transition to parenthood. *Dissertation Abstracts International: Section B. The Sciences and Engineering, 69*(7-B), 4465.

Lenhart, A. (2009, December 15). *Teens and sexting.* PewResearch Internet Project.

Lenhart, A., & Duggan, M. (2014, February 11). *Couples, the internet, and social media.* PewResearch Internet Project.

Lenhart, A., Madden M., Smith A., & MacGill, A. (2007). *Teens and social media.* PewResearch Internet Project.

Lenhart, A., Rainie, L., & Lewis, O. (2001). *Teenage life online.* Pew Internet and American Life Project.

Lerner, H. (2005). *The dance of anger: A woman's guide to changing the patterns of intimate relationships.* New York, NY: Perennial Currents.

Lerner, R. M., Rothbaum, F., Boulos, S., & Castellino, D. R. (2002). Developmental systems perspective on parenting. In M. Bornstein (Ed.), *Handbook of parenting: Vol. 2. Biology and ecology of parenting* (2nd ed., pp. 315–344). Mahwah, NJ: Erlbaum.

Leung, C., & Lewkowicz, J. (2013). Language communication and communicative competence: A view from contemporary classrooms. *Language & Education: An International Journal, 27,* 398–414.

Levine, R. V. (1988). The pace of life across cultures. In J. E. McGrath (Ed.), *The social psychology of time* (pp. 39–60). Newbury Park, CA: Sage.

Levine, R. V., & Norenzayan, A. (1999). The pace of life in 31 countries. *Journal of Cross-Cultural Psychology, 30,* 178–205.

Levine, R. V., Reysen, S., & Ganz, E. (2008). The kindness of strangers revisited: A comparison of 24 US cities. *Social Indicators Research, 85,* 461–481.

Levine, T. R., Aune, K., & Park, H. (2006). Love styles and communication in relationships: Partner preferences, initiation, and intensification. *Communication Quarterly, 54*, 465–486.

Lewandowski, G. W., Aron, A., & Gee, J. (2007). Personality goes a long way: The malleability of opposite-sex physical attractiveness. *Personal Relationships, 14*, 571–585.

Lewis, M. H., & Reinsch, N. L., Jr. (1988). Listening in organizational environments. *Journal of Business Communication, 25*, 49–67.

Lewis, M. P., Simons, G. F., & Fennig, C. D. (Eds.). (2013). *Ethnologue: Languages of the world* (17th ed.). Dallas, TX: SIL International.

Lewis, T., & Manusov, V. (2009). Listening to another's distress in everyday relationships. *Communication Quarterly, 57*, 282–301.

Lieberman, M. D., Eisenberger, N. I., Crockett, M. J., Tom, S., Pfeifer, J. H., & Way, B. M. (2007). Putting feelings into words: Affect labeling disrupts amygdala activity to affective stimuli. *Psychological Science, 18*, 421–428.

Lieberson, S. (2000). *A matter of taste: How names, fashions, and culture change.* New Haven, CT: Yale University Press.

Lillian, D. L. (2007). A thorn by any other name: Sexist discourse as hate speech. *Discourse & Society, 18*, 719–740.

Lim, G. Y., & Roloff, M. E. (1999). Attributing sexual consent. *Journal of Applied Communication Research, 27*, 1–23.

Lim, L. L. (2009). The influences of harmony motives and implicit beliefs on conflict styles of the collectivist. *International Journal of Psychology, 44*, 401–409.

Limon, M. S., & LaFrance, B. H. (2005). Communication traits and leadership emergence: Examining the impact of argumentativeness, communication apprehension, and verbal aggressiveness in work groups. *Southern Communication Journal, 70*, 123–133.

Lin, M., Hummert, M., & Harwood, J. (2004). Representation of age identities in on-line discourse. *Journal of Aging Studies, 18*, 261–274.

Lippert, T., & Prager, K. J. (2001). Daily experiences of intimacy: A study of couples. *Personal Relationships, 8*, 283–298.

Lippincott, J. A., & German, N. (2007). From blue collar to ivory tower: Counseling first-generation, working-class students. In J. A. Lippincott & R. B. Lippincott (Eds.), *Special populations in college counseling: A handbook for mental health professionals* (pp. 89–98). Alexandria, VA: American Counseling Association.

Littlejohn, S. W. (2008). *Theories of human communication* (9th ed.). Boston, MA: Cengage.

Litwin, A. H., & Hallstein, L. O. (2007). Shadows and silences: How women's positioning and unspoken friendship rules in organizational settings cultivate difficulties among some women at work. *Women's Studies in Communication, 30*, 111–142.

Liu, J., Hu, J., & Furutan, O. (2013). The influence of student perceived professors' "hotness" on expertise, motivation, learning outcomes, and course satisfaction. *Journal of Education for Business, 88*, 94–100.

Lo, S. (2008). The nonverbal communication functions of emoticons in computer-mediated communication. *CyberPsychology & Behavior, 11*, 595–597.

Locatelli, S. M., Kluwe, K., & Bryant, F. B. (2012). Facebook use and the tendency to ruminate among college students: Testing meditational hypotheses. *Journal of Educational Computing Research, 46*, 377–394.

Locher, M. A. (2010). Relational work, politeness, and identity construction. In D. Matsumoto (Ed.), *APA handbook of interpersonal communication* (pp. 111–138). Washington, DC: American Psychological Association.

Lock, C. (2004, July 31). Deception detection: Psychologists try to learn how to spot a liar. *Science News, 16*, 72.

Lo Coco, A., Ingoglia, S., & Lundqvist, L. (2014). The assessment of susceptibility to emotional contagion: A contribution to the Italian adaptation of the Emotional Contagion Scale. *Journal of Nonverbal Behavior, 38*, 67–87.

Lombardo, M. V., Chakrabarti, B., Bullmore, E. T., Wheelwright, S. J., Sadek, S. A., Suckling J., & Baron-Cohen S. (2010). Shared neural circuits for mentalizing about the self and others. *Journal of Cognitive Neuroscience, 22*, 1623–1635.

Long, E. C. J., Angera, J. J., Carter, S. J., Nakamoto, M., & Kalso, M. (1999). Understanding the one you love: A longitudinal assessment of an empathy training program for couples in romantic relationships. *Family Relations: Interdisciplinary Journal of Applied Family Studies, 48*, 235–242.

Lorenzo, G. L., Biesanz, J. C., & Human, L. J. (2010). What is beautiful is good and more accurately understood: Physical attractiveness and accuracy in first impressions of personality. *Psychological Science, 21*, 1777–1782.

Lount, R., Jr. (2013). The impact of positive mood on trust in interpersonal and intergroup interactions. *Journal of Personality and Social Psychology, 98*, 420–433.

Loving, T. J., & Slatcher, R. B. (2013). Romantic relationships and health. In J. A. Simpson & L. Campbell (Eds.), *The Oxford handbook of close relationships* (pp. 617–637). New York, NY: Oxford University Press.

Loyd, D. L., Phillips, K. W., Whitson, J., & Thomas-Hunt, M. C. (2010). Expertise in your midst: How congruence between status and speech style affects reactions to unique knowledge. *Group Processes & Intergroup Relations, 13*, 379–395.

Lubrano, A. (2004). *Limbo: Blue-collar roots, white-collar dreams*. Hoboken, NJ: John Wiley and Sons.

Lucas, K. (2011). The working class promise: A communicative account of mobility-based ambivalences. *Communication Monographs, 78*, 347–369.

Lucas, R. E., Le, K., & Dyrenforth, P. S. (2008). Explaining the extraversion/positive affect relation: Sociability cannot account for extraverts' greater happiness. *Journal of Personality, 76*, 385–414.

Luft, J. (1969). *Of human interaction*. Palo Alto, CA: National Press Books.

Lundqvist, L.-O. (2008). The relationship between the biosocial model of personality and susceptibility to emotional contagion: A structural equation modeling approach. *Personality and Individual Differences, 45*, 89–95.

Lunkenheimer, E. S., Shields, A. M., & Cortina, K. S. (2007). Parental emotion coaching and dismissing in family interaction. *Social Development, 16*, 232–248.

Luo, S., & Zhang, G. (2009). What leads to romantic attraction: Similarity, reciprocity, security, or beauty? Evidence from a speed-dating study. *Journal of Personality, 77*, 933–964.

Luo, S., Zhang, G., Watson, D., & Snider, A. G. (2010). Using cross-sectional couple data to disentangle the causality between positive partner perceptions and marital satisfaction. *Journal of Research in Personality, 44*, 665–668.

Lustig, M. W., & Koester, J. (1999). *Intercultural competence: Interpersonal communication across cultures* (3rd ed.). New York, NY: Longman.

Lustig, M. W., & Koester, J. (2005). *Intercultural competence: Interpersonal communication across cultures* (4th ed.). Upper Saddle River, NJ: Allyn & Bacon.

Lutgen-Sandvik, P., Riforgiate, S., & Fletcher, C. (2011). Work as a source of positive emotional experiences and the discourses informing positive assessment. *Western Journal of Communication, 75*, 2–27.

Lydon, J. E., & Quinn, S. K. (2013). Relationship maintenance processes. In J. A. Simpson & L. Campbell (Eds.), *The Oxford handbook of close relationships* (pp. 573–588). New York, NY: Oxford University Press.

Ma, R., & Chuang, R. (2001). Persuasion strategies of Chinese college students in interpersonal contexts. *Southern Communication Journal, 66*, 267–278.

Ma, Z., & Jaeger, A. M. (2010). A comparative study of the influence of assertiveness on negotiation outcomes in Canada and China. *Cross Cultural Management, 17*, 333–346.

MacGeorge, E. L., Feng, B., & Burleson, B. R. (2011). Supportive communication. In M. L. Knapp & J. A. Daly (Eds.), *The Sage handbook of interpersonal communication* (4th ed., pp. 317–354). Thousand Oaks, CA: Sage.

MacGeorge, E. L., Feng, B., & Thompson, E. R. (2008). "Good" and "bad" advice: How to advise more effectively. In M. T. Motley (Ed.), *Studies in applied interpersonal communication* (pp. 145–164). Thousand Oaks, CA: Sage.

MacGeorge, E. L., Samter, W., Feng, B., Gillihan, S. J., & Graves, A. R. (2004). Stress, social support, and health among college students after September 11, 2001. *Journal of College Student Development, 45*, 655–670.

MacGeorge, E. L., & Wilkum, K. (2012). Predicting comforting quality in the context of miscarriage. *Communication Reports, 25*, 62–74.

MacIntyre, P. D., & Thivierge, K. A. (1995). The effects of speaker personality on anticipated reactions to public speaking. *Communication Research Reports, 12*, 125–133.

MacNeil, S., & Byers, E. S. (2009). Role of sexual self-disclosure in the sexual satisfaction of long-term heterosexual couples. *Journal of Sex Research, 46*, 3–14.

Macrae, C. N., & Bodenhausen, G. V. (2001). Social cognition: Categorical person perception. *British Journal of Psychology, 92*, 239–256.

Madden, M., & Smith, A. (2010, May 26). *Reputation management and social media*. PewResearch Internet Project. Retrieved from http://pewinternet.org/Reports/2010/Reputation-Management.aspx

Madlock, P. E. (2012). The influence of power distance and communication on Mexican workers. *Journal of Business Communication, 49*, 169–184.

Madlock, P. E., & Kennedy-Lightsey, C. (2010). The effects of supervisors' verbal aggressiveness and mentoring on their subordinates. *Journal of Business Communication, 47*, 42–62.

Maisel, N. C., Gable, S. L., & Strachman, A. (2008). Responsive behaviors in good times and bad. *Personal Relationships, 15*, 317–338.

Mak, B., & Chui, H. (2013). A cultural approach to small talk: A double-edged sword of sociocultural reality during socialization into the workplace. *Journal of Multicultural Discourses, 8*, 118–133.

Makin, V. S. (2004). Face management and the role of interpersonal politeness variables in euphemism production and comprehension. *Dissertation Abstracts*

International: Section B. The Sciences and Engineering, 64(8-B), 4077.

Malachowski, C. C., & Dillow, M. R. (2011). An examination of relational uncertainty, romantic intent, and attraction on communicative and relational outcomes in cross-sex friendships. *Communication Research Reports, 28,* 356–368.

Mallalieu, S. D., Hanton, S., & Jones, G. (2003). Emotional labeling and competitive anxiety in preparation and competition. *The Sport Psychologist, 17,* 157–174.

Mann, S., Ewens, S., Shaw, D., Vrij, A., Leal, S., & Hillman, J. (2013). Lying eyes: Why liars seek deliberate eye contact. *Psychiatry, Psychology and Law, 20,* 452–461.

Mansson, D. H., & Myers, S. A. (2011). An initial examination of college students' expressions of affection through Facebook. *Southern Communication Journal, 76,* 155–168.

Marangoni, C., & Ickes, W. (1989). Loneliness: A theoretical review with implications for measurement. *Journal of Social and Personal Relationships, 6,* 93–128.

Marek, C. I., Wanzer, M. B., & Knapp, J. L. (2004). An exploratory investigation of the relationship between roommates' first impressions and subsequent communication patterns. *Communication Research Reports, 21,* 210–220.

Maricchiolo, F., Gnisci, A., Bonaiuto, M., & Ficca, G. (2009). Effects of different types of hand gestures in persuasive speech on receivers' evaluations. *Language and Cognitive Processes, 24,* 239–266.

Marsh, A. A., Elfenbein, H. A., & Ambady, N. (2003). Nonverbal "accents": Cultural differences in facial expressions of emotion. *Psychological Science, 14,* 373–376.

Marshall, T. (2012). Facebook surveillance of former romantic partners: Associations with postbreakup recovery and personal growth. *Cyberpsychology, Behavior, and Social Networking, 15,* 521–526.

Marshall, T. C. (2008). Cultural differences in intimacy: The influence of gender-role ideology and individualism-collectivism. *Journal of Social and Personal Relationships, 25,* 143–168.

Marshall, T. C. (2010). Love at the cultural crossroads: Intimacy and commitment in Chinese Canadian relationships. *Personal Relationships, 17,* 391–411.

Martin, A., Jacob, C., & Gueguen, N. (2013). Similarity facilitates relationships on social networks: A field experiment on Facebook. *Psychological Reports, 113,* 217–220.

Martin, M. M., Dunleavy, K. N., & Kennedy-Lightsey, C. (2010). Can verbally aggressive messages in the instructor-student relationship be constructive? *College Student Journal, 44,* 726–736.

Martin, R. C., Coyier, K. R., VanSistine, L. M., & Schroeder, K. L. (2013). Anger on the Internet: The perceived value of rant-sites. *Cyberpsychology, Behavior, and Social Networking, 16,* 119–122.

Martz, J. M., Verette, J., Arriaga, X. B., Slovik, L. F., Cox, C. L., & Rusbult, C. E. (1998). Positive illusion in close relationships. *Personal Relationships, 5,* 159–181.

Mashek, D., & Sherman, M. (2004). Desiring less closeness with intimate others. In D. Mashek & A. Aron (Eds.), *The handbook of closeness and intimacy* (pp. 343–356). Mahwah, NJ: Erlbaum.

Maslow, A. H. (1968). *Toward a psychology of being.* New York, NY: Van Nostrand Reinhold.

Massengill, J., & Nash, M. (2009, May). *Ethnocentrism, intercultural willingness to communicate, and international interaction among U.S. college students.* Paper presented at the conference of the International Communication Association, Chicago, IL.

Mast, M. S., & Hall, J. A. (2004). Who is the boss and who is not? Accuracy of judging status. *Journal of Nonverbal Behavior, 28,* 145–165.

Matsumoto, D. (1993). Ethnic differences in affect intensity, emotion judgments, display rule attitudes, and self-reported emotional expression in an American sample. *Motivation and Emotion, 17,* 107–123.

Matsumoto, D. (2006). Culture and nonverbal behavior. In V. Manusov & M. L. Patterson (Eds.), *The Sage handbook of nonverbal communication* (pp. 219–235). Thousand Oaks, CA: Sage.

Matsumoto, D., & Hwang, H. C. (2013). Cultural similarities and differences in emblematic gestures. *Journal of Nonverbal Behavior, 37,* 1–27.

Mattingly, B. A., Lewandowski, G. W., Jr., & McIntyre, K. P. (2014). "You make me a better/worse person": A two-dimensional model of relationship self-change. *Personal Relationships, 21,* 176–190.

Matveev, A. V. (2004). Describing intercultural communication competence: In-depth interviews with American and Russian managers. *Qualitative Research Reports in Communication, 5,* 55–62.

Mayne, T. J. (1999). Negative affect and health: The importance of being earnest. *Cognition and Emotion, 13,* 601–635.

McCain, J. (1999). *Faith of my fathers.* New York, NY: Random House.

McCallum, N. L., & McGlone, M. S. (2011). Death be not profane: Mortality salience and euphemism use. *Western Journal of Communication, 75,* 565–584.

McClure, J., Meyer, L. H., Garisch, J., Fischer, R., Weir, K. F., & Walkey, F. H. (2011). Students' attributions for their best and worst marks: Do they relate to achievement? *Contemporary Educational Psychology, 36,* 71–81.

McCornack, S. A., & Levine, T. R. (1990). When lies are uncovered: Emotional and relational outcomes of discovered deception. *Communication Monographs, 57,* 119–138.

McCroskey, J. C. (2009). Communication apprehension: What have we learned in the last four decades. *Human Communication, 12,* 157–171.

McCroskey, J. C., & Richmond, V. P. (1996). *Fundamentals of human communication: An interpersonal perspective.* Prospect Heights, IL: Waveland.

McCroskey, J. C., Richmond, V. P., Heisel, A. D., & Hayhurst, J. L. (2004). Eysenck's Big Three and communication traits: Communication traits as manifestations of temperament. *Communication Research Reports, 21,* 404–410.

McCroskey, J. C., & Wheeless, L. (1976). *Introduction to human communication.* Boston, MA: Allyn & Bacon.

McCullough, M. E., Root, L. M., Tabak, B. A., & Witvliet, C. van O. (2009). Forgiveness. In S. J. Lopez & C. R. Snyder (Eds.), *Oxford handbook of positive psychology* (2nd ed., pp. 427–435). New York, NY: Oxford University Press.

McEwan, B., & Guerrero, L. K. (2010). Freshman engagement through communication: Predicting friendship formation strategies and perceived availability of network resources from communication skills. *Communication Studies, 61,* 445–463.

McEwan, B., & Zanolla, D. (2013). When online meets offline: A field investigation of modality switching. *Computers in Human Behavior, 29,* 1565–1571.

McGinn, M. M., McFarland, P. T., & Christensen, A. (2009). Antecedents and consequences of demand/withdraw. *Journal of Family Psychology, 23,* 749–757.

McGlone, M. S., Beck, G., & Pfiester, A. (2006). Contamination and camouflage in euphemisms. *Communication Monographs, 73,* 261–282.

McGoldrick, M., Watson, M., & Benton, W. (1999). Siblings through the life cycle. In B. Carter & M. McGoldrick (Eds.), *The expanded family life cycle: Individual, family, and social perspectives* (3rd ed., pp. 153–168). Needham Heights, MA: Allyn & Bacon.

McGuire, K. C., & Kinnery, T. A. (2010). When distance is problematic: Communication, coping, and relational satisfaction in female college students' long-distance dating relationships. *Journal of Applied Communication Research, 38,* 27–46.

McLuhan, M. (1962). *The Gutenberg galaxy.* Toronto, Ontario, Canada: University of Toronto Press.

McNamee, L. G., Peterson, B. L., & Pena, J. (2010). A call to educate, participate, invoke, and indict: Understanding the communication of online hate groups. *Communication Monographs, 77,* 257–280.

McPherson, M., Smith-Lovin, L., & Brashears, M. E. (2006). Social isolation in America: Changes in core discussion networks over two decades. *American Sociological Review, 71,* 353–375.

McPherson, M. B., & Young, S. L. (2004). What students think when teachers get upset: Fundamental attribution error and student-generated reasons for teacher anger. *Communication Quarterly, 52,* 357–369.

Mehdizadeh, S. (2010). Self-presentation 2.0: Narcissism and self-esteem on Facebook. *Cyberpsychology, Behavior, and Social Networking, 13,* 357–364.

Mehl, M. R., Vazire, S., Holleran, S. E., & Clark, C. S. (2010). Eavesdropping on happiness: Well-being is related to having less small talk and more substantive conversations. *Psychological Science, 21,* 539–541.

Mehrabian, A. (1972). *Nonverbal communication.* Chicago. IL: Aldine-Atherton.

Mehrabian, A. (2001). Characteristics attributed to individuals on the basis of their first names. *Genetic, Social, and General Psychology Monographs, 127,* 59–88.

Mehrabian, A. (2008). Communication without words. In C. D. Mortensen (Ed.), *Communication theory* (2nd ed., pp. 193–200). Piscataway, NJ: Transaction Publishers.

Mehrabian, A., & Blum, J. S. (2003). Physical appearance, attractiveness, and the mediating role of emotions. In N. J. Pallone (Ed.), *Love, romance, sexual interaction: Research perspectives from current psychology* (pp. 1–29). New Brunswick, NJ: Transaction.

Mehrabian, A., & Weiner, M. (1967). Decoding of inconsistent communications. *Journal of Personality and Social Psychology, 6,* 109–114.

Meir, I., Sandler, W., Padden, C., & Aronoff, M. (2010). Emerging sign languages. In M. Marshark & P. E. Spencer (Eds.), *The Oxford handbook of deaf studies, language, and education* (Vol. 2, pp. 267–280). New York, NY: Oxford University Press.

Meissner, W. W. (2008). The role of language in the development of the self I: Language acquisition. *Psychoanalytic Psychology, 25,* 26–46.

Mendes de Leon, C. F. (2005). Why do friendships matter for survival? *Journal of Epidemiology and Community Health, 59,* 538–539.

Merkin, R. S. (2006). Uncertainty avoidance and facework: A test of the Hofstede model. *International Journal of Intercultural Relations, 30,* 213–228.

Merkin, R. S. (2012). Sexual harassment indicators: The socio-cultural and cultural impact of marital status, age, education, race, and sex in Latin America. *Intercultural Communication Studies, 21,* 154–172.

Merkin, R. S., & Ramadan, R. (2010). Facework in Syria and the United States: A cross-cultural comparison.

International Journal of Intercultural Relations, 34, 661–669.

Merolla, A. J. (2008). Communicating forgiveness in friendships and dating relationships. *Communication Studies, 59,* 114–131.

Merolla, A. J. (2010). Relational maintenance and noncopresence reconsidered: Conceptualizing geographic separation in close relationships. *Communication Theory, 20,* 169–193.

Merolla, A. J., Weber, K. D., Myers, S. A., & Booth-Butterfield, M. (2004). The impact of past dating relationship solidarity on commitment, satisfaction, and investment in current relationships. *Communication Quarterly, 52,* 251–264.

Merrill, D. M. (1997). *Caring for elderly parents: Juggling work, family, and caregiving in middle and working class families.* Westport, CT: Auburn House/Greenwood.

Messman, S. J., & Mikesell, R. L. (2000). Competition and interpersonal conflict in dating relationships. *Communication Reports, 13,* 21–34.

Metts, S., & Cupach, W. R. (1990). The influence of relationship beliefs and problem-solving relationships on satisfaction in romantic relationships. *Human Communication Research, 17,* 170–185.

Metts, S., Cupach, W. R., & Bejllovec, R. A. (1989). "I love you too much to ever start liking you": Redefining romantic relationships. *Journal of Social and Personal Relationships, 6,* 259–274.

Metts, S., Cupach, W. R., & Imahori, T. T. (1992). Perceptions of sexual compliance-resisting messages in three types of cross-sex relationships. *Western Journal of Communication, 56,* 1–17.

Metts, S., & Grohskopf, E. (2003). Impression management: Goals, strategies, and skills. In B. Burleson & J. O. Greene (Eds.), *Handbook of communication and social interaction skills* (pp. 357–399). Mahwah, NJ: Erlbaum.

Miczo, N., & Burgoon, J. K. (2008). Facework and nonverbal behavior in social support interactions within romantic dyads. In M. T. Motley (Ed.), *Studies in applied interpersonal communication* (pp. 245–266). Thousand Oaks, CA: Sage.

Mignault, A., & Chaudhuri, A. (2003). The many faces of a neutral face: Head tilt and perception of dominance and emotion. *Journal of Nonverbal Behavior, 27,* 111–132.

Miller, J. K., Westerman, D. L., & Lloyd, M. E. (2004). Are first impressions lasting impressions? An exploration of the generality of the primacy effect in memory for repetitions. *Memory & Cognition, 32,* 1305–1315.

Miller, K. I., & Koesten, J. (2008). Financial feeling: An investigation of emotion and communication in the workplace. *Journal of Applied Communication Research, 36,* 8–32.

Miller, L. C., Cooke, L. L., Tsang, J., & Morgan, F. (1992). Should I brag? Nature and impact of positive and boastful disclosures for women and men. *Human Communication Research, 18,* 364–399.

Miller, M. S. (2010). Epistemology and people who are Deaf: Deaf worldviews, views of the Deaf world, or my parents are hearing. *American Annals of the Deaf, 15,* 479–485.

Miller, P., Niehuis, S., & Huston, T. L. (2006). Positive illusions in marital relationships: A 13-year longitudinal study. *Personality and Social Psychology Bulletin, 32,* 1579–1594.

Miller-Ott, A. E., & Kelly, L. (2013). Communication of female relational aggression in the college environment. *Qualitative Research Reports in Communication, 14,* 19–27.

Miller-Ott, A. E., Kelly, L., & Duran, R. L. (2012). The effects of cell phone usage rules on satisfaction in romantic relationships. *Communication Quarterly, 60,* 17–34.

Miller-Ott, A. E., & Linder, A. (2013). Romantic partners' use of facework and humor to communicate about sex. *Qualitative Research Reports in Communication, 14,* 69–78.

Miró, E., Cano, M. C., Espinoza-Fernández, L., & Beula-Casal, G. (2003). Time estimation during prolonged sleep deprivation and its relation to activation measures. *Human Factors, 45,* 148–159.

Miwa, Y., & Hanyu, K. (2006). The effects of interior design on communication and impressions of a counselor in a counseling room. *Environment and Behavior, 38,* 484–502.

Modesti, S. (2012). Invitation accepted: Integrating invitational rhetoric in educational contexts. *Current Issues in Education, 15,* 1–12.

Moeller, S. K., Robinson, M. D., Wilkowski, B. M., & Hanson, D. M. (2012). The big chill: Interpersonal coldness and emotion-labeling skills. *Journal of Personality, 80,* 703–724.

Mongeau, P. A., & Henningsen, M. L. M. (2008). Stage theories of relationship development. In L. A. Baxter & D. O. Braithewaite (Eds.), *Engaging theories in interpersonal communication: Multiple perspectives* (pp. 363–375). Thousand Oaks, CA: Sage.

Mongeau, P. A., Knight, K., Williams, J., Eden, J., & Shaw, C. (2013). Identifying and explicating variation among friends with benefits relationships. *Journal of Sex Research, 50,* 37–47.

Montgomery, B. M. (1993). Relationship maintenance versus relationship change: A dialectical dilemma. *Journal of Social and Personal Relationships, 10,* 205–223.

Montoya, R., & Horton, R. S. (2013). A meta-analytic investigation of the processes underlying the similarity-attraction effect. *Journal of Social and Personal Relationships, 30,* 64–94.

Moore, J., & Mattson-Lauters, A. (2009). Coordinated management of meaning: Do established rules aid in chat room experiences? *American Communication Journal, 11*(2), 1–35.

Moore, S. A., Zoellner, L. A., & Mollenholt, N. (2008). Are expressive suppression and cognitive reappraisal associated with stress-related symptoms? *Behaviour Research and Therapy, 46,* 993–1000.

Morman, M. T., & Floyd, K. (2002). A "changing culture of fatherhood": Effects of affectionate communication, closeness, and satisfaction in men's relationships with their fathers and their sons. *Western Journal of Communication, 66,* 395–411.

Morris, D. (1973). *Intimate behavior.* New York, NY: Bantam.

Morris, T. L., Gorham, J., Cohen, S. H., & Huffman, D. (1996). Fashion in the classroom: Effects of attire on student perceptions of instructors in college classes. *Communication Education, 45,* 135–148.

Morrison, J. (2008). The relationship between emotional intelligence competencies and preferred conflict-handling styles. *Journal of Nursing Management, 16,* 974–983.

Morton, J. B., & Trehub, S. E. (2001). Children's understanding of emotion in speech. *Child Development, 72,* 834–843.

Motley, M. T. (1990). On whether one can(not) communicate: An examination via traditional communication postulates. *Western Journal of Speech Communication, 54,* 1–20.

Motley, M. T. (1992). Mindfulness in solving communicators' dilemmas. *Communication Monographs, 59,* 306–314.

MTV. (2009). *A thin line.* 2009 AP-MTV Digital Abuse Study. Retrieved from http://www.athinline.org/MTV-AP_Digital_Abuse_Study_Executive_Summary.pdf

Muise, A., Christofides, E., & Desmarais, S. (2009). More information than you ever wanted: Does Facebook bring out the green-eyed monster of jealousy? *Cyber-Psychology & Behavior, 12,* 441–444.

Muise, A., Christofides, E., & Desmarais, S. (2014). "Creeping" or just information seeking? Gender differences in partner monitoring in response to jealousy on Facebook. *Personal Relationships, 21,* 35–50.

Mulac, A. (2006). The gender-linked language effect: Do language differences really make a difference? In K. Dindia & D. J. Canary (Eds.), *Sex differences and similarities in communication* (2nd ed., pp. 211–231). Mahwah, NJ: Erlbaum.

Muñoz-Rivas, M. J., Graña, J. L., O'Leary, K. D., & González, M. P. (2007). Aggression in adolescent dating relationships: Prevalence, justification, and health consequences. *Journal of Adolescent Health, 40,* 298–304.

Murdock, G. P. (1965). *Social structure.* New York, NY: Free Press.

Mychalcewycz, P. (2009, February 12). *Breaking up via text message becoming commonplace, poll finds.* Retrieved from http://www.switched.com/2009/02/12/breaking-up-via-text-message-becoming-commonplace-poll-finds/

Myers, D. (1980, May). The inflated self. *Psychology Today, 14,* 16.

Myers, K. K., & Sadaghiani, K. (2010). Millennials in the workplace: A communication perspective on Millennials' organizational relationships and performance. *Journal of Business and Psychology, 25,* 225–238.

Myers, S. A. (1998). Students' self-disclosure in the college classroom. *Psychological Reports, 83*(3, Pt. 1), 1067–1070.

Myers, S. A. (2002). Perceived aggressive instructor communication and student state motivation, learning, and satisfaction. *Communication Reports, 15,* 113–121.

Myers, S. A. (2003). Sibling use of relational maintenance behaviors. In K. M. Galvin & P. J. Cooper (Eds.), *Making connections: Readings in relational communication* (pp. 300–308). Los Angeles, CA: Roxbury.

Myers, S., & Brann, M. (2009). College students' perceptions of how instructors establish and enhance credibility through self-disclosure. *Qualitative Research Reports in Communication, 10,* 9–16.

Myers, S. A., Byrnes, K. A., Frisby, B. N., & Mansson, D. H. (2011). Adult siblings' use of affectionate communication as a strategic and routine relational maintenance behavior. *Communication Research Reports, 28,* 151–158.

Myers, S. A., Edwards, C., Wahl, S. T., & Martin, M. M. (2007). The relationship between perceived instructor aggressive communication and college student involvement. *Communication Education, 56,* 495–508.

Myers, S. A., & Goodboy, A. K. (2013). Using equity theory to explore adult siblings' use of relational maintenance behaviors and relational characteristics. *Communication Research Reports, 30,* 275–281.

Myers, S. A., & Rocca, K. A. (2001). Perceived instructor argumentativeness and verbal aggressiveness in the college classroom: Effects on student perceptions of climate, apprehension, and state motivation. *Western Journal of Communication, 65,* 113–137.

Nabi, R. L., Prestin, A., & So, J. (2013). Facebook friends with (health) benefits? Exploring social network site use and perceptions of social support, stress, and well-being. *Cyberpsychology, Behavior, and Social Networking, 16,* 721–727.

Nagel, F., Maurer, M., & Reinemann, C. (2012). Is there a visual dominance in political communication? How verbal, visual, and vocal communication shape viewers' impressions of political candidates. *Journal of Communication, 62,* 833–850.

Nardone, G., & Watzlawick, P. (2005). *Brief strategic therapy: Philosophy, techniques, and research.* Lanham, MD: Jason Aronson.

National Association of Colleges and Employers. (2010, November). *Job outlook 2011.* Bethlehem, PA: Author. Retrieved from http://career.pages.tcnj.edu/files/2011/07/Job_Outlook_2011_Full_Report_PDF1.pdf

National Association of Colleges and Employers. (2013, November). *Job outlook 2014.* Bethlehem, PA: Author. Retrieved from https://www.naceweb.org/surveys/job-outlook.aspx

National Communication Association. (1999). *How Americans communicate* [online]. Retrieved from http://www.natcom.org/research/Roper/how_americans_communicate.htm

National Crime Prevention Council. (2007, February 28). *Teens and cyberbullying.* Executive Summary of a Report on Research Conducted for National Crime Prevention Council (NCPC).

National Institute of Mental Health. (2013). *The numbers count: Mental disorders in America.* Retrieved from http://www.nimh.nih.gov/health/publications/the-numbers-count-mental-disorders-in-america/index.shtml

Neenan, M., & Dryden, W. (2006). *Rational emotive behaviour therapy in a nutshell.* London, England: Sage.

Nellermoe, D. A., Weirich, T. R., & Reinstein, A. (1999). Using practitioners' viewpoints to improve accounting students' communications skills. *Business Communication Quarterly, 62*(2), 41–60.

Nelson D. (2009). Feeling good and open-minded: The impact of positive affect on cross cultural empathic responding. *Journal of Positive Psychology, 4,* 53–63.

Nelson, T. D. (2005). Ageism: Prejudice against our feared future self. *Journal of Social Issues, 61,* 207–221.

Neuliep, J. W. (1996). The influence of theory X and Y management style on the perception of ethical behavior in organizations. *Journal of Social Behavior and Personality, 11,* 301–311.

Ng, S. H., & Bradac, J. J. (1993). *Power in language: Verbal communication and social influence.* Newbury Park, CA: Sage.

Nguyen, H.-H. D., Le, H., & Boles, T. (2010). Individualism-collectivism and co-operation: A cross-society and cross-level examination. *Negotiation and Conflict Management Research, 3,* 179–204.

Nichols, M. P. (2009). *The lost art of listening: How learning to listen can improve relationships* (2nd ed.). New York, NY: Guilford Press.

Nie, N. H., & Erbring, L. (2000, February 17). *Internet and society: A preliminary report.* Stanford, CA: Stanford Institute for the Quantitative Study of Society (SIQSS).

Noakes, M. A., & Rinaldi, C. M. (2006). Age and gender differences in peer conflict. *Journal of Youth and Adolescence, 35,* 881–891.

Noller, P. (1995). Parent-adolescent relationships. In M. A. Fitzpatrick & A. L. Vangelisti (Eds.), *Explaining family interactions* (pp. 77–111). Thousand Oaks, CA: Sage.

Noller, P., & Fitzpatrick, M. A. (1993). *Communication in family relationships.* Englewood Cliffs, NJ: Prentice-Hall.

Nosko, A., Wood, E., & Molema, S. (2010). All about me: Disclosure in online social networking profiles: The case of Facebook. *Computers in Human Behavior, 26,* 406–418.

Notarius, C. I., & Herrick, L. R. (1988). Listener response strategies to a distressed other. *Journal of Social and Personal Relationships, 5,* 97–108.

Nummenmaa, L., Glerean, E., Hari, R., & Hietanen, J. K. (2014). Bodily maps of emotions. *PNAS, 111,* 646–651.

Oatley, K. (2010). Two movements in emotions: Communication and reflection. *Emotion Review, 2,* 29–35.

O'Barr, W. M. (1982). *Linguistic evidence: Language, power, and strategy in the courtroom.* New York, NY: Academic Press.

Ocana, A., & Hindman, D. (2004, May). *Unacquainted roommates, conflict style, and relational outcomes.* Paper presented at the meeting of the International Communication Association, New Orleans, LA.

O'Connor, S. S., Whitehill, J. M., King, K. M., Kernic, M. A., Boyle, L., Bresnahan, B. W., . . . Ebel, B. E. (2013). Compulsive cell phone use and history of motor vehicle crash. *Journal of Adolescent Health, 53,* 512–519.

Oduro-Frimpong, J. (2007). Semiotic silence: Its use as a conflict-management strategy in intimate relationships. *Semiotica, 167,* 283–308.

Oetzel, J. G. (1998). The effects of self-construals and ethnicity on self-reported conflict styles. *Communication Reports, 11,* 133–144.

Oetzel, J. G., & Ting-Toomey, S. (2003). Face concerns in interpersonal conflict: A cross-cultural empirical test of the face negotiation theory. *Communication Research, 30,* 599–625.

Officer, S. A., & Rosenfeld, L. B. (1985). Self-disclosure to male and female coaches by high school female athletes. *Journal of Sport Psychology, 7,* 360–370.

Ogden, C. K., & Richards, I. A. (1923). *The meaning of meaning.* New York, NY: Harcourt Brace.

Ogolsky, B. G., & Bowers, J. R. (2013). A meta-analytic review of relationship maintenance and its correlates. *Journal of Social and Personal Relationships, 30,* 343–367.

Ohbuchi, K., & Atsumi, E. (2010). Avoidance brings Japanese employees what they care about in conflict management: Its functionality and "good member" image. *Negotiation and Conflict Management Research, 3,* 117–129.

Ohse, D. M., & Stockdale, M. S. (2008). Age comparisons in workplace sexual harassment perceptions. *Sex Roles, 59,* 240–253.

Olson, D. H. (2000). Circumplex model of marital and family systems. *Journal of Family Therapy, 22*(2), 144–167.

Olson, L. N. (2002). "As ugly and painful as it was, it was effective." Individuals' unique assessment of communication competence during aggressive conflict episodes. *Communication Studies, 53,* 171–188.

Olson, L. N., & Braithwaite, D. O. (2004). "If you hit me again, I'll hit you back": Conflict management strategies of individuals experiencing aggression during conflicts. *Communication Studies, 55,* 271–285.

O'Meara, D. (1989). Cross-sex friendship: Four basic challenges of an ignored relationship. *Sex Roles, 21,* 525–543.

O'Neill, O. A. (2009). Workplace expression of emotions and escalation of commitment. *Journal of Applied Social Psychology, 39,* 2396–2424.

Oosterwijk, S., Rotteveel, M., Fischer, A. H., & Hess, U. (2009). Embodied emotion concepts: How generating words about pride and disappointment influences posture. *European Journal of Social Psychology, 39,* 457–466.

Orbe, M. P., & Everett, M. A. (2006). Interracial and interethnic conflict and communication in the United States. In J. G. Oetzel & S. Ting-Toomey (Eds.), *The Sage handbook of conflict communication* (pp. 575–626). Thousand Oaks, CA: Sage.

Orbe, M. P., & Groscurth, C. R. (2004). A co-cultural theoretical analysis of communicating on campus and at home: Exploring the negotiation strategies of first generation college (FGC) students. *Qualitative Research Reports in Communication, 5,* 41–47.

Orbe, M. P., & Spellers, R. E. (2005). From the margins to the center: Utilizing co-cultural theory in diverse contexts. In W. B. Gudykunst (Ed.), *Theorizing about intercultural communication* (pp. 173–192). Thousand Oaks, CA: Sage.

Orcutt, H. K. (2006). The prospective relationship of interpersonal forgiveness and psychological distress symptoms among college women. *Journal of Counseling Psychology, 53,* 350–361.

Osterman, K. (2001). Students' need for belonging in the school community. *Review of Educational Research, 70,* 323–367.

O'Sullivan, P. B. (2000). What you don't know won't hurt me: Impression management functions of communication channels in relationships. *Human Communication Research, 26,* 403–431.

O'Sullivan, P. B., & Flanagin, A. J. (2003). Reconceptualizing "flaming" and other problematic messages. *New Media and Society, 5,* 69–94.

Otondo, R. F., Van Scotter, J. R., Allen, D. G., & Palvia, P. (2008). The complexity of richness: Media, message, and communication outcomes. *Information & Management, 45,* 21–30.

Overall, N. C., & Sibley, C. G. (2008). Attachment and attraction toward romantic partners versus relevant alternatives within daily interactions. *Personality and Individual Differences, 44,* 1126–1137.

Owen, J., & Fincham, F. D. (2012). Friends with benefits relationships as a start to exclusive romantic relationships. *Journal of Social and Personal Relationships, 29,* 982–996.

Pachankis, J. E. (2007). The psychological implications of concealing a stigma: A cognitive-affective-behavioral model. *Psychological Bulletin, 133,* 328–345.

Pahl, S., & Eiser, J. R. (2007). How malleable is comparative self-positivity? The effects of manipulating judgmental focus and accessibility. *European Journal of Social Psychology, 37,* 617–627.

Palmer, M. T., & Simmons, K. B. (1995). Communicating intentions through nonverbal behaviors: Conscious and nonconscious encoding of liking. *Human Communication Research, 22,* 128–160.

Palomares, N. A. (2008). Explaining gender-based language use: Effects of gender identity salience on references to emotion and tentative language in intra- and intergroup contexts. *Human Communication Research, 34,* 263–286.

Palomares, N. A., & Lee, E. (2010). Virtual gender identity: The linguistic assimilation to gendered avatars in computer-mediated communication. *Journal of Language and Social Psychology, 29,* 5–23.

Pam, A., & Pearson, J. (1998). *Splitting up: Enmeshment and estrangement in the process of divorce.* New York, NY: Guilford Press.

Papadakis, M. (2003). Data on family and the Internet: What do we know and how do we know it. In J. Turow & A. L. Kavanaugh (Eds.), *The wired homestead* (pp. 121–140). Cambridge, MA: MIT Press.

Papp, L. M., Danielewicz, J., Cayemberg, C. (2012). Are we Facebook official? Implications of dating partners' Facebook use and profiles for intimate relationship satisfaction. *CyberPsychology, Behavior & Social Networking, 15,* 85–90.

Parisse, C. (2005). New perspectives on language development and the innateness of grammatical knowledge. *Language Sciences, 27,* 383–401.

Park, H. S., Levine, T. R., McCornack, S. A., Morrison, K., & Ferrara, M. (2002). How people really detect lies. *Communication Monographs, 69,* 144–157.

Parker, J. A., Keefer, K. V., & Wood, L. M. (2011). Toward a brief multidimensional assessment of emotional intelligence: Psychometric properties of the Emotional Quotient Inventory–Short Form. *Psychological Assessment, 23,* 762–777.

Parker-Pope, T. (2010). *For better: The science of a good marriage.* New York, NY: Dutton.

Parks, J. B., & Roberton, M. A. (2000). Development and validation of an instrument to measure attitudes toward sexist/nonsexist language. *Sex Roles, 42,* 415–438.

Parks, J. B., & Roberton, M. A. (2008). Generation gaps in attitudes toward sexist/nonsexist language. *Journal of Language & Social Psychology, 27,* 276–283.

Parmelee, J. H., & Bichard, S. L. (2012). *Politics and the Twitter revolution: How tweets influence the relationship between political leaders and the public.* New York, NY: Lexington Books.

Parton, S., Siltanen, S. A., Hosman, L. A., & Langenderfer, J. (2002). Employment interviews outcomes and speech style effects. *Journal of Language and Social Psychology, 21,* 144–161.

Passalacqua, S. A., & Harwood, J. (2012). VIPS communication skills training for paraprofessional dementia caregivers: An intervention to increase person-centered dementia care. *Clinical Gerontologist: The Journal of Aging and Mental Health, 35,* 425–445.

Patrick, V. M., & Hagtvedt, H. (2012). "I don't" versus "I can't": When empowered refusal motivates goal-directed behavior. *Journal of Consumer Research, 39,* 371–381.

Pausch, R. (2008). *The last lecture.* New York, NY: Hyperion.

Pawlowski, D. R. (1998). Dialectical tensions in marital partners' accounts of their relationships. *Communication Quarterly, 46,* 396–416.

Pearce, W. B. (2005). The Coordinated Management of Meaning (CMM). In W. B. Gudykunst (Ed.), *Theorizing about intercultural communication* (pp. 35–54). London, England: Sage.

Pearce, W. B., & Cronen, V. (1980). *Communication, action, and meaning.* New York, NY: Praeger.

Pearson, J. C. (2000). Positive distortion: "The most beautiful woman in the world." In K. M. Galvin & P. J. Cooper (Eds.), *Making connections: Readings in relational communication* (2nd ed., pp. 184–190). Los Angeles, CA: Roxbury.

Pence, M. E., & Vickery, A. J. (2012). The roles of personality and trait emotional intelligence in the active-empathic listening process: Evidence from correlational and regression analyses. *International Journal of Listening, 26,* 159–174.

Pennebaker, J. (2004). *Writing to heal: A guided journal for recovering from trauma and emotional upheaval.* Oakland, CA: New Harbinger.

Pennebaker, J. W. (1997). *Opening up: The healing power of expressing emotions* (Rev. ed.). New York, NY: Guilford Press.

Pennebaker, J. W. (2011). *The secret lives of pronouns: What our words say about us.* New York, NY: Bloomsbury.

Peper, M. (2000). Awareness of emotions: A neuropsychological perspective. In R. D. Ellis & N. Newton (Eds.), *The caldron of consciousness: Motivation, affect and self-organization—An anthology* (pp. 243–269). Philadelphia, PA: John Benjamins.

Perry, A., Rubinsten, O., Peled, L., & Shamay-Tsoory, S. G. (2013). Don't stand so close to me: A behavioral and ERP study of preferred interpersonal distance. *Neuroimage, 83,* 761–769.

Peterson, C. (2006). *A primer in positive psychology.* New York, NY: Oxford University Press.

Petronio, S. (2000). The boundaries of privacy: Praxis of everyday life. In S. Petronio (Ed.), *Balancing the secrets of private disclosures* (pp. 37–49). Mahwah, NJ: Erlbaum.

Petronio, S. (2002). *Boundaries of privacy: Dialectics of disclosure.* Albany: State University of New York Press.

Petronio, S. (2007). Translational research endeavors and the practices of communication privacy management. *Journal of Applied Communication Research, 35,* 218–222.

Petronio, S. (2013). Brief status report on communication privacy management theory. *Journal of Family Communication, 13,* 6–14.

Peyton, A., & Goei, R. (2013). The effectiveness of explicit demand and emotional expression apology cues in predicting victim readiness to accept an apology. *Communication Studies, 64,* 411–430.

Pflug, J. (2011). Contextuality and computer-mediated communication: A cross cultural comparison. *Computers in Human Behavior, 27,* 131–137.

Phillips, L., & Slessor, G. (2011). Moving beyond basic emotions in aging research. *Journal of Nonverbal Behavior, 35,* 279–286.

Piercey, M. (2000). Sexism in the English language. *TESL Canada Journal/La revue TESL du Canada, 17*(2), 110–115.

Pilgeram, R. (2007). "Ass-kicking" women: Doing and undoing gender in a US livestock auction. *Gender, Work and Organization, 14,* 572–595.

Pillet-Shore, D. (2011). Doing introductions: The work involved in meeting someone new. *Communication Monographs, 78,* 73–95.

Planalp, S. (1998). Communicating emotion in everyday life: Cues, channels, and processes. In P. A. Anderson & L. A. Guerrero (Eds.), *Handbook of communication and emotion: Research, theory, applications, and contexts* (pp. 29–48). San Diego, CA: Academic Press.

Planalp, S., Fitness, J., & Fehr, B. (2006). Emotion in theories of close relationships. In A. L. Vangelisti & D. Perlman (Eds.), *The Cambridge handbook of personal relationships* (pp. 369–384). New York, NY: Cambridge University Press.

Plander, K. L. (2013). Checking accounts: Communication privacy management in familial financial caregiving. *Journal of Family Communication, 13,* 17–31.

Pollack, W. (1999). *Real boys: Rescuing our sons from the myths of boyhood.* New York, NY: Owl Books.

Porter, S., Brinke, L., & Wallace, B. (2012). Secrets and lies: Involuntary leakage in deceptive facial expressions as a function of emotional intensity. *Journal of Nonverbal Behavior, 36,* 23–37.

Powell, J. (1969). *Why am I afraid to tell you who I am?* Niles, IL: Argus Communications.

Powell, M. B., Hughes-Scholes, C. H., & Sharman, S. J. (2012). Skill in interviewing reduces confirmation bias. *Journal of Investigative Psychology and Offender Profiling, 9,* 126–134.

Powers, W. G., & Witt, P. L. (2008). Expanding the theoretical framework of communication fidelity. *Communication Quarterly, 56,* 247–267.

Prager, K. J., & Buhrmester, D. (1998). Intimacy and need fulfillment in couple relationships. *Journal of Social and Personal Relationships, 15,* 435–469.

Prentice, C. (2009). Relational dialectics among in-laws. *Journal of Family Communication, 9,* 67–89.

Prentice, C. M., & Kramer, M. W. (2006). Dialectical tensions in the classroom: Managing tensions through communication. *Southern Communication Journal, 71,* 339–361.

Prentice, W. E. (2005). *Therapeutic modalities in rehabilitation.* New York, NY: McGraw-Hill.

Preparing the workers of today for the jobs of tomorrow. (2009, July). Executive Office of the President, Council of Economic Advisors. Retrieved from http://www.whitehouse.gov/administration/eop/cea/Jobs-of-the-Future

Prewitt-Freilino, J. L., Caswell, T., & Laakso, E. K. (2012). The gendering of language: A comparison of gender equality in countries with gendered, natural gender, and genderless languages. *Sex Roles, 66,* 268–281.

Price, D. (2012). *The heart of money: A couple's guide to creating true financial intimacy.* Novato, CA: New World Library.

Proctor, R. F. (1989). Responsibility or egocentrism? The paradox of owned messages. *Speech Association of Minnesota Journal, 26,* 57–69.

Proctor, R. F., & Wilcox, J. R. (1993). An exploratory analysis of responses to owned messages in interpersonal communication. *ETC: A Review of General Semantics, 50,* 201–220.

Przybylski, A. K., & Weinstein, N. (2013). Can you connect with me now? How the presence of mobile communication technology influences face-to-face conversation quality. *Journal of Social and Personal Relationships, 30,* 237–246.

Putnam, R. D. (2000). *Bowling alone.* New York, NY: Touchstone.

Qiu, L., Lin, H., Leung, A. K., & Tov, W. (2012). Putting their best foot forward: Emotional disclosure on Facebook. *Cyberpsychology, Behavior, and Social Networking, 15,* 569–572.

Quartana, P. J., & Burns, J. W. (2010). Emotion suppression affects cardiovascular responses to initial and subsequent laboratory stressors. *British Journal of Health Psychology, 15,* 511–528.

Quinto-Pozos, D. (2008). Sign language contact and interference: ASL and LSM. *Language in Society, 37,* 161–189.

Rabby, M. K., & Walther, J. B. (2003). Computer-mediated communication effects on relationship formation and maintenance. In D. J. Canary & M. Dainton (Eds.), *Maintaining relationships through communication: Relational, contextual, and cultural variations* (pp. 141–162). Mahwah, NJ: Erlbaum.

Ragins, B. R. (2008). Disclosure disconnects: Antecedents and consequences of disclosing invisible stigmas across life domains. *The Academy of Management Review, 33,* 194–215.

Ragins, B. R., & Singh, R. (2007). Making the invisible visible: Fear and disclosure of sexual orientation at work. *Journal of Applied Psychology, 92,* 1103–1118.

Raider, E., Coleman, S., & Gerson, J. (2006). Teaching conflict resolution skills in a workshop. In M. Deutsch, P. T. Coleman, & E. C. Marcus (Eds.), *The handbook of conflict resolution: Theory and practice* (2nd ed., pp. 695–725). Hoboken, NJ: Wiley.

Rains, S. A., & Keating, D. M. (2011). The social dimension of blogging about health: Health blogging, social support, and well-being. *Communication Monographs, 78,* 511–553.

Rakow, L. F. (1992). Don't hate me because I'm beautiful. *Southern Communication Journal, 57,* 132–142.

Ralph, B. C. W., Thomson, D. R., Cheyne, J., & Smilek, D. (2013). Media multitasking and failures of attention in everyday life. *Psychological Research.* doi:10.1007/s00426-013-0523-7

Ramirez, A., & Zhang, S. (2007). When online meets offline: The effect of modality switching on relational communication. *Communication Monographs, 74,* 287–310.

Rancer, A. S., & Avtgis, T. A. (2006). *Argumentative and aggressive communication: Theory, research, and application.* Thousand Oaks, CA: Sage.

Rancer, A. S., Kosberg, R. L., & Baukus, R. A. (1992). Beliefs about arguing as predictors of trait argumentativeness: Implications for training in argument and conflict management. *Communication Education, 41,* 375–387.

Randall, A. K., Post, J. H., Reed, R. G., & Butler, E. (2013). Cooperating with your romantic partner: Associations with interpersonal emotion coordination. *Journal of Social and Personal Relationships, 30,* 1072–1095.

Rawlins, W. K. (1992). *Friendship matters: Communication, dialectics, and the life course.* New York, NY: Aldine De Gruyter.

Rehman, U. S., Ebel-Lam, A., Mortimer, A., & Mark, K. (2009). Self-confirmation strivings in depression: An extension to the affective domain using an experimental design. *European Journal of Social Psychology, 39,* 900–908.

Rehman, U. S., & Holtzworth-Munroe, A. (2007). A cross-cultural examination of the relation of marital communication behavior to marital satisfaction. *Journal of Family Psychology, 21,* 759–763.

Reich, S. M., Subrahmanyam, K., & Espinoza, G. (2012). Friending, IMing, and hanging out face-to-face: Overlap in adolescents' online and offline social networks. *Developmental Psychology, 48,* 356–368.

Reid, C. A., Davis, J. L., & Green, J. D. (2013). The power of change: Interpersonal attraction as a function of attitude similarity and attitude alignment. *Journal of Social Psychology, 153,* 700–719.

Reid, S. A., & Ng, S. H. (1999). Language, power, and intergroup relations. *Journal of Social Issues, 55,* 119–139.

Reis, H. T., & Clark, M. S. (2013). Responsiveness. In J. A. Simpson & L. Campbell (Eds.), *The Oxford handbook of close relationships* (pp. 400–426). New York, NY: Oxford University Press.

Reis, H. T., Smith, S. M., Carmichael, C. L., Caprariello, P. A., Tsai, F., Rodrigues, A., & Maniaci, M. R. (2010). Are you happy for me? How sharing positive events with others provides personal and interpersonal benefits. *Journal of Personality and Social Psychology, 99,* 311–329.

Reissman, C. K. (1990). *Divorce talk: Women and men make sense of personal relationships.* New Brunswick, NJ: Rutgers University Press.

Rennels, J. L., & Cummings, A. J. (2013). Sex differences in facial scanning: Similarities and dissimilarities between infants and adults. *International Journal of Behavioral Development: Special Issue on Development of Face Processing, 37,* 111–117.

Renner, K.-H., & Schütz, A. (2008). The psychology of personal web sites. In S. Kelsey & K. Amant (Eds.), *Handbook of research on computer mediated communication* (Vols. 1–2, pp. 267–282). Hershey, PA: Information Science Reference/IGI Global.

Rentfrow, P. J. (2014). Geographical differences in personality. In P. J. Rentfrow (Ed.), *Geographical psychology: Exploring the interaction of environment and behavior* (pp. 115–137). Washington, DC: American Psychological Association.

Rentscher, K. E., Rohrbaugh, M. J., Shoham, V., & Mehl, M. R. (2013). Asymmetric partner pronoun use and demand-withdraw interaction in couples coping with health problems. *Journal of Family Psychology, 27,* 691–701.

Reyes, A. (2005). Appropriation of African American slang by Asian American youth. *Journal of Sociolinguistics, 9,* 509–532.

Reznik, R. M., & Roloff, M. E. (2011). Getting off to a bad start: The relationship between communication during an initial episode of a serial argument and argument frequency. *Communication Studies, 62,* 291–306.

Rheingold, H. (1988). *They have a word for it*. New York, NY: Tarcher/Putnam.

Rhode, D. L. (2010). *The beauty bias: The injustice of appearance in law and life*. New York, NY: Oxford University Press.

Richman, J. (2002, September 16). The news journal of the life scientist. *The Scientist, 16*, 42.

Richmond, V., Gorham, J. S., & Furio, B. J. (1987). Affinity-seeking communication in collegiate female-male relationships. *Communication Quarterly, 35*, 334–348.

Richmond, V. P., McCroskey, J. C., & Johnson, A. D. (2003). Development of the Nonverbal Immediacy Scale (NIS): Measures of self- and other-perceived nonverbal immediacy. *Communication Quarterly, 51*, 504–517.

Rick, S. I., Small, D. A., & Finkel, E. J. (2011). Fatal (fiscal) attraction: Spendthrifts and tightwads in marriage. *Journal of Marketing Research, 48*, 228–237.

Ridley, C. A., Wilhelm, M. S., & Surra, C. A. (2001). Married couples' conflict responses and marital quality. *Journal of Social and Personal Relationships, 18*, 517–534.

Rifkin, J. (2009). The empathic civilization: The race to global consciousness in a world in crisis. New York, NY: Tarcher.

Riggio, H. R., & Kwong, W. Y. (2009). Social skills, paranoid thinking, and social outcomes among young adults. *Personality and Individual Differences, 47*, 492–497.

Riggio, R. E. (2006). Nonverbal skills and abilities. In V. Manusov & M. L. Patterson (Eds.), *The Sage handbook of nonverbal communication* (pp. 79–95). Thousand Oaks, CA: Sage.

Righetti, F., Rusbult, C., & Finkenauer, C. (2010). Regulatory focus and the Michelangelo phenomenon: How close partners promote one another's ideal selves. *Journal of Experimental Social Psychology, 46*, 972–985.

Rill, L., Baiocchi, E., Hopper, M., Denker, K., & Olson, L. N. (2009). Exploration of the relationship between self-esteem, commitment, and verbal aggressiveness in romantic dating relationships. *Communication Reports, 22*, 102–113.

Riordan, M. A., Markman, K., M., & Stewart, C. O. (2013). Communication accommodation in instant messaging: An examination of temporal convergence. *Journal of Language & Social Psychology, 32*, 84–95.

Rittenour, C. E., Myers, S. A., & Brann, M. (2007). Commitment and emotional closeness in the sibling relationship. *Southern Communication Journal, 72*, 169–183.

Rius-Ottenheim, N., Mast, R., Zitman, F. G., & Giltay, E. J. (2013). The role of dispositional optimism in physical and mental well-being. In A. Efklides & D. Moraitou (Eds.), *A positive psychology perspective on quality of life* (pp. 149–173). New York, NY: Springer.

Roach, K. D. (1997). Effects of graduate teaching assistant attire on student learning, misbehaviors, and ratings of instruction. *Communication Quarterly, 45*, 125–141.

Robbins, S. A., & Merrill, A. F. (2014). Understanding posttransgressional relationship closeness: The roles of perceived severity, rumination, and communication competence. *Communication Research Reports, 31*, 23–32.

Roberto, A. J., Carlyle, K. E., & Goodall, C. E. (2007). Communication and corporal punishment: The relationship between self-report parent verbal and physical aggression. *Communication Research Reports, 24*, 103–111.

Roberto, A. J., Eden, J., Savage, M. W., Ramos-Salazar, L., & Deiss, D. M. (2014). Prevalence and predictors of cyberbullying perpetration by high school seniors. *Communication Quarterly, 62*, 97–114.

Robins, R. W., Mendelsohn, G. A., Connell, J. B., & Kwan, V. S. Y. (2004). Do people agree about the causes of behavior? A social relations analysis of behavior ratings and causal attributions. *Journal of Personality and Social Psychology, 86*, 334–344.

Robinshaw, H. (2007). Acquisition of hearing, listening and speech skills by and during key stage 1. *Early Child Development and Care, 177*, 661–678.

Robinson, W. P., Shepherd, A., & Heywood, J. (1998). Truth, equivocation/concealment, and lies in job applications and doctor-patient communication. *Journal of Language and Social Psychology, 17*, 149–164.

Rochat, P. (2001). Origins of self-concept. In G. Bremner & A. Fogel (Eds.), *Blackwell handbook of infant development* (pp. 191–212). Malden. MA: Blackwell.

Rochman, G. M., & Diamond, G. M. (2008). From unresolved anger to sadness: Identifying physiological correlates. *Journal of Counseling Psychology, 55*, 96–105.

Rochmis, J. (2000). Study: Humans do many things. *Wired* (online).

Rockwell, P. (2007a). The effects of cognitive complexity and communication apprehension on the expression and recognition of sarcasm. In A. M. Columbus (Ed.), *Advances in psychology research* (Vol. 49, pp. 185–196). Hauppauge, NY: Nova Science Publishers.

Rockwell, P. (2007b). Vocal features of conversational sarcasm: A comparison of methods. *Journal of Psycholinguistic Research, 36*, 361–369.

Rodero, E. (2011). Intonation and emotion: Influence of pitch levels and contour type on creating emotions. *Journal of Voice, 25*(1), 25–34.

Rodriguez, H. P., Rodday, A. C., Marshall, R. E., Nelson, K. L., Rogers, W. H., & Safran, D. G. (2008). Relation of patients' experiences with individual physicians to malpractice risk. *International Journal for Quality in Health Care, 20*, 5–12.

Rodway, P., Schepman, A., & Lambert, J. (2013). The influence of position and context on facial attractiveness. *Acta Psychologica, 144*, 522–529.

Roets, A., & Soetens, B. (2010). Need and ability to achieve closure: Relationships with symptoms of psychopathology. *Personality and Individual Differences, 48*, 155–160.

Rogers, L. E. (2001). Relational communication in the context of family. *Journal of Family Communication, 1*, 25–35.

Rohn, U. (2014). Social networking sites across cultures and countries: Proximity and network effects. *Qualitative Research Reports in Communication, 14*, 28–34.

Roloff, M. E., Janiszewski, C. A., McGrath, M. A., Burns, C. S., & Manrai, L. A. (1988). Acquiring resources from intimates: When obligation substitutes for persuasion. *Human Communication Research, 14*, 364–396.

Romaine, S. (1999). *Communicating gender*. Mahwah, NJ: Erlbaum.

Rose, A. J., Carlson, W., & Waller, E. M. (2007). Prospective associations of co-rumination with friendship and emotional adjustment: Considering the socioemotional trade-offs of co-rumination. *Developmental Psychology, 43*, 1019–1031.

Rosenfeld, J., & Ribner, D. S. (2011). *The newlywed's guide to physical intimacy*. Jerusalem, Israel: Gefen Publishing House Ltd.

Rosenfeld, L. B. (2000). Overview of the ways privacy, secrecy, and disclosure are balanced in today's society. In S. Petronio (Ed.), *Balancing the secrets of private disclosures* (pp. 3–17). Mahwah, NJ: Erlbaum.

Rosenfeld, L. B., & Bowen, G. L. (1991). Marital disclosure and marital satisfaction: Direct-effect versus interaction-effect models. *Western Journal of Speech Communication, 55*, 69–84.

Rosenfeld, L. B., & Richman, J. M. (1999). Supportive communication and school outcomes: Part II. Academically at-risk low income high school students. *Communication Education, 48*, 294–307.

Rosenthal, R., & Jacobson, L. (1968). *Pygmalion in the classroom*. New York, NY: Holt, Rinehart & Winston.

Ross, D. (1996). In their own words: Mixed-heritage children in the United States. *Dissertation Abstracts International: Section A. Humanities and Social Sciences, 56*(11-A), 4329.

Ross, J. B., & McLaughlin, M. M. (Eds.). (1949). *A portable medieval reader*. New York, NY: Viking.

Ruben, B. D. (1989). The study of cross-cultural competence: Traditions and contemporary issues. *International Journal of Intercultural Relationships, 13*, 229–240.

Rubin, L. B. (1983). *Intimate strangers*. San Francisco, CA: Harper & Row.

Rubin, L. B. (1985). *Just friends: The role of friendship in our lives*. New York, NY: Harper & Row.

Rubin, R. B., & Graham, E. E. (1988). Communication correlates of college success: An exploratory investigation. *Communication Education, 37*, 14–27.

Rubin, R. B., Perse, E. M., & Barbato, C. A. (1988). Conceptualization and measurement of interpersonal communication motives. *Human Communication Research, 14*, 602–628.

Rui, J., & Stefanone, M. A. (2013). Strategic self-presentation online: A cross-cultural study. *Computers in Human Behavior, 29*, 110–118.

Rusbult, C. E., Finkel, E. J., & Kumashiro, M. (2009). The Michelangelo phenomenon. *Current Directions in Psychological Science, 18*, 305–309.

Rusbult, C. E., & Martz, J. M. (1995). Remaining in an abusive relationship: An investment model analysis of nonvoluntary commitment. *Personality and Social Psychology Bulletin, 21*, 558–571.

Rusbult, C. E., & Van Lange, P. A. M. (1996). Interdependence processes. In E. T. Higgins & A. W. Kruglanski (Eds.), *Social psychology: Handbook of basic principles* (pp. 564–596). New York, NY: Guilford Press.

Russell, G. M., & Bohan, J. S. (2005). The gay generational gap: Communicating across the LGBT generational divide. *Institute for Gay and Lesbian Strategic Studies, 8*, 1–8.

Rymer, R. (1993). *Genie: An abused child's flight from silence*. New York, NY: HarperCollins.

Sagarian, E. (1976, March). The high cost of wearing a label. *Psychology Today, 10*, 25–27.

Sager, K. L. (2008). An exploratory study of the relationships between Theory X/Y assumptions and superior communicator style. *Management Communication Quarterly, 22*, 288–312.

Sahlstein, E., & Dun, T. (2008). "I wanted time to myself and he wanted to be together all the time": Constructing breakups as managing autonomy-connection. *Qualitative Research Reports in Communication, 9*, 37–45.

Salimi, S.-H., Mirzamani, S.-H., & Shahiri-Tabarestani, M. (2005). Association of parental self-esteem and expectations with adolescents' anxiety about career and education. *Psychological Reports, 96*, 569–578.

Salimkhan, G., Manago, A., & Greenfield, P. (2010). The construction of the virtual self on MySpace. *Cyberpsychology: Journal of Psychosocial Research on Cyberspace, 4*, article 1. Retrieved from http://cyberpsychology.eu/view.php?cisloclanku=2010050203&article=1

Saltz, R. (2012, March 23). An encounter with Simone Weil. *New York Times*, p. 8.

Samar, S. M., Walton, K. E., & McDermut, W. (2013). Personality traits predict irrational beliefs. *Journal of Rational-Emotive & Cognitive-Behavior Therapy, 31*, 231–242.

Samovar, L. A., & Porter, R. E. (2004). *Communication between cultures* (5th ed.). Belmont, CA: Wadsworth.

Samovar, L. A., Porter R. E., & McDaniel, E. R. (2007). *Communication between cultures* (6th ed.). Belmont, CA: Wadsworth.

Samovar, L. A., Porter R. E., & McDaniel, E. R. (2010). *Communication between cultures* (7th ed.). Belmont, CA: Wadsworth.

Samovar, L. A., Porter, R. E., & McDaniel, E. R. (2013). *Communication between cultures* (8th ed.). Boston, MA: Wadsworth.

Samp, J. A., Wittenberg, E., & Gillett, D. L. (2003). Presenting and monitoring a gender-defined self on the Internet. *Communication Research Reports, 20*, 1–12.

Samter, W., & Burleson, B. R. (2005). The role of communication in same-sex friendships: A comparison among African Americans, Asian Americans, and European Americans. *Communication Quarterly, 53*, 265–283.

Samter, W., & Cupach, W. R. (1998). Friendly fire: Topical variations in conflict among same- and cross-sex friends. *Communication Studies, 49*, 121–138.

Sandberg, J. G., Busby, D. M., Johnson, S. M., & Yoshida, K. (2012). The Brief Accessibility, Responsiveness, and Engagement (BARE) Scale: A tool for measuring attachment behavior in couple relationships. *Family Process, 51*, 512–526.

Sandel, T. L. (2004). Narrated relationships: Mothers-in-law and daughters-in-law justifying conflicts in Taiwan's Chhan-chng. *Research on Language and Social Interaction, 37*, 265–299.

Sanders, A. (2013). Performing positive emotion for prospective students: Emotional labor and customer service in an undergraduate admissions department. *Ohio Communication Journal, 51*, 78–102.

Sanderson, C. A., & Karetsky, K. H. (2002). Intimacy goals and strategies of conflict resolution in dating relationships: A mediational analysis. *Journal of Social and Personal Relationships, 19*, 317–337.

Sandler, W. (2013). Vive la différence: Sign language and spoken language in language evolution. *Language & Cognition, 5*, 189–203.

Sanford, A. A. (2010). "I can air my feelings instead of eating them": Blogging as social support for the morbidly obese. *Communication Studies, 61*, 567–584.

Santilli, V., & Miller, A. N. (2011). The effects of gender and power distance on nonverbal immediacy in symmetrical and asymmetrical power conditions: A cross-cultural study of classrooms and friendships. *Journal of International & Intercultural Communication, 4*, 3–22.

Sapadin, L. A. (1988). Friendship and gender: Perspectives of professional men and women. *Journal of Social and Personal Relationships, 5*, 387–403.

Sargent, J. (2002). Topic avoidance: Is this the way to a more satisfying relationship? *Communication Research Reports, 19*, 175–182.

Saslow, L. R., Muise, A., Impett, E. A., & Dubin, M. (2013). Can you see how happy we are? Facebook images and relationship satisfaction. *Social Psychological and Personality Science, 4*, 411–418.

Saulny, S. (2011, October 12). In strangers' glances at family, tensions linger. *The New York Times*. Retrieved from http://mobile.nytimes.com/2011/10/13/us/for-mixed-family-old-racial-tensions-remain-part-of-life.html

Savin-Williams, R. C. (2001). *Mom, dad. I'm gay. How families negotiate coming out*. Washington, DC: American Psychological Association.

Schachter, S. (1959). *The psychology of affiliation*. Stanford, CA: Stanford University Press.

Schade, L. C., Sandberg, J., Bean, R., Busby, D., & Coyne, S. (2013). Using technology to connect in romantic relationships: Effects on attachment, relationship satisfaction, and stability in emerging adults. *Journal of Couple & Relationship Therapy, 12*, 314–338.

Schaefer, M. T., & Olson, D. H. (1981). Assessing intimacy: The PAIR Inventory. *Journal of Marital and Family Therapy, 7*, 47–60.

Schandorf, M. (2013). Mediated gesture: Paralinguistic communication and phatic text. *Convergence: The Journal of Research into New Media Technologies, 19*, 319–344.

Scharlott, B. W., & Christ, W. G. (1995). Overcoming relationship-initiation barriers: The impact of a computer-dating system on sex role, shyness, and appearance inhibitions. *Computers in Human Behavior, 11*, 191–204.

Schiefenhövel, W. (1997). Universals in interpersonal interactions. In U. C. Segerstråle & P. Molnár (Eds.),

Nonverbal communication: Where nature meets culture (pp. 61–85). Hillsdale, NJ: Erlbaum.

Schmidt, J. J. (2006). *Social and cultural foundations of counseling and human services: Multiple influences on self-concept development*. Boston, MA: Pearson/Allyn and Bacon.

Schmitt, D. P., Jonason, P. K., Byerley, G. J., Flores, S. D., Illbeck, B. E., O'Leary, K. N., & Qudrat, A. (2012). A reexamination of sex differences in sexuality: New studies reveal old truths. *Current Directions in Psychological Science, 21,* 135–139.

Schneider, J. P., Weiss, R., & Samenow, C. (2012). Is it really cheating? Understanding the emotional reactions and clinical treatment of spouses and partners affected by cybersex infidelity. *Sexual Addiction & Compulsivity, 19,* 123–139.

Schnell, K., Bluschke, S., Konradt, B., & Walter, H. (2013). Functional relations of empathy and mentalizing: An fMRI study on the neural basis of cognitive empathy. *Neuroimage, 54,* 1743–1754.

Schotter, E. R., Berry, R. W., McKenzie, C. R. M., & Rayner, K. (2010). Gaze bias: Selective encoding and liking effects. *Visual Cognition, 18,* 1113–1132.

Schrodt, P. (2009). Family strength and satisfaction as functions of family communication environments. *Communication Quarterly, 57,* 171–186.

Schrodt, P., & Carr, K. (2012). Trait verbal aggressiveness as a function of family communication patterns. *Communication Research Reports, 29,* 54–63.

Schrodt, P., Turman, P. D., & Soliz, J. (2006). Perceived understanding as a mediator of perceived teacher confirmation and students' ratings of instruction. *Communication Education, 55,* 370–388.

Schrodt, P., Witt, P. L., & Messersmith, A. S. (2008). A meta-analytical review of family communication patterns and their associations with information processing, behavioral, and psychosocial outcomes. *Communication Monographs, 75,* 248–269.

Schrodt, P., Witt, P. L., & Shimkowski, J. R. (2014). A meta-analytical review of the demand/withdraw pattern of interaction and its associations with individual, relational, and communicative outcomes. *Communication Monographs, 81,* 28–58.

Schrodt, P., Witt, P. L., Turman, P. D., Myers, S. A., Barton, M. H., & Jernberg, K. A. (2009). Instructor credibility as a mediator of instructors' prosocial communication behaviors and students' learning outcomes. *Communication Education, 58,* 350–371.

Schroeder, J. A. (2010). Sex and gender in sensation and perception. In J. C. Chrisler & D. R. McCreary (Eds.), *Handbook of gender research in psychology* (Vol. 1, pp. 235–257). New York, NY: Springer.

Schubert, T. W., & Koole, S. L. (2009). The embodied self: Making a fist enhances men's power-related self-conceptions. *Journal of Experimental Social Psychology, 45,* 828–834.

Schütz, A. (1999). It was your fault! Self-serving biases in autobiographical accounts of conflicts in married couples. *Journal of Social and Personal Relationships, 16,* 193–208.

Schwartz, H. A., Eichstaedt, J. C., Kern, M. L., Dziurzynski, L., Ramones, S. M., Agrawal, M., . . . Ungar, L. H. (2013). Personality, gender, and age in the language of social media: The open-vocabulary approach. *PLoS ONE, 8,* e73791.

Scott, C., & Myers, K. K. (2005). The socialization of emotion: Learning emotion management at the fire station. *Journal of Applied Communication Research, 33,* 67–92.

Scott, G. G. (2010). *Playing the lying game: Detecting and dealing with lies and liars, from occasional fibbers to frequent fabricators*. Santa Barbara, CA: Praeger.

Scudder, J. N., & Andrews, P. H. (1995). A comparison of two alternative models of powerful speech: The impact of power and gender upon the use of threats. *Communication Research Reports, 12,* 25–33.

Seabrook, J. (1994, June 6). My first flame. *New Yorker, 71,* 70–79.

Sedikides, C., Campbell, W. K., Reeder, G. D., & Elliot, A. J. (1998). The self-serving bias in relational context. *Journal of Personality and Social Psychology, 74,* 378–386.

Segrin, C. (1993). The effects of nonverbal behavior on outcomes of compliance gaining attempts. *Communication Studies, 44,* 169–187.

Segrin, C., Hanzal, A., & Domschke, T. J. (2009). Accuracy and bias in newlywed couples' perceptions of conflict styles and the association with marital satisfaction. *Communication Monographs, 76,* 207–233.

Seider, B. H., Hirschberger, G., Nelson, K. L., & Levenson, R. W. (2009). We can work it out: Age differences in relational pronouns, physiology, and behavior in marital conflict. *Psychology and Aging, 24,* 604–613.

Seidman, B. (June 25, 2011). *Do not operate this marriage while drowsy*. Retrieved at http://www.pbs.org/wnet/need-to-know/the-daily-need/do-not-operate-this-marriage-while-drowsy/9839.

Self, W. R. (2009). Intercultural and nonverbal communication insights for international commercial arbitration. *Human Communication, 12,* 231–237.

Seligman, M. E. P. (2006). *Learned optimism*. New York. NY: Vintage.

Semlak, J. L., & Pearson, J. C. (2011). Big macs/peanut butter and jelly: An exploration of dialectical contradictions experienced by the sandwich generation. *Communication Research Reports, 28,* 296–307.

Semmer, N. K., Elfering, A., Jacobshagen, N., Perrot, T., Beehr, T. A., & Boos, N. (2008). The emotional meaning of instrumental social support. *International Journal of Stress Management, 15,* 235–251.

Servaes, J. (1989). Cultural identity and modes of communication. In J. A. Anderson (Ed.), *Communication yearbook 12* (pp. 383–416). Newbury Park, CA: Sage.

Shafer, D. N. (2007). Hearing loss hinders relationships. *ASHA Leader, 12*(9), 5–7.

Shafir, T., Taylor, S. F., Atkinson, A. P., Langenecker, S. A., & Zubieta, J. (2013). Emotion regulation through execution, observation, and imagery of emotional movements. *Brain and Cognition, 82,* 219–227.

Shamay, S. G., Tomer, R., & Aharon-Peretz, J. (2002). Deficit in understanding sarcasm in patients with prefrontal lesion is related to impaired empathic ability. *Brain and Cognition, 48,* 558–563.

Shargorodsky, J., Curhan, S. G., Curhan, G. C., & Eavey, R. (2010). Change in prevalence of hearing loss in US adolescents. *Journal of the American Medical Association, 304,* 772–778.

Shattuck, R. (1980). *The forbidden experiment: The story of the Wild Boy of Aveyron.* New York, NY: Farrar, Straus & Giroux.

Shaw, C., & Hepburn, A. (2013). Managing the moral implications of advice in informal interaction. *Research on Language & Social Interaction, 46,* 344–362.

Shearman, S. M., Dumlao, R., & Kagawa, N. (2011). Cultural variations in accounts by American and Japanese young adults: Recalling a major conflict with parents. *Journal of Family Communication, 11,* 105–125.

Shechory Bitton, M., & Shaul, D. (2013). Perceptions and attitudes to sexual harassment: An examination of sex differences and the sex composition of the harasser–target dyad. *Journal of Applied Social Psychology, 43,* 2136–2145.

Sheeks, M. S., & Birchmeier, Z. P. (2007). Shyness, sociability, and the use of computer-mediated communication in relationship development. *CyberPsychology & Behavior, 10,* 64–70.

Shepperd, J., Malone, W., & Sweeny, K. (2008). Exploring causes of the self-serving bias. *Social and Personality Psychology Compass, 2,* 895–908.

Sherman, S. M., & Dumlao, R. (2008) A cross-cultural comparison of family communication patterns and conflict between young adults and parents. *Journal of Family Communication, 8,* 186–211.

Shimanoff, S. B. (1985). Rules governing the verbal expression of emotions between married couples. *Western Journal of Speech Communication, 49,* 149–165.

Shimanoff, S. B. (1988). Degree of emotional expressiveness as a function of face-needs, gender, and interpersonal relationship. *Communication Reports, 1,* 43–53.

Shiota, M. N., & Levenson, R. W. (2007). Birds of a feather don't always fly farthest: Similarity in big five personality predicts more negative marital satisfaction trajectories in long-term marriages. *Psychology and Aging, 22,* 666–675.

Shirley, J. A., Powers, W. G., & Sawyer, C. R. (2007). Psychologically abusive relationships and self-disclosure orientations. *Human Communication, 10,* 289–301.

Shonbeck, K. (2011). Communicating in a connected world. In K. M. Galvin (Ed.), *Making connections: Readings in relational communication* (5th ed., pp. 393–400). New York, NY: Oxford University Press.

Shuler, S., & Sypher, B. D. (2000). Seeking emotional labor: When managing the heart enhances the work experience. *Management Communication Quarterly, 14,* 51–89.

Sieberg, E., & Larson, C. (1971, April). *Dimensions of interpersonal response.* Paper presented at the meeting of the International Communication Association, Phoenix, AZ.

Siegman, A. W., & Snow, S. C. (1997). The outward expression of anger, the inward experience of anger and CVR: The role of vocal expression. *Journal of Behavioral Medicine, 1,* 29–45.

Sigler, K., Burnett, A., & Child, J. T. (2008). A regional analysis of assertiveness. *Journal of Intercultural Communication Research, 37,* 89–104.

Sillars, A., Holman, A. J., Richards, A., Jacobs, K. A., Koerner, A., & Reynolds-Dyk, A. (2014). Conversation and conformity orientations as predictors of observed conflict tactics in parent-adolescent discussions. *Journal of Family Communication, 14,* 16–31.

Sillence, E. (2013). Giving and receiving peer advice in an online breast cancer support group. *Cyberpsychology, Behavior, and Social Networking, 16,* 480–485.

Simmons, J., Lowery-Hart, R., Wahl, S. T., & McBride, M. C. (2013). Understanding the African-American student experience in higher education through a relational dialectics perspective. *Communication Education, 62,* 376–394.

Simmons, R. A., Gordon, P. C., & Chambless, D. L. (2005). Pronouns in marital interaction: What do "you" and "I" say about marital health? *Family Process, 47,* 405–419.

Simon, V. A., Kobielski, S. J., & Martin, S. (2008). Conflict beliefs, goals, and behavior in romantic relationships during late adolescence. *Journal of Youth and Adolescence, 37,* 324–335.

Simonsohn, U. (2011). Spurious? Name similarity effects (implicit egotism) in marriage, job, and moving decisions. *Journal of Personality and Social Psychology, 101,* 1–24.

Singer, M. (1998). *Perception and identity in intercultural communication.* Yarmouth, ME: Intercultural Press.

Singh, M., & Woods, S. (2008). Predicting general well-being from emotional intelligence and three broad personality traits. *Journal of Applied Social Psychology, 38,* 635–646.

Singh, R., Simons, J. J. P., Young, D. P. C. Y., Sim, B. S. X., Chai, X. T., Singh, S., & Chiou, S. (2009). Trust and respect as mediators of the other- and self-profitable trait effects on interpersonal attraction. *European Journal of Social Psychology, 39,* 1021–1038.

Singleton, R. A., Jr., & Vacca, J. (2007). Interpersonal competition in friendships. *Sex Roles, 57,* 617–627.

Skowron, E., Stanley, K., & Shapiro, M. (2009). A longitudinal perspective on differentiation of self, interpersonal and psychological well-being in young adulthood. *Contemporary Family Therapy: An International Journal, 31,* 3–18.

Slatcher, R. B., Vazire, S., & Pennebaker, J. W. (2008). Am "I" more important than "we"? Couples' word use in instant messages. *Personal Relationships, 15,* 407–424.

Slotter, E. B., & Gardner, W. L. (2009). Where do you end and I begin? Evidence for anticipatory, motivated self–other integration between relationship partners. *Journal of Personality and Social Psychology, 96,* 1137–1151.

Smith, A. (2014, February 3). *6 new facts about Facebook.* Pew Research Center. Retrieved from http://www.pewresearch.org/fact-tank/2014/02/03/6-new-facts-about-facebook/

Smith, A., & Duggan, M. (2013, October 21). *Online dating & relationships.* PewResearch Internet Project.

Smith, D. E., Gier, J. A., & Willis, F. N. (1982). Interpersonal touch and compliance with a marketing request. *Basic and Applied Social Psychology, 3,* 35–38.

Smith, L., Heaven, P. C. L., & Ciarrochi, J. (2008). Trait emotional intelligence, conflict communication patterns, and relationship satisfaction. *Personality and Individual Differences, 44,* 1314–1325.

Smith, M. (2010). Hearing into being. *Women at Heart.* Retrieved from http://www.women-at-heart.com/effective-communication.html

Smith, P. B. (2011). Cross-cultural perspectives on identity. In S. J. Schwartz, K. Luyckx, & V. L. Vignoles (Eds.), *Handbook of identity theory and research* (Vols. 1 & 2, pp. 249–265). New York, NY: Springer Science + Business Media.

Smith-McLallen, A., Johnson, B. T., Dovidio, J. F., & Pearson, A. R. (2006). Black and white: The role of color bias and implicit race bias. *Social Cognition, 24,* 46–73.

Snell, J. (2013). Dialect, interaction and class positioning at school: From deficit to difference to repertoire. *Language & Education: An International Journal, 27,* 110–128.

Sobel, A. (2009, July 27). *Interview etiquette: Lessons from a first date.* The Ladders.

Social Security Administration. (2013). *Top 10 baby names for 2012.* Retrieved from http://www.ssa.gov/OACT/babynames/

Solomon, S., & Knafo, A. (2007). Value similarity in adolescent friendships. In T. C. Rhodes (Ed.), *Focus on adolescent behavior research* (pp. 133–155). Hauppauge, NY: Nova Science Publishers.

Sommer, K. L., Williams, K. D., Ciarocco, N. J., & Baumeister, R. F. (2001). When silence speaks louder than words: Explorations into the intrapsychic and interpersonal consequences of social ostracism. *Basic and Applied Social Psychology, 23,* 225–243.

Sommer, R. (1969). *Personal space: The behavioral basis of design.* Englewood Cliffs, NJ: Prentice-Hall.

Sommer, R. (2002). Personal space in a digital age. In R. B. Bechtel & A. Churchman (Eds.), *Handbook of environmental psychology* (pp. 647–660). New York, NY: Wiley.

Sopow, E. (2008). The communication climate change at RCMP. *Strategic Communication Management, 12,* 20–23.

Sousa, L. A. (2002). The medium is the message: The costs and benefits of writing, talking aloud, and thinking about life's triumphs and defeats. *Dissertation Abstracts International: Section B. The Sciences and Engineering, 62*(7-B), 3397.

Spears, R. (2001). The interaction between the individual and the collective self: Self-categorization in context. In C. Sedikides & M. B. Brewer (Eds.), *Individual self, relational self, collective self* (pp. 171–198). New York, NY: Psychology Press.

Speicher, H. (1999). Development and validation of intimacy capability and intimacy motivation measures. *Dissertation Abstracts International: Section B. The Sciences and Engineering, 59*(9-B), 5172.

Spielmann, S. S., MacDonald, G., & Tackett, J. L. (2012). Social threat, social reward, and regulation of investment in romantic relationhips. *Personal Relationships, 19,* 601–622.

Spitzberg, B. H. (1991). An examination of trait measures of interpersonal competence. *Communication Reports, 4,* 22–29.

Spitzberg, B. H. (1994). The dark side of (in)competence. In W. R. Cupach & B. H. Spitzberg (Eds.), *The dark side of interpersonal communication* (pp. 25–50). Hillsdale, NJ: Erlbaum.

Spitzberg, B. H. (2000). What is good communication? *Journal of the Association for Communication Administration, 29,* 103–119.

Sporer, S. L., & Schwandt, B. (2007). Moderators of nonverbal indicators of deception: A meta-analytic synthesis. *Psychology, Public Policy, and Law, 13*(1), 1–34.

Sprecher, S. (2014). Effects of actual (manipulated) and perceived similarity on liking in get-acquainted interactions: The role of communication. *Communication Monographs, 81,* 4–27.

Sprecher, S., Treger, S., & Wondra, J. D. (2013). Effects of self-disclosure role on liking, closeness, and other impressions in get-acquainted interactions. *Journal of Personal and Social Relationships, 30,* 497–514.

Sprecher, S., Treger, S., Wondra, J. D., Hilaire, N., & Wallpe, K. (2013). Taking turns: Reciprocal self-disclosure promotes liking in initial interactions. *Journal of Experimental Social Psychology, 49,* 860–866.

Sprecher, S., Wenzel, A., & Harvey, J. (Eds.). (2008). *Handbook of relationship initiation.* New York, NY: Psychology Press.

Spreng, R., McKinnon, M. C., Mar, R. A., & Levine, B. (2009). The Toronto Empathy Questionnaire: Scale development and initial validation of a factor-analytic solution to multiple empathy measures. *Journal of Personality Assessment, 91,* 62–71.

Stadler, S. (2013). Cultural differences in the orientation to disagreement and conflict. *China Media Research, 9*(4), 66–75.

Stafford, L. (2005). *Maintaining long-distance and cross-residential relationships.* Mahwah, NJ: Erlbaum.

Stafford, L. (2008). Social exchange theories. In L. A. Baxter & D. O. Braithewaite (Eds.), *Engaging theories in interpersonal communication: Multiple perspectives* (pp. 377–389). Thousand Oaks, CA: Sage.

Stamp, G. H., Vangelisti, A. L., & Daly, J. A. (1992). The creation of defensiveness in social interaction. *Communication Quarterly, 40,* 177–190.

Steen, S., & Schwartz, P. (1995). Communication, gender, and power: Homosexual couples as a case study. In M. A. Fitzpatrick & A. L. Vangelisti (Eds.), *Explaining family interactions* (pp. 310–343). Thousand Oaks, CA: Sage.

Steil, L. K. (1996). Listening training: The key to success in today's organizations. In M. Purdy & D. Borisoff (Eds.), *Listening in everyday life: A personal and professional approach* (2nd ed., pp. 213–237). Lanham, MD: University Press of America.

Stephens, C., & Long, N. (2000). Communication with police supervisors and peers as a buffer of work-related traumatic stress. *Journal of Organizational Behavior, 21,* 407–424.

Stephens, K. K., Cho, J. K., & Ballard, D. I. (2012). Simultaneity, sequentiality, and speed: Organizational messages about multiple-task completion. *Human Communication Research, 38,* 23–47.

Stephens, K. K., Houser, M. L., & Cowan, R. L. (2009). R U able to meat me: The impact of students' overly casual email messages to instructors. *Communication Education, 58,* 303–326.

Stephenson-Abetz, J., & Holman, A. (2012). Home is where the heart is: Facebook and the negotiation of "old" and "new" during the transition to college. *Western Journal of Communication, 76,* 175–193.

Stern, R. (2007). *The gaslight effect: How to spot and survive the hidden manipulations other people use to control your life.* New York, NY: Morgan Road.

Sternberg, R. J. (2004). A triangular theory of love. In H. T. Reis & C. E. Rusbult (Eds.), *Close Relationships* (pp. 258–276). New York, NY: Psychology Press.

Stets, J. E., & Cast, A. D. (2007). Resources and identity verification from an identity theory perspective. *Sociological Perspectives, 50,* 517–543.

Steves, R. (n.d.). Culture shock and wiggle room. *Rick Steves' Europe.* Retrieved from https://www.ricksteves.com/watch-read-listen/read/articles/culture-shock-and-wiggle-room

Stevens, B. (2005). What communication skills do employers want? Silicon Valley recruiters respond. *Journal of Employment Counseling, 42,* 2–9.

Stewart, G. L., Dustin, S. L., Barrick, M. R., & Darnold, T. C. (2008). Exploring the handshake in employment interviews. *Journal of Applied Psychology, 93,* 1139–1146.

Stiff, J. B., Dillard, J. P., Somera, L., Kim, H., & Sleight, C. (1988). Empathy, communication, and prosocial behavior. *Communication Monographs, 55,* 198–213.

Stiles, W. B., Walz, N. C., Schroeder, M. A. B., Williams, L. L., & Ickes, W. (1996). Attractiveness and disclosure in initial encounters of mixed-sex dyads. *Journal of Social and Personal Relationships, 13,* 303–312.

Strachan, H. (2004). Communication. *Research and Theory for Nursing Practice: An International Journal, 18,* 7–10.

Straus, M. A., & Field, C. J. (2003). Psychological aggression by American parents: National data on prevalence, chronicity, and severity. *Journal of Marriage and Family, 65,* 795–808.

Strong, C. M. (2005). The role of exposure to media-idealized male physiques on men's body image.

Dissertation Abstracts International: Section B. The Sciences and Engineering, 65(8-B), 4306.

Sturman, E. D., & Mongrain, M. (2008). The role of personality in defeat: A revised social rank model. *European Journal of Personality, 22,* 55–79.

Suler, J. R. (2002). Identity management in cyberspace. *Journal of Applied Psychoanalytic Studies, 4,* 455–459.

Sullins, E. S. (1991). Emotional contagion revisited: Effects of social comparison and expressive style on mood convergence. *Personality and Social Psychology Bulletin, 17,* 166–174.

Sullivan, A. (2012, July 2). Anderson Cooper: "The fact is, I'm gay." *The Dish.* Retrieved from http://dish.andrewsullivan.com/2012/07/02/anderson-cooper-the-fact-is-im-gay/

Sullivan, C. F. (1996). Recipients' perceptions of support attempts across various stressful life events. *Communication Research Reports, 13,* 183–190.

Sullivan, P. (2004). Communication differences between male and female team sport athletes. *Communication Reports, 17,* 121–128.

Suls, J., Martin, R., & Wheeler, L. (2002). Social comparison: Why, with whom, and with what effect? *Current Directions in Psychological Science, 11,* 159–163.

Sumter, S. R., Valkenburg, P. M., & Peter, J. (2013). Perceptions of love across the lifespan: Differences in passion, intimacy, and commitment. *International Journal of Behavioral Development, 37,* 417–427.

Supiano, B. (2013, April 10). Employers want broadly educated new hires, survey finds. *Chronicle of Higher Education.* Retrieved from http://chronicle.com/article/Employers-Want-Broadly/138453

Suter, E. A., Bergen, K. M., Daas, K. L., & Durham, W. T. (2006). Lesbian couples' management of public-private dialectical contradictions. *Journal of Social & Personal Relationships, 23,* 349–365.

Suter, E. A., Daas, K. L., & Bergen, K. (2008). Negotiating lesbian family identity via symbols and rituals. *Journal of Family Issues, 29,* 26–47.

Sutton, R. I. (2010, June 18). Is it sometimes useful to cuss when you are at work?: The strategic use of swear words. *Psychology Today.* Retrieved from http://www.psychologytoday.com/blog/work-matters/201006/is-it-sometimes-useful-cuss-when-you-are-work

Swain, S. (1989). Covert intimacy in men's friendships: Closeness in men's friendships. In B. J. Risman & P. Schwartz (Eds.), *Gender in intimate relationships: A microstructural approach* (pp. 71–86). Belmont, CA: Wadsworth.

Swami, V., & Allum, L. (2012). Perceptions of the physical attractiveness of the self, current romantic partners, and former partners. *Scandinavian Journal of Psychology, 53,* 89–95.

Swami, V., & Furnham, A. (2008). *The psychology of physical attraction.* New York: Routledge/Taylor & Francis.

Takaku, S., Weiner, B., & Ohbuchi, K (2001). A cross-cultural examination of the effects of apology and perspective-taking on forgiveness. *Journal of Language & Social Psychology, 20,* 144–167.

Tanaka, A., Koizumi, A., Imai, H., Hiramatsu, S., Hiramoto, E., & de Gelder, B. (2010). I feel your voice: Cultural differences in the multisensory perception of emotion. *Psychological Science, 21,* 1259–1262.

Tannen, D. (1986). *That's not what I meant! How conversational style makes or breaks your relations with others.* New York, NY: William Morrow.

Tannen, D. (1990). *You just don't understand: Women and men in conversation.* New York, NY: William Morrow.

Tannen, D. (1994). *Talking from 9 to 5: Women and men in the workplace: Language, sex and power.* New York, NY: William Morrow.

Tannen, D. (2001). But what do you mean? Women and men in conversation. In J. M. Henslin (Ed.), *Down to earth sociology: Introductory readings* (11th ed., pp. 168–173). New York, NY: Free Press.

Tashiro, T., & Frazier, P. (2003). "I'll never be in a relationship like that again": Personal growth following romantic relationship breakups. *Personal Relationships, 10,* 113–128.

Tavris, C., & Aronson, E. (2007). *Mistakes were made (but not by me).* Orlando, FL: Harcourt.

Taylor, A. F., Wiley, A., Kuo, F. E., & Sullivan, W. C. (1998). Growing up in the inner city: Green spaces as places to grow. *Environment and Behavior, 30,* 3–27.

Taylor, D. A., & Altman, I. (1987). Communication in interpersonal relationships: Social penetration processes. In M. E. Roloff & G. R. Miller (Eds.), *Interpersonal processes: New directions in communication research* (pp. 257–277). Newbury Park, CA: Sage.

Taylor, P. (2014, April 10). *The next America.* Pew Research Center. Retrieved from http://www.pewresearch.org/packages/the-next-america/

Taylor, S., & Mette, D. (1971). When similarity breeds contempt. *Journal of Personality and Social Psychology, 20,* 75–81.

Ten things everyone should know about race. (2003). *RACE—The power of an illusion.* Public Broadcasting System. Retrieved from http://www.pbs.org/race/000_About/002_04-background-01-x.htm

Teven, J. J. (2010). The effects of supervisor nonverbal immediacy and power use on employees' ratings of credibility and affect for the supervisor. *Human Communication, 13,* 69–85.

Teven, J. J., & Comadena, M. E. (1996). The effects of office aesthetic quality on students' perceptions of teacher credibility and communicator style. *Communication Research Reports, 13*, 101–108.

Teven, J. J., Richmond, V. P., McCroskey, J. C., & McCroskey, L. L (2010). Updating relationships between communication traits and communication competence. *Communication Research Reports, 27*, 263–270.

Tezer, E., & Demir, A. (2001). Conflict behaviors toward same-sex and opposite-sex peers among male and female late adolescents. *Adolescence, 36*(143), 525–533.

The many ways to say "I" in Japanese. (2009, November 28). *Nihonshock.* Retrieved from http://nihonshock.com/2009/11/the-many-ways-to-say-i/

Theiss, J. A., & Solomon, D. H. (2007). Communication and the emotional, cognitive, and relational consequences of first sexual encounters between partners. *Communication Quarterly, 55*, 179–206.

Thibaut, J. W., & Kelley, H. H. (1959). *The social psychology of groups.* New York, NY: Wiley.

Thomas, D. E., Bierman, K. L., & Powers, C. J. (2011). The influence of classroom aggression and classroom climate on aggressive–disruptive behavior. *Child Development, 82*, 751–757.

Thomas, K. W., & Kilmann, R. (1978). Comparison of four instruments measuring conflict behavior. *Psychological Report, 42*, 1139–1145.

Thomas, K. W., & Kilmann, R. H. (2007). *Thomas-Kilmann Conflict Mode Instrument.* Mountain View, CA: Xicom, a subsidiary of CPP, Inc. (Original work published 1974)

Thorson, A. R., & Horstman, H. A. K. (2014). Buy now, pay later: Family communication patterns theory, parental financial support, and emerging adults' openness about credit card behaviors. *Journal of Family Communication, 14*, 53–71.

Thourlby, W. (1978). *You are what you wear.* New York, NY: New American Library.

Tidwell, N. D., Eastwick, P. W., & Finkel, E. J. (2013). Perceived, not actual, similarity predicts initial attraction in a live romantic context: Evidence from the speed-dating paradigm. *Personal Relationships, 20*, 199–215.

Timmerman, L. M. (2002). Comparing the production of power in language on the basis of sex. In M. Allen, R. W. Preiss, B. M. Gayle, & N. Burrell (Eds.), *Interpersonal communication research: Advances through meta-analysis* (pp. 73–88). Mahwah, NJ: Erlbaum.

Timmons, J. M. (2009). *Financial intimacy: How to create healthy relationships with your money and your mate.* Chicago, IL: Chicago Review Press.

Ting-Toomey, S. (1999). *Communicating across cultures.* New York, NY: Guilford Press.

Ting-Toomey, S., Oetzel, J., & Yee-Jung, K. (2001). Self-construal types and conflict management styles. *Communication Reports, 14*, 87–104.

Todorov, A., Chaiken, S., & Henderson, M. D. (2002). The heuristic-systematic model of social information processing. In J. P. Dillard & M. Pfau (Eds.), *The persuasion handbook: Developments in theory and practice* (pp. 195–211). Thousand Oaks, CA: Sage.

Tohidian, I. (2009). Examining linguistic relativity hypothesis as one of the main views on the relationship between language and thought. *Journal of Psycholinguistic Research, 38*(1), 65–74.

Tolar, T. D., Lederberg, A. R., Gokhale, S., & Tomasello, M. (2008). The development of the ability to recognize the meaning of iconic signs. *Journal of Deaf Studies and Deaf Education, 13*(1), 71–86.

Tolhuizen, J. H. (1989). Communication strategies for intensifying dating relationships: Identification, use and structure. *Journal of Social and Personal Relationships, 6*, 413–434.

Toller, P. (2011). Bereaved parents' experiences of supportive and unsupportive communication. *Southern Communication Journal, 76*, 17–34.

Tolman, E. (2011). Instructors' corner: Communication competence and cell phone use. *Communication Currents, 6*, 1–2.

Toma, C., & Hancock, J. T. (2010). Looks and lies: The role of physical attractiveness in online dating self-presentation and deception. *Communication Research, 37*, 335–351.

Toma, C. L., & Hancock, J. T. (2013). Self-affirmation underlies Facebook use. *Personality and Social Psychology Bulletin, 39*, 321–331.

Toma, C. L., Hancock, J. T., & Ellison, N. B. (2008). Separating fact from fiction: An examination of deceptive self-presentation in online dating profiles. *Personality and Social Psychology Bulletin, 34*, 1023–1036.

Tomlinson, E. C. (2013). The role of invention in digital date side profile composition. *Computers and Composition, 30*, 115–128.

Tong, S. (2013). Facebook use during relationship termination: Uncertainty reduction and surveillance. *Cyberpsychology, Behavior, and Social Networking, 16*, 788–793.

Tong, S. T., Van Der Heide, B., Langwell, L., & Walther, J. B. (2008). Too much of a good thing? The relationship between number of friends and interpersonal impressions on Facebook. *Journal of Computer-Mediated Communication, 13*, 531–549.

Tong, S. T., & Walther, J. B. (2011). Just say "No thanks": The effects of romantic rejection across computer-mediated communication. *Journal of Personal and Social Relationships, 28,* 488–506.

Tong, S. T., & Walther, J. B. (2011). Relational maintenance and computer-mediated communication. In K. B. Wright & L. M. Webb (Eds.), *Computer mediated communication and personal relationships* (pp. 98–118). New York: Peter Lang.

Tracy, J. L., & Randles, D. (2011). Four models of basic emotions: A review of Ekman and Cordaro, Izard, Levenson, and Panksepp and Watt. *Emotion Review, 3,* 397–405.

Tracy, J. L., & Robins, R. W. (2008). The nonverbal expression of pride: Evidence for cross-cultural recognition. *Journal of Personality & Social Psychology, 94,* 516–530.

Tracy, L. (1991). *The secret between us: Competition among women.* Boston, MA: Little, Brown.

Tracy, S. J. (2002). When questioning turns to face threat: An interactional sensitivity in 911 call-taking. *Western Journal of Communication, 66,* 129–157.

Tracy, S. J. (2005). Locking up emotion: Moving beyond dissonance for understanding emotion labor discomfort. *Communication Monographs, 72,* 261–283.

Tracy, S. J., & Trethewey, A. (2005). Fracturing the real-self-fake-self dichotomy: Moving toward crystallized organizational identities. *Communication Theory, 15,* 168–195.

Trees, A. R., Kerssen-Griefp, J., & Hess, J. A. (2009). Earning influence by communicating respect: Facework's contributions to effective instructional feedback. *Communication Education, 58,* 397–416.

Triandis, H. C. (1975). Culture training, cognitive complexity and interpersonal attitudes. In R. Brislin, S. Bichner, & W. Lonner (Eds.), *Cross-cultural perspectives on learning* (pp. 39–77). New York, NY: Wiley.

Triandis, H. C. (1990). Cross-cultural studies of individualism and collectivism. In J. Berman (Ed.), *Nebraska symposium on motivation* (pp. 41–133). Lincoln: University of Nebraska Press.

Triandis, H. C. (1994). *Culture and social behavior.* New York, NY: McGraw-Hill.

Triandis, H. C. (1995). *Individualism and collectivism.* Boulder, CO: Westview.

Tripp, G., Schaughency, E. A., Lanlands, R., & Mouat, K. (2007). Family interactions in children with and without ADHD. *Journal of Child and Family Studies, 16,* 385–400.

Trompenaars, F. (1994). *Riding the waves of culture.* New York: McGraw-Hill/Irwin.Troy, A. S., Shallcross, A. J., & Mauss, I. B. (2013). A person-by-situation approach to emotion regulation: Cognitive reappraisal can either help or hurt, depending on the context. *Psychological Science, 24,* 2505–2514.

Tsai, J. L., Knutson, B., & Fung, H. H. (2006). Cultural variation in affect valuation. *Journal of Personality and Social Psychology, 90,* 288–307.

Tsang, J.-A. (2006). The effects of helper intention on gratitude and indebtedness. *Motivation and Emotion, 30,* 199–205.

Tuckett, A. G. (2005). The care encounter: Pondering caring, honest communication and control. *International Journal of Nursing Practice, 11*(2), 77–84.

Turkle, S. (2011). *Alone together: Why we expect more from technology and less from each other.* New York, NY: Basic Books.

Turman, P. D. (2008). Coaches' immediacy behaviors as predictors of athletes' perceptions of satisfaction and team cohesion. *Western Journal of Communication, 72,* 162–179.

Turnage, A. K. (2007). Email flaming behaviors and organizational conflict. *Journal of Computer-Mediated Communication, 13,* 43–59.

Turnley, W. H., & Bolino, M. C. (2001). Achieving desired images while avoiding undesired images: Exploring the role of the self-monitoring in impression management. *Journal of Applied Psychology, 86,* 351–360.

Uchino, B. N. (2004). *Social support and physical health: Understanding the health consequences of relationships.* New Haven, CT: Yale University Press.

Ulrey, K. L. (2001). Intercultural communication between patients and health care providers: An exploration of intercultural communication effectiveness, cultural sensitivity, stress, and anxiety. *Health Communication, 13,* 449–463.

Underwood, M. K. (2003). *Social aggression among girls.* New York, NY: Guilford Press.

Usunier, J., & Roulin, N. (2010). The influence of high- and low-context communication styles on the design, content, and language of business-to-business Web sites. *Journal of Business Communication, 47,* 189–227.

Utz, S. (2007). Media use in long-distance friendships. *Information, Communication & Society, 10,* 694–713.

Utz, S., & Beukeboom, C. J. (2011). The role of social network sites in romantic relationships: Effects on jealousy and relationship happiness. *Journal of Computer-Mediated Communication, 16,* 511–527.

Valentine, C. A., & Saint Damian, B. (1988). Communicative power: Gender and culture as determinants of the ideal voice. In C. A. Valentine & N. Hoar (Eds.), *Women and communicative power: Theory, research, and practice* (pp. 42–68). Washington, DC: National Communication Association.

Van Boven, L., Judd, C. M., & Sherman, D. K. (2012). Political polarization projection: Social projection of partisan attitude extremity and attitudinal processes. *Journal of Personality and Social Psychology, 103,* 84–100.

vanDellen, M. R., Bradfield, E. K., & Hoyle, R. H. (2010). Self-regulation of state self-esteem following threat: Moderation by trait self-esteem. In R. H. Hoyle (Ed.)., *Handbook of personality and self-regulation* (pp. 430–446). Hoboken, NJ: Wiley-Blackwell.

van den Bos, K., Brockner, J., Stein, J. H., Steiner, D. D., Van Yperen, N. W., & Dekker, D. M. (2010). The psychology of voice and performance capabilities in masculine and feminine cultures and contexts. *Journal of Personality and Social Psychology, 99,* 638–648.

VanderDrift, L. E., Wilson, J. E., & Agnew, C. R. (2013). On the benefits of valuing being friends for nonmarital romantic partners. *Journal of Social and Personal Relationships, 30,* 115–131.

Vandergriff, I. (2013). Emotive communication online: A contextual analysis of computer-mediated communication cues. *Journal of Pragmatics, 51,* 1–12.

Vangelisti, A. (Ed.). (2004). *Handbook of family communication.* Mahwah, NJ: Erlbaum.

Vangelisti, A. L., & Beck, G. (2007). Intimacy and fear of intimacy. In L. L'Abate (Ed.), *Low-cost approaches to promote physical and mental health: Theory, research, and practice* (pp. 395–414). New York, NY: Springer Science 1 Business Media.

Vangelisti, A. L., Caughlin, J. P., & Timmerman, L. (2001). Criteria for revealing family secrets. *Communication Monographs, 68,* 1–27.

Vangelisti, A. L., & Crumley, L. P. (1998). Reactions to messages that hurt: The influence of relational contexts. *Communication Monographs, 65,* 173–196.

Vangelisti, A. L., Knapp, M. L., & Daly, J. A. (1990). Conversational narcissism. *Communication Monographs, 57,* 251–274.

van Leeuwen, M. L., & Macrae, C. N. (2004). Is beautiful always good? Implicit benefits of facial attractiveness. *Social Cognition, 22,* 637–649.

Van Swol, L. M. (2003). The effects of nonverbal mirroring on perceived persuasiveness, agreement with an imitator, and reciprocity in a small group discussion. *Communication Research, 30,* 461–480.

Vaquera, E., & Kao, G. (2005). Private and public displays of affection among interracial and intra-racial adolescent couples. *Social Science Quarterly, 86,* 484–508.

Venetis, M. K., Greene, K., Magsamen-Conrad, K., Banerjee, S. C., Checton, M. G., & Bagdasarov, Z. (2012). "You can't tell anyone but . . .": Exploring the use of privacy rules and revealing behaviors. *Communication Monographs, 79,* 344–365.

Veroff, J., Douvan, E., Orbuch, T. L., & Acitelli, L. K. (1998). Happiness in stable marriages: The early years. In T. N. Bradbury (Ed.), *The developmental course of marital dysfunction* (pp. 152–179). New York, NY: Cambridge University Press.

Versfeld, N. J., & Dreschler, W. A. (2002). The relationship between the intelligibility of time-compressed speech and speech-in-noise in young and elderly listeners. *Journal of the Acoustical Society of America, 111*(1, Pt. 1), 401–408.

Vilhauer, R. P. (2009). Perceived benefits of online support groups for women with metastatic breast cancer. *Women & Health, 49,* 381–404.

Villadsen, L. S. (2008). Speaking on behalf of others: Rhetorical agency and epideictic functions in official apologies. *RSQ: Rhetoric Society Quarterly, 38,* 25–45.

Villaume, W. A., & Bodie, G. D. (2007). Discovering the listener within us: The impact of trait-like personality variables and communicator styles on preferences for listening style. *International Journal of Listening, 21,* 102–123.

Vitak, J., Ellison, N., & Steinfield, C. (2011). The ties that bond: Re-examining the relationship between Facebook use and bonding social capital. In *Proceedings of the 44th Annual Hawaii International Conference on System Sciences* [CD-ROM]. Computer Society Press. Retrieved from http://vitak.files.wordpress.com/2009/02/hicss-social-provisions-revised-final.pdf

Vocate, D. R. (1994). Self-talk and inner speech: Understanding the uniquely human aspects of intrapersonal communication. In D. R. Vocate (Ed.), *Intrapersonal communication: Different voices, different minds* (pp. 3–31). Hillsdale, NJ: Erlbaum.

Vohs, K. D., & Heatherton, T. F. (2004). Ego threats elicits different social comparison process among high and low self-esteem people: Implications for interpersonal perceptions. *Social Cognition, 22,* 168–191.

Von Briesen, P. D. (2007). Pragmatic language skills of adolescents with ADHD. *Dissertation Abstracts International: Section B, The Sciences and Engineering, 68*(5-B), 3430.

Vrij, A. (2006). Nonverbal communication and deception. In V. Manusov & M. L. Patterson (Eds.), *The Sage handbook of nonverbal communication* (pp. 341–360). Thousand Oaks, CA: Sage.

Vrij, A., Edward, K., Roberts, K. P., & Bull, R. (2000). Detecting deceit via analysis of verbal and nonverbal behavior. *Journal of Nonverbal Behavior, 24,* 239–263.

Waara, E., & Shaw, P. (2006). Male and female witnesses' speech in Swedish criminal trials. *Journal of Language and Communication Studies, 36*, 129–156.

Wade, N. G., & Worthington, E. L., Jr. (2005). In search of a common core: A content analysis of interventions to promote forgiveness. *Psychotherapy: Theory, Research, Practice, Training, 42*, 160–177.

Waldron, V. R., & Kelley, D. L (2005). Forgiving communication as a response to relational transgressions. *Journal of Social and Personal Relationships, 22*, 723–742.

Wallace, H. M., Exline, J. J., & Baumeister, R. F. (2008). Interpersonal consequences of forgiveness: Does forgiveness deter or encourage repeat offenses? *Journal of Experimental Social Psychology, 44*, 453–460.

Wallace, H. M., & Tice, D. M. (2012). Reflected appraisal through a 21st-century looking glass. In M. R. Leary & J. P. Tangney (Eds.), *Handbook of self and identity* (2nd ed., pp. 124–140). New York, NY: Guilford.

Wallace, J. C., Edwards, B. D., Shull, A., & Finch, D. M. (2009). Examining the consequences in the tendency to suppress and reappraise emotions on task-related job performance. *Human Performance, 22*, 23–43.

Walster, E., Aronson, E., Abrahams, D., & Rottmann, L. (1966). Importance of physical attractiveness in dating behavior. *Journal of Personality and Social Psychology, 4*, 508–516.

Walters, R. (1984). Forgiving: An essential element in effective living. *Studies in Formative Spirituality, 5*, 365–374.

Walther, J. B. (2007). Selective self-presentation in computer-mediated communication: Hyperpersonal dimensions of technology, language, and cognition. *Computers in Human Behavior, 23*, 2538–2557.

Walther, J. B. (2009). Nonverbal dynamics in computer-mediated communication or :(and the net :('s with you, :) and you :) alone. In V. Manusov & M. L. Patterson (Eds.), *The Sage handbook of nonverbal communication* (pp. 461–479). Thousand Oaks, CA: Sage.

Walther, J. B., & Bazarova, N. N. (2007). Misattribution in virtual groups: The effects of member distribution on self-serving bias and partner blame. *Human Communication Research, 33*, 1–26.

Walther, J. B., & Ramirez, A., Jr. (2010). New technologies and new directions in online relating. In S. W. Smith & S. R. Wilson (Eds.), *New directions in interpersonal communication research* (pp. 264–284). Thousand Oaks, CA: Sage.

Waltman, M., & Haas, J. (2011). *The communication of hate.* New York, NY: Peter Lang Publishing.

Walton, S., & Rice, R. E. (2013). Mediated disclosure on Twitter: The roles of gender and identity in boundary impermeability, valence, disclosure, and stage. *Computers in Human Behavior, 29*, 1465–1474.

Wang, Q., Fink, E. L., & Cai, D. A. (2012). The effect of conflict goals on avoidance strategies: What does not communicating communicate? *Human Communication Research, 38*, 222–252.

Wänke, M., Samochowiec, J., & Landwehr, J. (2013). Facial politics: Political judgment based on looks. In J. P. Forgas, K. Fiedler, & C. Sedikides (Eds.), *Social thinking and interpersonal behavior* (pp. 143–160). New York, NY: Psychology Press.

Waring, E. M. (1981). Facilitating marital intimacy through self-disclosure. *American Journal of Family Therapy, 9*, 33–42.

Warren, K., Schoppelrey, S., & Moberg, D. (2005). A model of contagion through competition in the aggressive behaviors of elementary school students. *Journal of Abnormal Child Psychology, 33*, 283–292.

Watkins, L., & Johnston, L. (2000). Screening job applicants: The impact of physical attractiveness and application quality. *International Journal of Selection and Assessment, 8*, 76–84.

Watt, D. (2007). Toward a neuroscience of empathy: Integrating affective and cognitive perspectives. *Neuro-Psychoanalysis, 9*, 119–140.

Watts, R. E., Peluso, P. R., Lewis, T. F., Anderson, R. N., & Rasmussen, P. R. (2005). Psychological strategies. *Journal of Individual Psychology, 61*, 380–387.

Watzlawick, P. (1984). *The invented reality: How do we know what we believe we know?* New York, NY: Norton.

Watzlawick, P. (1990). Reality adaptation or adapted "reality"? Constructivism and psychotherapy. In P. Watzlawick (Ed.), *Münchausen's pigtail: Or psychotherapy and "reality." Essays and lectures.* New York, NY: Norton.

Watzlawick, P. (2005). Self-fulfilling prophecies. In J. O'Brien & P. Kollock (Eds.), *The production of reality* (4th ed., pp. 382–394). Thousand Oaks, CA: Sage.

Watzlawick, P., Beavin, J., & Jackson, D. (1967). *Pragmatics of human communication: A study of interactional patterns, pathologies, and paradoxes.* New York, NY: Norton.

Weaver, J. B., & Kirtley, M. D. (1995). Listening styles and empathy. *Southern Communication Journal, 60*, 131–140.

Weder, M. (2008). Form and function of metacommunication in CMC. In S. Kelsey & K. St. Amant (Eds.), *Handbook of research on computer mediated communication* (Vols. 1–2, pp. 570–586). Hershey, PA: Information Science Reference/IGI Global.

Weger, H. (2005). Disconfirming communication and self-verification in marriage: Associations among the demand/withdraw interaction pattern, feeling understood, and marital satisfaction. *Journal of Social & Personal Relationships, 22,* 19–31.

Weger, H., Bell, G. C., Minei, E. M., & Robinson, M. C. (2014). The relative effectiveness of active listening in initial interactions. *International Journal of Listening, 28,* 13–31.

Weger, H., Jr., Castle, G. R., & Emmett, M. C. (2010). Active listening in peer interviews: The influence of message paraphrasing on perceptions of listening skill. *International Journal of Listening, 24,* 34–49.

Weger, H., & Emmett, M. C. (2009). Romantic intent, relationship uncertainty, and relationship maintenance in young adults' cross-sex friendships. *Journal of Personal and Social Relationships, 26,* 964–988.

Weider-Hatfield, D. (1981). A unit in conflict management skills. *Communication Education, 30,* 265–273.

Weigel, D. J. (2008). Mutuality and the communication of commitment in romantic relationships. *Southern Communication Journal, 73,* 24–41.

Weigel, D. J., Brown, C., & O'Riordan, C. K. (2011). Everyday expressions of commitment and relational uncertainty as predictors of relationship quality and stability over time. *Communication Reports, 24,* 38–50.

Weigert, A. J., & Gecas, V. (2003). Self. In N. J. Herman-Kinney & L. T. Reynolds (Eds.), *Handbook of symbolic interactionism* (pp. 267–288). Walnut Creek, CA: AltaMira Press.

Weisbuch, M., Ambady, N., Clarke, A. L., Achor, S., & Weele, J. V.-V. (2010). On being consistent: The role of verbal-nonverbal consistency in first impressions. *Basic and Applied Social Psychology, 32,* 261–268.

Weisskirch, R. S. (2012). Women's adult romantic attachment style and communication by cell phone with romantic partners. *Psychological Reports, 111,* 281–288.

Weisskirch, R. S., & Delevi, R. (2013). Attachment style and conflict resolution skills predicting technology use in relationship dissolution. *Computers in Human Behavior, 29,* 2530–2534.

Werking, K. (1997). *We're just good friends: Women and men in nonromantic relationships.* New York, NY: Guilford.

Wester, S. R., Vogel, D. L., Pressly, P. K., & Heesacker, M. (2002). Sex differences in emotion: A critical review of the literature and implications for counseling psychology. *Counseling Psychologist, 30,* 630–652.

Whaley, L. J. (1997). *Introduction to typology: The unity and diversity of language.* Thousand Oaks, CA: Sage.

Whited, M. C., Wheat, A. L., & Larkin, K. T. (2010). The influence of forgiveness and apology on cardiovascular reactivity and recovery in response to mental stress. *Journal of Behavioral Medicine, 33,* 293–304.

Whitty, M. T. (2005). The realness of cybercheating: Men's and women's representations of unfaithful Internet relationships. *Social Science Computer Review, 23,* 57–67.

Whitty, M. T. (2007). Manipulation of self in cyberspace. In B. H. Spitzberg & W. R. Cupach (Eds.), *The dark side of interpersonal communication* (2nd ed., pp. 93–120). London, England: Routledge.

Whorf, B. L. (1956). The relation of habitual thought and behavior to language. In J. B. Carroll (Ed.), *Language, thought, and reality: Selected writings of Benjamin Lee Whorf* (pp. 134–159). Cambridge, MA: MIT Press.

Wiemann, J. M., & Knapp, M. L. (2008). Turn-taking in conversations. In C. D. Mortensen (Ed.), *Communication theory* (2nd ed., pp. 226–245). Piscataway, NJ: Transaction Publishers.

Wildermuth, S. M., & Vogl-Bauer, S. (2007). We met on the net: Exploring perceptions of online romantic relationship participants. *Southern Communication Journal, 72,* 211–227.

Wilkerson, A., Carlson, N. E., Yen, I. H., & Michael, Y. L. (2012). Neighborhood physical features and relationships with neighbors: Does positive physical environment increase neighborliness? *Environment and Behavior, 44,* 595–615.

Williams, L., & Russell, S. T. (2013). Shared social and emotional activities within adolescent romantic and non-romantic sexual relationships. *Archives of Sexual Behavior, 42,* 649–658.

Williams-Baucom, K. J., Atkins, D. C., Sevier, M., Eldridge, K. A., & Christensen, A. (2010). "You" and "I" need to talk about "us": Linguistic patterns in marital interactions. *Personal Relationships, 17,* 41–56.

Wilmot, W. W. (1987). *Dyadic communication* (3rd ed.). New York, NY: Random House.

Wilmot, W. W. (1995). *Relational communication* (5th ed.). New York, NY: McGraw-Hill.

Wilmot, W. W., & Hocker, J. L. (2013). *Interpersonal conflict* (9th ed.). New York, NY: McGraw-Hill.

Wilson, T. D. (2011). *Redirect: The surprising new science of psychological change.* New York, NY: Little, Brown.

Wire, J. (2010, October 9). 20 awesomely untranslatable words from around the world. *Matador Abroad.* Retrieved from http://matadornetwork.com/abroad/20-awesomely-untranslatable-words-from-around-the-world/

Wiseman, R. (2003). *Queen bees and wannabes: Helping your daughter survive cliques, gossip, boyfriends, and other realities of adolescence*. New York, NY: Three Rivers Press.

Wolf, A. (2000). Emotional expression online: Gender differences in emoticon use. *CyberPsychology & Behavior, 3,* 827–833.

Wolfram, W., & Schilling-Estes, N. (2006). *American English: Dialects and variation* (2nd ed.). Malden, MA: Blackwell.

Wolvin, A. D. (1984). Meeting the communication needs of the adult learner. *Communication Education, 33,* 267–271.

Wood, J. T. (2005). Feminist standpoint theory and muted group theory: Commonalities and divergences. *Women and Language, 28*(2), 61–65.

Wood, J. T. (2013). *Gendered lives: Communication and gender* (10th ed.). Belmont, CA: Wadsworth.

Wood, J. T., & Inman, C. C. (1993). In a different mode: Masculine styles of communicating closeness. *Journal of Applied Communication Research, 21,* 279–295.

Wood, J. V., Heimpel, S. A., Manwell, L. A., & Whittington, E. J. (2009). This mood is familiar and I don't deserve to feel better anyway: Mechanisms underlying self-esteem differences in motivation to repair sad moods. *Journal of Personality & Social Psychology, 96,* 363–380.

Woodin, E. M. (2011). A two-dimensional approach to relationship conflict: Meta-analytic findings. *Journal of Family Psychology, 25,* 325–335.

Woodward, M. S., Rosenfeld, L. B., & May, S. K. (1996). Sex differences in social support in sororities and fraternities. *Journal of Applied Communication Research, 24,* 260–272.

Wright, C. N., Holloway, A., & Roloff, M. E. (2007). The dark side of self-monitoring: How high self-monitors view their romantic relationships. *Communication Reports, 20,* 101–114.

Wright, C. N., & Roloff, M. E. (2009). Relational commitment and the silent treatment. *Communication Research Reports, 26,* 12–21.

Wu, S., & Keysar, B. (2007). Cultural effects on perspective taking. *Psychological Science, 18,* 600–606.

Yan, W., Wu, Q., Liang, J., Chen, Y., & Fu, X. (2013). How fast are the leaked facial expressions: The duration of micro-expressions. *Journal of Nonverbal Behavior, 37,* 217–230.

Ybarra, M. L., & Mitchell, K. J. (2007). Prevalence and frequency of Internet harassment instigation: Implications for adolescent health. *Journal of Adolescent Health, 41,* 189–195.

Ybarra, O., Burnstein, E., Winkielman, P., Keller, M. C., Manis, M., Chan, E., & Rodriguez, J. (2008). Mental exercising through simple socializing: Social interaction promotes general cognitive functioning. *Personality and Social Psychology Bulletin, 34,* 248–259.

Ybarra, O., Rees, L., Kross, E., & Sanchez-Burks, J. (2011). Social context and the psychology of emotional intelligence: A key to creating positive organizations. In K. Cameron & G. Spreitzer (Eds.), *Handbook of positive organizational scholarship* (pp. 201–214). New York, NY: Oxford University Press.

Yee, N., & Bailenson, J. N. (2006, August). Walk a mile in digital shoes: The impact of embodied perspective-taking on the reduction of negative stereotyping in immersive virtual environments. *Proceedings of PRESENCE 2006: The 8th Annual International Workshop on Presence.* Cleveland, OH. Retrieved from http://www.temple.edu/ispr/prev _conferences/proceedings/2006/confindex.html

Yeh, J. B. (2010). Relations matter: Redefining communication competence from a Chinese perspective. *Chinese Journal of Communication, 3,* 64–75.

Yen, J., Yen, C., Chen, C., Wang, P., Chang, Y., & Ko, C. (2012). Social anxiety in online and real-life interaction and their associated factors. *Cyberpsychology, Behavior, and Social Networking, 15,* 7–12.

Yingling, J. (1994). Constituting friendship in talk and metatalk. *Journal of Social and Personal Relationships, 11,* 411–426.

Yopyk, D. J. A., & Prentice, D. A. (2005). Am I an athlete or a student? Identity salience and stereotype threat in student-athletes. *Basic and Applied Social Psychology, 27,* 329–336.

Young, S. L. (2004). What the _____ is your problem?: Attribution theory and perceived reasons for profanity usage during conflict. *Communication Research Reports, 21,* 338–447.

Young, S. L. (2009). The function of parental communication patterns: Reflection-enhancing and reflection-discouraging approaches. *Communication Quarterly, 57,* 379–394.

Young, S. L., Kelsey, D. M., & Lancaster, A. L. (2011). How email builds student-teacher ties. *Communication Currents, 6,* 18–19.

Yuki, M., Maddux, W. W., & Masuda, T. (2007). Are the windows to the soul the same in the East and West? Cultural differences in using the eyes and mouth as cues to recognize emotions in Japan and the United States. *Journal of Experimental Social Psychology, 43,* 303–311.

Yurtsever, G., & de Rivera, J. (2010). Measuring the emotional climate of an organization. *Perceptual and Motor Skills, 110,* 501–516.

Zapf, D., & Holz, M. (2006). On the positive and negative effects of emotion work in organizations. *European Journal of Work and Organizational Psychology, 15,* 1–28.

Zebrowitz, L. A., & Montepare, J. M. (2008). First impressions from facial appearance cues. In N. Ambady & J. J. Skowronski (Eds.), *First impressions* (pp. 171–204). New York, NY: Guilford.

Zeman, B. (2010). Beyond choice theory: Using language to take effective control of your life. *International Journal of Choice Theory and Reality Theory, 30,* 36–40.

Zenmore, S. E., Fiske, S. T., & Kim, H. J. (2000). Gender stereotypes and the dynamics of social interaction. In T. Eckes & H. M. Trautner (Eds.), *The developmental social psychology of gender* (pp. 207–241). Mahwah, NJ: Erlbaum.

Zhang, S. (2009). Sender-recipient perspectives of honest but hurtful evaluative messages in romantic relationships. *Communication Reports, 22,* 89–101.

Zhang, S., & Stafford, L. (2008). Perceived face threat of honest but hurtful evaluative messages in romantic relationships. *Western Journal of Communication, 72,* 19–39.

Zhang, S., & Stafford, L. (2009). Relational ramifications of honest but hurtful evaluative messages in close relationships. *Western Journal of Communication, 73,* 481–501.

Zhang, Y., Fang, Y., Wei, K., & Wang, Z. (2012). Promoting the intention of students to continue their participation in e-learning systems: The role of the communication environment. *Information Technology & People, 25,* 356–375.

Zhang, Y. B., Harwood, J., & Hummert, M. L. (2005). Perceptions of conflict management styles in Chinese intergenerational dyads. *Communication Monographs, 72,* 71–91.

Zhang, Z., Zhang, Y., & Wang, M. (2011). Harmony, illusory relationship costs, and conflict resolution in Chinese contexts. In A. Y. Leung, C. Chiu, & Y. Hong (Eds.), *Cultural processes: A social psychological perspective* (pp. 188–209). New York, NY: Cambridge University Press.

Zhong, J., Wang, A., Qian, M., Zhang, L., Gao, J., Yang, J., Li, B. & Chen, P. (2008). Shame, personality, and social anxiety symptoms in Chinese and American nonclinical samples: A cross-cultural study. *Depression and Anxiety, 25,* 449–460.

Zhu, Z., Ho, S. Y., & Bonanno, G. A. (2013). Cultural similarities and differences in the perception of emotional valence and intensity: A comparison of Americans and Hong Kong Chinese. *The American Journal of Psychology, 126,* 261–273.

Zick, A., Granieri, M., & Makoul, G. (2007). First-year medical students' assessment of their own communication skills: A video-based, open-ended approach. *Patient Education and Counseling, 68,* 161–166.

Zimbardo, P. G. (1971). *The psychological power and pathology of imprisonment.* Statement prepared for the U.S. House of Representatives Committee on the Judiciary, Subcommittee No. 3, Robert Kastemeyer, Chairman. Unpublished manuscript, Stanford University, Stanford, CA.

Zimbardo, P. G. (1977). *Shyness: What it is, what to do about it.* Reading, MA: Addison-Wesley.

Zimbardo, P. G. (2007, March 30). Revisiting the Stanford prison experiment: A lesson in the power of situation. *Chronicle of Higher Education, 53,* B6.

Zimbler, M., & Feldman, R. S. (2011). Liar, liar, hard drive on fire: How media context affects lying behavior. *Journal of Applied Social Psychology, 41,* 2492–2507.

Zimmerman, B. J. (1995). Self-efficacy and educational development. In A. Bandura (Ed.), *Self-efficacy in changing societies* (pp. 202–231). New York, NY: Cambridge University Press.

Zimmermann, J., Wolf, M., Bock, A., Peham, D., & Benecke, C. (2013). The way we refer to ourselves reflects how we relate to others: Associations between first-person pronoun use and interpersonal problems. *Journal of Research in Personality, 47,* 218–225.

Zorn, T. E., & Gregory, K. W. (2005). Learning the ropes together: Assimilation and friendship development among first-year male medical students. *Health Communication, 17,* 211–231.

Zuckerman, M., & Driver, R. E. (1989). What sounds beautiful is good: The vocal attractiveness stereotype. *Journal of Nonverbal Behavior, 13,* 67–82.

Zuckerman, M., Miserandino, M., Bernieri, F., Manusov, V., Axtell, R. E., Wiemann, J. M., . . . Gallois, C. (1999). Creating impressions and managing interaction. In L. K. Guerrero, J. A. DeVito, & M. L. Hecht (Eds.), *The nonverbal communication reader: Classic and contemporary readings* (2nd ed., pp. 379–422). Prospect Heights, IL: Waveland Press.

Credits

CARTOONS

Page 14: © Bruce Eric Kaplan/The New Yorker Collection/The Cartoon Bank

Page 32: © Liam Walsh/The New Yorker Collection/The Cartoon Bank

Page 58: DILBERT © 1991 Scott Adams. Used by permission of UNIVERSAL UCLICK. All rights reserved.

Page 78: © Edward Frascino/The New Yorker Collection/The Cartoon Bank

Page 85: DILBERT © 2013 Scott Adams. Used by permission of UNIVERSAL UCLICK. All rights reserved.

Page 99: ZITS © 2004 Zits Partnership, Dist. by King Features

Page 109: ZITS © 2001 Zits Partnership, Dist. by King Features

Page 120: © Edward Koren/The New Yorker Collection/The Cartoon Bank

Page 124: © Laughingstock Licensing Inc.

Page 132: © William Steig/The New Yorker Collection/The Cartoon Bank

Page 142: © Laura Hobbes LeGault/yourmometer.com

Page 145: © Drew Dernavich/The New Yorker Collection/The Cartoon Bank

Page 175: DILBERT © 2002 Scott Adams. Used by permission of UNIVERSAL UCLICK. All rights reserved.

Page 178: Zits: © 2013 Zits Partnership. Distributed by King Features Syndicate

Page 199: © 2011 Malcom Evans

Page 206: CartoonStock www.CartoonStock.com

Page 215: © William Haefeli/The New Yorker Collection/The Cartoon Bank

Page 222: CartoonStock www.CartoonStock.com

Page 242: © Peter Steiner/The New Yorker Collection/The Cartoon Bank

Page 255: Zits: © 1999 Zits Partnership. Distributed by King Features Syndicate

Page 271: © Erik Hilgerdt/The New Yorker Collection/The Cartoon Bank

Page 291: © Leo Cullum/The New Yorker Collection/The Cartoon Bank

Page 292: Jeroen Vanstiphout – www.kartoen.be

Page 296: PEARLS BEFORE SWINE © 2010 Stephan Pastis. Reprinted by permission of Universal Uclick for UFS. All rights reserved.

Page 304: © King Features Syndicate (Sally Forth cartoon)

Page 313: Everyday People Cartoons by Cathy Thorne

Page 316: © Sam Gross/The New Yorker Collection/The Cartoon Bank

Page 331: © Dan Piraro, distributed by King Features Syndicate (Bizarro cartoon)

Page 345: © John Caldwell/The New Yorker Collection/ The Cartoon Bank

Page 356: PEARLS BEFORE SWINE © 2012 Stephan Pastis. Reprinted by permission of Universal UClick for UFS.

Page 374: © Leo Cullum/The New Yorker Collection/The Cartoon Bank

Page 376: CALVIN AND HOBBES © 1993 Watterson. Reprinted with permission of UNIVERSAL UCLICK. All rights reserved.

PHOTOS

Page 2: © CoolR/Shutterstock

Page 7: © Leila Cutler/Alamy

Page 15: Imagerymajestic/Alamy

Page 25: Courtesy of Steven Weiss

Page 36: © PRILL Mediendesign/Alamy

Page 56: Patrick Harbron/© Netflix/courtesy Everett Collection

Page 68: iStock.com/SeanShot

Page 74: © CJG - Technology/Alamy

Page 80: © iStock.com/audioundwerbung

Page 82: blickwinkel/Alamy

Page 84: © Rogue Pictures/courtesy Everett Collection

Page 87: © Glasshouse Images/Alamy

Page 110: iStock.com/jeancliclac

Page 128: © Jose Luis Stephens/Alamy

Page XXX: PRNewsfoto/AP Images

Page 133: Bernhard Classen/Alamy

Page 141: Photograph by Christopher Voelker From *See What I'm Saying: The Deaf Entertainers Documentary* © Worldplay, Inc.

Page 147: digitalskillet/Getty Images

Page 150: NBC/Getty Images

Page 166: sjscreens/Alamy

Page 170: imageBROKER/Alamy

Page 172: The Kobal Collection at Art Resource, NY

Page 173: Jupiterimages/Getty Images

Page 179: © Vladimir Wrangel/Shutterstock

Page 183: Image Source/Alamy

Page 184: The Kobal Collection at Art Resource, NY

Page 187: Ryan Lane/Getty Images

Page 194: Cultura RM/Alamy

Page 202: Jerome Tisne/Getty Images

Page 208: Philip Lee Harvey/Getty Images

Page 214: © iStock.com/George Clerk

Page 220: AP Photo/Amy Sancetta

Page 234: AP Photo/Reed Saxon

Page 243: Michael Yarish / © AMC / Courtesy: Everett Collection

Page 248: robert hyrons/Alamy

Page 257: Getty Images

Page 261: B.A.E. Inc./Alamy

Page 264: Gallo Images/Alamy

Page 276: The Kobal Collection at Art Resource, NY

Page 281: Jim West/Alamy

Author Index

Subject Index